Lecture Notes in Computer Science 3086

Commenced Publication in 1973
Founding and Former Series Editors:
Gerhard Goos, Juris Hartmanis, and Jan van Leeuwen

Springer
Berlin
Heidelberg
New York
Hong Kong
London
Milan
Paris
Tokyo

Martin Odersky (Ed.)

ECOOP 2004 – Object-Oriented Programming

18th European Conference
Oslo, Norway, June 14-18, 2004
Proceedings

Springer

Volume Editor

Martin Odersky
École Polytechnique Fédérale de Lausanne (EPFL)
School of Computer and Communication Sciences
1015 Lausanne, Switzerland
E-mail: martin.odersky@epfl.ch

Library of Congress Control Number: 2004106985

CR Subject Classification (1998): D.1, D.2, D.3, F.3, C.2, K.4, J.1

ISSN 0302-9743
ISBN 3-540-22159-X Springer-Verlag Berlin Heidelberg New York

Springer-Verlag is a part of Springer Science+Business Media

springeronline.com

Printed in Germany

Typesetting: Camera-ready by author, data conversion by PTP-Berlin, Protago-TeX-Production GmbH
Printed on acid-free paper SPIN: 11012146 06/3142 5 4 3 2 1 0

Preface

ECOOP is the premier forum in Europe for bringing together practitioners, researchers, and students to share their ideas and experiences in a broad range of disciplines woven with the common thread of object technology. It is a collage of events, including outstanding invited speakers, carefully refereed technical papers, practitioner reports reflecting real-world experience, panels, topic-focused workshops, demonstrations, and an interactive posters session.

The 18th ECOOP 2004 conference held during June 14–18, 2004 in Oslo, Norway represented another year of continued success in object-oriented programming, both as a topic of academic study and as a vehicle for industrial software development. Object-oriented technology has come of age; it is now the commonly established method for most software projects. However, an expanding field of applications and new technological challenges provide a strong demand for research in foundations, design and programming methods, as well as implementation techniques. There is also an increasing interest in the integration of object-orientation with other software development techniques. We anticipate therefore that object-oriented programming will be a fruitful subject of research for many years to come.

This year, the program committee received 132 submissions, of which 25 were accepted for publication after a thorough reviewing process. Every paper received at least 4 reviews. Papers were evaluated based on relevance, significance, clarity, originality, and correctness. The topics covered include: programming concepts, program analysis, software engineering, aspects and components, middleware, verification, systems and implementation techniques. These were complemented by two invited talks, from Matthias Felleisen and Tom Henzinger. Their titles and abstracts are also included in these proceedings.

The success of a major conference such as ECOOP is due to the dedication of many people. I would like to thank the authors for submitting a high number of quality papers; selecting a subset of papers to be published from these was not easy. I would also like to thank the 22 members of the program committee for producing careful reviews, and for sometimes lengthy discussions during the program committee meeting, which was held February 5th and 6th in Lausanne. I thank the general chair of the conference, Birger Møller-Pedersen, and the local organizer, Arne Maus, for productive collaborations in planning the conference and for helping on a number of logistical issues. The AITO Executive Board gave useful guidance. Richard van de Stadt provided invaluable computer-assisted support for the electronic reviewing process, the PC meeting, as well as the production of these proceedings. Finally, Yvette Dubuis at EPFL provided administrative and logistic assistance for running the PC meeting.

April 2004 Martin Odersky

Organization

ECOOP 2004 was organized by the University of Oslo, the Norwegian Computing Center and Sintef, under the auspices of AITO (Association Internationale pour les Technologies Objets), and in cooperation with ACM SIGPLAN.

Executive Committee

Conference Chair
  Birger Møller-Pedersen (University of Oslo)
Program Chair
  Martin Odersky (École Polytechnique Fédérale de Lausanne)
Organizing Chair
  Arne Maus (University of Oslo)

Organizing Committee

Workshop Chairs
  Jacques Malenfant (Université Pierre et Marie Curie)
  Bjarte M. Østvold (Norwegian Computing Center)
Tutorial Chairs
  Arne-Jørgen Berre (Sintef)
  Hanspeter Mössenböck (Johannes Kepler Universität)
PhD Workshop/Doctoral Symposium Chairs
  Susanne Jucknath (Technische Universität Berlin)
  Eric Jul (University of Copenhagen)
Poster/Exhibition/Demonstration Chair
  Ole Smørdal (University of Oslo)
Practitioners' Reports Chair
  Egil P. Andersen (DNV Software)
Memorial Exhibition
  Håvard Hegna (Norwegian Computing Center)
Room Allocation
  Stein Krogdahl (University of Oslo)
Treasurer
  Øystein Haugen (University of Oslo)
Webmaster, Student Volunteers
  Dag Langmyhr (University of Oslo)

Program Committee

Uwe Assmann	Linköpings Universitet, Sweden
Don Batory	University of Texas at Austin, USA
Gilad Bracha	Sun Microsystems, USA
Luca Cardelli	Microsoft Research Cambridge, UK
Charles Consel	LaBRI/INRIA, France
Giuseppe Castagna	École Normale Supérieure, France
Peter Dickman	University of Glasgow, UK
Sophia Drossopoulou	Imperial College, UK
Erik Ernst	University of Aarhus, Denmark
Manuel Fähndrich	Microsoft Research, USA
Giovanna Guerrini	University of Pisa, Italy
Urs Hölzle	Google, USA
Mehdi Jazayeri	Technical University of Vienna, Austria
Shriram Krishnamurthi	Brown University, USA
Doug Lea	SUNY Oswego, USA
Mira Mezini	Darmstadt University of Technology, Germany
Oscar Nierstrasz	University of Bern, Switzerland
Atushi Ohori	JAIST, Japan
Douglas Schmidt	Vanderbilt University, USA
Luís Rodrigues	Universidade de Lisboa, Portugal
Clemens Szyperski	Microsoft Research, USA
Philip Wadler	University of Edinburgh, UK

Referees

Peter von der Ahé
Jonathan Aldrich
Eric Allen
Davide Ancona
Christopher Anderson
Pedro Antunes
Filipe Araujo
Gabriela Arévalo
Kenichi Asai
David F. Bacon
Thomas Ball
Véronique Benzaken
Alexandre Bergel
Lorenzo Bettini
Andrew P. Black
Viviana Bono
Ruth Breu
Kim Bruce
Michele Bugliesi
João Cachopo
Denis Caromel
Luis Carriço
Robert Chatley
Yoonsik Cheon
Jong-Deok Choi
Dave Clarke
Gregory Cobena
Alessandro Coglio
Dario Colazzo
Alexandre di Costanzo
William Cook
Greg Cooper
Erik Corry
Manuvir Das
Rob DeLine
Giorgio Delzanno
Amer Diwan
Damien Doligez
Alan Donovan
Karel Driesen
Stéphane Ducasse
Dominic Duggan
Michael Eichberg
Susan Eisenbach
Sonia Fagorzi
Pascal Fenkam
Robby Findler
Bernd Fischer
Kathleen Fisher
Markus G"alli
Jacques Garrigue
Tudor Girba
Patrice Godefroid
Georges Gonthier
Mark Grechanik
Orla Greevy
Thomas Gschwind
Masahito Hasegawa
Johannes Henkel
Michael Hind
Tom Hirschowitz
Pete Hopkins
Haruo Hosoya
Jim Hugunin
Atsushi Igarashi
Paul Kelly
Graham Kirby
Günter Kniesel
Juliana Küster-Filipe
Giovanni Lagorio
Patrick Lam
Michele Lanza
James Larus
Rustan Leino
Dan Licata
Adrian Lienhard
Jørgen Lindskov Knudsen
Roberto Lopez-Herrejon
Darko Marinov
Francisco Martins
Brian McNamara
Erik Meijer
Marco Mesiti
Todd Millstein
Hugo Miranda
Kjeld H. Mortensen
Gilles Muller
Curran Nachbar

Markus Noga
Isabel Nunes
Robert O'Callahan
Klaus Ostermann
Ulrik Pagh Schultz
Jens Palsberg
David Pearce
João Pedro Neto
Randy Pollack
Laura Ponisio
Seth Proctor
Shaz Qadeer
Sean Quinlan
Gianna Reggio
Jakob Rehof
Geral Reif
Lukas Renggli
Martin Rinard
António Rito-Silva
Kenneth Russell
Alexandru Salcianu
Don Sannella
Nathanael Schärli
Michael I. Schwartzbach
Nahid Shahmehri
Yannis Smaragdakis
V.C. Sreedhar
John Tang Boyland
Tachio Terauchi
Peter Thiemann
Michel Tilman
Mads Torgersen
Vasco T. Vasconcelos
Jan Vitek
Aino Vonge Corry
Jérôme Vouillon
David Walker
Dan Wallach
Stephanie Weirich
Lisa Wells
Toshiaki Yasue
Masahiro Yasugi
Steve Zdancewic
Ying Zhang
Elena Zucca

Table of Contents

Invited Talk 1

Middleware

Types

Verification

Invited Talk 2

Systems

Ownership Domains: Separating Aliasing Policy from Mechanism

Jonathan Aldrich[1] and Craig Chambers[2]

[1] Carnegie Mellon University, Pittsburgh, PA 15217, USA,
jonathan.aldrich@cs.cmu.edu
[2] University of Washington, Seattle, WA, 98195, USA,
chambers@cs.washington.edu

Abstract. Ownership types promise to provide a practical mechanism for enforcing stronger encapsulation by controlling aliasing in object-oriented languages. However, previous ownership type proposals have tied the aliasing policy of a system to the mechanism of ownership. As a result, these proposals are too weak to express many important aliasing constraints, yet also so restrictive that they prohibit many useful programming idioms.

In this paper, we propose *ownership domains*, which decouple encapsulation policy from the mechanism of ownership in two key ways. First, developers can specify multiple ownership domains for each object, permitting a fine-grained control of aliasing compared to systems that provide only one ownership domain for each object. Second, developers can specify the permitted aliasing between each pair of domains in the system, providing more flexibility compared to systems that enforce a fixed policy for inter-domain aliasing. Because it decouples policy from mechanism, our alias control system is both more precise and more flexible than previous ownership type systems.

1 Introduction

One of the primary challenges in building and evolving large object-oriented systems is reasoning about aliasing between objects. Unexpected aliasing can lead to broken invariants, mistaken assumptions, security holes, and surprising side effects, which in turn may cause defects and complicate software evolution.

Ownership types are one promising approach to addressing the problems of uncontrolled aliasing [23,13,10,4,8,11]. With ownership types, the developer of an abstract data type can encapsulate objects used in the internal representation of the ADT, and use static typechecking to ensure that clients of the ADT cannot access its representation.

Despite the potential of ownership types, current ownership type systems have serious limitations, both in the kinds of aliasing constraints they can express and in their ability to support important programming idioms. These limitations

M. Odersky (Ed.): ECOOP 2004, LNCS 3086, pp. 1–25, 2004.

can be understood by looking at ownership types as a combination of a *mechanism* for dividing objects into hierarchical groups, and a *policy* for constraining references between objects in those groups.

In previous ownership type systems, each object defines a single group to hold its private state. We will call these groups *ownership domains*. The ownership mechanism is useful for separating the internals of an abstract data type from clients of the ADT, but since each object defines only one ownership domain, ownership types cannot be used to reason about aliasing between different subsystems within an object.

The aliasing policy in previous ownership type systems is fixed: the private state of an object can refer to the outside world, but the outside world may not refer to the private state of the object. This policy is known as owners-as-dominators, because it implies that all paths to an object in a system must go through that object's owner.

This fixed policy is useful for ensuring that clients cannot access the internals of an abstract data type. However, the policy is too restrictive to support common programming idioms such as iterator objects or event callbacks. In these idioms, the iterator or event callback objects must be outside of the ADT so that clients can use them, but they must be able to access the internals of the ADT to do their jobs. Thus, iterators or callbacks create paths to the inside of an ADT that do not go through the ADT object itself, violating owners-as-dominators.

In this paper, we propose ownership domains, an extension of ownership types that separates the alias control policy of a system from the mechanism of ownership. Our system generalizes the mechanism of ownership to permit multiple ownership domains in each object. Each domain represents a logically related set of objects. Thus, developers can use the ownership domain mechanism to divide a system object into multiple subsystems, and can separately specify the policy that determines how those subsystems can interact.

Instead of hard-wiring an aliasing policy into the ownership mechanism, our system allows engineers to specify in detail the permitted aliasing relationships between domains. For example, a Sequence ADT can declare one domain for its internal representation, and a second domain for its iterators. The aliasing policy for the Sequence ADT can be written to allow clients to access the iterators, and to allow the iterators to access the internal representation of the Sequence, while prohibiting clients from accessing the internal representation directly.

As a result of separating the mechanism for dividing objects into domains from the policy of how objects in those domains may interact, our system is both more precise and more flexible than previous ownership type systems. It is more precise in allowing developers to control aliasing between the sub-parts of an object. Furthermore, while our system can be used to statically enforce the owners-as-dominators property, it also supports more flexible alias control policies that permit idioms like iterators or events.

The rest of this paper is organized as follows. In the next section we introduce ownership domains by example, showing how they can express aliasing policies and code idioms that were not expressible in previous systems. We have im-

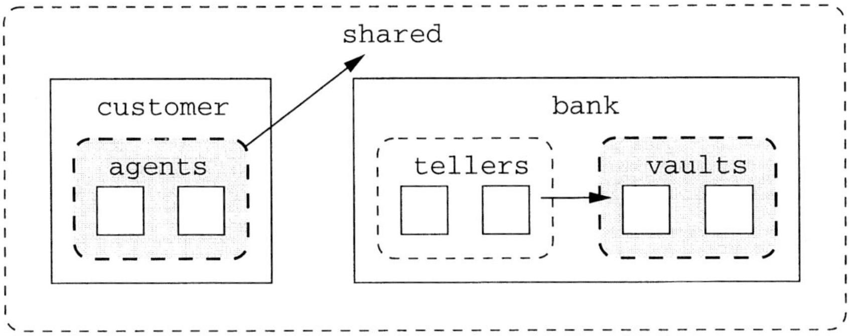

Fig. 1. A conceptual view of AliasJava's ownership domain model. The rounded, dashed rectangles represent domains, with a gray fill for private domains. Solid rectangles represent objects. The top-level `shared` domain contains the highest-level objects in the program. Each object may define one or more domains that in turn contain other objects.

plemented ownership domains in the open-source AliasJava compiler [4], which is freely available at `http://www.archjava.org/`. Section 3 presents our proposal more formally as an extension of Featherweight Java [18], and proves that our type system enforces the aliasing specifications given by the programmer. Section 4 discusses related work, and Section 5 concludes.

2 Ownership Domains

We illustrate ownership domains in the context of AliasJava, an extension to the Java programming language that adds support for a variety of alias specifications [4]. Figure 1 illustrates the ownership domain model used in AliasJava. Every object in the system is part of a single ownership domain. There is a top-level ownership domain denoted by the keyword `shared`. In addition, each object can declare one or more domains to hold its internal objects.

The example shows two objects in the `shared` domain: a `bank` and a `customer`, denoted by rectangles. The customer declares a domain denoting the customer's agents; the domain has two (unnamed) agent objects in it. The bank declares two domains: one for the tellers in the bank, and one for the bank's vaults. In this example, there are two tellers and two bank vaults.

Each object can declare a policy describing the permitted aliasing among objects in its internal domains, and between its internal domains and external domains. Our system supports two kinds of policy specifications:

- A `link` from one domain to another, denoted with an arrow in the diagram, allows objects in the first domain to access objects in the second domain.
- A domain can be declared `public`, denoted by a thinner dashed rectangle with no shading. Permission to access an object automatically implies permission to access its public domains.

```
class Class {
  domain owned;
  owned List signers;

  /* clients cannot call a method returning an owned list */
  owned List getSigners() {
    return signers;
  }
}
```

Fig. 2. In an early version of the JDK, the `Class.getSigners` method returned the internal list of signers rather than a copy, allowing untrusted clients to pose as trusted code. In an ownership type system, the list could be declared `owned`, and the typechecker would have caught this error at compile time.

For example, the `customer` object declares a link from its `agent` domain to the `shared` domain, allowing the customer's agents to access the bank. The bank declares a link from its `tellers` domain to its `vaults` domain, allowing the tellers to access the vaults. Finally, the bank declares its `tellers` domain to be `public`, allowing the customer and the customer's agents (and any other object that can access the bank) to also access the `tellers`. Note that permissions in our model are *not* transitive, so that the customer and the agents cannot access the bank's vaults directly; they must go through the bank or its tellers.

In addition to the explicit policy specifications mentioned above, our system includes the following implicit policy specifications:

- An object has permission to access other objects in the same domain.
- An object has permission to access objects in the domains that it declares.

The first rule allows the customer to access the bank (and vice versa), while the second rule allows the customer to access its agents and the bank to access its tellers and vaults. Any aliasing relationship not explicitly permitted by one of these rules is prohibited, according to the principle of least privilege.

2.1 Domain Declarations

Figure 2 illustrates ownership domains by showing how they could have been used to catch a security hole in an early release of the JDK, version 1.1. In this somewhat simplified example[1], the security system function `Class.getSigners` returns a pointer to an internal list, rather than a copy. Clients can then modify the list, compromising the Java security model and potentially allowing malicious applets to pose as trusted code.

[1] The real bug was of the same form but involved native code and arrays, not Java code and lists. In an earlier paper, we show how ownership can be integrated with arrays [4].

The code in Figure 2 has been annotated with ownership domain information in order to document the permitted aliasing relationships and prevent bugs like the one described above. Each `Class` instance contains a private domain `owned` that is distinct from the `owned` domain of all other `Class` instances.

In our system, the owner of an object is expressed as part of its type, appearing before the class part of the type. For example, the `signers` field refers to a list that is in the `owned` domain, expressing the fact that the list must not be shared with clients.

According to the typing rules of ownership domains, only objects that have access to the `owned` domain of a `Class` object can access its `signers` field or call the `getSigners` method. Since the `owned` domain is private, only the `Class` object itself can access these members–it would be a typechecking error if client code tried to call `getSigners`.

Although the `signers` field is intended to be private, we would like clients to be able to get the signers of a class, as long as they cannot modify the internal list holding the signers. Thus, a more appropriate return type for `getSigners` would be `shared List`, where the `shared` domain represents a set of globally visible objects. If we were to give `getSigners` this return type and leave the implementation as is, we would get a type error, because the actual list returned by the function has domain `owned`, not `shared`. The correct solution is the one used to fix this bug in the actual JDK: allocating a new list each time `getSigners` is called, copying the signers into the new list and returning the result.

This example shows that using ownership domains to protect internal state from clients enforces a stronger invariant than `private` declarations, because the latter only protect the field, not the object in the field. Thus, ownership domains are a useful tool for enforcing the internal invariants of a system, including security invariants like the one in this example.

2.2 Parameterized Types

Figure 3 illustrates how a `Sequence` abstract data type can be expressed with ownership domains. The `Sequence` must have internal references to the elements in the sequence, but the elements are typically part of the domain of some client. Following Flexible Alias Protection [23] and Featherweight Generic Confinement [24], we leverage Java's generics mechanism to specify the ownership information of a type parameter along with the name. Therefore, we parameterize the `Sequence` class by some type `T`, which includes the class of the elements as well as the domain they are in.

Since the sequence must maintain internal pointers to its elements, the compiler must typecheck it assuming that the sequence object has permission to access the domain of `T`. This assumption is expressed with an `assumes` clause stating that the special domain `owner` (meaning the owner of the current object) has permission to access `T.owner`, the domain of `T`. Whenever `Sequence` is instantiated with type parameter `T`, and is placed in some owner domain, this assumption is checked. For example, in Figure 5 a client instantiates the sequence,

```
class Sequence<T> assumes owner -> T.owner /* default */ {
  domain owned;          /* default */
  link owned -> T.owner; /* default */
  owned Cons<T> head;    /* owned is default here */
  void add(T o) {
    head = new Cons<T>(o,head)
  }

  public domain iters;
  link iters -> T.owner, iters -> owned;
  iters Iterator<T> getIter() {
    return new SequenceIterator<T, owned>(head);
  }
}

class Cons<T> assumes owner -> T.owner /* default */  {
  Cons(T obj, owner Cons<T> next) { this.obj=obj; this.next=next; }
  T obj;
  owner Cons<T> next;
}
```

Fig. 3. A Sequence abstract data type that uses a linked list for its internal representation. The Sequence declares a publicly accessible iters domain representing its iterators, as well as a private owned domain to hold the linked list. The link declarations specify that iterators in the iter domain have permission to access objects in the owned domain, and that both domains can access owner of the type parameter T.

passing in the type state Object for the type parameter T and placing the sequence in the state domain. Since the state domain (like every other domain) is considered to be linked to itself, the assumption is valid in this example.

In practice, nearly all objects need assume clauses linking their owner domain to their domains of their parameter types, so these clauses are defaults in our system and may be omitted.

The code in Figure 3 represents the sequence internally as a linked list. Clients of the Sequence should not be able to access the list directly, so the Sequence stores the linked list in a private domain called owned. Because the links in the list need to be able to refer to the elements of the sequence, the code includes a link declaration specifying that objects in the owned domain can refer to objects in the T.owner domain.

The Cons class represents a link in the linked list. In the example, Cons is also parameterized by the element type T. The cons cell declares that the next field is owned by the owner of the current cell, so that all the links in the list have the same owning domain. Back in the Sequence class, the head field has type owned Cons<T>, meaning that the field refers to a Cons object in the owned domain with the type parameter T.

```
interface Iterator<T> {
  T next();
  boolean hasNext();
}

class SequenceIterator<T, domain list> implements Iterator<T>
          assumes list -> T.owner {
  SequenceIterator<T, domain list>(list Cons<T> head) { current = head; }
  list Cons<T> current;

  boolean hasNext() { return current != null; }
  T next() {
    T obj = current.obj;
    current = current.next;
    return obj;
  }
}
```

Fig. 4. An iterator interface and a sequence iterator that implements the interface

In our proposed system, not only is the assumption `owner -> T.owner` a default, but every object has a `owned` domain by default that is linked to each of the domains of type parameters (such as `T.owner`). Also, every field of an object is `owned` by default. This means that in Figure 3, most of the ownership declarations may be omitted. The only declarations that are necessary are the `owner` annotations on `next` in `Cons`, and the declarations that have to do with iterators (discussed below). Thus, in the common case where a single domain per object is sufficient, and where domain parameters match the type parameters of Generic Java, there is very little programming overhead to using our system.

2.3 Expressing Iterators

It is typical for abstract data types like `Sequence` to provide a way for clients to iterate over their contents, but expressing iterators in previous ownership type systems presents a problem. If the iterator is part of a client's ownership domain, then it cannot access the links in the list, and so it cannot be implemented. However, if the iterator is part of the internal `owned` domain, the iterator will be useless because clients cannot access it. Previous solutions to this problem have been ad-hoc and often restrictive: for example, allowing iterators on the stack but not on the heap [11] or supporting iterator-like functionality only if the iterators are implemented as inner classes [10,8].

Intuitively, the iterators are part of the public interface of the sequence: they should be accessible to clients, but they should also be able to access the internals of the sequence [22]. With ownership domains, this intuition can be expressed in a straightforward manner. A second domain, `iters`, is declared to hold the

```
class SequenceClient {
  domain state;
  final state Sequence<state Object> seq = new Sequence<state Object>();

  void run() {
    state Object obj = ...
    seq.add(obj);

    seq.iters Iterator<state Object> i = seq.getIter();
    while (i.hasNext()) {
      state Object cur = i.next();
      doSomething(cur);
    }
  }
}
```

Fig. 5. A client of the Sequence

iterators of the sequence. So that clients can use the iterator objects, we make the `iters` domain public. In our system, permission to access the sequence implies permission to access its public domains.

In order to allow the iterator to access the elements and links in the sequence, we link the `iters` domain to the `T.owner` and `owned` domains. Then we can write a `getIter` method that creates a new `SequenceIterator` object and returns it as part of the `iters` domain.

The definitions of the `Iterator` interface and the concrete `SequenceIterator` class are shown in Figure 4. The `Iterator` interface has a single type parameter `T` to capture the class and owner of the elements over which it iterates. The `SequenceIterator` class has the type parameter `T` and also a *domain parameter* `list`, because its internal implementation must be able to refer to the `Cons` objects in the sequence. The domain parameter is just like a type parameter except it holds only a domain, not a full type. The `list` domain is used within the `SequenceIterator` to refer to the owner of the `Cons` cells.

The `SequenceIterator` class assumes that the `list` domain parameter has permission to refer to objects in the `T.owner` domain. This assumption is needed to fulfill the assumptions that `Cons` makes.

2.4 Using Sequence

Figure 5 shows a client of the `Sequence` ADT. The client declares some domain, `state`, which holds both the sequence and its elements. Thus the `Sequence` type is parameterized by the type `state Object`, meaning objects of class `Object` that are part of the `state` domain. The `run` method creates an object in the `state` domain, and adds it to the sequence. It then calls `getIter` to get an iterator for the sequence. The iterator is in the `iters` domain of the sequence.

Since each sequence has its own `iters` domain, we need to prefix the domain name by the object that declared it. In order to ensure type safety, the program source can only refer to domains of `final` variables such as `seq`–otherwise, we could assign another sequence to the `seq` variable and the type system would lose track of the relationship between a sequence object and its iterators.

2.5 Properties: Link Soundness

Our type system ensures *link soundness*, the property that the domain and link declarations in the system conservatively describe all aliasing that could take place at run time. Here we define link soundness in precise but informal language; section 3.5 defines link soundness formally and proves that our type system enforces the property.

To state link soundness precisely, we need a few preliminary definitions. First, we say that object o *refers to* object o' if o has a field that points to o', or else a method with receiver o is executing and some expression in that method evaluates to o'. We will say that object o declares a domain d or a link between domains d and d' if the class of o declares a domain or a link between domains that, when o is instantiated, refer to d and d'. Finally, we say that object o *has permission to access* domain d if one of the following conditions holds:

1. o is in domain d', and some object declares a link of the form `link` d' `->` d.
2. o has permission to access object o', and o' declares a public domain d.
3. o is part of domain d.
4. d is a domain declared by o.

These rules simply state the conditions in the introduction to section 2 more precisely. We can now define link soundness using the definitions above:

Definition 1 (Link Soundness). *If an object o refers to object o' and o' is in domain d, then o has permission to access domain d.*

Discussion. In order for link soundness to be meaningful, we must ensure that objects can't use `link` declarations or auxiliary objects to violate the intent of linking specifications. For example, in Figure 1, the `customer` should not be able to give itself access to the `bank`'s `vaults` domain. We can ensure this with the following restriction:

- Each `link` declaration must include a locally-declared domain.

Furthermore, even though the `agents` domain is local to the `customer` object, the `customer` should not be able to give the `agents` any privileges that the `customer` does not have itself. The following rules ensure that local domains obey the same restrictions as their enclosing objects or domains:

- An object can only link a local domain to an external domain d if the `this` object has permission to access d.
- An object can only link an external domain d to a local domain if d has permission to access the `owner` domain.

Finally, the customer should not be able to get to the bank's `vaults` domain by creating its own objects in the `tellers` domain:

- An object o can only create objects in domains declared by o, or in the `owner` domain of o, or in the `shared` domain.

Unlike many previous ownership type systems, our system does not have a rule giving an object permission to access all enclosing domains. This permission can be granted using `link` declarations if needed, but developers can constrain aliasing more precisely by leaving this permission out.

Relation to Previous Work. Previous ownership type systems have enforced the owners-as-dominators property: all paths to an object in a system must go through that object's owner. The link soundness property is more flexible than owners-as-dominators, since it can express examples like the `Iterator` in section 2.3 that violate the owners-as-dominators constraint. However, ownership domains can be used to enforce owners-as-dominators if programmers obey the following guidelines:

- Never declare a public domain.
- Never link a domain parameter to an internal domain.

These guidelines ensure that the rules for link declarations and public domains (rules #1 and #2 above) cannot be used to access internal domains. Rule #3 does not apply, and the only other way to access internal domains is through the object that declared them (rule #4), which is what owners-as-dominators requires.

These guidelines show that previous ownership type systems are essentially a special case of ownership domains. Thus, ownership domains provide a tradeoff between reasoning and expressiveness. Engineers can use ownership domains to enforce owners-as-dominators when this property is needed, but can also use a more flexible alias-control policy in order to express idioms like iterators.

2.6 Listener Callbacks

The listener idiom, an instance of the subject-observer design pattern [14], is very common in object-oriented libraries such as the Java Swing GUI. This pattern is often implemented as shown in Figure 6, where a `Listener` object creates a callback object that is invoked when some event occurs in the event `Generator` being observed. Expressing this idiom is impossible in ownership type systems that enforce owners-as-dominators, since the callback object is visible from the `Generator` but keeps internal references to the state of the `Listener`.

Using ownership domains, we can express this example as shown in Figure 6. The `ListenerSystem` declares domains representing the `generator` and `listener`, and links the `generator` domain to the `listener` domain so that it can pass the listener's callback to the generator. The `Generator` class needs to

```
class ListenerSystem {
   domain generator, listener;
   link generator->listener;
   generator Generator<l.callbacks Callback> s;
   final listener Listener l;
   ... s.callback = l.getCallback(); ...
}

class Generator<CB> {
   CB callback;
   ... callback.notify(data) ...
}

class Listener {
   public domain callbacks;
   domain state;
   link callbacks -> state;
   callbacks Callback getCallback() {
      return new ListenerCB<state>(...)
   }
}

interface Callback { void notify(int data); }
class ListenerCB<domain state> implements Callback {
   void notify(int data) { /* modify state */ }
}
```

Fig. 6. A Listener system.

store a reference to the callback object, so it is parameterized by the callback type CB.

Like the `Sequence` class described earlier, the `Listener` declares a private domain for its internal state and a public one for its callback objects, linking the `callback` domain to the `state` domain. The `ListenerCB` object implements the `Callback` interface, storing a reference to the listener's state and performing some action on that state when the `notify` method is invoked.

2.7 Expressing Architectural Constraints

One of our goals in designing ownership domains was to express aliasing constraints between different components in the architecture of a program. Figure 7 shows how the aliasing constraints in two different architectural styles can be expressed with ownership domains. The code in the first example represents a layered architecture [15] by creating an ownership domain for each layer. The link specifications express the constraint that objects in each layer can only refer to objects in the layer below.

```
class LayeredArchitecture {
   domain layer1, layer2, layer3;
   link layer2->layer1, layer3->layer2;
   ...
}

class MediatorArchitecture {
   domain component1, component2, component3;
   domain mediator;
   link component1->mediator, component2->mediator, component3->mediator;
   link mediator->component1, mediator->component2, mediator->component3;
}
```

Fig. 7. A layered architecture and a mediator architecture

The second example shows an architecture in which three different components communicate through a mediator component [26]. Again, the three components and the mediator are represented with domains. However, in this case, the aliasing pattern forms a star with the mediator in the center and the components as the points of the star. The link soundness property can then be used to guarantee that the individual components communicate only indirectly through the mediator. This property is crucial to gain the primary benefit of the mediator style: components in the system can be developed, deployed, and evolved independently from each other.

In both examples, the ability to create multiple ownership domains in one object and to specify aliasing constraints between them is crucial for specifying the architectural structure of the system. The use of ownership domains to specify architectural aliasing complements our earlier work specifying architectural interfaces and control flow in a different extension of Java [3].

2.8 Extensions

The AliasJava compiler includes an implementation of ownership domains as well as a number of useful extensions. A `unique` annotation indicates that there is only one persistent external reference to an object (we allow internal references to unique objects, providing *external uniqueness* [12] in the more flexible setting of ownership domains). Unique objects can later be assigned to a domain, at which point the type system verifies the object's linking assumptions that relate the owner domain to the parameter domains (in order to do this check soundly, we also verify that the domain parameters of a unique object are not "forgotten" by subsumption).

A `lent` annotation indicates a temporary reference to an object. A `unique` or `owned` object can be passed as a `lent` argument of a function, giving that function temporary access to the object but ensuring that the function does not store a persistent reference to the object. AliasJava supports method parameterization (and the corresponding `assumes` clauses) in addition to class parameterization. In the future, we may add support for package-level domains (generalizing confinement [7]) and for readonly types [21].

3 Formalizing Ownership Domains

We would like to use formal techniques to prove that our type system is safe and preserves the intended aliasing invariants. A standard technique, exemplified by Featherweight Java [18], is to formalize a core language that captures the key typing issues while ignoring complicating language details. We have formalized ownership domains as Featherweight Domain Java (FDJ), a core language based on Featherweight Java (FJ).

Featherweight Domain Java makes a number of simplifications relative to the full Java language. As in FJ, the model omits interfaces, inner classes, and some statement and expression forms, since these constructs can be written in terms of more fundamental ones. In order to focus exclusively on ownership domains, FDJ omits other constructs like `shared` that can be modeled with syntactic sugar. These omissions make the formal system simple enough to permit effective reasoning, while still capturing the core constructs of ownership domains.

Although Featherweight Java has been extended with type parameters [18], we model only domain parameters in order to simplify the system. The user-level system can be translated into the formal one by replacing each type parameter with a domain parameter, by replacing uses of the type parameter with the domain parameter applied to class `Object`, and by inserting casts where necessary.

3.1 Syntax

Figure 8 shows the syntax of FDJ. The metavariable C ranges over class names; T ranges over types; f ranges over fields; v ranges over values; e ranges over expressions; x ranges over variable and domain names; n ranges over values and variable names; S ranges over stores; ℓ ranges over locations in the store, α and β range over formal ownership domain parameters, and m ranges over method names. As a shorthand, an overbar is used to represent a sequence.

In FDJ, classes are parameterized by a list of ownership domains, and extend another class that has a subsequence of its domain parameters. An `assumes` clause states the linking assumptions that a class makes about its domain parameters. Our formal system does not have the default linking assumptions that are present in the real system; thus all assumptions must be specified explicitly. Each class defines a constructor and sets of fields, domains, link specifications, and methods. The canonical class constructor just assigns the constructor arguments to the fields of the class, while methods use standard Java syntax. We assume a predefined class `Object` that has no fields, domains, or methods.

Source-level expressions e_s include object creation expressions, field reads, casts, and method calls. Although FDJ is a pure language without field assignment, we want to reason about aliasing, and so we use locations to represent

$$
\begin{aligned}
CL &::= \texttt{class } C\texttt{<}\overline{\alpha},\overline{\beta}\texttt{>} \texttt{ extends } C'\texttt{<}\overline{\alpha}\texttt{>} \texttt{ assumes } \overline{\gamma} \rightarrow \overline{\delta} \; \{ \; \overline{T} \; \overline{f}; \; K \; \overline{D} \; \overline{L} \; \overline{M} \; \} \\
K &::= C(\overline{T'} \; \overline{f'}, \overline{T} \; \overline{f})\{\texttt{super}(\overline{f'}); \texttt{this}.\overline{f} = \overline{f};\} \\
D &::= [\texttt{public}] \; \texttt{domain } x; \\
L &::= \texttt{link } d \rightarrow d';
\end{aligned}
$$

$$
\begin{aligned}
M &::= T_R \; m(\overline{T} \; \overline{x}) \; \{ \; \texttt{return } e; \; \} \\
e_s &::= x \mid \texttt{new } C\texttt{<}\overline{\alpha}\texttt{>}(\overline{e}) \\
&\quad \mid \; e.f \mid (T)e \mid e.m(\overline{e}) \\
e &::= e_s \mid \ell \mid \ell > e \mid \texttt{error} \\
n &::= x \mid v \\
T &::= C\texttt{<}\overline{d}\texttt{>} \mid \texttt{ERROR} \\
d &::= \alpha \mid n.x
\end{aligned}
$$

$$
\begin{aligned}
v, \ell &\in \mathit{locations} \\
S &::= \ell \mapsto C\texttt{<}\overline{\ell.x}\texttt{>}(\overline{v}) \\
\Gamma &::= x \mapsto T \\
\Sigma &::= \ell \mapsto T
\end{aligned}
$$

Fig. 8. Featherweight Domain Java Syntax

object identity. A store S maps locations ℓ to their contents: the class of the object, the actual ownership domain parameters, and the values stored in its fields. We will write $S[\ell]$ to denote the store entry for ℓ and $S[\ell, i]$ to denote the value in the ith field of $S[\ell]$. Adding an entry for location ℓ to the store is abbreviated $S[\ell \mapsto C\texttt{<}\overline{\ell.x}\texttt{>}(\overline{\ell'})]$.

Several method calls may be executing on the stack at once, and to reason about ownership we will need to know the receiver of each executing call. Therefore, there are additional expression forms e that can occur during reduction, including locations ℓ. The expression form $\ell > e$ represents a method body e executing with a receiver ℓ. An explicit `error` expression is used to represent the result of a failed cast.

The result of computation is a location ℓ, which is sometimes referred to as a value v. The class of names n includes both values and variables. The set of variables includes the distinguished variable `this` used to refer to the receiver of a method. A domain is either one of the domain parameters α of the class, or else a pair of a name n (which can be `this`) and a domain name x. Neither the `error` expression, nor locations, nor $\ell > e$ expressions may appear in the source text of the program; these forms are only generated during reduction.

A type in FDJ is a class name and a set of actual ownership domain parameters. We simplify the formal system slightly by treating the first domain parameter of a class as its owning domain. We use a slightly different syntax in the practical system to emphasize the semantic difference between the owner domain of an object and its domain parameters.

$$\frac{l \notin domain(S) \qquad S' = S[\ell \mapsto C\texttt{<}\overline{d}\texttt{>}(\overline{v})]}{S \vdash \texttt{new}\ C\texttt{<}\overline{d}\texttt{>}(\overline{v}) \mapsto \ell, S'} \ \textit{R-New}$$

$$\frac{S[\ell] = C\texttt{<}\overline{d}\texttt{>}(\overline{v}) \qquad fields(C\texttt{<}\overline{d}\texttt{>}) = \overline{T}\ \overline{f}}{S \vdash \ell.f_i \mapsto v_i, S} \ \textit{R-Read}$$

$$\frac{S[\ell] = C\texttt{<}\overline{d}\texttt{>}(\overline{v}) \qquad C\texttt{<}\overline{d}\texttt{>} <: T}{S \vdash (T)\ell \mapsto \ell, S} \ \textit{R-Cast}$$

$$\frac{S[\ell] = C\texttt{<}\overline{d}\texttt{>}(\overline{v}) \qquad C\texttt{<}\overline{d}\texttt{>} \not<: T}{S \vdash (T)\ell \mapsto \texttt{error}, S} \ \textit{E-Cast}$$

$$\frac{S[\ell] = C\texttt{<}\overline{d}\texttt{>}(\overline{v}) \qquad mbody(m, C\texttt{<}\overline{d}\texttt{>}) = (\overline{x}, e_0)}{S \vdash \ell.m(\overline{v}) \mapsto \ell > [\overline{v}/\overline{x}, \ell/\texttt{this}]e_0, S} \ \textit{R-Invk}$$

$$\frac{}{S \vdash \ell > v \mapsto v, S} \ \textit{R-Context}$$

Fig. 9. Dynamic Semantics

We assume a fixed class table CT mapping classes to their definitions. A program, then, is a tuple (CT, S, e) of a class table, a store, and an expression.

Expressiveness. While FDJ has been simplified considerably from the full semantics of ownership domains in Java, it is still quite expressive. The example code in Figures 3-7 can be expressed in FDJ with some minor rewriting. For example, the FDJ `Cons` class below differs from the code in Figure 3 in that the `owner` parameter is explicit; the type parameter `T` is replaced with domain parameter `elemOwner`; and the `extends` clause is explicit. In addition, the owner domain of the field and method argument types is specified as the first parameter instead of appearing before the type name.

```
class Cons<owner, elemOwner> extends Object<owner>
          assumes owner -> elemOwner {
  Cons(Object<elemOwner> obj, Cons<owner,elemOwner> next) {
    this.obj=obj; this.next=next;
  }
  Object<elemOwner> obj;
  Cons<owner,elemOwner> next;
}
```

3.2 Reduction Rules

The evaluation relation, defined by the reduction rules given in Figure 9, is of the form $S \vdash e \mapsto e', S'$, read "In the context of store S, expression e reduces to expression e' in one step, producing the new store S'." We write $\mapsto^*$ for the

$$\frac{CT(C) = \texttt{class}\ C\texttt{<}\overline{\alpha,\beta}\texttt{>}\ \texttt{extends}\ C'\texttt{<}\overline{\alpha}\texttt{>} \ldots}{C\texttt{<}\overline{d,d'}\texttt{>}\ <:\ C'\texttt{<}\overline{d}\texttt{>}}\ \textit{Subtype-Class}$$

$$\frac{}{T <: T}\ \textit{Subtype-Reflex} \qquad \frac{T <: T' \quad T' <: T''}{T <: T''}\ \textit{Subtype-Trans}$$

$$\frac{}{\texttt{ERROR} <: T}\ \textit{Subtype-Error}$$

Fig. 10. Subtyping Rules

reflexive, transitive closure of $\mapsto$. Most of the rules are standard; the interesting features are how they track ownership domains.

The *R-New* rule reduces an object creation expression to a fresh location. The store is extended at that location to refer to a class with the specified ownership parameters, with the fields set to the values passed to the constructor.

The *R-Read* rule looks up the receiver in the store and identifies the ith field using the $fields$ helper function (defined in Figure 14). The result is the value at field position i in the store. As in Java (and FJ), the *R-Cast* rule checks that the cast expression is a subtype of the cast type. Note, however, that in FDJ this check also verifies that the ownership domain parameters match, doing an extra run-time check that is not present in Java. If the run-time check in the cast rule fails, however, then the cast reduces to the `error` expression, following the cast error rule *E-Cast*. This rule shows how the formal system models the exception that is thrown by the full language when a cast fails.

The method invocation rule *R-Invk* looks up the receiver in the store, then uses the *mbody* helper function (defined in Figure 14) to determine the correct method body to invoke. The method invocation is replaced with the appropriate method body, where all occurrences of the formal method parameters and `this` are replaced with the actual arguments and the receiver, respectively. Here, the capture-avoiding substitution of values $\overline{v}$ for variables $\overline{x}$ in e is written $[\overline{v}/\overline{x}]e$. Execution of the method body continues in the context of the receiver location.

When a method expression reduces to a value, the *R-Context* rule propagates the value outside of its method context and into the surrounding method expression. As this rule shows, expressions of the form $\ell > e$ do not affect program execution, and are used only for reasoning about invariants that are necessary for link soundness. The full definition of FDJ, in a companion technical report [2], also includes congruence rules that allow reduction to proceed within an expression in the the order of evaluation defined by Java. For example, the read rule states that an expression $e.f$ reduces to $e'.f$ whenever e reduces to e'.

3.3 Typing Rules

FDJ's subtyping rules are given in Figure 10. Subtyping is derived from the immediate subclass relation given by the `extends` clauses in the class table CT.

$$\frac{}{\Gamma, \Sigma, n_{this} \vdash x : \Gamma(x)}\ \textit{T-Var} \qquad \frac{}{\Gamma, \Sigma, n_{this} \vdash \ell : \Sigma(\ell)}\ \textit{T-Loc}$$

$$\frac{\begin{array}{cc} \Gamma, \Sigma, n_{this} \models \textit{assumptions}(C\texttt{<}\overline{d}\texttt{>}) & \Gamma, \Sigma, n_{this} \vdash \overline{e} : \overline{T'} \\ \textit{fields}(C\texttt{<}\overline{d}\texttt{>}) = \overline{T}\ \overline{f} \quad \overline{T'} <: \overline{T} & \Gamma, \Sigma, n_{this} \vdash n_{this} : T_{this} \\ \multicolumn{2}{c}{\textit{owner}(C\texttt{<}\overline{d}\texttt{>}) \in (\textit{domains}(T_{this}) \cup \textit{owner}(T_{this}))} \end{array}}{\Gamma, \Sigma, n_{this} \vdash \texttt{new}\ C\texttt{<}\overline{d}\texttt{>}(\overline{e}) : C\texttt{<}\overline{d}\texttt{>}}\ \textit{T-New}$$

$$\frac{}{\Gamma, \Sigma, n_{this} \vdash \texttt{error} : \texttt{ERROR}}\ \textit{T-Error}$$

$$\frac{\Gamma, \Sigma, n_{this} \vdash e_0 : T_0 \qquad \textit{fields}(T_0) = \overline{T}\ \overline{f}}{\Gamma, \Sigma, n_{this} \vdash e_0.f_i : T_i}\ \textit{T-Read}$$

$$\frac{\Gamma, \Sigma, n_{this} \vdash e : T'}{\Gamma, \Sigma, n_{this} \vdash (T)\ e : T}\ \textit{T-Cast}$$

$$\frac{\begin{array}{cc} \Gamma, \Sigma, n_{this} \vdash e_0 : T_0 & \Gamma, \Sigma, n_{this} \vdash \overline{e} : \overline{T_a} \\ \textit{mtype}(m, T_0) = \overline{T} \to T_R & \overline{T_a} <: [\overline{e}/\overline{x}, e_0/\texttt{this}]\ \overline{T} \end{array}}{\Gamma, \Sigma, n_{this} \vdash e_0.m(\overline{e}) : [\overline{e}/\overline{x}, e_0/\texttt{this}]\ T_R}\ \textit{T-Invk}$$

$$\frac{\Gamma, \Sigma, \ell \vdash e : T}{\Gamma, \Sigma, n_{this} \vdash \ell > e : T}\ \textit{T-Context}$$

Fig. 11. Typechecking

The subtyping relation is reflexive and transitive, and it is required that there be no cycles in the relation (other than self-cycles due to reflexivity). The ERROR type is a subtype of every type.

Typing judgments, shown in Figure 11, are of the form $\Gamma, \Sigma, n_{this} \vdash e : T$, read, "In the type environment Γ, store typing Σ, and receiver n_{this}, expression e has type T."

The *T-Var* rule looks up the type of a variable in Γ. The *T-Loc* rule looks up the type of a location in Σ. The object creation rule verifies that any assumptions (see Figure 14) that the class being instantiated makes about its domain parameters are justified based on the current typing environment. The entailment relation $\models$ for linking assumptions will be defined below in Figure 13. The creation rule also checks that the parameters to the constructor have types that match the types of that class's fields. Finally, it verifies that the object being created is part of the same domain as n_{this} or else is part of the domains declared by n_{this} (the *domains* function is defined in Figure 14, and the *owner* function gets the owner of n_{this} by extracting the first owner parameter from T).

The typing rule for `error` assigns it the type ERROR. The rule for field reads looks up the declared type of the field using the *fields* function defined in Figure 14. The cast rule simply checks that the expression being cast is well-typed; a run-time check will determine if the value that comes out of the expression

$$\frac{\begin{array}{c}\overline{M}\ OK\ in\ C \qquad fields(C'{<}\overline{\alpha}{>}) = \overline{T'}\ \overline{g} \qquad \overline{L}\ OK\ in\ C{<}\overline{\alpha},\overline{\beta}{>} \\ \{\mathtt{this} : C{<}\overline{\alpha},\overline{\beta}{>}\},\ \emptyset,\ \mathtt{this} \models (\mathtt{this} \rightarrow owner(\overline{T})) \\ K = C{<}\overline{\alpha},\overline{\beta}{>}(\overline{T'}\ \overline{g},\ \overline{T}\ \overline{f})\ \{\ super(\overline{g});\ this.\overline{f} = \overline{f};\ \}\end{array}}{\mathtt{class}\ C{<}\overline{\alpha},\overline{\beta}{>}\ \mathtt{extends}\ C'{<}\overline{\alpha}{>}\ \mathtt{assumes}\ \overline{\gamma} \rightarrow \overline{\delta}\ \{\ \overline{T}\ \overline{f};\ K\ \overline{D};\ \overline{L};\ \overline{M};\}\ OK}\ \textit{ClsOK}$$

$$\frac{\begin{array}{c}CT(C) = \mathtt{class}\ C{<}\overline{\alpha},\overline{\beta}{>}\ \mathtt{extends}\ C'{<}\overline{\alpha}{>}\ldots \\ override(m, C'{<}\overline{\alpha}{>}, \overline{T} \rightarrow T_R) \\ \{\overline{x} : \overline{T},\ \mathtt{this} : C{<}\overline{\alpha},\overline{\beta}{>}\},\ \emptyset,\ \mathtt{this} \vdash e : T_R \qquad T_R <: T \\ \{\overline{x} : \overline{T},\ \mathtt{this} : C{<}\overline{\alpha},\overline{\beta}{>}\},\ \emptyset,\ \mathtt{this} \models (\mathtt{this} \rightarrow owner(\overline{T}))\end{array}}{T_R\ m(\overline{T}\ \overline{x})\ \{\ \mathtt{return}\ e;\ \}\ OK\ in\ C}\ \textit{MethOK}$$

$$\frac{\begin{array}{c}\{d_1, d_2\} \cap domains(C{<}\overline{\alpha}{>}) \neq \emptyset \\ d_1 \notin domains(C{<}\overline{\alpha}{>}) \implies (\mathtt{this} : C{<}\overline{\alpha}{>}, \emptyset, \mathtt{this} \models d_1 \rightarrow owner(C{<}\overline{\alpha}{>})) \\ d_2 \notin domains(C{<}\overline{\alpha}{>}) \implies (\mathtt{this} : C{<}\overline{\alpha}{>}, \emptyset, \mathtt{this} \models \mathtt{this} \rightarrow d_2)\end{array}}{\mathtt{link}\ d_1 \rightarrow d_2\ OK\ in\ C{<}\overline{\alpha}{>}}\ \textit{LinkOK}$$

$$\frac{\forall \ell \in domain(\Sigma)\ \emptyset, \Sigma, \ell \models assumptions(\Sigma[\ell]))}{\Sigma\ OK}\ \textit{T-Assumptions}$$

$$\frac{\begin{array}{c}domain(S) = domain(\Sigma) \qquad S[\ell] = C{<}\overline{\ell'.x}{>}(\overline{v}) \iff \Sigma[\ell] = C{<}\overline{\ell'.x}{>} \\ (S[\ell, i] = \ell'') \wedge (fields(\Sigma[\ell]) = \overline{T}\ \overline{f}) \implies (\Sigma[\ell''] <: T_i) \qquad \Sigma\ OK \\ (S[\ell, i] = \ell'') \implies (\emptyset, \Sigma, \ell \models \ell \rightarrow owner(\Sigma[\ell'']))\end{array}}{\Sigma \vdash S}\ \textit{T-Store}$$

Fig. 12. Class, Method and Store Typing

matches the type of the cast. Our cast rule is simpler than Featherweight Java's in that we omit the check for "stupid casts."

Rule *T-Invk* looks up the invoked method's type using the *mtype* function defined in Figure 14, and verifies that the actual argument types are subtypes of the method's argument types. The method's nominal argument and result types must have actual parameter values substituted for formals, so that domain names that are qualified by a formal parameter are compared properly in the calling context. Finally, the *T-Context* typing rule for an executing method checks the method's body in the context of the new receiver ℓ.

Finally, for each rule of the form $\Gamma, \Sigma, n_{this} \vdash e : T$ we include an implicit check that $T \neq \mathtt{ERROR} \implies \Gamma, \Sigma, n_{this} \models n_{this} \rightarrow owner(T)$. This implicit check verifies that the current object named by n_{this} has permission to access the owning domain of the expression.

Figure 12 shows the rules for typing classes, declarations within classes, and the store. The typing rules for classes and declarations have the form "class C is OK," and "method/link declaration is OK in C." The class rule checks that the

$$\frac{(d_1 \to d_2) \in links(\Sigma[\ell])}{\Gamma, \Sigma, n_{this} \models (d_1 \to d_2)} \quad \textit{T-DynamicLink}$$

$$\frac{\Gamma, \Sigma, n_{this} \vdash n_{this} : T \qquad (d_1 \to d_2) \in linkdecls(T)}{\Gamma, \Sigma, n_{this} \models (d_1 \to d_2)} \quad \textit{T-DeclaredLink}$$

$$\frac{}{\Gamma, \Sigma, n_{this} \models (n \to n.x)} \quad \textit{T-ChildRef} \qquad \frac{}{\Gamma, \Sigma, n_{this} \models (d \to d)} \quad \textit{T-SelfLink}$$

$$\frac{\Gamma, \Sigma, n_{this} \vdash n : T \qquad \Gamma, \Sigma, n_{this} \models (owner(T) \to d)}{\Gamma, \Sigma, n_{this} \models (n \to d)} \quad \textit{T-LinkRef}$$

$$\frac{\Gamma, \Sigma, n_{this} \vdash n : T \qquad \Gamma, \Sigma, n_{this} \models (d \to owner(T)) \qquad public(x)}{\Gamma, \Sigma, n_{this} \models (d \to n.x)} \quad \textit{T-PublicLink}$$

$$\frac{\Gamma, \Sigma, n_{this} \vdash n : T \qquad \Gamma, \Sigma, n_{this} \models (n_s \to owner(T)) \qquad public(x)}{\Gamma, \Sigma, n_{this} \models (n_s \to n.x)} \quad \textit{T-PublicRef}$$

Fig. 13. Link Permission Rules

methods and links in the class are well-formed, and that the "this" references is allowed to access the domains of the fields in the class.

The rule for methods checks that the method body is well typed, and uses the *override* function (defined in Figure 14) to verify that methods are overridden with a method of the same type. It also verifies that the "this" reference has permission to access the domains of the arguments of the method.

The link rule verifies that one of the two domains in the link declaration was declared locally, preventing a class from linking two external domains together. The rule also ensures that if the declaration links an internal and an external domain, there is a corresponding linking relationship between `this` and the external domain.

The store typing rule ensures that the store type gives a type to each location in the store's domain that is consistent with the classes and ownership parameters in the actual store. For every value in a field in the store, the type of the value must be a subtype of the declared type of the field. The check $\Sigma\ OK$, defined by the *T-Assumptions* rule, verifies that all the linking assumptions made for each object in the store are justified based on actual link declarations in the source code. Finally, the last check verifies link soundness for the store: if object ℓ refers to object ℓ'' in it's ith field, then the link declarations implied by the store type Σ imply that ℓ has permission to access the domain of ℓ''.

Figure 13 shows the rules for determining whether an object named by n or a domain d has permission to access another domain d'. These rules come in two forms: $\Gamma, \Sigma, n_{this} \models (n \to d)$ and $\Gamma, \Sigma, n_{this} \models (d \to d')$. The first form of rule is read, "Given the type environment Γ, the store type Σ, and a name for the current object n_{this}, the object named by n has permission to access domain

d." The second form is similar, except that the conclusion is that any object in domain d has permission to access domain d'. The two forms allow us to reason about access permission both on a per-object basis and on a per-domain basis.

The *T-DynamicLink* rule can be used to conclude that two domains are linked if there is an object in the store that explicitly linked them. The *T-DeclaredLink* rule allows the type system to rely on any links that are declared or assumed in the context of the class of n_{this}. The *T-ChildRef* rule states that any object named by n has permission to access one of its own domains $n.x$. The *T-SelfLink* rule states that every domain can access itself. The *T-LinkRef* rule allows the object named by n to access a domain if the owner of n can access that domain. The *T-PublicLink* and *T-PublicRef* rules allow objects and domains to access the public domain of some object in a domain they already have access to.

Figure 14 shows the definitions of many auxiliary functions used earlier in the semantics. These definitions are straightforward and in many cases are derived directly from rules in Featherweight Java. The Aux-Public rule checks whether a domain is public. The next few rules define the *domains*, *links*, *assumptions*, and *fields* functions by looking up the declarations in the class and adding them to the declarations in superclasses. The *linkdecls* function just returns the union of the *links* and *assumptions* in a class, while the *owner* function just returns the first domain parameter (which represents the owning domain in our formal system).

The *mtype* function looks up the type of a method in the class; if the method is not present, it looks in the superclass instead. The *mbody* function looks up the body of a method in a similar way. Finally, the *override* function verifies that if a superclass defines method m, it has the same type as the definition of m in a subclass.

3.4 Properties

In this section, we state type soundness and link soundness for Featherweight Domain Java. The full proofs are straightforward but tedious, and so we relegate them to a companion technical report [2].

Theorem 1 (Type Preservation).
If $\emptyset, \Sigma, n_{this} \vdash e : T$, $\Sigma \vdash S$, *and* $S \vdash e \mapsto e', S'$, *then there exists* $\Sigma' \supseteq \Sigma$ *and* $T' <: T$ *such that* $\emptyset, \Sigma', n_{this} \vdash e' : T'$ *and* $\Sigma' \vdash S'$.

Proof. By induction over the derivation of $S \vdash e \mapsto e', S'$.

Theorem 2 (Progress).
If $\emptyset, \Sigma, n_{this} \vdash e : T$ *and* $\Sigma \vdash S$ *then either* e *is a value or* e *has an* `error` *subexpression or* $S \vdash e \mapsto e', S'$.

Proof. By induction over the derivation of $\emptyset, \Sigma, n_{this} \vdash e : T$.

$$\frac{CT(C) = \texttt{class}\ C\texttt{<}\overline{\alpha},\overline{\beta}\texttt{>}\ \ldots\ \{\ \overline{T}\ \overline{f};\ \overline{D};\ \overline{L};\ \overline{M};\ \} \quad (\texttt{public domain}\ x) \in \overline{D}}{public(x)}\ \textit{Aux-Public}$$

$$\frac{CT(C) = \texttt{class}\ C\texttt{<}\overline{\alpha},\overline{\beta}\texttt{>}\ \texttt{extends}\ C'\texttt{<}\overline{\alpha}\texttt{>}\ \ldots\ \{\ \overline{T}\ \overline{f};\ \overline{D};\ \overline{L};\ \overline{M};\ \} \quad \overline{D} = \overline{\texttt{public}_{opt}\ \texttt{domain}\ x} \quad domains(C'\texttt{<}\overline{d}\texttt{>}) = \overline{d'}}{domains(C\texttt{<}\overline{d},\overline{d'}\texttt{>}) = \overline{this.x},\overline{d'}}\ \textit{Aux-Domains}$$

$$\frac{CT(C) = \texttt{class}\ C\texttt{<}\overline{\alpha},\overline{\beta}\texttt{>}\ \texttt{extends}\ C'\texttt{<}\overline{\alpha}\texttt{>}\ \ldots\ \{\ \overline{T}\ \overline{f};\ \overline{D};\ \overline{L};\ \overline{M};\ \} \quad \overline{L} = \overline{\texttt{link}\ d_c \rightarrow d'_c} \quad links(C'\texttt{<}\overline{d}\texttt{>}) = \overline{d_s} \rightarrow \overline{d'_s}}{links(C\texttt{<}\overline{d},\overline{d'}\texttt{>}) = ([\overline{d}/\overline{\alpha},\overline{d'}/\overline{\beta}]\ (\overline{d_c} \rightarrow \overline{d'_c})),\ \overline{d_s} \rightarrow \overline{d'_s}}\ \textit{Aux-Links}$$

$$\frac{CT(C) = \texttt{class}\ C\texttt{<}\overline{\alpha},\overline{\beta}\texttt{>}\ \texttt{extends}\ C'\texttt{<}\overline{\alpha}\texttt{>}\ \texttt{assumes}\ \overline{\gamma} \rightarrow \overline{\delta}\ldots \quad assumptions(C'\texttt{<}\overline{d}\texttt{>}) = \overline{d_s} \rightarrow \overline{d'_s}}{assumptions(C\texttt{<}\overline{d},\overline{d'}\texttt{>}) = ([\overline{d}/\overline{\alpha},\overline{d'}/\overline{\beta}]\ (\overline{\gamma} \rightarrow \overline{\delta})),\overline{d_s} \rightarrow \overline{d'_s}}\ \textit{Aux-Assume}$$

$$\frac{CT(C) = \texttt{class}\ C\texttt{<}\overline{\alpha},\overline{\beta}\texttt{>}\ \texttt{extends}\ C'\texttt{<}\overline{\alpha}\texttt{>}\ \ldots\ \{\ \overline{T}\ \overline{f};\ \overline{D};\ \overline{L};\ \overline{M};\ \} \quad fields(C'\texttt{<}\overline{d}\texttt{>}) = \overline{T'}\ \overline{f'}}{fields(C\texttt{<}\overline{d},\overline{d'}\texttt{>}) = ([\overline{d}/\overline{\alpha},\overline{d'}/\overline{\beta}]\ \overline{T}\ \overline{f}),\overline{T'}\ \overline{f'}}\ \textit{Aux-Fields}$$

$$\frac{}{linkdecls(C\texttt{<}\overline{d}\texttt{>}) = links(C\texttt{<}\overline{d}\texttt{>}) \cup assumptions(C\texttt{<}\overline{d}\texttt{>})}\ \textit{Aux-LinkDecls}$$

$$\frac{}{owner(C\texttt{<}\overline{d}\texttt{>}) = d_1}\ \textit{Aux-Owner}$$

$$\frac{CT(C) = \texttt{class}\ C\texttt{<}\overline{\alpha}\texttt{>}\ \ldots\ \{\ \overline{T}\ \overline{f};\ \overline{D};\ \overline{L};\ \overline{M};\ \} \quad (T_R\ m(\overline{T}\ \overline{x})\ \{\ \texttt{return}\ e;\ \}) \in \overline{M}}{mtype(m,C\texttt{<}\overline{d}\texttt{>}) = [\overline{d}/\overline{\alpha}]\ \overline{T} \rightarrow T_R}\ \textit{Aux-MType1}$$

$$\frac{CT(C) = \texttt{class}\ C\texttt{<}\overline{\alpha},\overline{\beta}\texttt{>}\ \texttt{extends}\ C'\texttt{<}\overline{\alpha}\texttt{>}\ \ldots\ \{\ \overline{T}\ \overline{f};\ \overline{D};\ \overline{L};\ \overline{M};\ \} \quad m\ is\ not\ defined\ in\ \overline{M}}{mtype(m,C\texttt{<}\overline{d},\overline{d'}\texttt{>}) = mtype(m,C'\texttt{<}\overline{d}\texttt{>})}\ \textit{Aux-MType2}$$

$$\frac{CT(C) = \texttt{class}\ C\texttt{<}\overline{\alpha}\texttt{>}\ \ldots\ \{\ \overline{T'}\ \overline{f};\ \overline{D};\ \overline{L};\ \overline{M};\ \} \quad (T_R\ m(\overline{T}\ \overline{x})\ \{\ \texttt{return}\ e;\ \}) \in \overline{M}}{mbody(m,C\texttt{<}\overline{d}\texttt{>}) = [\overline{d}/\overline{\alpha}]\ (\overline{x},\ e)}\ \textit{Aux-MBody1}$$

$$\frac{CT(C) = \texttt{class}\ C\texttt{<}\overline{\alpha},\overline{\beta}\texttt{>}\ \texttt{extends}\ C'\texttt{<}\overline{\alpha}\texttt{>}\ \ldots\ \{\ \overline{T}\ \overline{f};\ \overline{D};\ \overline{L};\ \overline{M};\ \} \quad m\ is\ not\ defined\ in\ \overline{M}}{mbody(m,C\texttt{<}\overline{d},\overline{d'}\texttt{>}) = mbody(m,C'\texttt{<}\overline{d}\texttt{>})}\ \textit{Aux-MBody2}$$

$$\frac{(mtype(m,C\texttt{<}\overline{d}\texttt{>}) = \overline{T'} \rightarrow T') \Longrightarrow (\overline{T} = \overline{T'} \wedge T = T')}{override(m,C\texttt{<}\overline{d}\texttt{>},\overline{T} \rightarrow T)}\ \textit{Aux-Override}$$

Fig. 14. Auxiliary Definitions

Together, Type Preservation and Progress imply that the type system for FDJ is sound. We also wish to state a link soundness property for FDJ. First, we define link soundness for the heap: if one object refers to another, then it has permission to do so.

Theorem 3 (Heap Link Soundness).
If $\Sigma \vdash S$ *and* $S[\ell, i] = \ell''$ *then* $\emptyset, \Sigma, \ell \models \ell \rightarrow owner(\Sigma[\ell''])$.

Proof. This property is enforced by the store typing rule *T-Store.*

In practice, it is important that link soundness hold not only for field references in the system, but also for expressions in methods. The intuition behind expression link soundness is that if a method with receiver object n_{this} is currently executing, it should only be able to compute with objects that n_{this} has permission to access.

Theorem 4 (Expression Link Soundness).
If $\emptyset, \Sigma, n_{this} \vdash e : T$ *and* $T \neq \texttt{ERROR}$ *then* $\emptyset, \Sigma, n_{this} \models (n_{this} \rightarrow owner(T))$.

Proof. As stated earlier, this condition is implicitly enforced by each typing rule of the form $\emptyset, \Sigma, n_{this} \vdash e : T$.

As a result of link soundness, developers using ownership domains can be confident that the linking specifications are an accurate representation of run time aliasing in the system.

4 Related Work

Ownership type systems. A number of early research projects, including Islands [17] and Balloons [5], provided a way to encapsulate one object within another. The term "ownership" is due to the Flexible Alias Protection project [23,13], which added ownership parameters in order to support object-oriented idioms like collection classes. These early systems all enforced the owners-as-dominators property (or even more restrictive properties).

A number of researchers have proposed solutions to the long-recognized problem of expressing iterators in ownership type systems. One solution is to allow dynamic aliases to internal ownership domains [11], breaking the owners-as-dominators property for variables on the stack. Since iterators are generally used only on the stack, this solution is sufficient for most uses of iterators. However, it has two drawbacks: *any* external object–not only trusted iterators–can access objects in private domains. In addition, this solution does not support idioms like event callback objects, which are generally used in a way that requires references to callback objects on the heap.

A more expressive, but somewhat ad-hoc solution was proposed by Clarke [10] and later adopted by Boyapati et al. [8]. This solution allows inner classes to violate the owners-as-dominators property, while enforcing it for all regular classes. This technique supports both iterators and event callbacks, but places some restrictions on implementors, because all iterators and callbacks must be implemented as inner classes (as they often, but not always, are in practice).

Our own previous work, AliasJava, uses a capability-based encapsulation model instead of owners-as-dominators [4]. In this model, the domain parameters of an object are capabilities allowing the object to access the objects in that domain. Thus, developers can reason about access permission by examining the parameterization of objects. Although this solution is more flexible than either of the solutions described above, reasoning about capabilities is not as straightforward as reasoning about object containment.

More recently, Potanin et al. propose a way to provide capability-based encapsulation with no changes to Java's syntax, instead enforcing a stylized use of Java's generics [24]. We build on their ideas (as well as those of Noble et al. [23]) to integrate genericity with ownership, but we introduce some new syntax in order to support stronger and more flexible alias-control policies.

Ownership domains, as presented in this paper, represent the first solution that supports flexible implementations of iterator and event idioms while also preserving clear reasoning about inter-domain aliasing. In addition, the ability to define multiple ownership domains per object and specify a fine-grained policy controlling inter-domain aliasing allows ownership domains to express architectural constraints that cannot be described in previous systems.

Several systems build on the owners-as-dominators property to provide secondary properties including safe concurrency [8], safe memory management [9], reasoning about effects [11], and abstraction [6]. Since ownership domains can be used to enforce owners-as-dominators, our system can support similar kinds of reasoning in a more flexible setting.

Clarke's thesis presents an object calculus that allows multiple *ownership contexts* to be defined for each object, similar to our ownership domains [10]. We build on this work with a concrete language design and increase expressiveness by by specifying aliasing policy separately from containment.

Other related work. Our previous work on ArchJava allows developers to document architectural designs similar to those described in Figure 7 [3]. The original ArchJava system provided a more detailed description of component interactions than ownership domains do, but did not constrain aliasing between components. The first author's dissertation demonstrates adding ownership domains to ArchJava in order to reason about data sharing between components as well [1]. Lam and Rinard express design information using tokens that are somewhat similar to ownership domains, but their system does not support hierarchical designs or important object-oriented constructs like inheritance [19].

Confined types [7] restrict aliases of an object to within a particular package, a weaker but more lightweight notion compared to the object-based encapsulation provided by ownership domains. The Universes system provides both object-based encapsulation and package-based encapsulation [21]. Systems like alias types [27] and separation logic [25] provide a finer control of aliasing compared to ownership domains, but are also much more heavyweight, requiring many more declarations to gain the same level of reasoning about aliasing.

Leino et al.'s data groups [20] and Greenhouse et al.'s regions [16] are similar to ownership domains. Here groups and regions refer to sets of fields rather than sets of objects, and are used to reason about effects rather than aliasing.

5 Conclusion and Future Work

This paper generalizes previous work on ownership type systems to support ownership domains. By separating alias-control policy from the ownership mechanism, we gain two primary benefits. First, programmers can express more flexible aliasing policies that naturally support common object-oriented idioms such as iterators and events. Second, programmers can specify high-level design information by declaring multiple ownership domains per object and specifying the aliasing relationship among these domains. Thus, ownership domains are both more flexible and more precise than previous ownership-based encapsulation mechanisms. In the future, we intend to perform case studies that will provide insights into the usability and benefits of ownership domains.

Acknowledgements. We would like to thank Donna Malayeri, John Boyland, Neel Krishnaswami, Aaron Greenhouse, members of the Cecil group, and the anonymous reviewers for their comments and suggestions. This work was supported in part by NSF grants CCR-9970986, CCR-0073379, and CCR-0204047, and gifts from Sun Microsystems and IBM.

References

1. J. Aldrich. *Using Types to Enforce Architectural Structure.* PhD thesis, University of Washington, August 2003.
2. J. Aldrich and C. Chambers. Ownership Domains: Separating Aliasing Policy from Mechanism. Carnegie Mellon Technical Report CMU-ISRI-04-110, available at http://www.cs.cmu.edu/~aldrich/papers/, April 2004.
3. J. Aldrich, C. Chambers, and D. Notkin. Architectural Reasoning with ArchJava. In *European Conference on Object-Oriented Programming*, June 2002.
4. J. Aldrich, V. Kostadinov, and C. Chambers. Alias Annotations for Program Understanding. In *Object-Oriented Programming Systems, Languages, and Applications*, November 2002.
5. P. S. Almeida. Balloon Types: Controlling Sharing of State in Data Types. In *European Conference on Object-Oriented Programming*, June 1997.
6. A. Banerjee and D. A. Naumann. Representation Independence, Confinement, and Access Control. In *Principles of Programming Languages*, January 2002.
7. B. Bokowski and J. Vitek. Confined Types. In *Object-Oriented Programming Systems, Languages, and Applications*, November 1999.
8. C. Boyapati, R. Lee, and M. Rinard. Ownership Types for Safe Programming: Preventing Data Races and Deadlocks. In *Object-Oriented Programming Systems, Languages, and Applications*, November 2002.

9. C. Boyapati, A. Salcianu, J. William Beebee, and M. Rinard. Ownership Types for Safe Region-Based Memory Mangement in Real-Time Java. In *Programming Language Design and Implementation*, June 2003.
10. D. Clarke. *Object Ownership & Containment*. PhD thesis, University of New South Wales, July 2001.
11. D. Clarke and S. Drossopoulou. Ownership, Encapsulation, and the Disjointness of Type and Effect. In *Object-Oriented Programming Systems, Languages, and Applications*, November 2002.
12. D. Clarke and T. Wrigstad. External Uniqueness is Unique Enough. In *European Conference on Object-Oriented Programming*, July 2003.
13. D. G. Clarke, J. M. Potter, and J. Noble. Ownership Types for Flexible Alias Protection. In *Object-Oriented Programming Systems, Languages, and Applications*, October 1998.
14. E. Gamma, R. Helm, R. Johnson, and J. Vlissides. *Design Patterns: Elements of Reusable Object-Oriented Software*. Addison-Wesley, 1994.
15. D. Garlan and M. Shaw. An Introduction to Software Architecture. In V. Ambriola and G. Tortora, editors, *Advances in Software Engineering and Knowledge Engineering, I*, 1993.
16. A. Greenhouse and J. Boyland. An Object-Oriented Effects System. In *European Conference on Object-Oriented Programming*, June 1999.
17. J. Hogg. Islands: Aliasing Protection in Object-Oriented Languages. In *Object-Oriented Programming Systems, Languages, and Applications*, October 1991.
18. A. Igarashi, B. Pierce, and P. Wadler. Featherwieght Java: a Minimal Core Calculus for Java and GJ. In *Object-Oriented Programming Systems, Languages, and Applications*, November 1999.
19. P. Lam and M. Rinard. A Type System and Analysis for the Automatic Extraction and Enforcement of Design Information. In *European Conference on Object-Oricnted Programming*, July 2003.
20. K. R. M. Leino, A. Poetzsch-Heffter, and Y. Zhou. Using Data Groups to Specify and Check Side Effects. In *Programming Language Design and Implementation*, June 2002.
21. P. Muller and A. Poetzsch-Heffter. Universes: A Type System for Controlling Representation Exposure. In A. Poetzsch-Heffter and J. Meyer, editors, *Programming Languages and Fundamentals of Programming*, 1999.
22. J. Noble, R. Biddle, E. Tempero, A. Potanin, and D. Clarke. Towards a Model of Encapsulation. In *Intercontinental Workshop on Aliasing, Confinement and Ownership in Object-Oriented Programming*, July 2003.
23. J. Noble, J. Vitek, and J. Potter. Flexible Alias Protection. In *European Conference on Object-Oriented Programming*, 1998.
24. A. Potanin, J. Noble, D. Clarke, and R. Biddle. Featherweight Generic Confinement. In *Foundations of Object-Oriented Languages*, January 2004.
25. J. C. Reynolds. Separation Logic: a Logic for Shared Mutable Data Structures. In *Logic in Computer Science*, July 2002.
26. K. Sullivan and D. Notkin. Reconciling Environment Integration and Software Evolution. *Transactions on Software Engineering and Methodology*, 1(3), July 1992.
27. D. Walker and G. Morrisett. Alias Types for Recursive Data Structures. In *International Workshop on Types in Compilation*, September 2000.

Composable Encapsulation Policies

Nathanael Schärli[1], Stéphane Ducasse, Oscar Nierstrasz, and Roel Wuyts[2]

[1] Software Composition Group
University of Bern
www.iam.unibe.ch/$\sim$scg
[2] Lab for Software Composition and Decomposition
Université Libre de Bruxelles
http://homepages.ulb.ac.be/$\sim$rowuyts/

Abstract. Given the importance of encapsulation to object-oriented programming, it is surprising to note that mainstream object-oriented languages offer only limited and fixed ways of encapsulating methods. Typically one may only address two categories of clients, users and heirs, and one must bind visibility and access rights at an early stage. This can lead to inflexible and fragile code as well as clumsy workarounds. We propose a simple and general solution to this problem in which encapsulation policies can be specified separately from implementations. As such they become composable entities that can be reused by different classes. We present a detailed analysis of the problem with encapsulation and visibility mechanisms in mainstream OO languages, we introduce our approach in terms of a simple model, and we evaluate how our approach compares with existing approaches. We also assess the impact of incorporating encapsulation policies into Smalltalk.

1 Introduction

Encapsulation is widely acknowledged as being one of the cornerstones of object-oriented programming [11]. Nevertheless, the term *encapsulation* is often used in inconsistent ways.

At the very least, encapsulation refers to the *bundling together of data and the operations that manipulate them*. That is, *information hiding* is not necessarily an essential component of encapsulation. At the same time, the terms *encapsulation boundary* and *violation of encapsulation* suggest that information hiding is typically, albeit not necessarily, implied by encapsulation. In practice, depending on the programming language in use, or the programming conventions being applied, different *policies* concerning encapsulation may be in effect.

Snyder, in a classic paper [14], defines encapsulation as follows.

> Encapsulation is a technique for minimizing interdependencies among separately-written modules by defining strict external interfaces. The external interface of a module serves as a contract between the module and its clients, and thus between the designer of the module and other designers.

M. Odersky (Ed.): ECOOP 2004, LNCS 3086, pp. 26–50, 2004.

We feel this definition captures the essence of encapsulation, but we observe (as did Snyder) that present day object-oriented programming languages are surprisingly weak in terms of the mechanisms they offer programmers to establish the encapsulation policies that a class offers to its clients. In particular, we identify the following three weaknesses as being endemic to OO languages:

1. *Access rights are inseparable from classes:* access rights to methods are specified as part of their implementation. As a consequence, it is neither possible to apply the same policies in a reusable way to different classes, nor is it possible to apply different policies to the same class.
2. *Client categories are fixed:* existing languages offer only the possibility to specify access rights for a fixed set of client categories, typically users and heirs (*i.e.*, instances using a fixed, public interface, and subclasses).
3. *Access rights are not customizable:* the onus is on the provider to specify the access rights. It can be hard or impossible for a client to adapt certain encapsulation decisions once they are fixed by the providing class.

We propose to address these problems by turning encapsulation policies into separate entities that can be composed. We characterize our approach as follows:

- A class consists of an implementation and a number of *encapsulation policies.*
- An encapsulation policy is a mapping from method signatures to *access rights.*
- The set of access rights may be language-specific, but will typically express whether a method may be *called*, *implemented* or *overridden.*
- Encapsulation policies can be *composed.* One may *merge* available policies, thus combining their access rights, or *refinc* a policy to obtain a more restrictive one.
- A client can use a class through a default encapsulation policy, explicitly select one of the available policies, or a specify a customized policy.

We claim that this simple model of composable encapsulation policies addresses the weaknesses we have identified above in a fundamental way. Encapsulation policies not only give the programmer freedom to specify multiple usage contracts for different classes of clients, but they allow certain critical decisions to be delayed until the client is ready to bind them. Furthermore, encapsulation policies subsume other, less general, mechanisms, such as interfaces, and visibility mechanisms.

The contributions of this paper include:

- an analysis of the weaknesses in the encapsulation mechanisms of mainstream OO languages,
- a proposal for a new encapsulation mechanism based on composable encapsulation policies,
- a simple formalization of this mechanism,
- a detailed discussion of how we applied this model to Smalltalk,
- an evaluation of the proposed mechanism, including a comparison with mainstream OO languages.

This paper is structured as follows: In section 2 we motivate this work by presenting a detailed analysis of the shortcomings of present encapsulation mechanisms. In section 3 we propose encapsulation policies by means of a simple, set-theoretic model. In section 4 we present how this model can be applied to Smalltalk based on the experiences with our prototype implementation. We then evaluate our proposal with respect to the identified problems and provide some discussion in section 5. We review related work in section 6, and we conclude in section 7 with some remarks on future and ongoing work.

2 Problem Statement

In this section, we motivate our work by analyzing the limitations of the encapsulation mechanisms offered by mainstream object-oriented programming languages such as Java, C++, C#, and Eiffel.

2.1 Access Rights Are Inseparable from Classes

In most object-oriented languages, the access rights to classes are tightly bound to their implementation. In languages like Java, C++, and C#, methods may be annotated with certain access rights by using keywords such as public, private or protected. Since the access rights are inseparable from the methods they are applied to, they cannot be reused independently. It is consequently impossible to express, for example, that methods >, <, <=, *etc.* should be public in all classes that implement the magnitude protocol. Instead, the programmer has to express this information on a per-method basis and duplicate it in each class that implements these methods.

Illustration. As a concrete example, consider the two classes Collection and Path that each implement a collection protocol which typically consists of a few dozen methods such as add:, addAll:, remove:, do:, and select:. Path inherits from GraphicalObject and Collection inherits from Object, so they are not related by inheritance. In current languages, *both* of these classes must individually specify their encapsulation attributes for these methods (*i.e.*, which should be public, private, or protected). It is not possible to express these attributes in a sharable way.

The situation is worse if there are subclasses of Collection and Path in which only a subset (or a superset) of these methods should be accessible to a client, because the programmer is again forced to specify the new access rights on a per-method basis and duplicate this information to make it available in both subclasses.

2.2 Client Categories Are Fixed

Most object-oriented languages such as Java and C# offer a set of keywords (*i.e.*, private, public, and protected) that essentially allow the designer of a class to assign encapsulation policies for just two fixed categories of clients (*i.e.*, users and heirs) corresponding to two different modes of use (*i.e.*, instantiation and inheritance) [14].

This approach restricts modularity because it does not take into account that different clients within the same category may need to access a class in different ways [2]. By forcing the designer of a component to fix the encapsulation policy for each category of client, one takes away the freedom of the client to choose which mode of use is more appropriate, and one loses the ability to distinguish between different needs of clients within such a category.

Illustration. The class Morph is the root of all the graphical objects in the user interface framework of Squeak [4] and implements several hundred methods, most of which are internal auxiliary methods. Since this framework is designed to be extended by inheritance, Morph has many subclasses with a variety of different needs for encapsulation.

The vast majority of subclasses, exemplified by SketchMorph, specialize how the Morph is drawn on a graphical canvas. This means that they typically override only a very small set of designated hook methods such as drawOn: and draw-PostscriptOn:, which are then called by other methods such as fullDrawOn: and refreshOn: that are part of the "drawing protocol" of Morph. However, there are also other kinds of subclasses that override more than these hook methods. The class PluggableListMorph, for example, specializes other drawing methods to implement smooth scrolling and overrides the submorph management methods since it uses a list as a model and therefore does not need to explicitly store submorphs.

Several other kinds of subclasses of Morph exist, and each needs to customize certain methods of Morph. But unfortunately, encapsulation models like the one of Java are not expressive enough to address the needs of these different categories of subclasses. Instead, the designer of the class Morph has to declare practically all internal methods as public or as protected, in order not to restrict the most demanding clients from specializing the functionality of Morph according to their needs.

However, such a "one-size-fits-all" encapsulation policy is not appropriate for the majority of subclasses that just want to customize some designated hook methods or add some special purpose methods. This is because it *forces* all these subclasses to access the class through an extremely wide and error prone interface that unnecessarily restricts their freedom of choosing names for local auxiliary methods and makes them unnecessarily fragile with respect to changes in Morph (*e.g.*, introducing a new protected method in Morph will break any subclass that incidentally uses the same name for an own internal method).

This fragility is *unnecessary* because most subclasses neither need nor want to override any of these protected methods in Morph, but because the same encapsulation policy must be shared by all subclasses, they cannot explicitly declare this.

Existing Solutions. Eiffel addresses this problem by allowing the designer of a class to declare the classes that are allowed to access a certain method. However, this solution is very limited, because the designer has to take an up-front decision on the clients that will have access. Clients that are not known when the class is written (and are not subclasses of known clients) cannot be taken into account and so can never have access. Furthermore, it cannot be used to discriminate between different heirs, which means that all heirs access the class through a completely unrestricted interface.

C++ addresses this problems with the friend construct that allows a class to grant other functions or classes access to its internal members. Like the Eiffel approach, this is a very limited solution because the clients have to be known upfront. Furthermore, it is not fine-grained enough because a friend is always allowed to access *all* the otherwise private methods and fields, without distinction. Similarly, private and protected inheritance do not generally solve these problems: they allow a programmer to make either all or none of the methods available in a subclass, but are not fine-grained enough to address the precise needs of different subclasses.

In Java and C#, methods and fields can be defined to be accessible within the current package and the current assembly, respectively. However, this approach is also not flexible enough because it allows programmers to establish only one additional category of clients, which is given by the physical organization of classes and underlies therefore many constrictions. For example, each Java class can only be part of exactly one package.

2.3 Access Rights Are Not Customizable

It is clear that it is primarily the responsibility of the designer to define how a class should be encapsulated. But even if a language allowed the designer to specify an arbitrary number of encapsulation policies, it would neither be possible nor reasonable for the designer to provide a policy that precisely addresses the individual needs of each client. Therefore, a language should allow a client to customize the encapsulation policy according to its individual needs as long as it does not violate the restrictions defined by the designer of the component. This means that a client should be allowed to make the interface granted by an encapsulation policy smaller, but not larger.

Unfortunately, current languages offer at best only limited support for such customization. Java, for example, does not allow the client of a class to customize the encapsulation policy specified by its designer, whereas C++ offers only very coarse-grained and limited mechanisms (*i.e.*, public, private, and protected inheritance). This not only prevents unanticipated reuse, it also prevents a client from using a class through a customized encapsulation policy that minimizes the risk of inappropriate method accesses and reduces fragility with respect to changes in the used class.

To avoid unnecessarily fragile class hierarchies, the programmer of a subclass should, for example, have the means to decline the override right for all methods but the ones that effectively need to be overridden. This makes the new subclass invulnerable to the problem of unintended name clashes that can occur when the implementor of a superclass changes its internal implementation and adds some new auxiliary methods. Even if one of the new methods incidentally has a signature that is already used in the subclass, the absence of the override access right guarantees that the methods do not interfere.

Illustration. Consider a C++ class Point where the method == is implemented by comparing the two coordinates x and y. Furthermore consider a method moveTo(Point) that uses == and is implemented as follows:

```
void moveTo(Point other) {
    if (this == other) return;
    x = other.x;
    y = other.y;
    coordinatesChanged();   // Notify my clients
}
```

To allow another programmer to override the method == in a specialized subclass such as LargeIntegerPoint, == is declared as virtual, which grants subclasses the right to override this method. But since this encapsulation policy cannot be adapted by the subclass, it does not only *allow* a subclass to override this method, but it also *prevents* subclasses from accessing the method in another way; once the designer of Point has decided that this method will be dynamically bound, heirs can no longer customize this decision and make it statically bound.

In particular, this means that it is not possible for a client to implement a new method == without having all the calls to == in Point be bound to this new method. As a consequence, this encapsulation decision significantly restricts the freedom of all direct and indirect subclasses of Point because it does not allow them to use the method == in a way that does not fully conform to the original implementation.

It is for example not possible to implement a subclass ColoredPoint of Point where == takes into account both the color and the coordinates without breaking moveTo and all the other methods in Point that call == and expect that it just compares the coordinates.

Existing Solutions. Both Eiffel and C# address this problem and allow a subclass to resolve such unintended name captures. In Eiffel this is done by allowing a subclass to consistently rename arbitrary methods of the superclass. C# allows the programmer to assign the keyword new (rather than override) to a method to declare that it is used for a different concept than in the superclass and that all calls in the superclass should therefore be statically bound to the local method.

However, these solutions are not as flexible as they should be. Eiffel only allows the subclass to *resolve* unintended name captures that are apparent when the subclass is written, but it does not allow the subclass to *protect* itself from unintended name clashes that may occur later, for instance when the superclass is modified and new methods are added. This is because only existing superclass methods can be renamed in a subclass.

In C#, this limitation is avoided because the keywords new and override can also be used for methods that do not (yet) have a corresponding method in the superclass[1]. However, the C# approach suffers from the same limitations as described in section 2.1, which means that the only way to protect internal methods from such unintended name clashes is to explicitly assign the keyword new to the *implementation* of each of these methods. It is not possible for a programmer to declare a *reusable* policy that declines the override right for *all but* the methods where this right is effectively needed and then share this policy among a family of subclasses that need to override the same superclass methods but may use different internal methods that should all be protected from unintended name clashes that can arise when the superclass is modified.

Another limitation is that these solutions only allow a subclass to decline the right to override a method, but they do not allow *any* client to decline *any* access right that is granted by an encapsulation policy. Thus, it is for instance not possible for a subclass to declare that certain internal superclass methods cannot be called because they are inappropriate in a specific usage scenario.

3 Encapsulation Policies

In this section we present a new model for specifying encapsulation policies for object-oriented programming languages. We use a simple, set-theoretic approach to describe the model in a language-independent way. For concreteness, we use the terminology of class-based languages with inheritance and instantiation as the only two modes of use for a class. Note however that the concept of composable encapsulation policies is very general and could also be applied to prototype-based languages as well as languages that support non-standard composition mechanisms such as automated delegation [5][18] or trait composition [13].

3.1 Design Rationale and Overview

As we have seen in section 2, most of the weaknesses in present encapsulation mechanisms arise from the fact that encapsulation policies are inseparable from the implementation. We propose to tackle this problem essentially by introducing encapsulation policies as separate entities, which can be individually selected, composed and applied. We apply the following principles:

- An *encapsulation policy* expresses how a client can access the methods of a class, independent of the particular mode of use (*i.e.*, instantiation or subclassing).
- The designer can associate an arbitrary number of encapsulation policies to a class. Each policy represents a set of encapsulation decisions that correspond to a certain usage scenario.
- The client can independently decide which encapsulation policy to apply and in which way the class will be used. The chosen policy may be one that is provided by the class, or one that is *stricter* than a provided one.

[1] This causes a compiler warning but not an error.

Note that we only consider methods in the encapsulation policy, since we assume that instance variables are never accessible from the outside of an object.

3.2 Modelling Encapsulation Policies

We now present a simple model of encapsulation policies.

An *encapsulation policy* $P : \mathcal{S} \mapsto 2^{\mathcal{A}}$ is a mapping from method signatures to potentially empty sets of access attributes. P represents a contract between the class and its client. This means that a client accessing a class through P may only access a method m with signature s according to the set of attributes $P(s)$.

A signature $s \in \mathcal{S}$ identifies a method provided by the class. This may simply represent a method name, for dynamically typed languages like Smalltalk, or might include type information for statically typed languages with overloading, like Java and C++.

The access attributes represent the policy in effect that constrains how clients may use the method. The actual set of available access attributes may depend on the particular programming language. For the purpose of illustration, we will consider three kinds of access attributes, namely **c**, **r** and **o**, which specify, respectively, that the associated method may be *called*, *reimplemented* or *overridden*.

A word of explanation may be in order. We draw an important distinction between *reimplementing* and *overriding* a method in a subclass. If a subclass overrides a method, this means that all existing calls to this method in the superclass are *dynamically bound* to the overriding method. If a subclass does not override but only reimplements a method, existing calls in the superclass continue to be *statically bound* to the old version of the method. In Java, for example, a subclass may reimplement a method that has been declared as `private` in its superclass, but one cannot override it — the new method is not visible from the context of the superclass and all the calls remain statically bound to the local version of the method. By contrast, a subclass can neither reimplement nor override a method that is declared as `final` in its superclass.

Access attributes express rights that are conceptually *orthogonal*. We consider the access rights **c**, **r** and **o** to be orthogonal since each can logically occur in isolation independently of the others, whether or not all combinations are sensible or desirable. In most programming languages, only certain combinations may make sense, or might be expressible using the mechanisms available. For example, `protected` in Java corresponds to the rights $\{\mathbf{c}, \mathbf{o}\}$ — a heir may call `protected` methods and may override them, but may not simply reimplement them.

3.3 Composing Encapsulation Policies

We now define operators and relations over encapsulation policies that enable us to compose them and express constraints on their composition.

Suppose that P and Q are arbitrary encapsulation policies and s is an arbitrary method signature. Then we define the following:

- The policy $P + Q$ is the *merge* of P and Q:

$$(P + Q)(s) \stackrel{\text{def}}{=} P(s) \cup Q(s)$$

- The policy $P * Q$ is the *intersection* of P and Q:

$$(P * Q)(s) \stackrel{\text{def}}{=} P(s) \cap Q(s)$$

- The policy $P - Q$ is the *reduction* of P by Q:

$$(P - Q)(s) \stackrel{\text{def}}{=} P(s) - Q(s)$$

- For a set of selectors $S \subseteq \mathcal{S}$, the policy $P|S$ is the *restriction* of P to S:

$$(P|S)(s) \stackrel{\text{def}}{=} \begin{cases} P(s) & \text{if } s \in S \\ \emptyset & \text{otherwise} \end{cases}$$

- P is *stricter* than Q if all rights granted by P are also granted by Q:

$$P \leq Q \stackrel{\text{def}}{\Leftrightarrow} P(s) \subseteq Q(s), \forall s \in \mathcal{S}$$

- $P[a]$ is the set of method signatures for which right $a \in \mathcal{A}$ is granted:

$$P[a] \stackrel{\text{def}}{=} \{s \in \mathcal{S} \mid a \in P(s)\}$$

- The policy $P \setminus A$ is the result of *removing* the access rights $A \subseteq \mathcal{A}$ from P:

$$(P \setminus A)(s) \stackrel{\text{def}}{=} P(s) - A$$

3.4 Encapsulation Constraints

In class-based languages, clients use classes via two kinds of operations: inheritance and instantiation. With our approach, both of these operations are parameterized with an encapsulation policy that imposes certain constraints on the client.

Inheritance. Consider a chain of subclasses $C_0, C_1, \ldots, C_n$ where C_0 is the root of the class hierarchy, C_n is a concrete class, and the class C_i is defined as the subclass of C_{i-1} using the encapsulation policy P_i, for all $i \in \{1, \ldots, n\}$. For any class C, the term $pol(C)$ denotes the set of encapsulation policies offered by C, and $meth(C)$ denotes the set of methods implemented in C. Furthermore, we use $sig(C)$ to denote the signatures of the methods in $meth(C)$, we use $self(C)$ to denote the set of signatures that are sent to self in any of the methods in $meth(C)$, and we use $super(C)$ to denote the set of signatures that are sent to super in any of the methods in $meth(C)$.

For the concrete class C_n to be *valid*, the following encapsulation constraints must be fulfilled for all $k \in \{1, \ldots, n\}$.

$$\exists Q \in pol(C_{k-1}) : P_k \leq Q \quad (1)$$
$$sig(C_k) \cap \bigcup_{i<k} sig(C_i) \subseteq P_k[\mathbf{r}] \cup P_k[\mathbf{o}] \quad (2)$$
$$self(C_k) \cap \bigcup_{i<k} sig(C_i) \subseteq \bigcup_{n \geq i \geq k} sig(C_i) \cup P[\mathbf{c}] \quad (3)$$
$$super(C_k) \subseteq P[\mathbf{c}] \quad (4)$$
$$\forall Q \in pol(C_k) : Q|(\mathcal{S} - sig(C_k)) \leq \sum_{Q' \in pol(C_{k-1})} Q' \quad (5)$$

The first constraint guarantees that the policy P_k through which the client C_k uses the class C_{k-1} can only grant access rights that are also granted by a certain encapsulation policy Q offered by C_{k-1}. The second constraint makes sure that the class C_k only implements methods with signatures that are not defined in any of its superclasses, are allowed to be reimplemented by P_k, or are allowed to be overridden by P_k. The third constraint ensures that there are only self-sends to methods that are inherited from P_{k-1} if they are declared as callable by the policy P. Note that self-sends to methods implemented in C_k or one of its subclasses are always allowed, even if they have the same signature as a method implemented in a superclass of C_k. The fourth constraint ensures that there are only super-sends to methods that are declared as callable by the policy P_k.

Finally, the fifth constraint guarantees that for all the method signatures that are not implemented in C_k, the encapsulation policies $pol(C_k)$ offered by C_k can only grant access rights that are also granted by at least one of the policies $pol(C_{k-1})$ of the superclass C_{k-1}. This is important because it guarantees that the encapsulation restrictions that the designer of the class C_{k-1} assigned to its methods cannot be bypassed in indirect subclasses. Note that the subclass C_k is free to grant arbitrary access rights for all the methods $meth(C_k)$ that are implemented locally.

Note that these constraints do not prevent a subclass C_k from offering its clients a policy that grants more rights on the methods obtained from C_{k-1} than the policy P_k, through which the class C_k inherits from C_{k-1}. This is important because it allows a class C_k to access its superclass C_{k-1} through a *minimal* policy P_k without preventing its future clients from accessing the methods obtained from C_{k-1} through a policy that grants more rights. Also note that these constraints do not guarantee that the class C_k is correct (*i.e.*, that there are no calls to methods that are not available) nor are they concerned with issues related to subtyping (see section 5.4). Instead, they only ensure that the encapsulation restrictions are not violated.

Instantiation. Instantiation is also parameterized with an encapsulation policy, which means that each new instance o of the concrete class C_n is created through an encapsulation policy P. For such an instantiation and subsequent calls on o to the selector s to be *valid*, the following encapsulation constraints must be fulfilled.

$$\exists Q \in pol(C_n) : P \leq Q \quad (1)$$
$$s \in P[\mathbf{c}] \quad (2)$$

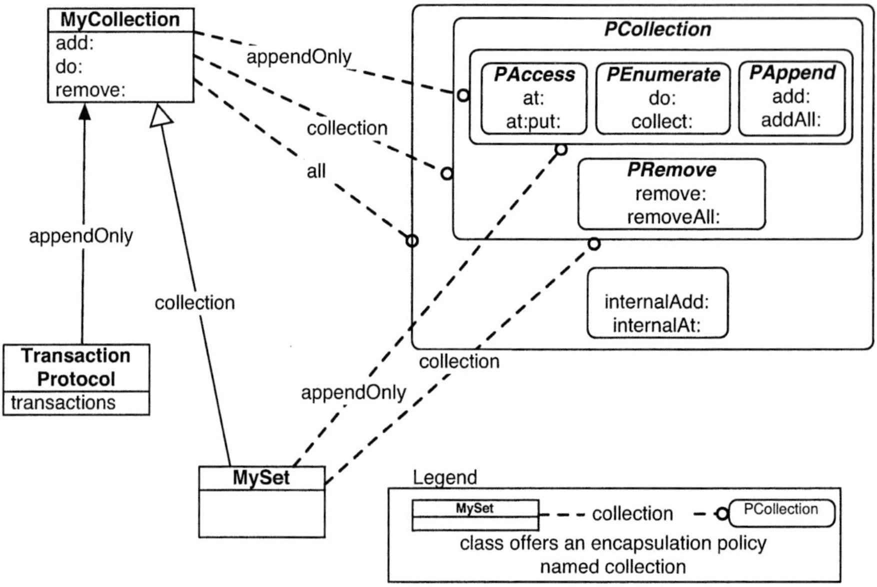

Fig. 1. Encapsulation policies at work

The first constraint is the same as for inheritance and it says that the policy P can only grant access rights that are also granted by a certain policy Q offered by C_n. The second constraint says that the only method signatures that are allowed to be called on the instance o are the ones that are marked as callable in P.

3.5 Example

In the example shown in figure 1, the class MyCollection offers three different encapsulation policies that are available under the names appendOnly, collection and all. Note that each of these three policies is composed from several stricter policies, some of which are shared.

The class MyCollection has two clients. One client is the subclass MySet, which inherits from MyCollection through the encapsulation policy collection and in turn offers the same policy as well as the policy appendOnly to its clients. The other client is the class TransactionProtocol, which uses an instance of MyCollection through the encapsulation policy appendOnly to store its transactions. To be usable, the class TransactionProtocol must also offer at least one encapsulation policy, but this is not shown in the figure.

4 Encapsulation Policies in Smalltalk

In the previous section we have introduced the model of encapsulation policies in a language independent way. Now we show how this model can be applied to Smalltalk. This section is based on our proof of concept implementation in the Smalltalk dialect Squeak [4]. However, we will present the examples in a somewhat simplified syntax to ease the reading of the paper, especially for readers who are not familiar with Smalltalk. In particular, we use bold face for symbols rather than the prefix #.

4.1 Representing Encapsulation Policies

Following the Smalltalk tradition of making everything an object, encapsulation policies are instances of the class Policy. Each policy object can contain some local definitions, which are represented as a dictionary of associations from method selectors (*i.e.*, symbols) to access attributes, and can refer to other encapsulation policies which it is composed from.

Creating Encapsulation Policies. In the previous section, we have pointed out that the actual set of access attributes may depend on the programming language. Since Smalltalk is dynamically typed and inheritance is often used for sharing implementation in unanticipated ways, we believe that it does not make much sense to declare a method that cannot be reimplemented in a subclass. Therefore, we define that a method can *always* be reimplemented, and consequently, our Smalltalk encapsulation policies only manage the access attributes callable (**c**) and overridable (**o**).

For convenience, we provide a literal way of creating encapsulation policies. This is done by putting the selectors between brackets [] and prefixing them with either ↑ or ↓ to indicate the associated access rights. The meaning of such a literal policy is defined as follows:

- No prefix means that the selector is fully accessible ({**c**, **o**})
- The prefix ↑ means that the selector is callable but not overridable ({**c**})
- The prefix ↓ means that the selector overridable but not callable ({**o**})
- All selectors that do not appear in the policy definition are neither callable nor overridable ({})

As an example, the expression [foo ↑bar ↓check] returns a policy that allows full access to the selector **foo**, allows the selector **bar** to be called but not overridden, and allows the selector **check** to be overridden but not called. All the other selectors are neither allowed to be called nor overridden. All selectors are allowed to be reimplemented.

Manipulating Encapsulation Policies. Since encapsulation policies are first-class objects, they can be manipulated by messages. If p and q are arbitrary encapsulation policies, the most common messages and their semantics are as follows:

– + is the merge operator, which means that the expression p + q returns a new policy that grants all the access rights granted by either p or q.

– * is the intersection operator, which means that the expression p * q returns a new policy that grants only the access rights that are granted by both P and Q.
– - is the reduction operator, which means that the expression p - q returns a new policy that grants the access rights granted by p without the rights granted by q.
– The expression p noOverride returns a new policy that is the same as p except that no selector can be overridden:

$$\mathsf{p\ noOverride} \equiv \mathsf{p} - \{\mathbf{o}\}$$

4.2 Associating Encapsulation Policies with Classes

A key feature of the model is that a programmer can associate an arbitrary number of encapsulation policies with a class. In our Smalltalk implementation, this is done by sending the message policyAt:put: to a class. This message takes a symbol and a policy as an argument and then associates the policy with the class under the identifier represented by the symbol. All the identifiers associated with encapsulation policies are local to the class, and they allow a client to refer to a certain encapsulation policy that is offered by the class. As an example, we can define a collection class OrderedCollection as follows:

```
(Collection subclass: OrderedCollection)
    instanceVariableNames: 'array offset';
    policyAt: basicUse put: [add: addAll: removeAt: ...];
    policyAt: basicExtend put: basicUse + [growBy: compact ...]
```

This creates the class OrderedCollection as a subclass of Collection, defines the two instance variables array and offset, and associates two encapsulation policies with the identifiers **basicUse** and **basicExtend**. Note that it is possible to define a policy that refers to another policy associated with the class by using its identifier in the policy definition. In our example, the expression **basicUse** + [growBy: compact ...] refers to the policy **basicUse** and merges it with the policy [growBy: compact ...].

The order of the policyAt:put: messages is only relevant as far as later messages override policies that have been bound to the same identifier by earlier messages. However, the order is not relevant for the meaning of the policy definition (*i.e.*, the second argument). This is because references to other policies are not evaluated when the expression is executed. Instead, these references remain part of the policy definition, which means that the relationship between the different policies remains valid even if one of the involved policies gets modified. Note that circular references in policy definitions are not allowed and result in an error.

4.3 Using Encapsulation Policies

When creating a subclass or an instance of class, the programmer can select which of the encapsulation policies offered by the class should be applied. This is done by passing the symbol selecting the encapsulation policy as an additional argument to the message that creates the new subclass or instance. The following code illustrates how the message newWithPolicy: is used to create a new instance of the class OrderedCollection using the encapsulation policy **basicUse**:

```
Morph>>initialize
    super initialize.
    submorphs := OrderedCollection newWithPolicy: basicUse.
    ...
```

As a consequence, the ordered collection submorphs responds only to the messages that are declared as callable by the policy **basicUse** in the class OrderedCollection. Sending any other messages leads to a runtime error.

Default Policies. To improve ease of use without sacrificing the flexibility of having multiple encapsulation policies, our implementation features the concept of *default policies.* The designer of a class can specify two default policies for a class by associating ordinary encapsulation policies with the identifiers **basicUse** and **basicExtend**. When a client uses this class and does not explicitly specify another policy, these default policies are then used for creating new instances and subclasses, respectively. This means that in the previous example, we could have used the simpler expression OrderedCollection new to create an instance that implicitly uses the default policy **basicUse**.

4.4 Sharing Encapsulation Policies

Although it is possible to define anonymous policies using the [] notation, it is often more appropriate to declare *named policies* and then share them among different classes. Because of the lack of namespace facilities in Squeak, we store policies in the same namespace as classes and just use the convention that we prefix policy names with the letter P.

In the following example, we first define encapsulation policies named PEnumeration, PAppend, and PRemove. Then we merge these policies to define a policy named PCollection, which is then shared between the classes Collection and Path described in section 2.1.

```
Policy named: PEnumeration
    is: [do: select: detect: collect: reject: ...].
Policy named: PAppend
    is: [add: addAll: ...].
Policy named: PRemove
    is: [remove: removeAll: ...].
Policy named: PCollection
    is: PEnumeration + PAppend + PRemove.
```

```
(Object subclass: Collection)
    instanceVariableNames: '';
    policyAt: basicUse put: PCollection

(GraphicalObject subclass: Path)
    instanceVariableNames: 'points';
    policyAt: basicUse put: PCollection + [draw drawOn: length segmentCount ...]
```

Note that neither classes Path nor Collection specify a policy to access their respective superclass, which means that the default policy **basicExtend** is applied.

Special Policies. The policy PProtoObject is defined so that it allows all the methods that are implemented in the class ProtoObject to be called. To guarantee that every object responds at least to this common set of system messages such as == and isNil, this policy is implicitly added to any policy that is assigned to a class (*e.g.*, using the message policyAt:put:). This means that the policy of the class Collection in the above example is in fact equivalent to PCollection + PProtoObject.

Traditionally, all methods in Smalltalk are public, and therefore many Smalltalk programmers enjoy the freedom of not having to deal with encapsulation decisions if they do not want to. We support this style of programming with a policy PAll, which allows full access to any valid method selector. As a consequence, it is possible to make a class fully accessible from the outside by simply associating the policy PAll to the default identifiers **basicUse** and **basicExtend**.

4.5 Encapsulation Policies in Subclasses

In section 3.4, we have formally defined the constraint that applies to encapsulation policies offered by subclasses (constraint 5). In our implementation, we ensure this by implicitly restricting each policy that is assigned to a class (*e.g.*, using the message policyAt:put:) so that it does not grant any access right for inherited methods that are not also granted by the union of the policies offered by the superclass.

To allow a programmer to create subclasses that have less encapsulation policies than their superclass, policies that are assigned to a class are not automatically available in subclasses. However, a programmer can "inherit" the policies offered by a superclass by sending the message addSuperPolicies to the newly created class. Note that these inherited policies are overridden by equivalently named policies that are explicitly assigned to the class using the message policyAt:put:.

Furthermore, a programmer can use the keyword super to refer to the superclass policy from within the definition of a policy that is assigned to the subclass using the message policyAt:put:. Note that super always refers to the superclass policy with the name of the newly added policy (*i.e.*, the first argument to the message policyAt:put:).

As an example, consider the class Morph and its subclass SketchMorph described in section 2.2. Since SketchMorph needs to override only the two drawing methods, it uses its superclass through the encapsulation policy **drawingHooks**. However, it still offers all the encapsulation policies specified by Morph so that it does not unnecessarily restrict its clients. This is done by using the message addSuperPolicies. In addition, SketchMorph overrides the inherited policy drawingHooks so that it also contains the method selector drawPDF:.

```
(Object subclass: Morph)
    instanceVariableNames: 'submorphs owner color bounds';
    policyAt: basicUse put: PMorph;
    policyAt: basicExtend put: PAll;
    policyAt: drawingHooks put: PAll noOverride + [drawOn: drawPostscriptOn:];
    policyAt: symbsubmorphManagement put: PAll noOverride + [addFront: addBack: ...]

(Morph subclass: SketchMorph withPolicy: drawingHooks)
    instanceVariableNames: 'form';
    addSuperPolicies;
    policyAt: drawingHooks put: super + [drawPDF:]
```

4.6 Customizing Encapsulation Policies

An important feature of encapsulation policies is that the client is not only allowed to select a policy offered by a class but can also customize the selected policy according to its needs. In our implementation, this is done by sending the messages -, *, and noOverride to the symbol corresponding the selected policy. As an example, assume that the class Point described in section 2.3 is defined as follows:

```
(Object subclass: Point)
    instanceVariableNames: 'x y';
    policyAt: basicUse put: [x y moveTo: radius degrees dotProduct: = ...];
    policyAt: basicExtend put: PAll
```

Although both encapsulation policies offered by this class declare the method = as overridable, we can still define a subclass ColoredPoint where implementing the method = does not override the superclass method. We do this by first selecting the policy **basicUse** and then customizing it so that it allows the method = to be called but not to be overridden.

```
((Point subclass: ColoredPoint withPolicy: basicUse - [↓=])
    instanceVariableNames: 'rgb';
    addSuperPolicies
```

Note that in our implementation, the programmer of the subclass decides whether the method = should override or simply reimplement the superclass method by means of specifying the encapsulation policy: the method = implemented in the subclass overrides the superclass method if and only if the encapsulation policy allows it. This means that the encapsulation policy not only specifies whether a method *can* override the superclass version but also whether it *will* override the superclass version.

5 Evaluation and Discussion

In section 2 we identified a set of limitations that are caused by the encapsulation models of state of the art object-oriented programming languages. In the following, we present a point-by-point evaluation of how composable encapsulation policies solve these problems in a simple and elegant way. Furthermore, we briefly discuss additional constraints for defining encapsulation policies in subclasses and compare encapsulation policies to Java interfaces.

5.1 Access Rights Are Inseparable from Classes

Encapsulation policies are separate and independent from the implementation of a class. This allows us to express encapsulation policies in a reusable way and share them between arbitrary classes. Since these policies are not only sharable but also composable, it is possible to define new policies by combining, modifying and extending existing policies.

This significantly raises the level of abstraction because a programmer does not have to explicitly associate encapsulation attributes with the implementation of every single method. Furthermore, it reduces implementation and maintenance overhead because encapsulation decisions do not have to be duplicated in the first place and are therefore much easier to adapt if necessary.

Illustration. Let us reconsider the example of section 2.1. When we implement the classes Collection and Path with this approach, we do not have to assign any encapsulation attributes to the implementation of their methods. Instead, we can create a named encapsulation policy PCollection that contains all the accessible collection methods as well as the corresponding access rights and then use it as an encapsulation policy for both Collection and Path. In our Smalltalk implementation, this could be done as shown in section 4.4.

Besides the fact that we do not have to duplicate the encapsulation decisions for the collection protocol, this example illustrates also other advantages of encapsulation policies:

- Since encapsulation policies specify only accessible methods, the classes Path and Collection can use different internal method names (*e.g.*, internalAt: *vs.* basicAt: and unsafeAdd: *vs.* privateAdd:) and still use the same encapsulation policy. Furthermore, a programmer can add, remove or rename such internal methods in either class without having to change the encapsulation policy.
- The encapsulation policy PCollection can also be shared if a certain method, for example removeAll:, should only be accessible for clients of Collection but not of Path. This can be done by using the policy PCollection - [removeAll:] in Path.
- The encapsulation policy PCollection can be used in any class that provides the collection protocol. This means that independent of how such a class is implemented, the programmer does not have to deal with encapsulation on a per-method level and can instead just reuse the policy PCollection.

This stands in contrast to the interface-based approaches of languages like Java and C#, which do not support reuse of encapsulation decisions even if multiple classes implement the same interface (see section 5.5 and the remark about .NET CAS in section 6).

5.2 Client Categories Are Fixed

We avoid this problem by allowing the designer to specify an arbitrary number of independent encapsulation policies for a given class. This allows a designer to implement a class with multiple usage scenarios in mind and to explicitly *specify* and *document* this by giving each of these scenarios a descriptive name and assigning it to an encapsulation policy. Another programmer can immediately see which usage scenarios a given class supports and then select the encapsulation policy corresponding to the usage scenario that is most appropriate.

In contrast to existing approaches, the designer can specify these encapsulation policies in a way that is independent of a particular mode of use. This raises the level of abstraction because it allows the programmer to think in a conceptual rather than an operational way. It is based on the realization that as long as it is not possible to sidestep such a conceptual policy, it is not relevant for the designer of a class whether a client uses the class by inheritance, instantiation, or any other mode of use such as automated delegation.

The fact that a particular encapsulation policy can be applied for both inheritance and instantiation gives a client the freedom to choose the mode of use that is most appropriate for its needs. In particular, it avoids those situations where a programmer is forced to inherit from a class just because this is the only way to obtain certain access rights, even if this is from a design point of view not appropriate (*e.g.*, when Stack inherits from OrderedCollection just to be able to access some internal methods of the collection) or not possible (*e.g.*, in a language that does not offer multiple inheritance).

Illustration. With our approach the limitation of a fixed set of categories can be avoided by associating different encapsulation policies with the class Morph. In our Smalltalk implementation, the class Morph and its subclass SketchMorph could be defined as shown in section section 4.5.

Another scenario in which it is useful to be able to assign multiple encapsulation policies to a class is when changes to the implementation of a class should be accessible for new clients without breaking existing ones. As an example, suppose that a vendor of a graphics framework ships a class GraphicalObject that is extensively subclassed by its customers. At a later point, the vendor would like to add the capability of *alpha-blending* to this class and therefore needs to add a few more internal methods such as transformAlpha:.

With traditional encapsulation approaches, these methods would be declared as protected since it should be possible to override them in new subclasses. However, doing this can break existing subclasses [15] because they may have introduced the same method name for another purpose! In our model, this dilemma can be solved by leaving the existing encapsulation policies as they are and instead assigning the class a new encapsulation policy (*e.g.*, under the name withAlphaBlending) that contains these new methods. As a consequence, the new methods are completely invisible to all the existing subclasses that use the class through an old policy, whereas they are available for new clients that want to take advantage of them.

5.3 Access Rights Are Not Customizable

We allow a client not only to select the most appropriate reuse policy, but also to customize this policy so that it best matches its individual needs as long as it does not violate the restrictions defined by the designer of the class.

This allows one to reuse a class in a way that may not have been anticipated by the designer. Furthermore, it allows a client to specify a customized encapsulation policy that contains only the access rights that are effectively necessary, and it therefore *minimizes* the interdependencies between the class and its client. Minimizing these interdependencies is important because each access right that is granted by a policy comes together with a *risk* (*e.g.*, to accidentally and inappropriately call or override a method), *restricts the freedom* of the client (*e.g.*, in Java, a subclass cannot use the name of a protected superclass method for a method that represents a different concept), and makes the code more *fragile* with respect to changes in the used class (*e.g.*, unintended name clashes that can occur when a new internal method is added to the used class).

Illustration. In section 4.6, we have already shown how customizing encapsulation policies allow a programmer to solve the problem introduced in section 2.3, even if the designer of the class Point did not anticipate a client such as ColoredPoint that needs to implement a method == that is not compatible to the original implementation.

As another illustration, consider the class Morph introduced in section 2.2 and assume that its designer only provided the encapsulation policy PAll, which exposes the complete interface to its clients. Now suppose that another programmer would like to make a subclass TurtleMorph that overrides the method drawOn: and implements the turtle-specific methods go: and pointNorth using the methods position: and rotate:. To minimize the interdependencies to Morph, the programmer of TurtleMorph can still access Morph through a minimal policy that grants only the rights that are needed. This is done by using the intersection of the policy basicExtend and the policy that allows the selectors position: and rotate: to be called and grants full access to the selector drawOn:.

```
((Morph subclass: TurtleMorph withPolicy: basicExtend * [↑position: ↑rotate: drawOn:])
    instanceVariables: '';
    ...
```

5.4 Constraints for Encapsulation Policies in Subclasses

In section 3.4, we formally stated the constraints that encapsulation policies impose on the clients of a class, and we have pointed out that these constraints guarantee only that the encapsulation restrictions expressed by the designer of a class can never be violated in a direct or indirect client.

This has the advantage that a subclass can always assign *fewer* access rights to inherited methods, which is very useful in the dynamically typed language Smalltalk where implementation inheritance is a common practice [17] and every method is traditionally fully accessible. For instance, it allows a programmer to create a class that can only be accessed through a restricted encapsulation policy even if the superclass (which may have been designed by another programmer) declares all the methods as fully accessible (*e.g.*, by using the policy PAll).

However, the price for this expressiveness is that it sacrifices substitutability of subclasses for superclasses. This means that if a superclass C offers a policy under the name p that grants full access rights to the method signature s, it may be that the policy that is offered by the subclass D under the same name does not grant any access rights for s. In fact, it may even be that the subclass D does not even provide a policy under the name p!

In a language like Java where subclassing implies subtyping, it may therefore be more appropriate to introduce additional constraints for the encapsulation policies offered by a subclass. For example, we could define that encapsulation policies are "inherited" and that a subclass cannot make these inherited policies stricter. This guarantees substitutability of subclasses for superclasses because every method signature that can be accessed through a policy named p in a class C can also be accessed through the policy p in all its subclasses.

Note that this additional constraint does not affect the ability to freely choose and customize a policy when creating a subclass nor does it prevent the designer of a subclass from offering additional policies (*i.e.*, policies that were not inherited from the superclass) that do not underly this constraint. Therefore, the programmer still enjoys all the conceptual benefits of encapsulation policies that are described in this paper.

5.5 Comparison to Java Interfaces

At a first glance, our notion of encapsulation policies resembles Java interfaces as they both specify a set of callable method signatures. However, aside from this structural resemblance, they are used for quite different purposes. Whereas the primary purpose of encapsulation policies is to express a usage contract between a component and its client, the purpose of Java interfaces is to declare subtype relationships in a way that is independent from subclassing.

As a consequence, Java interfaces are neither designed nor able to capture the encapsulation aspects of a class and separate them from the implementation. Instead, all the access attributes (*e.g.*, public, private, and protected) of methods are still declared together with their implementation. This means that regarding encapsulation, the information provided by interfaces is redundant because the definition of the methods in the class already defines all the encapsulation-related information.

Nevertheless, it may seem that Java interfaces offer a way for clients to reuse a class through different encapsulation policies by simply creating an instance of the class and then using type casts to restrict access to this instance to an interface that is associated with the class. However, this sort of "policy" is not comparable to the one expressed with our approach because of the following limitations:

1. *Policies cannot be enforced.* Even if a client reuses a class C through an instance that has been type casted to the interface I, there is no way to enforce that this instance is not accessed through the complete interface defined by C. This is because it is always possible to use a downcast to convert the instance back to the type C.
2. *Policies can only be defined for one category of clients.* The policies defined by Java interfaces are only available to instances but not to subclasses. This means that all subclasses always have to reuse the class through the unchangeable policy that is defined by the access attributes in the implementation of the class.
3. *Policies cannot be defined independently.* The policies defined by Java interfaces are interdependent with the encapsulation decisions specified within the implementation of the class. This is because an interface can only be applied to a class that declares all the method specified by the interface as public, but this in turn makes it impossible to provide another policy that does not allow full access to these methods.

Realizing that Java interfaces are not expressive enough to be used as encapsulation policies, the other interesting question is whether encapsulation policies are expressive enough to be used as types, *i.e.*, whether encapsulation policies subsume interfaces. Even though we have neither formalized nor implemented a type system based on encapsulation policies, we strongly believe that this is possible.

Our belief that this is possible stems from the fact that encapsulation policies contain a superset of the information expressed by interfaces. In fact, both types of entities define a set of method signatures that are allowed to be called. The only difference is that encapsulation policies also capture all the other encapsulation aspects such as which of these methods are allowed to be overridden and reimplemented. Also the relationship of encapsulation policies and classes is quite similar to the relationship of interfaces and classes. In fact, a programmer can associate several possibly nested encapsulation policies to a class to express that the class conforms to the "interface" that is expressed by such a policy.

6 Related Work

We have already discussed the encapsulation mechanisms of the languages Java, C++, C#, and Eiffel in section 2. In this Section, we briefly discuss encapsulation mechanisms of other languages as well as some related research.

The encapsulation model of CLOS and Dylan follow the tradition of Lisp-based object-oriented languages such as Flavors (with the notable exception of CommonObjects [14]). There is no direct access to slots as in Java or Smalltalk. The access is always performed via accessors that can be generated automatically from the class description. However, it is always possible to access a slot value using the function slot-value[2]. There is no encapsulation of methods, which means that they are all public and late-bound.

Ada [1] uses packages as a module system. These packages have a separated *definition* and *body*. Besides importing and exporting definitions, Ada 9X [16] also allows sharing of packages. This is used for constructing hierarchical libraries, and solves the problem of private types only providing coarse control of visibility and the inability to extend packages without recompiling them. Hierarchical libraries are built by adding *child packages* to existing packages. The child packages can add definitions to their parent package and can see the internal body of their parent. Child packages can be made private, which means that they are only visible within the subtree of the hierarchy whose root is its parent. Moreover, within that tree, a private child package is not visible to the specifications of any non-private sibling (although it is visible to their bodies).

Ada also has protected types that are used for concurrent tasks. Protected types consist of a *specification*, where the access protocol is specified, and a *body*, where the implementation details are provided. Protected types contain a notion of visibility (clients can only use the procedures as defined in the access protocol), but they also control the access to the data these procedures work with: calls from clients to subprograms within a protected body are mutually exclusive.

Modula-3 is a statically typed, object-oriented language with single inheritance, and modules that consist of separate interface and implementation files. Modula-3 sports *partial revelation* [3], which is a technique that allows one to inherit from a class without making all its features visible in the subclass. This is done by dividing class definitions across multiple files, which specify (partial) types for the class. Partial revelation allows a program unit to import only the relevant aspects of a class by selecting the corresponding type; the other aspects of the class are still available and can be revealed elsewhere in the program. Similar to encapsulation policies, this addresses the problem that different kinds of subclasses need to access a class in different ways.

However, there are many conceptual differences between the two approaches. For example, the Modula-3 types are more like Java interfaces and do not model different access attributes: a feature is either visible (*i.e.*, fully accessible) or hidden; it is not possible to distinguish between more fine-grained access rights such as callable, overridable, and reimplementable. Partial revelation does also not allow one to compose (*e.g.*, merge, restrict, intersect) types: it is only possible to use partial and full revelations to derive a new type (that reveals more

[2] In CLOS, slot-value is in fact calling slot-value-using-class, which is an entry point of the MOP that allows controlling of slot accesses. Therefore it is possible to define a different encapsulation mechanism than the default one.

features) from another type. Furthermore, it is not possible for a subclass to customize (*i.e.*, restrict) the type through which it inherits from a superclass.

The object-oriented programming language Beta [7] is a block-scoped language where the visibility is given by the nesting of the blocks. There are no explicit visibility attributes that can be granted beyond that. However, Beta allows one to declare *virtual* patterns that can be extended in subpatterns. Furthermore, virtual patterns can be finalized (*i.e.*, made non-virtual) in a subpattern. For programming in the large, Beta also has a hierarchical module system to declare interface modules and implementation modules. The module system allows different implementation modules to be associated with the same interface module (so-called *variants*). Module visibility is also controlled by nesting.

C# and other .NET languages allow one to place CAS attributes on methods of interfaces and thereby reuse the constraint attributes across all classes implementing these interfaces [10]. However, the *security* constraints that are expressed by CAS attributes and then checked at runtime by the .NET CLR are conceptually different from the *encapsulation* constraints that are expressed by our approach and C#'s access modifiers.

Wolczko also argues that existing class-based languages do not provide sufficient support for encapsulation [19]. This is addressed by a Smalltalk-based research language called MUST, which offers additional features such as two types of self-sends and super-sends. This allows a programmer to express additional encapsulation issues in a very fine-grained way, by extending the language with additional mechanisms. In contrast, our approach is of a conceptual and language independent nature: it does not specify exactly what encapsulation issues (*i.e.*, access attributes) should be modelled, but it suggests to separate these encapsulation issues from the implementation and to make them first class.

The Jigsaw modularity framework, developed by Bracha in his doctoral dissertation [2], defines module composition operators hide, show, and freeze to control how attributes of a module are encapsulated. Whereas hide eliminates the argument attributes from the interface of a module, show eliminates everything but the argument attributes from the interface of a module. The operator freeze allows one to control how attributes of a module are bound. It takes an attribute as an argument and produces a new module in which all references to the argument attribute are statically bound.

Altogether, these operators give a programmer fine-grained control over how a module should be encapsulated. Similar to our approach, they also allow the client of a module to decline access rights by hiding or statically binding attributes. However, the Jigsaw framework cannot capture such encapsulation decisions as separate, reusable entities, associate them to modules and apply them when a module is used.

Caesar's collaboration interfaces extend the concept of interfaces to include the declaration of expected methods, *i.e.*, the methods that a class must provide when bound to an interface [8]. However, they do not address the encapsulation problems that are addressed in this paper.

Sadeh and Ducasse present the introduction of *dynamic* interfaces in Smalltalk [12]. These interfaces represent a list of message selectors which are causally connected to the class that implements them. The system can be dynamically queried to get the classes implementing a given interface. Dynamic interfaces can be derived from other interfaces or included in other interfaces. As Smalltalk is dynamically typed, dynamic interfaces mainly serve as documentation purpose. Contrary to encapsulation policies, dynamic interfaces do not deal with encapsulation aspects.

To avoid the fragile base class problem [9], researchers developed better ways to describe the contract between a class and its subclasses. Lamping proposes a limited specialization interface that expresses the calling relationships between the methods in the superclass [6]. Reuse Contracts [15] bring the idea a step further by proposing a model in which the operations of class evolution are analyzed in the context of the calling dependencies in the superclass. Hence the evolution problems are categorized and detected with finer precision.

7 Conclusion and Future Work

In this paper we have proposed composable encapsulation policies as a way to improve the flexibility and expressiveness of object-oriented programming languages and to reduce the fragility of the resulting programs. Explicit encapsulation policies enable the expression of different usage scenarios for different classes of clients, they enable reuse of policies, and they enable client-specific customizations in a straightforward way.

We have outlined a general, language-independent model of encapsulation policies, and we have described a proof-of-concept prototype for Smalltalk that demonstrates the feasibility of the idea. Encapsulation policies can be incorporated into a language in such a way that there is an additional syntactic burden only when one wishes to make use of the feature. In other cases, default policies mimic the conventional approach offered by the language.

We are working on extending our proof-of-concept prototype to a full implementation of encapsulation policies in Smalltalk as well as Smalltalk with Traits. This will serve as the basis for a more detailed evaluation of the advantages of our approach in languages that feature non-standard composition mechanisms such as trait composition or automated delegation. Furthermore, we plan to investigate the impact of replacing the traditional encapsulation mechanisms of languages like Java with encapsulation policies. In particular, it seems that there could be interesting synergies if the notion of encapsulation policies would also be used as a type and could hence replace the notion of interfaces.

Acknowledgments. We gratefully acknowledge the financial support of the Swiss National Science Foundation for the projects "Tools and Techniques for Decomposing and Composing Software" (SNF Project No. 2000-067855.02, Oct. 2002 - Sept. 2004) and "RECAST: Evolution of Object-Oriented Applications" (SNF Project No. 620-066077, Sept. 2002 - Aug. 2006).

References

1. American National Standards Institute, Inc. *The Programming Language Ada Reference Manual*, volume 155 of *LNCS*. Springer-Verlag, 1983.
2. Gilad Bracha. *The Programming Language Jigsaw: Mixins, Modularity and Multiple Inheritance.* Ph.D. thesis, Dept. of Computer Science, University of Utah, March 1992.
3. Steve Freeman. Partial revelation and Modula-3. *Dr. Dobb's Journal*, 20(10):36–42, October 1995.
4. Dan Ingalls, Ted Kaehler, John Maloney, Scott Wallace, and Alan Kay. Back to the future: The story of Squeak, A practical Smalltalk written in itself. In *Proceedings OOPSLA '97*, pages 318–326. ACM Press, November 1997.
5. Günter Kniesel. Type-safe delegation for run-time component adaptation. In R. Guerraoui, editor, *Proceedings ECOOP '99*, volume 1628 of *LNCS*, pages 351–366, Lisbon, Portugal, June 1999. Springer-Verlag.
6. John Lamping. Typing the specialization interface. In *Proceedings OOPSLA '93, ACM SIGPLAN Notices*, volume 28, pages 201–214, October 1993.
7. Ole Lehrmann Madsen, Birger Moller-Pedersen, and Kristen Nygaard. *Object-Oriented Programming in the Beta Programming Language.* Addison Wesley, Reading, Mass., 1993.
8. Mira Mezini and Klaus Ostermann. Integrating independent components with on-demand remodularization. In *Proceedings OOPSLA 2002*, pages 52–67, November 2002.
9. Leonid Mikhajlov and Emil Sekerinski. A study of the fragile base class problem. In *Proceedings of ECOOP'98*, number 1445 in Lecture Notes in Computer Science, pages 355–383, 1998.
10. The Microsoft Developer Network. http://msdn.microsoft.com/.
11. Oscar Nierstrasz. A survey of object-oriented concepts. In W. Kim and F. Lochovsky, editors, *Object-Oriented Concepts, Databases and Applications*, pages 3–21. ACM Press and Addison Wesley, Reading, Mass., 1989.
12. Benny Sadeh and Stéphane Ducasse. Adding dynamic interface to Smalltalk. *Journal of Object Technology*, 1(1), 2002.
13. Nathanael Schärli, Stéphane Ducasse, Oscar Nierstrasz, and Andrew Black. Traits: Composable units of behavior. In *Proceedings ECOOP 2003*, volume 2743 of *LNCS*, pages 248–274. Springer Verlag, July 2003.
14. Alan Snyder. Encapsulation and inheritance in object-oriented programming languages. In *Proceedings OOPSLA '86, ACM SIGPLAN Notices*, volume 21, pages 38–45, November 1986.
15. Patrick Steyaert, Carine Lucas, Kim Mens, and Theo D'Hondt. Reuse contracts: Managing the evolution of reusable assets. In *Proceedings of OOPSLA '96 Conference*, pages 268–285. ACM Press, 1996.
16. S. Tucker Taft. Ada 9x: From abstraction-oriented to object-oriented. In *Proceedings OOPSLA '93*, volume 28, pages 127–143, October 1993.
17. Antero Taivalsaari. On the notion of inheritance. *ACM Computing Surveys*, 28(3):438–479, September 1996.
18. John Viega, Paul Reynolds, and Reimer Behrends. Automating delegation in class-based languages. In *Proceedings of TOOLS 34'00*, pages 171–182, July 2000.
19. Mario Wolczko. Encapsulation, delegation and inheritance in object-oriented languages. *IEEE Software Engineering Journal*, 7(2):95–102, March 1992.

Demand-Driven Type Inference with Subgoal Pruning: Trading Precision for Scalability

S. Alexander Spoon and Olin Shivers

Georgia Institute of Technology

Abstract. After two decades of effort, type inference for dynamically typed languages scales to programs of a few tens of thousands of lines of code, but no further. For larger programs, this paper proposes using a kind of demand-driven analysis where the number of active goals is carefully restricted. To achieve this restriction, the algorithm occasionally *prunes* goals by giving them solutions that are trivially true and thus require no further subgoals to be solved; the previous subgoals of a newly pruned goal may often be discarded from consideration, reducing the total number of active goals. A specific algorithm **DDP** is described which uses this approach. An experiment on **DDP** shows that it infers precise types for roughly 30% to 45% of the variables in a program with hundreds of thousands of lines; the percentage varies with the choice of *pruning threshold*, a parameter of the algorithm. The time required varies from an average of one-tenth of one second per variable to an unknown maximum, again depending on the pruning threshold. These data suggest that 50 and 2000 are both good choices of pruning threshold, depending on whether speed or precision is more important.

1 Introduction

While dynamic programming languages have many advantages, *e.g.*, supporting productive environments such as Smalltalk [1,2] and the Lisp Machine [3], they share the fundamental weakness that less information about programs is immediately apparent before the program runs. This lack of information affects both programmers and their tools. Programmers require more time tracing through a program in order to answer questions such as "what kind of object is the 'schema' parameter of this method?" Tools such as refactoring browsers [4] and compilers [5,6] are similarly hampered by the lack of type information. Refactoring browsers cannot make as many safe refactorings, and compilers cannot optimize as much.

To counteract this lack of information, there have been a number of attempts to *infer* types as often as possible for programs written in dynamically typed languages [6,7,8,9,10,11]. The algorithms from this body of work are quite successful for programs with up to tens of thousands of lines of code, but do not scale to larger programs with hundreds of thousands of lines.

For analyzing programs with hundreds of thousands of lines, this paper proposes modifying existing algorithms in two ways: (1) make them *demand-driven*,

M. Odersky (Ed.): ECOOP 2004, LNCS 3086, pp. 51–74, 2004.

and (2) make them *prune subgoals*. The rest of this paper describes this approach in more detail, describing a specific algorithm **DDP** which instantiates the approach, and giving experimental results showing **DDP**'s effectiveness.

2 Previous Work

2.1 Type Inference in Dynamic Languages

The type-inference problem is similar for various dynamic languages, including Smalltalk, Self, Scheme, Lisp, and Cecil. Algorithms that are effective in one language are effective in the others. As pointed out by Shivers [12], all of these languages share the difficulty that the analysis of control and data flow is interdependent; all of these language have and use dynamic dispatch on types and have data-dependent control flow induced by objects or by higher-order functions.

Efforts on this problem date back at least two decades. Suzuki's work in 1981 is the oldest published work that infers types in Smalltalk without any type declarations [7]. More recently, in 1991, Shivers identified *context selection*, called *contour selection* in his description, as a central technique and a central design difference among type-inference algorithms [6]. The core of Agesen's "Cartesian Products Algorithm" (**CPA**) is the insight of choosing contexts in a type-specific way [9]. **CPA** selects contexts as tuples of parameter types; the algorithm gets its name because the tuples are chosen as cartesian products of the possible argument types for each method. More recently yet, Flanagan and Felleisen have increased the speed and scalability of type-inference algorithms by isolating part of the algorithm to work on individual modules; thus, their algorithm spends less time analyzing the entire program [10]. Most recently of all, Garau has developed a type inference algorithm for a subset of Smalltalk [11]. However, the algorithm does not accurately model two important features of Smalltalk: multiple variables may refer to the same object, and objects may reference each other in cycles. Thus Garau's algorithm supports a much smaller subset of the full language than is usual, and it cannot be directly compared to other work in this area.

Unfortunately, the existing algorithms do not scale to dynamic programs with hundreds of thousands of lines. Certainly, no successful results have been reported for such large programs. Grove, *et al.*, implemented a wide selection of these algorithms as part of the Vortex project, and they report them to require an unreasonable amount of time and memory for larger Cecil programs. [5] Their experimental results for analyzing Cecil are summarized in Table 1. Clearly, **0-CFA** is the only algorithm of these that has any hope for larger programs; the various context-sensitive algorithms tend to fail even on programs with twenty thousand lines of code. However, even **0-CFA**, a context-insensitive algorithm that is faster but less precise, seems to require an additional order of magnitude of improvement to be practical for most applications. With the single order of magnitude in speed available today over the test machine of this study (a Sun Ultra 1 running at 170 MHz), and with the cubic algorithmic complexity of **0-CFA**[13], one can expect a program with one hundred thousand lines to be

Table 1. Type-inference performance data from Grove, *et al.* [5]. Each box gives the running time and the amount of heap consumed for one algorithm applied to one program. A ∞ entry means attempted executions that did not complete in 24 hours on the test machine.

	b-CPA	**SCS**	**0-CFA**	**1,0-CFA**	**1,1-CFA**	**2,2-CFA**	**3,3-CFA**
richards (0.4 klocs)	4 sec 1.6 MB	3 sec 1.6 MB	3 sec 1.6 MB	4 sec 1.6 MB	5 sec 1.6 MB	5 sec 1.6 MB	4 sec 1.6 MB
deltablue (0.65 klocs)	8 sec 1.6 MB	7 sec 1.6 MB	5 sec 1.6 MB	6 sec 1.6 MB	6 sec 1.6 MB	8 sec 1.6 MB	10 sec 1.6 MB
instr sched (2.0 klocs)	146 sec 14.8 MB	83 sec 9.6 MB	67 sec 5.7 MB	99 sec 9.6 MB	109 sec 9.6 MB	334 sec 9.6 MB	1,795 sec 21.0 MB
typechecker (20.0 klocs)	∞ ∞	∞ ∞	947 sec 45.1 MB	13,254 sec 97.4 MB	∞ ∞	∞ ∞	∞ ∞
new-tc (23.5 klocs)	∞ ∞	∞ ∞	1,193 sec 62.1 MB	9,942 sec 115.4 MB	∞ ∞	∞ ∞	∞ ∞
compiler (50.0 klocs)	∞ ∞	∞ ∞	11,941 sec 202.1 MB	∞ ∞	∞ ∞	∞ ∞	∞ ∞

analyzed in about 2.7 hours and to require 1600 MB of memory. A program with two hundred thousand lines would require 21 hours and 13 GB of memory. While one might quibble over the precise definition of "scalable", **0-CFA** is at best near the limit. Grove, *et al.*, agree with this assessment:

> The analysis times and memory requirements for performing the various interprocedurally flow-sensitive algorithms on the larger Cecil programs strongly suggest that the algorithms do not scale to realistically sized programs written in a language like Cecil [5].

2.2 Concrete Type Inference in Static Languages

Type inference (by which we mean "concrete type inference" or "class analysis") is a much easier problem in languages like Java and C which have static type information available, and there are already scalable analyses for these languages. It is not a trivial problem, because better types may be inferred than the type system provides, but it is nevertheless a much easier problem.

One way the problem is easier is that context sensitivity is not necessary. For example, Tip and Palsberg have developed an effective analysis that does not need context [14]. In fact, Tip and Palsberg argue that existing context-sensitive algorithms in Java should be abandoned as impractical:

> In practice, the scalability of the algorithms at either end of the spectrum is fairly clear. The CHA and RTA algorithms at the low end of the range scale well and are widely used. The k-CFA algorithms (for $k > 0$) at the high end seem not to scale well at all.[14]

It appears that the static types in static languages are helping by bounding the distance that an imprecise type may flow. For some intuition about this effect, consider the following example. Suppose we define an identity method, `yourself`, in Smalltalk—a simple polymorphic method that returns whatever is passed to it. Consider this use of the `yourself` message:

```
x := x yourself
```

This statement has no effect on the value of x, much less its type. With a context-free analysis, however, every invocation of `yourself` must be assigned the same result type, and thus the presence of this statement causes the type of x to be polluted by the types of every other sender of `yourself` in the entire program. Contrast this result to a context-sensitive analysis. With **CPA**, the `yourself` method is analyzed multiple times, once for each type of argument supplied to it. With **1-CFA** [6], the method is analyzed once for each place it is called from. In either case, the type of x will remain the same whether this statement is present or not.

To contrast, consider the same code converted to Java, where `yourself()` is an identity method and `Foo` is some class:

```
Object yourself(Object o) {return o;}
 ...
Foo x;
 ...
x = (Foo) yourself(x)
```

In this case, any context-free analysis is sufficient. The type of the expression `yourself`(x) will still be polluted just as in Smalltalk, but the cast will protect the type of x itself from being polluted. The statement may cause x's type to become less precise, but it will not become less precise than `Foo`.

The example generalizes well beyond identity methods. This situation arises with *any* polymorphic method that is called by monomorphic code. In Java, the monomorphic code will still get precise types, because there will always be casts to keep the imprecise types of the polymorphic code from polluting the monomorphic code. In dynamic languages there is no such protection, and only the use of context can keep the imprecise types at bay. Unfortunately, as described in the previous section, the known context-sensitive algorithms do not scale to hundred-thousand line programs in dynamically typed languages.

3 A Scalable Approach

To scale type inference to larger programs, this paper proposes two techniques: the algorithms are *demand-driven*, and they *prune subgoals*. Each technique is described below.

3.1 Demand-Driven Analysis

Demand-driven algorithms find information "on demand:" instead of finding information about every construct in an entire program, they find information that is specifically requested. Several demand-driven versions of data-flow algorithms have been developed [15,16,17,18,19].

Demand-driven algorithms are organized around *goals*. A client posts *goals* that the algorithm is to solve, *e.g.*, "what is the type of x?" To find a correct response to a goal, the algorithm may itself post subgoals. For example, in response to the query "what is the type of x?", it may ask "what is the type of y?" if there is a statement "x := y" in the program. As the algorithm progresses, it has a number of goals it is trying to solve; when it finishes, it has solved some number of those goals.

There are two main advantages to using demand-driven analysis instead of the usual exhaustive analysis. First, a demand-driven algorithm analyzes a subset of the program for each goal. For a particular goal, often only a small number of subgoals are needed and only a limited portion of the program is analyzed. Thus a demand-driven algorithm typically has much less work to do and can finish each execution much more quickly than an entire exhaustive analysis can complete. Since it is frequently the case that program-manipulation tools such as compilers and development environments only sparsely probe the program with queries, having an algorithm that doesn't require exhaustively computing the answer to *every* query just to provide answers for *some* queries can pay off handsomely.

Second, demand-driven algorithms can adaptively trade off between precision of results and speed of execution. If the algorithm completes quickly, then it can try more ambitious subgoals that would lead to more precise information about the target goal. Likewise, if the algorithm is taking too long, it can give up on some subgoals and accept less precise information. The latter idea is explored in Sect. 3.2.

The main disadvantage of a demand-driven analysis is that it only finds information about those constructs for which goals have been posted. If an application *does* need the answers for all possible queries of a given program, then an exhaustive algorithm (if one is available) can be faster than running the demand-driven algorithm once for each query, as the exhaustive algorithm may be able to share information across the various queries being processed.

3.2 Subgoal Pruning

A goal is pruned by giving it an immediate solution which is correct (albeit probably lacking in precision) independent of the answer to any other goals. In other words, a pruned goal has no subgoals. By carefully choosing goals to prune, an algorithm may reduce the number of goals that are relevant to the target goal. In turn, having fewer goals tends to speed up the algorithm. Thus, pruning subgoals is a technique for trading precision for speed.

Pruning subgoals is not itself a new idea. It is an instance of *heuristic search*, a well-known technique of artificial intelligence [20]. However, the technique is rare in published program analyses. Published work tends to insist on optimal solutions within some rules of inference, even though these rules are themselves typically approximate, *e.g.*, data-flow analyses include flow paths in their meet-over-paths specification that may never occur at run time. Some researchers have designed clever techniques that adaptively *increase* the number of goals to gain more precision when time allows [19]. We know of no published work in program analysis that adaptively *reduces* the number of goals in response to resource limitations.

3.3 Synthesis

The combination of being demand-driven and of adaptively pruning subgoals yields a nice synthesis where precise information is found in two different situations. First, precise information is found whenever ambitious context-sensitive expansion of subgoals is both effective and inexpensive. Note that just because context-sensitive expansion *allows* a huge number of subgoals to be generated, the expansion does not *always* do so. Second, precise information is found whenever context is not necessary. Each goal being analyzed gets both opportunities, and different subgoals can use different opportunities within a single execution of the analysis. Intuitively, the synthesis might be described as: *aim high but tolerate less.* For the algorithm designer, the benefit is that context-sensitive justification rules can be added without much worry about the worst cases of subgoal explosion.

4 The DDP Algorithm

We have designed an algorithm using these principles to perform type analysis of programs written in a dynamically-typed object-oriented language such as Smalltalk. This algorithm is named **DDP**, because it is demand-driven and it prunes subgoals.

DDP searches backwards from a root goal g, which is the original request. We essentially build a proof tree, in a goal-directed manner, using Agesen's CPA abstraction. This abstraction provides for an analytic space that is finite, albeit intractably large for large programs. However, let us assume for the moment that we have unbounded computational resources at hand for this search (we'll fix this assumption later). Were this the case, we could explore the proof tree backwards, terminating the search at (1) axioms (that is, leaf nodes), and (2) circular dependencies. An example of an axiom would be an assertion that the type of the value produced by sending a `new:` message to a class C in some context has type $\{C\}$. An example of a circular dependency would be found by searching backwards through a loop or recursion. The presence of circular dependencies means that our proof tree is actually a rooted graph, of course. Note that this proof graph, for a particular request or root goal, might quite likely make reference to only a subset of the entire program under consideration. (That, at least, is our hope.)

Once this proof graph had been determined by backwards search, we would then propagate information *forwards* from the axioms. Circular dependencies in the graph are handled by iterating to convergence. However, flowing information forwards may trigger the creation of further subgoals in our graph. This is in the nature of higher-order control-flow analysis: as we discover values of new types flowing to the receiver position of a message-send statement, determining the value produced by the entire statement will require establishing new subgoals for message sends to objects of the newly-discovered classes for the receiver. Thus backwards search and forwards information flow are interleaved.

The facts that concern our proof graph (type and control-flow assertions) have a lattice structure; a fixed point is a valid solution (which is how we account for cycles in the proof graph). By valid, we mean that any possibility that might arise during the execution of the program is described by the asserted type or flow fact. Note that even the least fixed-point solution to the proof graph might also include possibilities that never arise during actual program execution; this fundamental limitation is typical for this kind of analysis. Further, any value above the least fixed point is also valid, in that it will be a less precise approximation admitting all the possibilities of the least fixed-point solution, and others as well.

With this structure in mind, let's now adjust the algorithm to account for our need to do analysis in the presence of bounded computational resources. As we search backwards, recursively expanding out the proof graph, we associate with each node in our proof graph a current value from our fact lattice. For a newly-created goal, this fact starts out as the bottom fact. At all times, this value is $\sqsubseteq$ the fixed-point value we would compute if we had unbounded resources. That is, we are always consistent with the fixed-point value, but possibly more precise than it is (*i.e.*, *too* precise)—the current value at a node might not account for all the cases that the final fixed-point value would cover. As our search uncovers new sources of information, we flow this information forward through the graph.

If we are fortunate enough for this entire process to settle out and terminate within some previously established resource budget, then we can halt with a fixed-point solution that provides our final answer. If, however, we exhaust time or space, then we may choose to prune subgoals. This is a standard technique from the AI community, which has long dealt with the problem of search in intractably large spaces. We can choose a fringe of unsatisfied nodes in the tree, and simply assert the top fact for these nodes—the fact that is so pessimistically or conservatively general that it *must* cover the actual run-time behavior described by the goal in question. Hopefully, if this fact occurs deep in the search tree, it will not have too large an effect on the precision of the fact produced at the root of the tree.

Introducing top values in place of more precise facts to elide search means that our final result must now be above the least fixed-point solution we would

```
procedure InferType(var) {
  rootgoal := typegoal(var)
  worklist := { rootgoal }
  while worklist ≠ ∅ do
    if resource bounds unexhausted
    then Search1()
    else Prune()
}
procedure Search1() {
  Remove g from worklist
  changed? := Update(g)
  if changed? then
    deps := Depends_on(g)
    worklist := worklist ∪ deps
}
procedure Prune() {
  for g ∈ ChoosePrunes() do
    prune g
  worklist := Relevant(rootgoal)
}
```

Fig. 1. The top-level structure of the **DDP** algorithm.

have found with our simple, unbounded-resource algorithm. So this is where we introduce approximation to handle resource bounds on the analysis.

Note that the bidirectionality of the analysis means that simply trimming the search tree and asserting top facts does not give us an immediate solution. Recall that forward flow of facts that are high in the lattice may require us to create new subgoals higher in the search tree. However, taking a large step upwards in the fact lattice certainly moves us closer to an eventual fixed point.

This, in a nutshell, is the essence of our algorithm. The rest is simply filling in the particulars of our particular analysis problem (OO type inference) and finite abstraction (Agesen's CPA).

4.1 Overall Algorithm

The top-level structure of the algorithm is shown in Figure 1. The algorithm is based on a worklist; it commences by initializing the worklist to the initial top-level goal. The worklist-processing loop, however, is sensitive to resource usage.

As long as resources (either time or space) have not been exhausted, the basic loop removes a work item g from the worklist and processes it. Each work item corresponds to a node in the proof graph we are constructing. Each such node has associated with it a current tentative solution in the fact lattice, the set of nodes on which it is dependent, and the set of nodes that depend on it. First, we update g, recalculating its value in the fact lattice from the current nodes in the proof graph upon which it is dependent (change in these nodes was the reason for g being added to the worklist). If the justification requires subgoals that do not exist, then new goals are created and added to the worklist. New goals are always given a maximally optimistic tentative solution, *e.g.*, $\bot$ for type goals. Once all the necessary subgoals have been created or located, and g's solution is consistent with all its subgoals, we may remove g from the worklist and proceed. However, if any of this processing has caused g's current value to rise in the fact lattice, then any goal depending on g must be revisited. These goals are added to the worklist. In this way, the graph is searched backwards, in a goal-directed fashion, and values are propagated forwards through this graph; when we arrive at a fixed point, the worklist will be exhausted.

Once the search has proceeded beyond pre-set resource limits, however, a pruning step is triggered. The pruning step selects some number of nodes to prune, assigns to each one the appropriate top value, and performs a graph search starting at the root goal in order to find the goals that are still relevant. Those goals found in the graph search become the new contents of the worklist.

4.2 Mini-smalltalk

DDP analyzes full Smalltalk, but many of the details are more tedious than interesting. In this paper, **DDP** is described as an analysis of Mini-Smalltalk, a minimal language that captures the essence of Smalltalk.

A program in Mini-Smalltalk has a list of global variables and a class hierarchy with single inheritance. Each class has a list of instance variables and a list of methods. Each method has a selector and a main block. A block, including the main block of a method, has a list of parameters, a list of local variables, and a list of statements.

A statement in Mini-Smalltalk is of one of the following forms:

- *var* := *literal*. This statement assigns a literal to the specified variable. The precise set of literals is unimportant, except to note that method selectors are valid literals.
- *var* := *rvar*. This statement assigns one variable to another.
- *var* := `self`. This statement assigns the current receiver to the variable *var*.
- *var* := `new` *class*. This statement creates a new object with the specified class, and it sets all of the new object's instance variables to `nil`.
- *var* := `send`(*rcvrvar*, *selector*, $argvar_1$, ... , $argvar_m$). This statement initiates a message send. When the invoked method completes, the result will be stored into *var*.
- *var* := `sendvar`(*rcvrvar*, *selvar*, $argvar_1$, ... , $argvar_m$). This statement also invokes a method, with the difference that the selector is read from a variable instead of being specified in the syntax. In Smalltalk, this functionality is invoked with the `perform:` family of methods.
- `return` *var*. This statement returns a value to the calling method.

- *var* := *block*. This statement creates a new block, which has its own parameters, local variables, and statements, and assigns that block to a variable. A block statement is the same as a lambda expression in a functional language. A block captures any variable bindings in its surrounding lexical scope, it can be passed around the program as a first-class value, and it can be evaluated later.
- *var* := `beval`(*blockvar*, $argvar_1$, ... , $argvar_m$). This statement reads a block from a variable and invokes the block with the specified parameters.
- `breturn` *var*. This statement returns a value from a block. Note that `breturn` and `return` are not the same: the latter will return from the whole method, and thus may simultaneously pop multiple levels of the runtime call stack.

It is assumed that all variable names in a Mini-Smalltalk program are distinct. Since variables are statically bound in Smalltalk, this causes no loss of generality.

Most program constructs in full Smalltalk can be translated to Mini-Smalltalk. Variables may be renamed to be unique because all variable references are statically bound. A compound expression may be rewritten as a series of simple statements that assign subexpressions to fresh temporary variables. The primitive `value` method for evaluating a block may be replaced by a single Mini-Smalltalk method that executes a `beval` on `self`. Likewise the `perform:` method can be replaced using a `sendvar` statement. Note that the Mini-Smalltalk `new` statement is not intended to model the full effect of sending a `new` message to some class; that is handled by the full body of the class's corresponding method. The Mini-Smalltalk `new` statement simply provides for the primitive allocation part of such a computation.

A few items are missing from Mini-Smalltalk, but cause no fundamental difficulty if they are added back. The `super` keyword is missing, but if `super` message sends are added back, they can be treated in the same way normal message sends are treated, only with a different and simpler method lookup algorithm. Primitive methods are missing, but if they are added, a type inferencer can analyze most of them in a straightforward fashion so long as a few descriptive functions are available for the primitives of interest. These descriptive functions give information such as what return type the primitive has when it is supplied with various input types. Primitives without descriptive functions may still be analyzed soundly by using conservative approximations.

There are remaining primitives in full Smalltalk which cause difficulties. For example, one such primitive, analogously to the `eval` function of Lisp, creates a new method from an arbitrary list of bytecodes. Such methods are inherently very difficult for static analysis. However, it is quite rare to see these capabilities used outside of program-development environments. Most applications stay away from such powerful and difficult-to-analyze reflection facilities: they can make programs hard for humans to understand, for the same reasons that they make them difficult for compilers to analyze and optimize. Thus a static analysis is still useful if it ignores such constructs, and in fact ignoring such constructs is par for most static analyses to date.

4.3 Goals

The algorithm has five kinds of goals. Informally they are:

- type goals, *e.g.*, "what is the type of x?"
- transitive flow goals, *e.g.*, "where can objects flow, if they start in x?"
- simple flow goals, *e.g.*, "where can objects flow after just one program step, if they start in x?"
- senders goals, *e.g.*, "what statements can invoke the method named + in class SmallInteger?"
- responders goals, *e.g.*, "what methods are invoked by [x := 2 + 2] ?"

Each goal is answered by its own kind of *judgement*. For example, the type goal "what is the type of x" could be answered by a type judgement "x is of type Integer."

This section will describe these kinds of goals and judgements in more detail, but first it is necessary to describe *types*, *contexts*, and *flow positions*.

Types. A *type* describes a set of objects. The following kinds of types are available:

- $\{c\}$, a *class type* including all instances of class c. A class type does *not* include instances of subclasses.
- $S\{sel\}$, a *selector type* including the sole instance of the method selector *sel*. (Selector types are included in the list so that `sendvar` statements can be handled.)
- $B\{blk\}_{ctx}$, a *block type*, including all block objects which were created from a block statement $[v := blk]$ in context ctx (contexts are described below).
- $t_1 \sqcup t_2 \sqcup \cdots \sqcup t_n$, a union of two or more types of the above kinds.
- $\top$, a type including every object.
- $\bot$, a type including no objects.

As usual, one type may be a subtype of another, $t_1 \sqsubseteq t_2$, if all objects in t_1 are also in t_2. For example, every type is a subtype of $\top$. Further, the union of two types, $t_1 \sqcup t_2$, is the set of objects included in either t_1 or t_2. Note, that subclasses are not included in class types, *e.g.*, {Object} is *not* a supertype of {Integer}.

Contexts. A *context* specifies a subset of possible execution states. It does so by specifying a block or method and by placing restrictions on the types of the parameters of the current method or block, and possibly by restricting the type of the current message receiver. A valid context may only restrict parameters that are visible within the specified block. A valid context cannot, for example, restrict the types of parameters from two different methods (as methods do not lexically nest). Further restrictions on valid contexts are described further below.

Most contexts are written as follows:

$$<: (\textbf{Foo.addBar:})\ \texttt{self} = \{\text{Foo}\},\ \ \texttt{x} = \{\text{Bar}\} :>$$

This context matches execution states for which all of the following are true:

– The block that is executing is either the main block of the method named `addBar:` in class Foo, or is a block nested within that method.
– The receiver, *i.e.*, `self` in Smalltalk, is a member of type {Foo}.
– The parameter named `x` holds an object of type {Bar}.

Additionally, the context $\top_{ctx}$ matches any execution state, and the context $\bot_{ctx}$ matches no execution state.

Like types, contexts may be compared with each other; $ctx_1 \sqsubseteq ctx_2$ if every state matched by ctx_1 is also matched by ctx_2. Furthermore, $ctx_1 \sqcap ctx_2$ is a context which matches a state if the both ctx_1 and ctx_2 also match it. Likewise, $ctx_1 \sqcup ctx_2$ matches states that either ctx_1 or ctx_2 match.

There is a mutual recursion between the definitions of types and contexts, and it is desirable that only a finite number of types and contexts be available. Otherwise, the algorithm might have what Agesen terms "recursive customization" [9]. To gain this property, a technical restriction is imposed: the context of a block type $B\{blk\}_{ctx}$ is not allowed to mention, either directly or indirectly, another block type whose block is *blk*. The restriction is enforced whenever the algorithm is about to create a new block type: a recursive traversal of the context is performed and any context mentioning *blk* is replaced by $\top_{ctx}$. While this approach is surely suboptimal, it does not appear to be an issue in practice.

Flow Positions. A *flow position* describes a set of locations in the program that can hold a value. The following kinds of flow positions are used by **DDP**:

– $[\!:V\ var :\!]_{ctx}$ is a *variable flow position*, and it describes the variable *var* while execution is in context *ctx*.
– $[\!:S\ meth :\!]_{ctx}$ is a *self flow position*, and it describes the current receiver while the method *meth* is executing under the context *ctx*.
– $fp_1 \sqcup fp_2 \sqcup \cdots \sqcup fp_n$ is a union of a finite number of flow positions, and it describes the locations described by any of $fp_1, \ldots, fp_n$. Each fp_i must be a flow position of one of the above kinds.
– $\top_{fp}$ is the universal flow position. It includes every possible location in the program.
– $\bot_{fp}$ is the empty flow position. It includes no locations.

Type Goals. A *type goal* asks what the type of some variable is, when the variable appears in some context. It looks like:

$$var :_{ctx} ?$$

The solution to this type goal is some *type judgement* $var :_{ctx} type$. This judgement declares that as the program executes, the variable *var*, whenever it appears in a context matching *ctx*, will only hold objects of type *type*.

Flow Goals. A *simple flow goal* asks where values may flow in one program step, given a starting flow position. It looks like:

$$fp_1 \rightarrow ?$$

The solution to a simple flow goal is some *simple flow judgement* $fp_1 \rightarrow fp_2$. This judgement claims that after any one step of execution, an object that was at flow position fp_1 may only now be found in either positions fp_1 and fp_2. fp_1 is a possibility because the judgement claims that the object *may* flow to fp_2, not that it *will*.

A *transitive flow goal* asks the same question except that any number of program steps is allowed. A transitive flow goal looks like:

$$fp_1 \rightarrow^* ?$$

The solution to this transitive flow goal is a *transitive flow judgement* $fp_1 \rightarrow^* fp_2$. This judgement claims that if an object is located only in position fp_1, then after any number of program steps, it may only be found in position fp_2.

Senders Goals. A *senders goal* asks what statements may invoke a specified method or block.

$$blk_{ctx} \xleftarrow{send} ?$$

The solution to this senders goal is a *senders judgement* $blk_{ctx} \xleftarrow{send} ss$. This judgement claims that whenever a step of execution will invoke the block blk, there must be a statement/context pair $(stat, ctx) \in ss$ such that the invoking statement is $stat$ and the invoking execution state is matched by ctx.

Alternatively, ss may be $\top_s$, in which case the judgement makes no claim about which statements may invoke the block.

Responders Goals. A *responders goal* asks what methods or blocks may be invoked by a specified statement. It looks like:

$$stat_{ctx} \xrightarrow{send} ?$$

The solution to this responders goal is a *responders judgement* $stat_{ctx} \xrightarrow{send} rs$. Typically, rs is a set of block/context pairs. The judgement claims that whenever $stat$ executes in context ctx, it will invoke a block b in some context $bctx$ such that $(b, bctk) \in rs$. If $stat$ is a `send` or `sendvar` statement, then all of the blocks in rs will be main blocks of methods. If $stat$ is a `beval` statement, then all of the blocks will instead be blocks created by block statements.

Alternatively, rs may be $\top_r$, in which case the judgement makes no claim about which blocks might be invoked by $stat$.

Valid Contexts. We have already seen that a valid context may only specify the types of parameters that are lexically visible within the block specified by the context. An additional restriction appears in each place that a context is used.

- The context for a variable flow position may only specify a block that declares the variable, or which lexically encloses a block declaring the variable. Note we *don't* mean contexts nested *within* the scope of the variable (*i.e.*, the scope in which the variable is visible), but the contexts within which it is nested itself—these are the allocated contexts that are known to exist when the variable is bound itself.
- The context for a self flow position may only specify the main block of the method.
- The context for a block type may only specify a block that encloses the statement which creates the block.
- The context for a type goal may only specify a block that lexically encloses the variable whose type is to be inferred.

If a context is invalid for its intended usage, it can be broadened until it meets the necessary restrictions. The notation $\lceil ctx \rceil$ denotes a context that is less restrictive than *ctx* and which is valid for the intended purpose (as described above). That intended purpose will be clear from the context of discussion. For example, one might write:

$$var :_{\lceil ctx \rceil} type$$

In this type judgement, the context is a valid context at least as inclusive as *ctx*, and if that context is other than $\top_{ctx}$, then it specifies a block that either declares *var* itself or encloses the block that does.

4.4 Justification Rules

When **DDP** updates a goal (see Sect. 4.1), it assigns a new tentative solution to the goal and references one *justification rule* to justify it. The rules available to **DDP** have been chosen, for the most part, to be as simple as possible. The main choice is that the algorithm uses the kind of context sensitivity that **CPA** does.

Unfortunately, as straightforward as the rules are, they still require 17 pages to describe in the current working document giving the formal definition of **DDP**. With five kinds of judgements and ten kinds of statements, the details simply add up. Thus, instead of listing all of the justification rules, we describe only a few representative rules in this section. The full set are straightforwardly derived from the application of Agesen's **CPA** in a backwards-search context.

Usually, a judgement is justified by accounting for every statement that the program might execute in a program $\mathcal{P}$:

$$\frac{\text{J-ALLSTATS} \quad \forall stat \in \mathbf{statements}(\mathcal{P}) : \quad stat \ \rhd \ j}{\rhd \ j}$$

The notation $\rhd\ j$ claims that judgement j is justified without qualification. The notation $stat\ \rhd\ j$ claims that the judgement j accounts for the possible execution of statement $stat$.

Here is the justification rule for type judgements that is used to account for variable-assignment statements:

$$\text{T-VAR}\quad \frac{\begin{array}{c}\rhd\ v_2 :_{\lceil ctx \rceil} t_2 \\ t_2 \sqsubseteq t\end{array}}{[v_1 := v_2]\ \rhd\ v_1 :_{ctx} t}$$

Informally, this justification rule requires the type of v_1 to be a supertype of that for v_2.

Note that using T-VAR requires a subgoal to be satisfied. Whenever the T-VAR rule is used as part of the justification for a solution to the goal $v_1 :_{ctx} ?$, there is a subgoal generated to also find and justify a solution to the goal $v_2 :_{\lceil ctx \rceil} ?$. The solution to the subgoal will be some judgement $v_2 :_{\lceil ctx \rceil} t_2$ that can be used to satisfy the assumptions in T-VAR. This pattern is general: judgements in the assumption list of a justification rule, correspond to subgoals that **DDP** generates.

A more complex rule is used to show that a type judgement accounts for a message send statement:

$$\text{T-SEND}\quad \frac{\begin{array}{c} stat = [v := \mathtt{send}(v_{rcvr}, sel, v_1, \ldots, v_m)] \\ \rhd\ stat_{ctx} \xrightarrow{send} \{(m_1, c_1), \ldots, (m_p, c_p)\} \\ \forall i \in 1 \ldots p : \forall\ v_{ret} \in \mathbf{ret\_vars}(m_i) : \\ \exists t' : (\rhd\ v_{ret} :_{\lceil c_i \rceil} t')) \wedge (t' \sqsubseteq t) \end{array}}{v := \mathtt{send}(v_{rcvr}, sel, v_1, \ldots, v_m)\ \rhd\ v :_{ctx} t}$$

Informally, this rule finds the methods that may respond to the statement, it finds a type for each return statement in those methods, and then it requires that t be a supertype of all of the returned types.

In more detail, the rule first requires that there is a justified responders judgement $stat_{ctx} \xrightarrow{send} \ldots$. This judgement identifies the methods that can respond to this `send` statement along with the contexts those methods can be invoked under. For each tuple (m_i, c_i) of a responding method and context, the function **ret_vars** is used to find the variables returned by a return statement in m_i. For each such variable v_{ret}, the rule requires that there exists a justified type judgement $v_{ret} :_{\lceil c_i \rceil} t'$ giving a type t' for the object returned. Each such t' must be a subtype of t, the type in the type judgement that is being justified.

Finally, here is the main justification rule is used to find the invokers of a block:

S-BEVAL

$$\frac{\begin{array}{c} stat = [v := \texttt{beval}(v_{beval}, v_1, \ldots, v_m)] \\ [v_{blk} := blk] \in \textbf{statements}(\mathcal{P}) \\ \triangleright [: V\ v_{blk} :]_{\lceil ctx \rceil} \rightarrow^* f_b \\ f_b \sqcap [: V\ v_{beval} :]_{\top_{ctx}} = [: V\ v_{beval} :]_{bctx_1} \sqcup \cdots \sqcup [: V\ v_{beval} :]_{bctx_p} \\ \forall i \in 1 \ldots p: \ \ (stat, bctx_i) \in ss \end{array}}{[v := \texttt{beval}(v_{beval}, v_1, \ldots, v_m)] \ \triangleright \ blk_{ctx} \xleftarrow{send} ss}$$

The goal of this justification rule is to justify that a senders judgement accounts for a particular `beval` statement. Informally, this rule requires that the block has been traced forward through the program, and that the senders set accounts for each way (if any) the block can reach the `beval` statement.

In detail, the rule first finds the unique statement $[v_{blk} := blk]$ that creates the block. The rule then requires that there is a justified transitive flow judgement $[: V\ v_{blk} :]_{\lceil ctx \rceil} \rightarrow^* f_b$. This flow judgement claims that the only locations the block can reach are those in the flow position f_b. Next, the rule picks out the portions of f_b which is for variable v_{beval}, the variable the `beval` statement is reading its block from. For each such portion $[: V\ v_{beval} :]_{bctx_i}$, the senders set ss must include an entry for the `beval` statement under context $bctx_i$.

4.5 Subgoal Pruning

A complete algorithm must specify *how* to prune, *when* to prune, *which* goals to prune, and how to *garbage collect* goals that are no longer needed. **DDP** has straightforward choices for all of these.

To prune a goal, **DDP** chooses the appropriate $\top$ value for the goal: $\top$ for type goals, $\top_{fp}$ for flow goals, $\top_r$ for responders goals, and $\top_s$ for senders goals. In any case, the goal is immediately justified without depending on any subgoals.

DDP prunes goals when either many goal updates have happened since the last pruning, or many new goals have been added since the last pruning. Specifically, there is a threshold `Thresh`, and if the sum of the number of new updates plus the number of new goals surpasses that threshold, then **DDP** makes a number of prunings and then garbage collects.

Before choosing which goals to prune, **DDP** chooses which goals to keep: it keeps the first `Thresh` goals it encounters during a breadth-first traversal of the proof graph. The goals it chooses to prune are then the goals which are kept but which have subgoals that are not kept.

Garbage collection is then straightforward: any node not to be kept is removed from consideration.

4.6 Example Execution

Figure 2 gives a short fragment of a program. Suppose the type inferencer tries to infer a type for `x`. A goal is posted for the type of `x`, and after a few updates goals for `h` and `doc` are posted, reaching the goal table shown in Table 2.

```
x := 0
doc := (something complicated)
h := send(doc, documentHeight)
x := h
```

Fig. 2. An example program fragment

Note that each assigned type includes {UndefinedObject}, the type of `nil`, because all variable bindings other than parameters are initialized with `nil`. **DDP** makes no effort to determine whether a variable is used before it is initialized, and thus {UndefinedObject} must be included for correctness.

At this point, the algorithm will spend many updates working on the type of `doc`. Eventually the algorithm will give up on `doc` and prune it, leading to the goal table in Table 3. The type of `doc` has been lost, but now the calculation for the type of `h` may proceed. Since only one method in the program has selector `documentHeight` (let us presume), losing the type of `doc` causes no harm. Suppose the one `documentHeight` method has a single return statement returning variable `height`. Then, after a few more steps, the goal table reaches the state shown in Table 4, and a precise type of `x` has been found.

5 Experimental Evaluation

We have implemented **DDP** and performed an experiment with two objectives: to measure the algorithm's overall performance, and to determine a good pruning threshold for the algorithm. This section describes the experiment in more detail, gives the data it produced, and interprets the results.

DDP was implemented in Squeak 2.8, one version of a single large program written in Smalltalk. This implementation was then used to analyze portions of a combined program with Squeak 2.8 plus **DDP** plus the Refactoring Browser[1] as ported to Squeak.[2] (The Refactoring Browser was included because it is used in the implementation of **DDP**). This combined program has 313,775 non-blank lines of code, 1901 classes, and 46,080 methods. Table 5 summarizes the components of this program that were targeted for analysis.

The implementation was given a series of queries, with the queries ranging over (1) instance variables from one of the above packages, and (2) a pruning threshold between 50 and 5000 goals. We ran our tests on a Linux IA32 system with a 2.0 GHz Athlon processor and 512Mb of RAM. The speed of the inferencer is summarized in Table 6, and the precision of the inferencer is summarized in Table 7.

To compute the precision percentages, each type inferred for a variable in a given component was hand classified as either *precise* or *imprecise*. We hand classified results using the following rules:

– $\top$ is imprecise.

1 |http://www.refactory.com/RefactoringBrowser—

2 |http://minnow.cc.gatech.edu/squeak/227

Table 2. Example goal table after a few goal updates

Goal Number	Goal	Current Solution	Subgoals
1	x $:\top_{ctx}$?	{SmallInteger} $\sqcup$ {UndefinedObject}	2
2	h $:\top_{ctx}$?	{UndefinedObject}	3
3	doc $:\top_{ctx}$?	{UndefinedObject}	*many* ...
⋮	⋮	⋮	⋮

Table 3. Example goal table after pruning goal 3

Goal Number	Goal	Current Solution	Subgoals
1	x $:\top_{ctx}$?	{SmallInteger} $\sqcup$ {UndefinedObject}	2
2	h $:\top_{ctx}$?	{UndefinedObject}	3,100
3	doc $:\top_{ctx}$?	$\top$	*none*
100	height $:\top_{ctx}$?	{UndefinedObject}	...
⋮	⋮	⋮	⋮

Table 4. Example goal table at finish

Goal Number	Goal	Current Solution	Subgoals
1	x $:\top_{ctx}$?	{SmallInteger} $\sqcup$ {UndefinedObject}	2
2	h $:\top_{ctx}$?	{SmallInteger} $\sqcup$ {UndefinedObject}	3,100
3	doc $:\top_{ctx}$?	$\top$	*none*
100	height $:\top_{ctx}$?	{SmallInteger} $\sqcup$ {UndefinedObject}	...
⋮	⋮	⋮	⋮

- $\perp$ is precise. ($\perp$ means that the variable is never instantiated at all.)
- Any simple class type, selector type, or block type is precise.
- A union type is precise if, according to human analysis, at least half of its component simple types may arise during execution. For this analysis, the exact values of arithmetic operations are not considered; *e.g.*, any operation might return a negative or positive result, and any integer operation might overflow the bounds of SmallInteger.
- If none of the above rules apply, then the type is imprecise.

Table 5. The components of the program analyzed in the experiment.

Name	Instance variables	Description
rbparse	56	Refactoring browser's parser.
mail	70	Mail reader distributed with Squeak
synth	183	Package for synthesis and manipulation of digital audio
irc	58	Client for IRC networks
browser	23	Smalltalk code browser
interp	207	In-Squeak simulation of the Squeak virtual machine
games	120	Collection of small games for Morphic GUI
sunit	14	User interface to an old version of SUnit
pda	44	Personal digital assistant

Table 6. Speed of the inferencer. Entries gives the average speed in seconds for inferences of instance variables in one component, using the given pruning threshold. The "overall" entries on the last line are averaged across all individual type inferences; thus, they are weighted averages of the component averages, weighted by the number of instance variables within each component.

	50 nodes	150 nodes	500 nodes	1000 nodes	1500 nodes	2000 nodes	2500 nodes	3000 nodes	4000 nodes	5000 nodes
rbparse	0.16	0.57	2.76	5.57	15.43	16.4	25.33	26.02	33.94	61.33
mail	0.13	0.72	3.12	9.6	17.32	18.45	21.38	32.32	42.73	60.45
synth	0.17	0.75	3.07	6.45	9.3	13.5	33.17	25.93	36.13	79.56
irc	0.1	0.56	2.53	2.83	5.5	7.56	10.04	14.17	20.86	20.94
browser	0.14	0.46	2.64	3.82	7.16	8.88	19.1	14.55	85.74	180.29
interp	0.07	0.33	1.3	2.58	4.96	7.13	11.88	18.44	18.63	23.99
games	0.11	0.44	1.68	3.01	5.23	6.91	8.95	11.77	17.54	16.41
sunit	0.26	1.1	2.26	3.65	6.3	7.24	7.68	10.09	9.24	7.21
pda	0.08	0.76	2.54	5.86	7.65	11.07	16.46	22.16	30.31	38.49
Overall	0.12	0.56	2.27	4.67	8.18	10.6	18.54	20.6	28.53	46.86

There is clearly some subjectivity in the fourth rule. However, we believe that we have been at least as conservative as any reasonable experimenter would be; when in doubt, we classified a type as imprecise. Further, the following types, which are obviously precise, comprise 87.0% of the inferences that were classified as precise:

- (56.3%) $\{C\} \sqcup \{\text{UndefinedObject}\}$, for some class C.
- (13.7%) $\{\text{UndefinedObject}\}$, *i.e.*, the variable is never initialized from the code.
- (10.3%) $\{\text{True}\} \sqcup \{\text{False}\} \sqcup \{\text{UndefinedObject}\}$
- (6.7%) $\{\text{SmallInt}\} \sqcup \{\text{LargePosInt}\} \sqcup \{\text{LargeNegInt}\} \sqcup \{\text{UndefObject}\}$[3]

[3] Class names have been abbreviated.

For external validation, a complete listing of the type inferred for each variable is available on the net [21], and will be included in the longer report describing this work [22].

The precision varies from 31.0% to 43.7%, depending on the pruning threshold. This level of precision is clearly enough to be useful for many purposes, *e.g.*, program understanding tools which present type information directly to the programmer. The speed varies from 0.12 seconds to 46.86 seconds on average, again depending on the pruning threshold. Again, this level of performance is clearly high enough to be useful in various tools.

The best choice of pruning threshold depends on whether speed or precision is more important. If speed is the most important, then the extreme choice of a mere 50 nodes appears like the best choice. The inferences are very rapid, while precision is a reasonable 31.7%. If precision is more important, then the data suggest that 2000 nodes is a good choice; thresholds above 2000 nodes use much more time while yielding only a small improvement in precision. Of course, the best choice depends on the application; if precision is extremely useful and time is cheap, then higher thresholds would still make sense.

6 Future Work

While **DDP** is effective as it stands, there are several areas of investigation that remain open: extending the algorithm for exhaustive analysis, augmenting the justification rules, and studying pruning techniques.

Table 7. Precision of the inferencer. Entries give the percentage of inferred types considered by a human as "precise" for instance variables in one component using one pruning threshold. As in Table 6, the "overall" entries are averaged across inferences, not averaged across the averages in the table.

	50 nodes	150 nodes	500 nodes	1000 nodes	1500 nodes	2000 nodes	2500 nodes	3000 nodes	4000 nodes	5000 nodes
rbparse	33.9	33.9	30.4	32.1	33.9	35.7	39.3	33.9	35.7	39.3
mail	28.6	35.7	31.4	38.6	40.0	38.6	41.4	35.7	38.6	37.1
synth	25.1	27.3	32.8	35.5	36.1	36.1	35.5	35.5	36.6	36.1
irc	37.9	41.4	41.4	50.0	50.0	48.3	51.7	56.9	53.4	62.1
browser	8.7	8.7	13.0	13.0	13.0	8.7	13.0	13.0	13.0	13.0
interp	23.7	24.6	23.7	23.7	24.6	34.8	35.7	34.3	35.3	34.8
games	55.0	64.2	63.3	63.3	63.3	75.0	75.0	74.2	74.2	75.0
sunit	21.4	42.9	35.7	28.6	28.6	42.9	42.9	50.0	50.0	50.0
pda	31.8	34.1	31.8	36.4	36.4	38.6	38.6	38.6	38.6	38.6
Overall	31.0	34.7	34.8	37.0	37.6	42.3	43.3	42.4	43.0	43.7

6.1 Exhaustive Analysis

The approach of this paper allows an analysis of the entire program, but not efficiently: one could execute the algorithm against every variable in the program, one by one. The major inefficiency in this approach is that much information is calculated but then discarded: most queries require a type for multiple variables to be calculated, not just the type of the target variable.

For an efficient exhaustive analysis, it is desirable to keep old results and to reuse them in later queries. However, subgoal pruning adds a complication: distant subgoals of the target goal are more strongly affected by pruning, and thus have relatively low precision. At the extreme, if a subgoal is distant enough that it was in fact pruned, then there is no benefit from reusing it. Thus, it is important to consider how close to the target a goal was before it is reused.

Additionally, it is probably desirable to run multiple queries simultaneously. To choose the queries to run, one could start with an individual query and then promote the first k subgoals created to additional target goals. With this approach, all $k+1$ target goals are likely to contribute to each other and to need similar subgoals. Thus a small increase in the pruning threshold should allow $k+1$ targets to be computed simultaneously.

6.2 Justification Rules

The presence of subgoal pruning allows *speculative* justification tactics to be used, because if they are too expensive, the algorithm will eventually prune them away. Thus, subject to the constraints of soundness, an analysis designer can add more tactics at whim—one tactic for any situation that seems reasonably likely to occur. The algorithm can try the most ambitious available tactic first, and if that is too expensive, it can fall back on other tactics.

One particular way the justification tactics should be augmented is to account for *data polymorphism*. Data polymorphism, in object-oriented languages, is the use of a single class to reference different other classes at different points in a program. In particular, collection classes exhibit data polymorphism. In **DDP**, values retrieved from most collections have type $\top$, because the analysis does not track which additions to collections match which removals from collections. It may be possible to adapt the extension of **CPA** reported by Wang and Smith[23] to work with **DDP**.

A smaller way the justification tactics should probably be augmented is to add a second "senders-of" justification tactic. When finding the type of a parameter, or the flow through a return statement, it is often necessary to find which methods invoke a particular method. Note that while an exhaustive algorithm such as **CPA** may efficiently accumulate call-graph information in the course of analyzing type information, in a demand-driven algorithm the call graph must be queried specifically.

The only senders-of tactic that **DDP** uses is, first, to find all message-send expressions whose selector matches the current method, and then to find and check the type of the receiver of each one. This tactic fails when there are a very large number of `send` statements with a matching selector. An alternative tactic would be to reverse the order of the search: instead of finding all message-send expressions with the correct selector and then filtering those by the receiver type, one could find all variables with a proper receiver type and then filter those by looking at the message selectors sent to that variable. That first step of the query might be called an "inverse type query," because it asks which variables hold a particular type. Such queries would seem straightforward to implement for many classes: start from mentions of the class, then trace flow forward to instantiations, and finally trace flow forward from there. There are complications, such as classes that arise from language constructs other than instantiation, and it does not always work, *e.g.*, if the flow trace leads to $\top_{fp}$, but the general approach seems promising.

6.3 Pruning Algorithm

The pruning algorithm of **DDP** is a not sophisticated. A better algorithm could prefer to prune type goals that only contribute to the call graph; such a pruning has a relatively graceful effect. Further, a better pruner could attempt to make choice prunings that would remove large numbers of subgoals at once. Finally, it may help to prune goals that are already very imprecise. Such goals are unlikely to be useful; additionally, the individual computations on large union types are more expensive than computations on singular $\top$ tokens. The time could better be spent on goals that are more likely to yield a useful result.

6.4 Other Analysis Problems

DDP infers types for Smalltalk, but it could just as well be used for other data-flow problems and other languages. For example **DDP** would likely perform well at escape analysis in Java, or call graph construction in Scheme.

7 Conclusion

This work shows that practical type inference is possible for dynamically typed programs that are hundreds of thousands of lines long. The path to scalability relies upon *demand-driven analysis* to focus the search, and *subgoal pruning* to manage resources. **DDP** is a straightforward instantiation of this approach that works.

However, we'd like to conclude with a message larger than the specifics of **DDP**: the potential of applying AI-based, resource-bounded search techniques to intractable program-analysis problems. The key attraction of these techniques is their ability to match the computational resources available for a task to the specific complexity of different instances of that task. We applied this notion to the task of reasoning about Smalltalk programs because we are personally enthusiastic about this style of language and programming. But it may well be applicable to other programming languages and other analytic tasks, as well.

Thus the manner in which we solved our problem, and the general outline of its solution, is quite likely to be of broader interest than the particulars of our intended application.

Acknowledgements. We are grateful to our anonymous reviewers for comments that have contributed to the clarity of the paper.

References

1. American National Standards Institute: ANSI NCITS 319-1998: Information Technology — Programming Languages — Smalltalk. American National Standards Institute, 1430 Broadway, New York, NY 10018, USA (1998)
2. Kay, A.C.: The early history of smalltalk. In: The second ACM SIGPLAN conference on History of programming languages, ACM Press (1993) 69–95
3. Kogge, P.M.: The Architecture of Symbolic Computers. McGraw-Hill (1991)
4. Opdyke, W.F.: Refactoring object-oriented frameworks. PhD thesis, University of Illinois at Urbana-Champaign (1992)
5. Grove, D., Defouw, G., Dean, J., Chambers, C.: Call graph construction in object-oriented languages. In: ACM Conference on Object-Oriented Programming, Systems, Language, and Applications (OOPSLA). (1997)
6. Shivers, O.: The semantics of scheme control-flow analysis. In: Partial Evaluation and Semantic-Based Program Manipulation. (1991) 190–198
7. Suzuki, N.: Inferring types in smalltalk. In: Conference record of the 8th ACM Symposium on Principles of Programming Languages (POPL). (1981) 187–199
8. Barnard, A.J.: From types to dataflow: code analysis for an OO language. PhD thesis, Manchester University (1993)
9. Agesen, O.: The cartesian product algorithm: Simple and precise type inference of parametric polymorphism. In: Proc. of ECOOP. (1995)
10. Flanagan, C., Felleisen, M.: Componential set-based analysis. ACM Transactions on Programming Languages and Systems (TOPLAS) **21** (1999) 370–416
11. Garau, F.: Inferencia de tipos concretos en squeak. Master's thesis, Universidad de Buenos Aires (2001)
12. Shivers, O.: Control-Flow Analysis of Higher-Order Languages. PhD thesis, Carnegie Mellon University (1991)
13. Heintze, N., McAllester, D.A.: On the cubic bottleneck in subtyping and flow analysis. In: Logic in Computer Science. (1997) 342–351
14. Tip, F., Palsberg, J.: Scalable propagation-based call graph construction algorithms. ACM SIGPLAN Notices **35** (2000) 281–293
15. Reps, T.W.: Demand interprocedural program analysis using logic databases. In: Workshop on Programming with Logic Databases (Book), ILPS. (1993) 163–196
16. Duesterwald, E., Gupta, R., Soffa, M.L.: Demand-driven computation of interprocedural data flow. In: Symposium on Principles of Programming Languages. (1995) 37–48
17. Agrawal, G.: Simultaneous demand-driven data-flow and call graph analysis. In: ICSM. (1999) 453–462
18. Heintze, N., Tardieu, O.: Demand-driven pointer analysis. In: SIGPLAN Conference on Programming Language Design and Implementation. (2001) 24–34

19. Dubé, D., Feeley, M.: A demand-driven adaptive type analysis. In: Proceedings of the Seventh ACM SIGPLAN International Conference on Functional Programming, ACM Press (2002) 84–97
20. Rich, E.: Artificial Intelligence. McGraw-Hill Book Company (1983)
21. Spoon, S.A., Shivers, O.: Classification of inferred types in ddp experiment. |http://www.cc.gatech.edu/˜lex/ti— (2003)
22. Spoon, S.A.: Subgoal Pruning in Demand-Driven Analysis of a Dynamically Typed Object-Oriented Language. PhD thesis, Georgia Institute of Technology (forthcoming)
23. Wang, T., Smith, S.F.: Precise constraint-based type inference for Java. Lecture Notes in Computer Science **2072** (2001) 99–117

Efficiently Verifiable Escape Analysis

Matthew Q. Beers, Christian H. Stork, and Michael Franz

School of Information and Computer Science
University of California, Irvine
Irvine, CA 92717-3425, United States
{mbeers,cstork,franz}@uci.edu

Abstract. Escape analysis facilitates better optimization of programs in object-oriented programming languages such as Java, significantly reducing memory management and synchronization overhead. Unfortunately, existing escape analysis algorithms are often too expensive to be applicable in just-in-time compilation contexts. We propose to perform the analysis ahead of time and ship its results as code annotations. We present an interprocedural, flow insensitive, static escape analysis that is less precise than traditional escape analyses, but whose result can be transported and verified efficiently. Unlike any other escape analysis that we know of, our method optionally provides for dynamic class loading, which is necessary for full Java compatibility. Benchmarks indicate that, when compared to Whaley and Rinard's elaborate escape analysis, our simple analysis can pinpoint 81% of all captured allocation sites (69% when dynamic loading is supported), with negligible space overhead for the transport of annotations and negligible time overhead for the verification.

1 Introduction

Just-in-time compilation systems for mobile code do not always use the best available optimization algorithms. Many of the analyses and optimizations that are commonplace in off-line compilers are simply too time-consuming to perform while an interactive user is waiting for program execution to commence. As a result, most just-in-time compilers are skewed towards compilation speed rather than code quality.

Annotation-guided optimization systems [1,2,3,4,5,6] try to resolve this conflict between compilation speed and code quality. In these systems, analyses are performed off-line and appended to the mobile code as program annotations. This reduces the just-in-time compilation overhead at the code consumer and enables optimizations that would otherwise be too time consuming to perform on-line.

Escape analysis [7,8,9], a technique that identifies objects that can be allocated on the stack as opposed to on the heap, is a good candidate for annotation-guided optimizations. Escape analysis can also reveal when objects are accessible only to a single thread. This information can then be used to eliminate unnecessary synchronization overhead.

M. Odersky (Ed.): ECOOP 2004, LNCS 3086, pp. 75–95, 2004.

An elaborate escape analysis is time consuming and requires lots of memory for the internal graph representation of each method in a program [7,8,9]. Benchmarks indicate, however, that its use can result in substantial performance gains, even in case of simpler linear-time analyses [10]. Ideally, we would annotate programs with escape analysis information that can be transported with the program and exploited by an annotation-aware just-in-time compilation system at the target site.

However, there are two primary drawbacks to the use of such annotations for escape analysis: first, they introduce transfer overhead (for the extra annotation information); and second—and more seriously—their use is *unsafe*. That is, if someone accidentally or maliciously changed the escape-analysis result recorded for an allocation site from "heap allocatable" to "stack allocatable", then the memory safety of the whole target system is potentially in jeopardy.

Hence, one needs to *verify* such annotations, similar to the way that Java bytecode is verified. Verification of traditional escape analysis annotations, however, would essentially be as demanding as performing the original analysis in the first place, negating the original objective of reducing the workload on the code consumer. We are not aware of any prior work on *safe* annotations of escape analysis that would be applicable to Java, i.e., annotations that could actually be verified at the target. All published annotation-based solutions in this domain [2, 3,4] are unsafe.

In this paper, we introduce and evaluate an escape analysis that

- can be performed by the code producer in linear time,
- has a very small space overhead for the annotations,
- can be verified with little time overhead by the code consumer, and
- optionally supports dynamic class loading without the need for deoptimization.

Outline. The rest of the paper is organized as follows. Section 2 introduces our escape analysis. Section 3 explains how to annotate programs and how to efficiently verify these annotations. Section 4 presents our experimental results. Section 5 lists related work. A concluding section summarizes our contributions.

2 Escape Analysis

Escape analysis identifies *captured objects*, i.e., objects with lifetimes that do not exceed that of the method in which they are created. Identification of captured objects enables several optimizations. Most importantly, captured objects can be allocated on the stack avoiding the overhead of heap allocation and garbage collection. Furthermore, all synchronization of captured objects can be eliminated since only a single thread can ever access a captured object. Both optimizations have been shown to improve program performance [7,8,9] noticeably. Capturedness also enables additional minor optimizations, for example, dead store removal and object inlining, i.e., replacing objects by local variables that represent their fields [10,11,12].

Commonly, escape analysis is achieved by constructing a variant of a *points-to-graph* that models object lifetimes and object aliasing. Based on this model, the analysis indicates which objects are captured by the method in which they are created. Whaley and Rinard's escape analysis [7] follows this approach.

We propose a different escape analysis technique, one that considers *variables*[1] that are bound to objects instead of the objects proper. Variables are classified as *local variables* or *formal variables* (also called *parameters*). Intuitively, we consider a variable *captured* if it is never returned from its defining method, is passed only to captured parameters of called methods, and is never assigned to an escaping variable. If an object during its lifetime is only ever referenced by captured variables, then the object is captured in the traditional sense. So, given an allocation site

v = new C();

the allocated *object* o is captured if the *variable* v is captured. This holds because by our definition "no object can escape through v" and v is the initial reference to o; therefore o cannot escape. This does not imply that objects that are pointed to by the fields of o are also captured. Indeed, we conservatively assume that all field references $v.f$ escape.

Arrays are handled like objects and array elements are treated as object fields. Therefore, a one-dimensional array can be captured, but its elements escape, and multi-dimensional arrays can only be captured in their first dimension since they are modelled as nested one-dimensional arrays in Java. An array allocation site

v = new C[];

allocates a captured array—just like for regular objects—if v is captured according to our analysis.

For the rest of our analysis it is beneficial to consider slightly transformed source code rather than the original Java source code. The transformation is illustrated in Table 1. First, we make the otherwise implicit declaration of the `this` parameter explicit in order to treat all parameters uniformly. See the transformations for instance method declarations and constructor declarations. Instance method invocations are changed correspondingly. Second, assignments of freshly constructed objects to variables are transformed by splitting the creation of new objects into two consecutive statements akin to the treatment of constructor calls in Java bytecode. The first statement returns a reference to the allocated and zeroed object; the second statement calls the corresponding initializer with the otherwise implicit `this` reference as first argument. This allows us to treat initializer calls formally as regular method calls.[2]

---

[1] Also often called *references*.

[2] If a constructor body does not begin with an explicit constructor invocation we consider the implicit super class constructor call as part of the constructor body unless we are at the root of the class hierarchy.

Table 1. Conceptual source code transformations

	Before	After

Instance Method Declaration	`class` C `{...`
	  $C_{\mathtt{ret}}$ m`(`C_{p_1} p_1`,...){`
	  `...}`
	`...}`
		`class` C `{...`
		  $C_{\mathtt{ret}}$ m`(`C **`this`**`,` C_{p_1} p_1`,...){`
		  `...}`
		`...}`

Instance Method Call	v_0`.`m`(`v_1`,...)`	m`(`v_0`,`v_1`,...)`

Constructor Declaration	`class` C `{...`
	  C`(`C_{p_1} p_1`,...){`
	  `...}`
	`...}`
		`class` C `{...`
		  `void` $init_C$`(`C **`this`**`,` C_{p_1} p_1`,...){`
		  `...}`
		`...}`

Constructor Call	v_0 `= new` C`(`v_1`,...`v_n`)`	v_0 `= new` C`;` $init_C$`(`v_0`,`v_1`,...`v_n`)`

2.1 Run-Time Type Constraints

Generally speaking, our analysis consists of two passes. Each pass builds and then solves a constraint system, which is a set of inequalities simply referred to as *constraints.* The first pass generates constraints for the run-time type $rtt(v)$ of variables v. The second pass uses the results of the first pass to generate constraints for the escape predicates $esc(v)$; the second pass is the subject of the next section.

The value of the run-time type property $rtt(v)$ is either a class C, uninitialized ($\bot$), or initialized but unknown ($\top$). These elements form a flat lattice with partial order $\leq$ and $\top$ being the least upper bound of any two distinct elements. The meaning of $rtt(v) = \top$ is "v's run-time type is its declared type or any subtype thereof".

The run-time type property must obey certain constraints that are generated according to the rules given in Table 2. Assigning a new object of class C to a variable v lifts $rtt(v)$ to at least C. Therefore, if our analysis encounters another assignment of a new instance of class B to v, then $rtt(v)$ becomes $\top$ unless $B = C$.

Our analysis makes no assumptions about what is passed into a method. Consequently, the run-time type of formal parameters is unknown. We assume conservatively that the run-time type of fields, array elements, and method results is also unknown.

The run-time type constraint corresponding to an assignment v_0 `=` v_1 enforces that "v_0 has at least v_1's run-time type". Note that assigning the `null` reference to a variable does not generate any constraint. This means, for example, if v is exclusively assigned the `null` reference then $rtt(v)$ keeps its default value $\bot$ and every use of v could be replaced by `null`.

Each constraint variable $rtt(v)$ in the constraint system that our analysis builds is initialized with the trivial constraint $rtt(v) \geq \bot$. The remaining constraints are produced by traversing the code and generating the constraints corre-

Table 2. Representative statements with their corresponding constraints where v, v_i stand for local variables or formal parameters, s for static fields, f for instant fields, m for methods, C for classes, and C_i for arbitrary types.

Run-Time Type Constraints	
v = new C	$rtt(v) \geq C$
$C_0\ m(C_1\ p_1, \ldots)\{\ldots\}$	$\forall$ parameters p_i: $rtt(p_i) = \top$
v = s	$rtt(v) = \top$
v_0 = $v_1.f$	$rtt(v_0) = \top$
v_0 = v_1[...]	$rtt(v_0) = \top$
v_0 = v_1	$rtt(v_0) \geq rtt(v_1)$
v_0 = $m(v_1, v_2, \ldots v_n)$	$rtt(v_0) = \top$
Escape Constraints	
return v	$esc(v) = \top$
throw v	$esc(v) = \top$
s = v	$esc(v) = \top$
$v_0.f$ = v_1	$esc(v_1) = \top$
v_0[...] = v_1	$esc(v_1) = \top$
v_0 = v_1	$esc(v_0) \Rightarrow esc(v_1)$
v_0 = $m(v_1, v_2, \ldots v_n)$	$esc(v_0) = \top \ \wedge$ $\forall$ parameters $p_i^{m'}$ of methods m' invokable as m: $esc(p_i^{m'}) \Rightarrow esc(v_i)$

sponding to the statements. The run-time type constraints system then consists of inequalities of simple terms: constraint variables $rtt(v)$ and constants C_i, $\top$, and $\bot$. Note that $rtt(v) = \top$ is equivalent to $rtt(v) \geq \top$.

We are trying to find the solution to the constraint system that has the most specific information, i.e., the minimal solution to the constraint system. We know that a unique minimal solution exists and that we can find it in linear time since the constraint system is a definite and simple constraint set as defined in [13]. In order to find the minimal solution, we employ a standard worklist algorithm to lift the values according the given constraints. Since the values of the constraint variables change only monotonically and since the lattice height is constant (three in this case) the number of property value changes is linear in the number of constraints. Using pending lists to efficiently implement the processing of dependencies, the overall complexity for finding the minimal solution is linear in the number of constraints.

2.2 Escape Constraints

Our analysis specifies the boolean predicate $esc(v)$ for local variables or parameters v. We write $esc(v) = \top$ if the escape predicate is true and $esc(v) = \bot$ if it is false, thereby interpreting the boolean values as a two-point lattice. If $esc(v)$ is false we say that v is *captured*. Note the difference from most other escape

Table 3. Determining the constraints of escape predicates $esc(v_i)$ for arguments v_i of method calls $m(v_1, v_2, \ldots v_n)$ based on invokable declarations of m. If m is non-static, then the dynamic dispatch is based on v_1's run-time type. If $rtt(v_1) = C$, then we refer to m's only invokable method declaration as m_C, otherwise ($rtt(v_1) = \top$) we refer to the potentially multiple invokable methods as $m_{\leq D}$ where D stands for v_1's declared (compile-time) type (We have not yet implemented the special treatment of package protected methods within sealed packages in the open world case)

<table>
<tr><td>final, private, or static methods m</td><td colspan="2">$\forall$ parameters p_i of the only invokable method m':
$esc(p_i) \Rightarrow esc(v_i)$</td></tr>
<tr><td>$rtt(v_1) = C$</td><td colspan="2">$\forall$ parameters p_i of method m_C:
$esc(p_i) \Rightarrow esc(v_i)$</td></tr>
<tr><td>package protected methods m within a sealed package P</td><td colspan="2">$\forall$ parameters $p_i^{m_{\leq D}}$ of methods $m_{\leq D}$ within package P:
$esc(p_i^{m_{\leq D}}) \Rightarrow esc(v_i)$</td></tr>
<tr><td>all other methods m</td><td>Open World
$\forall$ variables v_i:
$esc(v_i) = \top$</td><td>Closed World
$\forall$ parameters $p_i^{m_{\leq D}}$ of methods $m_{\leq D}$ invokable as m within the whole program:
$esc(p_i^{m_{\leq D}}) \Rightarrow esc(v_i)$</td></tr>
</table>

analyses, which model capturedness of objects, not variables. The meaning of $esc(v) = \top$ is roughly "an object could escape through v". Therefore, if an object o is only referenced by captured variables, then o is captured. This does not mean that a captured variable always references a captured object! For example, it is perfectly in accordance with our analysis to assign an escaping variable to a captured variable.

The escape constraints for the relevant source code statements are also given in Table 2. The first five escape constraints define our notion of "directly escaping". References escape if they are returned, thrown, or assigned to static variables, fields, or array elements. We exclude the assignment of a captured variable to an escaped one since such an assignment might cause the escape of the object through the captured variable.

We assume that all method results escape and we ensure that passing a variable v_i as an argument to method m lets this variable escape if the corresponding parameter p_i escapes. For a language with dynamic method dispatch such as Java, the former necessitates knowledge of the type hierarchy to determine all method declarations m' that could be invoked when calling m. We chose a relatively conservative approximation of what we mean by "invokable". Table 3 summarizes our notion of invokable methods and the accompanying constraints. Whichever condition of the left column applies first causes the generation of the escape constraints to the right. If m is a static, private, or final method then there is exactly one invokable implementation; otherwise the invokable methods depend on the run-time type property $rtt(v_1)$ of the target reference. $rtt(v_1)$ is either a specific class C, in which case only C's declaration of m is invokable, or $rtt(v_1)$ is unknown, i.e., $\top$, in which case all implementations of m for v_1's declared type or subtypes thereof are invokable. Note that $rtt(v_1)$ cannot be uninitialized due to Java's definite assignment rules.

This is the only place in our analysis where supporting dynamic class loading makes a difference. In a *closed world* without dynamic loading, a whole-program analysis can inspect all subclasses of v_1's declared type. In an *open world* in which additional classes can be added dynamically at any time, this is not possible. We have to assume the worst case, so all arguments of m escape.

There is one exception to this worst-case scenario. Java's sealed packages ensure that package protected methods, i.e., methods with default access, can be overridden only by the package's classes that are part of their containing JAR file. In the context of our analysis, this results in a closed world assumption for package protected methods within sealed packages. We have not yet taken advantage of this additional knowledge since the expected gain is rather small — only 4% of our benchmarks' methods are declared package protected and similarly approximately 4% of all method invocation sites are package protected.

Note that the run-time type information of the previous pass is needed to determine the implications that depend on the set of invokable methods; this is the sole purpose of the run-time type property in our framework. The second pass also requires knowledge of the class hierarchy, more specifically, of the call graph to determine the invokable methods in cases where $rtt(v_1) \neq C$.

Given that $esc(v_0) \Rightarrow esc(v_1)$ is equivalent to $esc(v_0) \leq esc(v_1)$, the escape constraint system can be solved just as the previous constraint system. In the open world scenario, the number of generated constraints is linear in the size N of the program.[3] In the closed world scenario, the number of constraints is linear in the size N of the program plus the size G of the call graph measured as the total number of corresponding argument/parameter pairs at all call sites.

2.3 Example

We demonstrate the generation of constraints by means of the code excerpt in Figure 1. The example consists of two Java methods, which are part of an enclosing class `MyClass` (not shown) and which implement a rather typical collection traversal in public method `transformMap` using Java's iterator interface. `transformMap` has a private helper method `transformVal`, which is contrived to demonstrate our analysis. `transformVal` instantiates a `Transformer t` and it invokes its `do` method to transform the `val` object. A `token` object is handed through `transformMap` and through `transformVal` to `t`'s `do` method. Our analysis shows that `token` and `t` will not escape assuming that the `do` method does not let them escape.

[3] This ignores the sealed package option mentioned earlier.

```
public Map transformMap(Map m, Object token)
{
    Iterator iter;
    Object key;
    Object val;

    iter = m.keySet().iterator();
    while (iter.hasNext())
    {
        key = iter.next();
        val = m.get(key);
        m.put(key, transformVal(val, token));
    }
    return m;
}

private Object transformVal(Object val, Object token)
{
    Transformer t = new Transformer();
    return t.do(val, token);
}
```

Fig. 1. Example Java source code excerpt

3 Annotations and Verification

In order to transport the analysis results, we annotate local and formal variables v at their declaration site with their $esc(v)$ predicate and their run-time type property $rtt(v)$. Figure 2 shows the annotations resulting from the solved constraint system of our running example. Note again that it is not necessary to annotate the captured allocation sites proper (line 26 of Figure 2).

Verifying the annotations only involves generating and verifying the constraints according to Table 2 while traversing the code. Of course, the run-time system needs to provide access to invokable methods for the check of escape constraints of method arguments. Note that verification can happen incrementally and on-demand, minimizing interference with a JIT compiler. If, during verification, one of the constraints fails to be satisfied by the provided annotations, then this implies that the program or the annotations have been tampered with after the analysis was performed.

Verification ensures only that the annotations are a valid solution of the constraint system. The code consumer will not notice if the received annotations are suboptimal, or even just the trivial solution where everything escapes.

In both the open and the closed world scenarios we analyze the appropriate library methods that are called by the subject program and we require that their parameter annotations satisfy the constraints of the subject program at verifi-

```
public Map transformMap(
    MyClass this,            // Annotation: esc(this) = ⊥, rtt(this) = ⊤
    Map m,                   // Annotation: esc(m) = ⊤, rtt(m) = ⊤
    MyToken token)           // Annotation: esc(token) = ⊥, rtt(token) = ⊤
{
    Iterator iter;           // Annotation: esc(iter) = ⊤, rtt(iter) = ⊤
    Object key;              // Annotation: esc(key) = ⊤, rtt(key) = ⊤
    Object val;              // Annotation: esc(val) = ⊤, rtt(val) = ⊤

    iter = iterator(keySet(m));
    while (hasNext(iter))
    {
        key = next(iter);
        val = get(m, key);
        put(m, key, transformVal(this, val, token));
    }
    return m;
}

private Object transformVal(
    MyClass this,            // Annotation: esc(this) = ⊥, rtt(this) = ⊤
    Object val,              // Annotation: esc(val) = ⊥, rtt(val) = ⊤
    MyToken token)           // Annotation: esc(token) = ⊥, rtt(token) = ⊤
{
    Transformer t;           // Annotation: esc(t) = ⊥, rtt(t) = Transformer
    t = new Transformer;
    init_Transformer(t);
    return do(t, val, token);
}
```

Fig. 2. Example with annotations for local and formal variables that result from solving the constraints of Table ??

cation time. In practice, this means that the authors of libraries have to commit to certain escape analysis annotations in order to maintain binary compatibility with respect to the escape analysis. Of course, the run-time system can always revert to the "everything escapes" worst-case assumption if it encounters an unmet constraint; but due to cascading effects in our analysis this can result in potentially disruptive deoptimization of the system.

Even though our implementation augments canonicalized abstract syntax trees, the annotations should be easily adaptable to Java classfiles. This would provide a low-impact addition of escape analysis optimizations for existing JVMs.

4 Evaluation

To evaluate our framework, we first compared the accuracy of our escape analysis to that of the most precise known escape analysis, namely that of Whaley

Table 4. Description of benchmarks

JavaGrande Benchmarks		SPECjvm Benchmarks	
crypt	IDEA encryption	jess	Java Expert Shell System
heapsort	Integer sorting	raytrace	3-dimensional ray tracer
fft	Fast Fourier Transform	db	Database benchmark
lufact	LU Factorization	javac	Java compiler
sor	Successive over-relaxation	jack	Java parser generator
sparse	Sparse matrix multiplication		
series	Fourier coefficient analysis		
euler	Computational fluid dynamics		
moldyn	Molecular dynamics simulation		
montecarlo	Monte Carlo simulation		
raytracer	3-dimensional ray tracer		
search	Alpha-beta pruned search		

and Richard [7]. To do this, we compared the number of static allocation sites generated by both techniques. This comparison also discusses allocations within loops and measuring static versus dynamic allocations. Next we estimate the overhead incurred by adding our annotations to standard Java classfiles. We conclude the experimental section by examining the speed of verification.

We based our evaluation on a series of standard benchmarks. We chose sections 2 and 3 of JavaGrande [14] and a subset of SPECjvm98 [15] as listed in Table 4. These are the benchmarks for which source code was readily available or for which we were able to derive the source code from the provided class files. Section 1 of the JavaGrande benchmarks was not analyzed because it evaluates the performance of specific virtual machine features and is therefore not a representative benchmark.

We perform a rather Java-specific transformation on string concatenations in order to attain more comparable results with the Java bytecode-based implementation of Whaley and Rinard. The standard way of dealing with string concatenation in Java bytecode is to generate a series of `append` method calls to an anonymously allocated `StringBuffer` object. Given the statement

```
String s = s1 + s2;
```

the concatenation operation creates a new `String` object `s` that is the string concatenation of `s1` and `s2`. Primarily for efficiency purposes, the Java compiler converts the above statement into the following:

```
String s = new StringBuffer(s1).append(s2).toString();
```

The latter statement necessitates the allocation of a `StringBuffer`, creating an additional allocation site, which is not present in our canonicalized abstract syntax tree. However, since we need a common basis for a precise comparison of our analysis to Whaley and Rinard, we perform the same transformation and, knowing that the `StringBuffer` does not escape, mark the newly allocated object as captured.

Table 5. Comparison of captured allocation sites

Benchmark	Whaley & Rinard		Our Analysis			Rel. Capt.	
	Sites	Closed W.	Sites	Closed W.	Open W.	C.W.	O.W.
crypt	11	4 (36%)	11	3 (27%)	3 (27%)	75 %	75 %
fft	8	5 (63%)	8	5 (63%)	5 (63%)	100%	100%
heapsort	5	3 (60%)	5	2 (40%)	2 (40%)	67 %	67 %
lufact	8	3 (38%)	8	3 (38%)	3 (38%)	100%	100%
series	10	8 (80%)	10	8 (80%)	8 (80%)	100%	100%
sor	5	2 (40%)	5	2 (40%)	2 (40%)	100%	100%
sparsematmult	8	2 (25%)	8	2 (25%)	2 (25%)	100%	100%
euler	39	11 (28%)	39	10 (26%)	10 (26%)	91 %	91 %
moldyn	7	2 (29%)	7	2 (29%)	2 (29%)	100%	100%
montecarlo	41	22 (54%)	41	18 (44%)	13 (32%)	82 %	59 %
raytracer	46	9 (20%)	46	6 (13%)	5 (11%)	67 %	56 %
search	18	8 (44%)	19	8 (42%)	8 (42%)	95 %	95 %
raytrace	129	55 (43%)	129	29 (22%)	13 (10%)	53 %	24 %
jess	433	164 (38%)	436	155 (36%)	141 (32%)	94 %	85 %
db	41	30 (73%)	41	28 (68%)	21 (51%)	93 %	70 %
jack	209	123 (59%)	214	114 (53%)	105 (49%)	91 %	83 %
javac	760	200 (26%)	750	145 (19%)	121 (16%)	73 %	61 %
Total	1777	651 (36%)	1777	540 (30%)	464 (26%)	81 %	69 %

4.1 Efficacy

Our method is by design less accurate than more traditional escape analyses at denoting captured objects. This loss of precision is acceptable because we gain verifiability. Likewise, by introducing an open world assumption, we lose accuracy, but gain the ability to dynamically load classes without invalidating our escape analysis annotations. We base our comparison with Whaley and Rinard on static coverage of allocation sites because this seems to be the best basis for for a meaningful comparison. (We will discuss the omission of dynamic numbers at the end of this section.) As explained in Section 2, we consider an allocation site as captured if the new object is assigned to a captured variables. Each benchmark was analyzed under both closed and open world assumptions.

The results of Whaley and Rinard's analysis were obtained by inserting a custom counting pass into the `PointerAnalysis` package of the FLEX research compiler [16]. This custom counting pass utilized the points-to-graph to determine the escapedness for each analyzed allocation site. The FLEX compiler infrastructure begins its analysis with the `main` method of a Java classfile, and only analyzes methods that are reachable from there. We have attempted to limit our analysis to only these methods to present a more accurate comparison. Semantic differences between source and bytecode cause a small variation in the total number of allocation sites between their results and ours.

Table 5 shows the number of allocation sites that allocate captured objects relative to the total number of allocation sites. On average, Whaley and Rinard mark 36% of the static allocation sites as captured.

As expected, their comprehensive analysis marks a higher percentage of static allocation sites captured. Our escape analysis fares quite well, however, marking on average 30% allocation sites captured. Perhaps more interesting is how well the algorithm performed in the open world case, covering an average of 26% of the static allocation sites.

The final columns of Table 5 show the coverage our algorithm achieves when compared with Whaley and Rinard. For each benchmark, the percentage is the number of allocation sites that our analysis marks as captured compared against the number of sites their analysis marks as captured. On average, we cover 81% of the static allocation sites in the closed world, and 69% in the open world. This means that even with dynamic class loading, we can still find and potentially optimize about two thirds of the allocation sites that Whaley and Rinard's analysis finds—and transmit this information to a just-in-time compiler in a verifiable manner.

Whaley and Rinard's algorithm explicitly tracks objects through potentially many method calls, which contributes to its higher costs. However, even compared against our analysis under the open world assumption, these higher costs do not seem to materialize in a proportional advantage.

Allocations Inside Loops. Object allocations inside loops warrant extra attention since they are potentially executed many more times then allocations outside of loops. To better understand how our analysis performs with respect to loops, we compare the relative number of captured allocation sites inside and outside of loops. (We consider only whether an allocation site is located inside a loop or not, that is, we ignore the nesting level of loops.)

The results in Tables 6 and 7 show the percentage of captured allocation sites located inside versus outside of loops under the closed and open world assumptions, respectively. We found that the percentage of allocation sites captured inside of loops is markedly higher than those captured outside of loops. We believe that this is partly due to our choice of benchmarks. However, it still appears as if objects are normally more short-lived within loops and that our analysis benefits from this. This indicates that the dynamic allocations of captured objects should be higher than our overall averages indicate.

Stack-Allocatability. We refrained from trying to obtain dynamic allocation numbers for two reasons. First, we lack the appropriate infrastructure for such experiments. Second, adapting an existing VM would have required us to modify its allocation strategy in a way that allows a meaningful comparison with currently published dynamic allocation measurements. This is not trivial because there are additional factors to consider for stack-allocatability in specific VMs.

To illustrate this point, Gay and Steensgaard [10] used their escape analysis results to implement stack allocation of captured objects in the Marmot VM [17], which prefers a constant frame size. Therefore they introduced an extra predicate, which depends on their use of SSA, to indicate overlapping life ranges of

Table 6. Distribution of captured allocation sites within loops under the closed world assumption

Benchmark	Allocations in loop (AIL)	Alloc. outside loop (AOL)	Captured AIL	Captured AOL	CAIL /AIL	CAOL /AOL
crypt	3 (27%)	8 (73%)	3	0	100%	0%
fft	0 (0%)	8 (100%)	0	5	—	63%
heapsort	2 (40%)	3 (60%)	2	0	100%	0%
lufact	0 (0%)	8 (100%)	0	3	—	38%
series	3 (30%)	7 (70%)	3	5	100%	71%
sor	0 (0%)	5 (100%)	0	2	—	40%
sparsematmult	0 (0%)	8 (100%)	0	2	—	25%
euler	7 (18%)	32 (82%)	0	10	0%	31%
moldyn	2 (29%)	5 (71%)	0	2	0%	40%
montecarlo	6 (15%)	35 (85%)	5	13	83%	37%
raytracer	2 (4%)	44 (96%)	0	6	0%	14%
search	3 (16%)	16 (84%)	3	5	100%	31%
raytrace	14 (11%)	115 (89%)	1	28	7%	24%
jess	71 (16%)	365 (84%)	27	128	38%	35%
db	8 (20%)	33 (80%)	5	23	63%	70%
jack	56 (26%)	158 (74%)	44	70	79%	44%
javac	132 (18%)	618 (82%)	26	119	20%	19%
Total	309 (17%)	1468 (83%)	119	421	39%	29%

Table 7. Distribution of captured allocation sites within loops under the open world assumption

Benchmark	Allocations in loop (AIL)	Alloc. outside loop (AOL)	Captured AIL	Captured AOL	CAIL /AIL	CAOL /AOL
crypt	3 (27%)	8 (73%)	3	0	100%	0%
fft	0 (0%)	8 (100%)	0	5	—	63%
heapsort	2 (40%)	3 (60%)	2	0	100%	0%
lufact	0 (0%)	8 (100%)	0	3	—	38%
series	3 (30%)	7 (70%)	3	5	100%	71%
sor	0 (0%)	5 (100%)	0	2	—	40%
sparsematmult	0 (0%)	8 (100%)	0	2	—	25%
euler	7 (18%)	32 (82%)	0	10	0%	31%
moldyn	2 (29%)	5 (71%)	0	2	0%	40%
montecarlo	6 (15%)	35 (85%)	4	9	67%	26%
raytracer	2 (4%)	44 (96%)	0	5	0%	11%
search	3 (16%)	16 (84%)	3	5	100%	31%
raytrace	14 (11%)	115 (89%)	0	13	0%	11%
jess	71 (16%)	365 (84%)	24	117	34%	32%
db	8 (20%)	33 (80%)	5	16	63%	48%
jack	56 (26%)	158 (74%)	44	61	79%	39%
javac	132 (18%)	618 (82%)	15	106	11%	17%
Total	309 (17%)	1468 (83%)	103	361	33%	25%

loop allocations. Whaley and Rinard described an implementation of stack allocation based on the Jalapeño compiler [18]. Objects were only stack allocated if the allocation site is executed at most once per invocation of the method. This was to prevent a statically unbounded number of objects from being created on the stack. Both approaches were unsuitable for us since we would have had to provide additional verifiable annotations to guarantee stack-allocatability within a fixed-size stack frame. Neither of these approaches attempted to allocate arrays on the stack since their size is also potentially dynamic.

The most simplistic way to stack allocate all captured objects would be to allow the stack to grow during a method's lifetime. However, this leads to an unbounded frame size and necessitates an additional frame pointer, which is uncommon among current VMs. Alternatively, one could consider implementing dynamic regions, which are heap-allocated stacks for each method. In either case, these simpler solutions do not produce dynamic allocation results comparable to published work since they stack-allocate more objects.

Table 8 illustrates the difference between how many objects could be allocated on a static frame size stack versus a dynamic frame size stack. The static frame size numbers are determined by finding all allocation sites that are not contained within a loop and are not array allocations. The dynamic frame size numbers are given as increments over the static numbers and reflect those allocation sites that are within loops, or allocate an array. These results are given for the open and closed world scenarios. In both scenarios it seems that almost one third of the captured allocation sites requires dynamic stack frames in order to be exploitable.

4.2 Annotation Size

The size of the annotations required to encode the escape and run-time type annotations for local variables and formal parameters varies widely depending on which framework is used for the encoding.

A naive implementation based on the annotation framework provided by the Java class file format [19] needs six bytes per method for the `attribute_info` data structure. For each annotated variable, we need to encode the predicate $esc(v)$, which requires one bit (if we are willing to go through the associated decoding process), and the property $rtt(v)$, which can either be encoded as a four byte long reference into the class file's constant table or as one bit, based on the following remarks.

Assuming we allow for some simple code transformations, the property $rtt(v)$ can actually be turned into a boolean predicate $rtt_{bool}(v)$ with an approximate meaning of "v's run-time type is equal to its declared type D". The meaning of $rtt(v) = \bot$ is that v is not the target of a non-`null` assignment in the program and all of v's occurrences in the program could be replaced by `null`. This transformation allows us therefore to ignore the case of $rtt(v) = \bot$. Now, if $rtt(v) = C \neq D$ then C has to be a subclass of D and all assignments to v are—by definition of our constraints—of run-time type C. Therefore the program is still valid after changing v's declared type to C. Given the previous and

Table 8. Comparison of captured object allocation sites that could be stack allocated given static stack frames versus dynamic stack frames in both the closed and open world assumptions

Benchmark	Alloc. Sites	Closed World Static Frame	Closed World Dyn. Frame	Open World Static Frame	Open World Dyn. Frame
crypt	11	0 (0%)	+ 3 (27%)	0 (0%)	+ 3 (27%)
fft	8	3 (37%)	+ 2 (25%)	3 (37%)	+ 2 (25%)
heapsort	5	0 (0%)	+ 2 (40%)	0 (0%)	+ 2 (40%)
lufact	8	2 (25%)	+ 1 (12%)	2 (25%)	+ 1 (12%)
series	10	0 (0%)	+ 8 (80%)	0 (0%)	+ 8 (80%)
sor	5	1 (20%)	+ 1 (20%)	1 (20%)	+ 1 (20%)
sparsematmult	8	1 (12%)	+ 1 (12%)	1 (12%)	+ 1 (12%)
euler	39	9 (23%)	+ 1 (2%)	9 (23%)	+ 1 (2%)
moldyn	7	1 (14%)	+ 1 (14%)	1 (14%)	+ 1 (14%)
montecarlo	41	12 (29%)	+ 6 (14%)	8 (19%)	+ 5 (12%)
raytracer	46	4 (8%)	+ 2 (4%)	3 (6%)	+ 2 (4%)
search	19	0 (0%)	+ 8 (42%)	0 (0%)	+ 8 (42%)
raytrace	129	18 (13%)	+ 11 (8%)	4 (3%)	+ 9 (6%)
jess	436	123 (28%)	+ 32 (7%)	115 (26%)	+ 26 (5%)
db	41	19 (46%)	+ 9 (21%)	16 (39%)	+ 5 (12%)
jack	214	68 (31%)	+ 46 (21%)	59 (27%)	+ 46 (21%)
javac	750	112 (14%)	+ 33 (4%)	102 (13%)	+ 19 (2%)
Total	1777	373 (20%)	+167 (9%)	324 (18%)	+140 (7%)

Table 9. Approximate size of escape annotations (in bytes) relative to the size of the original and uncompressed class file

Benchmark	Original Classfile Size	1 Bit + 4 Bytes Encoding	2 Bits Encoding
crypt	5018	338 (7%)	106 (2%)
fft	5164	404 (8%)	104 (2%)
heapsort	2892	202 (7%)	86 (3%)
lufact	6031	684 (11%)	144 (2%)
series	3238	222 (7%)	87 (3%)
sor	2873	216 (8%)	70 (2%)
sparsematmult	3298	200 (6%)	69 (2%)
euler	22447	906 (4%)	186 (1%)
moldyn	10586	462 (4%)	136 (1%)
montecarlo	35793	1600 (4%)	629 (2%)
raytracer	18334	1208 (7%)	379 (2%)
search	10872	538 (5%)	163 (1%)
raytrace	57000	3290 (6%)	1111 (2%)
jess	396393	10194 (3%)	3140 (1%)
db	12087	838 (7%)	227 (2%)
jack	130889	5640 (4%)	1961 (1%)
javac	561462	25652 (5%)	7791 (1%)
Total	1284377	52594 (4%)	16389 (1%)

Table 10. Time (in milliseconds) to perform the analysis and verification in the closed world case

Benchmark	Analysis Time	Verification Time	No-op Time
crypt	41.37	3.27	0.44
euler	73.28	21.14	3.48
fft	46.57	4.60	0.43
heapsort	39.23	2.08	0.24
lufact	39.60	3.88	0.96
moldyn	49.79	4.40	0.64
montecarlo	111.79	26.10	3.29
raytracer	78.29	12.68	0.81
search	48.11	5.62	0.71
series	39.47	2.40	0.27
sor	40.89	1.90	0.26
sparsematmult	42.14	2.17	0.25
jess	369.28	63.88	9.34
raytrace	141.29	34.68	4.05
db	79.91	12.93	1.20
javac	550.62	137.06	11.23
jack	187.42	55.36	5.39
Total	1979.04	394.15	43.00

the latter transformations, $rtt(v)$ is either the declared type D or the unspecified type $\top$, which are mapped to $rtt_{bool}(v)$ being true or false, respectively. We have not implemented this optimization yet, nevertheless we will consider it for our estimate of annotation overhead.

Table 9 shows the approximate overhead of including annotations in a regular Java classfile. (We are not accounting for the fact that class files are normally compressed as part of a JAR file prior to distribution.) As expected, the numbers indicate that the size increase is relatively insignificant.

4.3 Verification

Verification is the most time critical operation, since it is performed by many code receivers under potentially high time pressure, whereas the analysis is only performed by one code producer under arguably lower time pressure. To demonstrate efficiency of verification, we constructed a verifier that performs all the necessary steps to validate the correctness of the annotations. Table 10 compares the time needed to perform the closed world escape analysis versus time needed to verify the annotations.[4] Since we argue that verification can easily be integrated into another pass over the code we also provide the timings for a no-op pass that only traverses the program without performing any operations.

[4] All measurements were performed on a P4/1.8GHz/512MB PC running Java 2 (Blackdown 1.4.1_01 without special flags) on Linux Kernel 2.4.22.

Therefore, we could look instead at the difference between the verification and no-op times.

On average the verification time is only one fourth of the analysis time. We expect the verification time to drop further after the verification is integrated into the run-time environment. Furthermore, the verifier is simplistic, and could be improved. This comparison does not take into account that, in contrast to the analysis, the verification can be performed in a just-in-time fashion for each method.

5 Related Work

Lifetime analysis as dealt with in this paper was first described by Ruggieri and Murtagh [20]. The term *escape analysis* was coined by Park and Goldberg [21] in the context of functional languages. Their research spawned work on algorithms which represent the escaping objects by integers [22,23]. In contrast, the most precise escape analyses for Java use augmented points-to-graphs to model a program's behavior [8,7].

With the exception of Gay and Steensgaard's analysis [10], our (closed world) analysis is the only one we know of that can be performed in time $O(N + G)$ where N is program size and G is the size of the call graph. Overall, our analysis can be viewed as a simple non-SSA variant of Gay and Steensgaard's algorithm. In comparison, our analysis has less precision. This is mostly due to the fact that they require SSA form and we do not. Their freshness analysis relies crucially on the single assignment property. It is, however, in spirit, close to our run-time type analysis. We employ the run-time type property solely for reducing the potentially invokable methods, whereas they use freshness of returned objects to allocate them on the stack. (In our previous example, their analysis would be able to identify the `iter` variable as captured.) In contrast to us, they suggest employing a whole program analysis such as Rapid Type Analysis to determine the run-time type of the variable on which the method dispatch is performed. While it seems that their analysis is as suitable for the safe transportation of efficiently verifiable annotations as ours, they apparently did not consider this. Furthermore, the use of Rapid Type Analysis hinders the process of just-in-time verification, because it requires the whole program to be available before the analysis can begin.

Our approach is also similar to the phase 1 analysis in Bogda and Hölzle [9] with the major difference that Bogda and Hölzle deal with alias sets instead of variables.

Hartmann et al. [11] enable safe object inlining by extending their SafeTSA code format to include escape analysis annotations. The core difference to our analysis is their assumption about what is known of the run-time environment. We assume knowledge of the libraries used by the code receiver insofar as we presuppose the escape analysis results for these libraries. (Allowing for dynamic class loading in the open world scenario is orthogonal to this assumption.) In contrast, Hartmann et al. assume no knowledge beyond the given program. Within the given program they use a more coarse-grain static analysis, but they compensate for this loss in precision by providing a third kind of type annotation, "may-escape". In principle, they mark variables as "may-escape" which we mark as escaped in the open world and as captured in the closed world. Of course, to determine their final status these variables require a form of escape analysis at load time and classes loaded later might cause dynamic deoptimization of the whole program.

Hummel et al. [2] employ annotations for register allocation hints in order to improve compilation time and run-time performance. Verifiability is addressed by associating a virtual register with a type and integrating the verification step with the bytecode verifier. Similarly, Jones et al. [3] describe an annotation for register allocation; however, verifiability of these annotations is not addressed. Finally, Krintz et al. [1] propose an annotation framework, and describe a series of annotations, that are focused on reducing the overhead of dynamic compilation, primarily through hints indicating "hot" methods. Verifiability is not a concern in this framework, because none of the annotations could lead to an incorrect program; at worst, the dynamic compiler will not efficiently optimize the program. Other annotation systems [5,6] do not address verifiability at all.

The fact that our annotations are verifiable in the same sense that an explicit proof of certain properties, e.g., type safety, is checkable, lies at the heart of similarities with techniques that utilize more explicit proofs. Our verification process does not directly relate to proof-carrying code [24] or certifying compilation [25] since we employ neither verification conditions nor general theorem provers. Our approach is more directly related to credible compilation [26,27] and translation validation [28] even though these approaches use techniques that are much more comprehensive and more heavyweight than ours. A credible compiler provides for each successfully compiled program a proof showing that the compilation preserved the semantics of the program. Rinard and Marinov [26,27] employ a two stage process to prove the correctness of program transformations performed by a certifying compiler. The first stage proves the correctness of the analysis results and the second stage establishes the correctness of program transformations utilizing the result of the first stage. Our annotations are essentially a transmission of first stage analysis results. In our case the proof is so simple that we are not transmitting it, instead it is implied.

6 Conclusion

In this paper, we have presented and evaluated a verifiable escape analysis for object-oriented languages such as Java. We have introduced a simple and flow-insensitive escape analysis that uses an inexpensive intraprocedural type analysis to enhance the interprocedural escape analysis proper. For this analysis, we have introduced low-overhead annotations to communicate the analysis results to the code consumer in an efficiently verifiable manner. Analysis, annotations, and low-cost verification together enable a shift of analysis costs from code consumer to code producer. We have provided experimental evidence that our analysis has an acceptable efficacy compared to other state-of-the-art analyses and that transport and verification are indeed efficiently achievable.

We have presented an open world variant of our escape analysis that is not invalidated in the presence of dynamic class loading and that is, therefore, amenable for integration into standard-conforming Java virtual machines. To our knowledge, no other escape analysis provides this feature.

Acknowledgements. This work evolved out of earlier joint work with Chandra Krintz and Vivek Haldar [29]. We are thankful to Alexandru Sălcianu for his help with the FLEX compiler and to Urs Hölzle, the anonymous referees, Peter Fröhlich, Cristian Petrescu-Prahova, Christian Probst, Jeffery von Ronne, and Vasanth Venkatachalam for their comments.

This effort is partially funded by the Defense Advanced Research Projects Agency (DARPA) and Air Force Research Laboratory, Air Force Materiel Command, USAF, under agreement number F30602-99-1-0536, by the National Science Foundation under grants CCR-0205712 and CCR-0105710, and by the Office of Naval Research under grant N00014-01-1-0854.

Any opinions, findings, and conclusions or recommendations expressed in this material are those of the authors and should not be interpreted as necessarily representing the official views, policies or endorsements, either expressed or implied, of Defense Advanced Research Projects Agency (DARPA), the National Science foundation (NSF), the Office of Naval Research (ONR), or any other agency of the U.S. Government.

References

1. Krintz, C., Calder, B.: Using annotations to reduce dynamic optimization time. In: Proceedings of the ACM SIGPLAN '01 Conference on Programming Language Design and Implementation, Snowbird, Utah (2001) 156–167 *SIGPLAN Notices,* 36(5), May 2001.
2. Azevedo, A., Nicolau, A., Hummel, J.: Java annotation-aware just-in-time compilation system. In: ACM Java Grande Conference. (1999) 142–151
3. Jones, J., Kamin, S.: Annotating Java class files with virtual registers for performance. Concurrency: Practice and Experience **12** (2000) 389–406
4. Pominville, P., Qian, F., Vallee-Rai, R., Hendren, L., Verbrugge, C.: A framework for optimizing Java using attributes. In: Sable Technical Report No. 2000-2. (2000)
5. Grant, B., Mock, M., Philipose, M., Chambers, C., Eggers, S.J.: DyC: an expressive annotation-directed dynamic compiler for C. Theoretical Computer Science **248** (2000) 147–199
6. Reig, F.: Annotations for portable intermediate languages. In Benton, N., Kennedy, A., eds.: Electronic Notes in Theoretical Computer Science. Volume 59., Elsevier Science Publishers (2001)
7. Whaley, J., Rinard, M.: Compositional pointer and escape analysis for Java programs. In: Proceedings of the 14th Annual ACM SIGPLAN Conference on Object-Oriented Programming Systems, Languages, and Applications, Denver, CO (1999)

8. Choi, J., Gupta, M., Serrano, M., Shreedhar, V., Midkiff, S.: Escape analysis for Java. In: ACM SIGPLAN Conference on Object-Oriented Programming Systems, Languages, and Applications (OOPSLA). (1999)
9. Bogda, J., Hölzle, U.: Removing unnecessary synchronization in Java. In: ACM SIGPLAN Conference on Object-Oriented Programming Systems, Languages, and Applications (OOPSLA). (1999)
10. Gay, D., Steensgaard, B.: Fast escape analysis and stack allocation for object-based programs. In: Compiler Construction 2000, Berlin, Germany (2000)
11. Hartmann, A., Amme, W., von Ronne, J., Franz, M.: Code annotation for safe and efficient dynamic object resolution. Electronic Notes in Theoretical Computer Science **82** (2003)
12. Lhoták, O., Hendren, L.: Run-time evaluation of opportunities for object inlining in Java. In: Proceedings of the 2002 joint ACM-ISCOPE conference on Java Grande (JGI-02), New York, ACM Press (2002) 175–184
13. Rehof, J., Mogensen, T.Æ.: Tractable constraints in finite semi-lattices. In Cousot, R., Schmidt, D.A., eds.: Third International Static Analysis Symposium (SAS). Volume 1145 of Lecture Notes in Computer Science., Springer (1996) 285–301
14. Java Grande Forum: The Java Grande Forum benchmark suite (2003)
15. Standard Performance Evaluation Corporation: SPEC JVM98 benchmarks. See online at http://www.spec.org/osg/jvm98 for more information (1998)
16. Sălcianu, A.: Pointer analysis and it applications for Java programs. Master's thesis, Massachusetts Institute of Technology, Cambridge, MA (2001)
17. Fitzgerald, R., Knoblock, T.B., Ruf, E., Steensgaard, B., Tarditi, D.: Marmot: an optimizing compiler for Java. Software—Practice and Experience **30** (2000) 199–232
18. Alpern, B., Attanasio, C.R., Barton, J.J., Cocchi, A., Hummel, S.F., Lieber, D., Ngo, T., Mergen, M., Shepherd, J.C., Smith, S.: Implementing Jalapeño in Java. In: Proceedings of the ACM SIGPLAN '99 Conference on Object-Oriented Programming Systems, Languages and Applications (OOPSLA). (1999)
19. Lindholm, T., Yellin, F.: The Java Virtual Machine Specification. Second edn. Addison-Wesley, Reading, MA, USA (1999)
20. Ruggieri, C., Murtagh, T.P.: Lifetime analysis of dynamically allocated objects. In: Conference Record of the Conference on Principles of Programming Languages, ACM SIGACT and SIGPLAN, ACM Press (1988) 285–293
21. Park, Y.G., Goldberg, B.: Escape analysis on lists. In: Proceedings of the 5th ACM SIGPLAN Conference on Programming Language Design and Implementation. (1992) 116–127
22. Deutsch, A.: On the complexity of escape analysis. In: Conference Record of POPL '97: The 24TH ACM SIGPLAN-SIGACT Symposium on Principles of Programming Languages, ACM SIGACT and SIGPLAN, ACM Press (1997) 358–371
23. Blanchet, B.: Escape Analysis for Java(TM). Theory and Practice. ACM Transactions on Programming Languages and Systems **25** (2003) 713–775
24. Necula, G.C.: Proof-carrying code. In: Proceedings of the ACM SIGPLAN-SIGACT Symposium on Principles of Programming Languages (POPL), Paris, France (1997) 106–119
25. Necula, G.C., Lee, P.: The design and implementation of a certifying compiler. In: Proceedings of the ACM SIGPLAN'98 Conference on Programming Language Design and Implementation (PLDI), Montreal, Canada (1998) 333–344 *SIGPLAN Notices* 33(5), May 1998.
26. Rinard, M.: Credible compilation. Technical Report MIT/LCS/TR-776, MIT (1999)

27. Rinard, M., Marinov, D.: Credible compilation with pointers. In: Proceedings of the FLoC Workshop on Run-Time Result Verification, Trento, Italy (1999)
28. Necula, G.C.: Translation validation for an optimizing compiler. ACM SIGPLAN Notices **35** (2000) 83–94
29. Franz, M., Krintz, C., Haldar, V., Stork, C.H.: Tamper-proof annotations, by design. Technical report, Department of Information and Computer Science, University of California, Irvine (2002)

Pointer Analysis in the Presence of Dynamic Class Loading*

Martin Hirzel[1], Amer Diwan[1], and Michael Hind[2]

[1] University of Colorado, Boulder, CO 80309, USA
{hirzel,diwan}@cs.colorado.edu
[2] IBM Watson Research Center, Hawthorne, NY 10532, USA
hind@watson.ibm.com

Abstract. Many optimizations need precise pointer analyses to be effective. Unfortunately, some Java features, such as dynamic class loading, reflection, and native methods, make pointer analyses difficult to develop. Hence, prior pointer analyses for Java either ignore these features or are overly conservative. This paper presents the first non-trivial pointer analysis that deals with all Java language features. This paper identifies all problems in performing Andersen's pointer analysis for the full Java language, presents solutions to those problems, and uses a full implementation of the solutions in Jikes RVM for validation and performance evaluation. The results from this work should be transferable to other analyses and to other languages.

1 Introduction

Pointer analysis benefits many optimizations, such as inlining, load elimination, code movement, stack allocation, and parallelization. Unfortunately, dynamic class loading, reflection, and native code make ahead-of-time pointer analysis of Java programs impossible.

This paper presents the first non-trivial pointer analysis that works for all of Java. Most prior papers assume that all classes are known and available ahead of time (e.g., [39,40,47,60]). The few papers that deal with dynamic class loading assume restrictions on reflection and native code [7,36,44,45]. Prior work makes these simplifying assumptions because they are acceptable in some contexts, because dealing with the full generality of Java is difficult, and because the advantages of the analyses often outweigh the disadvantages of only handling a subset of Java.

This paper describes how to overcome the restrictions of prior work in the context of Andersen's pointer analysis [3], so the benefits become available in the general setting of an executing Java virtual machine. This paper:

* This work is supported by NSF ITR grant CCR-0085792, an NSF Career Award CCR-0133457, an IBM Ph.D. Fellowship, an IBM faculty partnership award, and an equipment grant from Intel. Any opinions, findings and conclusions or recommendations expressed in this material are the authors' and do not necessarily reflect those of the sponsors.

M. Odersky (Ed.): ECOOP 2004, LNCS 3086, pp. 96–122, 2004.

(a) identifies all problems of performing Andersen's pointe s for the full Java language,
(b) presents a solution for each of the problems,
(c) reports on a full implementation of the solutions in Jikes R source research virtual machine from IBM [2],
(d) validates, for our benchmark runs, that the list of problems is co pen- solutions are correct, and the implementation works, and
(e) evaluates the efficiency of the implementation.

The performance results show that the implementation is efficient enough stable long-running applications. However, because Andersen's algorithm has c bic time complexity, and because Jikes RVM, which is itself written in Java, leads to a large code base even for small benchmarks, performance needs improvements for short-running applications. Such improvements are an open challenge; they could be achieved by making Andersen's implementation in Jikes RVM more efficient, or by using a cheaper analysis.

The contributions from this work should be transferable to

- Other analyses: Andersen's analysis is a whole-program analysis consisting of two steps: modeling the code and computing a fixed-point on the model. Several other algorithms follow the same pattern, such as VTA [54], XTA [57], or Das's one level flow algorithm [15]. Algorithms that do not require the second step, such as CHA [16,20] or Steensgaard's unification-based algorithm [52], are easier to perform in an online setting. Andersen's analysis is flow-insensitive and context-insensitive. While this paper should also be helpful for performing flow-sensitive or context-sensitive analyses online, these pose additional challenges (multithreading and exceptions, and multiple calling contexts) that need to be addressed.
- Other languages: This paper shows how to deal with dynamic class loading, reflection, and native code in Java. Other languages have similar features, which pose similar problems for pointer analysis.

2 Motivation

Java features such as dynamic class loading, reflection, and native methods prohibit static whole-program analyses. This paper identifies all Java features that create challenges for pointer analysis; this section focuses just on class loading, and discusses why it precludes static analysis.

2.1 It Is Not Known Statically *Where* a Class Will Be Loaded from

Java allows user-defined class loaders, which may have their own rules for where to look for the bytecode, or even generate it on-the-fly. A static analysis cannot analyze those classes. User-defined class loaders are widely used in production-strength commercial applications, such as Eclipse [56] and Tomcat [55].

2.2 …Known Statically *Which* Class Will Be Loaded

…alysis that restricts itself to the subset of Java without *user-* …ss loaders cannot be fully static, because code may still load stati- …known classes with the *system* class loader. This is done by invoking …*orName*(String *name*), where *name* can be computed at runtime. For ex- …le, a program may compute the localized calendar class name by reading … environment variable. One approach to dealing with this issue would be to assume that all calendar classes may be loaded. This would result in a less precise solution, if, for example, at each customer's site, only one calendar class is loaded. Even worse, the relevant classes may be available only in the execution environment, and not in the development environment. Only an online analysis could analyze such a program.

2.3 It Is Not Known Statically *When* a Given Class Will Be Loaded

If the classes to be analyzed are available only in the execution environment, but Class.*forName* is not used, one could imagine avoiding *static* analysis by attempting a whole-program analysis during JVM *start-up*, long before the analyzed classes will be needed. The Java specification says it should appear to the user as if class loading is lazy, but a JVM could just pretend to be lazy by showing only the effects of lazy loading, while actually being eager. This is difficult to engineer in practice, however. One would need a deferral mechanism for various visible effects of class loading. An example for such a visible effect would be a static field initialization of the form

static HashMap *hashMap* = **new** HashMap(Constants.CAPACITY);

Suppose that Constants.CAPACITY has the illegal value −1. The effect, an ExceptionInInitializerError, should only become visible when the class containing the static field is loaded. Furthermore, *hashMap* should be initialized after CAPACITY, to ensure that the latter receives the correct value. Loading classes eagerly and still preserving the proper (lazy) class loading semantics is challenging.

2.4 It Is Not Known Statically *Whether* a Given Class Will Be Loaded

Even if one ignores the order of class loading, and handles only a subset of Java without *explicit* class loading, *implicit* class loading still poses problems for static analyses. A JVM implicitly loads a class the first time executing code refers to it, for example, by creating an instance of the class. Whether a program will load a given class is undecidable, as Figure 1 illustrates: a run of "`java Main`" does not load class C; a run of "`java Main anArgument`" loads class C, because Line 5 creates an instance of C. We can observe this by whether Line 10 in the static initializer prints its message. In this example, a static analysis would have to conservatively assume that class C will be loaded, and to analyze it. In general, a static whole-program analysis would have to analyze many more classes than necessary, making it inefficient (analyzing more classes costs time and space) and less precise (the code in those classes may exhibit behavior never encountered at runtime).

```
class Main {
    public static void main(String[] argv) {
        C v = null;
        if (argv.length > 0)
            v = new C();
    }
}
class C {
    static {
        System.out.println("loaded class C");
    }
}
```

Fig. 1. Class loading example.

3 Related Work

This paper shows how to enhance Andersen's pointer analysis to analyze the full Java programming language. Section 3.1 puts Andersen's pointer analysis in context. Section 3.2 discusses related work on online, interprocedural analyses. Section 3.3 discusses related work on using Andersen's analysis for Java. Finally, Section 3.4 discusses work related to our validation methodology.

3.1 Static Pointer Analyses

The body of literature on pointer analyses is vast [30]. At one extreme, exemplified by Steensgaard [52] and type-based analyses [18,25,57], the analyses are fast, but imprecise. At the other extreme, exemplified by shape analyses [29, 49], the analyses are slow, but precise enough to discover the shapes of many data structures. In between these two extremes there are many pointer analyses, offering different cost-precision tradeoffs.

The goal of our research was to choose a well-known analysis and to extend it to handle all features of Java. This goal was motivated by our need to build a pointer analysis to support connectivity-based garbage collection, for which type-based analyses are too imprecise [32]. Liang et al. [41] report that it would be very hard to significantly improve the precision of Andersen's analysis without biting into the much more expensive shape analysis. This left us with a choice between Steensgaard's [52] and Andersen's [3] analysis. Andersen's analysis is less efficient, but more precise [31,50]. We decided to use Andersen's analysis, because it poses a superset of the Java-specific challenges posed by Steensgaard's analysis, leaving the latter (or points in between) as a fall back option.

3.2 Online Interprocedural Analyses

An *online* interprocedural analysis is an interprocedural analysis that occurs during execution, and thus, can correctly deal with dynamic class loading.

Demand-driven interprocedural analyses. A number of pointer analyses are demand-driven, but not online [1,9,10,27,38,59]. All of these analyses build a representation of the static whole program, but then compute exact solutions only for parts of it, which makes them more scalable. None of these papers discuss issues specific to dynamic class loading.

Incremental interprocedural analyses. Another related area of research is incremental interprocedural analysis [8,14,23,24]. The goal of this line of research is to avoid a reanalysis of the complete program when a change is made after an interprocedural analysis has been performed. This paper differs in that it focuses on the dynamic semantics of the Java programming language, not programmer modifications to the source code.

Extant analysis. Sreedhar, Burke, and Choi [51] describe extant analysis, which finds parts of the static whole program that can be safely optimized ahead of time, even when new classes may be loaded later. It is not an online analysis, but reduces the need for one in settings where much of the program is available statically.

Analyses that deal with dynamic class loading. Below, we discuss some analyses that deal with dynamic class loading. None of these analyses deals with reflection or JNI, or validate their analysis results. Furthermore, all are less precise than Andersen's analysis.

Pechtchanski and Sarkar [44] present a framework for interprocedural whole-program analysis and optimistic optimization. They discuss how the analysis is triggered (when newly loaded methods are compiled), and how to keep track of what to de-optimize (when optimistic assumptions are invalidated). They also present an example online interprocedural type analysis. Their analysis does not model value flow through parameters, which makes it less precise, as well as easier to implement, than Andersen's analysis.

Bogda and Singh [7] and King [36] adapt Ruf's escape analysis [48] to deal with dynamic class loading. Ruf's analysis is unification-based, and thus less precise than Andersen's analysis. Escape analysis is a simpler problem than pointer analysis because the impact of a method is independent of its parameters and the problem doesn't require a unique representation for each heap object [11]. Bogda and Singh discuss tradeoffs of when to trigger the analysis, and whether to make optimistic or pessimistic assumptions for optimization. King focuses on a specific client, a garbage collector with thread-local heaps, where local collections require no synchronization. Whereas Bogda and Singh use a call graph based on capturing call edges at their first dynamic execution, King uses a call graph based on rapid type analysis [6].

Qian and Hendren [45], in work concurrently with ours, adapt Tip and Palsberg's XTA [57] to deal with dynamic class loading. The main contribution of their paper is a low-overhead call edge profiler, which yields a precise call graph on which XTA is based. Even though XTA is weaker than Andersen's analysis, both have separate constraint generation and constraint propagation steps, and thus pose similar problems. Qian and Hendren solve the problems posed by dynamic class loading similarly to the way we solve them; for example, their approach to unresolved references is analogous to our approach in Section 4.5.

3.3 Andersen's Analysis for Static Java

A number of papers describe how to use Andersen's analysis for Java [39,40,47, 60]. None of these deal with dynamic class loading. Nevertheless, they do present solutions for various other features of Java that make pointer analyses difficult (object fields, virtual method invocations, etc.).

Rountev, Milanova, and Ryder [47] formalize Andersen's analysis for Java using set constraints, which enables them to solve it with BANE (Berkeley ANalysis Engine) [19]. Liang, Pennings, and Harrold [40] compare both Steensgaard's and Andersen's analysis for Java, and evaluate trade-offs for handling fields and the call graph. Whaley and Lam [60] improve the efficiency of Andersen's analysis by using implementation techniques from CLA [28], and improve the precision by adding flow-sensitivity for local variables. Lhoták and Hendren [39] present SPARK (Soot Pointer Analysis Research Kit), an implementation of Andersen's analysis in Soot [58], which provides precision and efficiency tradeoffs for various components.

Prior work on implementing Andersen's analysis differs in how it represents constraint graphs. There are many alternatives, and each one has different cost/benefit tradeoffs. We will discuss these in Section 4.2.

3.4 Validation Methodology

Our validation methodology compares points-to sets computed by our analysis to actual pointers at runtime. This is similar to limit studies that other researchers have used to evaluate and debug various compiler analyses [18,37,41].

4 Algorithm

Section 4.1 presents the architecture for performing Andersen's pointer analysis online. The subsequent sections discuss parts of the architecture that deal with: constraint finding (4.2), call graph building (4.3), constraint propagation (4.4), type resolution (4.5), and other constraint generating events (4.6).

4.1 Architecture

As mentioned in Section 1, Andersen's algorithm has two steps: finding the constraints that model the code semantics of interest, and propagating these constraints until a fixed point is reached. In an offline setting, the first step requires a scan of the program and its call graph. In an online setting, this step is more complex, because parts of the program are "discovered" during execution of various VM events. Figure 2 shows the architecture for performing Andersen's pointer analysis online. The events during virtual machine execution (left column) generate inputs to the analysis. The analysis (dotted box) consists of four components (middle column) that operate on shared data structures (right column). Clients (bottom) trigger the constraint propagator component of the analysis, and consume the outputs. The outputs are represented as points-to sets in the constraint graph. In an online setting, the points-to sets conservatively describe the pointers in the program until there is an addition to the constraints.

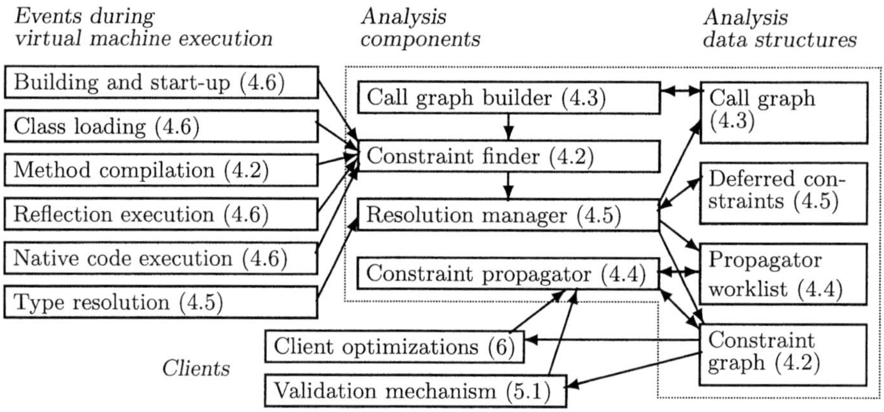

Fig. 2. Architecture for performing Andersen's pointer analysis online. The numbers in parentheses refer to sections in this paper.

When used offline, Andersen's analysis requires only a part of the architecture in Figure 2. In an offline setting, the only input comes from method compilation. It is used by the constraint finder and the call graph builder to create a constraint graph. After that, the constraint propagator finds a fixed-point on the constraint graph. The results are consumed by clients.

Four additions to the architecture make Andersen's analysis work online:

Building the call graph online. Andersen's analysis relies on a call graph for interprocedural constraints. This paper uses an online version of CHA (class hierarchy analysis [16,20]) for the call graph builder. CHA is an offline whole-program analysis, Section 4.3 describes how to make it work online.

Supporting re-propagation. Method compilation and other constraint-generating events happen throughout the execution. Where an offline analysis can propagate once after all constraints have been found, the online analysis has to propagate whenever a client needs points-to information and new constraints have been created since the last propagation. Section 4.4 describes how the propagator starts with its previous solution and a worklist of changed parts in the constraint graph to avoid incurring the full propagation cost every time.

Supporting unresolved types. The constraint finder may find constraints that involve as-yet unresolved types. But both the call graph builder and the propagator rely on resolved types for precision; for example, the propagator filters points-to sets by types. Section 4.5 describes how the resolution manager defers communicating constraints from the constraint finder to other analysis components until the involved types are resolved.

Capturing more input events. A pointer analysis for Java has to deal with features such as reflection and native code, in addition to dynamic class loading. Section 4.6 describes how to handle all the other events during virtual machine execution that may generate constraints.

4.2 Constraint Finder

Section 4.2 describes the constraint graph data structure, which models the data flow of the program. Section 4.2 describes how code is translated into constraints at method compilation time. Our approach to representing the constraint graph and analyzing code combines ideas from various earlier papers on offline implementation of Andersen's analysis.

Constraint graph. The constraint graph has four kinds of nodes that participate in constraints. The constraints are stored as sets at the nodes. Table 1 describes the nodes, introducing the notation that is used in the remainder of this paper, and shows which sets are stored at each node. The node kinds in "[· · ·]" are the kinds of nodes in the set.

Table 1. Constraint graph representation.

Node kind	Represents concrete entities	Flow sets	Points-to sets
h-node	Set of heap objects, e.g., all objects allocated at a particular allocation site	none	none
v-node	Set of program variables, e.g., a static variable, or all occurrences of a local variable	flowTo[v], flowTo[$v.f$]	pointsTo[h]
$h.f$-node	Instance field f of all heap objects represented by h	none	pointsTo[h]
$v.f$-node	Instance field f of all h-nodes pointed to by v	flowFrom[v], flowTo[v]	none

Flow-to sets (Column 3 of Table 1) represent a flow of values (assignments, parameter passing, etc.), and are stored with v-nodes and $v.f$-nodes. For example, if $v'.f \in \text{flowTo}(v)$, then v's pointer r-value may flow to $v'.f$. Flow-from sets are the inverse of flow-to sets. In the example, we would have $v \in \text{flowFrom}(v'.f)$.

Points-to sets (Column 4 of Table 1) represent the set of objects (r-values) that a pointer (l-value) may point to, and are stored with v-nodes and $h.f$-nodes. Since it stores points-to sets with $h.f$-nodes instead of $v.f$-nodes, the analysis is *field sensitive* [39].

The constraint finder models program code by v-nodes, $v.f$-nodes, and their flow sets. Based on these, the propagator computes the points-to sets of v-nodes and $h.f$-nodes. For example, if a client of the pointer analysis is interested in whether a variable p may point to objects allocated at an allocation site a, it checks whether the h-node for a is an element of the points-to set of the v-node for p.

Each h-node has a map from fields f to $h.f$-nodes (i.e., the nodes that represent the instance fields of the objects represented by the h-node). In addition to language-level fields, each h-node has a special node $h.f_{\text{td}}$ that represents the field containing the reference to the type descriptor for the heap node. A type descriptor is implemented as an object in Jikes RVM, and thus, must be modeled by the analysis. For each h-node representing arrays of references, there is a special node $h.f_{\text{elems}}$ that represents all of their elements. Thus, the analysis does not distinguish between different elements of an array.

There are many alternatives for storing the flow and points-to sets. For example, we represent the data flow between v-nodes and $h.f$-nodes implicitly, whereas BANE represents it explicitly [22,47]. Thus, our analysis saves space compared to BANE, but may have to perform more work at propagation time. As another example, CLA [28] stores reverse points-to sets at h-nodes, instead of storing forward points-to sets at v-nodes and $h.f$-nodes. The forward points-to sets are implicit in CLA and must therefore be computed after propagation to obtain the final analysis results. These choices affect both the time and space complexity of the propagator. As long as it can infer the needed sets during propagation, an implementation can decide which sets to represent explicitly. In fact, a representation may even store some sets redundantly: for example, to obtain efficient propagation, our representation uses redundant flow-from sets.

Finally, there are many choices for how to implement the sets. The SPARK paper evaluates various data structures for representing points-to sets [39], finding that hybrid sets (using lists for small sets, and bit-vectors for large sets) yield the best results. We found the shared bit-vector implementation from CLA [26] to be even more efficient than the hybrid sets used by SPARK.

Method compilation. The left column of Figure 2 shows the various events during virtual machine execution that invoke the constraint finder. This section is only concerned with finding intraprocedural constraints during method compilation; later sections discuss other kinds of events.

The intraprocedural constraint finder analyzes the code of a method, and models it in the constraint graph. It is a flow-insensitive pass of the optimizing compiler of Jikes RVM, operating on the high-level register-based intermediate representation (HIR). HIR decomposes access paths by introducing temporaries, so that no access path contains more than one pointer dereference.

Column "Actions" in Table 2 gives the actions of the constraint finder when it encounters the statement in Column "Statement". Column "Represent constraints" shows the constraints implicit in the actions of the constraint finder using mathematical notation.

Table 2. Intraprocedural constraint finder.

Statement		Actions	Represent constraints
$v' = v$	(move $v \to v'$)	flowTo(v).add(v')	pointsTo(v) $\subseteq$ pointsTo(v')
$v' = v.f$	(load $v.f \to v'$)	flowTo($v.f$).add(v')	$\forall h \in$ pointsTo(v) : pointsTo($h.f$) $\subseteq$ pointsTo(v')
$v'.f = v$	(store $v \to v'.f$)	flowTo(v).add($v'.f$), flowFrom($v'.f$).add(v)	$\forall h \in$ pointsTo(v') : pointsTo(v) $\subseteq$ pointsTo($h.f$)
ℓ: $v =$ **new**...	(alloc $h_\ell \to v$)	pointsTo(v).add(h_ℓ)	$\{h_\ell\} \subseteq$ pointsTo(v)

In addition to the actions in Table 2, the analysis needs to address some more issues during method compilation.

Unoptimized code. The intraprocedural constraint finder is implemented as a pass of the Jikes RVM optimizing compiler. However, Jikes RVM compiles some methods only with a baseline compiler, which does not use a representation that is amenable to constraint finding. We handle such methods by running the constraint finder as part of a truncated optimizing compilation. Other virtual machines, where some code is not compiled at all, but interpreted, can take a similar approach.

Recompilation of methods. Many JVMs, including Jikes RVM, may recompile a method (at a higher optimization level) if it executes frequently. The recompiled methods may have new variables or code introduced by optimizations (such as inlining). Since each inlining context of an allocation site is modeled by a separate h-node, the analysis generates new constraints for the recompiled methods and integrates them with the constraints for any previously compiled versions of the method.

Magic. Jikes RVM has some internal "magic" operations, for example, to allow direct manipulation of pointers. The compilers expand magic in special ways directly into low-level code. Likewise, the analysis expands magic in special ways directly into constraints.

4.3 Call Graph Builder

For each call-edge, the analysis generates constraints that model the data flow through parameters and return values. Parameter passing is modeled as a move from actuals (at the call-site) to formals (of the callee). Each return statement in a method m is modeled as a move to a special v-node $v_{\text{retval}(m)}$. The data flow of the return value to the call-site is modeled as a move to the v-node that receives the result of the call.

We use CHA (Class Hierarchy Analysis [16,20]) to find call-edges. A more precise alternative to CHA is to construct the call graph on-the-fly based on the results of the pointer analysis. We decided against that approach because prior work indicated that the modest improvement in precision does not justify the cost in efficiency [39]. In work concurrent with ours, Qian and Hendren developed an even more precise alternative based on low-overhead profiling [45].

CHA is a static whole-program analysis, but to support Andersen's analysis online, CHA must also run online, i.e., deal with dynamic class loading. The key to solving this problem is the observation that for each call-edge, either the call-site is compiled first, or the callee is compiled first. The constraints for the call-edge are added when the second of the two is compiled. This works as follows:

- When encountering a method $m(v_{\text{formal}_1(m)}, \ldots, v_{\text{formal}_n(m)})$, the call graph builder
  - creates a tuple $I_m = \langle v_{\text{retval}(m)}, v_{\text{formal}_1(m)}, \ldots, v_{\text{formal}_n(m)} \rangle$ for m as a callee,
  - finds all corresponding tuples for matching call-sites that have been compiled in the past, and adds constraints to model the moves between the corresponding v-nodes in the tuples, and
  - stores the tuple I_m for lookup on behalf of call-sites that will be compiled in the future.
- When encountering a call-site $c : v_{\text{retval}(c)} = m(v_{\text{actual}_1(c)}, \ldots, v_{\text{actual}_n(c)})$, the call graph builder
  - creates a tuple $I_c = \langle v_{\text{retval}(c)}, v_{\text{actual}_1(c)}, \ldots, v_{\text{actual}_n(c)} \rangle$ for call-site c,
  - looks up all corresponding tuples for matching callees that have been compiled in the past, and adds constraints to model the moves between the corresponding v-nodes in the tuples, and
  - stores the tuple I_c for lookup on behalf of callees that will be compiled in the future.

Besides parameter passing and return values, there is one more kind of interprocedural data flow that our analysis needs to model: exception handling. Exceptions lead to flow of values (the exception object) between the site that throws an exception and the catch clause that catches the exception. For simplicity, our initial prototype assumes that any throws can reach any catch clause; type filtering eliminates many of these possibilities later on. One could easily imagine making this more precise, for example by assuming that throws can only reach catch clauses in the current method or its (transitive) callers.

4.4 Constraint Propagator

The propagator propagates points-to sets following the constraints that are implicit in the flow sets until the points-to sets reach a fixed point. In order to avoid wasted work, our algorithm maintains two pieces of information, a worklist of v-nodes and isCharged-bits on $h.f$-nodes, that enable it to propagate only the changed points-to sets at each iteration (rather than propagating all points-to sets). The worklist contains v-nodes whose points-to sets have changed and thus need to be propagated, or whose flow sets have changed and thus the points-to sets need to be propagated to additional nodes. The constraint finder initializes the worklist.

The algorithm in Figure 3, which is a variation of the algorithm from SPARK [39], implements the constraint propagator component of Figure 2.

```
1: while worklist not empty, or isCharged(h.f) for any h.f-node
2:     while worklist not empty
3:         remove node v from worklist
4:         for each v' ∈ flowTo(v)                                    // move v → v'
5:             pointsTo(v').add(pointsTo(v))
6:             if pointsTo(v') changed, add v' to worklist
7:         for each v'.f ∈ flowTo(v)                                  // store v → v'.f
8:             for each h ∈ pointsTo(v')
9:                 pointsTo(h.f).add(pointsTo(v))
10:                if pointsTo(h.f) changed, isCharged(h.f) ← true
11:        for each field f of v,
12:            for each v' ∈ flowFrom(v.f)                            // store v' → v.f
13:                for each h ∈ pointsTo(v)
14:                    pointsTo(h.f).add(pointsTo(v'))
15:                    if pointsTo(h.f) changed, isCharged(h.f) ← true
16:            for each v' ∈ flowTo(v.f)                              // load v.f → v'
17:                for each h ∈ pointsTo(v)
18:                    pointsTo(v').add(pointsTo(h.f))
19:                    if pointsTo(v') changed, add v' to worklist
20:    for each v.f
21:        for each h ∈ pointsTo(v), if isCharged(h.f)
22:            for each v' ∈ flowTo(v.f)                              // load v.f → v'
23:                pointsTo(v').add(pointsTo(h.f))
24:                if pointsTo(v') changed, add v' to worklist
25:    for each h.f
26:        isCharged(h.f) ← false
```

Fig. 3. Constraint propagator

The propagator puts a v-node on the worklist when its points-to set changes. Lines 4-10 propagate the v-node's points-to set to nodes in its flow-to sets. Lines 11-19 update the points-to set for all fields of objects pointed to by the v-node. This is necessary because for the h-nodes that have been newly added to v's points-to set, the flow to and from $v.f$ carries over to the corresponding $h.f$-nodes. Line 12 relies on the redundant flow-from sets.

The propagator sets the isCharged-bit of an $h.f$-node to true when its points-to set changes. To discharge an $h.f$-node, the algorithm needs to consider all flow-to edges from all $v.f$-nodes that represent it (lines 20-24). This is why it does not keep a worklist of charged $h.f$-nodes: to find their flow-to targets, it needs to iterate over $v.f$-nodes anyway. This is the only part of the algorithm that iterates over all ($v.f$-) nodes: all other parts of the algorithm attempt to update points-to sets while visiting only nodes that are relevant to the points-to sets being updated.

To improve the efficiency of this iterative part, the implementation uses a cache that remembers the charged nodes in shared points-to sets. The cache speeds up the loops at Lines 20 and 21 by an order of magnitude.

The propagator performs on-the-fly filtering by types: it only adds an h-node to a points-to set of a v-node or $h.f$-node if it represents heap objects of a subtype of the declared type of the variable or field. Lhoták and Hendren found that this helps keep the points-to sets small, improving both precision and efficiency of the analysis [39]. Our experiences confirm this observation.

The propagator creates $h.f$-nodes lazily the first time it adds elements to their points-to sets, in lines 9 and 14. It only creates $h.f$-nodes if instances of the type of h have the field f. This is not always the case, as the following example illustrates. Let A, B, C be three classes such that C is a subclass of B, and B is a subclass of A. Class B declares a field f. Let h_A, h_B, h_C be h-nodes of type A, B, C, respectively. Let v be a v-node of declared type A, and let v.pointsTo $= \{h_A, h_B, h_C\}$. Now, data flow to $v.f$ should add to the points-to sets of nodes $h_B.f$ and $h_C.f$, but there is no node $h_A.f$.

We also experimented with the optimizations partial online cycle elimination [19] and collapsing of single-entry subgraphs [46]. They yielded only modest performance improvements compared to shared bit-vectors [26] and type filtering [39]. Part of the reason for the small payoff may be that our data structures do not put $h.f$-nodes in flow-to sets (á la BANE [19]).

4.5 Resolution Manager

The JVM specification allows a Java method to have unresolved references to fields, methods, and classes [42]. A class reference is resolved when the class is instantiated, when a static field in the class is used, or when a static method in the class is called.

The unresolved references in the code (some of which may never get resolved) create two main difficulties for the analysis.

First, the CHA (class hierarchy analysis) that implements the call graph builder does not work when the class hierarchy of the involved classes is not yet known. Our current approach to this is to be conservative: if, due to unresolved classes, CHA cannot yet decide whether a call edge exists, the call graph builder adds an edge if the signatures match.

Second, the propagator uses types to perform type filtering and also for deciding which $h.f$-nodes belong to a given $v.f$-node. If the involved types are not yet resolved, this does not work. Therefore, the resolution manager defers all flow sets and points-to sets involving nodes of unresolved types, thus hiding them from the propagator:

– When the constraint finder creates an unresolved node, it registers the node with the resolution manager. A node is unresolved if it refers to an unresolved type. An h-node refers to the type of its objects; a v-node refers to its declared type; and a $v.f$-node refers to the type of v, the type of f, and the type in which f is declared.
– When the constraint finder would usually add a node to a flow set or points-to set of another node, but one or both of them are unresolved, it defers the information for later instead. Table 3 shows the deferred sets stored at unresolved nodes. For example, if the constraint finder finds that v should point to h, but v is unresolved, it adds h to v's deferred pointsTo set. Conversely, if h is unresolved, it adds v to h's deferred pointedToBy set. If both are unresolved, the points-to information is stored twice.

Table 3. Deferred sets stored at unresolved nodes.

Node kind	Flow	Points-to
h-node	none	pointedToBy[v]
v-node	flowFrom[v], flowFrom[$v.f$], flowTo[v], flowTo[$v.f$]	pointsTo[h]
$h.f$-node	there are no unresolved $h.f$-nodes	
$v.f$-node	flowFrom[v], flowTo[v]	none

– When a type is resolved, the resolution manager notifies all unresolved nodes that have registered for it. When an unresolved node is resolved, it iterates over all deferred sets stored at it, and attempts to add the information to the real model that is visible to the propagator. If a node stored in a deferred set is not resolved yet itself, the information will be added in the future when that node gets resolved.

With this design, some constraints will never be added to the model, if their types never get resolved. This saves unnecessary propagator work. Qian and Hendren developed a similar design independently [45].

Before becoming aware of the subtleties of the problems with unresolved references, we used an overly conservative approach: we added the constraints eagerly even when we had incomplete information. This imprecision led to very large points-to sets, which in turn slowed down our analysis prohibitively. Our current approach is both more precise and more efficient.

4.6 Other Constraint-Generating Events

This section discusses the remaining events in the left column of Figure 2 that serve as inputs to the constraint finder.

VM building and start-up. Jikes RVM itself is written in Java, and begins execution by loading a *boot image* (a file-based image of a fully initialized VM) of pre-allocated Java objects for the JIT compilers, GC, and other runtime services. These objects live in the same heap as application objects, so our analysis must model them.

Our analysis models all the *code* in the boot image as usual, with the intraprocedural constraint finder pass from Section 4.2 and the call graph builder from Section 4.3. Our analysis models the *data snapshot* of the boot image with special boot image h-nodes, and with points-to sets of global v-nodes and boot image $h.f$-nodes. The program that creates the boot image does not maintain a mapping from objects in the boot image to their actual allocation site, and thus, the boot image h-nodes are not allocation sites, instead they are synthesized at boot image writing time. Finally, the analysis propagates on the combined constraint system. This models how the snapshot of the data in the boot image may be manipulated by future execution of the code in the boot image.

Our techniques for correctly handling the boot image can be extended to form a general hybrid offline/online approach, where parts of the application are analyzed offline (as the VM is now) and the rest of the application is handled by the online analysis presented in this work. Such an approach could be useful for applications where the programmer asserts no use of the dynamic language features in parts of the application.

Class loading. Even though much of this paper revolves around making Andersen's analysis work for dynamic class loading, most analysis actions actually happen during other events, such as method compilation or type resolution. The only action that does take place exactly at class loading time is that the constraint finder models the ConstantValue bytecode attribute of static fields with constraints [42, Section 4.5].

Reflection execution. Java programs can invoke methods, access and modify fields, and instantiate objects using reflection. Although approaches such as String analysis [12] could predict which entities are manipulated in special cases, this problem is undecidable in the general case. Thus, when compiling code that uses reflection, there is no way of determining which methods will be called, which fields manipulated, or which classes instantiated at runtime.

One solution is to assume the worst case. We felt that this was too conservative and would introduce significant imprecision into the analysis for the sake of a few operations that were rarely executed. Other pointer analyses for Java side-step this problem by requiring users of the analysis to provide hand-coded models describing the effect of the reflective actions [39,60].

Our solution is to handle reflection when the code is actually executed. We instrument the virtual machine service that handles reflection with code that adds constraints dynamically. For example, if reflection stores into a field, the constraint finder observes the actual source and target of the store and generates a constraint that captures the semantics of the store at that time.

This strategy for handling reflection introduces new constraints when the reflective code does something new. Fortunately, that does not happen very often. When reflection has introduced new constraints and a client needs up-to-date points-to results, it must trigger a re-propagation.

Native code execution. The Java Native Interface (JNI) allows Java code to interact with dynamically loaded native code. Usually, a JVM cannot analyze that code. Thus, an analysis does not know (i) what values may be returned by JNI methods and (ii) how JNI methods may manipulate data structures of the program.

Our approach is to be imprecise, but conservative, for return values from JNI methods, while being precise for data manipulation by JNI methods. If a JNI method returns a heap allocated object, the constraint finder assumes that it could return an object from any allocation site. This is imprecise, but easy to implement. The constraint propagation uses type filtering, and thus, will filter the set of heap nodes returned by a JNI method based on types. If a JNI method manipulates data structures of the program, the manipulations must go through the JNI API, which Jikes RVM implements by calling Java methods that use reflection. Thus, JNI methods that make calls or manipulate object fields are handled precisely by our mechanism for reflection.

5 Validation

Implementing a pointer analysis for a complicated language and environment such as Java and Jikes RVM is a difficult task: the pointer analysis has to handle numerous corner cases, and missing any of the cases results in incorrect points-to sets. To help us debug our pointer analysis (to a high confidence level) we built a validation mechanism.

5.1 Validation Mechanism

We validate the pointer analysis results at GC (garbage collection) time. As GC traverses each pointer, we check whether the points-to set captures the pointer: (i) When GC finds a static variable p holding a pointer to an object o, our validation code finds the nodes v for p and h for o. Then, it checks whether the points-to set of v includes h. (ii) When GC finds a field f of an object o holding a pointer to an object o', our validation code finds the nodes h for o and h' for o'. Then, it checks whether the points-to set of $h.f$ includes h'. If either check fails, it prints a warning message.

To make the points-to sets correct at GC time, we propagate the constraints (Section 4.4) just before GC starts. As there is no memory available to grow points-to sets at that time, we modified Jikes RVM's garbage collector to set aside some extra space for this purpose.

Our validation methodology relies on the ability to map concrete heap objects to h-nodes in the constraint graph. To facilitate this, we add an extra header word to each heap object that maps it to its corresponding h-node in the constraint graph. For h-nodes representing allocation sites, we install this header word at allocation time. This extra word is only used for validation runs; the pointer analysis does not require any change to the object header.

5.2 Validation Anecdotes

Our validation methodology helped us find many bugs, some of which were quite subtle. Below are two examples. In both cases, there was more than one way in which bytecode could represent a Java-level construct. Both times, our analysis dealt correctly with the more common case, and the other case was obscure, yet legal. Our validation methodology showed us where we missed something; without it, we might not even have suspected that something was wrong.

Field reference class. In Java bytecode, a field reference consists of the name and type of the field, as well as a class reference to the class or interface "in which the field is to be found" ([42, Section 5.1]). Even for a static field, this may not be the class that declared the field, but a subclass of that class. Originally, we had assumed that it must be the exact class that declared the static field, and had written our analysis accordingly to maintain separate v-nodes for static fields with distinct declaring classes. When the bytecode wrote to a field using a field reference that mentions the subclass, the v-node for the field that mentions the superclass was missing some points-to set elements. That resulted in warnings from our validation methodology. Upon investigating those warnings, we became aware of the incorrect assumption and fixed it.

Field initializer attribute. In Java source code, a static field declaration has an optional initialization, for example, "**final static** String s = `"abc"`;". In Java bytecode, this usually translates into initialization code in the class initializer method *<clinit>*() of the class that declares the field. But sometimes, it translates into a ConstantValue attribute of the field instead ([42, Section 4.5]). Originally, we had assumed that class initializers are the only mechanism for initializing static fields, and that we would find these constraints when running the constraint finder on the *<clinit>*() method. But our validation methodology warned us about v-nodes for static fields whose points-to sets were too small. Knowing exactly for which fields that happened, we looked at the bytecode, and were surprised to see that the *<clinit>*() methods didn't initialize the fields. Thus, we found out about the ConstantValue bytecode attribute, and added constraints when class loading parses and executes that attribute (Section 4.6).

6 Clients

This section investigates two example clients of our analysis, and how they can deal with the dynamic nature of our analysis.

Method inlining can benefit from pointer analysis: if the points-to set elements of v all have the same implementation of a method m, the call $v.m()$ has only one possible target. Modern JVMs [4,13,43,53] typically use a dual execution strategy, where each method is initially either interpreted or compiled without optimizations. No inlining is performed for such methods. Later, an optimizing compiler that may perform inlining recompiles the minority of frequently executing methods. Because inlining is not performed during the initial execution, our analysis does not need to propagate constraints until the optimizing compiler needs to make an inlining decision.

Since the results of our pointer analysis may be invalidated by any of the events in the left column of Figure 2, an inlining client must be prepared to invalidate inlining decisions. Techniques such as code patching [13] and on-stack replacement [21,34] support invalidation. If instant invalidation is needed, our analysis must repropagate every time it finds new constraints. There are also techniques for avoiding invalidation of inlining decisions, such as pre-existence based inlining [17] and guards [5,35], that would allow our analysis to be lazy about repropagating after it finds new constraints.

CBGC (connectivity-based garbage collection) is a new garbage collection technique that requires pointer analysis [32]. CBGC uses pointer analysis results to partition heap objects such that connected objects are in the same partition, and the pointer analysis can guarantee the absence of certain cross-partition pointers. CBGC exploits the observation that connected objects tend to die together [33], and certain subsets of partitions can be collected while completely ignoring the rest of the heap.

CBGC must know the partition of an object at allocation time. However, CBGC can easily combine partitions later if the pointer analysis finds that they are strongly connected by pointers. Thus, there is no need to perform a full propagation at object allocation time. However, CBGC does need full conservative points-to information when performing a garbage collection; thus, CBGC needs to request a full propagation before collecting. Between collections, CBGC does not need conservative points-to information.

7 Performance

This section evaluates the efficiency of our pointer analysis implementation in Jikes RVM 2.2.1. Prior work (e.g., [39]) has evaluated the precision of Andersen's analysis. In addition to the analysis itself, our modified version of Jikes RVM includes the validation mechanism from Section 5. Besides the analysis and validation code, we also added a number of profilers and tracers to collect the results presented in this section. For example, at each yield-point (method prologue or loop back-edge), a stack walk determines whether the yield-point belongs to analysis or application code, and counts it accordingly. We performed all experiments on a 2.4GHz Pentium 4 with 2GB of memory running Linux, kernel version 2.4.

Since Andersen's analysis has cubic time complexity and quadratic space complexity (in the size of the code), optimizations that increase the size of the code can dramatically increase the constraint propagation time. In our experience, aggressive inlining can increase constraint propagation time by up to a factor of 5 for our benchmarks. In default mode, Jikes RVM performs inlining (and optimizations) only inside the hot application methods, but is more aggressive about methods in the boot image. We force Jikes RVM to be more cautious about inlining inside boot image methods by using a FastAdaptiveMarkSweep image and disabling inlining at build time. During benchmark execution, Jikes RVM does, however, perform inlining for hot boot image methods when recompiling them.

7.1 Benchmark Characteristics

Table 4 describes our benchmark suite; *null* is a dummy benchmark with an empty main method. Column "Analyzed methods" gives the number of methods analyzed. We analyze a method when it is part of the boot image, or when the program executes it for the first time. The analyzed methods include the benchmark's methods, library methods called by the benchmark, and methods belonging to Jikes RVM itself. The *null* benchmark provides a baseline: its data represents approximately the amount that Jikes RVM adds to the size of the application. This data is approximate because, for example, some of the methods called by the optimizing compiler may also be used by the application (e.g., methods on container classes). Column "Loaded classes" gives the number of classes loaded by the benchmarks. Once again, the number of loaded classes for the *null* benchmark provides a baseline. Finally, Column "Run time" gives the run time for our benchmarks using our configuration of the Jikes RVM.

Table 4. Benchmark programs.

Program	Command line arguments	Analyzed methods	Loaded classes	Run time
null	*none*	*15,598*	*1,363*	*1s*
javalex	`qb1.lex`	15,728	1,389	37s
compress	`-m1 -M1 -s100`	15,728	1,391	14s
db	`-m1 -M1 -s100`	15,746	1,385	28s
mtrt	`-m1 -M1 -s100`	15,858	1,404	14s
mpegaudio	`-m1 -M1 -s100`	15,899	1,429	27s
jack	`-m1 -M1 -s100`	15,962	1,434	21s
richards	none	15,963	1,440	4s
hsql	`-clients 1 -tpc 50000`	15,992	1,424	424s
jess	`-m1 -M1 -s100`	16,158	1,527	29s
javac	`-m1 -M1 -s100`	16,464	1,526	66s
xalan	`1 1`	17,057	1,716	10s

The Jikes RVM methods and classes account for a significant portion of the code in our benchmarks. Thus, our analysis has to deal with much more code than it would have to in a JVM that is not written in Java. On the other hand, writing the analysis itself in Java had significant software engineering benefits; for example, the analysis relies on garbage collection for its data structures. In addition, the absence of artifical boundaries between the analysis, other parts of the runtime system, and the application exposes more opportunities for optimizations. Current trends show that the benefits of writing system code in a high-level, managed, language are gaining wider recognition. For example, Microsoft is pushing towards implementing more of Windows in managed code.

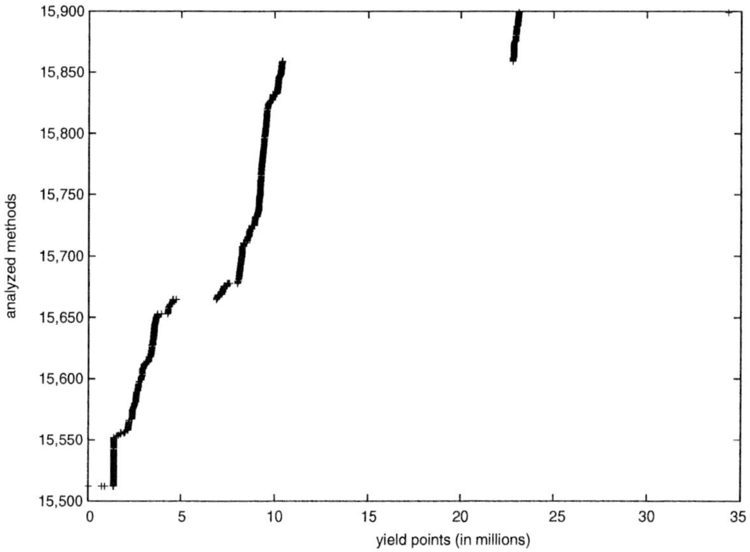

Fig. 4. Yield-points versus analyzed methods for *mpegaudio*. The first shown data point is the `main()` method.

Figure 4 shows how the number of analyzed method increase over a run of *mpegaudio*. The x-axis represents time measured by the number of thread yield-points encountered in a run. There is a thread yield-point in the prologue of every method and in every loop. We ignore yield-points that occur in our analysis code (this would be hard to do if we used real time for the x-axis). The y-axis starts at 15,500: all methods analyzed before the first method in this graph are in the boot image and are thus analyzed once for all benchmarks. The graphs for other benchmarks have a similar shape, and therefore we omit them.

From Figure 4, we see that there are two significant stages (around the 10 and 25 million yield-point marks) when the application is executing only methods that it has encountered before. At other times, the application encounters new methods as it executes. We expect that for longer running benchmarks (e.g., a webserver that runs for days), the number of analyzed methods stabilizes after a few minutes of run time. That point may be an ideal time to propagate the constraints and use the results to perform optimizations.

7.2 Analysis Cost

Our analysis has two main costs: constraint finding and constraint propagation. Constraint finding happens whenever we analyze a new method, load a new class, etc. Constraint propagation happens whenever a client of the pointer analysis needs points-to information. We define *eager* propagation to be propagation after every event from the left column of Figure 2, if it generated new constraints. We define *lazy* propagation to be propagation that occurs just once at the end of the program execution.

Cost in space. Table 5 shows the total allocation for our benchmark runs. Column "No analysis" gives the number of megabytes allocated by the program without our analysis. Column "No propagation" gives the allocation when the analysis generates, but does not propagate, constraints. Thus, this column gives the space overhead of just representing the constraints. Columns "Eager", "Lazy", and "At GC" give the allocation when using eager, lazy, and at GC propagation. The difference between these and the "No propagation" column represents the overhead of representing the points-to sets. Sometimes we see that doing more work actually reduces the amount of total allocation (e.g., *mpegaudio* allocates more without any analysis than with lazy propagation). This phenomenon occurs because our analysis is interleaved with the execution of the benchmark program, and thus the Jikes RVM adaptive optimizer optimizes different methods with our analysis than without our analysis.

Table 5. Total allocation (in megabytes)

Benchmark	Eager	At GC	Lazy	No propagation	No analysis
null	*48.5*	*48.1*	*48.8*	*13.5*	*9.7*
javalex	621.7	104.7	110.6	70.0	111.8
compress	416.2	230.0	167.0	129.3	130.2
db	394.4	213.8	151.0	112.7	113.6
mtrt	721.9	303.8	240.5	201.5	172.9
mpegaudio	755.9	145.8	83.1	42.8	137.0
jack	1,782.4	418.4	354.8	309.2	322.8
richards	1,117.8	61.3	67.7	26.6	12.6
hsql	4,047.0	3,409.6	3,343.8	3,291.1	3,444.6
jess	4,694.8	458.0	394.4	341.4	398.3
javac	2,023.0	450.4	381.3	328.2	429.3
xalan	6,074.9	166.4	200.4	131.5	37.6

Finally, since the boot image needs to include constraints for the code and data in the boot image, our analysis inflates the boot image size from 31.5 megabytes to 73.4 megabytes.

Table 6. Percent of execution time in constraint finding

Program	Analyzing methods	Resolving classes and arrays
null	*69.16%*	*3.68%*
javalex	2.02%	0.39%
compress	5.00%	1.22%
db	1.77%	0.39%
mtrt	7.68%	1.70%
mpegaudio	6.23%	6.04%
jack	6.13%	2.10%
richards	21.98%	5.88%
hsql	0.29%	0.09%
jess	5.59%	1.24%
javac	3.20%	1.60%
xalan	26.32%	8.66%

Cost of constraint finding. Table 6 gives the percentage of overall execution time spent in generating constraints from methods (Column "Analyzing methods") and from resolution events (Column "Resolving classes and arrays"). For these executions we did not run any propagations. Table 6 shows that generating constraints for methods is the dominant part of constraint generation. Also, as the benchmark run time increases, the percentage of time spent in constraint generation decreases. For example, the time spent in constraint finding is a negligible percentage of the run time for our longest running benchmark, *hsql*.

Cost of propagation. Table 7 shows the cost of propagation. Columns "Count" give the number of propagations that occur in our benchmark runs. Columns "Time" give the arithmetic mean ± standard deviation of the time (in seconds) it takes to perform each propagation. We included the lazy propagation data to give an approximate sense for how long the propagation would take if we were to use a static pointer analysis. Recall, however, that these numbers are still not comparable to static analysis numbers of these benchmarks in prior work, since, unlike them, we also analyze the Jikes RVM compiler and other system services.

Table 7 shows that the mean pause time due to eager propagation varies between 3.8 and 16.8 seconds for the real benchmarks. In contrast, a full (lazy) propagation is much slower. Thus, our algorithm is effective in avoiding work on parts of the program that have not changed since the last propagation.

Our results (omitted for space considerations) showed that the propagation cost did not depend on which of the events in the left column of Figure 2 generated new constraints that were the reason for the propagation.

Table 7. Propagation statistics (times in seconds)

	Eager		At GC		Lazy	
Program	Count	Time	Count	Time	Count	Time
null	*1*	*135.6±0.0*	*1*	*120.7±0.0*	*1*	*137.8±0*
javalex	166	13.6±22.0	1	120.7±0.0	1	158.4±0
compress	127	8.6±18.7	3	104.7±23.6	1	142.8±0
db	140	10.0±20.2	3	106.1±24.8	1	144.5±0
mtrt	262	5.5±14.4	3	106.8±24.7	1	148.0±0
mpegaudio	317	5.5±13.4	3	105.4±24.1	1	144.3±0
jack	392	10.9±17.8	3	114.4±33.8	1	161.8±0
richards	410	3.8±10.9	1	120.8±0.0	1	134.8±0
hsql	391	10.1±20.6	6	76.6±94.8	1	426.7±0
jess	734	16.8±20.5	3	117.7±38.5	1	182.4±0
javac	1,103	12.5±22.9	5	114.3±97.6	1	386.7±0
xalan	1,726	11.2±21.4	1	120.5±0.0	1	464.6±0

Figure 5 presents the spread of propagation times for *javac*. A point (x,y) in this graph says that propagation "x" took "y" seconds. Out of 1,107 propagations in *javac*, 524 propagations take under 1 second. The remaining propagations are much more expensive (10 seconds or more), thus increasing the average. We also discern that more expensive propagations occur later in the execution. The omitted graphs for other benchmarks have a similar shape. Although we present

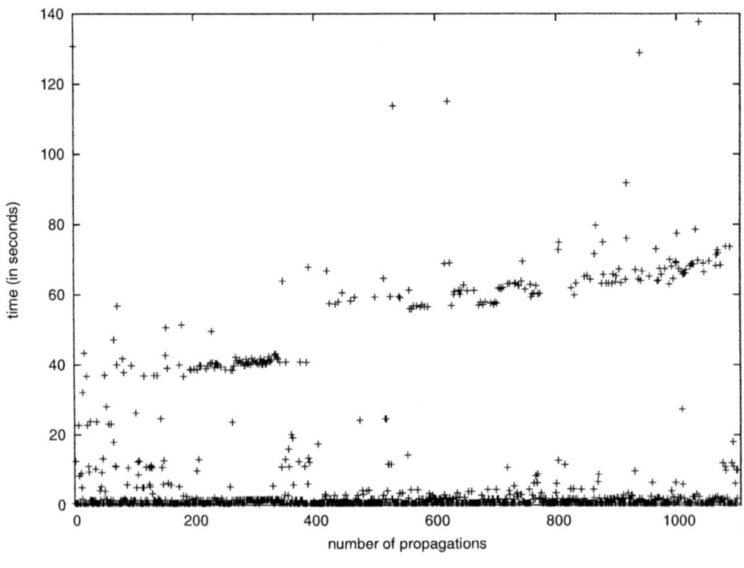

Fig. 5. Propagation times for *javac* (eager).

the data for eager propagation, clients of our analysis do not necessarily require eager propagation (Section 6).

As expected, the columns for propagation at GC in Table 7 show that if we propagate less frequently, the individual propagations are more expensive; they are still on average cheaper than performing a single full propagation at the end of the program run. Recall that, for Java programs, performing a static analysis of the entire program is not possible because what constitutes the "entire program" is not known until it executes to completion.

7.3 Understanding the Costs of Our Constraint Propagation

The speed of our constraint propagator (a few seconds to update points-to information) may be adequate for long-running clients, but may not be feasible for short-running clients. For example, a web server that does not touch new methods after a few minutes of running can benefit from our current analysis: once the web server stops touching new methods, the propagation time of our analysis goes down to zero. Since we did not have a server application in our suite, we confirmed this behavior by running two benchmarks (*javac* and *mpegaudio*) multiple times in a loop: after the first run, there was little to no overhead from constraint finding or constraint propagation (well under 1%). On the other hand, an application that only runs for a few minutes may find our analysis to be prohibitively slow. On profiling our analysis, we found that the worklist part (lines 2 to 19 in Figure 3) takes up far more of the propagation time than the iterative part (lines 20 to 26 in Figure 3). Thus, in our future work, we will first focus on the worklist part to improve propagator performance.

8 Conclusions

We describe and evaluate the first non-trivial pointer analysis that handles all of Java. Java features such as dynamic class loading, reflection, and native methods introduce many challenges for pointer analyses. Some of these prohibit the use of static pointer analyses. We validate the output of our analysis against actual pointers created during program runs. We evaluate our analysis by measuring many aspects of its performance, including the amount of work our analysis must do at run time. Our results show that our analysis is feasible and fast enough for server applications.

References

1. G. Agrawal, J. Li, and Q. Su. Evaluating a demand driven technique for call graph construction. In *Internat. Conference on Compiler Construction (CC)*, 2002.
2. B. Alpern, C. R. Attanasio, J. J. Barton, M. G. Burke, P. Cheng, J.-D. Choi, A. Cocchi, S. J. Fink, D. Grove, M. Hind, S. F. Hummel, D. Lieber, V. Litvinov, M. F. Mergen, T. Ngo, J. R. Russell, V. Sarkar, M. J. Serrano, J. C. Shepherd, S. E. Smith, V. C. Sreedhar, H. Srinivasan, and J. Whaley. The Jalapeño virtual machine. *IBM Systems Journal*, 39(1), 2000.

3. L. O. Andersen. *Program Analysis and Specialization for the C Programming Language.* PhD thesis, University of Copenhagen, 1994. DIKU report 94/19.
4. M. Arnold, S. Fink, D. Grove, M. Hind, and P. F. Sweeney. Adaptive optimization in the Jalapeño JVM. In *Obj.-Oriented Prog., Systems, Lang., and Applic. (OOPSLA)*, 2000.
5. M. Arnold and B. G. Ryder. Thin guards: A simple and effective technique for reducing the penalty of dynamic class loading. In *European Conference for Object-Oriented Prog. (ECOOP)*, 2002.
6. D. F. Bacon and P. F. Sweeney. Fast static analysis of C++ virtual function calls. In *Obj.-Oriented Prog., Systems, Lang., and Applic. (OOPSLA)*, 1996.
7. J. Bogda and A. Singh. Can a shape analysis work at run-time? In *Java Virtual Machine Research and Technology Symp. (JVM)*, 2001.
8. M. Burke and L. Torczon. Interprocedural optimization: Eliminating unnecessary recompilation. *Trans. on Prog. Lang. and Systems (TOPLAS)*, 1993.
9. R. Chatterjee, B. G. Ryder, and W. A. Landi. Relevant context inference. In *Principles of Prog. Lang. (POPL)*, 1999.
10. B.-C. Cheng and W.-m. W. Hwu. Modular interprocedural pointer analysis using access paths: design, implementation, and evaluation. In *Prog. Lang. Design and Impl. (PLDI)*, 2000.
11. J.-D. Choi, M. Gupta, M. Serrano, V. C. Sreedhar, and S. Midkiff. Escape analysis for Java. In *Obj.-Oriented Prog., Systems, Lang., and Applic. (OOPSLA)*, 1999.
12. A. S. Christensen, A. Møller, and M. I. Schwartzbach. Precise analysis of string expressions. In *Static Analysis Symposium (SAS)*, 2003.
13. M. Cierniak, G.-Y. Lueh, and J. M. Stichnoth. Practicing JUDO: Java under dynamic optimizations. In *Prog. Lang. Design and Impl. (PLDI)*, 2000.
14. K. D. Cooper, K. Kennedy, and L. Torczon. Interprocedural optimization: Eliminating unnecessary recompilation. *Trans. on Prog. Lang. and Systems (TOPLAS)*, 1986.
15. M. Das. Unification-based pointer analysis with directional assignments. In *Prog. Lang. Design and Impl. (PLDI)*, 2000.
16. J. Dean, D. Grove, and C. Chambers. Optimization of object-oriented programs using static class hierarchy analysis. In *European Conference for Object-Oriented Prog. (ECOOP)*, 1995.
17. D. Detlefs and O. Agesen. Inlining of virtual methods. In *European Conference for Object-Oriented Prog. (ECOOP)*, 1999.
18. A. Diwan, K. S. McKinley, and J. E. B. Moss. Using types to analyze and optimize object-oriented programs. *Trans. on Prog. Lang. and Systems (TOPLAS)*, 2001.
19. M. Fähndrich, J. S. Foster, Z. Su, and A. Aiken. Partial online cycle elimination in inclusion constraint graphs. In *Prog. Lang. Design and Impl. (PLDI)*, 1998.
20. M. F. Fernandez. Simple and effective link-time optimization of Modula-3 programs. In *Prog. Lang. Design and Impl. (PLDI)*, 1995.
21. S. J. Fink and F. Qian. Design, implementation, and evaluation of adaptive recompilation with on-stack replacement. In *Code Gen. and Optimization (CGO)*, 2003.
22. J. S. Foster, M. Fähndrich, and A. Aiken. Flow-insensitive points-to analysis with term and set constraints. Technical report, University of California at Berkeley, 1997.
23. D. P. Grove. *Effective Interprocedural Optimization of Object-Oriented Languages.* PhD thesis, University of Washington, 1998.

24. M. W. Hall, J. M. Mellor-Crummey, A. Carle, and R. G. Rodriguez. Fiat: A framework for interprocedural analysis and transformations. In *Workshop on Languages and Compilers for Parallel Computing (LCPC)*, 1993.
25. T. Harris. Early storage reclamation in a tracing garbage collector. *ACM SIGPLAN Notices*, 1999.
26. N. Heintze. Analysis of large code bases: The compile-link-analyze model. `http://cm.bell-labs.com/cm/cs/who/nch/cla.ps`, 1999.
27. N. Heintze and O. Tardieu. Demand-driven pointer analysis. In *Prog. Lang. Design and Impl. (PLDI)*, 2001.
28. N. Heintze and O. Tardieu. Ultra-fast aliasing analysis using CLA: A million lines of C code in a second. In *Prog. Lang. Design and Impl. (PLDI)*, 2001.
29. L. Hendren. *Parallelizing Programs with Recursive Data Structures.* PhD thesis, Cornell University, 1990.
30. M. Hind. Pointer analysis: Haven't we solved this problem yet? In *Workshop on Program Analysis for Software Tools and Engineering (PASTE)*, 2001.
31. M. Hind and A. Pioli. Which pointer analysis should I use? In *Internat. Symp. on Software Testing and Analysis (ISSTA)*, 2000.
32. M. Hirzel, A. Diwan, and M. Hertz. Connectivity-based garbage collection. In *Obj.-Oriented Prog., Systems, Lang., and Applic. (OOPSLA)*, 2003.
33. M. Hirzel, J. Henkel, A. Diwan, and M. Hind. Understanding the connectivity of heap objects. In *Internat. Symp. on Memory Management (ISMM)*, 2002.
34. U. Hölzle, C. Chambers, and D. Ungar. Debugging optimized code with dynamic deoptimization. In *Prog. Lang. Design and Impl. (PLDI)*, 1992.
35. U. Hölzle and D. Ungar. Optimizing dynamically-dispatched calls with run-time type feedback. In *Prog. Lang. Design and Impl. (PLDI)*, 1994.
36. A. C. King. Removing GC synchronization (extended version). `http://www.acm.org/src/subpages/AndyKing/overview.html`, 2003. Winner (Graduate Division) ACM Student Research Competition.
37. J. R. Larus and S. Chandra. Using tracing and dynamic slicing to tune compilers. University of Wisconsin Technical Report 1174, Aug. 1993.
38. C. Lattner and V. Adve. Data Structure Analysis: An Efficient Context-Sensitive Heap Analysis. Tech. Report UIUCDCS-R-2003-2340, Computer Science Dept., Univ. of Illinois at Urbana-Champaign, Apr 2003.
39. O. Lhoták and L. Hendren. Scaling Java points-to analysis using SPARK. In *Internat. Conference on Compiler Construction (CC)*, 2003.
40. D. Liang, M. Pennings, and M. J. Harrold. Extending and evaluating flow-insenstitive and context-insensitive points-to analyses for Java. In *Workshop on Program Analysis for Software Tools and Engineering (PASTE)*, 2001.
41. D. Liang, M. Pennings, and M. J. Harrold. Evaluating the precision of static reference analysis using profiling. In *Internat. Symp. on Software Testing and Analysis (ISSTA)*, 2002.
42. T. Lindholm and F. Yellin. *The Java virtual machine specification.* Addison-Wesley, second edition, 1999.
43. M. Paleczny, C. Vick, and C. Click. The Java HotSpot server compiler. In *Java Virtual Machine Research and Technology Symp. (JVM)*, 2001.
44. I. Pechtchanski and V. Sarkar. Dynamic optimistic interprocedural analysis: a framework and an application. In *Obj.-Oriented Prog., Systems, Lang., and Applic. (OOPSLA)*, 2001.
45. F. Qian and L. Hendren. Towards dynamic interprocedural analysis in JVMs. In *Java Virtual Machine Research and Technology Symp. (JVM)*, 2004.

46. A. Rountev and S. Chandra. Off-line variable substitution for scaling points-to analysis. In *Prog. Lang. Design and Impl. (PLDI)*, 2000.
47. A. Rountev, A. Milanova, and B. G. Ryder. Points-to analysis for Java using annotated constraints. In *Obj.-Oriented Prog., Systems, Lang., and Applic. (OOPSLA)*, 2001.
48. E. Ruf. Effective synchronization removal for Java. In *Prog. Lang. Design and Impl. (PLDI)*, 2000.
49. M. Sagiv, T. Reps, and R. Wilhelm. Parametric shape analysis via 3-valued logic. In *Principles of Prog. Lang. (POPL)*, 1999.
50. M. Shapiro and S. Horwitz. The effects of the precision of pointer analysis. In *Static Analysis Symp. (SAS)*, 1997.
51. V. C. Sreedhar, M. Burke, and J.-D. Choi. A framework for interprocedural analysis and optimization in the presence of dynamic class loading. In *Prog. Lang. Design and Impl. (PLDI)*, 2000.
52. B. Steensgaard. Points-to analysis in almost linear time. In *Principles of Prog. Lang. (POPL)*, 1996.
53. T. Suganuma, T. Yasue, M. Kawahito, H. Komatsu, and T. Nakatani. A dynamic optimization framework for a Java just-in-time compiler. In *Obj.-Oriented Prog., Systems, Lang., and Applic. (OOPSLA)*, 2001.
54. V. Sundaresan, L. J. Hendren, C. Razafimahefa, V.-R. Raja, P. Lam, E. Gagnon, and C. Godin. Practical virtual method call resolution for Java. In *Obj.-Oriented Prog., Systems, Lang., and Applic. (OOPSLA)*, 2000.
55. The Apache Tomcat Project. Apache Tomcat. `http://jakarta.apache.org/tomcat`.
56. The Eclipse Project. Eclipse. `http://www.eclipse.org`.
57. F. Tip and J. Palsberg. Scalable propagation-based call graph construction algorithms. In *Obj.-Oriented Prog., Systems, Lang., and Applic. (OOPSLA)*, 2000.
58. R. Vallée-Rai, E. Gagnon, L. Hendren, P. Lam, P. Pominville, and V. Sundaresan. Optimizing Java bytecode using the Soot framework: Is it feasible? In *European Conference for Object-Oriented Prog. (ECOOP)*, 2000.
59. F. Vivien and M. Rinard. Incrementalized pointer and escape analysis. In *Prog. Lang. Design and Impl. (PLDI)*, 2001.
60. J. Whaley and M. Lam. An efficient inclusion-based points-to analysis for strictly-typed languages. In *Static Analysis Symp. (SAS)*, 2002.

The Expression Problem Revisited

Four New Solutions Using Generics

Mads Torgersen

Computer Science Department
University of Aarhus
Aabogade 34, Aarhus, Denmark
madst@daimi.au.dk

Abstract. The expression problem (aka the extensibility problem) refers to a fundamental dilemma of programming: To which degree can your application be structured in such a way that both the data model and the set of virtual operations over it can be extended without the need to modify existing code, without the need for code repetition and without runtime type errors.

Over the years, many approaches to this problem have been proposed, each having different characteristics of type safety and reusability. While many of these rely on exotic or problem specific language extensions, this paper investigates the solution space within the framework of the soon-to-be mainstream generic extensions of C# and the Java programming language.

Four new solutions are presented which, though quite different, all rely on techniques that can be used in everyday programming.

1 Introduction

A typical structure found in application programs is the one represented by the *Composite* design pattern [1]: a recursive data structure defined by a number of interrelated classes, and a set of operations with specific behaviour for each class. The *expression problem* (or *extensibility problem*) is concerned with the issue of modular extensibility of such structures: Depending on the programming language and the organisation of the code, it is usually straightforward to add either new data types or new operations without changing the original program, but with the price that it is very hard to add the other kind. There are already many solutions to this problem, all with their own qualities and drawbacks. This paper presents no less than four new solutions, each with its own contributions to the subject area. While many previous approaches are linguistic in nature, introducing special purpose constructs to deal with the problem, the present solutions are all based on the new generic capabilities of C# and the Java programming language [2,3,4,5]. Furthermore we establish a terminology framework for assessing the multitude of solutions, using this to compare with a number of previous approaches.

M. Odersky (Ed.): ECOOP 2004, LNCS 3086, pp. 123–143, 2004.

1.1 The Expression Example

Although the issue has been known for many years, and was discussed by e.g. Reynolds in 1975 [6] and Cook in 1990 [7], the expression problem was named thus by Philip Wadler in 1998 [8] as a pun referring on the one hand to the challenges it poses to the expressive power of programming languages, and on the other to a classical domain in which programming language implementors often encounter it: when representing expressions of a language, along with operations to manipulate them, it is a very real dilemma whether to favor future extension with new expression kinds or new operations over them.

In this paper we shall follow the tradition and use as a running example a processor of a (very!) simple language with the following grammar:

$$\begin{aligned} \mathit{Exp} &::= \mathit{Lit} \mid \mathit{Add} \\ \mathit{Lit} &::= \textit{non-negative integer} \\ \mathit{Add} &::= \mathit{Exp}\ \text{'+'}\ \mathit{Exp} \end{aligned}$$

We name the language ALE from the initials of its constituent categories. Along with a representation of the data itself, from the outset the processor is to implement a print() operation to show expressions on screen.

To examine the expression problem we shall then want to try out different representations of ALE in the context of two "future" extensions: with a new operation, eval(), to evaluate expressions, and with a new kind of expression *Neg*:

$$\begin{aligned} \mathit{Exp} &::= \ldots \mid \mathit{Neg} \\ \mathit{Neg} &::= \text{'}-\text{'}\ \mathit{Exp} \end{aligned}$$

Of course this is a toy example, limited to the minimum necessary to illustrate the points in the paper. Note that this example differs slightly from the one put forth by Wadler to better highlight problematic issues (recursion in the base case) and weed out orthogonal issues (the handling of return values in visitors).

Given the small amount of application logic involved, it may seem that the amount of infrastructure needed in the examples is overwhelming in comparison. But one should keep in mind that real applications will involve a much larger proportion of application logic. Also, "legacy" client code of a *Composite* structure can also be made reusable by a nondestructive extension, and is therefore likely to constitute another major bulk of code that is spared the need to be hand updated or recompiled.

1.2 The Extensibility Dilemma

Given, in the manner of the *Composite* design pattern, a number of recursively defined classes describing the data, there are basically two ways of structuring the description of the operations around them, each with extensibility consequences:

Data-centered: Each operation may be defined as a virtual method in the common base class of the data, and overwritten in each specific data class. This is the straightforward object-oriented approach, and has the modular property that a new class may be easily added without modifications to the existing code. Adding a new operation, however, involves modifying every single data class to implement the data specific behaviour of the new operation.

Operation-centered: Instead the code may be structured according to the *Visitor* design pattern [1]: Each operation is represented by a separate visitor class, containing handler methods (or *visit* methods) for each datatype. All data classes are equipped once and for all with an *accept* method which calls the appropriate visit method of a given visitor with the data object itself as an argument. This structuring makes the data classes robust toward the addition of new operations in the form of new Visitor classes, but unfortunately the addition of a new data class requires all the visitor classes to extend their fixed list of visit methods so that they can deal with the new kind of data.

A straightforward data-centered implementation of ALE may look as in Figure 1. In order to use the code we just have to build instances of the data classes and start calling print() on them.

```
interface Exp { void print(); } class Lit implements Exp { public int value;
Lit(int v) { value = v; } public void print() { System.out.print(value); } } class
Add implements Exp { public Exp left, right; Add(Exp l, Exp r) { left = l; right
= r; } public void print() { left.print(); System.out.print('+'); right.print(); } }
```

Fig. 1. A class-based implementation

As can be seen in Figure 2, an operation-centered implementation requires a bit more setup. To use the implemented functionality, when we have created appropriate instances we have to call their accept() method with an instance of the AlePrint visitor class in order to get the desired output.

```
interface Exp { void accept(AleVisitor v); } class Lit implements Exp {
public int value; Lit(int v) { value = v; } public void accept(AleVisitor
v) { v.visitLit(this); } } class Add implements Exp { public Exp left, right;
Add(Exp l, Exp r) { left = l; right = r; } public void accept(AleVisitor
v) { v.visitAdd(this); } } interface AleVisitor { void visitLit(Lit lit); void
visitAdd(Add add); } class AlePrint implements AleVisitor { public void vis-
itLit(Lit lit) { System.out.print(lit.value); } public void visitAdd(Add add) {
add.left.accept(this); System.out.print('+'); add.right.accept(this); } }
```

Fig. 2. A visitor-based implementation

Adding a *Neg* expression to the data-centered code calls for a new data class which just has to implement the print() method. This requires no change to the existing code. In the operation-centered implementation, however, all existing visitor classes must be modified to contain a visitNeg() method, breaking the modularity of the extension.

When adding the eval() operation the situation is reversed. In the visitor-based implementation the operation easily fits in as a new implementation, AleEval, of the AleVisitor interface, but as a virtual eval() method in the data-centered implementation it would have to be added to all classes.

Thus, either choice seems to paint us into a corner, and that is the core of the expression problem. The approach of most solutions is to take one of the above structuring principles as a starting point, and then use various tricks and language constructs to "loosen up" the dilemma. Of the solutions in this paper, the first is fundamentally data-centered, whereas the second and third (which are closely related) are operation-centered. The fourth solution is a hybrid, using both approaches in one implementation.

1.3 A Note on Code Examples

Minimal as the solution examples may be, this is a paper about the structuring of code, and very often the twist undermining a whole approach is hidden in one of those tiny details that one is tempted to gloss over in presentations. Thus, in the interest of verifiability we have chosen to show the full code for the different solutions.

The solutions are all presented using the familiar syntax of the Java programming language, with the generic enhancements scheduled for the next release (JDK1.5) of the Java platform. The full java source code for the solutions can be accessed at `www.daimi.au.dk/~madst/ecoop04`. In the interest of uniformity, this is the case even for the fourth solution, which in fact does not work *as-is* in a Java setting, where runtime information of generic types is lacking, but would in the generic framework being added to C#. This solution has been hand-translated in a straightforward fashion to obtain a slightly less elegant but still working solution in Java. The solutions have all been compiled and tested using the prototype compiler available for evaluation from Sun Microsystems at `developer.java.sun.com/developer/earlyAccess/adding_generics/index.html`. Any errors are thus due to the formatting process.

1.4 Overview

The following section introduces a terminology framework for characterizing and evaluating solutions to the expression problem. The next four sections (3 to 6) develop and examine as many solutions. Section 7 concludes.

2 Solutions

Many solutions to the expression problem have been proposed over the years. On close scrutiny they differ considerably in their requirements to the language context, as well as in the degree of extensibility they offer, and the limitations they impose. In this section we set up a framework of terminology which can help to assess the characteristics of the many different solutions.

But first of all, let us define exactly what we mean by a "solution":

A solution to the expression problem is a combination of
- *a programming language*
- *an implementation of a Composite structure in that language, and*
- *a discipline for extension*

which allows both new data types and operations to be subsequently added
1. *any number of times*
2. *without modification of existing source code*
3. *without replication of non-trivial code*
4. *without risk of unhandled combinations of data and operations*

This definition is less restrictive than the one given by Philip Wadler in [8]. For one thing, he requires extensions to be made without the need to recompile existing source code, whereas we contend ourselves with the source code not being changed. Thus we include more approaches in the solution space, because some of these are realistic and interesting. In order to maintain a differentiation, below we classify the different solutions according to their degree of robustness – their "level of extensibility".

Another important difference is that Wadler includes only completely type safe (i.e. cast free) solutions. We have weakened this requirement to state that the solution must handle all combinations.

In his description of the expression problem [9], Kim Bruce goes a bit in the other direction from our definition, being content with "rewriting as little code as possible", whereas we stand firm on "no modifications". In practice, however, his paper is concerned primarily with non-modifying solutions.

2.1 Language Context

The expression problem is in fact not specific to an object-oriented setting, but has been discussed also in the context of functional languages. Here, the straightforward solution is to declare an algebraic datatype over the nodes and use type-casing (i.e. pattern matching) functions to express the operations. This is equivalent to the visitor-based solution above, in the sense that it is hard to add new data types modularly, whereas operations are easy. To complete the picture, functional languages may simulate the object-oriented approach using closures, so the same dichotomy of operation versus data extensibility remains.

There are some important differences, however, because functional solutions do not have to deal with statefulness and subclass substitutability. That this can have an impact on the solution is witnessed e.g. by the proposals in [9], many of which depend on a restriction of subclass substitutability for type safety. It is therefore not obvious that solutions from the functional world translate well to an object-oriented counterpart, and in this paper we will look only at proposals dealing with an object-oriented context.

Even so, most approaches depend strongly on the precise set of language constructs available in their environment, and oftentimes new mechanisms are proposed specifically for dealing with the expression problem. Examples of such linguistic approaches include "deep subtyping" [8], "classgroups" [9] and "extensible algebraic datatypes" [10]. Other solutions depend on general-purpose, but not so widespread mechanisms, such as virtual types or multi-methods.

The solutions in this paper are less linguistic. They highlight what can be done with existing or soon-to-be mainstream generics, and so the contributions are in the code structure rather than the mechanisms. Yet, they are still very dependent on the exact constructs available: the third solution makes use of the wildcard mechanism which occurs only in the Java implementation of generics, whereas the fourth solution depends on runtime reification of type variables, which, apart from some research dialects of Java (e.g. NextGen [11] and PolyJ [12]), is available only in the C# version of generics.

2.2 Level of Extensibility

A very important characteristic is the degree of reuse of existing code offered by the various approaches. To qualify as a solution we require that extensions fully reuse nontrivial application logic from the extended code. Thus, there should be no need to duplicate code except for whatever "scaffolding" is needed to set up the extension. We refer to this property as *source-level* extensibility.

As noted above, the definition in [8] requires that existing code need not even be recompiled. This is a much stronger requirement and clearly broadens the applicability of the solution. For instance, recompilation is a big problem in widely distributed code, on which independent third party operations have to be able to interact. We call this degree of reuse *code-level* extensibility. All the solutions in this paper have this property.

Additionally however, it is highly desirable that the data structures themselves, which may be large, persistently stored or part of an application that cannot be allowed to terminate and restart because of the extension, may continue to be usable after the extension has taken place. Thus, we want the objects created before the extension to survive and remain compatible afterward. We call this property *object-level* extensibility. The third and fourth of our solutions in this paper have that property.

2.3 Generative Programming

Recent years have seen a flourishing of so-called *generative* approaches to programming, in which higher level source code is used to direct the generation or manipulation of base level source code. A popular example is aspect-oriented programming, which e.g. allows extra methods to be added to a class from a separate unit of source code. This clearly solves the expression problem (in our definition), but leads to an under-the-hood mangling of the original class, that requires recompilation to a binary format.

In general, any discipline of destructive modification of a source code text can be automated, and thus turned into a generative approach. Of course an automated approach may be more safe than hand-editing, since it can be made to check that various invariants are maintained.

While generative programming seems to have its uses, it does however suffer from the need to deploy new binary code for every extension. Due to the focus of this paper on a generic Java and C# context, generative approaches are out of reach, and will not be further treated.

2.4 Basic Approach

Most proposals take as a starting point either a data-centered approach, making it hard to add new operations, or an operation-centered (visitor-based) approach, making it equally hard to add new data types. The choice may depend on various language specific issues, but one thing is certain: If object-level extensibility is desired, then the data-centered approach must be ruled out. This is because the addition of operations will then require new virtual methods to be added to all the classes representing data, e.g. by the use of subclassing. Old data objects created from the unmodified classes will not have the new methods, and will therefore not support the new operations.

With the operation-centered approach, however, there is hope that existing objects can be made to work with newly added or extended visitors. Of course, the converse restriction exists, that old visitor objects cannot survive the addition of new data types, because they have no appropriate visit method. But this problem is less grave because visitors represent operations, which we do not expect to be lasting, just as we do not expect to reuse the activation record of a method call.

Our first solution examines the data-centered approach, whereas the second is operation-centered. The third solution enhances the second in a manner that allows for object level extensibility with some drawbacks, whereas the fourth solution ventures a new *hybrid* approach which allows both data components *and* visitor objects to be reused across extensions.

2.5 Extension Graph

Most solutions assume that extensions happen linearly, one after the other, and that a given extension knows about the previous version. One might well imagine, however, that a given piece of software is extended independently by two different parties, and that one might later want to merge them.

The approach in [10] relies heavily on a linear extension discipline, because dispatching method calls are chained all the way up through the extension path.

There it is argued that a merge is rarely needed in practice, and that it can be handled by other means.

Our extension approaches rely on subclassing, and a merge of multiple extensions would require the inheritance mechanism to also be multiple. Thus the Java versions in this paper are restricted to linearity, but in other languages or dialects with e.g. mixins [13,14] they might not be.

2.6 Surrounding Code

An important but often overlooked aspect of solutions is the effect they have on the reusability of the surrounding code. There are two main sorts of external code that depend on the implementation of the *Composite* structure itself:

Creation code: The part of the application that is in charge of actually producing instances of the datatype classes. If a solution relies on defining new data types for each extension, then new constructors need to be called.

Client code: The code that calls the operations on the datatype classes. If the operations are represented by visitors, which get subclassed by new extensions, then we have the dual situation to the one described for creation code: we need to be able to create the right kinds of visitors.

Furthermore, both types of external code will have to be type parameterised, if the classes they depend on are. Due to space limitations the descriptions in the following sections on how to support reuse of surrounding code will not show the full code for doing so. The full code which has been used to test these approaches includes factories and similar infrastructure, as well as simple creation and client methods which are reused across extensions, in order to demonstrate the extensibility of surrounding code. As mentioned in Section 1 this Java code can be downloaded from `www.daimi.au.dk/~madst/ecoop04`.

2.7 Type Safety

As noted above, Wadler requires full type safety of solutions. The reality is, however, that a number of approaches make use of type casts, but still provide other interesting perspectives on the problem. For instance, neither of [15,10] is fully statically type safe, yet we wish to include those for comparison, rather than branding them as irrelevant *á priori* . To minimise the danger, both of these approaches propose language extensions handled by preprocessing, to ensure that casts are inserted using a safe discipline.

While the first three of our solutions in this paper are statically typed, the fourth one resorts to runtime type checks in exchange for other benefits. The casts occur only in an initial dispatching framework, so the extenders will not have to write unsafe code themselves. They will however have to stick to a linear extension discipline without the aid of a type checker to avoid "holes" of unhandled combinations of operations and data.

3 A Data-Centered Approach

We may note that the data-centered version of ALE in Figure 1 is considerably simpler than the visitor-based one in Figure 2, and perhaps more appealing from an object-oriented point of view. In this section we therefore investigate what it takes to equip it for code-level extensibility, and what the major challenges are.

Adding new kinds of data does not pose an immediate problem in this setting; what we have to deal with is how to add a new virtual method to all members of the type hierarchy. In our specific example, we wish to add an eval() method to the Exp interface and the classes Lit and Add. We can achieve this nondestructively by introducing a new interface EvalExp extending the Exp interface with an eval() method. New versions of Lit and Add must then extend the old ones while implementing the new interface. This will lead to e.g. a new class EvalAdd of the following form:

```
class EvalAdd extends Add implements EvalExp {
  public int eval() { return left.eval()+right.eval(); }
}
```

Immediately we are in trouble: the inherited instance variables left and right are of type Exp, and therefore do not have an eval() method to call recursively. Thus, the compiler fails to type check the above code.

As also pointed out in [9], we can attempt to address this with genericity: we may parameterise expressions with the type of their children. While Add will allow its type parameter to be any kind of Exp, EvalAdd may then restrict it to be a kind of EvalExp, thus ensuring that its children also have an eval() method. In both cases, the children must have the same child type as their parents, which we arrange by making use of *F-bounds* [16] in the declarations of the type variables i.e., the type variable occurs in its own bound. Figure 3 shows the parameterised code for ALE.

```
interface Exp<C extends Exp<C>> {   void print(); } class Lit<C extends Exp<C>>
implements Exp<C> {   public int value;   Lit(int v) { value = v; }   public void

print() { System.out.print(value); } } class Add<C extends Exp<C>> implements
Exp<C> {   public C left, right;   Add(C l, C r) { left = l; right = r; }   public void
print() { left.print(); System.out.print('+'); right.print(); } }
```

Fig. 3. A data-centered implementation of ALE with code-level extensibility

The extension with an eval() operation can now be undertaken in a type safe manner: in Figure 4, EvalAdd not only adds an eval() method implementation, but also expects a child type parameter that extends EvalExp.

Thus, a type safe extension has been achieved. The type bookkeeping is overwhelming, however, and it can be hard to spot the few lines of actual application logic. But there is one more twist: because all the classes are F-bounded, there

```
interface EvalExp⟨C extends EvalExp⟨C⟩⟩ extends Exp⟨C⟩ {  int eval(); }

class EvalLit⟨C extends EvalExp⟨C⟩⟩ extends Lit⟨C⟩ implements EvalExp⟨C⟩ {
  EvalLit(int v) { super (v); }  public int eval() { return value; } } class EvalAdd⟨C
extends EvalExp⟨C⟩⟩ extends Add⟨C⟩ implements EvalExp⟨C⟩ {  EvalAdd(C l, C
r) { super (l,r); }  public int eval() { return left.eval()+right.eval(); } }
```

Fig. 4. An extension of Figure 3 with eval() methods

does not at this point exist any class or interface that can be used as a type parameter for them.

In a manner typical of programming with F-bounds, we first have to create a new set of non-generic subclasses that *fix* the F-bound on themselves. This has to be done for every layer of extension that needs to be used in actual application code, since there is no other way of getting to construct instances of the classes. For the evaluation extension, the fixing classes can be seen in Figure 5.

```
interface EvalExpFix extends EvalExp⟨EvalExpFix⟩ {} class EvalLitFix extends
EvalLit⟨EvalExpFix⟩ implements EvalExpFix {  EvalLitFix(int v) { super (v);
} } class EvalAddFix extends EvalAdd⟨EvalExpFix⟩ implements EvalExpFix {
  EvalAddFix(EvalExpFix l, EvalExpFix r) { super (l,r); } }
```

Fig. 5. Fixed point classes for the F-bounds in Figure 4

The classes have trivial bodies and add no new semantics to our application, but simply "tie down" the F-bounds.

Finally, then, we have a set of eval()-enabled classes that can be instantiated in application code like this:

```
EvalExpFix e1 = new EvalLitFix(2);
EvalExpFix e2 = new EvalLitFix(3);
EvalExpFix e3 = new EvalAddFix(e1,e2);
e3.print(); System.out.println(" = " + e3.eval());
```

This is a type-safe data-centered code-level-extensible solution to the expression problem, and indeed the first in the literature to use only standard generics. Yet, the reader will have noticed that the initial simplicity of the data-centered approach has disappeared.

3.1 Surrounding Code

Using the techniques of the *Abstract Factory* design pattern, we can limit the complexity of object creation in this approach to the extension code itself, and keep it out of surrounding creation code. The following method, taken from the on-line code examples for this paper, demonstrates the point:

```
static ⟨C extends Exp⟨C⟩⟩ C build(AleFactory⟨C⟩ f) {
  return f.makeAdd(f.makeLit(2),f.makeLit(3));
}
```

The method builds a specific expression tree without heed to the operations its nodes contain. It is reusable across extensions because it is parameterised over the two kinds of things that extensions alter: The base expression type and the creation procedure for its instances.

Of course this means more work when extending with new data classes such as Neg, because a new NaleFactory interface extending AleFactory has to introduce a method for creating new Neg instances of the right kind.

Client code is made reusable simply by parameterizing it over the base expression type, as in:

```
static ⟨C extends Exp⟨C⟩⟩ void show(C exp) { exp.print(); }
```

3.2 Related Work

This solution is quite similar in structure to the solution by Bruce [9] using self types as the type of child nodes. This works only because of the rather peculiar semantics of self types in that work, where the self type in a class is not the class itself, but its nearest interface. Thus, the self type of Add would not be Add but Exp.

Compared to F-bounds, the problem with self types is that they cannot be fixed, and therefore may require type-exact references (i.e., no subsumption) to work properly.

On the other hand, F-bounds cannot fully express self types. We shall see an example of this shortcoming in the following section. Thus, independently of the expression problem, the lack of true self types in Java and C# leads to a less permissive type system in some situations.

4 An Operation-Centered Approach

Given the unexpected complexity of the data-centered solution, we now turn to the other, initially more complex viewpoint of the operation-centered approach. Starting from the visitor-based version of the ALE code in Figure 2, the hard problem now is to extend the language to NALE by adding an additional datatype Neg representing negation.

The argument runs somewhat dual to the data-centered approach: If we add the Neg class, we need to extend our visitors to handle it, and we can do so nondestructively only by subclassing:

```
interface NaleVisitor extends AleVisitor {
  void visitNeg(Neg neg);
}
class NalePrint extends AlePrint implements NaleVisitor {
  public void visitNeg(Neg neg) {
    System.out.print('−'); neg.exp.accept(this);
  }
class Neg implements Exp {
  public Exp exp;
  public void accept(AleVisitor v) { v.visitNeg(this); } //Type error!!!
}
```

Again we are in type checking trouble: this time the culprit is the accept() method of Neg, which expects an AleVisitor rather than a NaleVisitor. It has to, in order to implement the accept() method of Exp, but this means that v is not known to have a visitNeg() method.

Again we may resort to type parameterization of the datatype hierarchy in order to allow the accept() method of Neg to expect more of its visitor than its fellow expression types. Note however, that this time the data classes are not parameterised with themselves, which was what lead to all the hassle with F-bounds in the previous solution, but rather with the kind of Visitor they accept().

In the visitor classes, the visit methods must adjust to the fact that the classes they visit are now parameterised. We can obtain this by parameterizing the visit methods themselves over the visitor type of their argument expressions. For Add and its corresponding visit method in AlePrint, we would expect something like this to work:

```
class Add⟨V extends AleVisitor⟩ implements Exp⟨V⟩ {
  public Exp⟨V⟩ left, right;
  public void accept(V v) { v.visitAdd(this); }
}
class AlePrint implements AleVisitor {
  ...;
  public ⟨V extends AleVisitor⟩ void visitAdd(Add⟨V⟩ add) {
    add.left.accept(this); //Type error!!!
    System.out.print('+');
    add.right.accept(this); //Type error!!!
  }
}
```

Surprisingly, however, this does not type check. Because now the AlePrint visitor does not know that the *children* of add will actually accept() it. All we know from the signature of the visitAdd() method is that they will accept V's, but we do not know at this point in the code that **this** is a V.

It *is*, though. Because of the structure of the *Visitor* pattern, visitAdd() is invoked only from a single point in the whole program, and that is in the accept()

method of Add. There, we *do* know that the visitor called is one that both the Add object itself *and* its children are able to accept(), simply because the children by definition accept the same visitor type V as their parent. So how can we pass this knowledge on to the visitAdd() method?

No amount of F-bounded self-parameterization of the visitor classes will help us here. It is a well known shortcoming of F-bounds that they cannot express true self types. To the best of our knowledge there is no way in the generic type system of the forthcoming Java release to get '**this**' in the visitAdd() method typed as a V. This is where [9] has to give up, and the solution presented by Wadler in [8] was later found to be unsafe because of this same issue.

There is a trick, however, which, considering the pain caused by this hurdle, is provocatively simple. We observe that, although the visitAdd() method of AlePrint needs a V object to work on, it does not need to know that this object is indeed **this** object. We may therefore simply add as an extra argument to visitAdd() the visitor to use for recursive calls, and then let the accept() method of Add pass the visitor object *to itself* in the call of visitAdd(). The full ALE implementation with this approach is shown in Figure 6.

```
interface Exp⟨V extends AleVisitor⟩ { void accept(V v); } class Lit⟨V ex-
tends AleVisitor⟩ implements Exp⟨V⟩ { public int value; Lit(int v) { value
= v; } public void accept(V v) { v.visitLit(this); } } class Add⟨V extends
AleVisitor⟩ implements Exp⟨V⟩ { public Exp⟨V⟩ left, right; Add(Exp⟨V⟩ l,
Exp⟨V⟩ r) { left = l; right = r; } public void accept(V v) { v.visitAdd(this,
v); } } interface AleVisitor { ⟨V extends AleVisitor⟩ void visitLit(Lit⟨V⟩ lit);
⟨V extends AleVisitor⟩ void visitAdd(Add⟨V⟩ add, V self); } class AlePrint
implements AleVisitor { public ⟨V extends AleVisitor⟩ void visitLit(Lit⟨V⟩
lit) { System.out.print(lit.value); } public ⟨V extends AleVisitor⟩ void
visitAdd(Add⟨V⟩ add, V self) { add.left.accept(self); System.out.print('+');
add.right.accept(self); } }
```

Fig. 6. An operation-based implementation of ALE with code-level extensibility

Despite its simplicity, this trick is one of the major contributions of this paper, because it finally moves the visitor-based approach to the expression problem into the realm of static type safety.

Finally we now have the scaffolding needed to extend the set of expressions with a Neg class, using the same trick once more for the visitNeg() method. See Figure 7 for the full code.

4.1 Surrounding Code

Creation code is easily made reusable across extensions by parameterizing it with the Visitor kind of its products and then using the constructors directly, as in:

```
class Neg⟨V extends NaleVisitor⟩ implements Exp⟨V⟩ { public Exp⟨V⟩ exp;
  Neg(Exp⟨V⟩ e) { exp = e; } public void accept(V v) { v.visitNeg(this, v);
} } interface NaleVisitor extends AleVisitor { ⟨V extends NaleVisitor⟩ void
visitNeg(Neg⟨V⟩ neg, V self); } class NalePrint extends AlePrint implements Nale-
Visitor { public ⟨V extends NaleVisitor⟩ void visitNeg(Neg⟨V⟩ neg, V self) {
  System.out.print("−("); neg.exp.accept(self); System.out.print(")"); } }
```

Fig. 7. An extension of Figure 6 adding a Neg class

```
static ⟨V extends AleVisitor⟩ Exp⟨V⟩ build() {
  return new Add⟨V⟩(new Lit⟨V⟩(2), new Lit⟨V⟩(3));
}
```

Reusable client code can be obtained by using a variation of the *Abstract Factory* pattern to abstract over the creation of appropriate visitors for handling the operations.

4.2 Related Work

A special case of client code is the operations themselves, when calling the same or other operations recursively on substructures of the data. In our simple examples we have assumed that there is only a need to call recursively with the same visitor object. Krishnamurthi et.al. [15] propose dealing with the more general situation by using factory methods [1], unfortunately in a type-unsafe manner.

5 Object-Level Extensibility Using Wildcards

The solution above effectively divides the node classes of the different phases into separate, incompatible families, each characterised, in the form of a type parameter, by the specific brand of Visitor they are capable of accepting. Wildcards, a new mechanism to appear with generics in the forthcoming version of the Java platform (JDK1.5/Tiger), aim at allowing the programmer to bridge the gap between such separate families of classes [17]. Wildcards (represented by question marks) abstract over different instantiations of a given parameterised class, guided by given bounds on the type parameters. For instance

```
Exp⟨? super NaleVisitor⟩ e;
```

declares a variable e which may contain objects of type Exp⟨T⟩ for *any* T that is a supertype of NaleVisitor. Thus, it may for example be assigned an instance of Add⟨AleVisitor⟩. To maintain static type safety, the type rules for wildcards impose certain restrictions on method calls, but none of these apply in the given situation.

To obtain object-level extensibility, we should be able to continue to use old ALE expression trees after an extension to NALE has occurred. Already, NaleVisitors can be accepted by instances of Exp⟨AleVisitor⟩, simply because of subclassing. However, we would like for the old trees also to be usable as subtrees of new composite expressions, e.g., of Add⟨NaleVisitor⟩. We can obtain this by using wildcards in the types of children:

```
class Add<V extends AleVisitor> implements Exp<V> {
  public Exp<? super V> left, right;
  public void accept(V v) { v.visitAdd(this, v); }
}
```

Defining composite nodes like this, subtrees with a more general visitor type than V are allowed. As a consequence, not only can we reuse old trees, but we also lift the requirement on leaf nodes to have a type parameter they do not use, only for the purpose of being allowed into the company of like-parameterised classes. Thus, with a few minor changes, in Figure 8 we have modified the solution of the previous section to provide object-level extensibility. Figure 9 shows the modified Neg extension. Only the Neg class itself has changed, the visitors are as in Figure 7.

```
interface Exp<V extends AleVisitor> { void accept(V v); } class Lit implements
Exp<AleVisitor> { public int value; Lit(int v) { value = v; } public void ac-
cept(AleVisitor v) { v.visitLit(this); } } class Add<V extends AleVisitor> implements
Exp<V> { public Exp<? super V> left, right; Add(Exp<? super V> l, Exp<? su-
per V> r) { left = l; right = r; } public void accept(V v) { v.visitAdd(this, v);
} } interface AleVisitor { void visitLit(Lit lit); <V extends AleVisitor> void
visitAdd(Add<V> add, V self); } class AlePrint implements AleVisitor { public
void visitLit(Lit lit) { System.out.print(lit.value); } public <V extends AleVisitor>
void visitAdd(Add<V> add, V self) { add.left.accept(self); System.out.print('+');
add.right.accept(self); } }
```

Fig. 8. A modification of Figure 6 using wildcards to obtain object-level extensibility

```
class Neg<V extends NaleVisitor> implements Exp<V> { public Exp<? super
V> exp; Neg(Exp<? super V> e) { exp = e; } public void accept(V v) {
v.visitNeg(this, v); } }
```

Fig. 9. An extension of Figure 8 adding a Neg class. Visitors are identical to Figure 7 and have been omitted

There is a price to pay for this change, though: With the wildcard type on child nodes, we lose the exact knowledge about the child type of the children themselves – the "grandchild type" as it were. Thus, it is effectively disallowed to write into them anything other than expressions of the original unextended framework, in this case Exp⟨AleVisitor⟩s. This means that we cannot in general write visitors that *change* the structure of a given tree. If we could, we might accidentally store new NALE nodes inside old ALE trees, and any code still using old AleVisitors would be prone to a runtime type error when traversing it.

Depending on the type of application, this limitation may or may not be a problem. In compilers for programming languages, it is rare to see a destructive update of the structure of syntax trees. However, in a small step evaluator for e.g., lambda expressions, tree manipulation is at the core of the semantics, and this restriction would be a real showstopper.

5.1 Surrounding Code

The surrounding code is where we reap the benefits of this approach: code written at a certain time may keep global references to expressions around, which stay valid even across extensions. Old code will continue to work, and new code is sure not to violate the integrity of the old expression objects. Thus extension is a much less destructive endeavour than in the previous approaches.

6 A Hybrid Approach

We now turn to a completely different approach. The solution presented here is based on the following idea: if using either a data-centered or an operation-centered approach leads to so much difficulty, can we find a sweet spot in between?

More precisely, one might view the extensibility problems with both approaches as deriving from the need to "backpatch" existing code when new is added. Virtual methods avoid backpatching of operations when data types are added, whereas visitors avoid backpatching of data types when operations are added. So why not combine these approaches to use virtual methods when adding data types, *and* use visitors when adding operations?

This would require any given operation to be represented both as a virtual method and a visitor. When a new operation is added, it provides functionality for existing data types by means of a visitor, but it also defines a new specialised expression interface with the operation added as a method. Subsequently added data types must then implement this interface, and furthermore provide a new specialised visitor interface with visit methods for the new data types.

This approach is attractive because both data and visitor instances remain valid across new extensions. Compared to the previous solution, which used wildcards to soften the boundaries between the type families originating from the different phases of extension, in this approach there *are* no separate families. As a result there is no need for type parameterization of child types of composite nodes, wherefore the limitations of the wildcard approach on modification of the tree structure are gone.

This sounds almost too good to be true, and sure enough there is a major catch: we cannot implement it without casts. The hard part turns out to be the dispatch of operation calls. Given an expression and a visitor object, we need to figure out whether the operation:

- should be called as a method on the expression,
- should be called as a visit method on the visitor, or
- neither apply and we need to call a default method on the visitor.

We have been able to think of nothing better than to use type tests (using instanceof in Java) for this dispatch. To stop the type unsafe code from spilling out all over the extensions, we parameterise visitors with the kind of data types having the corresponding operation as a method, and we parameterise data types with the kind of visitors that have visit methods for them. In this way we can implement the type testing once and for all in a framework of base classes, as can be seen in Figure 10.

```
interface Exp { void handle(Visitor v); } interface Visitor { void ap-
ply(Exp e); void default(Exp e); } abstract class Node⟨V extends Visitor⟩ im-
plements Exp { public final void handle(Visitor v) { if (v instanceof V)
accept((V)v); else v.default(this); } abstract void accept(V v); } abstract
class Op⟨E extends Exp⟩ implements Visitor { public final void apply(Exp e) {
    if (e instanceof E) call((E)e); else e.handle(this); } abstract void
call(E e); public void default(Exp e) { throw new IllegalArgumentExcep-
tion("Expression problem occurred!"); } }
```

Fig. 10. A dispatch framework for a hybrid solution with full object-level extensibility

The dispatch starts with the apply() method of visitors. It is implemented in the abstract Op class (which all concrete visitors will extend) to call the proper method on its argument expression, if it exists, or otherwise ask the expression to do the dispatch using the handle() method. This in turn will check if the visitor has a proper visit method, or otherwise call the default() method of the visitor, which, by default, throws an exception.

Figure 11 shows how ALE can be implemented in this framework. The expression classes implement the print() operation using the class-based approach, but also have accept() methods to deal with future additions. The Print visitor, on the other hand, is trivial, since no expression will ever need a visit() method on it. An AleVisitor interface is provided for future extension.

In Figure 12 an eval() operation is added. It provides visit methods for the already existing data classes, and an interface EvalExp for future extension.

```
interface PrintExp extends Exp { void print(Print print); } class Print extends
Op⟨PrintExp⟩ implements Visitor { void call(PrintExp e) { e.print(this); } } class
Lit extends Node⟨AleVisitor⟩ implements PrintExp { public int value; Lit(int
v) { value = v; } public void print(Print print) { System.out.print(value); } void
accept(AleVisitor v) { v.visitLit(this); } } class Add extends Node⟨AleVisitor⟩ im-
plements PrintExp { public Exp left, right; Add(Exp l, Exp r) { left = l; right
= r; } public void print(Print print) { print.apply(left); System.out.print('+');
print.apply(right); } void accept(AleVisitor v) { v.visitAdd(this); } } interface
AleVisitor extends Visitor { void visitLit(Lit lit); void visitAdd(Add add); }
```

Fig. 11. A hybrid implementation of ALE based on the framework of Figure 10

```
class Eval extends Op⟨EvalExp⟩ implements AleVisitor { int result; public
final int eval(Exp e) { apply(e); return result; } void call(EvalExp e) { result =
e.eval(this); } public void visitLit(Lit lit) { result = lit.value; } public void
visitAdd(Add add) { result = eval(add.left) + eval(add.right); } } interface EvalExp
extends PrintExp { int eval(Eval eval); }
```

Fig. 12. An extension of Figure 11 with an eval() operation

The addition of a Neg class in Figure 13 is quite symmetric to this. Methods are implemented for existing operations, and a NaleVisitor defined for future extension.

```
class Neg extends Node⟨NaleVisitor⟩ implements EvalExp { public Exp
exp; Neg(Exp e) { exp = e; } public void print(Print print) {
System.out.print("−("); print.apply(exp); System.out.print(")"); } public
int eval(Eval eval) { return −eval.eval(exp); } void accept(NaleVisitor v) {
v.visitNeg(this); } } interface NaleVisitor extends AleVisitor { void visitNeg(Neg
neg); }
```

Fig. 13. A further extension of Figure 12 with a Neg class

In the forthcoming release of the Java platform, it is not possible to use casts and the instanceof operation on type variables. This is one of the few essential differences between the generic frameworks of C# and the Java programming language, and comes down to differences in implementation techniques. In this case, however, the limitation in Java is not grave. We can simulate the two operations by adding the following methods to the Node class:

```
abstract boolean isV(Visitor v);
abstract V asV(Visitor v);
```

and the following methods to the Op class:

```
abstract boolean isE(Exp e);
abstract E asE(Exp e);
```

Both must be implemented in the subsequent concrete specialisations of the two classes, when the type parameters are fixed to specific classes on which the runtime type operations work. This is similar to the automated translation performed by NextGen [11] to make up for these shortcomings of generic Java.

6.1 Surrounding Code

Reuse of surrounding code in this approach is almost for free. Creation code just instantiates the data classes directly. Client code may directly instantiate operation objects, and apply() them to expression objects. Both data and visitor objects may be kept around as global data, and will still work when new data and operation types are added.

In summary, the previous three approaches allow the *extender* of the data types and operations the safety of a type checked extension discipline, while putting a certain burden of parameterization on the *user* of these structures, along with limitations on object reuse. The present solution requires more discipline of the extender, who must make sure to always extend the latest previous version, without the aid of the type checker. But in return it completely liberates the user from the worries of the expression problem, essentially allowing any usage patterns of the naive non-extensible approaches of Figure 1 and 2.

6.2 Related Work

Odersky and Zenger [10] make use of *defaults* to handle the situations that "fall through" due to the lack of static safety, so that operations are called on data for which they are not defined. It is argued that this approach is useful in the setting they have investigated, an extensible compiler for Java-like languages. However, it is not obvious that there will always be a sensible default action for unhandled nodes in other domains, and throwing a runtime exception explicitly is hardly better than getting a runtime type error.

This approach is reminiscent of what may be achieved with *multimethods* (see e.g. [18]), which dispatch at runtime to the most specific implementation fitting their arguments. If a most-general fallback implementation is supplied, no runtime type errors can occur, as argued by Castagna in the context of a related problem [19]. However, the practical problem of providing meaningful such defaults remains.

In our solution above, the type checker ensures that defaults will not need to be called unless the extender has broken the discipline of linear extension, so the situation is somewhat less severe.

7 Conclusion

The scene of mainstream object-oriented programming languages is ever evolving, and genericity in the form of parameterised classes is becoming a standard component of most popular platforms. This calls for a re-evaluation of old problems and apparent dichotomies in the new context.

In this paper we have shown by examples that standard parametric genericity is a powerful means to obtain type safe solutions. Furthermore we have shown that the features peculiar to the two main language contenders in the market, namely Java's wildcards and C#'s reified type parameters, both have a real impact in terms of extensibility.

A number of novel concrete techniques have been proposed, which are constructive and general, and may be readily applied in real world settings. Thus, they can have a great impact on the extensibility and safety of future applications making use of the *Composite* structure.

A "full and final" solution to expression problem would combine the complete and straightforward object-level extensibility of our hybrid solution with full static type safety. This is still an important challenge for the future, and is unlikely to be achieved only with the linguistic means employed in this paper. Yet we hope that this paper has brought us closer to this ideal, and that it will inspire others to pursue it.

Acknowledgments. Thanks are due to Gilad Bracha, Philip Wadler and the anonymous reviewers for helpful comments and corrections.

References

1. Gamma, E., Helm, R., Johnson, R., Vlissides, J.: Design Patterns: Abstraction and Reuse of Object-Oriented Designs. Addison-Wesley (1994)
2. Gosling, J., Joy, B., Steele, G., Bracha, G.: The Java Language Specification – Third Edition. Third. edn. Addison-Wesley (2004)
3. Bracha, G., Odersky, M., Stoutamire, D., Wadler, P.: Making the future safe for the past: Adding genericity to the java programming language. [20]
4. ECMA: C# language specification. `http://www.ecma-international.org/publications/standards/Ecma-334.htm` (2002)
5. Kennedy, A., Syme, D.: Design and implementation of generics for the .NET common language runtime. In Norris, C., Fenwick, J.J.B., eds.: Proceedings of the ACM SIGPLAN '01 Conference on Programming Language Design and Implementation (PLDI-01). Volume 36.5 of ACM SIGPLAN Notices., N.Y., ACMPress (2001) 1–12
6. Reynolds, J.C.: User-defined types and procedural data as complementary approaches to data abstraction. In Schuman, S.A., ed.: New Directions in Algorthmic Languages. INRIA (1975) Reprinted in D. Gries, ed, Programming Methodology, Springer-Verlag, 1978 and in C. A. Gunter and J. C. Mitchell, eds, Theoretical Aspects of Object-Oriented Programmig, MIT Press, 1994.

7. Cook, W.R.: Object-oriented programming versus abstract data types. In: REX Workshop on Foundations of Object-oriented Languages. Number 489 in LNCS, Springer-Verlag (1990)
8. Wadler, P.: The expression problem. Posted on the Java Genericity mailing list (1998)
9. Bruce, K.B.: Some challenging typing issues in object-oriented languages. In Bono, V., Bugliesi, M., eds.: Electronic Notes in Theoretical Computer Science. Volume 82., Elsevier (2003)
10. Zenger, M., Odersky, M.: Extensible algebraic datatypes with defaults. In: Proceedings of the International Conference on Functional Programming. (2001)
11. Cartwright, R., Steele, G.L.: Compatible genericity with runtime-types for the Java programming language. [20]
12. Myers, A., Bank, J., Liskov, B.: Parameterized types for Java. In: Conf. Proceedings of the 24th ACM SIGPLAN-SIGACT Symposium on Principles of Programming Languages (POPL), Paris, France, POPL97, ACM Press. Neil D. Jones, editor. (1997)
13. Bracha, G., Cook, W.: Mixin-based inheritance. In: Object Oriented Programming: Systems, Languages and Applications/European Conference on Object-Oriented Programming, Ottawa, Canada, OOPSLA/ECOOP90, ACM Press. Norman K. Meyrowitz, editor. (1990) 303–311
14. Flatt, M., Krishnamurthi, S., Felleisen, M.: Classes and mixins. In: Principles of Programming Languages, San Diego, California, POPL98, ACM Press. David MacQueen, editor. (1998) 171–183
15. Krishnamurthi, S., Felleisen, M., Friedman, D.P.: Synthesizing object-oriented and functional design to promote re-use. In: European Conference on Object-Oriented Programming, Brussels, Belgium, ECOOP98, LNCS 1445, Springer Verlag. Eric Jul, editor. (1998) 91–113
16. Canning, P., Cook, W., Hill, W., Olthoff, W., Mitchell, J.: F-bounded polymorphism for object-oriented programming. In: ACM Conference on Functional Programming and Computer Architecture, ACM Press (1990) 273–280
17. Torgersen, M., Hansen, C.P., Ernst, E., von der Ahé, P., Bracha, G., Gafter, N.: Adding wildcards to the java programming language. In: Proceedings of the ACM Symposium of Applied Computing. (2004)
18. Bobrow, D.G., DeMichiel, L.G., Gabriel, R.P., Keene, S.E., Kiczales, G., Moon, D.A.: Common lisp object system specification. ACM Sigplan Notices, special issue **23** (1988)
19. Castagna, G.: Covariance and contravariance: Conflict without a cause. ACM Transactions on Programming Languages and Systems **17** (1995) 431–447
20. Object Oriented Programming: Systems, Languages and Applications, Vancouver, BC, ACM Press. Craig Chambers, editor. (1998)

Rewritable Reference Attributed Grammars

Torbjörn Ekman and Görel Hedin

Department of Computer Science, Lund University, Sweden
(torbjorn|gorel)@cs.lth.se

Abstract. This paper presents an object-oriented technique for rewriting abstract syntax trees in order to simplify compilation. The technique, Rewritable Reference Attributed Grammars (ReRAGs), is completely declarative and supports both rewrites and computations by means of attributes. We have implemented ReRAGs in our aspect-oriented compiler compiler tool JastAdd II. Our largest application is a complete static-semantic analyzer for Java 1.4. ReRAGs uses three synergistic mechanisms for supporting separation of concerns: inheritance for model modularization, aspects for cross-cutting concerns, and rewrites that allow computations to be expressed on the most suitable model. This allows compilers to be written in a high-level declarative and modular fashion, supporting language extensibility as well as reuse of modules for different compiler-related tools. We present the ReRAG formalism, its evaluation algorithm, and examples of its use. Initial measurements using a subset of the Java class library as our benchmarks indicate that our generated compiler is only a few times slower than the standard compiler, javac, in J2SE 1.4.2 SDK. This shows that ReRAGs are already useful for large-scale practical applications, despite that optimization has not been our primary concern so far.

1 Introduction

Reference Attributed Grammars (RAGs) have proven useful in describing and implementing static-semantic checking of object-oriented languages [1]. These grammars make use of *reference attributes* to capture non-local tree dependences like variable decl-use, superclass-subclass, etc., in a natural, yet declarative, way.

The RAG formalism is itself object-oriented, viewing the grammar as a class hierarchy and the abstract syntax tree (AST) nodes as instances of these classes. Behavior common to a group of language constructs can be specified in superclasses, and can be further specialized or overridden for specific constructs in the corresponding subclasses.

In plain RAGs, the complete AST is built prior to attribute evaluation. While this works well for most language constructs, there are several cases where the most appropriate tree structure can be decided only *after* evaluation of some of the attributes. I.e., the context-free syntax is not sufficient for building the desired tree, but contextual information is needed as well. By providing means for rewriting the AST based on a partial attribution, the specification of the remaining attribution can be expressed in a simpler and more natural way.

This paper presents ReRAGs, Rewritable Reference Attributed Grammars, which extend RAGs with the capability to rewrite the AST dynamically, during attribute evaluation, yet specified in a declarative way. ReRAGs form a conditional rewrite system

M. Odersky (Ed.): ECOOP 2004, LNCS 3086, pp. 144–169, 2004.

where conditions and rewrite rules may use contextual information through the use of attributes. We have implemented a static-semantics analyzer for Java using this technique. Based on this experience we exemplify typical cases where rewriting the AST is useful in practice.

ReRAGs are closely related to Higher-ordered Attribute Grammars (HAGs) [2], [3] and to the technique of forwarding in HAGs [4]. A major difference lies in the object-oriented basis of ReRAGs, where reference attributes are kept as explicit links in the tree and subtrees are rewritten in place. HAGs, in contrast, have a functional programming basis, viewing the AST as well as its attributes as structured values without identity.

ReRAGs also have similarities to tree transformation systems like Stratego [5], ASF+SDF [6], and TXL[7], but improves data acquisition support through the use of RAGs instead of embedding contextual data in rewrite rules. Rewrite application strategies differ in that ReRAGs only support the above described declarative approach while the above mentioned systems support user defined strategies. In Stratego and AST+SDF the rewrite application strategy is specified through explicit traversal strategies and in TXL the rewrite application order is implicitly defined as part of the functional decomposition of the transformation ruleset.

The plain RAG evaluation scheme is demand driven, evaluating an attribute only when its value is read. The ReRAG evaluation scheme extends this basic approach by rewriting parts of the AST as needed during the evaluation. We have designed different caching strategies to achieve performance optimization and evaluated the approach using a subset of the J2SDK 1.4.2 class library as our benchmark suite.

ReRAGs are implemented in our tool JastAdd II, a successor to our previous tool JastAdd that supported plain RAGs [8]. Several grammars have been developed for JastAdd II, the largest one being our Java grammar that implements static-semantics checking as specified in the Java Language Specification [9].

In addition to RAG/ReRAG support, the JastAdd systems support static aspect-oriented specification and integration with imperative Java code. Specifications are aspect-oriented in that sets of attributes and equations concerning a particular aspect, such as name analysis, type checking, code generation, etc., can be specified in modules separate from the AST classes. This is similar to the static introduction feature of AspectJ [10] where fields, methods, and interface implementation clauses may be specified in modules separate from the original classes.

Integration with imperative Java code is achieved by simply allowing ordinary Java code to read attribute values. This is useful for many problems that are more readily formulated imperatively than declaratively. For example, a code emission module may be written as ordinary Java code that reads attribute values from the name and type analysis in order to emit the appropriate code. These modules are also specified as static introduction-like aspects that add declarations to the existing AST classes. The ReRAG examples given in this paper are taken from our experience with the Java grammar and utilize the separation of concerns given by the aspect-oriented formulation, as well as the possibility to integrate declarative and imperative modules.

The rest of this paper is structured as follows. Section 2 introduces some typical examples of when AST rewriting is useful. Section 3 gives background information on RAGs and ASTs. Section 4 introduces ReRAG rewriting rules. Section 5 discusses how

ReRAGs are evaluated. Section 6 describes the algorithms implemented in JastAdd II. Section 7 discusses ReRAGs from both an application and a performance perspective. Section 8 compares with related work, and Section 9 concludes the paper.

2 Typical Examples of AST Rewriting

From our experience with writing a static-semantics analyzer for Java, we have found many cases where it is useful to rewrite parts of the AST in order to simplify the compiler implementation. Below, we exemplify three typical situations.

2.1 Semantic Specialization

In many cases the same context-free syntax will be used for language constructs that carry different meaning depending on context. One example is names in Java, like `a.b`, `c.d`, `a.b.c`, etc. These names all have the same general syntactic form, but can be resolved to a range of different things, e.g., variables, types, or packages, depending on in what context they occur. During name resolution we might find out that `a` is a class and subsequently that `b` is a static field. From a context-free grammar we can only build generic `Name` nodes that must capture all cases. The attribution rules need to handle all these cases and therefore become complex. To avoid this complexity, we would like to do *semantic specialization*. I.e., we would like to replace the general `Name` nodes with more specialized nodes, like `ClassName` and `FieldName`, as shown in Figure 1. Other computations, like type checking, optimization, and code generation, can benefit from this rewrite by specifying different behavior (attributes, equations, fields and methods) in the different specialized classes, rather than having to deal with all the cases in the general `Name` class.

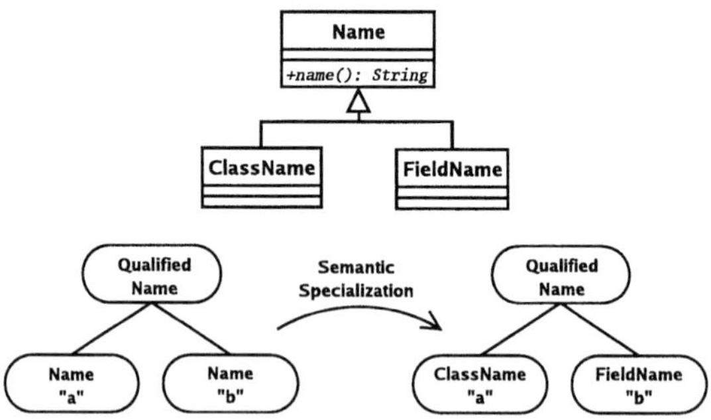

Fig. 1. Semantic specialization of name references.

2.2 Make Implicit Behavior Explicit

A language construct sometimes has *implicit behavior* that does not need to be written out by the programmer explicitly. An example is the implicit constructors of Java classes. If a class in Java has no constructors, this corresponds to an implicit constructor taking no arguments. The implicit behavior can be made explicit by rewriting the AST, see Figure 2. This simplifies other computations, like code generation, which do not have to take the special implicit cases into account.

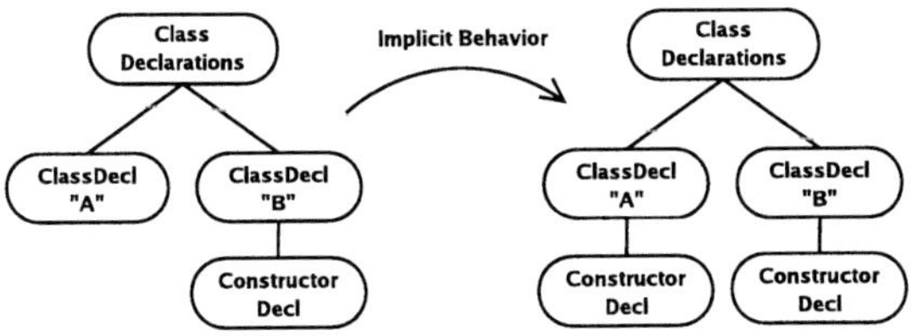

Fig. 2. The implicit constructor in class "A" is made explicit.

2.3 Eliminate Shorthands

Some language constructs are shorthands for specific combinations of other, more basic, constructs. For example, string concatenation in Java can be written using the binary addition operator (e.g., `a+b`), but is actually implemented as an invocation of the `concat` method in the `String` class (e.g., `a.concat(b)`). The AST can be rewritten to eliminate such shorthands, as shown in Figure 3. The AST now reflects the semantics rather than the concrete syntax, which simplifies other computations like optimizations and code generation.

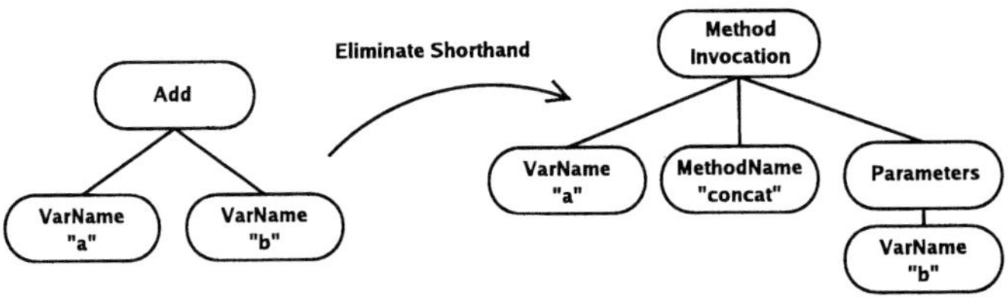

Fig. 3. Eliminate shorthand and reflect the semantic meaning instead.

3 Background

3.1 AGs and RAGs

ReRAGs are based on Reference Attributed Grammars (RAGs) which is an object-oriented extension to Attribute Grammars (AGs) [11]. In plain AGs each node in the

AST has a number of *attributes*, each defined by an *equation*. The right-hand side of the equation is an expression over other attribute values and defines the value of the left-hand side attribute. In a consistently attributed tree, all equations hold, i.e., each attribute has the same value as the right-hand side expression of its defining equation.

Attributes can be *synthesized* or *inherited*. The equation for a synthesized attribute resides in the node itself, whereas for an inherited attribute, the equation resides in the parent node. From an OO perspective we may think of attributes as fields and of equations as methods for computing the fields. However, they need not necessarily be implemented that way. Note that the term *inherited attribute* refers to an attribute defined in the parent node, and is thus a concept unrelated to the inheritance of OO languages. In this article we will use the term *inherited attribute* in its AG meaning.

Inherited attributes are used for propagating information downwards in the tree (e.g., propagating information about declarations down to use sites) whereas synthesized attributes can be accessed from the parent and used for propagating information upwards in the tree (e.g. propagating type information up from an operand to its enclosing expression).

RAGs extend AGs by allowing attributes to have reference values, i.e., they may be object references to AST nodes. AGs, in contrast, only allow attributes to have primitive or structured algebraic values. This extension allows very simple and natural specifications, e.g., connecting a use of a variable directly to its declaration, or a class directly to its superclass. Plain AGs connect only through the AST hierarchy, which is very limiting.

3.2 The AST Class Hierarchy

The nodes in an AST are viewed as instances of Java classes arranged in a subtype hierarchy. An AST class correponds to a nonterminal or a production (or a combination thereof) and may define a number of children and their declared types, corresponding to a production right-hand side. In an actual AST, each node must be *type consistent* with its parent according to the normal type-checking rules of Java. I.e., the node must be an instance of a class that is the same or a subtype of the corresponding type declared in the parent. Shorthands for lists, optionals, and lexical items are also provided. An example definition of some AST classes in a Java-like syntax is shown below.

```
// Expr corresponds to a nonterminal
ast Expr;
// Add corresponds to an Expr production
ast Add extends Expr ::= Expr leftOp, Expr rightOp;
// Id corresponds to an Expr production, id is a token
ast Id extends Expr ::= <String id>;
```

Aspects can be specified that define attributes, equations, and ordinary Java methods of the AST classes. An example is the following aspect for very simple type-checking.

```
// Declaration of an inherited attribute env of Expr nodes
inh Env Expr.env();
// Declaration of a synthesized attribute type of Expr nodes
// and its default equation
syn Type Expr.type() = TypeSystem.UNKNOWN;
```

```
// Overriding the default equation for Add nodes
eq Add.type() = TypeSystem.INT;
// Overriding the default equation for Id nodes
eq Id.type() = env().lookup(id()).type();
```

The corresponding Java API is shown in the following UML diagram. It includes methods for accessing child nodes like `leftOp` and `rightOp`, tokens like `id` and user-defined attributes like `env` and `type`. This API can be used freely in the right-hand sides of equations, as well as by ordinary Java code.

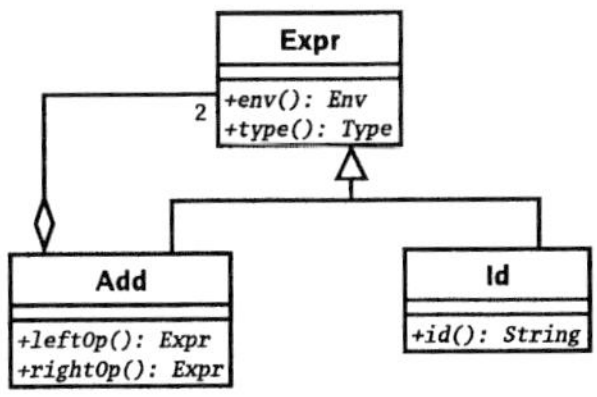

4 Rewrite Rules

ReRAGs extend RAGs by allowing rewrite rules to be written that automatically and transparently rewrite nodes. The rewriting of a node is triggered by the first access to it. Such an access could occur either in an equation in the parent node, or in some imperative code traversing the AST. In either case, the access will be captured and a reference to the final rewritten tree will be the result of the access. This way, the rewriting process is transparent to any code accessing the AST. The first access to the node will always go via the reference to it in the parent node. Subsequent accesses may go via reference attributes that refer directly to the node, but at this point, the node will already be rewritten to its final form.

A rewrite step is specified by a rewrite rule that defines the conditions when the rewrite is applicable, as well as the resulting tree. For a given node, there may be several rewrite rules that apply, which are then applied in a certain order. It may also be the case that after the application of one rewrite rule, more rewrite rules become applicable. This allows complex rewrites to be broken down into a series of simple small rewrite steps.

A rewrite rule for nodes of class N has the following general form:

```
rewrite N {
  when (cond)
  to R result;
}
```

This specifies that a node of type N may be replaced by another node of type R as specified in the result expression *result*. The rule is applicable if the (optional) boolean condition *cond* holds and will be applied if there are no other applicable rewrite rules of higher priority (priorites will be discussed later). Furthermore, all rewrite rules must be type consistent in that the replacement will result in a type consistent AST regardless of the context of the node, as will be discussed in Section 4.2. In a consistently attributed tree, all equations hold and all rewrite conditions are false.

4.1 A Simple Example

As an example, consider replacing an Add node with a StringAdd node in case both operands are strings [1]. This can be done as follows.

```
ast StringAdd extends Expr ::= Expr leftOp, Expr rightOp;
rewrite Add {
   when (childType().equals(TypeSystem.STRING))
   to StringAdd new StringAdd(leftOp(), rightOp());
}
syn Type Add.childType() = ...;
```

Note that in the creation of the new right-hand side, the previous children `leftOp()` and `rightOp()` are used. These accesses might trigger rewrites of these nodes in turn.

Avoiding repeated applications. `StringAdd` nodes might have much in common with `Add` nodes, and an alternative way of handling this rewrite would be to define `StringAdd` as a subclass of `Add`, rather than as a sibling class. In this case, the rewrite should apply to all `Add` nodes, except those that are already `StringAdd` nodes, and can be specified as follows.

```
ast StringAdd extends Add;
rewrite Add {
   when (childType().equals(TypeSystem.STRING)
      and !(this instanceOf StringAdd))
   to StringAdd new StringAdd(leftOp(), rightOp());
}
syn Type Add.childType() = ...;
```

Note that the condition includes a type test to make sure that the rule is not applied to nodes that are already of type StringAdd. This is necessary since the rule would otherwise still be applicable after the rewrite, resulting in repeated applications of the same rule and thereby nontermination. In general, whenever the rewrite results in the same type or a subtype, it is advicable to reflect over if the condition might hold also after the rewrite and in that case if the condition should be tightened in order to avoid nontermination.

Solutions that refactor the AST class hierarchy. A third alternative solution could be to keep `Add` and `StringAdd` as sibling classes and to factor out the common parts into a superclass as follows.

```
ast Expr:
ast GeneralAdd extends Expr ::= Expr leftOp, Expr rightOp;
ast Add extends GeneralAdd;
ast StringAdd extends GeneralAdd;
```

This solution avoids the type test in the rewrite condition. However, it requires that the grammar writer has access to the original AST definition of `Add` so that it can be refactored.

[1] In Section 4.4 we will instead rewrite addition of strings as method calls.

4.2 Type Consistency

As mentioned above, rules must be *type consistent*, i.e., the replacing node must always be type consistent with any possible context. This is checked statically by the JastAdd II system. Consider the rewrite rule that replaces an `Add` node by a sibling `StringAdd` node using the grammar described above. The expected child type for all possible contexts for `Add` nodes is `Expr`. Since both `Add` and `StringAdd` are subclasses of `Expr` the rule is type consistent. However, consider the addition of the following AST class.

```
ast A ::= Add:
```

In this case the rewrite rule would not be type consistent since the rewrite could result in an `A` node having a `StringAdd` node as a child although an `Add` node is expected. Similarly, in the second rewrite example in Section 4.1 where `StringAdd` is a subclass of `Add`, that rewrite rule would not be type consistent if the following classes were part of the AST grammar.

```
ast B ::= C:
ast C extends Add;
```

In this case, the rewrite rule could result in a `B` node having a `StringAdd` node as a child which would not be type consistent.

Theorem 1. *A rule* `rewrite` *A...*`to` *B... is type consistent if the following conditions hold: Let C be the first common superclass of A and B. Furthermore, let $\mathcal{D}$ be the set of classes that occur on the right-hand side of any production class. The rule is type consistent as long as there is no class D in $\mathcal{D}$ that is a subclass of C, i.e., $D \nless C$.*

Proof. The rewritten node will always be in a context where its declared type D is either the same as C, or a supertype thereof, i.e. $C \leq D$. The resulting node will be of a type $R \leq B$, and since $B \leq C$, then consequently $R \leq D$, i.e., the resulting tree will be type consistent. □

4.3 Rewriting Descendent Nodes

The tree resulting from a rewrite is specified as an expression which may freely access any of the current node's attributes and descendents. Imperative code is permitted, using the syntax of a Java method body that returns the resulting tree. This imperative code may reuse existing parts in the old subtree in order to build the new subtree, but may have no other externally visible side effects. This can be used to rewrite descendent nodes, returning an updated version of the node itself as the result.

As an example, consider a Java class declaration `class A { ... }`. Here, `A` is given no explicit superclass which is equivalent to giving it the superclass `Object`. In order to simplify further attribution (type checking, etc.), we would like to change the AST and insert the superclass as an explicit node. This can be done by the following rewrite rule:

```
ast ClassDecl extends Decl ::=
   <String classId>, [ TypeRef superClass ], Body body;
rewrite ClassDecl {
   when (!hasSuperClass() && !name().equals("Object"))
```

```
    to ClassDecl {
        setSuperClass(new TypeRef("Object"));
        return this;
    }
}
```

Note that the rewrite rule updates a descendent node and returns itself, as illustrated in the figure below.

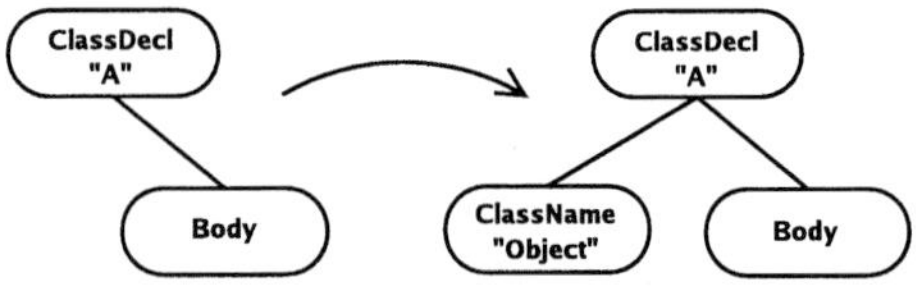

As seen from the specification above, the condition for doing this rewrite is that the class has no explicit superclass already, and that it is another class than the root class `Object`. The result type is the same as the rewritten type, which means we should reflect on possible nontermination due to repeated applications of the same rule. However, it is clear that the rewrite will not be applicable a second time since the rewrite will result in a node where the condition is no longer met.

4.4 Combining Rules

It is often useful to rewrite a subtree in several steps. Consider the following Java-like expression

```
a+"x"
```

Supposing that a is a reference to an non-null `Object` subclass instance, the semantic meaning of the expression is to convert a into a string, convert the string literal `"x"` into a string object, and to concatenate the two strings by the method `concat`. It can thus be seen as a shorthand for the following expression.

```
a.toString().concat(new String(new char[ ] {'x'} ))
```

To simplify code generation we would like to eliminate the shorthand notation by rewriting the AST. This can be accomplished by a number of rewrite rules, each taking care of a single subproblem:

1. replace the right operand of an Add node by a call to `toString` if the left operand is a string, but the right is not
2. replace the left operand of an Add node by a call to `toString` if the right operand is a string, but the left is not
3. replace an Add node by a method call to `concat` if both operands are strings
4. replace a string literal by an expression creating a new string object

Suppose the original `Add` node is accessed from its parent. This will cause the AST to be rewritten in the following steps. First, it will be checked which rules are applicable for `Add`. This will involve accessing its left and right operands, which triggers the rewrite of these nodes in turn. In this case, the right operand will be rewritten according to rule 4. It is now found that rule 2 is applicable for `Add`, and it is applied, replacing the left operand by a `MethodCall`. This causes rule 3 to become applicable for `Add`, replacing it too by a `MethodCall`. Now, no more rules are applicable for the node and a reference is returned to the parent. Figure 4 illustrates the steps applied in the rewrite.

Rule priority. In general, it is possible that more than one rule applies to a node. Typically, this happens when there are two rewrite rules in a node, each rewriting different parts of the substructure of the node. For example, in a class declaration there may be one rewrite rule that takes care of making an implicit constructor explicit, and another rule making an implicit superclass explicit. Both these rules can be placed in the `ClassDecl` AST class, and may be applicable at the same time. In this particular case, the rules are *confluent*, i.e., they can be applied in any order, yielding the same resulting tree. So far, we have not found the practical use for nonconfluent rules, i.e., where the order of application matters. However, in principle they can occur, and in order to obtain a predictable result also in this case, the rules are prioritized: Rules in a subclass have priority over rules in superclasses. For rules in the same class, the lexical order is used as priority.

5 ReRAG Evaluation

5.1 RAG Evaluation

An attribute evaluator computes the attribute values so that the tree becomes consistently attributed, i.e., all the equations hold. JastAdd uses a demand-driven evaluation mechanism for RAGs, i.e., the value of an attribute is not computed until it is read [8]. The implementation of this mechanism is straight-forward in an object-oriented language [12]. Attributes are implemented as methods in the AST classes where they are declared. Accessing an attribute is done simply by calling the corresponding method. Also equations are translated to methods, and are called as appropriate by the attribute methods: The method implementing an inherited attribute will call an equation method in the parent node. The method implementing a synthesized attribute calls an equation method in the node itself. JastAdd checks statically that all attributes in the grammar have a defining equation, i.e., that the grammar is well-formed. For efficiency, the value of an attribute is cached in the tree the first time it is computed. All tree nodes inherit generic accessor methods to its parent and possible children through a common superclass. As a simple example, consider the following RAG fragment:

```
ast Expr;
ast Id extends Expr ::= <String id>;
inh Env Expr.env();
syn Type Expr.type();
eq Id.type() = env().lookup(id()).type();
```

This is translated to the following Java code:

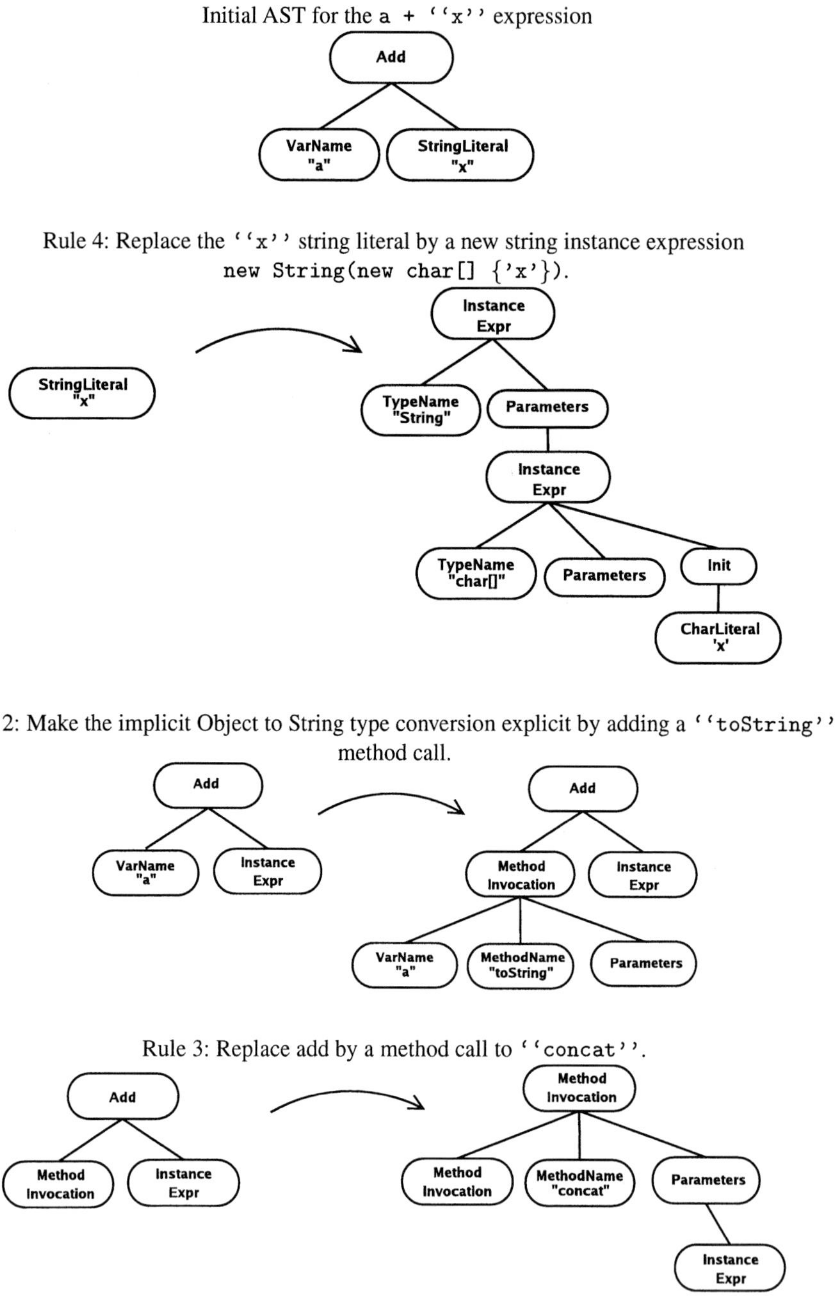

Fig. 4. Combine several rules to eliminate the shorthand for String addition and literals in a Java like language.

```
class Expr extends ASTNode {    // inherit generic node access
  Env env_value = null;          // cached attribute value
  boolean env_cached = false;    // flag true when cached
  Env env() {                   // method for inherited attribute
    if(!env_cached) {
      env_value = ((HasExprSon)parent()).env_eq(this);
      env_cached = true; }
    return env_value; }
  Type type_value = null;        // cached attribute value
  boolean type_cached = false;   // flag true when cached
  Type type() {                 // method for synthesized attribute
    if(!type_cached) {
      type_value = type_eq();
      type_cached = true; }
    return type_value; }
  abstract Type type_eq(); }
interface HasExprSon {
  Env env_eq(Expr son); }
class Id extends Expr {
  String id() { ... }
  Type type_eq() {               // method for equation defining
    return env().lookup(id()).type() // synthesized attribute
  } }
```

This demand-driven evaluation scheme implicitly results in topological-order evaluation (evaluation order according to the attribute dependences). See [1] for more details.

Attribute evaluation using this scheme will often follow complex tree traversal patterns, often visiting the same node multiple times in order to evaluate all the attributes that a specific attribute depends on. For example, consider the evaluation of the attribute *Id.type* above. This involves finding the declaration of the identifier, then finding the declaration of the type of the identifier, and during this process, possibly finding the declarations of classes in the superclass chain where these declarations may be located. In this process, the same block nodes and declaration nodes may well be visited several times. However, once a certain attribute is evaluated, e.g., the reference from a class to its superclass, that computation does not need to be redone since the attribute value is cached. The traversals do therefore not always follow the tree structure, but can also follow reference attributes directly, e.g., from subclass to superclass or from variable to declaration.

5.2 Basic Rewrite Strategy

To handle ReRAGs, the evaluator is extended to rewrite trees in addition to evaluating attributes, resulting in a consistently attributed tree where all equations hold and all rewrite conditions are false. A demand-driven rewriting strategy is used. When a tree node is visited, the node is rewritten iteratively. In each iteration, the rule conditions are evaluated in priority order, and the first applicable rule will be applied, replacing the node (or parts of the subtree rooted at the node). The next iteration is applied to the root of the new subtree. The iteration stops when none of the rules are applicable (all the conditions are false), and a reference to the resulting subtree is then returned to the visiting node. The subtree may thus be rewritten in several steps before the new subtree is returned to the visiting node. Since the rewrites are applied implicitly when visiting a node, the rewrite is transparent from a node traversal point of view.

The figure below shows how the child node *B* of *A* is accessed for the first time and iteratively rewritten into the resulting node *D* that is returned to the parent *A*. The subscript *v* indicates that a node has been visited and *r* that a rewrite is currently being evaluated. When *B* is visited a rewrite is triggered and the node is rewritten to a *C* node that in turn is rewritten to a *D* node. No rewrite conditions for the *D* node are true, and the node is returned to the parent *A* that need not be aware of the performed rewrite.

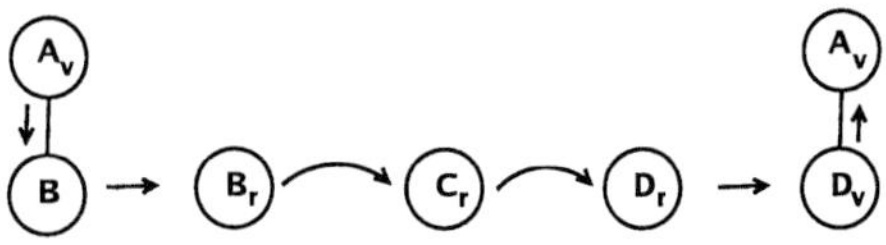

5.3 Nested and Multi-level Rewrites

When evaluating a condition or a result expression in a rewrite rule, attributes may be read that trigger a visit to another node. That visit may in turn trigger a second rewrite that is executed before the first may continue its evaluation. This nesting of rewrites results in several rewrites being active at the same time. Since attributes may reference distant subtrees, the visited nodes could be anywhere in the AST, not necessarily in the subtree of the rewritten tree.

The following figure shows an example of nested rewrites. The subscript *v* indicates that a node has been visited and *r* that a rewrite is currently being evaluated. The rewrites are numbered in the order they started.

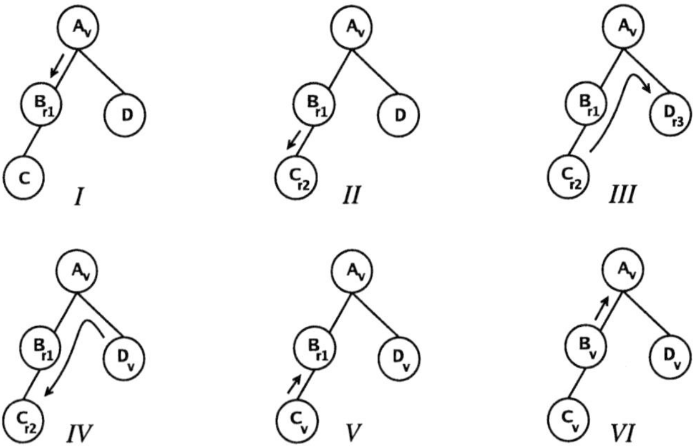

An initial rewrite, *r1*, is triggered when *A* visits its child *B* in stage *I*. A visit to *C*, that is caused by accessing a synthesized attribute during rewrite condition checking, triggers a second rewrite *r2* in stage *II*. That rewrite triggers a visit to a distant node *D* by reading an inherited attribute and initiates a third rewrite *r3* in stage *III*. When no conditions in D are true the result of the inherited attribute is calculated and returned to C in stage *IV*. The synthesized attribute is calculated and returned to B in stage *V*. The resulting node B is finally returned to A in stage *VI*. Notice that the rewrites terminate in the opposite order that they were initiated.

As discussed in Section 5.1, most non-trivial attribute grammars are multi-visit in that a node may have to be visited multiple times to evaluate an attribute. A common situation is when a child node has an inherited attribute, and the equation in the parent node depends on a synthesized attribute that visits the child node again. The situation is illustrated in the figure below. A visits B and a rewrite is initiated in stage *I*. During condition evaluation the inherited attribute *y()* is read and A is visited to evaluate its equation in stage *II*. That equation contains the synthesized attribute *x()* that in turn depends on *z()* in B and a second visit is initiated in stage *III*.

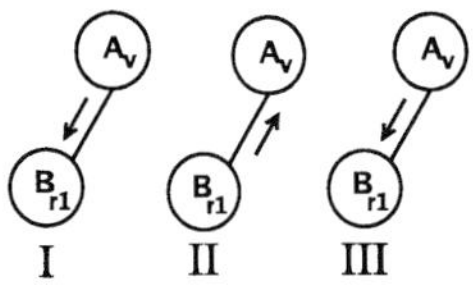


```
ast A ::= B child;
inh Type B.y();
eq A.child().y() = x();
syn Type A.x() = child().z();
syn Type B.z() = ... ;
```

Such multi-visits complicate the rewrite and attribute evaluation process somewhat. Should the second visit to a node that is being rewritten start a second rewrite? No. The attributes read in a node that is being rewritten should reflect the current tree structure. Otherwise, the definition of rewrites would be circular and evaluation would turn into an endless loop. Therefore, when visiting a node that is already being rewritten, the current node is returned and no new rewrite is triggered.

Note that attribute values that depend on nodes that are being rewritten, might have different values during the rewrite than they will have in the final tree. Therefore, such attributes will not be cached until all the nodes they depend on have reached their final form. We will return to this issue in Section 6.3.

Note also that a node may well be rewritten several times, provided that the previous rewrite has completed. This can happen if the rewrites are triggered by the rewriting of another node. For example, suppose we are rewriting a node A. During this process, we visit its son node S which is then rewritten to S'. After this rewrite of S, the conditions of S' are all false (the rewrite of S completes). We then complete one iteration of rewriting A, replacing it with a new node A'(but keeping the son S'). In the next iteration of rewriting A', it may be found that S' needs to be rewritten again since the conditions of S' may give other results after replacing A by A'. This will also be discussed more in Section 6.2.

6 Implementation Algorithm

6.1 Basic Algorithm

As discussed in Section 3.2, a Java class is generated for each node type in the AST. All classes in the class hierarchy descend from the same superclass, *ASTNode*, providing generic traversal of the AST by the generic *parent()* and *child(int index)* methods. These methods are used in the implementation of attribute and equation methods, as discussed in Section 5.1.

We have implemented our rewriting algorithm by extending the existing JastAdd RAG evaluator as an AspectJ [10] aspect. In particular, the *child* method is extended to trigger rewrites when appropriate. To start with, we consider the case when no RAG attributes are cached. The handling of cached attributes in combination with rewriting is treated in Section 6.3.

Rewrite rules for each node type are translated into a corresponding Java method, *rewriteTo()*, that checks rewrite rule conditions and returns the possibly rewritten tree. This method is iteratively invoked until no conditions are true. If all conditions in one node's rewriteTo() method are false, then rewriteTo() in the node's superclass is invoked. The generated Java method for the first example in Section 4 is shown below.

```
ASTNode Add.rewriteTo() {
  if(childType().equals(TypeSystem.STRING))
    return new StringAdd(leftOp(), rightOp())
  return super.rewriteTo();
}
```

To determine when no conditions are true and iteration should stop, a flag is set when the rewriteTo() method in ASTNode is reached, indicating that no overriding rewriteTo method has calculated a result tree. A flag is used since a simple comparison of the returned node is not sufficient because the rewrite may have rewritten descendent nodes only. In order to handle nested rewrites, a stack of flags is used.

Figure 5 shows an AspectJ aspect implementing the above described behaviour:

(1) The stack used to determine when no conditions are true
(2) Iteratively apply rewrite until no conditions are true
(3) Push *false* on the stack to guess that a rewrite will occur
(4) Bind the rewritten tree as a child to the parent node.
(5) Set top value on stack to *true* when rewriteTo in ASTNode is reached (no rewrite occurred)
(6) Define a pointcut when the child method is called.
(7) Each call to child is extended to also call rewrite.

As discussed in Section 5.3 a tree node currently in rewrite may be visited again during that rewrite when reading attributes. When a node that is in rewrite is visited, the current tree state should be returned instead of initiating a new rewrite. That behaviour is implemented in the aspect shown in Figure 6:

(1) A flag, inRewrite, is added to each node to indicate whether the node is in rewrite or not.
(2) Add advice around each call to the rewriteTo method.
(3) The flag is set when a rewrite is initiated.
(4) The flag is reset when a rewrite is finished.
(5) Add advice around the rewrite loop in the previous aspect.
(6) When a node is in rewrite then the current tree is returned instead of initiating a new rewrite.

```
    public aspect Rewrite {
(1)   protected static Stack noRewrite = new Stack();
(2)   ASTNode rewrite(ASTNode parent, ASTNode child, int index) {
        do {
(3)       noRewrite.push(Boolean.FALSE);
          child = child.rewriteTo();
(4)       parent.setChild(index, child);
        } while(noRewrite.pop() == Boolean.FALSE);
        return child; }
(5)   ASTNode ASTNode.rewriteTo() {
        noRewrite.pop();
        noRewrite.push(Boolean.TRUE);
        return this; }
(6)   pointcut child(int index, ASTNode parent) :
        call(ASTNode ASTNode.child(int)) &&
        args(index) && target(parent);
(7)   ASTNode around (int index, ASTNode parent) :
            child(index, parent) {
        ASTNode child = proceed(index, parent):
        return rewrite(parent, child, index); }
    }
```

Fig. 5. Aspect Rewrite: Iteratively rewrite each visited tree node

```
     public aspect ReVisit {
(1)    boolean ASTNode.inRewrite = false;
(2)  ASTNode around(ASTNode child)
      : execution(ASTNode ASTNode+.rewriteTo()) && target(child) {
(3)    child.inRewrite = true;
       ASTNode newChild = proceed(child);
(4)    child.inRewrite = false;
       return newChild; }
(5)  ASTNode around(ASTNode child)
       : execution(ASTNode Rewrite.rewrite(ASTNode, ASTNode, int)
       && args(*, child, *) {
(6)    if(child.inRewrite)
         return child;
       return proceed(child);
     }
```

Fig. 6. Aspect ReVisit: Pass through re-visit to a node already in rewrite

6.2 Optimization of Final Nodes

As mentioned, a node may be rewritten several times. We are interested in detecting when no further rewriting of it is possible so we know that it has reached its final identity. By detecting final nodes, we can avoid the needless checking of their rewrite conditions (since they will all be false). This performance improvement can be significant for nodes with expensive conditions, e.g., when extracting a property by visiting all the children of the node. We can also use the concept of final nodes to cache attributes, as will be discussed in Section 6.3.

Definition 1. *A node is said to be* final *when i) all its rewrite conditions evaluate to false, and ii) future evaluations of its rewrite conditions cannot yield other values, and iii) it cannot be rewritten by any other node.*

Clearly, no further rewriting of final nodes is possible: i) and ii) guarantee that the node itself cannot trigger any rewriting of it, and iii) that it cannot be rewritten by any other node.

To find out when a node is final, we first recall (from Section 4) which nodes may be changed by a rewrite rule. Consider a node N which is the root of a subtree T. The rewrite rule will result in replacing T by T', where T' consists of a combination of newly created nodes and old nodes from T. I.e., the rewrite may not change nodes outside T. From this follows that a node can only be rewritten by rules in the node itself or rules in nodes on the path to the AST root node.

This allows us to state that

Lemma 1. *If a node is final, all its ancestor nodes are final.*

Proof. Otherwise the node may be rewritten by an ancestor node, in which case it is not final.

From Lemma 1 follows that at any point during evaluation, the final nodes of the AST will constitute a connected region that includes a path to the root, the *final region*. Initially, the evaluator visits only nodes in the final region, and is said to be in *normal* mode. But as soon as a non-final node is accessed from normal mode, the evaluator enters *rewrite* mode and that non-final node is said to be a *candidate*. When the iterative rewriting of the candidate has finished it turns out that it is final (see Theorem 2, and the evaluator returns to normal mode, completing the rewrite session. This way the final region is successively expanded. During a rewrite session, other non-final nodes may be visited and rewritten, but these are not considered candidates and will not become final during that rewrite session. There is only one candidate per rewrite session.

Note that during a rewrite session, the evaluator may well visit non-final nodes outside of the candidate subtree, and non-final nodes may be visited several times, the candidate included. For example, let us say we are rewriting a class String to add an explicit superclass reference to class Object. This means we will visit and trigger a rewrite of class Object. The rewrite of Object includes adding an explicit constructor. This involves searching through the methods of Object for a constructor. Suppose there is a method String toString() in Object. When this method is traversed, this will trigger rewriting of the identifier String to a type reference that directly refers to the String class. This in turn will involve a second visit to the String class (which was the candidate).

Theorem 2. *At the end of a rewrite session, the candidate* c *is final.*

Proof. At the end of the rewrite session, all rewrite conditions of c have just been evaluated to false. Furthermore, all ancestors of c are final, so no other node can rewrite c. What remains to be shown (see Definition 1) is that future evaluations of the rewrite conditions cannot yield other values. To see this we must consider the set of all other non-final nodes N that were visited in order to evaluate the rewrite conditions of c. This has involved evaluating all the rewrites conditions of these nodes in turn, also yielding false for all these conditions, and without triggering any rewrites of those nodes. Otherwise, another iteration of rewrite of c would have been triggered and we would not be at the end of the rewriting session. Since all these conditions evaluate to false, and there is no other node that can rewrite any of the nodes in N (since their ancestors outside N are final), none of these conditions can change value, and not only c, but in fact all nodes in N are final. □

In keeping track of which nodes are final, we add a flag isFinal to each node. In principle, we could mark both c and all the nodes in N as final at the end of the rewriting session. However, it is sufficient to mark c since any subsequent visits to a node in N will immediately mark that node as final, since all its rewrite conditions are false. An aspect introducing the isFinal flag is implemented in the aspect shown in Figure 7:

(1) A flag, isFinal, is added to each node to indicate whether the node is final or not.
(2) Add advice around the rewrite loop in the Rewrite aspect.
(3) When a node is final no rule condition checking is necessary and the node is returned immediately.
(4) When a node is entered during normal mode it becomes the next node to be final and we enter rewrite mode. On condition checking completion the node is final and we enter normal mode.
(5) A rewrite during rewrite mode continues as normal.

```
    public aspect FinalNodes {
(1)   boolean ASTNode.isFinal = false;
(2)   boolean normalMode = true;
(2)   ASTNode around(ASTNode parent, ASTNode child)
        : execution(ASTNode Rewrite.rewrite(ASTNode, ASTNode, int))
        && args(parent, child, *) {
(3)     if(child.isFinal)
          return child;
(4)     if(normalMode) {
          normalMode = false;
          child = proceed(parent, child);
          child.isFinal = true;
          normalMode = true;
          return child; }
(5)     return proceed(parent, child); }
    }
```

Fig. 7. Aspect FinalNodes: Detect final nodes and skip condition evaluation

6.3 Caching Attributes in the Context of Rewrites

In plain RAGs, attribute caching can be used to increase performance by ensuring that each attribute is evaluated only once. When introducing rewrites the same simple technique cannot be used. A rewrite that changes the tree structure may affect the value of an already cached attribute that must then be re-evaluated. There are two principle approaches to ensure that these attributes have consistent values. One is to analyze attribute dependences dynamically in order to find out which attributes need to be reevaluated due to rewriting. Another approach is to cache only those attributes that cannot be affected by later rewrites. In order to avoid extensive run-time dependency analysis, we have chosen the second approach.

We say that an attribute is *safely cachable* when its value cannot be affected by later rewrites. Because final nodes cannot be further rewritten, an attribute will be safely cachable if all nodes visited during its evaluation are final.

A simple solution is to only cache attributes whose evaluation is started when the evaluator is in normal mode, i.e., not in a rewriting session. These attributes will be safely cachable. To see this, we can note that

i) the node where the evaluation starts is final (since the evaluator is in normal mode)

ii) any node visited during evaluation will be in its final form before its attributes are accessed, since any non-final node encountered will cause the evaluator to enter rewrite mode, returning the final node after completing that rewriting session.

It is possible to cache certain attributes during rewriting, by keeping track dynamically of if all visited nodes are final. However, this optimization has not yet been implemented.

As mentioned earlier, the ReRAG implementation is implemented as aspects on top of the plain RAG implementation. The RAG implementation caches attributes, so we need to disable the caching whenever not in normal mode in order to handle ReRAGs. This is done simply by advice on the call that sets the cached-flag. Figure 8 shows how this is done.

```
public aspect DisableCache {
  Object around() : set(boolean ASTNode+.*_cached) {
    if(!FinalNodes.normalMode)
      return false;
    return proceed(); }
}
```

Fig. 8. Aspect DisableCache: Disable caching of attributes when not in normal mode

7 Implementation Evaluation

7.1 Applicability

We have implemented ReRAGs in our tool JastAdd II and performed a number of case studies in order to evaluate their applicability.

Full Java static-semantics checker. Our largest application is a complete static-semantic analyzer for Java 1.4. The grammar is a highly modular specification that follows the Java Language Specificaton, second edition[9], with modules like name binding, resolving ambiguous names, type binding, type checking, type conversions, inheritance, access control, arrays, exception handling, definite assignment and unreachable statements.

An LALR(1) parser using a slightly modified grammar from the Java Language Specification [9], is used to build the initial abstract syntax tree. The AST is rewritten during the analysis to better capture the semantics of the program and simplify later computations. Some examples where rewrites were useful are:

- for resolving ambiguous names and for using semantic specialization for bound name references.
- for making implicit constructs explict by adding (as appropriate) empty constructors, supertype constructor accesses, type conversions and promotions, and inheritance from *java.lang.Object*.
- for eliminating shorthands such as splitting compound declarations of fields and variables to a list of single declarations.

Java to C compiler. Our collegue, Anders Nilsson, has implemented a Java to C compiler in ReRAGs [13], based on an older version of the Java checker. The generated C code is designed to run with a set of special C runtime systems that support real-time garbage collection, and is interfaced to through a set of C macros. ReRAGs are used in the back end for adapting the AST to simplify the generation of code suitable for these runtime systems. For example, all operations on references are broken down to steps of only one indirection, generating the macro calls to the runtime system. ReRAGs are also used for optimizing the generated code size by eliminating unused classes, methods, and variables. They are also used for eliminating shorthands, for example to deal with all the variants of loops in Java.

Worst-case execution time analyzer. The Java checker was extended to also compute worst-case execution times using an annotation mechanism. The extension could be done in a purely modular fashion.

Automation Language. The automation language *Structured Text* in IEC-61131-3 has been modeled in ReRAGs and extended with an object-oriented type system and instance references. The extended language is translated to the base language by flattening the class hierarchies using iterative rewriting. Details will appear in a forthcoming paper.

7.2 Performance

We have implemented ReRAGs in our aspect-oriented compiler compiler tool JastAdd II. To give some initial performance measurements we benchmark our largest application, a complete static-semantic analyzer for Java 1.4. After parsing and static-semantic analysis the checked tree is pretty printed to file. Since code generation targeted for the Java virtual machine, [14], is fairly straight forward once static-semantic analysis is performed we believe that the work done by our analyzer is comparable to the work done by a java to byte-code compiler. We therefore compare the execution time of our analyzer to the standard java compiler, javac, in J2SE JDK.

Two types of optimizations to the basic evaluation algorithm were discussed in Section 6.2 and Section 6.3. The first disables condition checking for nodes that are final and the second caches attribute values that only depend on attributes in final nodes. To verify that these optimizations improve performance we benchmark our analyzer with and without optimizations. The execution times when analysing a few files of the *java.lang* package are shown in Figure 9. These measurements show that both attribute caching and condition checking disabling provide drastic performance improvements when applied individually and even better when combined. Clearly, both optimizations should be used to get reasonable execution times.

The execution times do not include parsing that took 3262ms without attribute caching and slightly more, 3644ms, when caching attributes. We believe the increase is due to the larger tree nodes used when caching attributes.

	condition checking	no condition checking
no attribute caching	546323 ms	61882 ms
attribute caching	21216 ms	2016 ms

Fig. 9. Comparison of analysis execution time with and without optimizations

To verify that the ReRAG implementation scales reasonably we compare execution times with a traditional Java compiler, javac, see Figure 10. We are using a subset of the Java class library, the *java.lang, java.util, java.io* packages, as our benchmarks. Roughly 100.000 lines of java source code from J2SE JDK 1.4.2 are compiled, and the ReRAG-based compiler uses both the optimizations mentioned above. The comparison is not completely fair because javac generates byte code whereas the ReRAG compiler only performs static-semantic analysis and then pretty-prints the program. However, generating byte code from an analyzed AST is very straight-forward and should be roughly comparable to pretty-printing. The comparison shows that the ReRAG-based compiler is only a few times slower than javac. Considering that the ReRAG-based compiler is generated from a declarative specification, we find this highly encouraging. This shows that ReRAGs are already useful for large-scale practical applications.

	total	JVM init	parsing	analysis and prettyprinting
ReRAG compiler	22801ms	600ms	7251ms	14950ms
javac	6112ms			

Fig. 10. Compile time for the *java.lang, java.util, java.io* packages using the ReRAG-based compiler and javac.

8 Related Work

Higher-ordered Attribute Grammars. ReRAGs are closely related to Higher-ordered Attribute Grammars (HAGs) [2], [3] where an attribute can be *higher-order*, in that it has the structure of an AST and can itself have attributes. Such an attribute is also called an *ATtributable Attribute* (ATA). Typically, there will be one equation defining the bare AST (without attributes) of the ATA, and other equations that define or use attributes of the ATA, and which depend on the evaluation of the ATA equation.

In ReRAGs each node in the AST is considered to be the root of a *rewritable attribute* of its parent node and may be rewritten to an alternative subtree during attribute evaluation. The rewriting is done conditionally, in place (replacing the original subtree during evaluation), and may be done in several steps, each described by an individual rewrite rule. This is contrast to the ATAs of HAGs which are constructed unconditionally, in one step, and where the evaluation does not change previously existing parts of the AST (the new tree is stored as a previously unevaluated attribute).

A major difference lies in the object-oriented basis of ReRAGs, where reference attributes are kept as explicit links in the tree and subtrees are rewritten in place. HAGs, in contrast, have a functional programming basis, viewing the AST as well as its attributes as structured values without identity. This is in our view less intuitive where, for instance, cross references in the AST have to be viewed as infinite values.

HAGs + Forwarding. Forwarding [4] is an attribute grammar technique used to forward attribute equations in one node to an equation in another node. This is transparent to other attribute equations and when combined with ATAs that use contextual information it allows later computations to be expressed on a more suitable model in a way similar to ReRAGs. To simulate a nested and multi-level rewrite there would, however, conceptually have to be a new tree for each step in the rewrite.

Visitors. The Visitor pattern is often used in compiler construction for separation of concerns when using object-oriented languages. Visitors can only separate crosscutting methods while the weaving technique used in JastAdd can be used for fields as well. This is superior to the Visitor pattern in that there is no need to rely on a generic delegation mechanism resulting in a cleaner more intuative implementation and also provide type-safe parameter passing during tree traversal. ReRAGs also differ in that traversal strategies need not be specified explicitly since they are implicitly defined by attribute dependences. The use of attributes provide better separation of concerns in that contextual information need not be included in the traversal pattern but can be declared separately.

Rewrite Systems. ReRAGs also have similarities to tree transformation systems like *Stratego* [5], *ASF+SDF* [6], and *TXL* [7] but improves data acquisition support through the use of RAGs instead of embedding contextual data in rewrite rules or as global variables. *Stratego* uses Dynamic Rewrite Rules [15] to separate contextual data acquisition from rewrite rules. A rule can be generated at run-time and include data from the context where it originates. That way contextual data is included in the rewrite rule and need not be propagated explicitly by rules in the grammar. ReRAGs provide an even cleaner separation of rewrite rule and contextual information by the use of RAGs that also are superior in modeling complex non-local dependences. The rewrite application order differs in that ReRAGs only support the described declarative approach while the other systems support user defined strategies. In *Stratego* and *ASF+SDF* the user can define explicit traversal strategies that control rewrite application order. Transformation rules in *TXL* are specified through a pattern to be matched and a replacement to substitute for it. The pattern to be matched may be guarded by conditional rules and the replacement may be a defined as a function of the matched pattern. A function used in a transformation rule may in turn be a composed from other functions. The rewrite application strategy in *TXL* is thus implicitly defined as part of the functional decomposition of the transformation ruleset, which controls how and in which order subrules are applied. Dora [16] supports attributes and rewrite rules that are defined using pattern matching to select tree nodes for attribute definitions, equation, and as rewrite targets. Attribute equations and rewrite results are defined through Lisp expressions. Composition rules are used to define how to combine and repeat rewrites and the order the tree is traversed. The approach is similar to ReRAGs in that attribute dependences are computed dynamically at run-time but there is no support for remote attributes and it is not clear how attributes read during rewriting are handled.

Dynamic reclassification of objects. Semantic specialization is similar to dynamic reclassification of objects, e.g. Wide Classes, Predicate Classes, FickleII, and Gilgul. All of these approaches except Gilgul differ from ReRAGs in that they may only specialize a single object compared to our rewritten sub-trees. *Wide Classes* [17] demonstrates the use of dynamic reclassification of objects to create a more suitable model for compiler computations. The run-time type of an object can be changed into a super- or a sub-type by explicitly passing a message to that object. That way, instance variables can be dynamically added to objects when needed by a specific compiler stage, e.g., code optimization. Their approach differs from ours in that it requires run-time system support and the reclassification is explicitly invoked and not statically type-safe. In *Predicate Classes* [18], an object is reclassified when a predicate is true, similar to our rewrite conditions. The reclassification is dynamic and lazy and thus similar to our demand-driven rewriting. The approach is, however, not statically type-safe. *FickleII* [19] has strong typing and puts restrictions on when an object may be reclassified to a super type by using specific state classes that may not be types of fields. This is similar to our restriction on rewriting nodes to supertypes as long as they are not used in the right hand side of a production rule as discussed in Section 4.2. The reclassification is, however, explicitly invoked compared to our declarative style. *Gilgul* [20] is an extension to Java that allows dynamic object replacement. A new type of classes, implementation-only classes, that can not be used as types are introduced. Implementation-only instance may not only be replaced by subclass instances but also by instances of any class that has the same least non implementation-only superclass. Object replacement in Gilgul is similar to our appraoch in that no support from the run-time system is needed. Gilgul uses an indirection scheme to be able to simultaneously update all object references through a single pointer re-assignment. The ReRAGs implementation uses a different approach and ensures that all references to the replaced object structure are recalculated dynamically on demand.

9 Conclusions and Future Work

We have introduced a technique for declarative rewriting of attributed ASTs, supporting conditional and context-dependent rewrites during attribution. The generation of a full Java static-semantic analyzer demonstrates the practical use of this technique. The grammar is highly modular, utilizing all three dimensions of separation of concerns: inheritance for separating the description of general from specific behavior of the language constructs (e.g., general declarations from specialized declarations like fields and methods); aspects for separating different computations from each other (e.g., type checking from name analysis); and rewriting for allowing the computations to be expressed on suitable forms of the tree. This results in a specification that is easy to understand and to extend. The technique has been implemented in a general system that generates compilers from a declarative specification. Attribute evaluation and tree transformation are performed automatically according to the specification.The running times are sufficiently low for practical use. For example, parsing, analyzing, and prettyprinting roughly 100.000 lines of Java code took approximately 23 seconds as compared to 6 seconds for the javac compiler on the same platform.

We have identified several typical ways of transforming an AST that are useful in practice: Semantic Specialization, Make Implicit Behavior Explicit, and Eliminate Shorthands. The use of these transformations has substantially simplified our Java implementation as compared to having to program this by hand, or having to use a plain RAG on the initial AST constructed by the parser.

Our work is related to many other transformational approaches, but differs in important ways, most notably by being declarative, yet based on an object-oriented AST model with explicit references beween different parts. This gives, in our opinion, a very natural and direct way to think about the program representation and to describe computations.

Many other transformational systems apply transformations in a predefined sequence, making the application of transformations imperative. In contrast, the ReRAG transformations are applied based on conditions that may read the current tree, resulting in a declarative specification.

There are many interesting ways to continue this research.

Optimization. The caching strategies currently used can probably be improved in a variety of ways, allowing more attributes to be cached, resulting in better performance.

Termination. Our current implementation does not deal with possible non-termination of rewriting rules (i.e., the possibility that the conditions never become false). In our experience, it can easily be seen (by a human) that the rules will terminate, so this is usually not a problem in practice. However, techniques for detecting possible non-termination, either statically from the grammar or dynamically, during evaluation, could be useful for debugging.

Circular ReRAGs. We plan to combine earlier work on Circular RAGs [21] with our work on ReRAGs. We hope this can be used for running various fixed-point computations on ReRAGs, with applications in static analysis.

Language extensions. Our current studies on generics indicate that the basic problems in GJ [22] can be solved using ReRAGs. Extending our Java 1.4 to handle new features in Java 1.5 like generics, autoboxing, static imports, and type safe enums is a natural next step. This will also further illustrate how language extensions can be modularized using ReRAGs.

Acknowledgements. We are grateful to John Boyland and to the other reviewers (anonymous) for their valuable feedback on the first draft of this paper.

References

1. Hedin, G.: Reference Attributed Grammars. Informatica (Slovenia) **24** (2000)
2. Vogt, H.H., Swierstra, S.D., Kuiper, M.F.: Higher order attribute grammars. In: Proceedings of the SIGPLAN '89 Programming language design and implementation, ACM Press (1989)
3. Saraiva, J.: Purely functional implementation of attribute grammars. PhD thesis, Utrecht University, The Netherlands (1999)
4. Van Wyk, E., Moor, O.d., Backhouse, K., Kwiatkowski, P.: Forwarding in attribute grammars for modular language design. In: Proceedings of Compiler Construction Conference 2002. Volume 2304 of LNCS., Springer-Verlag (2002) 128–142
5. Visser, E.: Stratego: A language for program transformation based on rewriting strategies. System description of Stratego 0.5. In: Proceedings of Rewriting Techniques and Applications (RTA'01). Volume 2051 of LNCS., Springer-Verlag (2001) 357–361
6. van den Brand et al., M.: The ASF+SDF Meta-Environment: a Component-Based Language Development Environment. In: Proceedings of Compiler Construction Conference 2001. Volume 2027 of LNCS., Springer-Verlag (2001)
7. Cordy, J.R.: Txl: A language for programming language tools and applications. In: Proceedings of the 4th Workshop on Language Descriptions, Tools, and Applications (LDTA'04) at ETAPS 2004. (2004)
8. Hedin, G., Magnusson, E.: JastAdd: an aspect-oriented compiler construction system. Science of Computer Programming **47** (2003) 37–58
9. Gosling, J., Joy, B., Steele, G., Bracha, G.: The Java Language Specification Second Edition. Addison-Wesley, Boston, Mass. (2000)
10. Kiczales, G., Hilsdale, E., Hugunin, J., Kersten, M., Palm, J., Griswold, W.G.: An overview of AspectJ. LNCS **2072** (2001) 327–355
11. Knuth, D.E.: Semantics of context-free languages. Mathematical Systems Theory **2** (1968) 127–145 Correction: *Mathematical Systems Theory* 5, 1, pp. 95-96 (March 1971).
12. Hedin, G.: An object-oriented notation for attribute grammars. In: the 3rd European Conference on Object-Oriented Programming (ECOOP'89). BCS Workshop Series, Cambridge University Press (1989) 329–345
13. Nilsson, A.: Compiling Java for Real-Time Systems. Licentiate thesis, Department of Computer Science, Lund Institute of Technology (2004) In preparation.
14. Lindholm, T., Yellin, F.: Java Virtual Machine Specification. Addison-Wesley Longman Publishing Co., Inc. (1999)
15. Visser, E.: Scoped dynamic rewrite rules. Electronic Notes in Theoretical Computer Science **59** (2001)
16. Boyland, J., Farnum, C., Graham, S.L.: Attributed transformational code generation for dynamic compilers. In Giegerich, R., Graham, S.L., eds.: Code Generation - Concepts, Tools, Techniques. Workshops in Computer Science. Springer-Verlag (1992) 227–254
17. Serrano, M.: Wide classes. In: Proceedings of ECOOP'99. Volume 1628 of LNCS., Springer-Verlag (1999) 391–415
18. Chambers, C.: Predicate classes. In: Proceedings of ECOOP'93. Volume 707 of LNCS., Springer-Verlag (1993) 268–296
19. Drossopoulou, S., Damiani, F., Dezani-Ciancaglini, M., Giannini, P.: More dynamic object reclassification: FickleII;. ACM Trans. Program. Lang. Syst. **24** (2002) 153–191

20. Costanza, P.: Dynamic object replacement and implementation-only classes. In: 6th International Workshop on Component-Oriented Programming (WCOP 2001) at ECOOP 2001. (2001)
21. Magnusson, E., Hedin, G.: Circular reference attributed grammars - their evaluation and applications. Electronic Notes in Theoretical Computer Science **82** (2003)
22. Bracha, G., Odersky, M., Stoutamire, D., Wadler, P.: Making the future safe for the past: Adding genericity to the Java programming language. In: Proceedings of Object Oriented Programming: Systems, Languages, and Applications (OOPSLA. (1998) 183–200

Finding and Removing Performance Bottlenecks in Large Systems

Glenn Ammons[1], Jong-Deok Choi[2], Manish Gupta[2], and Nikhil Swamy[3]

[1] IBM T. J. Watson Research Center,
Hawthorne, New York, USA,
ammons@us.ibm.com

[2] IBM T. J. Watson Research Center,
Yorktown Heights, New York, USA,
{jdchoi,mgupta}@us.ibm.com

[3] Department of Computer Science, University of Maryland,
College Park, Maryland, USA,
nswamy@cs.umd.edu

Abstract. Software systems obey the 80/20 rule: aggressively optimizing a vital few execution paths yields large speedups. However, finding the vital few paths can be difficult, especially for large systems like web applications. This paper describes a novel approach to finding bottlenecks in such systems, given (possibly very large) profiles of system executions. In the approach, for each kind of profile (for example, call-tree profiles), a tool developer implements a simple profile interface that exposes a small set of primitives for selecting summaries of profile measurements and querying how summaries overlap. Next, an analyst uses a search tool, which is written to the profile interface and thus independent of the kind of profile, to find bottlenecks. Our search tool (BOTTLENECKS) manages the bookkeeping of the search for bottlenecks and provides heuristics that automatically suggest likely bottlenecks. In one case study, after using BOTTLENECKS for half an hour, one of the authors found 14 bottlenecks in IBM's WebSphere Application Server. By optimizing some of these bottlenecks, we obtained a throughput improvement of 23% on the Trade3 benchmark. The optimizations include novel optimizations of J2EE and Java security, which exploit the high temporal and spatial redundancy of security checks.

1 Introduction

J. M. Juran's Pareto principle [19,16] (also known as the 80/20 rule) admonishes, "Concentrate on the vital few, not the trivial many". For software systems, the Pareto principle says that aggressively optimizing a few execution paths yields large speedups. The principle holds even for large systems like web applications, for which finding the "vital few" execution paths is especially difficult. Consequently, finding bottlenecks in such systems has been the focus of much previous work [27,22,1].

M. Odersky (Ed.): ECOOP 2004, LNCS 3086, pp. 170–194, 2004.

This paper describes a novel approach to finding bottlenecks, given (possibly extremely large) profiles of one or more executions of a system. In our approach, for each kind of profile (for example, call-tree profiles), one implements a simple interface that supports searching for bottlenecks. Next, an analyst uses a search tool, which is independent of the kind of profile, to find bottlenecks. The tool manages the bookkeeping of the search and provides heuristics that automatically suggest likely bottlenecks.

Our search tool is called BOTTLENECKS. In one case study, after using BOTTLENECKS for half an hour, one of the authors found 14 bottlenecks in IBM's WebSphere Application Server (WAS) [30]; optimizing six of these bottlenecks yielded a 23% improvement in throughput on the Trade3 benchmark [29]. Although the author was already familiar with several of these bottlenecks from spending many days inspecting call-tree and call-graph profiles without the aid of BOTTLENECKS, by using BOTTLENECKS, the author quickly verified the familiar bottlenecks and found new bottlenecks. Moreover, one of the new bottlenecks suggested a new optimization of Java 2 security.

```
Cost: 25% of total
Context:
  CCommandImpl.execute
  calls TCI.setOutputProperties
  calls AC.doPrivileged
  calls TCommandImpl$1.run
  calls Class.checkMemberAccess
  calls SM.checkMemberAccess
  calls SM.getClassContext
```

```
Cost: 13% of total
Context:
  EJSSecurityCllbrtr.preInvoke
  calls AC.doPrivileged
  calls EJSSecurityCollaborator$1.run
  calls CurrentImpl.get_credentials
  calls SM.checkPermission
  calls SM.checkPermission
  calls AC.checkPermission
  calls AC.getStackACC
```

Fig. 1. Two WAS bottlenecks, which we found with BOTTLENECKS. Each bottleneck summarizes execution-cost measurements by the calling context in which they were taken. Method and class names have been shortened to fit on a line.

Finding bottlenecks in large systems by hand is hard because of two related problems: choosing the best way to summarize execution-cost measurements, and keeping track of overlap among bottlenecks. The bottlenecks in Figure 1 illustrate the problems. These bottlenecks are real bottlenecks in WAS, which we found with BOTTLENECKS. Each bottleneck lists a sequence of calls, and summarizes execution-cost measurements taken in calling contexts that contain the sequence. In this example, execution-cost measurements record the instruction-count overhead of enabling security in WAS; for example, if the application executes one billion more instructions when security is enabled than it does when security is disabled, then the bottlenecks in the figure account for 250 million and 130 million of those instructions, respectively.

There are two reasons to summarize measurements: efficiency and understandability. For efficiency, profilers summarize measurements on-line, as the system runs. For example, flat profiles keep one summary per basic block, control-flow edge, or method; call-tree or calling-context-tree profiles [2] keep one summary per calling context; call-graph profiles keep one summary per call-graph edge; and Ball-Larus path profiles [4] keep one summary per intraprocedural, acyclic path.

Understandability of measurements is also crucial because human analysts cannot comprehend large numbers of measurements without summaries. In fact, profilers are usually distributed with report-generation tools that can reduce profiles to flat profiles, no matter how the profiler summarizes measurements internally.

The problem with summarization is that no summarization scheme suffices to find all bottlenecks. For example, neither a call-tree nor a call-graph profile is adequate for finding the bottlenecks in Figure 1. A call-tree profile is inadequate because both bottlenecks occur in many different calling contexts, and so in many different locations in the tree; a call-graph profile is inadequate because it has one summary for `doPrivileged`, while finding the bottlenecks requires a summary for `doPrivileged` when called by `setOutputProperties` and another summary for `doPrivileged` when called by `preInvoke`.

Two bottlenecks *overlap* if both summarize measurements of some common cost. Keeping track of overlap among bottlenecks is the second problem in finding bottlenecks.

For example, the bottlenecks in Figure 1 have no overlap with one another, because no execution-cost measurements occurred in a calling context that contained both the call sequence on the left and the call sequence on the right. On the other hand, both bottlenecks overlap with `doPrivileged`, because a calling context that contains either sequence in the figure also contains a call of `doPrivileged`.

Computing overlap manually is difficult in large profiles, but without computing overlap it is impossible to estimate the potential speedup of optimizing a set of bottlenecks. Because of overlap, while optimizing bottlenecks separately may yield performance improvements in each case, optimizing bottlenecks together might not yield the sum of their separate improvements.

Our method for finding bottlenecks addresses both the summarization problem and the overlap problem. In our method, a profile interface defines a small set of primitives that support constructing summaries of execution-cost measurements and computing the overlap of summaries. The interface associates summaries with execution paths (for example, call sequences), instead of summarizing according to a fixed summarization scheme like call-graphs or call-trees. Of course, any given profiler *will* use some fixed summarization scheme; however, the interface presents a flexible mechanism for automatic tools or human analysts to summarize further. And, because the interface makes overlap explicit, speedup can be estimated directly from any collection of summaries.

Because the profile interface can be implemented for any profile that associates execution-cost measurements with paths, it isolates analysis tools from details of the profiles. In fact, by including two implementations of the profile interface, BOTTLENECKS supports analyzing call-tree profiles in two very different ways.

The first implementation supports finding expensive call sequences by analyzing call-tree profiles. This implementation provides the full precision of the call-tree profile only where it is needed; where precision is not needed, measurements are summarized just as fully as they are in a flat profile, without losing the ability to estimate speedup.

The second implementation is comparative: it supports finding call sequences that are significantly more expensive in one call-tree profile than in another call-tree profile. For example, if a system is slower in one configuration than another, the cause can be found by comparing a profile of the slow configuration with a profile of the fast configuration.

No matter which implementation is in use, BOTTLENECKS presents the same user interface to the performance analyst. This interface manages the bookkeeping of the search and provides simple heuristics that automatically suggest likely bottlenecks.

Contributions. This paper makes the following contributions:

- A novel method for finding performance bottlenecks, given program execution profiles.
- Two instances of the method, both of which we have implemented within BOTTLENECKS. One instance supports finding expensive call sequences in call-tree profiles, while the second supports finding call sequences that are significantly more expensive in one call-tree profile than in another call-tree profile.
- A report on the bottlenecks we found with BOTTLENECKS and optimizations that remove them. Among the latter are novel optimizations that remove much of the overhead of enabling the security features of WAS. These optimizations exploit two properties: the same security checks are made several times in close succession (that is, they have high *temporal redundancy*) and the same checks are made repeatedly on the same code paths (that is, they have high *spatial redundancy*).

2 Finding Bottlenecks

We started the BOTTLENECKS project after a painful experience in analyzing large profiles of WAS with traditional tools. Based on that experience, and on the observations in Section 1, we had three goals for a better method:

Adequate power. The method must allow an analyst (human or machine) to vary how profiles are summarized and to account accurately for overlap among summaries.

Profile independence. The method must place as few requirements on input profiles as possible.

Extensibility. Because finding bottlenecks is not a well-understood problem, it must be easy to improve the method iteratively by inventing and validating new interfaces and algorithms to support the search for bottlenecks.

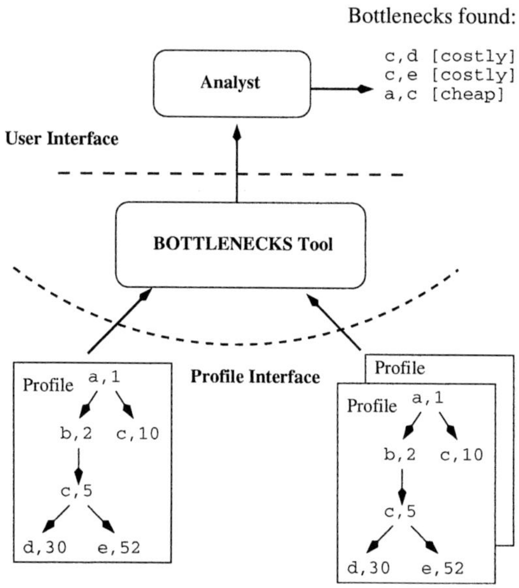

Fig. 2. The architecture of BOTTLENECKS.

Figure 2 is an overview of our BOTTLENECKS tool, which satisfies these goals. BOTTLENECKS has two parts: the *profile interface* and the *user interface*.

The profile interface defines an abstraction with adequate power for navigating and analyzing profiles. Specifically, the interface provides primitives for constructing various summaries (with associated execution paths) and for computing the overlap among summaries. The interface is profile independent, because these primitives can be implemented for any profile that associates a metric with paths; as the figure shows, BOTTLENECKS has one implementation for call-tree profiles and another for comparing two call-tree profiles.

The user interface is the abstraction that a human analyst sees. In its simplest usage mode, the user interface allows navigating a profile by inspecting summaries of longer and shorter execution paths. At this level, the tool helps the analyst by managing tedious bookkeeping such as remembering which summaries have been inspected. In addition, the user interface is designed to be extended with algorithms that suggest starting places for the analyst's search or that automate parts of the search.

The outline of the rest of this section is as follows. Section 2.1 discusses the profile interface. Section 2.2 explains how we implemented the interface for call-tree profiles and for comparing call-tree profiles. Finally, Section 2.3 describes the user interface and gives an example of its use.

2.1 The Profile Interface

The profile interface is a simple abstraction that supports constructing summaries and computing overlap among summaries. Specifically, the interface has functions to generate an initial set of summaries, given a profile; to query summaries; to construct new summaries from old summaries; and to compute overlap among summaries.

```
module type PROFILE_INTERFACE =
sig
  type t
  type profile_t
  val path_of : t -> string list
  val initial_summaries : profile_t -> t list   (* Construction. *)
  val top_extensions : t -> string list
  val bottom_extensions : t -> string list
  val extend_top : t -> string -> t
  val extend_bottom : t -> string -> t
  val trim_top : t -> t option
  val trim_bottom : t -> t option
  val base_of : t -> int64                      (* Metrics. *)
  val cum_of : t -> int64
  val total_base_of : t list -> int64
  val total_cum_of : t list -> int64
end
```

Fig. 3. The profile interface: a standard interface to profiles that associate a metric with paths.

Figure 3 lists Objective Caml [23] code for the profile interface. The type `t` is the type of summaries; the type `profile_t` is the type of the underlying profile. The code in the figure lists interface functions with their types but without their definitions—for example, the function `initial_summaries` accepts a profile as its sole argument and returns a list of summaries.

A central principle of the interface is that each summary corresponds to an execution path, which is simply a sequence that identifies a set of execution-cost measurements (for example, a call sequence). The function `path_of` returns a summary's execution path, which is assumed to be representable as a list of strings (for example, a list of method names).

The profile interface has seven functions for constructing summaries. Given a profile, the function `initial_summaries` returns a set of basic summaries, which, in a typical implementation, correspond to execution paths of length 1.

The other six functions enable constructing summaries that correspond to longer execution paths. These include functions to query the profile for the list of possible additions to the front or back of a summary's execution path (`top_extensions` and `bottom_extensions`), to create a new summary by adding a string at the front or back (`extend_top` and `extend_bottom`), and to create a new summary by trimming one string from the front or back (`trim_top` and `trim_bottom`).

The profile interface supports two metrics for each summary. We assume that the profile associates (implicitly or explicitly) a metric with each execution path. The function `base_of` returns this metric, which we call the *base* of a summary. Some profiles also have a concept of a cumulative metric; for example, the cumulative cost of a node in a call-tree profile is the cost of the node itself plus the cost of all its descendants. For such profiles, the function `cum_of` returns the cumulative metric of a summary's execution path, which we call the *cum* of the summary.

Finally, `total_base_of` and `total_cum_of` return the total base and cum of a list of summaries. The intent is that these functions should account for any overlap among the summaries: even if an execution-cost measurement belongs to more than one summary, it should be counted only once.

Other useful functions about overlap can be defined in terms of `total_base_of` and `total_cum_of`.[1] For example, this function returns the cum overlap of a summary s with a list of summaries S (in Objective Caml, the `::` operator conses a value onto the head of a list):

```
let cum_ol s S =
  (cum_of s) + (total_cum_of S) - (total_cum_of (s :: S))
```

The user interface of Bottlenecks assumes only that `base_of`, `cum_of`, `total_base_of`, and `total_cum_of` are implemented as functions of the right type. There are no other assumptions. In fact, comparative profiles violate many "common sense" assumptions (see Section 2.2): in comparative profiles, both base and cum may be negative and a summary's cum may be smaller than its base. Nonetheless, implementations should not return haphazard values; although Bottlenecks does not fix an interpretation of these metrics, a natural interpretation should exist. Section 2.2 explains what these functions compute in our implementations.

2.2 Implementations of the Profile Interface

This section describes two implementations of the profile interface: one for call-tree profiles and another for comparing two call-tree profiles.

[1] Even `cum_of` and `base_of` can be defined in terms of `total_base_of` and `total_cum_of`. For explanatory purposes, we give separate definitions.

Call-tree Profiles. To implement the profile interface for call-tree profiles, we must implement the types and functions in Figure 3. The following is a sketch of our implementation, which is both simple and fast enough to navigate call-tree profiles with over a million nodes.

The type `profile_t` is the type of call-tree profiles; a call-tree profile is a tree where

- each node is labeled with a method name and a cost; and
- for each calling context $m_0, \ldots, m_k$ that occurred during program execution, there is exactly one path $n_0, \ldots, n_k$ such that n_0 is the root of the tree and, for each $0 \leq i \leq k$, n_i is labeled with the method name m_i.

Intuitively, a node's cost summarizes all execution-cost measurements that occurred in the node's calling context. The profile that appears (twice) in Figure 2 is a call-tree profile.

Summaries consist of a call sequence and the list of all nodes that *root* the call sequence:

```
type t = { calls : string list ; roots : node list }
```

A node roots a call sequence iff the call sequence labels a path that begins at that node. For example, in Figure 2, the call sequence `[c]` has two roots: namely, the two nodes labeled `c`. By contrast, the only root of `[c;d]` is the left node labeled `c`.

The function `path_of` simply returns the `calls` component of a summary.

The function `initial_summaries` traverses the tree and creates a summary for each length-1 call sequence that occurs in the tree. For example, given the profile in Figure 2, `initial_summaries` creates five summaries: one each for `[a]`, `[b]`, `[c]`, `[d]`, and `[e]`.

Given a summary s, the function `top_extensions` returns all method names m such that m `::` `path_of(`s`)` labels at least one path in the tree; these names are easy to find by inspecting the parents of s`.roots`. For example, if s is the summary for `[c]` in Figure 2, then `top_extensions(`s`)` returns `a` and `b`.

Similarly, `bottom_extensions(`s`)` returns all method names m such that `path_of(`s`)` `@` `[`m`]` has at least one root (in Objective Caml, the `@` operator concatenates two lists); these names are easy to find by inspecting the children of all nodes reachable by following paths labeled s`.calls` from nodes in s`.roots`. For example, if s is the summary for `[c]` in Figure 2, then `bottom_extensions(`s`)` returns `d` and `e`.

Given a summary s and a top extender m of s, `extend_top` returns the summary s' for m `::` `path_of(`s`)`; s'`.roots` can be computed easily from s`.roots` and is never larger than s`.roots`. The definition of `extend_bottom` is similar.

We come now to the definitions of the base and cum metrics. For these, we need some auxiliary definitions (as usual, s is a summary):

paths(s). All paths labeled s`.calls` from nodes in s`.roots`.
along(s). All nodes that are along some path in paths(s).

interior(s)**.** All nodes that are along some path in paths(s) but *not* at the end of any such path.
final(s)**.** All nodes that are at the end of some path in paths(s).
descendants(s)**.** All nodes that are descendants of some node in final(s).

Note that our implementation does not necessarily compute these sets. In particular, descendants(s) can be the entire tree, so computing it for each summary is prohibitively expensive.

Given a summary s, the base of s is given by

$$\texttt{base\_of}(s) = \sum_{n \in \text{along}(s)} \text{cost of } n$$

For example, if s is the summary for `[c]` in Figure 2, then `base_of(`s`)` is 15.

The cum of s also includes the cost of all descendants of s:

$$\texttt{cum\_of}(s) = \sum_{n \in \text{along}(s) \cup \text{descendants}(s)} \text{cost of } n$$

For example, if s is the summary for `[c]` in Figure 2, then `cum_of(`s`)` is 97.

As mentioned above, computing descendants(s) is too expensive. Thus, when it loads a profile, our implementation precomputes a *cum-cost* for each node in the tree: the cum-cost of a node equals its cost plus the cost of its descendants. All cum-costs can be computed in one traversal of the tree. Given cum-costs, `cum_of(`s`)` can be implemented efficiently by evaluating this formula:

$$\sum_{\substack{n \in \text{interior}(s) \\ n \notin \text{descendants}(s)}} \text{cost of } n \quad + \sum_{\substack{n \in \text{final}(s) \\ n \notin \text{descendants}(s)}} \text{cum-cost of } n$$

This formula can be evaluated quickly because checking for membership of n in descendants(s) can be done in time proportional to the depth of n, by traversing tree edges backwards towards the root.

The reader may be asking why we exclude descendants of s from the sums in the last formula. The reason is that, in the presence of recursion, a node can be in interior(s) or final(s) and also have an ancestor in final(s). If such descendants were not excluded, the sums would count them twice.

To complete the implementation of the profile interface, we must implement `total_base_of` and `total_cum_of`. Intuitively, computing cum and base for a set of summaries S is the same as computing cum and base for a single summary, except that now all paths in S must be taken into account. So, we extend the auxiliary functions to functions over sets of summaries:

paths(S)**.** The union over all $s \in S$ of paths(s).
along(S)**.** All nodes that are along some path in paths(S).
interior(S)**.** All nodes that are along some path in paths(S) but *not* at the end of any such path.

final(S). All nodes that are at the end of some path in paths(S).
descendants(S). All nodes that are descendants of some node in final(S).

Then, the formulas for `total_base_of` and `total_cum_of` are the same as the formulas for `base_of` and `cum_of`, but with s replaced by S. For example, if S consists of the summary for `[a]` and the summary for `[c]` in Figure 2, then `total_base_of`(S) is 16 and `total_cum_of`(S) is 100.

Comparing Call-tree Profiles. It is sometimes useful to compare two profiles. For example, if a system is slower in one configuration than another, the cause can be found by comparing a profile in the slow configuration with a profile in the fast configuration—Section 3 discusses how we applied this technique to reduce the security overhead of WAS. This section describes an implementation of the profile interface that allows comparing two call-tree profiles.

Comparing two call-tree profiles requires deciding how to relate subtrees of the first profile to subtrees of the second profile. Our approach is based on the intuition that analysts are most interested in the cost of paths through programs. Thus, instead of (for example) explicitly constructing a map from subtrees of one profile to subtrees of the other profile, our implementation simply compares the cost of a call sequence in one profile with its cost in the other profile.

An advantage of this approach is that the comparative implementation can reuse most of the code of the implementation for single call-tree profiles. The type of summaries is a slight modification of the type of summaries for single call-tree profiles:

```
type t = { calls : string list ;
           a_roots : node list ; b_roots : node list }
```

Instead of one `roots` field, we now have an `a_roots` field that lists nodes in the first profile and a `b_roots` field that lists nodes in the second profile. Thus, a summary s denotes zero or more paths in one tree, and zero or more paths in a second tree.

The function `initial_summaries` traverses both trees and produces a list of paths of length 1, of the form

```
{ calls = [m] ; a_roots = a_ns ; b_roots = b_ns }
```

Here `a_ns` lists all roots of `[m]` in the first tree, while `b_ns` lists all roots of `[m]` in the second tree. At least one of these lists is not empty.

The other functions are defined in terms of the functions for a single call-tree profile. For example, if `Single.base_of` implements `base_of` for a single call-tree profile, then the comparative `base_of` is defined by

```
let base_of s =
  (Single.base_of ({ calls = s.calls ; roots = s.a_roots}))
  - (Single.base_of ({ calls = s.calls ; roots = s.b_roots}))
```

In general, functions that return numbers are implemented by subtracting the single-tree result for the second profile from the single-tree result for the first profile. Other functions combine the results in other natural ways. For example, `top_extensions` returns the union of the top extensions in the first and the second profile.

Due to the nature of comparing profiles, the comparative implementation lacks several "common sense" properties. For example, if a summary has a higher base in the second profile than it does in the first profile, then the summary has a *negative* base in the comparative profile. For similar reasons, the cum of a summary can be lower than its base. These paradoxes arise because of the nature of comparison; the best that an implementation can do is expose them, so that they can be dealt with at a higher level. In practice, we find that they are not problematic, at least when comparing trees that are more similar than they are different.

2.3 The User Interface

This section describes the user interface of BOTTLENECKS. This command-line interface provides three kinds of commands: *suggestion commands*, which request summaries at which to start a search for bottlenecks; a *navigation command*, which moves from one summary to another; and a *labeling command*, which assigns labels to summaries. Suggestion and navigation permit the human analyst to find summaries that explain bottlenecks well, without the limitations of fixed summarization schemes like call trees and call graphs; by design, they are also good points at which to introduce automation. The analyst uses labels to mark interesting summaries. Labels are also the mechanism for requesting overlap computations: during navigation, BOTTLENECKS prints the overlap of each summary with labeled summaries, so that the analyst can avoid investigating redundant summaries.

The rest of this section gives a simplified overview of the user interface and, as an example, demonstrates how to use BOTTLENECKS to uncover the bottleneck on the left side of Figure 1.

The analyst starts a search by picking a *suggester*:

<`set suggester` *name*>. Pick a suggester. A suggester generates an ordered list of starting summaries, based on the profile.

Next, the analyst views the suggestions:

<`suggest`>. Print the suggester's starting summaries.

In the future, as we discover better techniques for finding bottlenecks automatically, we will implement them as suggesters. At the moment, BOTTLENECKS has two simple suggesters:

HighCum. The HighCum suggester suggests summaries for paths of length 1 (that is, individual methods), with summaries ranked in descending order by their cum. These summaries are good starting points for a top-down search.

HighBase. The HighBase suggester also suggests summaries for paths of length 1, but with summaries ranked in descending order by their base. These summaries are good starting points for a bottom-up search.

BOTTLENECKS gives a number to every summary it prints. The analyst navigates from summary to summary by selecting them by number:

`<select n>`. Select the summary numbered n. The summary (call it s) becomes the *current summary*. BOTTLENECKS prints details about s:
- If s has been labeled, the labels of s.
- The cum and base metrics of s.
- For each unique label l that the analyst has assigned to one or more summaries, the overlap of s's cum and base metrics with summaries labeled l.
- The execution path associated with s.
- A numbered list of "nearby" summaries, which can be reached by applying summary construction functions (see Figure 3).

Generating the list of nearby summaries is another point at which the user interface can be extended with heuristics. BOTTLENECKS has two algorithms for producing this list. The first algorithm simply prints all 1-method extensions and trimmings of the current summary.

The second algorithm, called *zooming*, omits low-cost extensions and trimmings and greedily "zooms" through extensions and trimmings that concentrate the cost. The goal is to avoid printing uninteresting summaries: low-cost summaries are uninteresting because the user is unlikely to choose them, while summaries that concentrate the cost are uninteresting because the user is almost certain to choose them. In practice, zooming significantly reduces the time it takes to find useful bottlenecks.

Zooming depends on a user-settable cutoff ratio c, which is a positive real number (the default is 0.95). Zooming uses c both to identify low-cost summaries and to identify summaries that concentrate the cost. The following pseudocode shows how zooming finds nearby top extensions (bottom extensions and trimmings are similar):

```
Routine Zoom(s,c) = ZoomRec(s,c|cum_of(s)|)
Routine ZoomRec(s,C) =
  T  := top extensions of s, in descending order by |cum_of|
  Tz := first N summaries in T, where N > 0 is smallest s.t
          |total_cum_of(Tz)| ≥ C, or ∅ if no such N exists
  If |Tz| = 1 Then Return ZoomRec(first(Tz), C)
  Else Return Tz
```

Sorting T_z by the absolute value of `cum_of` [2] identifies low-cost summaries. The conditional tests for summaries that concentrate the cost: if the cost of a summary is at least C, then the user will almost certainly select it, so the algorithm zooms through it.

[2] Taking the absolute value is necessary for comparative profiles, in which a summary's cum can be negative.

For example, suppose that the current summary is for [cd] in Figure 2. If zooming were enabled, BOTTLENECKS would zoom to the 2-method top extension [abcd] instead of listing the 1-method top extension [bcd].

Finally, BOTTLENECKS provides a labeling command, which the analyst uses to mark interesting summaries:

<label *name*>. Assign the label *name* to the current summary.

Once labeled, a summary can be inspected later or saved to a file. More importantly, as the analyst searches for bottlenecks, BOTTLENECKS displays the overlap of the current summary with labeled summaries. Accounting for overlap is key to estimating the expected benefit of optimizing a particular bottleneck; therefore, after the first bottleneck has been found, the analyst must take overlap into account when selecting the next summary.

Note that BOTTLENECKS does not interpret labels; labels have meaning for the analyst, not for BOTTLENECKS.

An Example. Like other application servers, WAS is slower when its security features are enabled. To find the cause of this slowdown, we ran the Trade3 application server benchmark twice, the first time with security enabled and the second time with security disabled, and compared them with BOTTLENECKS, using the comparative implementation of the profile interface. Figure 1 lists two of the bottlenecks that we found. This section works through a session in which we find the bottleneck on the left side of the figure, using BOTTLENECKS and a bottom-up approach.

The first steps are to choose an appropriate suggester and list the highly ranked suggestions. The HighBase suggester is better for a bottom-up search:

```
set suggester HighBase
suggest
```

BOTTLENECKS prints the summaries with highest base. The highest-ranked summary is for the call sequence

[SM.getClassContext]

which has a base that accounts for 9.85% of the total security overhead—that is, 9.85% of the difference between the cost when security is enabled and the cost when security is disabled. As it happens, this method is never called when security is disabled. We look at this summary more closely:

```
select 0
```

This sets [SM.getClassContext] as the current summary (call it s). BOTTLENECKS prints s, the base and cum of s, and s's top and bottom extensions (with a number assigned to each one). In this case, there are no bottom extensions, and the top extension

[SM.checkMemberAccess ; SM.getClassContext]

(call this s') has a much higher cum than the other choices. This is extension number 0, and we look at it more closely:

```
select 0
```

This sets s' as the current summary and BOTTLENECKS prints s' and its metrics and extensions; the length of s' is greater than 1, so BOTTLENECKS also prints the summaries that result from trimming the top or bottom method of s' (the former is s again).

The next step is to extend s' at the top. In general, we repeatedly extend the current summary by choosing the extension with the highest cum. This process continues until all potential extensions have a low cum, or until there are many possible extensions, no one of which contributes substantially to the overhead. Note that, if we were using zooming, this process would be mostly automatic.

In this case, we continue extending at the top until we reach the summary on the left side of Figure 1. At this point, there are many top extensions (for various Trade3 commands) and none of them contribute substantially to the overhead. This summary contributes 25% of the total overhead, which is significant, so we decide that it is a bottleneck and label it:

```
label ''bottleneck''
```

3 Experience

This section presents our experience with BOTTLENECKS. Section 3.1 discusses bottlenecks we found in the implementation of the security model in IBM's WebSphere Application Server (WAS) and novel optimizations that target those bottlenecks. In Section 3.2, we evaluate how helpful BOTTLENECKS is for finding bottlenecks in two other object-oriented applications: the SPECjAppServer2002 [28] application server benchmark [3] and a program under development at IBM that is related to the optimization of XML.

3.1 Speeding up WAS Security

WAS implements J2EE, which is a collection of Java interfaces and classes for business applications. Most importantly, J2EE implementations provide a *container* that hosts Enterprise JavaBeans (EJBs). In J2EE, applications are constructed from EJBs; the container is like an operating system for EJBs, providing services such as database access and messaging, as well as managing resources like threads and memory.

Among these services is security. Security is optional: containers like WAS can be configured to bypass security checks. Enabling security entails some overhead.

[3] SPEC and the benchmark name SPECjAppServer2002 are registered trademarks of the Standard Performance Evaluation Corporation. In accord with the SPEC/OSG Fair Use Policy, this paper does not make competitive comparisons or report SPECjAppServer metrics. For more information, see http://www.spec.org.

For example, in our experiments, turning on full security reduced the throughput of IBM's Trade3 [29] benchmark by 30%.

To find the causes of this slowdown, we collected call-tree profiles of Trade3, running with security enabled and with security disabled, and compared the profiles with BOTTLENECKS, using the comparative implementation of the profile interface. The result was fourteen bottlenecks, which accounted for over 80% of the overhead of enabling security.

The rest of this section discusses four topics: what we mean by "WAS security" in this paper, our experimental setup, the bottlenecks we found in WAS security, and finally optimizations that target those bottlenecks.

Security in WAS. For our purposes here and at a high level, WAS supports two kinds of security:

Java 2 security. Java 2 security is the security model supported by Java 2, Standard Edition (J2SE) [15]. In this model, an application developer or system administrator associates permissions with Java code: that is, the model supports framing and answering questions of the form, "may this code access that resource?". For example, an administrator can use Java 2 security to prevent applets from accessing the local filesystem.

Global security. Global security is the security model supported by Java 2, Enterprise Edition (J2EE) [14], with extensions specific to WAS. Along with user authentication, the model supports framing and answering questions of the form, "may this user invoke that code?" A system administrator associates *roles* both with methods and with users: a user may invoke a method only if a role exists that is associated with both the user and with the method.

Experimental Setup. To measure WAS security overhead, we needed an application that uses security. We used IBM's Trade3 benchmark, which is a client-server application developed specifically to measure the performance of many features of WAS. Trade3 models an on-line stock brokerage, providing services such as login and logout, stock quotes, stock trades, and account details.

The standard version of Trade3 does not use WAS security, so we used a "secured" version, which defines one role that protects all bean methods. We assigned that role to two users and used one of those users to access the application; the other user was the WAS administrator.

Trade3 is a small application, with only 192 classes and 2568 methods. By comparison, WAS contains 23270 classes and 246903 methods. Still, Trade3 revealed significant security bottlenecks in WAS.

We analyzed the performance of Trade3 when hosted by version 5.0.0 of IBM's WAS implementation. We ran the benchmark on a single desktop computer, which had 1.5GB of RAM and a single 2.4GHz Intel Pentium 4 processor. The operating system was Red Hat Linux 7.3 [25], and the database system used was version 7.2 of IBM's DB2 [9]. The secured Trade3 also requires an LDAP server: we used version 4.1 of IBM's Directory Server [18].

Table 1. Characteristics of Trade3 ArcFlow profiles. **Nodes** lists the number of tree and leaf nodes in each call-tree profile; **Depth** lists the maximum and average (arithmetic mean) depth of tree nodes; **Out-degree** lists the maximum and average out-degree of interior nodes.

Security	Nodes		Depth		Out-degree	
	Total	Leaf	Max	Mean	Max	Mean
Disabled	413637	189386	135	59.9	69	1.84
Enabled	480994	230248	135	64.6	109	1.92

Table 2. Trade3 bottlenecks, and the time and number of BOTTLENECKS commands needed to find them. Time includes the user's "think" time.

Bottlenecks			Cost to find	
Number	Coverage	Mean length	Minutes	Commands
14	82.7%	14	32.4	151

To collect call-tree profiles, we used IBM's ArcFlow profiler [3]. ArcFlow builds a call-tree on-line by intercepting method entries and exits. ArcFlow can collect various metrics: we chose to collect executed instructions (as measured by the Pentium 4 performance counters) because ArcFlow can accurately account for its own perturbation of this metric. Time would have been a better metric, but all profilers available to us either perturb this metric too much or collect only flat profiles.

Bottlenecks in WAS Security. Using ArcFlow, we collected two call-tree profiles of Trade3: one from a run with WAS security enabled and one from a run with WAS security disabled. Both runs were otherwise as identical as we could make them (for example, both runs performed the same number of transactions). Then, one of the authors used BOTTLENECKS to find paths with high security overhead.

Table 1 lists some characteristics of the call-tree profiles. The profiles are bushy and deep: in both cases, roughly half of the nodes are leaf nodes and the average depth of a node is around 60. Thus, these profiles are not human-readable; an analyst would need a tool to make sense of them.

Table 2 shows how effective the author was at finding bottlenecks in these profiles with BOTTLENECKS. The author is, of course, an expert at using BOTTLENECKS. The author was also familiar with some of the bottlenecks in Trade3, because he had found them earlier without the aid of BOTTLENECKS.

BOTTLENECKS worked well on Trade3. Over 80% of the security overhead of Trade3 is covered by just fourteen bottlenecks. Also, these bottlenecks are useful: by optimizing six of them, we obtained a 23% improvement in throughput with security enabled.

Table 3. Optimizations suggested by Trade3 bottlenecks.

Optimization	Kind	Lines	Est. Impr.	Comment
CheckRole	temporal	216	0.07	Remove redundant role checks on bean method access. Applied to WAS.
DBReuse	temporal	343	0.04	Remove redundant comparisons and hashes for database connections. Applied to WAS.
GetCredentials	spatial	114	0.06	Remove doPrivileged and checkPermission on a hot path. Applied to WAS.
Reflection	spatial	157	0.11	Replace field access via reflection with direct access. Applied to Trade3.

In addition, the author found the bottlenecks quickly. By contrast, before BOTTLENECKS existed, it took the author over a week to find fewer and less specific bottlenecks by studying call-graph profiles and source code.

Security Optimizations. This section describes four optimizations inspired by the bottlenecks that we found in the Trade3 profiles. Together, these optimizations speed up Trade3 by 23% when security is enabled. Three of these optimizations were applied to WAS and apply directly to other WAS applications. In addition, all four optimizations exploit two general properties of Java security, and we believe that similar optimizations could be applied in other applications, or perhaps automatically in a just-in-time compiler.

Both properties have to do with the high redundancy of security checks. We distinguish two kinds of redundancy. A security check exhibits high *temporal redundancy* if the check makes the same decision based on the same data several times in close succession (for example, a check that repeatedly tests if the same user may invoke bean methods that are protected by the same role). A security check exhibits high *spatial redundancy* if the check frequently makes the same decision because it is reached by the same code path (for example, a `checkPermission` that is executed repeatedly in the same calling context).

Optimizations that exploit temporal redundancy are based on caching. The results of an expensive check are stored in a cache, which is indexed by the data that form the basis of the decision. The cache is consulted before making the check: if the decision is in the cache, the check is avoided. Note that caching is effective only when cache hits are sufficiently frequent and the cost of cache lookups and maintenance is sufficiently cheap.

Optimizations that exploit spatial redundancy are based on specialization. The frequent code path is copied, and the expensive check is replaced with a cheaper version tailored specifically to that path. Specialization is effective only when the benefit of the tailored check outweighs the cost of duplicating code.

Table 3 summarizes our optimizations. The CheckRole and DBReuse optimizations exploit temporal redundancy, while the GetCredentials and Reflection optimizations exploit spatial redundancy. The ease of implementing these optimizations varied: Reflection took less than an hour, DBReuse and GetCredentials less than a day. The CheckRole optimization took a few days, because we wrote three versions before finding a fast cache implementation. In general, the temporal optimizations were harder to implement than the spatial optimizations, because the temporal optimizations required implementing a cache. For the spatial optimizations, most of the lines we changed were merely copied from one place to another.

For each optimization, we estimated the potential improvement in throughput by comparing the overhead of the bottleneck(s) that the optimization exploited to the total security overhead. The estimates in Table 3 assume that all of the bottleneck's overhead can be eliminated, and that the instruction counts reported by ArcFlow correlate well with execution time. In fact, optimizations cannot normally eliminate all overhead, and ArcFlow misses the overhead of I/O. Thus, these estimates are overestimates; see below for the actual improvements in throughput.

Detailed descriptions of our optimizations follow.

CheckRole. The J2EE security model allows an administrator to associate roles with methods and with users. When global security is enabled, WAS inserts an access check before each bean method call. If there is a role that is associated with both the current user and with the method, then the call is allowed; otherwise, it is forbidden.

Our analysis found that role-checking is a bottleneck that accounts for 16% of the instruction-count overhead of security when running Trade3. By instrumenting the code, we discovered that these checks have high temporal redundancy, which we exploited by caching. Here is pseudocode for role-checking:

```
Routine CheckRole(User u, Method m) =
  Return UserRoles(u) ∩ MethodRoles(m) ≠ ∅
```

Our optimization introduces a *decision cache* (DC):

```
Routine CachingCheckRole(User u, Method m) =
  If DC.lookup(u, m) Then Return true
  ElseIf CheckRole(u, m) Then (DC.add(u, m) ; Return true)
  Else Return false
```

The decision cache is indexed by the user and by a set of roles. For fast lookups, we modified the WAS code to ensure a correspondence between users and objects representing users; there was already a correspondence between methods and objects representing methods. With this implementation, the cache can check equality simply by comparing references.

To further speed lookups, the decision cache is hierarchical. The cache contains a hash table that maps methods (which vary more frequently than do users) to 4-element arrays. Given a user and a method, a lookup starts by finding the 4-element array for the method; if the array exists, then the lookup scans it for a match with the user. The alternative of composing the user and method into a hash table key is significantly more expensive.

The CheckRole optimization is effective only when role checks have high temporal redundancy. Temporal redundancy is high for Trade3 because there is only one user and one role, so checks necessarily repeat. However, even if multiple users were configured, temporal redundancy in Trade3 should remain high, because each page request corresponds to seven bean method calls. We do not know if such behavior is common among J2EE applications: the more common it is, the more widely applicable is the CheckRole optimization.

DBReuse. Because creating a database connection is expensive, WAS reuses them: when a transaction starts, WAS assigns it a connection from a pool of available connections; when a transaction completes, its connection is returned to the pool so that it can be used again.

In J2EE, a Subject represents information about a user or other entity. When security is enabled, WAS associates a Subject with each database connection. This association complicates connection pooling, because WAS must ensure that a database connection that is opened on behalf of one user is never used on behalf of a different user. Our analysis found that the security checks necessary to provide this guarantee comprise three bottlenecks, which account for about 10% of the instruction-count overhead of security when running Trade3.

Once again, we used caching to remove this overhead. Most of the overhead of the check was related to checking equality of Subjects and computing hash codes for Subjects. These operations are expensive because Subjects contain private credentials, which cannot be read without first passing a permission check. Our caches avoid this expense by remembering the results of equality checks and hash code computations.

GetCredentials. Like DBReuse, this optimization speeds up an operation that depends on reading private credentials. However, while DBReuse is a temporal optimization, this optimization is spatial. The optimization is an instance of a general technique for removing Java 2 permission checks.

Permission checking in Java 2 security is complicated, but we can suppose that it provides two primitives: `checkPermission` and `doPrivileged`.

The `checkPermission` method receives a permission object as its only argument, and walks the call-stack to verify that the code has the permission represented by the object. Intuitively, on a call of `checkPermission`, the Java runtime visits each call on the call-stack, visiting each callee before its caller. At each call, the runtime consults a table (prepared by the administrator) to decide whether the invoked method has the permission or not. If the runtime finds a method that does not have the permission, it raises an exception.

A `doPrivileged` call is used to cut off the stack walk. If, while walking the stack, the runtime finds a `doPrivileged` call, it stops the walk. Thus, the walk's outcome cannot depend on the calling context of the `doPrivileged`.

Our optimization exploits this property. The following pseudocode illustrates the optimization, as we applied it to the bottleneck on the right side of Figure 1, which accounts for 13% of the instruction-count overhead of security when running Trade3:

```
Class PrivilegedClass
  Routine Invoker = doPrivileged ...GetCredentials()...
Class CheckingClass
  Routine GetCredentials() =
    checkPermission(constant) ; Return the secret credentials
```

We can optimize this code as follows:

```
Class CallingClass
  private Object secret
  private bool succeeded := false
  Routine checkSecret(Object o) = Return secret = o
  Routine Invoker =
    If succeeded Then creds := GetCredentials(secret)
    Else doPrivileged
           creds := GetCredentials()
           succeeded := true
Class CheckingClass
  private bool succeeded := false
  Routine GetCredentials(Object o) =
    If ¬ CallingClass.checkSecret(o) Then
      checkPermission(constant)
    ElseIf ¬ succeeded Then
      checkPermission(some constant)
      succeeded := true
    Return the secret credentials
```

The optimized code performs a full security check just once; if the check succeeds (the common case), then any further calls perform a fast security check. The fast check uses a secret object, known only to `CallingClass`, to verify that the caller is `CallingClass.Invoker`. Because the secret is private to `CallingClass` and escapes only to `GetCredentials`, it cannot be forged. So, if attacking code calls `GetCredentials`, its permissions will be checked in the normal, safe way.

There is a caveat: once the permission checked by `GetCredentials` is granted to `CallingClass.Invoker`, it must never be revoked. In this instance, the caveat is not problematic—if the code in question did not have the permission, then WAS would not work.

There are other ways to implement this optimization safely. First, the runtime could detect such redundant security checks and rewrite the compiled code (as we rewrote the source code) to avoid them. This solution would require no source changes at all and would automatically optimize away other occurences of the pattern. Second, one could add a module system to Java (such as MJ [8]), which would allow a programmer to say statically that `GetCredentials` may only be called by `Invoker`. Finally, instead of passing the secret as a parameter of `GetCredentials`, the secret could be stored in a thread-local variable. This last approach avoids changing the signature of `GetCredentials` but is slow on many JVMs, for which accessing thread-local storage is expensive.

Table 4. Performance benefit of the optimizations.

Optimization	Throughput (pages/s) Insecure	Secure	Improvement Insecure	Secure	Security Overhead
Original	101.1 ± 0.3	71.4 ± 0.2	0.00	0.00	29%
CheckRole	98.7 ± 0.4	74.1 ± 0.2	−0.02	0.04	25%
DBReuse	101.7 ± 0.3	72.3 ± 0.2	0.01	0.01	29%
GetCredentials	100.1 ± 0.3	71.1 ± 0.2	−0.01	0.00	29%
Reflection	102.8 ± 0.2	74.1 ± 0.3	0.02	0.04	28%
All	103.4 ± 0.3	88.1 ± 0.1	0.02	0.23	15%

Reflection. Java's reflection API allows programs to ask the runtime for the methods, fields, and other attributes of classes. Reflection is inherently expensive, and code that must be fast should avoid using it. Reflection is especially expensive when security is enabled, because the runtime must check that code that requests attributes of a class has appropriate permissions.

Our analysis found that Trade3 uses reflection unnecessarily on the code path on the left side of Figure 1, which accounts for 25% of the instruction-count overhead of security when running Trade3.

Benefits of Security Optimizations. Table 4 shows the performance of the original WAS and Trade3 code and the performance benefit of each optimization in isolation, all safe optimizations together (that is, all optimizations except GetCredentials), and all optimizations together. For each optimization, we rebuilt the Trade3 system from scratch and measured performance with security enabled and with security disabled. To obtain a measurement, we warmed up the system by requesting 50000 pages, and then measured the time for Trade3 to satisfy 20000 page requests, repeating the latter measurement ten times. The **Throughput** columns of the table report the mean and probable error (that is, 50% confidence interval) of these measurements, assuming a normal distribution. The **Improvement** columns report the mean improvement in throughput with respect to the unoptimized code. Finally, the **Overhead** column reports the overhead of enabling security after applying each optimization.

Overall, we obtained a 23% improvement in throughput (with security enabled) with all optimizations.

The performance benefit of all optimizations together exceeds the benefit of the optimizations separately. This is a reproducible effect, which we are not sure how to explain.

In general, the optimizations achieve a little more than half of the estimated improvement of Table 3. This indicates that the ArcFlow profiles, which measure executed instructions instead of time, miss some security overhead. Unfortunately, we are unaware of any profiling tools for Java that combine context-sensitivity (crucial for finding these bottlenecks) with sufficiently accurate measurements of execution time.

Table 5. Characteristics of ArcFlow profiles. **Nodes** lists the number of tree and leaf nodes in each call-tree profile; **Depth** lists the maximum and average (arithmetic mean) depth of tree nodes; **Out-degree** lists the maximum and average out-degree of interior nodes.

Application	Nodes		Depth		Out-degree	
	Total	Leaf	Max	Mean	Max	Mean
SPECjAppServer2002	1096416	516173	77	34.2	74	1.89
XML	24321	11107	86	21.9	62	1.84

3.2 Other Applications of BOTTLENECKS

This section evaluates the effectiveness of BOTTLENECKS on two more applications:

SPECjAppServer2002. SPECjAppServer2002 is a client-server application developed specifically to measure and compare the performance of J2EE application servers. At runtime, SPECjAppServer2002 consists of an application server, the EJBs that are hosted by the application server, a database system, and a driver and supplier emulator. The SPEC reporting rules require that the emulator run on a different machine than the other components, but, in our tests, we ran all components on the single computer described above.

XML. This is an internal IBM program, written in Java, and related to the optimization of XML. For this application, we had an ArcFlow profile from the developers but neither an executable nor the source code. Thus, this application represents an extreme case of performance analysis with very little information.

We used BOTTLENECKS to analyze ArcFlow profiles of both applications. We collected the SPECjAppServer2002 profile ourselves; the XML profile for XML was given to us by one of its developers.

Table 5 lists some characteristics of these profiles. The SPECjAppServer2002 profile was large, with over one million nodes, while the XML profile was relatively small. Both profiles are bushy and deep: in both cases, roughly half of the nodes are leaf nodes and the average depth of a node is 34.2 (SPECjAppServer2002) and 21.9 (XML). As was the case for the Trade3 profiles, these profiles are not human-readable.

Table 6 shows how effective one of the authors was at finding bottlenecks in these profiles with our tool. Once again, the author is an expert at using BOTTLENECKS, although he was not familiar a priori with the bottlenecks in SPECjAppServer2002 and XML.

BOTTLENECKS worked well on XML. The author quickly found thirteen bottlenecks that cover almost 90% of the executed instructions of XML. Also, these bottlenecks are useful: we reported them to one of the XML developers, who told us that they accurately identified the expensive paths in that application.

Table 6. Bottlenecks found for each application, and the time and number of BOTTLENECKS commands needed to find them. Time includes the user's "think" time.

Application	Bottlenecks			Cost to find	
	Number	Coverage	Mean length	Minutes	Commands
SPECjAppServer2002	13	35.8%	8.7	50	251
XML	13	88.7%	6.2	29.5	143

BOTTLENECKS was less effective on the SPECjAppServer2002 profile. The author quit analyzing the profile after about an hour: at this point, he had found thirteen bottlenecks that accounted for only 36% of the executed instructions. These bottlenecks were also less useful, primarily because the ArcFlow profile measures only executed instructions. By using a sampling-based profiler that measures time accurately but ignores calling context, the author found that SPECjAppServer2002 is I/O-bound, not compute-bound. Because ArcFlow does not measure execution time spent waiting on I/O, it is unlikely that optimizing the bottlenecks we found would significantly improve execution time.

4 Related Work

Our profile interface can be implemented for any profile that associates metrics with execution paths. A number of tools produce profiles that satisfy this assumption. Program tracers like QPT [7] record the control flow of an entire execution. Ball-Larus path profilers [4] record intraprocedural, acyclic control-flow paths. Interprocedural path profiles [21] generalize Ball-Larus path profiles. Whole program path profilers [17] record an execution trace in a compact, analyzable form. Calling-context trees [2] are space-efficient cousins of the call-tree profiles we use in this paper. ArcFlow [3], which we used for the experiments in this paper, constructs call-tree profiles on-line by intercepting method entries and exits. Stack sampling [12,13] is an alternative, lower overhead method. Finally, Ball, Mataga and Sagiv show that intraprocedural paths can be deduced, with significant accuracy, from edge profiles [6].

Many other tools exist for analyzing profiles. The closest to BOTTLENECKS is Hall's call-path refinement profiling [12,13]. The summary construction functions in Figure 3 are essentially special cases of Hall's call-path-refinement profiles, and Hall also describes a tool for navigating call sequences. However, our work differs from Hall in several ways. First, while our profile interface can be implemented for any profile that associates metrics with execution paths, Hall assumes a specific stack-sampling profiler. Second, Hall addresses the issue of overlap differently, by extending the user interface with the ability to prune away time spent either in or not-in given call paths. Finally, Hall's tools do not support comparing profiles.

Another closely related analysis tool is the Hot Path Browser [5] (HPB), a visualizer for Ball-Larus path profiles. HPB graphically shows overlap among intraprocedural Ball-Larus paths and allows the user to combine profiles by taking their union, intersection, and difference.

Fields and others [11] use *interaction cost* to find microarchitectural bottlenecks, while we use overlap to find bottlenecks in large applications. Overlap and interaction cost our closely related—in fact, they are arithmetic inverses of one another. In their work, interaction cost was important because processors perform tasks in parallel. In our work, overlap was important because the same execution-cost occurs in the context of many different call-sequences.

BOTTLENECKS assumes that profiles are not flat and can be analyzed off-line. For efficiency, performance analysis tools for large-scale parallel systems often violate one or both of these assumptions. For example, Paradyn [22] avoids collecting large amounts of data by interleaving measurement with interactive and automatic bottlenecks analysis. Paradyn's search strategy is top-down, although their DeepStart stack-sampling heuristic [26] can suggest starting points that are deep in the call-tree. Other tools for parallel systems, such as HPCView [20] and SvPablo [10], gather only flat profiles. Insofar as these compromises are necessary for analyzing parallel systems, they pose an obstacle to applying tools like BOTTLENECKS to such systems.

Our security optimizations that exploit temporal redundancy rely on identifying checks that repeatedly operate on the same data. When we suspected temporal redundancy, we verified it by instrumenting the code. Object equality profiling [24] might have discovered these opportunities more directly.

References

[1] Marcos K. Aguilera, Jeffrey C. Mogul, Janet L. Wiener, Patrick Reynolds, and Athicha Muthitacharoen. Performance debugging for distributed systems of black boxes. In *Proceedings of the Nineteenth ACM Symposium on Operating Systems Principles*, pages 74–89. ACM Press, 2003.

[2] Glenn Ammons, Thomas Ball, and James R. Larus. Exploiting hardware performance counters with flow and context sensitive profiling. In *Proceedings of the ACM SIGPLAN 1997 Conference on Programming Language Design and Implementation*, pages 85–96. ACM Press, 1997.

[3] Real-time ArcFlow. `http://www.ibm.com/developerworks/oss/pi`.

[4] Thomas Ball and James R. Larus. Efficient path profiling. In *Proceedings of the 29th Annual ACM/IEEE International Symposium on Microarchitecture*, pages 46–57. IEEE Computer Society, 1996.

[5] Thomas Ball, James R. Larus, and Genevieve Rosay. Analyzing path profiles with the Hot Path Browser. In *Workshop on Profile and Feedback-Directed Compilation*, 1998.

[6] Thomas Ball, Peter Mataga, and Shmuel Sagiv. Edge profiling versus path profiling: The showdown. In *Symposium on Principles of Programming Languages*, pages 134–148, 1998.

[7] Tom Ball and James R. Larus. Optimally profiling and tracing programs. *ACM Transactions on Programming Languages and Systems*, 16(3):1319–1360, July 1994.

[8] John Corwin, David F. Bacon, David Grove, and Chet Murthy. MJ: A rational module system for Java and its applications. In *Proceedings of the 18th ACM SIGPLAN Conference on Object-oriented Programming, Systems, Languages, and Applications*, pages 241–254. ACM Press, 2003.
[9] IBM DB2 Universal Database. `http://www.ibm.com/db2`.
[10] Luiz DeRose and Daniel A. Reed. SvPablo: A multi-language architecture-independent performance analysis system. In *Proceedings of the International Conference on Parallel Processing (ICPP'99)*, September 1999.
[11] Brian A. Fields, Rastislav Bodík, Mark D. Hill, and Chris J. Newburn. Using interaction costs for microarchitectural bottleneck analysis. In *Proceedings of the 36th Annual IEEE/ACM International Symposium on Microarchitecture (MICRO-36)*, pages 228–242, December 2003.
[12] Robert J. Hall. Call path refinement profiles. *IEEE Transactions on Software Engineering*, 21(6):481–496, June 1995.
[13] Robert J. Hall. CPPROFJ: Aspect-capable call path profiling of multi-threaded Java applications. In *Proceedings of the 17th IEEE International Conference on Automated Software Engineering (ASE'02)*, pages 107–116, September 2002.
[14] Java 2 Platform, Enterprise Edition (J2EE). `http://java.sun.com/j2ee`.
[15] Java 2 Platform, Standard Edition (J2SE). `http://java.sun.com/j2se`.
[16] Joseph M. Juran and A. Blanton Godfrey, editors. *Juran's Quality Handbook*. McGraw-Hill, New York, New York, USA, fifth edition, 1999.
[17] James R. Larus. Whole program paths. In *Proceedings of the ACM SIGPLAN 1999 Conference on Programming Language Design and Implementation*, pages 259–269. ACM Press, 1999.
[18] IBM Tivoli Directory Server. `http://www.ibm.com/tivoli`.
[19] Thomas J. McCabe and G. Gordon Schulmeyer. *Handbook of Software Quality Assurance*, chapter The Pareto Principle Applied to Software Quality Assurance, pages 178–210. Van Nostrand Reinhold Company, 1987.
[20] John Mellor-Crummey, Robert Fowler, Gabriel Marin, and Nathan Tallent. HPCView: A tool for top-down analysis of node performance. *The Journal of SuperComputing*, 23:81–101, 2002.
[21] David Melski and Thomas W. Reps. Interprocedural path profiling. In *Computational Complexity*, pages 47–62, 1999.
[22] Barton P. Miller, Mark D. Callaghan, Jonathan M. Cargille, Jeffrey K. Hollingsworth, R. Bruce Irvin, Karen L. Karavanic, Krishna Kunchithapadam, and Tia Newhall. The Paradyn parallel performance measurement tool. *IEEE Computer*, 28(11):37–46, 1995.
[23] Objective Caml. `http://www.ocaml.org`.
[24] Robert O'Callahan and Darko Marinov. Object equality profiling. In *Proceedings of the 18th ACM SIGPLAN Conference on Object-oriented Programming, Systems, Languages, and Applications (OOPSLA'03)*, pages 313–325, October 2003.
[25] Red Hat Linux. `http://www.redhat.com`.
[26] Philip C. Roth and Barton P. Miller. Deep start: A hybrid strategy for automated performance searches. In *Euro-Par 2002*, number 2400 in Lecture Notes in Computer Science, August 2002.
[27] G. Sevitsky, W. De Pauw, and R. Konuru. An information exploration tool for performance analysis of Java programs. In *Proceedings of TOOLS Europe*, 2001.
[28] SPECjAppServer2002. `http://www.specbench.org/jAppServer2002`.
[29] IBM Trade3 J2EE Benchmark Application. `http://www.ibm.com`.
[30] WebSphere Application Server. `http://www.ibm.com/websphere`.

Programming with Crosscutting Effective Views

Doug Janzen and Kris De Volder

University of British Columbia
201-2366 Main Mall
Vancouver, BC Canada
{dsjanzen,kdvolder}@cs.ubc.ca

Abstract. Aspect-oriented systems claim to improve modularity by providing explicit mechanisms that allow modularization of concerns which crosscut the object-oriented decomposition of a system in terms of classes. However, by modularizing concerns which crosscut classes, at the same time the structure and functionality associated with the classes themselves becomes scattered across the implementation of different aspects. This may hamper system understanding in other ways. In this paper we present a system that addresses this issue by allowing a developer to move fluidly between two alternative modular views on the decomposition of the program, editing the program either as decomposed into classes, or alternatively as decomposed into modules that crosscut classes. Thus developers gain the advantages of open classes, without having to give up the ability to edit the program directly in terms of classes.

1 Introduction

Aspect-oriented software development [1] addresses the issue of crosscutting concerns and how they can be more cleanly modularized and dealt with by developers. There are many different approaches towards this goal. What all the approaches have in common is that they attempt to provide explicit representations of crosscutting structure in software.

Language based approaches provide programming language extensions such as open classes, aspects, pointcuts and advice that allow concerns which cut across classes to be captured modularly. Some examples of this are systems like AspectJ [2], Caesar [3], and Aspectual Collaborations [4].

Tool-based approaches on the other hand make crosscutting structure explicit by constructing views on top of the code. In this way tools can make crosscutting structure which is implicit in the code explicitly visible and accessible to the developer. Examples of tool-based approaches are FEAT [5], AJDT [6], JQuery [7], AspectBrowser [8] and Stellation [9]. These tools can be loosely divided into two camps. On the one hand there are tools which work on legacy OO systems and try to show how implicit crosscutting concerns exist within the object-oriented program (examples: FEAT, JQuery, AspectBrowser, Stellation). On the other hand there are tools which try to do exactly the opposite: they try to produce

M. Odersky (Ed.): ECOOP 2004, LNCS 3086, pp. 195–218, 2004.

views that recover the object-oriented structure of the program which has been made implicit by the introduction of aspect-oriented features in the language (example: AJDT for AspectJ).

In both cases the fact that one of the views is explicit in the code and the other views are generated by tools implies a different level of support for working with those views. The view which has been made explicit in the code can be edited directly by editing the code. We call such a view an *effective* view. For example, for all programming languages which are based on textual syntax and the use of source files to store programs, the source code of a program represents an effective view, because editing the source code directly affects program structure. On the other hand, the views produced by most tools are non-effective because typically these views cannot be edited in such a way that the actual program structure is affected by the edits to the view. Instead, the typical usage profile for tool-based crosscutting views is that they serve as documentation or navigational aids for developers. But in order to make effective changes to program structure developers must edit the actual source code.

In this paper we present the Decal prototype. Decal is a tool that lets developers work simultaneously with two mutually crosscutting and *effective* source code views. Decal is atypical in that the views it produces are not derived from source code, they *are* source code. In some sense, Decal reverses the roles of tool-based views and source code as found in most tools. A typical tool produces a view *based on* source code. Decal maintains an internal, structured representation of the program and, from this, views are generated *in the form of* source code.

The current prototype is limited to two crosscutting views only but this could easily be extended. In section 7 we will discuss some possible extensions. For now we limit ourselves to a brief introduction to the two views supported by the current prototype.

The first of the two views is called the *modules view*. This view provides a decomposition of program structure in terms of modular units which crosscut classes in a way that is similar to open classes. The second view is called the *classes view* and is a more traditional object-oriented view, showing a decomposition of the program structure in terms of classes. The classes view crosscuts the modules view in a similar way that the modules view crosscuts the classes view. Every element in the program belongs simultaneously to both the classes view as well as the modules view. Both the modules view and the classes view are effective and editing the textual representation of either view impacts program structure. Consequently, when changes are made to one view, these changes are also automatically reflected in the other view. Figure 1 depicts this mutually crosscutting relationship between the two views.

To accomplish this bi-directional causal connection between the two views, Decal views are represented as *virtual source files* (VSFs). The term "virtual source file" was introduced in Stellation [9]. VSFs are dynamically generated ASCII files which can be browsed and edited by the developer with commonly available text editors. To be able to generate the VSFs dynamically and have

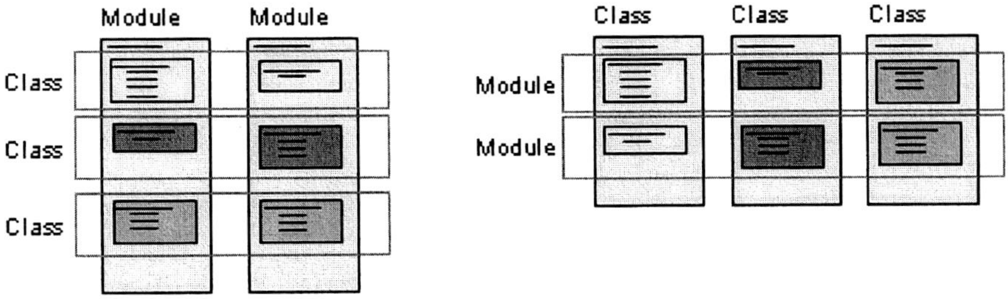

Fig. 1. The modules view crosscuts classes and the classes view crosscuts modules.

changes from one view be reflected in the other view, Decal internally maintains a single common representation of the program structure. After editing a VSF, the developer can commit the file back to Decal. The system will then translate the changes the developer made into corresponding changes to the common representation. At this point, the VSF is "absorbed" back into the system and ceases to exist. This extract-edit-absorb cycle is depicted in Figure 2.

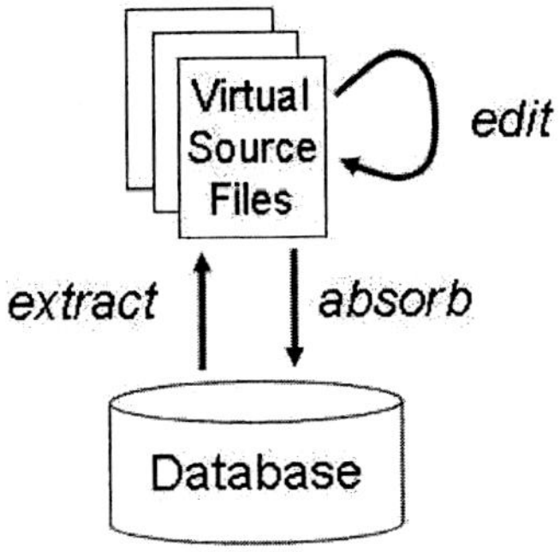

Fig. 2. The Extract-Edit-Absorb Cycle

Both the modules view and the classes view in Decal are, on their own, similar to conventional decompositions of program structure into source files. The classes view provides an effective, textual view similar to that of traditional object-oriented source files. The modules view provides an effective, textual view similar to that of a language that supports open classes. The contribution of this paper is to show that these mutually crosscutting effective views can be supported simultaneously.

An additional contribution this paper makes is to identify a number of issues and problems that are specific to a system that supports crosscutting effective views. We believe that the insights gained from the design and implementation of Decal, and the ways in which we have addressed them are valuable for the future design and implementation of similar systems.

The rest of this paper is structured as follows. In the following section, we present a motivating example. This example illustrates why it is desirable to provide an effective view for classes as well as modules at the same time. Section 3 presents the Decal system and its two different views. Section 4 describes the Decal database and issues surrounding its design. Section 5 looks at issues that arise when editing virtual source files. Section 6 describes the implementation of Decal. Section 7 discusses how the ideas explored in our prototype might be applied to a more realistic language. The last three sections describe future and related work and end with some concluding remarks.

2 Motivating Example

The example presented here is derived from a similar example in Tarr et. al. [10]. What the example tries to illustrate is that no matter how well designed a program may be and no matter how carefully developers may have considered the decomposition of their program to anticipate future evolution, the choice of any decomposition makes an implicit tradeoff, making certain tasks easier at the expense of making other tasks harder.

The example is phrased in the context of an implementation for an environment for working with programmatic expressions. The example is strongly simplified for presentation purposes. The class diagram in Figure 3 depicts a simplified version of the subsystem for representing expression abstract syntax trees. It depicts the most natural way to represent an AST in terms of a hierarchy of classes. This is also most naturally mapped onto an implementation in an object-oriented language such as Java, mapping every "class box" in the diagram to a compilation unit in the implementation language.

This natural object-oriented decomposition makes it hard to add new features to the system that require the implementation of new operations on AST structures. For example, suppose we wanted to extend our implementation with a pretty-printing feature. This would require the addition of one or more printing related methods to most, if not all, of the AST classes. Good designers may have anticipated the need for such extensions and included a Visitor pattern [11] in their design. The Visitor pattern comes at a price however because it introduces additional complexity into the program. In many ways the Visitor pattern is just a way of reifying a more procedural abstraction as an object/class, so that it can be represented with the available decomposition mechanism of classes.

Some languages, such as MultiJava [12] and AspectJ [2] provide the concept of open classes which leads to more flexibility in this regard. With open classes it is possible to declare methods outside of the class that they "belong to". Thus a developer may simply add additional operations on AST structures in a separate module and need not modify the original source code of the AST classes. With open classes, one may achieve a decomposition which has a modular

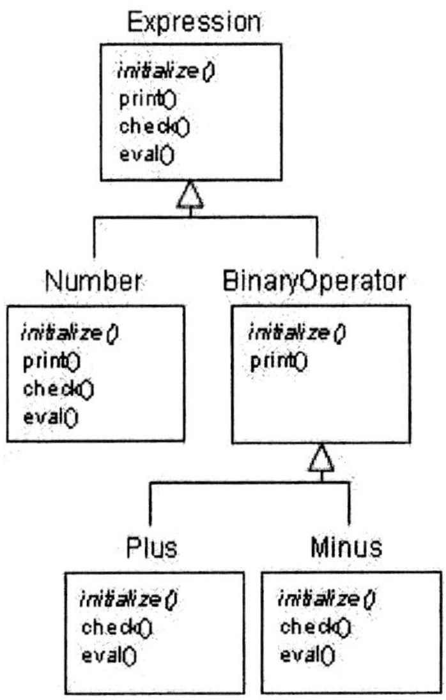

Fig. 3. Most natural OO decomposition for a simple AST implementation

structure similar to that of the Visitor pattern, but without the complications of implementing procedural abstractions in terms of closed classes. This situation is depicted in Figure 4.

Unfortunately, even the extra flexibility of open classes ultimately is not sufficient. When developers choose to structure modules around certain operations such as printing, type checking, etc. they are gaining more ease to maintain these types of abstractions, but at the same time they inevitably make it harder to do other types of extensions because the implementation of classes is scattered across multiple modules. This makes it harder to perform tasks that more naturally align with the class structure of the program. For example, suppose a future extension requires adding a new type of expression node to the AST. This task will be complicated because it will require making additions to several modules to implement all the required functionality for the new class, such as printing, type checking, etc.

Decal addresses this problem by letting developers alternate between editing the program in the modules view or the classes view. In the following sections we will explain each view in terms of the example from this section. At the end of the section we will show how the classes view eases the extensions of the AST implementation with new classes, while at the same time program structure is decomposed in terms of modules that crosscut those classes.

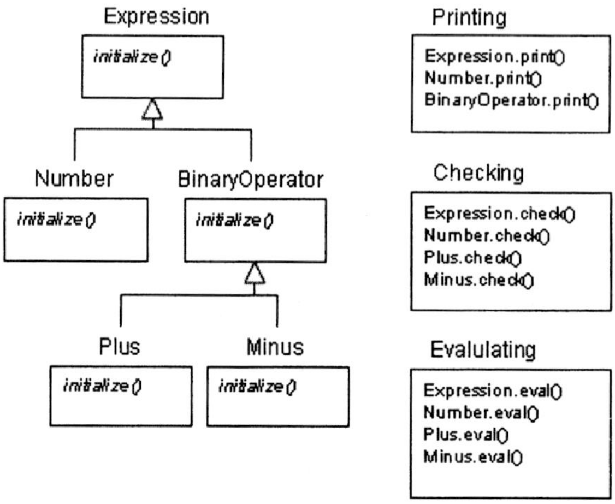

Fig. 4. A decomposition of a simple AST implementation with open classes

3 The Decal System

At the core of the Decal system is a simple object-oriented language with support for open classes. To keep the prototype lightweight and suitable for quick exploratory experiments we wanted to keep the language as simple as possible. The Decal language therefore supports only a minimal subset of object-oriented features. Specifically, it supports single inheritance with the ability to override operations, but does not support advanced features such as interfaces, overloading, static members and constructors[1].

To this basic object-oriented core language, Decal adds support for a simple form of open classes (but does not support multiple dispatch as in MultiJava). We consider open classes the simplest "flavor" of aspect-oriented programming [2]. Our current prototype does not support more advanced aspect-oriented language features such as pointcuts and advice.

The addition of more advanced object-oriented features would make the design and implementation of several components of the Decal system technically harder, but we do not believe it should pose fundamental problems. The situation is not as clear-cut for adding additional aspect-oriented features such as support for pointcuts and advice. In Section 7 we discuss how the choices made

[1] We assume reliance on ordinary methods and programming conventions for initializing objects as is also the case in, for example, Smalltalk[13]

[2] Some people might argue that open classes belong in the camp of traditional object-oriented languages because open classes do not include a mechanism of implicit invocation. What set of features makes a language aspect-oriented (or object-oriented for that matter) can of course be debated. Our view is that they are a simple form of aspect-orientation because they explicitly provide a mechanism to support a form of crosscutting modular structure.

in designing and simplifying the Decal language may affect the generalizability of our approach both in terms of object-oriented as well as aspect-oriented features.

3.1 The Modules View

The modules view in Decal allows programs to be edited according to a modular structure that may crosscut classes. Declarations related to a particular class may be spread across multiple modules, and each module may contain declarations related to more than one class. Figure 5 shows the `ast` module from our running example. It contains the "bare bones" declaration of several classes to represent a simple AST structure.

```
module ast {

   public class Expression {
   }

   public class Number extends Expression {
      public int value;
      public void initialize(int value) {:
         this.value = value;
      :}
   }

   public class BinaryOperator extends Expression {
      public Expression left;
      public Expression right;
      public String op;
      public void initialize(Expression left, String op, Expression right) {:
         this.left = left;
         this.op = op;
         this.right = right;
      :}
   }

   public class Plus extends BinaryOperator {
   }

   public class Minus extends BinaryOperator {
   }

}
```

Fig. 5. Example VSF: The `ast` module

Decal modules are a means to group declarations related to a specific concern. Each declaration can be marked `public` to indicate that it is visible outside the module or `private` to indicate that it is visible only within the same module.

Besides declaring classes of its own, a module may also introduce additional declarations into classes that are publicly defined in other modules. Figure 6 shows a `printing` module that provides an additional printing-related operation for the classes defined in the `ast` module. As with open classes, using the modules view in Decal allows programmers to work with concerns that crosscut the class structure in a modular way. All code related to the printing concern are brought together in the `printing` module. Similarly, it is possible to add operations related to semantic checking functionality to all the AST classes in a separate module VSF as well (this is not shown to save space).

```
module printing {

   import ast;

   Expression {
      public void print(Printer out);
   }

   Number {
      print {:
         out.printInt(value);
      :}
   }

   BinaryOperator {
      print {:
         left.print(out);
         out.printString(op);
         right.print(out);
      :}
   }
}
```

Fig. 6. Example VSF: The `printing` Module

Decal is similar to Java minus a number of features such as interfaces, static members, overloading and constructors. Besides these simplifications, there are a few other differences that are worth mentioning.

First, Decal makes a distinction between "operations" and "methods". We will have more to say on the reason for this distinction when we discuss program representation in Section 4. For now we merely explain the nature of the difference.

An operation represents an operational abstraction. For example, the `printing` module provides a declaration for an operation called `print` on `Expression`. A method declaration on the other hand provides a specific implementation for an operation on a specific class. A method declaration provides the method body that is to be executed in the event of an invocation of the operation on some specific type of object. Therefore, generally an operation is implemented by one or more method declarations. Methods are dispatched at run time according to the standard single dispatch semantics of overriding and inheritance.

In our example the `print` operation is implemented by two methods, for the `Number` and `BinaryOperator` classes respectively. Note that an operation declaration is where the signature of the operation resides, but that it is not repeated in the method declaration which only requires the name of the operation to identify it unambiguously (since there is no overloading in Decal). An alternative VSF syntax might redundantly repeat the operation signature with the method declaration, for the sake of readability. However, in this version, the syntax was designed to resemble the database representation as closely as possible and redundant information in the syntax is factored out, just as it is in the database representation.

3.2 The Classes View

The classes view in Decal contains the same declarations that are present in the modules view except that they are organized according to class membership rather than module membership. A VSF can be generated for each class in the system. Each VSF contains all the declarations related to the chosen class grouped in blocks according to which module they are declared in. Figure 7 shows what the VSF looks like for the `Number` class from our example.

Note that in conventional languages the boundaries of information hiding are typically defined in terms of lexical position. In Decal, where every declaration occurs simultaneously in two textual locations, a class VSF and a module VSF, this alignment of scope with textual nesting only really happens in the modules view. This is because we can think of the modules view as the "primary" view, which is most like the only textual view one would get if Decal was a conventional programming system. The classes view is conceived of as a secondary, derived view which is generated from the primary view. However, because both views are mutually effective this distinction between primary and secondary view is not all that clear. Scoping rules however, is one way in which there is still a clear qualitative difference between the nature of the two views. Classes, unlike modules, do not define a name space in Decal and do not have import statements. The names referred to in the code in the class VSF in Figure 7 therefore are to be interpreted in relation to the modules they belong to and to their respective import statements. For example, the `print` method and the `value` field are defined in the same class. However this alone is not sufficient to make a reference like `this.value` legal. It is further required that the name `value` can be resolved in terms of the import statements of the `printing` module (as it was shown in

```
public class ast.Number extends ast.Expression {

   module ast {
      public int value;
      public void initialize(int value) {:
         this.value = value;
      :}
   }

   module printing {
      print {:
         out.printInt(value);
      :}
   }

   module checking {
      check {:
         ...
      :}
   }

   module evaluating {
      eval {:
         ...
      :}
   }
}
```

Fig. 7. Example VSF: The `Number` class

Figure 6). Similarly, it would be legal for other modules to declare additional fields called `value` on the `Number` class. These fields would be considered as distinct. This is especially useful for private fields, providing modules with a safe way to add additional state to classes without having to worry about accidental name conflicts with extensions defined by other modules on the same class.

3.3 Motivating Example Revisited

Now let us return to the motivating example again. The explanations in the preceding sections already show how the modules view allows extending classes with new functionality, for example to modularize behavior such as printing, or checking across multiple classes. Let us now examine how the classes view aids in extending the system with an additional AST class, even when the system has been decomposed around behavior oriented modules as shown above.

For example, assume we needed to add a new class `UnaryOperator`. This can be conveniently accomplished in the classes view. Indeed, it can be done in a way very similar to what we might do if the program was written in a style similar to the most natural class-based decomposition shown in Figure 3. What we can do is — inspired by the assumption that `UnaryOperator` is most similar to `BinaryOperator` — extract the `BinaryOperator` class VSF and use it as a template. We create a new VSF for `UnaryOperator` and copy-paste the contents of the `BinaryOperator` class into the new VSF. Then we edit it at will into what we need. This works very well, because the `BinaryOperator` class will already have all the right pieces of functionality from various crosscutting modules in place, telling us exactly what functionality we also need to implement for a `UnaryOperator` and providing us with some convenient code snippets to base our implementation on. The task of adding a new AST class would be significantly harder in the modules view. This is true even in a fancy development environment that provides some additional non-effective tool-based views that show a view recovering the class structure. This is so because although a non-effective class view will help by telling us what we need to do, and where we need to do it, we would still need to add snippets of code in multiple different modules across the system. In Decal we get spared from this because we can directly edit the classes view and even meaningfully copy-paste code from one class VSF into another class VSF.

We can extend this example a little further. Assume that after considering the copy-pasting solution, we do not like the amount of code duplication that was introduced as a result. So we want to refactor this code and introduce a common superclass to capture the similarity between unary and binary operator expressions. This refactoring task is also more easily carried out on the class-based decomposition. We can do the refactoring by working with only three class VSFs, the class VSF for the new class, plus VSFs for the two classes to be refactored. It would be significantly harder to do this refactoring in the modules view because the functionality to be factored out into the superclass is scattered across many modules.

4 The Decal Database

To support multiple crosscutting effective views Decal uses a database as a single common representation of the program, from which all views are generated on-demand. We have chosen an RDBMS over other alternatives, not for any particularly significant reason, except perhaps that it is the most standard and commonly available type of database. In this section we provide some information about the design of the Decal program database.

4.1 Developing a Schema

The database schema of Decal is basically a fairly straightforward mapping of the structure of Decal's modules view into database tables. Some aspects of the schema design are non-obvious and, we believe, key to making Decal work. We refrain from discussing all the details of the schema but provide some information here about some key issues and design decisions.

Granularity. The core object-oriented structure of the database is made up of tables to represent classes, fields, operations, methods and the relationships between them. A key choice that we made in designing this part of the schema was to store method bodies as blocks of text, rather than explicitly representing every statement and expression as a separate fact. What is necessary for generating Decal VSFs is the relationship between high-level declarations, not the details of the AST structure of method bodies. A further motivation for this choice was the experience of the OMEGA project [14] which reported serious performance problems due to the number of queries required to generate the text of even simple programs.

Object IDs. The database representation makes an explicit distinction between the identity of an entity (module, class, operation, method, etc.) and its name. This is important because it is possible that several distinct entities exist that have the same name. For example multiple classes called `TraversalState` might be defined as helper classes in different modules for printing, checking etc. in the AST example. For convenience and efficiency (to avoid performing name lookup each time), references to program entities in database tables are represented in terms of some globally defined non-ambiguous object IDs (OIDs).

Soft keys. Another key feature of the schema design is the notion of "soft keys". In order to support incremental name resolution and error tolerance, an extra level of indirection was introduced to represent references that use names. For such references, rather than storing a direct link to an OID, a so called "soft-key" is stored. A soft key points to a table entry that stores what information is needed to resolve the reference and caches the OID of its target once it becomes resolved.

Soft keys provide a form of intentional name capture. Even if a reference can be resolved immediately, the target of the reference may later be deleted or renamed. By retaining the name used to resolve a reference, Decal can ensure that the reference can be resolved and unresolved many times as the program evolves while retaining, to some degree, the original intention of the programmer.

4.2 Impact of Schema Design on the Language

It is interesting to note that the design of Decal's database schema, has had an impact on the language design. In particular, in the process of designing the schema for the representation of method declarations we realized that information about method signatures would be represented redundantly. Standard normalization practices in database design suggest that this information should be factored out into an additional table. Refactoring the database tables in this fashion, we also decided to make the language itself reify the notion of an operation explicitly. Though we don't think this is essential to make our approach work, it leads to a cleaner correspondence between the database schema and the syntax of the language. As a result, the implementation of generation/absorption of VSFs from/to the database is more straightforward.

5 A Practical Editing System

In this section we will look at Decal's editing system. When we say editing system we mean more than just a tool for editing the text of a VSF. The editing system includes everything required to support the extract-edit-absorb cycle. The editing system of Decal, which is characterized by a complete separation between the editing format and storage format of programs, introduces some new issues that do not arise in traditional programming systems, where the editing format and the storage format are one and the same. In the following subsections we elaborate on some of those issues and how we have addressed them in Decal.

5.1 Editing Semantics

In a conventional programming system, where programs are stored as text files, and where developers can edit the stored program representation directly, the meaning of edits is unambiguously defined. However, when the text being edited is part of a virtual source file the meaning of the edits may not be as clear.

An important design decision that we made is that declarations can belong to only one module. For a brief moment we deliberated about supporting overlapping modules, so that one piece of information (e.g. a method declaration) would be represented simultaneously in multiple modules. We found this idea very appealing, because it would make it possible to support modules that not only crosscut classes, but also modules that crosscut each other. However, this raised the issue that the editing semantics of module VSFs are no longer intuitively unambiguous. For example, if a declaration can belong to more than one module VSF at the same time then it is not clear when a developer deletes a declaration if the intent is to delete the declaration from this module only, or from the system as a whole. Assuming that declarations belong to only one module naturally gives VSFs an editing semantics very similar to regular source files. I.e. it is intuitively clear that deleting declarations *must* remove them from the program altogether.

We call the property that a piece of information is represented in at most one VSF within a particular view, the *disjointness* property. It is a desirable property because it allows an editing semantics of VSFs which is intuitive, in that it is designed to behave similarly to what would be expected of "real" source files. Note that the converse property, completeness — that every a piece of information is represented in at least one VSF — is not as significant in defining the semantics of edits. It does however affect the usefulness of a view since it determines *what* information can be manipulated through it. This is not to say that incomplete views are necessarily less useful (they are more abstract in a sense).

In the case of ambiguity, it is of course possible to explicitly assign a semantics one way or another, or to design a mechanism to let developers explicitly state their intent. However it should be clear that the design of an editing semantics that would feel intuitive to developers becomes significantly more difficult in the absence of the disjointness property. Note that a similar problem of confusion around editing semantics does not arise because of overlapping VSFs that are in different views. The fact that the semantics of an edit is defined in one view automatically defines what it means in the other view as well.

We believe that studying mechanisms to deal with ambiguity in editing semantics is an interesting and important topic for future research. Indeed, resolving this issue is a necessary condition for supporting a more complex set of aspect-oriented language features, as will be discussed in Section 7.2. However we considered it outside the scope of the current paper.

5.2 Name Resolution

The generation of multiple views requires that the database provides the necessary connections to determine what VSFs (module or class) a specific element belongs to. The availability of that information in the database is dependent on the successful resolution of names. For example, in Figure 6 the identifier "Number" refers to the class `Number` as defined in the `ast` module. To generate the class VSF for class `Number` the system must resolve all references to `Number` from all the modules that add members to that class. This dependence on name resolution implies that in a system that supports multiple views, name resolution needs to be done as early as possible. Therefore, in Decal name resolution takes place each time a changed VSF is saved, rather than at compile time as is usual in traditional languages.

5.3 Error Tolerance

An additional complication arises because an incremental name resolution mechanism, as described above, needs to be tolerant of errors and incompleteness. During the process of constructing a program developers often leave parts of the program in an inconsistent state. This is not due to bad programming, but is simply a consequence of the fact that programmers can only do one thing at a time. It is often convenient for a programmer to work on one part of a program and refer to elements that he or she intends to define later on. Or sometimes a developer may wish to delete several parts of a program that contain references to each other. Thus it is highly impractical to force all names to be resolved before a VSF can be saved.

As mentioned earlier, we use a representation for name references that we call a soft key. Soft keys retain all the information needed to resolve a reference. This includes the name used to make the reference and the module from which the reference is being made. If the reference can be resolved then the OID of the target is also stored. As elements are added to the database, unresolved soft keys are checked to see if they refer to the new element. When an element is deleted, soft keys that point to the element have their OID removed, but retain all the information needed to resolve the reference again as new elements are created. The use of soft keys gives Decal VSFs a similar kind of flexibility that regular source files have while at the same time allowing the kinds of queries that depend on direct cross-referencing information.

Another place where tolerance of errors becomes an issue is when checking the syntax of VSFs at the time they are saved. It would be impractical to expect developers to remove all syntax errors just to be able to save their work. However some degree of syntactic correctness is necessary for Decal to be able to map regions of text back to the database. To minimize the impact of this requirement Decal does not force method bodies to be syntactically correct before they are saved. This can be easily supported thanks to our choice to store method bodies as blocks of text. Also, we have designed Decal's method declaration to have its body delimiters easy to recognize, by adding an additional colon next to the outer braces. This makes it easy to identify the textual area of the body without having to parse what is inside them.

5.4 Temporal Continuity of Views

In a conventional programming system, it is trivially true that a file saved at one time, when revisited at some later time, will look identical. However, in a system based on VSFs, this property does not automatically hold. The exact layout of a VSF depends on how it is generated. Since it is regenerated on each successive visit, the VSF layout may differ each time. We call this the issue of "temporal continuity of views".

The fact that the contents of a VSF may change between visits is a necessary property of the system, because it is what allows changes in one view to be reflected onto the other view as well. However, changes in a VSF between visits also have the potential for causing disorientation. This is because there is typically a lot of freedom in the use of indentation, whitespace and the order of declarations. This freedom is actively used by developers. It is therefore desirable that VSFs should look and feel as much as possible like "real" files, preserving not just the semantic content, but also non-semantically meaningful attributes of their textual layout.

In the current implementation of Decal we did not spend a great deal of effort on this issue. Our choice of representation for method bodies ensures that their formatting is retained in the database exactly as the programmer typed them, including comments. We also provide limited support for preserving comments outside of method bodies. Each element in Decal can have a Javadoc style comment attached to it that is stored with the element in the database. Other kinds of comments, such as single line comments, are not allowed outside method bodies as it is not always possible to determine which element they should be attached to in the database.

The order of declarations and white space between declarations are not currently retained. Instead we settled for maintaining a consistent use of white space and ordering (alphabetic). This guarantees some continuity: there will not be huge discrepancies in layout unless substantial edits are performed. Nevertheless, this implementation is clearly far from optimal since it takes away most of the freedom that developers have in conventional text-based editing systems in constructively using the layout of the source text.

Even in the limited setting where we have used Decal for toy examples, we found the "jumping text" behavior (on saves) to be disorienting. Therefore we believe that temporal view continuity is important for practical usability. We also believe it is technically feasible to make VSFs feel nearly the same as real files, by storing more information about their layout in the database. A good solution is not trivial to implement and requires detailed consideration about what additional information to store, but we believe it is mostly a technical implementation issue.

6 A Prototype Implementation

The user interface for our prototype is implemented as an Eclipse [15] plugin. Users can browse the contents of the database using two simple views that show the inheritance hierarchy of classes and the list of modules. Selecting a class or module from one of these views opens the corresponding VSF in the editor.

At the core of Decal is an API for manipulating Decal programs. This API uses a relational database called HSQLDB [16] to actually store the program information. HSQLDB is a lightweight embeddable database that can be distributed as part of Decal thus eliminating the need for users to install and maintain a full database management system. Its use of JDBC would make it relatively easy to switch to a more industrial strength database in the future.

The generation of virtual source files is built as a layer on top of the core API. This layer generates text and maps changes back to the database independently of how the text is edited. This makes it easier to integrate Decal into a variety of programming environments.

The prototype is still in an experimental stage and is not yet available to the general public. We are currently developing a third view whose VSFs correspond to proper Java source code suitable for compilation. Since Decal's name resolution mechanism is incompatible with Java packages all VSFs in this view are written to a single directory and a name mangling scheme is used to avoid name collisions. Thus it is not a VSF that can be edited and saved back to the database, but will allow us to compile and run programs written in Decal with a standard Java compiler.

Similarly we have done only a small amount of exploratory work on type checking Decal programs. Although type checking such a system is not a trivial issue, we did not think the implementation of the type checker would be a substantial contribution compared to other languages that support open classes, such as MultiJava and AspectJ. For this reason we decided to defer this work and focus on crosscutting effective views.

7 Supporting More Realistic Languages

The Decal prototype shows how multiple views can be implemented on a simplified language, but to be of practical value, our methods must be applicable to more realistic languages. Adding support for standard OO features would be a good first step, but the real power of multiple views is in their application to aspect-oriented languages.

7.1 Adding More OO Features to Decal

To extend Decal to include more advanced OO features such as interfaces, static members, constructors, overloading etc, the first thing that must be done is to design a more extensive database schema to represent the additional features. This is mostly a technical issue not a fundamental one.

Second, the additional features make the design of the Decal module system more complex. MultiJava has already proven that it is possible to support open classes in a clean way in conjunction with a rich set of core object-oriented language features, adding both open classes and multi-methods to Java in a way that is backwards compatible. Thus, the design of the module system is technically complex, but doesn't present any unsolvable problems.

Third, we have to consider potential complications that might arise with respect to editing semantics. Assuming that we design the language from the point of view of the modules view and consider the classes view as secondary, then the editing semantics of the modules view is automatically clearly defined. We also do not foresee any real complications with editing semantics of the generated classes view because adding conventional OO features only introduces new or more elaborate declarations that can be associated with a specific location in the class structure of the program. Therefore, they would not introduce information overlap within the classes view. As discussed before, the disjointness of different VSFs within a view implies that editing semantics can be unambiguously and intuitively defined to mimic the semantics of real source files.

7.2 Adding More Aspect-Oriented Features

Besides considering the extension of Decal to support a more complete set of conventional object-oriented features, we may also wish to consider extending its arsenal of features to express crosscutting in the language. For example, we may wish to include mechanisms for pointcuts and advice instead of just the simpler notion of open classes.

Presumably, the modules view would be augmented to show the system from an aspect-oriented point of view. Whereas the classes view would show where the aspects apply in terms of the class-based decomposition.

We believe this will pose more fundamental challenges than the addition of object-oriented features because the expressiveness of pointcuts and advice make the connection between the two views fundamentally more complicated. Intuitively, open classes provide only a very simple form of crosscutting, in the sense that any declaration in the modules view can be interpreted as applying to a single location in the classes view. This property, which guarantees an easy translation between the two views, is destroyed by the introduction of an expressive pointcut language. Pointcuts allow the application of advise to a large number of locations in the classes view, or even dynamically, in terms of properties that cannot necessarily be associated directly with static locations at all. This raises some issues with the generation of the classes view, such as how to represent dynamic advice. Additionally, independent of its dynamic nature, the fact that advice may apply to many locations in terms of the classes view destroys the disjointness property of the classes view: a single advice body may occur in multiple places in the classes view. This implies that we will have to tackle some complications with the editing semantics: for example, what does it mean to edit, add or delete advice from within the classes view?

8 Future Work

We believe that aspect-oriented languages which offer advanced features for expressing crosscutting structure would be exactly where support for multiple effective views would pay off the most. We believe that tackling the issues raised above, which complicate the design of the editing semantics is feasible. However it is a non-trivial problem which requires more research.

Another possible extension is to support additional effective views beyond the two that are currently supported. A natural view to add would be one that shows all the methods that implement a particular operation. Given that the concept of operations are already explicitly reified in the Decal language and also explicitly represented in the Decal program database, the addition of this view would be a very straightforward but potentially useful extension. There are numerous other views which might be worth exploring. For example the authors of this paper have frequently been frustrated with the fact that object-oriented inheritance makes it hard to get a complete view of a class, scattering its implementation over multiple superclasses. It would be possible to address this issue by providing an additional object-oriented view, in which the contents of superclasses is "unfolded" into the VSF of its subclasses. In fact, we consider it an interesting idea to explore different forms of this kind of "unfolding" or "expanding" of a VSF to include source code from "semantic neighbors". For example, we think this could be a very effective metaphor for user interface support that lets developers dynamically tailor and grow a VSF file to include exactly what they need to see and edit for a task. Simple versions of this idea are implemented in the Visual Studio [17] IDE, although in Visual Studio, understandably it is only possible to unfold/fold code within a single source file. So it can be used to elide details within a file, but not expand the current textual view into entities residing in different files. However, in a system where source files are virtual, and boundaries between files become much less real, exciting new possibilities for extending this simple but powerful idea present themselves.

Besides these somewhat futuristic ideas, there are also some more pressing needs to empirically validate the current ideas and approach in terms of a more realistic language and realistic code. Our next step therefore will likely be to explore how to extend the current implementation with a sufficiently rich set of

OO features, so that it is possible to import legacy Java code into the system and conduct some experiments on realistic code.

9 Related Work

The main contribution of this paper is to show how it is possible to construct an editing system that lets a developer alternate between editing a system through either one of two mutually crosscutting, effective views. This work is most closely related to tool-based aspect-oriented approaches that support the creation of crosscutting views on top of source code. Decal distinguishes itself from most of these other tools in that it produces *effective* textual views. In contrast, most other tools provide views which are non-effective. In such tools the main utility of the view is to serve as documentation and to support navigation. Some examples of tools which fit this description are AspectBrowser [8], JQuery [7], FEAT [5] and AJDT [6]. Of these tools, AJDT is the only one that is in the same camp as Decal, generating views that help developers to recover object-oriented structure which has been made implicit by the introduction of more aspect-like modularity in the language.

While the majority of tools provide only non-effective views, there are some notable exceptions. The oldest one is probably MasterScope in the Interlisp [18] development environment. In MasterScope, a developer may request the generation of a textual view by writing a query that identifies what declarations in the program are of interest. The declarations which match the query are returned in a textual, editable view and can then be edited as a group. A similar mechanism was provided more recently by the Stellation [9] system from which we adopted the idea of VSFs. In both cases, the views are textual and effective. The main difference is that in Decal, views are first class and have a well-defined intuitive semantics for all possible edit operations, whereas in Stellation and Interlisp, the views are arbitrary groupings of declarations and the editing system does not attach a specific semantics to the grouping of elements into a view. This has consequences for the semantics of additions and deletions of declarations to/from views which — in Stellation or MasterScope — don't have a clearly defined and intuitive editing semantics. Our example provided in section 3.3 illustrates the importance of this difference. The example relied on copying and pasting declarations between different class VSFs in order to effectively move or copy them from one class to another. This requires that insertion and deletion of declarations has the appropriate semantics with respect to the classes view in which these operations take place. Consequently, as far as the authors understand, this example would not work in either Stellation or MasterScope.

The *Smalltalk Envy* [19] programming environment is similar to Decal in a number of ways. The role of source code in Smalltalk differs from most other programming systems and is similar to Decal in that program structure is not stored as source code but in a more structured format, as a coarse grained object-oriented data structure. Smalltalk Envy also has a mechanism for packaging of applications, similar to Decal modules. The main difference is that Envy does not provide textual editable views of classes or application packages as a whole. Instead, views are created by, and manipulated through different GUI source code browsers. These browsers provide some level of effectiveness by providing refactoring and restructuring commands in menus. Decal on the other hand preserves the "illusion" of source files and lets developers edit source file views of classes or modules as a whole. We believe the GUI browser approach has advantages as well as disadvantages over a VSF-based editing metaphor. Moreover, they are complementary, in the sense that GUI browsers can be added to an editing environment based around VSFs, just as many modern IDEs provide browsers for real source files. Some advantages of GUI based refactoring and restructuring commands is that they allow developers to express their intent more clearly. This is one way of resolving ambiguity in editing semantics. Nevertheless, we believe it is hard to design and implement a "complete" set of GUI tools to support the refactoring-type of editing operations. Textual manipulation of source code seems to be still what developers always need to revert to when specific refactoring operations are not supported directly in the GUI. This is also true for Envy. Although the lower-level text editing operations do not capture the intent of the developer directly, all edits can be accomplished by copying, pasting and editing text. Moreover, editing programs in terms of source files is what the majority of developers are already most familiar with.

Intentional Programming (IP) [20], like Decal also uses a rich data structure to store programs and provides different kinds of views to edit this structure. However IP views can be graphical as well as textual. Furthermore, its main purpose is to facilitate language extensions of various kinds, not the creation of crosscutting views (though this might be a potential application of IP). The complexity of coordinating the interactions between several language extensions and visual editors make IP a much more ambitious project than ours. The Decal approach consequently is more lightweight. It uses a much coarser grained representation of programs, and requires only limited support from some fairly simple and cheap tools: a standard SQL engine, standard text editors and some simple VSF parsers and VSF code generators.

HyperJ [10] and its notion of multi-dimensional separation of concerns are closely related. In HyperJ's terminology, Decal could be characterized as "a system that supports two orthogonal dimensions of program decomposition simultaneously". Decal modules are similar to HyperSlices. The main differences are the following. First of all, Decal modules are true modules and have true support for encapsulation and information hiding (public and private), whereas HyperSlices have no mechanisms to hide internal structure[3]. Second, HyperJ focuses more on the composition of HyperSlices rather than the generation of views from existing program structure. To this end HyperJ provides a very complex mechanism of composition rules. In contrast, the composition rules for modules in Decal are embodied by a straightforward mechanism of name binding.

[3] HyperJ supports public and private to be used in HyperSlices, but these relate to the class structure and have no bearing on whether something is visible or not to another HyperSlice composed with it.

The concept of mixin layers [21] proposed by Smaragdkis and Batory are similar to Decal modules. The mixin layers approach focusses primarily on the complexity of composition of families of systems whereas our focus is not on the composition of modules into multiple systems but rather on supporting editing a single system simultaneously from multiple points of view. It is noteworthy that in a recent paper [22] Batory et. al. report they implemented and used an "unmixin" tool that allows a system composed from mixin layers to be edited directly, and the edits to be mapped back into the corresponding mixin layers. They report that the ability to edit from both a composed and uncomposed point of view was tremendously useful. They do not however provide any details or insights about issues such as editing semantics, temporal continuity of views, etc.

We used MultiJava's open classes and AspectJ's inter-type declarations as models for designing our module system. Both languages support more advanced kinds of modularity than just open classes. MultiJava includes support for multi-methods and AspectJ supports pointcuts and advice. We have already discussed in Section 7 what the possible implications of adding such features to Decal are.

The Decal extract-edit absorb cycle depicted in Figure 2 bears a remarkable similarity to the idea of roundtrip engineering as supported by many CASE tools [23,24]. The main difference, as we see it, between Decal and such roundtrip engineering tools is that Decal tranforms between (textual) representations that are both at the same level of abstraction – implementation – whereas CASE tools tranform between representations at different levels of abstraction, for example connecting design to implementation or architecture to design.

In his work on trying to define a theorethical framework for Automated Roundtrip Engineering (ARE) [25], Assmann has proposed a theorethical definition of an ARE system and a classification of AOP systems in the context of roundtrip engineering systems. In Assmann's terminology, Decal is *not* an ARE system, i.e. it does not provide a means to automatically generate an unweaver from a weaver. However, the Decal editing system's extract and absorb functions could be interpreted as hand crafted instances of what Assmann calls a bi-directional weaver, or "Beaver". Although Assmann provides good arguments why such bi-directionality is desirable, he does not provide a clear insight on how it can be achieved in practice.

Decal has some similarities with integrated environments as proposed by Garlan [26] and Herrmann and Mizini [27] where a common data structure is shared by a collection of tools. In these systems each tool is given its own view of the common data structure and is also able to keep its own data structures that are unique to its operation. Such integrated environments could be used to produce a variety of effective views, including something like Decal. However their focus is on the problems of tool coordination and integration, and they do not address the specific problems of working with virtual source files such as editing semantics.

10 Conclusion

We have presented the Decal system, an unconventional programming system which provides two mutually crosscutting, effective, textual views. One view, called the modules view lets developers decompose and edit program structure in a way similar to open classes. The second view, called the classes view, presents a more traditional object-oriented decomposition of the system into classes. Developers can alternate arbitrarily between the two views. Both views are presented as a collection of virtual source files (VSFs) and can be edited by developers to effect changes to the system. Both the modules view and the classes view in Decal are, on their own, similar to conventional decompositions of program structure into source files. The main contribution of this paper is to show that both views can be supported simultaneously, as effective views on the same program.

The design and implementation of a system which simultaneously supports several textual, crosscutting, effective views poses some unique challenges. Little or no work exists in the literature on how such systems should be designed and implemented. Thus, another contribution this paper makes is to identify some of the issues that arise in the design and implementation of such a system, and to describe specific principles and techniques we have used to address those issues.

Below, we provide a brief overview of the most important issues that were touched upon in different parts of the paper, and summarize what has been done in the context of Decal to address those issues.

Program Representation. A system that supports multiple views must perform early name resolution, be tolerant of errors, and have clearly defined editing semantics. Some form of a database is necessary to allow for efficient querying of program information. The Decal database uses a representation that is tolerant of unresolved references while at the same time allows efficient querying.

Editing Semantics. In a system where the storage format and the editing format of programs are separated, it becomes an issue to define the meaning of edits in terms of changes to the stored representation of the program. In Decal this issue is addressed by respecting the disjointness property which makes it possible to define editing semantics that mimick those of "real" source files.

Temporal Continuity of Views. In a system where source files are generated on the fly the layout of the generated text can change between editing sessions, resulting in a sense of disorientation for the developer. We believe it is technically feasible to design VSF generators that produce stable views by adding explicit information to the database about the textual structure of VSF files at the moment they are saved. We have not implemented this in the current version of Decal but leave it as a topic for future research.

Incrementality and Tolerance of Errors. To be able to generate one view from another a minimum of information about the structure of the program needs to be updated incrementally as developers edit VSFs. To support the typical editing patterns of developers this process must support a certain amount of error tolerance. When saving a VSF Decal tolerates syntax errors in method bodies by parsing and storing them as single tokens. Decal is also tolerant of unresolved names and supports incremental name resolution through the mechanism of soft keys in its database representation.

While the issues and solutions presented here stem only from the experience in designing and implementing a single prototype, and therefore do not necessarily generalize to all systems, we believe that our experience recorded in this paper will prove a valuable starting point for the design of other systems that support multiple crosscutting effective views simultaneously.

Acknowledgments. This work was supported in part by an IBM Eclipse Innovation Grant and the University of British Columbia. We thank Gregor Kiczales, Brian de Alwis and Mik Kersten for their valuable comments, insights and stimulating discussions which have greatly contributed to this paper.

References

1. Kiczales, G., Lamping, J., Mendhekar, A., Maeda, C., Lopes, C., Loingtier, J.M., Irwin, J.: Aspect-oriented programming. In: Proc. of European Conference on Object-Oriented Programming (ECOOP). Volume 1241 of Lecture Notes in Computer Science., Springer Verlag (1997) 220–242
2. Kiczales, G., Hilsdale, E., Huginim, J., Kersten, M., Palm, J., Griswold, W.G.: An overview of aspectj. In Knudsen, J.L., ed.: European Conference on Object-Oriented Programming. (2001) 327–353
3. Mezini, M., Ostermann, K.: Conquering aspects with caesar. In: Proceedings of the 2nd international conference on Aspect-oriented software development, ACM Press (2003) 90–99
4. Lieberherr K., L.D., J, O.: Aspectual collaborations – combining modules and aspects. The Computer Journal **46** (2003) 542–565
5. Robillard, M.P., Murphy, G.C.: Concern graphs: finding and describing concerns using structural program dependencies. In: Proceedings of the 24th international conference on Software engineering, ACM Press (2002) 406–416
6. AJDT: Aspectj development tools website. http://www.eclipse.org/ajdt/ (2003)
7. Janzen, D., De Volder, K.: Navigating and querying code without getting lost. In: Proceedings of the 2nd international conference on Aspect-oriented software development, ACM Press (2003) 178–187
8. W.G. Griswold, Y.K., Yuan, J.: Aspect browser: Tool support for managing dispersed aspects. In: First Workshop on Multi-Dimensional Separation of Concerns in Object-oriented Systems - OOPSLA 99). (1999)
9. Chu-Carroll, M.C., Wright, J., Shield, D.: Aspect-oriented programming: Supporting aggregation in fine grained software configuration management. In: Proceedings of the tenth ACM SIGSOFT symposium on Foundations of software engineering, ACM (2002) 99–108
10. Tarr, P.L., Ossher, H., Harrison, W.H., Jr., S.M.S.: N degrees of separation: Multidimensional separation of concerns. In: International Conference on Software Engineering. (1999) 107–119

11. Gamma, E., Helm, R., Johnson, R., Vlissides, J.: Design Patterns. Addison Wesley (1995)
12. Clifton, C., Leavens, G.T., Chambers, C., Millstein, T.: Multijava: modular open classes and symmetric multiple dispatch for java. In: Proceedings of the 15th ACM SIGPLAN conference on Object-oriented programming, systems, languages, and applications, ACM Press (2000) 130–145
13. Goldberg, A., Robson, D.: Smalltalk-80: The Language and its Implementation. Addison Wesley (1983)
14. Linton, M.A.: Implementing relational views of programs. In: Proceedings of the first ACM SIGSOFT/SIGPLAN software engineering symposium on Practical software development environments. (1984) 132–140
15. IBM: Eclipse website. http://www.eclipse.org/ (2003)
16. HSQLDB: Hsql database engine. http://hsqldb.sourceforge.net/ (2003)
17. Microsoft: Visual studio. http://msdn.microsoft.com/vstudio/ (2003)
18. W., T., L., M.: The interlisp programming environment. IEEE Computer **14** (1981) 25–33
19. Object Technology International Inc.: ENVY/Developer R3.01. (1995)
20. Simonyi, C.: The death of computer languages, the birth of intentional programming (1995)
21. Smaragdakis, Y., Batory, D.: Mixin layers: an object-oriented implementation technique for refinements and collaboration-based designs. ACM Trans. Softw. Eng. Methodol. **11** (2002) 215–255
22. Batory, D., Sarvela, J.N., Rauschmayer, A.: Scaling step-wise refinement. In: Proceedings of the 25th international conference on Software engineering, IEEE Computer Society (2003) 187–197
23. Borland: Together CASE tool. http://www.borland.com/together/ (2003)
24. IBM: Rational software. http://www.ibm.com/software/rational/ (2003)
25. Aßmann, U.: Automatic Roundtrip Engineering. In Aßmann, U., Pulverm ller, E., Cointe, P., Bouraquadi, N., Cointe, I., eds.: Proceedings of Software Composition (SC) – Workshop at ETAPS 2003. Volume 82 of Electronic Notes in Theoretical Computer Science (ENTCS)., Warshaw, Elsevier (2003)
26. Garlan, D.: Views for tools in integrated environments. In: An international workshop on Advanced programming environments, Springer-Verlag (1986) 314–343
27. Herrmann, S., Mezini, M.: Pirol: a case study for multidimensional separation of concerns in software engineering environments. In: Proceedings of the 15th ACM SIGPLAN conference on Object-oriented programming, systems, languages, and applications, ACM Press (2000) 188–207

AspectJ2EE = AOP + J2EE

Towards an Aspect Based, Programmable and Extensible Middleware Framework

Tal Cohen* and Joseph (Yossi) Gil**

Department of Computer Science
Technion—Israel Institute of Technology
Technion City, Haifa 32000, Israel
{ctal,yogi}@cs.technion.ac.il

Abstract. J2EE is a middleware architecture augmented with supporting tools for developing large scale client/server and multi-tier applications. J2EE uses Enterprise JavaBeans as its component model. The realization of these components by a J2EE application server can be *conceptually* decomposed into distinct aspects such as persistence, transaction management, security, and load balancing. However, current servers do not employ aspect-oriented programming in their implementation. In this paper, we describe a new aspect language, AspectJ2EE, geared towards the generalized implementation of J2EE application servers, and applications within this framework. AspectJ2EE can be easily employed to extend the fixed set of services that these servers provide with new services such as logging and performance monitoring. Even *tier-cutting concerns* like encryption, data compression, and memoization can be added while avoiding the drags of cross-cutting and scattered code.

AspectJ2EE is less general (and hence less complicated) than AspectJ, yet demonstrably powerful enough for the systematic development of large scale (and distributed) applications. The introduction of *parameterized aspects* makes aspects in AspectJ2EE more flexible and reusable than aspects in AspectJ.

AspectJ2EE also generalizes the process of binding services to user applications in the application server into a novel *deploy-time* weaving of aspects. Deploy-time weaving is superior to traditional weaving mechanisms, in that it preserves the object model, has a better management of aspect scope, and presents a more understandable and maintainable semantic model.

1 Introduction

The term *enterprise applications* is used to describe the large-scale software programs used to operate and manage large organizations. The world's largest and most important software systems are enterprise applications; this includes the programs used to run government organizations, banks, insurance companies, financial institutes, hospitals, and so forth. Enterprise applications make the world go around.

---

* Contact author

** Research supported in part by the IBM faculty award

M. Odersky (Ed.): ECOOP 2004, LNCS 3086, pp. 219–243, 2004.

In many cases, enterprise applications are based on a heterogeneous platform configuration, connecting various independent systems (called *tiers*) into a coherent whole. The various tiers of an enterprise application can include, e.g., legacy mainframe servers, dedicated database servers, personal computers, departmental servers, and more.

The core functionality served by enterprise applications is often quite simple. It does not involve overly elaborate computation or pose complex algorithmic demands. However, developing enterprise applications is considered a daunting task, due to orthogonal requirements presented by most of these applications: uncompromising reliability, unyielding security, and complete trustworthiness.

The staggering demand for rapid development of enterprise applications initiated a series of component-based *middleware architectures*. A prime example of these, and emphasizing client/server and multi-tier structures, is *Java 2, Enterprise Edition* (J2EE) [1] which uses Enterprise JavaBeans (EJB) [2] as its component model.

Aspect-oriented programming (AOP) [3], the methodology which encapsulates the code relevant to any distinct non-functional concern in *aspect* modules, can also be thought of as answering the same demand [4, 5]. As it turns out, the functionality of J2EE application servers can be *conceptually* decomposed into distinct aspects such as persistence, transaction management, security, and load balancing. The effectiveness of this decomposition is evident from Kim and Clarke's case study [6], which indicates that the EJB framework drastically reduces the need for generic AOP language extensions and tools.

Yet, as we shall see here, the EJB support for functional decomposition is limited and inflexible. In cases where the canned EJB solution is insufficient, applications resort again to a tangled and highly scattered implementation of cross-cutting concerns. Part of the reason is that current J2EE servers do not employ AOP in their implementation, and do not enable developers to decompose new non-functional concerns that show up during the development process.

A natural quest then is for a harmonious integration of middleware architectures and AOP. Indeed, there were several works on an AOP-based implementation of J2EE servers and services (see e.g., the work of Choi [7]).

The new approach and main contribution of this paper is in drawing from the lessons of J2EE and its implementation to design a new AOP language, AspectJ2EE, geared towards the generalized implementation of J2EE application servers and applications within this framework. In particular, AspectJ2EE generalizes the process of binding services to user applications in the J2EE application server into a novel *deploy-time* weaving mechanism. Deploy-time weaving is superior to traditional weaving mechanisms in that it preserves the object model, has a better management of aspect scope, and presents a more understandable and maintainable semantic model.

As a consequence of its particular weaving method, and of staying away from specialized JVMs and bytecode manipulation for aspect-weaving, AspectJ2EE is similar to, yet (slightly) less general than, the *AspectJ* programming language [8]. Nevertheless, standing on the shoulders of the J2EE experience, we can argue that AspectJ2EE is highly suited to systematic development of enterprise applications. Perhaps the main limitation of AspectJ2EE when compared to ApsectJ is that it does not directly support *field* read and write join points, and hence cannot be employed for low-level debugging or nit-picking logging. If however the design of a software solution is such that the management of a certain field can be decomposed into several aspects, then this field can be realized as a J2EE *attribute*, with join points at its retrieval and setting.

The semantic model of applying an aspect to a class in AspectJ2EE is shown to be conceptually similar to the application of a generic type definition to a class, yielding a new type. This has both theoretical and practical implications, since maintaining the standard object model makes AspectJ2EE easier to understand and master, a crucial consideration for the widespread adoption of any new technology in the field of enterprise application development[1]. Despite the similarities, we show that AspectJ2EE aspects are more flexible and expressive than generics when used to extend existing types.

AspectJ2EE also introduces *parameterized aspects*. These constructs, combined with AspectJ2EE's aspect binding language, make aspects in AspectJ2EE more reusable than AspectJ aspects.

We stress that unlike previous implementations of aspects within the standard object model, AspectJ2EE does not merely support "before" and "after" advices and "method execution" join points. AspectJ2EE supports "around" advices, and a rich set of join points, including control-flow based, conditional, and object- and class-initialization.

Using AspectJ2EE, the fixed set of standard J2EE services is replaced by a library of core aspects. These services can be augmented with new ones, such as logging and performance monitoring. Moreover, the AspectJ2EE language has specific support for the composition of aspects that are scattered across program tiers (*tier-cutting concerns*), such as encryption, data compression, and memoization.

Terminology. The article assumes basic familiarity with standard AOP terms, including *join point* (a well-defined point in the program's execution), *pointcut* (a specification of a set of join points), *advice* (code that is added at specified join points), *weaving* (the process of applying advices to join points), and *aspect* (a language construct containing advices).

Outline. Section 2 makes the case for AspectJ2EE by explaining in greater detail how J2EE services can be thought of as aspects. Discussing the benefits of using AOP for these services, we present the main points in which the design of AspectJ2EE is different than standard AOP. The deploy time weaving strategy is discussed in Sect. 3. Section 4 shows how the AspectJ2EE approach introduces AOP into the OOP model without breaking it. Section 5 introduces some of the fine points and innovations in the language, and discusses implementation details. Section 6 lists several possible innovative uses for AspectJ2EE, some of which can lead to substantial performance benefits. Section 7 concludes.

---

[1] Historically, the developers of enterprise applications are slow to adopt new technologies; a technology has to prove itself again and again, over a long period of time, before the maintainers of such large-scale applications will even consider adopting it for their needs. It is not a coincidence that many large organizations still use and maintain software developed using some technologies, such as COBOL [9], that other sectors of the software industry view as thoroughly outdated.

2 The Case for AOP in J2EE

2.1 J2EE Services as Managers of Non-functional Concerns

Ideally, with the J2EE middleware framework (and to a lesser extent in other such frameworks), the developer only has to implement the domain-specific *business logic*. This "business logic" is none other than what the AOP community calls *functional concerns*. The framework takes charge of issues such as security, persistence, transaction management, and load balancing which are handled by *services* provided by the *EJB container* [10, Chap. 2]. Again, these issues are none other than *non-functional concerns* in AOP jargon.

Suppose for example that the programmer needs data objects whose state is mirrored in persistent storage. This storage must then be constantly updated as the object is changed during its lifetime, and vice versa. Automatic updates can be carried out by the *Container-Managed Persistence* (CMP) service of the EJB container. To make this happen, the objects should be defined as *entity beans* [2, Chap. 10]. Bean types are mapped to tables in a relational database with an appropriate XML configuration file. This *deployment descriptor* file also maps each bean attribute (persistent instance variable) to a field of the corresponding table.

Another standard J2EE service is security, using an approach known as *role-based security*. Consider, for example, a financial software system with two types of users: clients and tellers. A client can perform operations on his own account; a teller can perform operations on any account, and create new accounts. By setting the relevant values in the program's deployment descriptor, we can limit the account-creation method so that only users that were authenticated as tellers will be able to invoke it.

Other services provided by the EJB container handle issues such as transaction management and load balancing. The developer specifies which services are applied to which EJB. Deployment descriptors are used for setup and customization of these services. Thus, J2EE reduces the implementation of many non-functional concerns into mere configuration decisions; in many ways, they turn into *non-concerns*.

And while this work focuses on EJBs, the J2EE design guideline, according to which the developer configures various services via deployment descriptors, is not limited to EJBs only. It is also used in other parts of the J2EE platform. For example, servlets (server-side programs for web servers) also receive services such as security from their container, and access to specific servlets can be limited using role-based security. This is also true for Java Server Pages (JSPs), another key part of the J2EE architecture. Hence, in our financial software example, certain privileged web pages can be configured so that they will be only accessible to tellers and not to clients.

The various issues handled by EJB container services were always a prime target for being implemented as aspects in AOP-based systems [11, pp. 13–14]. For example, Soares *et. al.* [4] implement distribution, persistence and transaction aspects for software components using AspectJ. Security was implemented as an aspect by Hao *et. al.* [5]. The use of aspects reduces the risk of scattered or tangled code when any of these non-functional concerns is added to a software project.

Conversely, we find that J2EE developers, having the benefit of container services, do not require as much AOP. Indeed, Kim and Clarke [6] present a case study where they investigate the relevance of AOP to J2EE developers. The case study comprised of an e-voting system which included five non-functional concerns: (1) persistent storage of votes, (2) transactional vote updates, (3) secure database access, (4) user authentication, and (5) secure communications using a public key infrastructure [6, Table 1]. Of these five non-functional concerns, *not one* remained cross-cutting or introduced tangled code. The first three were handled by standard J2EE services, configured by setting the proper values in the deployment descriptors. The last two were properly modularized into a small number of classes (two classes in each case) with no code replication and no tangled code.

The implementation of services in J2EE also includes sophisticated mechanisms for combining each of the services, as configured by the deployment descriptors, with the user code. We will discuss these mechanisms, which can be though of as the equivalent of aspect weaving, in detail below (Sect. 3). Suffice to say at this point that the combination in J2EE is carried out without resorting to drastic means such as byte code patching and code preprocessing—means which may break the object model, confuse debuggers and other language tools, and even obfuscate the semantics.

2.2 Limitations of the Services-Based Solution

Even though the J2EE framework reduces the developer's need for AOP tools, there are limits to such benefits. The reason is that although the EJB container is configurable, it is neither extensible nor programmable. Pichler, Ostermann, and Mezini [12] refer to the combination of these two problems as *lack of tailorability*.

The container is *not extensible* in the sense that the set of services it offers is fixed. Kim and Clarke [6] explain why supporting logging in the framework would require scattered and tangled code. In general, J2EE lacks support for introducing new services for non-functional concerns which are not part of its specification. Among these concerns, we mention memoization, precondition testing, and profiling.

The container is *not programmable* in the sense that the implementation of each of its services cannot be easily modified by the application developer. For example, current implementations of CMP rely on a rigid model for mapping data objects to a relational database. The service is then useless in the case that data attributes of an object are drawn from several tables. Nor can it be used to define read-only beans that are mapped to a database view, rather than a table. The CMP service is also of no use when the persistent data is not stored in a relational database (e.g., when flat XML files are used).

Any variation on the functionality of CMP is therefore by *re-implementation* of object persistence, using what is called *Bean-Managed Persistence* (BMP). BMP support requires introducing callback methods (called *lifecycle methods* in EJB parlance) in each bean. Method `ejbLoad()` (`ejbStore()`) for example is invoked whenever memory (store) should be updated.

The implication is that the pure business logic of EJB classes is contaminated with unrelated I/O code. For example, the tutorial code of Bodoff *et. al.* [13, Chap. 5], demonstrates a mixup in the same bean of SQL queries and a Java implementation of functional concern. Conversely, we find that the code in charge of persistence is *scattered* across all entity bean classes, rather than being encapsulated in a single cohesive module.

Worse, BMP may lead to code *tangling*. Suppose for example that persistence is optimized by introducing a "dirty" flag for the object's state. Then, each business logic method which modifies state is tangled with code to update this flag.

Similar scattering and tangling issues rise with modifications to any other J2EE service. In our financial software example, a security policy may restrict a client to transfer funds only out of his own accounts. The funds-transfer method, which is accessible for both clients and tellers, acts differently depending on user authentication. Such a policy cannot be done by setting configuration options, and the method code must explicitly refer to the non-functional concern of security.

To summarize, whenever the canned solutions provided by the J2EE platform are insufficient for our particular purpose, we find ourselves facing again the problems of scattered, tangled and cross-cutting implementation of non-functional concerns. As Duclos, Estublier and Morat [14] state: "*clearly, the 'component' technology introduced successfully by EJB for managing non-functional aspects reaches its limits*".

2.3 Marrying J2EE with AOP

Having exposed some of the limitations of J2EE, it is important to stress that the framework enjoys extensive market penetration, commanding a multi-billion dollar market [15].

In contrast, AOP, with its elegant syntax and robust semantics, did not find its place yet in mainstream industrial production. It is only natural then to seek a reconciliation of the two approaches, in producing an aspect based, programmable and extensible middleware framework. Indeed, Pichler *et. al.* call for "a marriage of aspects and components" [12, Sect. 4].

Obviously, each of the services that J2EE provides should be expressed as an aspect. The collection of these services will be the *core aspect library*, which relying on J2EE success, would not only be provably useful, but also highly customizable. Developers will be able to add their own aspects (e.g., logging) or modify existing ones, possibly using inheritance in order to re-use proven aspect code.

The resulting aspects could then be viewed as stand-alone modules that can be re-used across projects. Another implication is that not all aspects must come from a single vendor; in the current J2EE market, all J2EE-standard services are provided by the J2EE application server vendor. If developers can choose which aspects to apply, regardless of the application server used, then aspects implemented by different vendors (or by the developers themselves) can all be used in the same project.

Choi [7] was the first to demonstrate that an EJB container can be built from the ground up using AOP methodologies, while replacing services with aspects which exist independently of the container. The resulting prototype server, called *AES*, allows developers to add and remove aspects from the container, changing the runtime behavior of the system.

Release 4.0 of JBoss [16], an open-source application server which implements the J2EE standard, supports aspects with no language extensions [17]. Aspects are implemented as Java classes which implement a designated interface, while pointcuts are defined in an XML syntax. These can be employed to apply new aspects to existing beans without introducing scattered code. Standard services however are not implemented with this aspect support.

Focal to all this prior work was the attempt to make an existing widespread framework more robust using AOP techniques. In this research, we propose a new approach to the successful marriage of J2EE and AOP in which the design of a new AOP language draws from the lessons of J2EE and its programming techniques. The main issues in which the AspectJ2EE language differs from AspectJ are:

1. *Aspect targets.* AspectJ can apply aspects to any class, whereas in AspectJ2EE aspects can be applied to *enterprise beans* only. In OOP terminology these beans are the core classes of the application, each of which represents one component of the underlying data model. As demonstrated by the vast experience accumulated in J2EE, aspects have great efficacy precisely with these classes. We believe that the acceptance of aspects by the community may be improved by narrowing their domain of applicability, which should also benefit understandability and maintainability.
2. *Weaving method.* Weaving the base class together with its aspects in AspectJ2EE relies on the same mechanisms employed by J2EE application servers to combine services with the business logic of enterprise beans. This is carried out entirely within the dominion of object oriented programming, using the standard Java language, and an unmodified Java virtual machine (JVM). In contrast, different versions of AspectJ used different weaving methods relying on preprocessing, specialized JVMs, and dedicated byte code generators, all of which deviate from the standard object model.
3. *Aspect parametrization.* Aspects in AspectJ2EE can contain two types of parameters that accept values at the time of aspect application: abstract pointcut definitions, and field values. Aspects that contain abstract pointcut definitions can be applied to EJBs, by providing (in the EJBs deployment descriptor) a concrete definition for each such pointcut. This provides significant flexibility by removing undesired cohesion between aspects and their target beans, and enables the development of highly reusable aspects. It creates, in AspectJ2EE, the equivalent of Caesar's [18] much-touted separation between aspect implementation and aspect binding. Field values, the other type of aspect parameters, also greatly increase aspect reusability and broaden each aspect's applicability.
4. *Support for tier-cutting concerns.* AspectJ2EE is uniquely positioned to enable the localization of concerns that cross not only program modules, but program tiers as well. Such concerns include, for example, encrypting or compressing the flow of information between the client and the server (processing the data at one end and reversing the process at the other). Even with AOP, the handling of tier-cutting concerns requires scattering code across at least two distinct program modules. We show that using AspectJ2EE, many tier-cutting concerns can be localized into a single, coherent program module.

3 Deployment and Deploy-Time Weaving

Weaving is the process of inserting the relevant code from various aspects into designated locations, known as *join points*, in the main program. In their original presentation of AspectJ [8], Kiczales *et. al.* enumerate a number of weaving strategies: "*aspect weaving can be done by a special pre-processor, during compilation, by a post-compile processor, at load time, as part of the virtual machine, using residual runtime instructions, or using some combination of these approaches*", each of which was employed in at least one aspect-oriented programming language implementation.

As noted before, AspectJ2EE uses its own peculiar *deploy-time weaving* strategy. In this section we motivate this strategy and explain it in greater detail.

3.1 Unbounded Weaving Considered Harmful

All weaving strategies mentioned in the quote above transgress the boundaries of the standard object model. Patching binaries, pre-processing, dedicated loaders or virtual machines, will confuse language processing tools such as debuggers, and may have other adverse effects on generality and portability.

However, beyond the intricacies of the implementation, weaving introduces a major conceptual bottleneck. As early as 1998, Walker, Baniassad and Murphy [19] noted the disconcert of programmers when realizing that merely reading the source of a code unit is not sufficient for understanding its runtime behavior[2].

3.2 Non-intrusive Explicit Weaving

The remedy suggested by Constantinides, Bader, and Fayad in their *Aspect Moderator* framework [20] was restricting weaving to the dominion of the OOP model. In their suggested framework, aspects and their weaving are realized using pure object oriented constructs. Thus, every aspect oriented program can be presented in terms of the familiar notions of inheritance, polymorphism and dynamic binding. Indeed, as Walker *et. al.* conclude: "*programmers may be better able to understand an aspect-oriented program when the effect of aspect code has a well-defined scope*".

Aspect Moderator relies on the PROXY design pattern [21] to create components that can be enriched by aspects. Each core class has a proxy which manages a list of operations to be taken before and after every method invocation. As a result, join points are limited to method execution only, and only `before()` and `after()` advices can be offered. Another notable drawback of this weaving strategy is that it is *explicit*, in the sense that every advice has to be manually registered with the proxy. Registration is carried out by issuing a plain Java instruction—there are no external or non-Java elements that modify the program's behavior. Therefore, long, tiresome and error-prone sequences of registration instructions are typical to Aspect Moderator programs.

The *Aspect Mediator* framework, due to Cohen and Hadad [22], ameliorates the problem by simplifying the registration process, and each of the registration instructions. Still, their conclusion is that the explicit weaving code should be generated by an automatic tool from a more concise specification. The AspectJ2EE language processor gives this tool, which generates the explicit registration sequence out of an AspectJ-like weaving specification.

---

[2] Further, Laddad [11, p. 441] notes that in AspectJ the runtime behavior cannot be deduced even by reading *all* aspects, since their application to the main code is governed by the command by which the compiler was invoked.

We stress that AspectJ2EE does not use any of the obtrusive weaving strategies listed above. True to the spirit of Aspect Mediator, it employs a weaving strategy that *does not break* the object model. Instead of modifying binaries (directly, or by pre-processing the source code), AspectJ2EE generates new classes that inherit from, rather than replace, the core program classes. Aspect application is carried out by subclassing, during the deployment stage, the classes that contain the business logic.

3.3 J2EE Deployment as a Weaving Process

Deployment is the process by which an application is installed on a J2EE application server. Having received the application binaries, deployment involves generating, compiling and adding additional support classes to the application. For example, the server generates *stub* and *tie* (skeleton) classes for all classes that can be remotely accessed, in a manner similar to, or even based on, the *remote method invocation* (RMI) compiler, `rmic` [23]. Even though some J2EE application servers (e.g., JBoss [16]) generate support class binaries directly (without going through the source), these always conform to the standard object model.

Figure 1 compares the development cycle of traditional and J2EE application. We see in the figure that deployment is a new stage in the program development process, which occurs after compilation but prior to execution. It is unique in that although new code is generated, it is not part of the development, but rather of user installation.

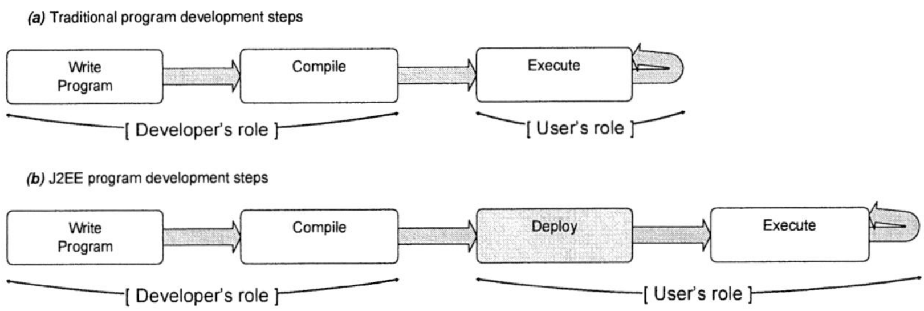

Fig. 1. (a) the development steps in a traditional application, **(b)** the development steps in a J2EE application.

Deployment is the magic by which J2EE services are welded to applications. Therefore, the generation of sub- and support classes is governed by deployment descriptors. The idea behind deploy-time weaving is to extend this magic, by placing rich AOP semantics in government of this process. Naturally, this extension also complicates the structure and inter-relationships between the generated support classes.

To better understand plain deployment, consider first Figure 2, which shows the initial hierarchy associated with an ACCOUNT CMP bean. This bean will serve as a running example for the rest of this article. While technically, it is defined as a CMP entity EJB, we shall see later that the use of AspectJ2EE completely blurs the lines between CMP and BMP entity beans, and between entity beans in general and session beans (both stateful and stateless). The nature of each bean is derived simply from the aspects that are applied to it.

Interface `Account` is written by the developer in support of the remote interface to the bean[3]. This is where client-accessible methods are declared.

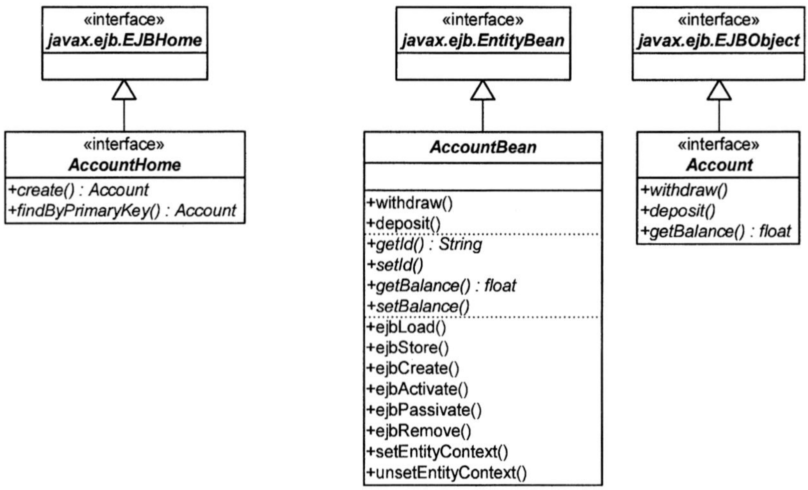

Fig. 2. Classes created by the programmer for defining the ACCOUNT EJB.

The developer's main effort is in coding the abstract class `AccountBean`. The first group of methods in this class consists the implementation of business logic methods (`deposit()` and `withdraw()` in the example).

In addition to regular fields, an EJB has *attributes*, which are fields that will be governed by the persistence service in the J2EE server. Each attribute *attr* is represented by abstract setter and getter methods, called `set`*Attr*`()` and `get`*Attr*`()` respectively. Attributes are not necessarily client accessible. By examining the second group of methods in this class, we see that ACCOUNT has two attributes: `id` (the primary key) and `balance`. From the `Account` interface we learn that `id` is invisible to the client, while `balance` is read-only accessible.

The third and last method group comprises a long list of mundane lifecycle methods, such as `ejbLoad()` and `ejbStore()`, most of which are normally empty when the CMP service is used. Even though sophisticated IDEs can produce a template implementation of these, they remain a developer's responsibility, contaminating the functional concern code. Later we shall see how deploy-time weaving can be used to remove this burden.

[3] For the sake of simplicity, we assume that ACCOUNT has a remote interface only, even though since version 2.0 of the EJB specification [2], beans can have either a local interface, a remote interface, or both.

Interface `AccountHome` declares a FACTORY [21] of this bean. Clients can only generate or obtain instances of the bean by using this interface.

Concrete classes to implement `AccountHome`, `Acount` and `AccountBean` are generated at deployment time. The specifics of these classes vary with the J2EE implementation. Figure 3 shows some of the classes generated by IBM's WebSphere Application Server (WAS) [24] version 5.0 when deploying this bean.

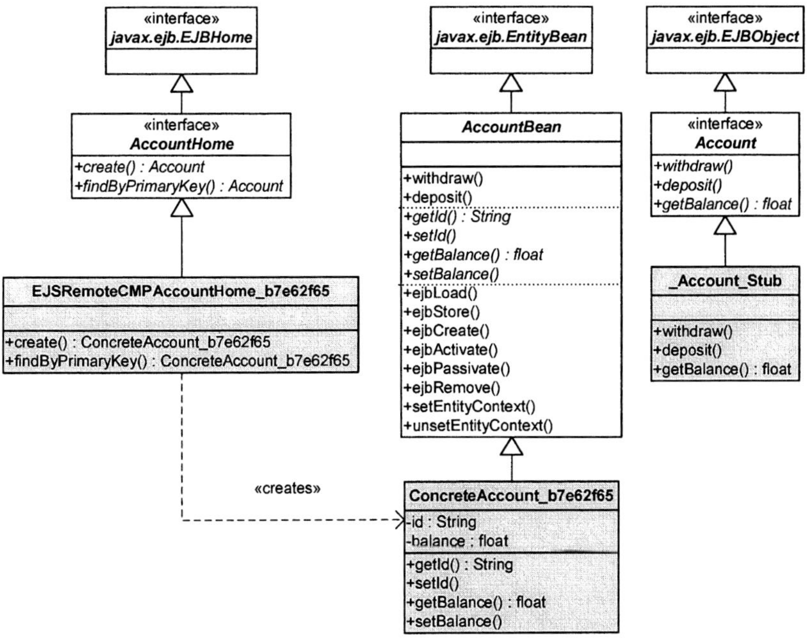

Fig. 3. UML diagram of the ACCOUNT EJB classes defined by the programmer, and a partial set of the support classes (in gray) generated by WebSphere Application Server during the deployment stage.

`ConcreteAccount_b7e62f65` is the *concrete bean class*, implementing the abstract methods defined in `AccountBean` as setters and getters for the EJB attributes. Instances of this class are handed out by class `EJSRemoteCMPAccountHome_b7e62f65`, which implements the factory interface `AccountHome`. Finally, `_Account_Stub` is a COBRA-compliant stub class to the bean, to be used by the bean's clients.

In support of the ACCOUNT bean, WAS deployment generates several additional classes which are not depicted in the figure: a stub for the home interface, ties for both stubs, and more. Together, the deployment classes realize various services that the EJB container provides to the bean: persistence, security, transaction management and so forth. However, as evident from the figure, all this support is provided within the standard object oriented programming model.

J2EE application servers offer the developer only minimal control over the generation of support classes. AspectJ2EE however, gives a full AOP semantics to the deployment process. With deploy-time weaving, the main code is unmodified, both at the source and the binary level. Further, the execution of this code is unchanged, and can be carried out on any standard JVM.

AspectJ2EE does not impose constraints on the base code, other than some of the dictations of the J2EE specification [10,2] on what programmers must, and must not, do while defining EJBs. These dictations are that attributes must be represented by abstract getter and setter methods, rather than by a standard Java class member; that instances must be obtained via the Home interface, rather than by directly invoking a constructor or any other user-defined method; business methods must not be `final` or `static`; and so forth.

4 An OOP-Compliant Implementation of AOP

Having described deployment as a weaving process, we are ready to explain how AspectJ2EE is implemented without breaking the object model.

Figure 4 shows how the application of four aspects to the ACCOUNT bean is realized. Comparing the figure to Fig. 3 we see that the definition of class `AccountBean` is simplified by moving the lifecycle methods to a newly defined class, `AdvAccount_Lifecycle`. In AspectJ2EE the programmer is not required to repeatedly write token implementations of the lifecycle methods in each bean. Instead, these implementations are packaged together in a standard `Lifecycle` aspect. Class `AdvAccount_Lifecycle` realizes the application of this aspect to our bean.

In general, for each application of an aspect to a class the deploy tool generates an *advised class*, so called since its generation is governed by the advices given in the aspect. There are three other advised classes in the figure: `AdvAccount_Persistence`, `AdvAccount_Security` and `AdvAccount_Transactions`, which correspond to the application of aspects `Persistence`, `Security` and `Transactions` to ACCOUNT.

The sequence of aspect applications is translated into a chain of inheritance starting at the main bean class. The *root advised class* is the first class in this chain (`AdvAccount_Lifecycle` in the example), while the *terminal advised class* is the last (`AdvAccount_Transactions` in the example). Fields, methods and inner classes defined in an aspect are copied to its advised class. *Advised methods* in this class are generated automatically based on the advices in the aspect.

The restriction of aspect targets to classes is one of the key features of AspectJ2EE which made it possible to reify *aspect application* as a class. In contrast, AspectJ is inclined to reify each *aspect* as a class, with rich and somewhat confusing semantics of instantiation controlled by a list of dedicated keywords (`perthis`, `pertarget`, `percflow`, `percflowbelow` and `issingleton`).

We note that although all the advised classes are concrete, only instances of the terminal advised class are created by the bean factory (the generated EJB home). In the figure for example, class `ConcreteRemoteAccountHome` creates all ACCOUNTS, which are always instances of `AdvAccount_Transactions`. It may be technically possible to construct instances of this bean in which fewer aspects are applied. There are however

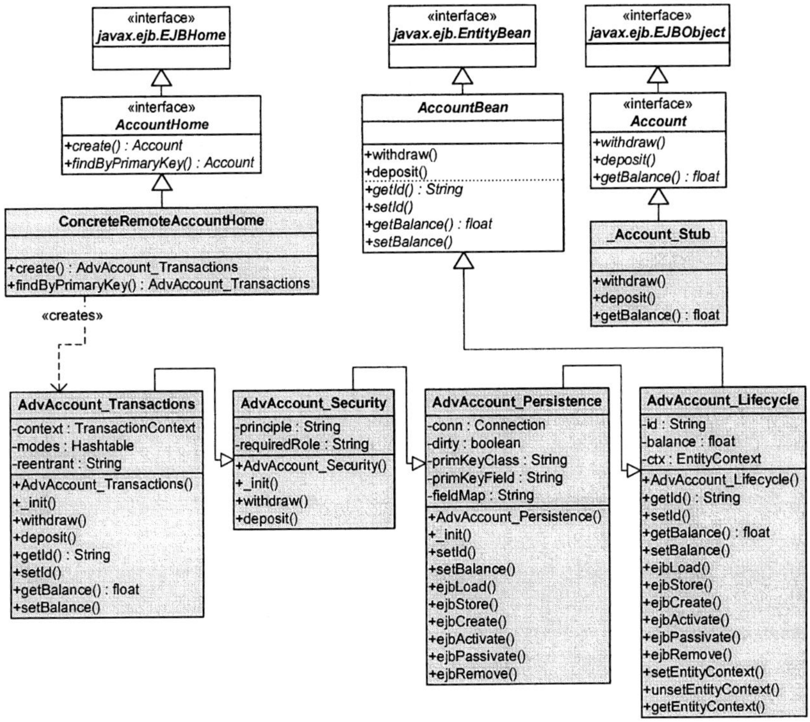

Fig. 4. The class hierarchy of bean ACCOUNT including programmer defined classes and interfaces and the support classes (in gray) generated by the AspectJ2EE deployment tool.

deep theoretical reasons for preventing this from happening. Suppose that a certain aspect applies to a software module such as a class or a routine, etc., in all but some exceptional incarnations of this module. Placing the tests for these exceptions at the point of incarnation (routine invocation or class instantiation) leads to scattered and tangled code, and defeats the very purpose of AOP. The bold statement that some accounts are exempt from security restrictions should be made right where it belongs—as part of the definition of the security aspect! Indeed, J2EE and other middleware frameworks do not support conditional application of services to the same business logic. A simple organization of classes in packages, together with Java accessibility rules, enforce this restriction and prevents clients from obtaining instances of non-terminal advised classes.

4.1 Aspects as Mixins and Generics

The AspectJ2EE approach draws power from being similar in concept to familiar mechanisms such as generics. In this interpretation, aspect `Persistence` is a generic class definition. The application of an aspect to a class is modelled then as the application of the corresponding generic definition to that class, yielding a concrete, instantiable class.

Thus, class `Lifecycle<AccountBean>` is the conceptual equivalent of applying aspect `Lifecycle` to `AccountBean`, class

```
Persistence<Lifecycle<AccountBean>>
```

corresponds to the application of aspect `Persistence` to the result, etc.

The generic declaration of an aspect `Aspect` would be written, in JDK 1.5-like[4] syntax, as

```
class Aspect<bean B> extends B { /*... */ }.                (1)
```

The form (1) allows us to draw parallels between the implementation of aspects in AspectJ2EE and another very familiar programming construct, namely *mixins* [25]. Curiously, Kiczales *et. al.* mention [8, Sect. 7.4] that mixins can be implemented with aspects. AspectJ2EE in effect shows the converse, namely that aspects can be implemented using a mixin-like mechanism, where the parallel drawn between `before()`, `after()` and `around()` advices and variations of overriding: "before" and "after" demons, and plain refining.

Interestingly, the programming pattern (1) was one of the prime motivations in the development of MixGen [26], a next-generation implementation of generics for Java and other OO languages. In extrapolating the evolution of generics mechanisms we see it supporting our embedding of aspects in the object model, while preserving the solid formal foundation.

4.2 Inheritance of Aspects, Abstract, and Parameterized Aspects

Despite the similarities, we note that AspectJ2EE aspects are more flexible and expressive than mixins and generics. The main difference is that the body of an aspect (the "`/*... */`" in (1)) may contain a pointcut definition, which may specify e.g., that a single advice applies to a range. In contrast, generics and mixins implementations do not allow specialization based on actual parameter.

We therefore rely on the form (1) as a conceptual model, which should help in understanding the semantics of AspectJ2EE, rather than any means for syntax definition. This form is beneficial for example in modelling aspect inheritance. An aspect `A1` inheriting from an aspect `A2` is simply written as

```
class A1<B> extends A2<B> { /*... */ }.                (2)
```

Furthermore, with this perspective we can easily distinguish between the two kinds of `abstract` aspects of AspectJ. Abstractness due to abstract methods is modelled by prefixing the class definition (1) with keyword `abstract`. The more interesting case of abstractness is when a pointcut is declared but not defined. In AspectJ, abstract aspects of this kind must be made concrete by way of inheritance before they are applied. In contrast, AspectJ2EE coins the term *parameterized aspects* for these, and allows missing

[4] Note that the Java SDK version 1.5 does not actually support this construct; the type parameter cannot serve as the superclass of the generic type.

pointcut definitions to be provided at application time, as modelled by the following form

$$\texttt{class Aspect<B,}\mathcal{P}_1,\ldots,\mathcal{P}_k\texttt{> extends B } \{\ \texttt{/*}\ldots\texttt{*/}\ \} \qquad (3)$$

where each $\mathcal{P}_i$, $i = 1, \ldots, k$, is a formal parameter to the aspect representing an abstract pointcut.

Parameterized aspects are similar to Caesar's *passive* pointcuts and advice [12], providing a separation between aspect implementation and aspect binding and hence enjoy similar reusability benefits. A typical example is that of a transaction management aspect with an `abstract` pointcut but specific advice for each of the transactional modes of methods. Such modes in the J2EE standard are `required` (method must execute within a database transaction; if no transaction exists, start one), `requiresnew` (the method must execute within a new transaction), etc.

The most crucial advantage of our approach over Caesar's is that in the sake of combat against scattered and tangled code problems, we forbid invocation and binding of aspects at runtime.

Parameterized aspects are not limited to abstract pointcut definitions. An abstract aspect can also include what can be thought of as an "abstract field"—a field whose initial value is specified at application time, as modelled by the form

$$\texttt{class Aspect<B,}\mathcal{P}_1,\ldots,\mathcal{P}_k,\mathcal{V}_1,\ldots,\mathcal{V}_n\texttt{> extends B } \{\texttt{/*}\ldots\texttt{*/}\} \qquad (4)$$

where each $\mathcal{V}_i$, $i = 1, \ldots, n$, is a formal parameter to the aspect representing an abstract field.

The form (4) makes it possible to apply the same aspect more than once to a single bean class, with each repeated application providing a distinct new extension. For example, consider a parameterized security aspect that accepts two parameters: a pointcut definition, specifying in which join points in the class should security checks be placed; and a field value, specifying the role to require at each of these join points. A single application of this aspect to the bean ACCOUNT could look like this:

`Security<Account,`P_{teller}`,"teller">`

where P_{teller} is a concrete pointcut definition specifying the execution of methods that require teller authorization. An additional application of the same aspect to the bean can then be used to specify which methods require client authoriation:

`Security<Security<Account,`P_{teller}`,"teller">,`P_{client}`,"client">`

where P_{client} is also a concrete pointcut definition.

5 The AspectJ2EE Programming Language

In this section we describe the implementation details of AspectJ2EE, and in particular how aspect application is described and how advice weaving is accomplished by way of subclassing.

5.1 The Aspect Binding Specification Language

One of the key issues in the design of an AOP language is the binding of aspects to the core functional code. This binding information includes the specification of the list of aspects which apply to each software module, their order of application, and even parameters to this application.

In AspectJ, this binding is specified in a declarative manner. However, the programmer, wearing the hat of the *application assembler* [2, Sect. 3.1.2], must take specific measures to ensure that the specified binding actually takes place, by compiling each core module with all the aspects that may apply to it. Thus, an aspect with global applicability may not apply to certain classes if these classes are not compiled with it. The order of application of aspects in AspectJ is governed by `declare precedence` statements; without explicit declarations, the precedence of aspects in AspectJ is undefined. Also, AspectJ does not provide any means for passing parameters to the application of aspects to modules.

In AspectJ2EE, aspect application is defined per bean class. The application also allows the application assembler to provide parameters to abstract aspects (including concrete pointcut definitions and initial field values).

Conceptually, aspect application in AspectJ2EE can be achieved using the generics-like syntax used in Sect. 4. However, when a large number of aspects is applied to a single bean (as is common in enterprise applications), the resulting syntactic constructs can be unwieldy. Hence, AspectJ2EE employs a semantically equivalent syntax based on XML deployment descriptors, following the tradition of using deployment descriptors to specify the application of services to EJBs in J2EE. Listing 1 gives an example.

Listing 1. A fragment of an EJB's deployment descriptor specifying the application of aspects to the ACCOUNT bean.

```
<entity id="Account">
    <ejb-name>Account</ejb-name>
    <home>aspectj2ee.demo.AccountHome</home>
    <remote>aspectj2ee.demo.Account</remote>
    <ejb-class>aspectj2ee.demo.AccountBean</ejb-class>
    <aspect>
        <aspect-class>aspectj2ee.core.Lifecycle</aspect-class>
    </aspect>
    <aspect>
        <aspect-class>aspectj2ee.core.Persistence</aspect-class>
        <value name="primKeyClass">java.lang.String</value>
        <value name="primKeyField">id</value>
        <value name="fieldMap">id:ID,balance:BALANCE</value>
    </aspect>
    <aspect>
        <aspect-class>aspectj2ee.core.Security</aspect-class>
        <pointcut name="secured">execution(*(..))</pointcut>
        <value name="requiredRole">User</value>
    </aspect>
    <aspect>
        <aspect-class>aspectj2ee.core.Transactions</aspect-class>
        <value name="reentrant">false</value>
        <pointcut name="requiresnew">execution(deposit(..)) ||
                                     execution(withdraw(..))</pointcut>
        <pointcut name="required">execution(*(..)) && !requiresnew()</pointcut>
    </aspect>
</entity>
```

As in the J2EE specification, bean ACCOUNT is defined by the `<entity>` XML element, and internal elements such as `<home>` specify the Java names that make this bean. In our extension of the deployment descriptor syntax, there is a new XML element, `<aspect>`, for each aspect applied to the bean. The `<pointcut>` element is used for binding any abstract pointcut, and the `<value>` element for specifying the initial value of fields.

As can be seen in the listing, four aspects are applied to our bean: `Lifecycle`, `Persistence`, `Security`, and `Transactions`. All four aspects are drawn from the `aspectj2ee.core` aspect library. Deploying this bean would result in the set of support classes depicted in Fig. 4.

The order of aspect specification determines the precedence of their application. Therefore, AspectJ2EE does not recognize the AspectJ statement `declare precedence`. The AspectJ2EE approach is more flexible, since it allows the developer to select a different order of precedence for the same set of aspects when applied to different beans, even in the same project. Intra-aspect precedence (where two or more advice from the same aspect apply to a single join point) is handled as per regular AspectJ.

Note that ACCOUNT can be viewed as an entity bean with container-managed persistence (CMP EJB) simply because it relies on the core persistence aspect, which parallels the standard J2EE persistence service. Should the developer decide to use a different persistence technique, that persistence system would itself be defined as an AspectJ2EE aspect, and applied to ACCOUNT in the same manner. This is parallel to bean-managed persistence beans (BMP EJBs) in the sense that the persistence logic is provided by the application programmer, independent of the services offered by the application server. However, it is completely unlike BMP EJBs in that the persistence code would not be tangled with the business logic and scattered across several bean and utility classes. In this respect, AspectJ2EE completely dissolves the distinction between BMP and CMP entity beans.

5.2 Implementing Advice Using Deploy-Time Weaving

AspectJ2EE supports each of the join point kinds defined in AspectJ, except for `handler` and `call`. We shall now describe how, for each supported type of join point, advice can be woven into the entity bean code.

Execution Join Points. The `execution(`*`methodSignature`*`)` join point is defined when a method is invoked and control transfers to the target method. AspectJ2EE captures `execution` join points by generating advised methods in the advised class, overriding the inherited methods that match the execution join point. Consider for example the advice in Listing 2 (a), whose pointcut refers to the execution of the `deposit()` method. This is a `before()` advice which prepends a printout line to matched join points. When applied to ACCOUNT, only one join point, the execution of `deposit()`, will match the specified pointcut. Hence, in the advised class, the `deposit()` method will be overridden, and the advice code will be inserted prior to invoking the original code. The resulting implementation of `deposit()` in the advised class appears in Listing 2 (b).

Recall that only instances of the terminal advised class exist in the system, so every call to the advised method (`deposit()` in this example) would be intercepted by means of regular polymorphism. Overriding and refinement can be used to implement

Listing 2. **(a)** Sample advice for `deposit()` execution, and **(b)** the resulting advised method.

(a)
```
before(float amount): execution(deposit(float)) && args(amount) {
    System.out.println("Depositing " + amount);
}
```

(b)
```
void deposit(float amount) {
    System.out.println("Depositing " + amount);
    super.deposit(amount);
}
```

`before()`, `after()` (including `after() returning` and `after() throwing`), and `around()` advice. With `around()` advice, the `proceed` keyword would indicate the location of the call to the inherited implementation.

The example in Listing 3 demonstrates the support for `after() throwing` advice. The advice, listed in part (a) of the listing, would generate a printout if the `withdraw()` method resulted in an `InsufficientFundsException`. The exception itself is re-thrown, i.e., the advice does not swallow it. The resulting advised method appears in part (b) of the listing. It shows how `after() throwing` advice are implemented by encapsulating the original implementation in a `try/catch` block.

Listing 3. **(a)** Sample `after() throwing` advice, applied to a method execution join point, and **(b)** the resulting advised method.

(a)
```
after() throwing (InsufficientFundsException ex)
    throws InsufficientFundsException:
    execution(withdraw(..)) {
    System.out.println("Withdrawal failed, exception message: "
                       + ex.getMessage());
    throw ex;
}
```

(b)
```
void withdraw(float amount) throws InsufficientFundsException {
    try {
        super.withdraw(amount);
    }
    catch (InsufficientFundsException ex) {
        System.out.println("Withdrawal failed, exception message: "
                           + ex.getMessage());
        throw ex;
    }
}
```

The execution join point cannot refer to `private` or `static` methods, since the invocation of these methods cannot be intercepted using polymorphism. The AspectJ2EE compiler issues a warning if a pointcut matches only the execution of such methods.

Constructor Execution Join Points. The constructor execution join point in AspectJ is defined using the same keyword as regular method execution. The difference lies in the method signature, which uses the keyword `new` to indicate the class's constructor. For example, the pointcut `execution(*.new(..))` would match the execution of any constructor in the class to which it is applied.

Unlike regular methods, constructors are limited with regard to the location in the code where the inherited implementation (`super()`) must be invoked. In particular, the invocation must occur before any field access or virtual method invocation. Hence, join points that refer to constructor signatures can be advised, but any code that executes before the inherited constructor (`before()` advice, or parts of `around()` advice that appear prior to the invocation of `proceed()`) must adhere to these rules.

An `around()` advice for constructor execution that does not contain an invocation of `proceed()` would be the equivalent of a Java constructor that does not invoke `super()` (the inherited constructor). This is tantamount to having an implicit call to `super()`, and is possible only if the advised class contains a constructor that does not take any arguments.

It is generally preferable to affect the object initialization process simply defining a constructor in the aspect, rather than by applying advice to constructor execution join points.

Class Initialization Join Points. EJBs must not contain read/write static fields, making static class initialization mostly mute. Still, the `staticinitialization(`*`typeSignature`*`)` join point can be used (with `after()` advice only), resulting in a static initialization block in the advised class.

Field Read and Write Access Join Points. Field access join points match references to and assignments of fields. In AspectJ2EE, field access join points apply to EJB *attributes* only. Recall that attributes are not declared as fields; rather, they are indicated by the programmer using abstract getter and setter methods in the bean class. These methods are then implemented in the concrete bean class (in J2EE) or in the root advised class (in AspectJ2EE).

If no advice is provided for a given attribute's read or write access, the respective method implementation in the root advised class would simply read or update the class field. The field itself is defined also in the root advised class. However, an attribute can be advised using `before()`, `around()` and `after()` advice, which would affect the way the getter and setter method are implemented.

Remote Call Join Points. The `remotecall` join point designator is a new keyword introduced in AspectJ2EE. Semantically, it is similar to AspectJ's `call` join point designator, defining a join point at a method invocation site. However, it only applies to remote calls to various methods; local calls are unaffected.

Remote call join points are implemented by affecting the stub generated at deploy time for use by EJB clients (such as `_Account_Stub` in Fig. 4). For example, the `around()` advice from Listing 4 (a) adds printout code both before and after the remote invocation of `Account.deposit()`. The generated stub class would include a `deposit()` method like the one shown in part (b) of that listing. Since the advised code appears in the stub, rather than in a server-side class, the output in this example will be generated by the client program.

Remote call join points can only refer to methods that are defined in the bean's remote interface. Advice using `remotecall` can be used to localize tier-cutting concerns, as detailed in Sect. 6.

5.3 Control-Flow Based Pointcuts

AspectJ includes two special keywords, `cflow` and `cflowbelow`, for specifying control-flow based limitations on pointcuts. Such limitations are used, for example, to prevent recursive application of advice. Both keywords are supported by AspectJ2EE.

Listing 4. **(a)** Sample advice for a method's `remotecall` join point, and **(b)** the resulting `deposit()` method generated in the RMI stub class.

(a)
```
around(): remotecall(* * Account.deposit(..)) {
    System.out.println("About to perform transaction.");
    proceed();
    System.out.println("Transaction completed.");
}
```

(b)
```
public void deposit(float arg0) {
    System.out.println("About to perform transaction.");
    // ... normal RMI/IIOP method invocation code ...
    System.out.println("Transaction completed.");
}
```

The manner in which control-flow limitations are enforced relies on the fact that deployment can be done in a completely platform-specific manner, since at deploy time, the exact target platform (JVM implementation) is known. Different JVMs use different schemes for storing a stack snapshot in instances of the `java.lang.Throwable` class [27] (this information is used, for example, by the method `java.lang.Exception.printStackTrace()`). Such a stack snapshot (obtained via an instance of `Throwable`, or any other JVM-specific means) can be examined in order to test for `cflow`/`cflowbelow` conditions at runtime.

5.4 The Core Aspects Library

AspectJ2EE's definition includes a standard library of core aspects. Four of these aspects were used in the ACCOUNT example, as shown in Fig. 4. Here is a brief overview of these four, and their effect on the advised classes:

1. The `aspectj2ee.core.Lifecycle` aspect (used to generated the root advised class) provides a default implementation to the J2EE lifecycle methods. The implementations of `setEntityContext()`, `unsetEntityContext`, and `getEntityContext()` maintain the entity context object; all other methods have an empty implementation. These easily-available common defaults make the development of EJBs somewhat easier (compared to standard J2EE development); the user-provided `AccountBean` class is now shorter, and contains strictly business logic methods[5].
2. The `aspectj2ee.core.Persistence` aspect provides a CMP-like persistence service. The attribute-to-database mapping properties are detailed in the parameters passed to this aspect in the deployment descriptor. This aspect advises some of the lifecycle methods, as well as the attribute setters (for maintaining a "dirty" flag), hence these methods are all overridden in the advised class.
3. The `aspectj2ee.core.Security` aspect can be used to limit the access to various methods based on user authentication. This is a generic security solution, on par with the standard J2EE security service. More detailed security decisions, such as role-based variations on method behavior, can be defined using project-specific aspects without tangling security-related code with the functional concern code.

[5] The fact that the fields used to implement the attributes, and the concrete getter and setter method for these attributes, appear in `AdvAccount_Lifecycle` (in Fig. 4) stems from the fact that this is the root advised class, and is not related to the `Lifecycle` aspect per se.

4. Finally, the `aspectj2ee.core.Transactions` aspect is used to provide transaction management capabilities to all business-logic methods. The parameters passed to it dictate what transactional behavior will be applied to each method.

6 Innovative Uses for AOP in Multi-tier Applications

The use of aspects in multi-tier enterprise applications can reduce the amount of cross-cutting concerns and tangled code. As discussed in Sect. 2, the core J2EE aspects were shown to be highly effective to this end, and the ability to define additional aspects (as well as alternative implementations to existing ones) increases this effectiveness and enables better program modularization.

But AspectJ2EE also allows developers to confront a different kind of cross-cutting non-functional concerns: aspects of the software that are implemented in part on the client and in part on the server. Here, the cross-cutting is extremely acute as the concern is implemented not just across several classes and modules, but literally across programs. We call these *tier-cutting concerns*.

The remainder of this section shows that a number of several key tier-cutting concerns can be represented as single aspect by using the `remotecall` join point designator. In each of these examples, the client code is unaffected; it is the RMI stub, which acts as a proxy for the remote object, which is being modified.

6.1 Client-Side Checking of Preconditions

Method preconditions [28] are commonly presented as a natural candidate for non-functional concerns being expressed cleanly and neatly in aspects. This allows preconditions to be specified without littering the core program, and further allows precondition testing to be easily disabled.

Preconditions should normally be checked at the method execution point, i.e., in the case of multi-tier applications, on the server. However, a precondition defines a contract that binds whoever invokes the method. Hence, by definition, precondition violations can be detected and flagged at the invocation point, i.e., on the client. In a normal program, this matters very little; but in a multi-tier application, trapping failed preconditions on the client can prevent the round-trip of a remote method invocation, which incurs a heavy overhead (including communications, parameter marshaling and un-marshaling, etc.).

Listing 5 presents a simple precondition that can be applied to the ACCOUNT EJB: neither `withdraw()` nor `deposit()` are ever supposed to be called with a non-positive amount as a parameter. If such an occurrence is detected, a `PreconditionFailed-Exception` is thrown. Using two named pointcut definitions, the test is applied both at the client and at the server.

In addition to providing a degree of safety, such aspects decrease the server load by blocking futile invocation attempts. In a trusted computing environment, if the preconditioned methods are invoked only by clients (and never by other server-side methods), the server load can be further reduced by completely disabling server-side tests.

When using aspects to implement preconditions, always bear in mind that preconditions test for logically flawed states, rather than states that are unacceptable from a

Listing 5. An aspect that can be used to apply precondition testing (both client- and server-side) to the ACCOUNT EJB.

```
public aspect EnsurePositiveAmounts {
    pointcut clientSide(float amount):
        (remotecall(public void Account.deposit(float)) ||
         remotecall(public void Account.withdraw(float))) && args(amount);

    pointcut serverSide(float amount):
        (execution(public void Account.deposit(float)) ||
         execution(public void Account.withdraw(float))) && args(amount);

    before(float amount): clientSide(amount) || serverSide(amount) {
        if (amount <= 0.0)
            throw new PreconditionFailedException("Non-positive amount: "+amount);
    }
}
```

business process point of view. Thus, preventing the withdrawal of excessive amounts should not be defined as a precondition, but rather as part of `withdraw()`'s implementation.

6.2 Symmetrical Data Processing

By adding code both at the sending and receiving ends of remotely-invoked methods, we are able to create what can be viewed as an additional layer in the communication stack. For example, we can add encryption at the stub and decryption at the remote tie, for increased security; or we can apply a compression scheme (compressing information at the client, decompressing it at the server) to reduce the communications overhead; and so forth.

Consider an EJB representing a university course, with the method `register()` accepting a `Vector` of names of students (`Strings`) to be registered to that course. The aspect in Listing 6 shows how the remote invocation of this method can be made more effective by applying compression. Assume that the class `CompressedVector` represents a `Vector` in a compressed (space-efficient) manner. Applying this aspect to the COURSE EJB would result in a new method, `registerCompressed()`, added to the advised class. Unlike most non-public methods, this one would be represented in the class's RMI stub, since it is invoked by code that is included in the stub itself (that code would reside in the advised stub for the `register()` method).

Listing 6. An aspect that can be used for sending a compressed version of an argument over the communications line, when applied to the COURSE EJB.

```
public aspect CompressRegistrationList {
    around(Vector v): remotecall(public void register(Vector)) && args(v) {
        CompressedVector cv = new CompressedVector(v);
        registerCompressed(cv);
    }

    void registerCompressed(CompressedVector cv) {
        Vector v = cv.decompress();
        register(v);
    }
}
```

Compression and encryption can be applied not only for arguments, but also for return values. In this case, the aspect should use `after() returning` advice for both the `remotecall` and `execution` join points. Advice for `after() throwing` can be used for processing exceptions (which are often information-laden, due to the embedded call stack, and would hence benefit greatly from compression).

6.3 Memoization

Memoization (the practice of caching method results) is another classic use for aspects. When applied to a multi-tier application, this should be done with care, since in many cases the client tier has no way to know when the cached data becomes stale and should be replaced. Still, it is often both possible and practical, and using AspectJ2EE it can be done without changing any part of the client program.

For example, consider a session EJB that reports international currency exchange rates. These rates are changed on a daily basis; for the sake of simplicity, assume that they are changed every midnight. The aspect presented in Listing 7 can be used to enable client-side caching of rates.

Listing 7. An aspect that can be used for caching results from a currency exchange-rates EJB.

```
public aspect CacheExchangeRates {
    class CacheData { int year; int dayOfYear; float value; }

    Hashtable cache = new Hashtable();

    pointcut clientSide(String currencyName):
        remotecall(public float getExchangeRate(String)) && args(currencyName);

    around(String currencyName): clientSide(currencyName) {
        Calendar now = Calendar.getInstance();
        int currentYear = now.get(Calendar.YEAR);
        int currentDayOfYear = now.get(Calendar.DAY_OF_YEAR);

        // First, try and find the value in the cache
        CacheData cacheData = (CacheData) cache.get(currencyName);
        if (cacheData != null) && currentYear = cacheData.year &&
            currentDayOfYear == cacheData.dayOfYear)
                return cacheData.value; // Value is valid; no remote invaocation

        float result = proceed(currencyName); // Normally obtain the value

        // Cache the value for future reference
        cacheData = new CacheData();          cacheData.year = currentYear;
        cacheData.dayOfYear = currentDayOfYear;  cacheData.value = result;

        cache.put(currencyName, cacheData);
    }
}
```

7 Conclusions and Future Work

We believe that AspectJ2EE opens a new world of possibilities to developers of EJB-based applications, allowing them to extend, enhance and replace the standard services provided by EJB containers with services of their own. EJB services can be distributed and used across several projects; libraries of services can be defined and reused.

Aspects in AspectJ2EE are less general, and have a more defined target, than their AspectJ counterparts. Also, even though the same aspect can be applied (possibly with different parameters) to several EJBs, each such application can only affect its specific EJB target. Therefore, we expect AspectJ2EE aspects should be more understandable, and the woven programs more maintainable.

By using deploy-time weaving, AspectJ2EE allows the programmer's code to be advised without being tampered with. Programmers can define methods that will provide business functionality while being oblivious to the various services (transaction management, security, etc.) applied to these methods.

And in addition to the familiar services provided by EJB containers, AspectJ2EE aspects can be used to unscatter and untangle tier-cutting concerns, which in many cases can improve an application server's performance.

Work is currently underway to implement AspectJ2EE as a new deployment process for the IBM WebSphere Application Server, version 5.0. We will then use AspectJ2EE to define every service currently provided by WebSphere as an aspect. Ideally, the result would be a standard-compliant J2EE server that can easily be extended using Aspect-Oriented Programming concepts.

References

1. Shannon, B., Hapner, M., Matena, V., Davidson, J., Davidson, J., Cable, L.: Java 2 Platform, Enterprise Edition: Platform and Component Specifications. Addison-Wesley (2000)
2. DeMichiel, L.G., Yalçinalp, L.U., Krishnan, S.: Enterprise JavaBeans specification, version 2.0. http://java.sun.com/j2ee/ (2001)
3. Kiczales, G., Lamping, J., Menhdhekar, A., Maeda, C., Lopes, C., Loingtier, J.M., Irwin, J.: Aspect-oriented programming. In Akşit, M., Matsuoka, S., eds.: Proceedings European Conference on Object-Oriented Programming. Volume 1241. Springer-Verlag, Berlin, Heidelberg, and New York (1997) 220–242
4. Soares, S., Laureano, E., Borba, P.: Implementing distribution and persistence aspects with AspectJ. In: Proceedings of OOPSLA'02, Object Oriented Programming Systems Languages and Applications, ACM Press (2002)
5. Hao, R., Boloni, L., Jun, K., Marinescu, D.C.: An aspect-oriented approach to distributed object security. In: Proceedings of The Fourth IEEE Symposium on Computers and Communications, IEEE Press (1999)
6. Kim, H., Clarke, S.: The relevance of AOP to an applications programmer in an EJB environment. First International Conference on Aspect-Oriented Software Development (AOSD) Workshop on Aspects, Components, and Patterns for Infrastructure Software (ACP4IS) (2002)
7. Choi, J.P.: Aspect-oriented programming with Enterprise JavaBeans. In: 4th International Enterprise Distributed Object Computing Conference (EDOC 2000), IEEE Computer Society (2000) 252–261
8. Kiczales, G., Hilsdale, E., Hugunin, J., Kersten, M., Palm, J., Griswold, W.G.: An overview of AspectJ. Lecture Notes in Computer Science **2072** (2001) 327–355
9. American National Standards Institute, Inc.: Programming language – COBOL, ANSI X3.23–1985 edition (1985)
10. Shannon, B.: Java 2 platform enterprise edition specification, v1.3. http://java.sun.com/-j2ee/1.3/download.html#platformspec (2001)
11. Laddad, R.: AspectJ in Action: Practical Aspect-Oriented Programming. Manning, Greenwich (2003)

12. Pichler, R., Ostermann, K., Mezini, M.: On aspectualizing component models. Software – Practice and Experience **33** (2003) 957–974
13. Bodoff, S., Green, D., Haase, K., Jendrock, E., Pawlan, M., Stearns, B.: The J2EE Tutorial. Addison-Wesley (2002)
14. Duclos, F., Estublier, J., Morat, P.: Describing and using non functional aspects in component based applications. In: Proceedings of the 1st International Conference on Aspect-Oriented Software Development (AOSD 2002). (2002) 22–26
15. Weinschenk, C.: The application server market is dead; long live the application server market. http://www.serverwatch.com/tutorials/article.php/2234311 (2003)
16. JBoss Group: JBoss product homepage. http://www.jboss.org/ (2003)
17. Burke, B., Brock, A.: Aspect-oriented programming and JBoss. http://www.onjava.com/-lpt/a/3878 (2003)
18. Mezini, M., Ostermann, K.: Conquering aspects with Caesar. In: Proceedings of the 2nd International Conference on Aspect-Oriented Software Development (AOSD 2003), ACM Press (2003)
19. Walker, R.J., Baniassad, E.L.A., Murphy, G.C.: An initial assessment of aspect-oriented programming. In: IEEE International Conference on Software Engineering (ICSE). (1999) 120–130
20. Constantinides, C.A., Elrad, T., Fayad, M.E.: Extending the object model to provide explicit support for crosscutting concerns. Software – Practice and Experience **32** (2002) 703–734
21. Gamma, E., Helm, R., Johnson, R., Vlissides, J.: Design Patterns: Elements of Reusable Object-Oriented Software. Professional Computing. Addison-Wesley (1995)
22. Cohen, T., Hadad, E.: An enhanced framework for providing explicit support for crosscutting concerns in object-oriented languages. Submitted to Software – Practice and Experience (2004)
23. Sun Microsystems, Inc.: rmic - the Java RMI compiler. http://java.sun.com/j2se/1.4.2/docs/-tooldocs/solaris/rmic.html (2003)
24. IBM Corp.: IBM WebSphere Application Server product family homepage. http://www-3.ibm.com/software/info1/websphere/index.jsp?tab=products/appserv (2003)
25. Bracha, G., Cook, W.: Mixin-based inheritance. In Meyrowitz, N., ed.: Proceedings of the Conference on Object-Oriented Programming: Systems, Languages, and Applications / Proceedings of the European Conference on Object-Oriented Programming, Ottawa, Canada, ACM Press (1990) 303–311
26. Allen, E., Bannet, J., Cartwright, R.: A first-class approach to genericity. In: Proceedings of OOPSLA'03, Object Oriented Programming Systems Languages and Applications, ACM Press (2003)
27. Chan, P., Lee, R., Kramer, D.: The Java Class Libraries. 2 edn. Volume 1. Addison-Wesley (1998)
28. Meyer, B.: Object-Oriented Software Construction. 2nd edn. Prentice-Hall (1997)

Use Case Level Pointcuts

Jonathan Sillito, Christopher Dutchyn,
Andrew David Eisenberg, and Kris De Volder

Department of Computer Science
University of British Columbia
Vancouver, BC, Canada
{sillito,cdutchyn,ade,kdvolder}@cs.ubc.ca

Abstract. Software developers create a variety of artifacts that model the behaviour of applications at different levels of abstraction; e.g. use cases, sequence diagrams, and source code. Aspect-oriented programming languages, such as AspectJ, support the modularization of crosscutting concerns at the source code level. However, crosscutting concerns also arise in other behavioural models of software systems. We provide a new aspect language, AspectU, which supports modularization of crosscutting concerns in the use-case model. Further, we provide a prototype tool that partially translates AspectU aspects into AspectJ aspects. To facilitate this translation we introduce a third aspect language, AspectSD, which targets the sequence-diagram model. AspectU together with our translation tool allows developers to express advice using use case level concepts while still affecting the runtime behaviour of a system, yielding a natural and intensional expression of some concerns.

1 Introduction

When limited to a hierarchical decomposition of a system as supported by object-oriented languages, some concerns of interest cannot be cleanly modularized. Instead, the implementation of the concern is scattered across multiple modules, tangled with the primary concerns of these modules. Aspect-Oriented Software Development (AOSD) has focused on improving the modularity of these *crosscutting concerns*. One prominent AOSD tool is *AspectJ* [9], a general-purpose aspect-oriented programming language. It extends the *Java*[1] programming language with join points, pointcuts, and advice [11]. These additions enable aspects to be written that gather the otherwise scattered and tangled source code into one location.

We believe crosscutting concerns exist in other behavioural models as well, including the use-case and sequence-diagram models. Existing aspect-oriented programming languages operate at the level of implementation and support pointcuts reflecting programming language constructs such as classes, methods, fields, and objects. When limited to such constructs, it can be difficult to understand the effects of the pointcuts in terms of other behavioural models.

[1] Java is a trademark of Sun Microsystems, Inc.

M. Odersky (Ed.): ECOOP 2004, LNCS 3086, pp. 244–266, 2004.

We present a new aspect language, *AspectU*, for modularizing crosscutting concerns within the use-case model. AspectU provides a join-point model based on elements in this model: use cases, steps, and extensions. Many crosscutting concerns that can be naturally expressed in terms of the use cases can be formally expressed using AspectU. AspectU aspects capture changes to a system's dynamic behaviour as expressed in its use cases. These behavioural changes are expressed as steps and extensions added to or replacing elements of the existing behaviour.

In addition, we present an exploration of aspect modularity between models. To this end, we have implemented a tool for partially translating between AspectU and AspectJ. In particular, the translation focuses on translating AspectU pointcuts. Our translation makes use of a third language, *AspectSD*, that targets the sequence diagram model. AspectSD bridges AspectU and AspectJ in the same way that sequence diagrams bridge the use-case model and the implementation. Our translation relies on a mapping between the use case model and the sequence-diagram model, as well as correspondence between the sequence-diagram model and the implementation. Given such a mapping, our tool translates an AspectU pointcut into an AspectSD representation, and then into AspectJ advice that identifies the join points in the implementation corresponding to the specified join points in the use case. In addition to identifying join points, the generated AspectJ advice can trigger user supplied Java code, bind objects for that code to operate on, and control the flow of the application in a number of ways.

Using AspectU and our translation tool together allow a developer to write aspects using use case level pointcuts—affecting both the use-case model and the behaviour of the running system. We claim that for many concerns such a pointcut will be more natural and intensional than a corresponding pointcut in AspectJ or another (source level) aspect-oriented programming language.

We present the AspectU language in detail in Section 2. Two complete AspectU examples are shown in Section 3. The AspectSD language is presented in Section 4. The details of our translation between aspect languages is in Section 5. We discuss the benefits of our approach in Section 6, and conclude with a discussion of related work in Section 7.

2 The AspectU Language

AspectU extends the use-case model with support for modularizing crosscutting behaviour. This support makes it possible to define additional behaviour at certain points in the model. Crosscutting in AspectU is based on a small set of constructs based on AspectJ's constructs: *join points*, which are points in the model, *pointcuts*, which are a means to identify join points, and *advice*, which is a means of affecting the behaviour at the join points. Taken together, these constructs define a *join-point model* that specifies how the crosscutting behaviour relates to the underlying use-case model.

Use Case: Entity establishes session *(session)*

Trigger: Entity connects to server *(entity connect)*

Main Success Scenario:
1. entity initiates stream *(entity initialize)*
2. server connects to entity and initiates stream *(server connect)*
3. entity authenticates with server *(authenticate)*
4. server handles message, presence and iq stanzas *(handle)*
5. entity sends terminates stream *(terminate)*
6. server terminates stream and closes connection *(close)*

Extensions:

⋆a. Stream level error
- ⋆a1. server sends error stanza to entity *(error)*
- ⋆a2. server terminates stream and closes connection *(close)*

3a. Authentication fails
- 3a1. server sends failure stanza to entity *(fail)*
- 3b2. server terminates stream and closes connection *(close)*

Fig. 1. Use case describing the behaviour of the system when an entity (a client or other server) establishes a session with a XMPP server.

This section contains several small examples targeting use cases (see Figures 1, 3, and 4) based on the XMPP [15] specification. This specification describes a set of client server-messaging protocols. The use cases we present in this paper describe parts of those protocols in terms of steps and extensions. More details on the XMPP specification, along with more complete examples are presented in Section 3. These use cases are simplified slightly for presentation convenience; primarily that not all use-case extensions are shown. Also, we provide an identifying name next to each step, each use case, and some extensions.

One use case, shown in Figure 1, indicates to the steps involved when a client or other server connects to a server. It consists of six steps: the first three involve the entity connecting and authenticating with the server. The fourth step handles each stanza, or communication unit, between the entity and the server. There are several different kinds of stanzas; each is handled in a different way as documented in separate use cases. Finally, when the entity wishes to disconnect, the last two steps are performed. This use case also contains two extensions. The first extension is triggered whenever there is a stream-level error anywhere in the use case, and ensures that the server attempts to cleanly terminate the connection. The second extension specifies that the session should be terminated when authentication fails.

2.1 Join Points

Use cases are a behavioural model of a system, and can be thought of as something that can be *executed*. Elements in the model are nested: a use case is made up of extensions and steps; an extension is made up of steps. This can be taken

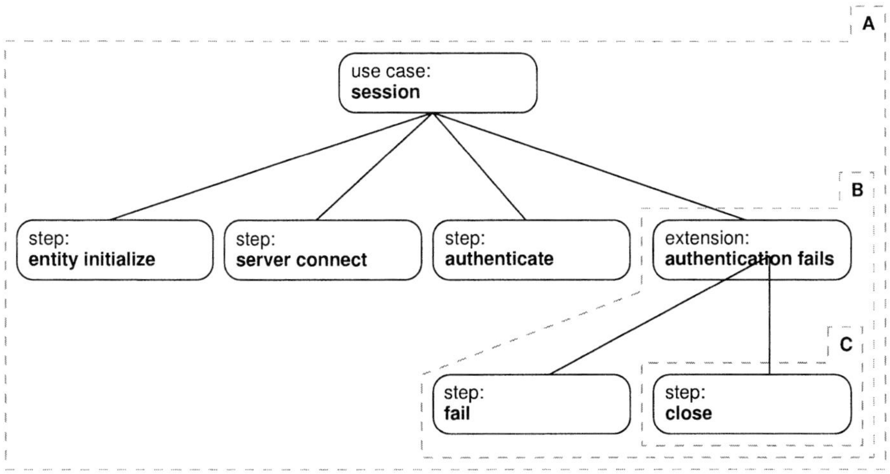

Fig. 2. A tree describing one possible execution of the *session* use case shown in Figure 1. The tree captures the execution corresponding to an authentication failure. The enclosed areas labelled **A**, **B** and **C** refer to three subtrees rooted at the use-case *session*, the extension *authentication fails* and the step *close* respectively.

further in that steps may be further elaborated as other use cases. Because of this nesting property of the model, each execution of a use case can be thought of as forming a tree. Execution order is represented in left-to-right, depth-first traversal of this tree.

As an example, one possible execution of the *session* use case (see Figure 1) is shown in Figure 2. In this particular execution, authentication fails and so steps **4**, **5**, and **6**, and extension ***a** are never executed. The system behaviour captured by this execution of the use case is broken down as three steps followed by one extension, which is is further broken down as two additional steps.

Join points in AspectU are elements in the execution of the use-case model. These points can be considered as subtrees in the execution of that model. In particular there are three types of join points: use-case, extension, and step join points. The entire subtree labelled **A** in Figure 2 corresponds to a join point of type use case; the subtree labelled **B** corresponds to a join point of type extension, and the subtree labelled **C** corresponds to a join point of type step.

2.2 Pointcuts

An AspectU pointcut identifies a set of join points. Pointcuts can be thought of in terms of matching certain join points (subtrees) in the execution. Three primitive pointcuts, which can be composed to form more sophisticated pointcuts, are defined:

1. `usecase(id)`—matches the join point for any *use-case* subtree with name matching `id`,

2. `extension(id)`—matches the join point for any *extension* subtree with name matching `id`, and
3. `step(id)`—matches the join point for any *step* subtree with name matching `id`.

The identifiers used as arguments in the above primitive pointcuts can contain the wild-card character `*`, which matches any substring. For example, `step(send*)` would match the join point for any step with a name beginning with *send*.

Pointcuts can be combined using *and* (`&&`) and *or* (||) operators. The *and* operator combines two pointcuts to build a new pointcut that matches any subtree matched by one of the pointcuts and lies *within* a subtree matched by the other pointcut. For example,

```
usecase(session) && extension(authentication fails)
```

identifies subtrees that are either (a) matched by the pointcut `usecase(session)` *and* lie within a subtree matched by the pointcut `extension(authentication fails)`, or (b) matched by the pointcut `extension(authentication fails)` *and* lie within a subtree matched by the pointcut `usecase(session)`. For the execution tree shown in Figure 2, the example pointcut identifies the subtree labelled **B**, because it is matched by `extension(authentication fails)` and is within a subtree matched by `usecase(session)` (i.e. it is withing subtree **A**).

The *or* operator combines two pointcuts to build a new one that matches execution trees where either subordinate pointcut matches. For example,

```
usecase(session) || extension(authentication fails)
```

identifies execution trees that are in use-case *session* or in extension *authentication fails*. For the execution tree shown in Figure 2, the previous pointcut identifies the subtree labelled **A** as well as the subtree labelled **B**.

The *and* and *or* pointcut combinators allow powerful effects when used in concert with wild cards. The pointcut

```
step(deliver*)
```

would apply to the execution subtrees corresponding to the *deliver presence* step in the *handle presence* use case (see Figure 4), as well as the *deliver message* step in the *handle message* use case (see Figure 3). However when this pointcut is combined as follows

```
usecase(handle message) && step(deliver*)
```

only execution trees corresponding to the *deliver message* step in the *handle message* use case are matched by the pointcut.

In addition to identifying join points, a pointcut can also provide access to values in the execution context of those join points. This is done using the `bind(bind-id, entity-id)` pointcut, which binds the use-case entity named `entity-id` to the identifier `bind-id`. This pointcut allows values associated with the matching join point to be available within the advice body. For example,

```
usecase(session) && bind(m,message)
```

provides a name, `m`, for the message entity within the *session* use case. As in this example, `bind` is most often used with *and* and *or* operators. For a complete example of this, see the privacy aspect in Figure 6, discussed in Section 3.

2.3 Advice

Advice is a mechanism used to declare that certain *additional* behaviour should execute at each of the join points in a pointcut. A piece of advice has three parts:

1. a pointcut indicating *where* the additional behaviour should be performed;
2. an advice body describing *what* the additional behaviour is, expressed in terms of steps and extensions; and,
3. a qualifier indicating *how* the additional behaviour combines with the behaviour at the join point.

AspectU supports three types of qualifiers, with meanings analogous to the corresponding AspectJ qualifiers. Each qualifier has a `binding-list` associated with it, which specifies the bound entities available in the advice body:

1. `before(binding-list)`—denotes advice to apply immediately before the execution of the matched subtrees,
2. `around(binding-list)`—denotes advice to apply around, and possibly instead of, the matched subtrees (more on this below), and
3. `after(binding-list)`—denotes advice to apply immediately after the execution of the matched subtrees.

A simple example of a complete piece of advice (with comments on the right identifying the advice parts) is

```
after(m) :                                          // qualifier
   step(handle*) && bind(m, message)                // pointcut
{                                                   // body
   steps:
      - server logs delivery of message m
}
```

The additional behaviour given in advice can combine with the pre-existing behaviour in three ways. First, advice can be strictly additive with respect to the normal execution. That is it can simply add behaviour at the join points identified by the pointcut. This can be done with `before` or `after` advice to specify additional steps to be applied at entry to or exit from a join point (subtree).

Second, advice can influence the behaviour in a way that is not strictly additive. To that end `around` advice has the special capability of selectively preempting the normal execution at the join point. An `around` advice can, alternatively, allow the execution to continue normally by including a step named `proceed`. This special step, analogous to AspectJ's `proceed()`, is used only in `around`

Use Case: Server handles message stanza *(handle message)*
Trigger: Entity sends message *(send)*
Main Success Scenario:
1. server processes and verifies message *(verify)*
2. server determines recipient of message *(determine recipient)*
3. server delivers message to recipient *(deliver message)*

Extensions:
2a. Non-local recipient
  2a1. route message *(route)*
2b. No such client
  2b1. reply with 'recipient unavailable' *(error)*
3a. Delivery failed *(delivery failed)*
  3a1. reply with 'recipient unavailable' *(error)*

Fig. 3. Use case describing how an XMPP server handles a message stanza: a simple push scheme is followed.

advice. A `proceed` step instructs the execution to proceed into the subtrees that the advice surrounds. An `around` advice lacking a `proceed` step replaces the original behaviour of the use case. One example of this is shown in the storage aspect (see Figure 5). That example's `around` advice introduces a step that executes in place of the execution of the *delivery failed* extension.

Third, advice can introduce use-case extensions. Like normal use-case extensions, this specifies behaviour that is executed when a certain condition is met. In AspectU, an added extension can end with a step named `rejoin`, which instructs the execution to return to (i.e. rejoin with) the use case at the location the advice was started from. If no `rejoin` is specified, the extension is understood to *terminate* the use case. The result is that the subtree corresponding to the extension is the last in that particular execution of the use case. An example of this is shown in the privacy aspect (see Figure 6). In the event that the privacy check fails, the control will pass to the added extension. As this extension does not rejoin, the remaining steps in the use case will be skipped.

Taken together, join points, pointcuts and advice support the expression of crosscutting behaviour. Aspects package these constructs in a modular way. Two complete example aspects are presented in the next section.

3 AspectU Examples

Throughout this paper we use examples based on a set of XML protocols and technologies that enable entities (clients and servers) to exchange communication units called stanzas. Stanzas can be messages, presence, and other structured information. The Internet Engineering Task Force has formalized the core protocols under the name *Extensible Messaging and Presence Protocol* (XMPP). The official documentation is in several parts or layers. The base specification is called *XMPP Core* [15].

Use Case: Server handles presence stanza. *(handle presence)*

Trigger: Entity sends presence *(send)*

Main Success Scenario:

1. server processes and verifies presence *(verify)*
2. server obtains entity's subscription information *(subscription)*
3. server determines recipients based on subscription information *(determine recipients)*
4. server delivers stanza to each recipient *(deliver presence)*

Extensions:

1a. Presence probe
    1a1. server determines target of probe *(determine target)*
    1a2. server obtains target's last reported presence *(obtain presence)*
    1a3. server replies to probe with this presence *(reply)*
4a. Non-local recipient
    4a1. route presence *(route)*

Fig. 4. Use case describing how an XMPP server handles presence stanza. The basic approach is based on a subscribe and broadcast scheme.

Based on XMPP Core specifications, we have developed several use cases. The first of these was presented in Section 2. Two more are given in Figures 3 and 4. The use case shown in Figure 3 details the steps taken to handle a message stanza sent by a connected entity. The *handle message* use case comprises three steps: verification, addressing, and delivery. If addressing indicates that a message cannot be locally delivered, extension **2a** is triggered to route the message to a remote location. Addressing could fail because the recipient does not exist, which is handled by extension **2b**. Delivery can fail because the recipient is not currently connected, which is handled by extension **3a**.

The use case shown in Figure 4 details the steps taken to handle presence stanzas sent by a connected entity. Presence stanzas are used for communicating status (e.g. online, offline, or away) between entities. While handling presence stanzas, the server follows a publish-subscribe scheme in which the information is sent to all subscribed entities. An exception to this is a presence probe which is a query for a particular entity's presence. Presence probes continue to be handled in extension **1a**.

XMPP Core is intended to provide a general framework for building messaging applications. One such application is instant messaging (IM) similar to AIM or ICQ. A separate specification document, XMPP Instant Messaging (XMPPIM) [16], extends XMPP Core with features needed to support such instant-messaging applications. In addition to adding more use cases the XMPPIM specification adds some concerns that crosscut the XMPP Core use cases. Two examples of such crosscutting concerns are from the *storage* and *privacy* features. We present each these as examples of AspectU aspects in the following two subsections. Expressing these concerns in AspectU, rather than directly modifying the affected use cases, is natural—it supports a modularization consistent with the specification.

```
aspect storage {
    around(stanza) : usecase(handle message) &&
        extension(delivery failed) && bind(stanza,message)
    {
      steps:
        - server stores stanza for later delivery (store)
    }

    before(client) : usecase(session) && step(handle) &&
        bind(client,entity)
    {
      steps:
         - server delivers any stored messages to client (deliver)
    }
}
```

Fig. 5. An AspectU aspect expressing the storage concern.

3.1 Storage Aspect

Message storage is a store-and-forward feature similar to that found in email servers. Describing the effect of this feature in terms of the *session* and *handle message* use cases described above is straightforward: when handling a message for a local recipient, if they are offline (i.e. in extension **3a**) then store the message; and, when a client connects to and successfully authenticates with the server (i.e. before the *handle* step) then deliver any stored messages.

This concern, written in AspectU, (see Figure 5) is similarly straightforward. It contains two pieces of advice, one for each new behaviour: the first stores undeliverable messages, and the other delivers deferred messages once a new connection is established. Each of the pieces of advice contains a `bind()` in the pointcut. In both cases this identifies objects that are referred to in the advice body. The `bind()` in the `around` advice, for example, states that the stanza referred to in the added step is the message object referred to in the use case. It is noteworthy that this advice does not contain a `proceed` step.

3.2 Privacy Aspect

The aspect in Figure 6 packages the behaviour needed to implement crosscutting associated with the privacy feature. Privacy, like the message storage concern, is introduced in the XMPPIM specification as a concern layered on top of the core protocol. The privacy concern deals with a client's ability to limit communication to or from other users. Supporting privacy requires the addition of several use cases for managing privacy lists, but these are already well modularized. But, it also introduces some additional required behaviour crosscutting the *handle message* and *handle presence* use cases shown in Figures 3 and 4 respectively. Rather than modify the affected use cases directly, AspectU supports modularization of these concerns.

```
aspect privacy {
   before (user, stanza) :
   (step(deliver message) && bind(user, recipient) &&
       bind(stanza, message)) ||
   (step(deliver presence) && bind(user, entity) &&
       bind(stanza, presence))
   {
     steps:
         - server verifies stanza against user's privacy settings
           (check privacy)

     extensions:
         - name: privacy check failed
           source: check privacy
           steps:
               - silently drop stanza (drop)
    }
}
```

Fig. 6. An AspectU aspect expressing the privacy concern.

The privacy aspect in Figure 6 implements this additional behaviour. The pointcut matches executions of the *deliver message* step from the *handle message* use case and executions of the *deliver presence* step from the *handle presence* use case. The body adds a step before each of the identified steps and also adds an associated extension. The inserted step involves verifying that the stanza can be sent without violating the appropriate privacy settings. The extension ensures that if the privacy check fails then the stanza is silently dropped rather than delivered.

The body of the privacy aspect is written in terms of a user and a stanza: the arguments to the qualifier. There are some differences between how privacy should be enforced in the *handle message* use case and in the *handle presence* use case. In the *handle message* use case, the check verifies that the privacy rules of the recipient allow the given message. In the *handle presence* use case, the check verifies that the privacy rules of the connecting entity allow the given presence notification to be sent. AspectU's name binding mechanism allows the body of the privacy aspect to be general enough to apply privacy in both of these cases. For handling messages the `bind` statements in the pointcut support this by mapping *recipient* to *user* and *message* to *stanza*. Similarly, for handling presence, *entity* is mapped to *user* and *presence* is mapped to *stanza*.

The AspectU language is supported by a tool that takes as input use cases (stored in a machine-readable format, based on the *yaml* [4] mark-up language) and AspectU aspects and produces transformed use cases. This tranformation process is sometimes called called *weaving*. Figure 7 shows the results of weaving both the privacy and storage concerns into the message handling use case. The steps and extensions shown in bold represent the additions made by the aspects.

Use Case: Server handles message stanza *(handle message)*
Trigger: Entity sends message *(send)*
Main Success Scenario:
1. server processes and verifies message *(verify)*
2. server determines recipient of message *(determine recipient)*
3. server verifies message against recipient's privacy settings (check privacy)
4. server delivers message to recipient *(deliver message)*

Extensions:
2a. Non-local recipient
  2a1. route message *(route)*
2b. No such client
  2b1. reply with 'recipient unavailable' *(error)*
3a. Privacy check failed
  3a1. silently drop message (drop)
4a. Delivery failed *(delivery failed)*
  4a1. server stores message for later delivery (store)

Fig. 7. Illustrates the effect of weaving the privacy and storage aspects into the *handle message* use case. Added behaviour added by the aspects is shown in bold.

Notice that in step number 3, *stanza* and *user* have been replaced by *message* and *recipient*.

While this can be a useful tool, ultimately the goal is not to modify the use case but rather to keep these concerns separate. Given this separation it is possible to pursue modularization between models, as discussed in the next two sections.

4 The AspectSD Language

For our purposes a *sequence diagram* is a sequence of messages along with the objects that send and receive them. Figure 8 contains a sample sequence diagram. During the design of a system, sequence diagrams may be used to refine the behaviour specified by the use cases in terms of object interactions.

Each sequence diagram corresponds to a single scenario of a use case and, therefore, to a single execution tree. For example, the sequence diagram shown in Figure 8 corresponds to the main success scenario of the *handle message* use case. Sequence diagrams can be viewed as a further elaboration of the behaviour captured by a use-case execution tree in terms of messages between objects.

Like use cases, we store sequence diagrams in a machine readable format based on the yaml mark-up language. Our format for storing sequence diagrams supports various annotations that document what sequences of messages correspond to which use-case steps. Given this mapping it is possible to think about a sequence diagram as the fringe of one execution tree. This is illustrated in Figure 9 where, for example, the execution of the *verify* step is decomposed as the execution of messages $m_1 \ldots m_4$.

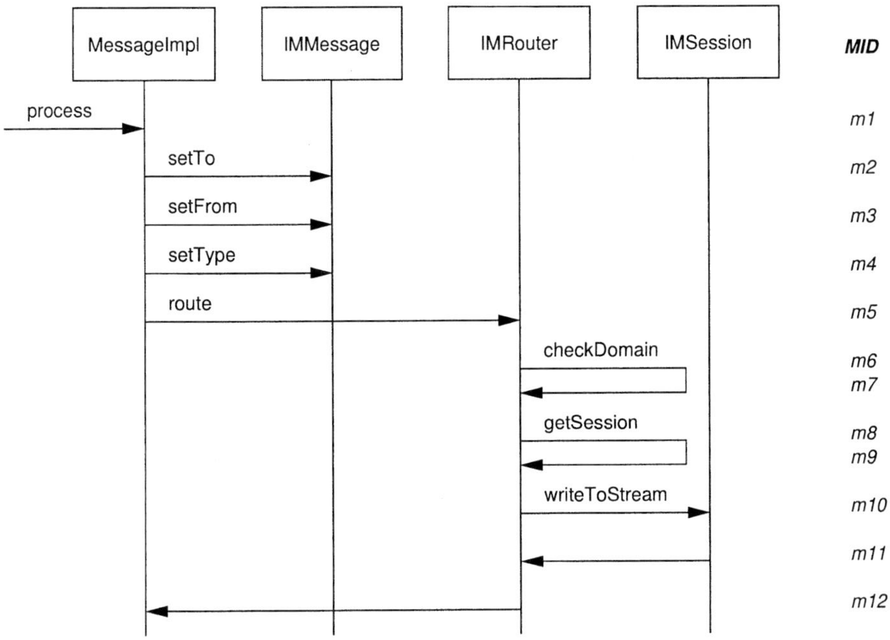

Fig. 8. Sequence diagram corresponding to the main success scenario of the *handle message* use case. A message identifier (MID) for each message is shown on the right of the diagram. We use simple MID's for presentation convenience.

This mapping provides a correspondence between use case subtrees and sequences of messages. Based on this correspondence, we present a join point model for AspectSD, a language that targets the sequence-diagram model. We use AspectSD as a bridge between AspectU and AspectJ in the same way that, during system design and development, sequence diagrams bridge the gap between use cases and source code. In this section we describe the AspectSD language, the mapping and translation between models is discussed more fully in Section 5.

The join points exposed by AspectSD are simply sequences of consecutive messages which correspond to the subtrees that form AspectU's join points. As an example consider the tree in Figure 9. In that particular execution tree, the AspectU join point for the *verify* use-case step, corresponds to the AspectSD join point (i.e. the message sequence) $m_1 \ldots m_4$.

AspectSD pointcuts identify join points using two primitive pointcuts. These pointcuts can be composed using the *and* (`&&`) and *or* (||) operators, which operate analogously to those in AspectU. The two primitive pointcuts in AspectSD are:

1. `messages(message-list)`—matches consecutive message sequences (join points) identical to the sequence of messages in `message-list`, and

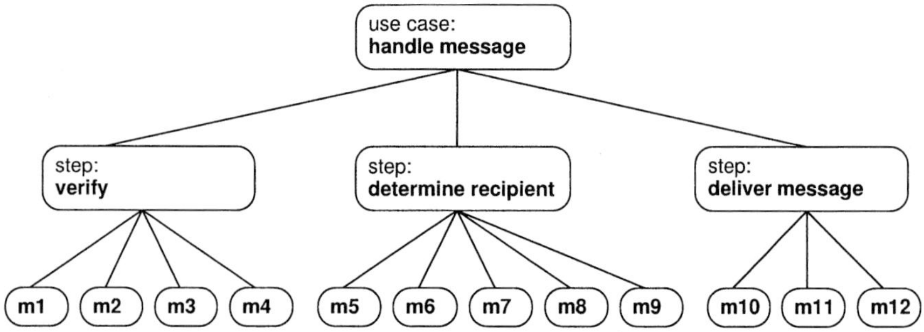

Fig. 9. An execution tree corresponding to the main success scenario of the *handle message* use case shown in Figure 3. The leaves of this tree correspond to the messages from the sequence diagram in Figure 8.

2. `in-flow(message-list)`—restricts the pointcut to match only immediately *after* the sequence of messages in `message-list` (in order) has occurred. This provides the context where the `messages` pointcut will match.

With these join points and pointcuts it is straightforward to map an AspectU pointcut to a corresponding AspectSD points. For example, with respect to the particular execution illustrated in Figure 9, the AspectU pointcut `step(determine recipient)` would correspond directly with the AspectSD pointcut

```
in-flow(m1,m2,m3,m4) && messages(m5,m6,m7,m8,m9)
```

This pointcut matches the sequence of messages $m_5 \ldots m_9$ when it occurs immediately after the sequence $m_1 \ldots m_4$. In general, AspectU pointcuts will correspond to multiple subtrees in multiple possible execution trees and so, multiple sequences of messages will correspond to a given AspectU pointcut.

In addition to identifying join points, an AspectSD pointcut can also provide access to values in the execution context of those join points. In the case of sequence diagram messages, values in the execution context include the sender of the message, the receiver of the message, the return value of the message and values passed as arguments to the message. Binding these values is done using the `bind(id, msg-id, entity-id)` pointcut, which provides a binding for the identifier `id` (part of the advice qualifier's `binding-list`) to the entity `entity-id` in message `msg-id`; `entity-id` can be any of `sender`, `receiver`, `argument_`n (where n is the nth argument), and `return-value`. For example,

```
bind(stanza, m2, receiver)
```

binds the receiver of message m_2 to the name *stanza*.

AspectSD advice, like AspectU advice, can have one of three qualifiers: `before`, `around`, and `after`. For each of these, the `message` sequence identifies the advised join point. When applying `after` advice this will be the sequence just seen. When applying `before` or `around` advice this will be the sequence about to begin. This implies that the `in-flow` sequence in the pointcut uniquely identifies the advised join point.

In our work we have only used AspectSD in the context of our translation process, rather than as a language a developer may use directly. As a result the body of a piece of AspectSD advice is of limited use. However, a developer can include sequences of messages to AspectSD advice. The primary use of this mechanism is to provide information for the translator described in the next section.

5 Translation between Models

We want to leverage AspectU in a way that allows us to affect a running system. To this end, we have implemented an AspectU to AspectJ translator. The inputs to the translator, all described in more detail below, are the system's use cases, several AspectU aspects based on those use cases, the system's sequence diagrams (including mapping information), and a small amount of Java code. Given this input, the tool generates an AspectJ aspect that is able to affect the system in a way consistent with the behavioural changes specified by the AspectU advice.

This translation is challenging for a number of reasons. The decomposition of the system generally will not match the decomposition of the use cases. The messages in the sequence diagram may be implemented as method calls, returns from methods or exceptions being thrown. Also, much of the behaviour (i.e. many of the method calls, etc.) of the running system will not be specified in the sequence diagrams.

The details of the translation are presented along with an example AspectU aspect (the privacy aspect introduced in Section 3.2) and an example system. The example system is OpenIM [1], which is a partial implementation of the XMPP specification. The use cases were derived from the specification and the sequence diagrams (including the annotations) were developed by investigating the source code of the system.

The translation is a two stage process: AspectU to AspectSD and then AspectSD to AspectJ. The implementation of the translation tool requires explicit traceability links between the use cases, sequence diagrams, and source code. Our format for storing sequence diagrams allows basic message information to be specified along with mapping information to support our translation. Basic information includes: sender, receiver and message name. The primary pieces of mapping information specify which use-case *step* or *condition* (i.e. a condition triggering an extension) the message relates to. Other information can map high-level objects mentioned in the use case to parts of messages: sender, receiver, arguments, and return values.

Figure 8 shows the sequence diagram that corresponds to the main success scenario of the *handle message* use case. The following is an example of the information that can be captured for a message in our sequence diagram format, it corresponds to message m_5 in Figure 8:

```
sender: MessageImpl
receiver: IMRouter
name: route
step: determine recipient
arguments: entity, message
```

The first three lines provide basic information about the message. The last two lines provide mapping information; this message contributes to the *determine recipient* use-case step and the arguments to the message correspond to the *entity* and *message* objects referred to in the use case. Put another way, the object passed as the first argument to the *route* message, in this scenario, corresponds to the *entity* discussed in the use case. While discovering and documenting this information was a manual process for us, techniques described in [5, 10,14] could be used to assist in the creation and maintenance of these explicit links either automatically or semi-automatically. Another approach to facilitate this mapping could involve work in the area of model-driven architectures [6].

The two stages of our translation process are described in the following subsections. The description of the process is based on the privacy-concern example introduced as an AspectU aspect in Section 3. The concern is converted from AspectU aspect to AspectSD aspect and then to an AspectJ aspect that was then applied to the OpenIM system. This yielded an extended and runnable application that contains the new features.

5.1 AspectU to AspectSD

The annotations attached to messages in our sequence-diagram format provide a mapping between use-case steps and the messages that implement those steps. For each distinct message (usually a triple: sender, receiver, and method) in a system's sequence diagrams, our translation tool assigns a *message identifier* (MID). For example, the messages in the sequence diagram shown in Figure 8 have been assigned the MID's $m_1 \ldots m_{12}$. As mentioned above, in order to map from use cases to sequence diagrams, sequences of messages can be annotated as participating in various use-case steps. Figure 9 shows how the messages correspond to one particular use case execution tree. The following is an alternative illustration of this scenario, which shows what use-case steps are implemented by what sequences of messages in this scenario:

$$\underbrace{m_1\ m_2\ m_3\ m_4}_{\textit{verify}}\ \underbrace{m_5\ m_6\ m_7\ m_8\ m_9}_{\substack{\textit{determine}\\ \textit{recipient}}}\ \underbrace{m_{10}\ m_{11}\ m_{12}}_{\substack{\textit{deliver}\\ \textit{message}}}$$

Section 4 described the correspondence between AspectU pointcuts and AspectSD pointcuts. Given all relevant sequence diagrams (appropriately annotated) and a piece of AspectU advice, the AspectU translator computes the effect of the added steps, added extensions, and replaced subtrees on the sequence diagrams. In the advice for the privacy aspect described in Section 3.2, we added one step (we will refer to this with message id $\mathbf{s}_1$) and one extension (we will refer to this by message id $\mathbf{e}_1$).

The translation process from AspectU to AspectSD comprises three steps.

1. Insert identifiers for steps—For each block of steps inserted by the AspectU advice body, the associated MID is inserted into each message sequence that matches the appropriate sequence of use-case steps.

For example, the step added by the privacy advice is intended to go *before* the *deliver message* step in the *handle message* use case. Therefore, the above sequence would be modified as follows:

$$\underbrace{m_1\ m_2\ m_3\ m_4}_{\textit{verify}}\ \underbrace{m_5\ m_6\ m_7\ m_8\ m_9}_{\substack{\textit{determine}\\ \textit{recipient}}}\ \mathbf{s}_1\ \underbrace{m_{10}\ m_{11}\ m_{12}}_{\substack{\textit{deliver}\\ \textit{message}}}$$

2. Insert identifiers for extensions—Next, the effect of adding extensions is computed. While adding steps expands a sequence of messages, adding an extension splits one sequence into two sequences: one where the extension does occur and one where it does not. Again from the privacy aspect, when the privacy check fails the extension is triggered, this corresponds to the following message sequence being added:

$$\underbrace{m_1\ m_2\ m_3\ m_4}_{\textit{verify}}\ \underbrace{m_5\ m_6\ m_7\ m_8\ m_9}_{\substack{\textit{determine}\\ \textit{recipient}}}\ \mathbf{s}_1\ \mathbf{e}_1$$

In this example, the use case is terminated by the extension $\mathbf{e}_1$; thus, ending the sequence. In situations where the added extension rejoins the scenario the modified sequence would be followed by the additional messages from the original sequence.

3. Translate `bind` designators—Next, the tool determines how `bind` designators are to be translated. For each matching bind in an AspectU advice's pointcut, our translation tool computes a corresponding AspectSD bind. This is done by considering all messages that preceded the match point, starting from the match point and working toward the start of the message sequence. In the case of the privacy example, the messages $m_9 \ldots m_1$ would be considered based on the sequence above.

For each of these messages, the tool searches for a message with a sender, receiver, argument or return value that matches the operand of the AspectU advice. In the case of the first AspectU `bind` in the privacy aspect the *recipient* matches with return value of message m_9 so the corresponding AspectSD pointcut is `bind(user, m9, return_value)`. For the second AspectU `bind` in the privacy aspect the *stanza* matches with the second argument of message m_5 so the AspectSD pointcut is `bind(user, m5, argument_2)`.

Once the modified sequences have been computed along with the associated bindings the AspectSD pointcut can be generated. The location identified by the pointcut for the privacy aspect (and the *handle message* use case) is the *deliver message* step, which corresponds to the message sequence m_{10} m_{11} m_{12}, corresponding to the entire AspectSD pointcut:

```
before(user,stanza) :
    in-flow(m1,m2,m3,m4,m5,m6,m7,m8,m9) &&
    messages(m10,m11,m12) &&
    bind(user, m9, return_value) &&
    bind(stanza, m5, argument_2)
```

We have shown one sequence diagram being modified along with one resulting AspectSD pointcut. In general translating a piece of AspectU advice will result in multiple sequence diagrams being modified. One AspectSD pointcut is generated for each of these modified points.

5.2 AspectSD to AspectJ

The translation from AspectU to AspectSD produces a description of how the the AspectU advice impacts a system in terms of its sequence diagrams. The goal of the second stage of the AspectU translator tool is to generate AspectJ advice that can appropriately impact the execution of the system.

To support the privacy feature, we wrote Java code to implement various parts of concern including code to check that a given message or presence stanza should be accepted. The translation process automatically determines when in the execution of the system the check should be performed along with binding the objects needed for the check (the *user* and *stanza* objects). So that the correct operation will be carried out at that point, we provide the translator with some minimal information about what to call. This is done by supplying to the translator one block of Java source for the steps in an advice body and one for each extension added by the advice. These blocks connect the generated AspectJ code and the Java code it is expected to trigger at the appropriate point in the execution. In the case of the *check privacy* step introduced by the privacy aspect the block simply contains a call to a static method:

```
{ UserPrivacy.accept(user, stanza); }
```

For each AspectU aspect, the output of our tool is one AspectJ aspect. In addition to advice (explained below), the aspect contains an `Event` class, an `eventList` field, a `post` method, a `match` method, and a `get` method. An event corresponds to the sending and receiving of one sequence-diagram message. These components of the generated aspect help manage these events.

- `Event`—instances of this class capture information about a particular message event such as its name (which is the MID of the corresponding message

as a `String`) and name-value pairs binding objects corresponding to the sender, receiver, arguments and return type of the message.
- `eventList`—a list that stores events in the order they occur[2].
- `void post(String messageName)`—pushes a new event onto the event list.
- `boolean match(String messageList)`—checks the event list to see if the messages in `messageList` exist in the same order at the top of the list.
- `Object get(String mid, String objectName)`—searches the list of events starting from the most recent event for the first event whose name matches `mid`; returns the object bound to the `objectName` in the matched event.

Also part of this generated aspect are three kinds of AspectJ advice: *tracing advice*, *triggering advice*, and *blocking advice*, which interact with the application at the source-code level. Each of these categories of advice are described below along with examples from the AspectJ aspect generated when applying the privacy AspectU aspect to the OpenIM system.

Tracing advice keeps track of messages as they occur. For each distinct message that appears in a system's sequence diagrams, a piece of AspectJ advice is generated that calls the `post` method when this message occurs. Name-value pairs are attached to the event to support the variable binding mechanism. The generated tracing advice for the m_1 message, part of the sequence diagram in Figure 8, looks like this:

```
before(MessageImpl receiver) :
    execution(* MessageImpl.process(..)) &&
    target(receiver)
{
    Event event = new Event("m1");
    event.set("receiver", receiver);
    post(event);
}
```

The above example shows the posting of an event that corresponds to a method being called. Tracing advice is also generated to capture events associated with returns from methods. It is possible that a return message specified in a sequence diagram could be associated with a specific value being returned or with a specific exception being thrown. For example, a scenario described in one sequence diagram may contain a return message that corresponds to an exception being thrown from a particular method, while a different scenario may contain a return message that corresponds to a normal return from the same method. We generate pieces of AspectJ advice to distinguish between various types of returns so that the appropriate event is posted.

[2] The event list can be viewed as unbounded, but for practical purposes, a maximum size can be enforced.

Triggering advice triggers the actual work of the AspectU advice body. It determines when the blocks of Java code supplied by the user get executed. The execution of this code is conditional on whether the appropriate sequence of messages has occurred.

In the special case where the sequence of messages correspond to nested method calls, AspectJ's `cflow` construct could be used to check the context. However, in the more general case, AspectJ provides no direct support for this kind of checking. As a result, our generated aspects rely on the event history supplied by the tracing aspects and stored in the `eventList`. This history is checked at runtime by calling the `match` method with a message pattern that captures the expected context. Only if that method call to `match` returns true is the block executed.

One piece of triggering advice will be generated for each situation in which a user-supplied block of Java code may need to be executed. The following is the triggering advice associated with the steps added by the AspectU privacy aspect (i.e. the actual check that the stanza should be accepted). As shown in Section 5.1, the check is intended to be done after the message sequence $m_1 \ldots m_9$. Before the advice is executed the `match` method is called to verify that the sequence has indeed occurred. Message m_9 corresponds to the return of the `getRegisteredSession` method call, as shown in the sequence diagram in Figure 8. As a result this generated piece of AspectJ advice is implemented as `after` advice on that call.

In addition to the call to the `match` method and the user supplied block of code, the generated advice contains a call to `post` to add the event associated with this portion of the AspectU advice (identified by the message id $\mathtt{s}_1$), and calls to the `get` method to bind the variables expected by the block.

```
after(IMRouterImpl receiver, IMRouterImpl sender) :
    call(* IMRouterImpl.getRegisteredSession(..)) &&
    this(sender) && target(receiver)
{
    // check context (pattern is in reverse order)
    if (match("m9,m8,m7,m6,m5,m4,m3,m2,m1")) {
        Event event = new Event("s1");
        post(event);

        // generated bindings
        Object user = get("m9","return_value");
        Object stanza = get("m5","argument_2");

        // user supplied source block
        UserPrivacy.accept(user, stanza);
    }
}
```

Blocking advice is the final type of generated advice. In situations where AspectU advice adds an extension that terminates the use case (i.e. an extension with no `rejoin`) or replaces part of the behaviour (due to `around` advice), there may be some remaining steps that should be skipped. One such situation is illustrated by the AspectU privacy aspect shown in Figure 6, which adds an extension to handle a privacy-check failure. In this case, the *deliver message* step should be skipped. As a result, the method calls implementing these steps should be blocked. Preventing these calls is handled by `around` advice on each method call that may need to be blocked. The `around` advice first checks whether or not the extension has been executed. If it has not, then the `proceed` is called, permitting the method to execute. Otherwise, the `proceed` is not called and the method call is skipped.

```
void around() :
    call(* net.java.dev.openim.IMSession.writeToStream(..))
{
    if (!match("e1,s1,m9,m8,m7,m6,m5,m4,m3,m2,m1")) {
        proceed();
    }
}
```

In the OpenIM application's privacy concern, this approach works well. However, in general there could be problems with this approach. If there is some code unrelated to the given use case that is tangled with the code that is blocked from executing, incorrect behaviour may result as the unrelated code will be blocked as well. The limitations of our approach are discussed further in the next Section.

6 Discussion

We have analyzed the storage and privacy instant messaging concerns, two concerns that crosscut a system's use cases and source code. The specification for XMPPIM describes instant messaging as a layer added on top of a general messaging protocol (XMPP Core). Following this separation of concerns, we presented storage and privacy as aspects that add IM features to a system implementing the core protocol. Describing the various parts of these concerns in terms of where they affect existing use cases is relatively straightforward:

- when delivery of a message fails because the client is not connected, store the message,
- when an entity connects to the server, before handling any message stanzas deliver any deferred messages,
- before delivering a message stanza check the recipient's privacy rules, and
- before forwarding a presence stanza check the sender's privacy rules.

The AspectU pointcut and advice body for expressing these concerns is similarly straightforward, in fact the advice reads almost like their English descriptions. For these concerns (and many others, we believe), expressing them at a use-case level is natural and makes the developer's intention clear. Further, our approach results in an aspect that captures the concern in a way that can be understood in terms of the use-case model; and, when combined with our translator, affects the runtime behaviour.

We believe that use cases and the types of concerns we have discussed, map naturally to sequences of method calls in the source code. Capturing such concerns in an aspect-oriented programming language like AspectJ can be difficult. This is because AspectJ does not provide direct support for pointcuts based on such sequences. An AspectJ implementation may require manually developing support for bindings and tracing along the lines of what is automatically generated by our translation tool. Furthermore, explicitly describing the concern in terms of these sequences is less intensional than expressing them in terms of use-case steps and extensions.

AspectU advice along with translation based on a mapping between models provides a level of indirection that provides a degree of independence from implementation details. However, this independence comes at the cost of creating and maintaining this mapping between models. If this cost is too high, our approach becomes impractical; hence, the full benefits depend on the extent to which this maintenance can be automated.

In addition to the benefits we experience from using use case level pointcuts, we have a natural mechanism for allowing high-level manipulation of the control flow of the system in some situations. In particular, our tool can automatically translate an AspectU extension that terminates a use case into AspectJ code that suppresses the remainder of the use case after it is terminated by the extension. However there are limitations with our approach in its ability to control the flow of an application. First, as discussed above, in some cases suppressing method calls could produce unintended side effects. Second, ideally an added extension would be able to rejoin at an arbitrary step in the use case (possibly repeating a previous step or skipping ahead to another). Supporting these arbitrary changes to the flow of the application is not feasible with our approach.

A different approach, that may not suffer this limitations could involve applying aspect languages similar to AspectU in the context of a model-driven approach [6]. Using such an approach, higher-level models are used to drive the generation of the source model. In this context, aspect languages based on the appropriate models could be used to influence the source code generation. This approach might give the AspectU aspects more control of the flow of the system, avoid the cost associated with maintaining a mapping between models, and overcome key limitations with our current approach.

The work we have presented has been inspired by the success of aspect-oriented languages in modularizing crosscutting concerns in source code. Our goal has been to extend these ideas beyond the source code to include other behavioural models; the use-case model, in particular. In addition to this, our approach allows a developer to express advice with use case level pointcuts while still affecting the runtime behaviour of the system modelled by the use cases.

7 Related Work

Much of the work in developing other aspect languages has been the foundation of our work with AspectU. *Hyper/J* [13] supports Multi-Dimensional Separation of Concerns [18] by allowing a software engineer to define separate, but overlapping hyperslices in a software system simultaneously. The *Caesar* aspect programming language [12] offers an alternative to AspectJ as an implementation language. It offers a higher-level module concept on top of join-point interception, helping with the encapsulation of aspects. However, like AspectJ, neither of these aspect languages help encapsulate higher-level concerns; they interact with the source code only.

Work by Jacobson [8] suggests that aspect-oriented programming can provide a link between use cases and implementation. In particular aspects could support a decomposition of a system based on use cases, including extension use cases. In contrast to this, our work focuses on modularizing concerns that crosscut the structure of the use-cases model and translating those to a form that can be applied to a system with a conventional decomposition.

Gray, et al. [7] introduce *Embedded Constraint Language*, a domain-specific aspect modelling language and tool that implement constraints as aspects. Like AspectU, their tool recognizes and weaves aspects that apply to non-code artifacts. While Gray's approach targets domain specific models, ours targets use cases.

Batory, et al. [2,3] add a notion of aspects to product-line architectures and domain specific languages so that features can be added or removed from a product by a simple reconfiguring of its architecture. Their technique targets cross-cutting concerns that can span multiple document types. Our approach also supports aspects that cross-cut behavioural models.

Our work is also related to work in Early Aspects, which refers to the identification and encapsulation of crosscutting concerns that occur in requirements and architecture. One example of work in this area is *Cosmos* as described in [17]. Cosmos offers an alternative means to encode the mapping between requirements level artifacts. It is a concern-modelling schema for creating a rich set of relationships between all types of software artifacts. However, Cosmos offers no means of applying advice on any of the concerns that it models.

References

1. A. Agahi. OpenIM Java jabber server, September 2003. http://openim.jabberstudio.org/.
2. D. Batory, J. N. Sarvela, and A. Rauschmayer. Scaling step-wise refinement. In *Proceedings of the 25th International Conference on Software Engineering (ICSE)*, pages 187–197. IEEE Computer Society Press, 2003.
3. D. S. Batory, C. Johnson, B. MacDonald, and D. von Heeder. Achieving extensibility through product-lines and domain-specific languages: a case study. *ACM Transactions on Software Engineering Methodolology (TOSEM)*, 11(2):191–214, 2002. http://doi.acm.org/10.1145/505145.505147.

4. O. Ben-Kiki, C. Evans, and B. Ingerson. Yaml ain't markup language (yaml™1.0). http://yaml.org/spec/.
5. A. Egyed and P. Grünbacher. Automating requirements traceability — beyond the record and replay paradigm. In *Proceedings 17th International Conference Automated Software Engineering (ASE)*, pages 163–171, September 2002. http://citeseer.nj.nec.com/egyed02automating.html.
6. D. Frankel. *Model Driven Architecture.* Wiley Publishing, Inc, 1 edition, 2003.
7. J. Gray, T. Bapty, S. Neema, and J. Tuck. Handling crosscutting constraints in domain-specific modeling. *Communications of the ACM (CACM)*, 44(10):87–93, 2001. http://doi.acm.org/10.1145/383845.383864.
8. I. Jacobson. Use cases and aspects – working seamlessly together. *Journal of Object Technology*, 2(4):7–28, July 2003.
9. G. Kiczales, E. Hilsdale, J. Hugunin, M. Kersten, J. Palm, and W. G. Griswold. An overview of AspectJ. In *Proceedings of the European Conference on Object-Oriented Programming (ECOOP)*, volume 2072, pages 327–355, 2001. http://citeseer.nj.nec.com/kiczales01overview.html.
10. K. Koskimies, T. Systä, J. Tuomi, and T. Männistö. Automated support for modelling OO software. *IEEE Software*, 15(1):87–94, January 1998.
11. H. Masuhara and G. Kiczales. Modelling crosscutting in aspect-Oriented mechanisms. In *European Conference on Object-Oriented Programming (ECOO[illegible]* July 2003.
12. M. Mezini and K. Ostermann. Conquering aspects with Caesar. In *Proceedings International Conference on Aspect-Oriented Software Development (AOSD '03)* 2003. http://citeseer.nj.nec.com/mezini03conquering.html.
13. H. Ossher and P. Tarr. Hyper/J: Multi-dimensional separation of concerns for Java. In *Proceedings of the 22nd International Conference on Software Engineering (ICSE)*, pages 734–737. ACM Press, 2000. http://doi.acm.org/10.1145/337180.337618.
14. Use case management with Rational Rose and Rational RequisitePro, 2000. http://www.therationaledge.com/content/feb_03/rdn.jsp.
15. P. Saint-Andre. XMPP core, September 2003. http://www.jabber.org/ietf/draft-ietf-xmpp-core-18.html.
16. P. Saint-Andre. XMPP instant messaging, September 2003. http://www.potaroo.net/ietf/ids/draft-ietf-xmpp-im-18.txt.
17. S. M. Sutton, Jr. and I. Rouvellou. Modeling of software concerns in Cosmos. In *Proceedings of the 1st International Conference on Aspect-Oriented Software Development (AOSD '02)*, pages 127–133. ACM Press, 2002. http://doi.acm.org/10.1145/508386.508402.
18. P. Tarr, H. Ossher, W. Harrison, and S. M. Sutton, Jr. N degrees of separation: Multi-dimensional separation of concerns. In *Proceedings of the 21st International Conference on Software Engineering (ICSE)*, pages 107–119. IEEE Computer Society Press, 1999.

Functional Objects

Matthias Felleisen

Northeastern University
Boston, Massachusetts

At first glance, object-oriented programming has little or nothing in common with functional programming. One grew out of the procedural tradition, providing means for representing real-world objects and mechanisms for encapsulating state. Computing proceeds via method calls. The other is a radical departure from conventional programming. It emphasizes a(n almost) purely mathematical approach. Programmers design systems of algebraic datatypes and functions, and a computation is the evaluation of an expression. Still, nobody can overlook the similarities of the two approaches considering the development of design patterns and notions of effective object-oriented programming practices.

In my talk, I will compare and contrast the two ideas of programming and programming language design. I will present and defend the thesis that good object-oriented programming heavily "borrows" from functional programming and that the future of object-oriented programming is to study functional programming and language design even more.

M. Odersky (Ed.): ECOOP 2004, LNCS 3086, p. 267, 2004.

Inheritance-Inspired Interface Versioning for CORBA

Skef Iterum[1] and Ralph Campbell[2]

[1] Seattle WA 98102, USA
skef@skef.org
[2] Sun Microsystems, Menlo Park CA 94025, USA
ralph.campbell@sun.com

Abstract. CORBA lacks a mature interface versioning system, which makes it difficult to use in the implementation of tightly-coupled distributed systems. There are patterns of inheritance that can substitute for specialized versioning support, but the programming model that results is cumbersome, particularly on the client side. We have enhanced the IDL specification of our ORB with two new features, one for minor (or upwardly compatible) changes and one for major (or incompatible) changes, which together give CORBA interface versioning support superior to that of most other distributed communication systems. The key to the design and implementation of these features is that each started with a pattern of inheritance that was then customized to address more specifically the problem of interface evolution. The new functionality can be used as part of a life-cycle methodology that guides the versioning of IDL interfaces across product releases.

1 Introduction

Using CORBA as the infrastructure for a distributed system has a number of advantages, including the ability to extend the reach of the object models of OOP languages while not being tied to any one of them. CORBA is a complex system to master but provides a very high level of functionality and flexibility when compared with many other distributed communication frameworks.

Unfortunately, CORBA's advantages come with significant problems in the areas of versioning and interface life-cycle. Some of this is due to the lack of consensus on how to version objects generally. In nondistributed contexts, the first step in making a change to an object is often convincing everyone who uses it to switch to the new interface at a single point in time. But in many distributed systems, particularly those in which resource availability is a primary requirement, there are no such points. Complex systems built on top of CORBA can become brittle once they are deployed, greatly slowing the amount of change possible and complicating bug fixes. In these respects simpler systems such as RPC that have basic versioning functionality [1] are superior. The long-standing absence of specialized versioning support in CORBA appears to stem from two

M. Odersky (Ed.): ECOOP 2004, LNCS 3086, pp. 268–290, 2004.

factors: the mistaken belief that inheritance, by itself, is sufficient for all versioning scenarios, and the lack of alternative designs that fit well into the CORBA framework.

In November 2000 our product group shipped Sun Cluster 3.0, which is partly based on technology originally developed for Spring, an operating system designed using OO principles and technology [2]. The heart of its communication infrastructure is an ORB with support for domains in both process and kernel contexts that allows invocations to be made freely between different nodes in a cluster. This infrastructure had been in development for many years, and seeing it put to good use by customers was very satisfying, but we soon realized we faced a huge problem. One of the two basic goals of the product was high availability (the other was scalability), and for a distributed system to provide availability in the long term it must include support for rolling upgrades, in which each node in turn is removed from the cluster, upgraded, and reintroduced. We knew there were specific areas of the product that would need work before changes to those areas could be made in a rolling upgrade, but we had underestimated how much difficulty would result from CORBA itself.

Writing good software requires two skills. The first is the ability to write code that, when compiled, causes a computer to perform actions that add up to a desired result. The second is the ability to structure code so that it can be understood by people. As projects get more complicated and more people work on them, the importance of the second skill looms larger. The value and importance of CORBA lies in this second area; the investment required to use it proficiently is significant, but it provides a model for structuring complex distributed systems so that they can be grasped, and this is what our project values most about it. When faced with the problem of interface evolution in the context of rolling upgrades, however, we found that the model broke down. We could imagine solutions that would allow each node of the cluster to achieve the desired results during and after a rolling upgrade, but each of these would add enough complexity to compromise our ability to understand our code.

Switching to a different infrastructure was possible, but we were not aware of alternatives that could provide a comparable level of clarity, and a change that significant would have caused a serious disruption in the stability of our product. Instead, we decided to investigate whether we could add functionality to CORBA that would support the simultaneous mixing of old and new interfaces in a way that preserved the OO methodology we were used to. Our group was in a particularly good position to develop a new versioning scheme because our ORB was not part of the public product interface; it was strictly private and did not fully comply with the CORBA specification because of the age of the code and the lack of need to keep up with the standard. This gave us the freedom to make whatever additions or changes we desired. Our ORB also lacks certain features, such as dynamic type discovery and value types, so there are issues that would need to be investigated before this versioning system could be ported into a fully compliant implementation.

This paper describes the result of our investigation: a semantic for IDL interface versioning that is consistent with CORBA and the object-oriented principles that inspired it. We understand that most groups are not in a position to modify their communication infrastructures and that adding incompatible features to a CORBA implementation is contrary to the spirit of the specification. However, as we discovered when we began our research, there is a dearth of information on compelling methods of versioning distributed objects in CORBA or in the more recent object frameworks, and we hope that by documenting our system we might influence the future functionality of CORBA, the newer infrastructures, or their successors.

2 Feature Design

Our survey of existing and proposed solutions for managing changes in CORBA readily divided into two categories. The first set of solutions outlined how versioning could be achieved using inheritance. These shared the advantage of not requiring modifications to CORBA and were available to all ORB implementations, but they had two problems. The programming model (that is, what developers actually had to write in IDL and their code) was awkward, and there was an implicit assumption that the model was strictly client-server and that all servers could be upgraded before all clients. We balked at the difficulty that would be introduced into our code and our minds if we used these solutions, and in any case some of our systems were explicitly distributed and others were client-server but on a service-by-service level, not on a node level. Thus, whatever cluster node was upgraded first would introduce new servers *and* new clients simultaneously.

The second set of solutions consisted of various possible enhancements to the CORBA model to address the problem of versioning. It is difficult to generalize about these as a group, so we will leave the detailed discussion to later sections. Here we simply note that some were insufficient, and others would have worked but had usability problems worse than the strict inheritance systems. A number of the designs would have been difficult to implement, and some introduced namespace clashes. The majority had never been implemented even in prototype form, calling their correctness and utility into question.

After considering the benefits and drawbacks of the various solutions in our survey we chose an intermediate path. We started with the example of the inheritance-based solutions, examined the related problems in detail, and then designed new language features that were similar to inheritance but addressed the problems. The result was a set of specific versioning features that, owing to their similarity with existing inheritance functionality, fit quite well into the CORBA model in both interface and implementation. In parallel, we developed an interface life-cycle model to guide use of the new features to make arbitrary changes in distributed systems built with object frameworks.

The inheritance-based solutions for maintaining upward compatibility are different from those for introducing locally incompatible changes, and our analogous features are also distinct and are discussed separately in the following two subsections. The phrase "upwardly compatible" is unwieldy, and there are some aspects of our design to which it might not apply, so we will use the term *minor versioning* to refer to this kind of change, and will therefore also use *major versioning* when referring to changes that introduce incompatibilities.

2.1 Minor Versioning

Minor, or upwardly compatible, versioning is the introduction of new functionality that retains completely the semantics of the existing functionality. In a client-server model, this means older clients must be able to use modified servers in the same way they used older servers. This requirement is very similar to the Liskov Substitution Principle [3], which can be paraphrased as:

Principle 1. *Liskov Substitution: A component with an object reference widened to a base type must be able to use a server that implements a derived type without knowing it is doing so.*

```
interface B {
  void b_i ();
};

interface D : B {
  void d_i ();
};
```

Fig. 1. An existing product type hierarchy

This similarity is the basis for a common inheritance-based solution to the minor versioning problem, in which derived types are used to add new functionality [4,5]. Assume that the type hierarchy illustrated in Fig. 1, in which D inherits from B, is part of an existing product.[1] In the next version of the product a new method is needed in B, and objects implementing D also need to support this new method, a different new method on D itself, and a new inheritance of interface O. These additions can be made by creating two new derived types, as shown in Fig. 2.

This object design achieves the desired goals: Instances of new_B can be widened to and passed as B, and instances of new_D can be widened to and passed as D. If all servers can be upgraded to use new_B and new_D before any clients are upgraded, all the old clients can use these new objects widened to the original interfaces. After all servers implement the new objects, clients can be upgraded to make use of the new interfaces and functionality.

[1] All examples in this paper have been simplified to remove everything not directly relevant to the semantics of the versioning features

```
interface new_B : B {
  void b_ii ();
};

interface new_D : D, O {
  void d_ii ();
};
```

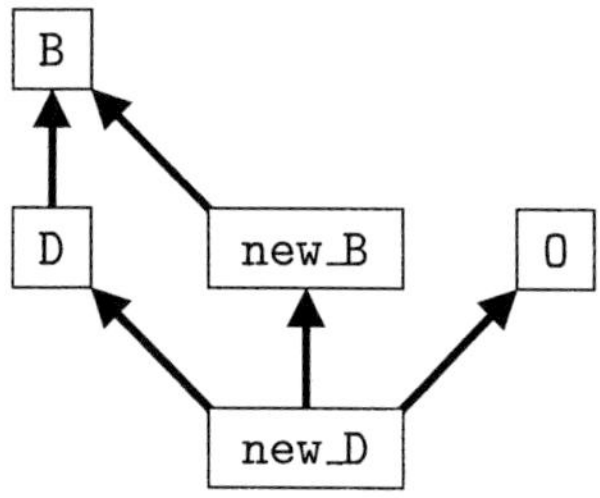

Fig. 2. Functionality added with inheritance

Unfortunately, this approach has a number of problems relating to the programming model and the assumptions made. Think of systems making use of the interfaces `D` and `new_D`.

- In many distributed systems, it is unreasonable to require that all servers are upgraded before any client. In CORBA systems this means that new clients must also be able to use servers implementing the original interfaces, making whatever compromises are necessary to work around the absence of the new functionality. When the inheritance-based approach is used, this leads to one of three designs:
  - The object is narrowed to and kept as `new_D` if possible, and `D` otherwise, using two different appropriately typed reference variables, one `nil` and one non-`nil` at any given time. The code for all method calls is modified to test for and use the appropriate variable.
  - All objects are narrowed to `D`, and new objects are also narrowed to `new_D`. Clients use the `D` reference to invoke old methods and the `new_D` reference to invoke new ones if possible.
  - The object is narrowed to and kept as the old interface, in this case `D`, and then narrowed to the new one, `new_D`, when the new methods must be called. If the narrow fails, the client code implements the appropriate workaround.

  None of these approaches is attractive. The first requires more storage and a test branch before *every* method call, old or new, and the second requires even more storage and complicates the reference counting code. The third solution is probably the best in terms of syntax but entails a narrow for every invocation of a new method. Narrow operations can be expensive, especially in those implementations in which the server-side must be checked whenever a narrow operation might fail in case the interfaces supported by the reference change, as is true in more recent CORBA specifications [6]. None of the syntaxes directly indicates that the potential lack of functionality is the result of a versioning issue. Finally, all of the problems with these approaches are magnified when clients are using multiple servers simultaneously (storing references in a list, for example) and when there are subsequent changes (`new_new_D`, `new_new_new_D`, and so on).

- More important, even when all servers can be upgraded before any client, there is the question of what interface type should be used to pass the object references. The original code will have passed the object as D, B, or CORBA::Object. If D was used, the new code could pass the new object as either D or new_D. If D is used for the new object, new clients must constantly narrow references to new_D as they are received, even many versions after any client or server is expecting or implementing only D. If new_D is used, a new method to hand out new_D references must be added to whatever interface implements the original method passing D. This design leads to a minor versioning cascade all the way out to whatever object is first passed as CORBA::Object, which is untenable. This problem is often missed by investigators who have not reduced their designs to practice.
- The system leads to an interface name explosion and an interface hierarchy with mostly nonlocal information. The information of what D objects are *for* is spread out among multiple interfaces that result not from design but from the details of when particular methods were introduced.

These problems conspire to make both IDL interface definitions and client-side code difficult to manage. They also make always passing objects using the CORBA::Object type more attractive, but doing so eliminates the many benefits of strong typing.

Our solution to these problems is to use the same basic structure as this inheritance-based solution but with a new semantic specifically for upwardly compatible changes. The first aspect of this semantic is that the related types (D and new_D, for instance) are maintained in the original interface, and therefore in a single point of the IDL namespace. New methods and inheritances are added to increasing versions of the interface, which are numbered explicitly.

```
interface B {
  void b_i ();
  void b_ii <1> ();
};

interface D : B, B <1:1>, O <1:0> {
  void d_i ();
  void d_ii <1> ();
};
```

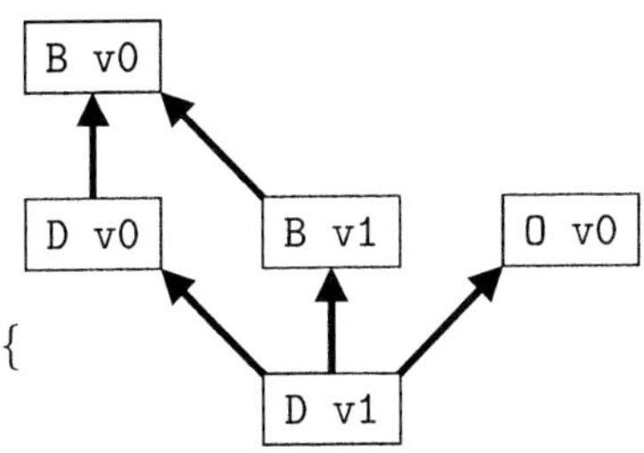

Fig. 3. Functionality added with minor versioning

Fig. 3 illustrates the new syntax for our example case: new_B becomes version 1 of B, and new_D becomes version 1 of D. The version numbers for new methods are specified after the method name and before the arguments. Inheritances are specified with two numbers: the first is the version of the interface the inheritance is being added to, and the second is the version number of the interface being inherited.[2] The numbering of interface versions starts at 0, and untagged methods are assumed to be part of version 0. Inheritances with no versioning are assumed to be both part of version 0 and to inherit version 0 of the other interface. This convention is upwardly compatible with all existing CORBA interface definitions.

In almost every respect our notation mirrors the inheritance-based solution, including the fact that version 1 of `D` must inherit version 1 of `B`; if that inheritance were omitted, `D` would not have method `b_ii` anywhere in its inheritance tree. The inheritance by each version of its predecessor is implicit. Interfaces change only as a result of making additions to the interface itself, and never as a result of changes to other interfaces, unless an existing version of an interface is changed in error.

The numbering scheme itself solves only the namespace explosion problem. The remaining problems are addressed by changes in CORBA semantics to take advantage of the fact that the related versions of interfaces are grouped together. First, the version numbers, once they have been placed in the IDL definitions, are of no concern to server implementations. Each server must implement all methods associated with the highest defined version. Second, the semantic of narrow operation (both explicit with the `_narrow` function and implicitly when references are passed in invocations) is adjusted: a reference can be narrowed to a CORBA interface if and only if version 0 of that interface exists somewhere in its type hierarchy. Any object implementing version 0 of an interface is considered to be a valid instance of that interface, and all other versions are optional. With this change, a client can use a single type of reference to point to both old and new implementations, and it is not necessary to choose between old and new interfaces when passing a reference because all versions coexist in the same point of the namespace.

With the inheritance-based system, clients could determine whether a server implemented the new methods by attempting to narrow a reference to the new interface type (`new_D`, for instance). With all interfaces collapsed into a single name, this is no longer possible, so we have added a new function called `_version`. Like `_narrow`, `_version` is implemented by the IDL compiler for each type and takes an object reference as an argument. Instead of a pointer it returns an integer specifying the highest version of the interface supported by the reference, or −1 if no version is supported.[3] This code fragment shows an example of how the `_version` function can be used.

[2] The colon notation for the version numbers is meant to reflect the existing inheritance notation, in which left inherits from right.

[3] This isn't strictly accurate. Our implementation actually returns the minimum of the highest version supported and the highest version known to the client code. This is because it is easy to write code such as "`if (D::_version(D_ref) == 1)`," which works fine until you try to create version 2 of `D`.

```
if (D::_version(D_ref) >= 1) {
  // Use version 1 method
} else {
  // Make do with version 0 equivalent
}
```

Because the properties of the inheritance system are retained, support of some version of an interface always implies support for all the types inherited by that version. In our example, if the `D::_version(D_ref)` function returns 1, the client is guaranteed that the object also supports (at least) version 1 of `B` and version 0 of `O`.

Our system also creates a new situation for client code, which is that a server might not implement some of the methods a client could invoke on a validly narrowed interface. A client that was compiled with knowledge of version 1 of `D` can invoke method `D_ii` even if the reference it was passed at run-time only supported version 0 of `D`. For this case, a new `VERSION` exception has been added. Clients invoking methods that are unsupported because the version implemented by a server is not high enough will receive a `VERSION` exception. This is a significant change from the existing CORBA specification in which all methods on a narrowed interface are assumed to be supported, but the new semantic mirrors the reality of servers with different levels of functionality and `VERSION` is not thrown at random; a client can determine exactly what methods are supported on a given object reference using the `_version` function. `VERSION` can also be thrown explicitly by a server implementation. We discuss that use of the exception in Sect. 3.

To summarize, this semantic retains the advantages of the object model, including inheritance. It adds a minor versioning semantic on a par with that provided by simpler systems such as RPC, and it is upwardly compatible with existing interfaces.

2.2 Major Versioning

Major versioning is introduction of new functionality that is not compatible with the semantics of existing functionality. In general, major versioning is a much broader category than minor versioning, as there are limitless ways in which systems can be changed so they are not compatible. At first glance it might seem unnecessary to address this issue at all, because such changes are, by definition, not going to cooperate. However, what is incompatible at the interface level is not necessarily incompatible at other levels. For instance, a subsystem could provide a new interface to its functionality, and both the old and the new interfaces could coexist until the old one is no longer needed.

Our feature addresses the aggregation of multiple interfaces into a single server implementation, which is the problem in major versioning most likely to be solved at the level of IDL interfaces. Assume that there is an interface `E` that is part of an existing product, and the designers have decided that it would make more sense to define a new interface `N` that provides access to the same functionality using different methods. Part of the overall design goal is the eventual removal of `E`, so it doesn't make sense to have `N` inherit from it. Instead, both interfaces would coexist for some number of releases, and eventually `E` would be removed.

Before we describe the inheritance-based solution to this problem, we need to address a specific approach that was part of some of the solutions we surveyed and that we rejected. These solutions added a version number space to some or all points in the CORBA IDL namespace, allowing multiple objects, generally of the same basic category, to be added to each point and then differentiated among by using the numbers. In some systems the number space had two levels, as in 1.4, and the first number was used for major versioning and the second for minor. Each interface would be specified separately, but presumably the IDL compiler could enforce upward compatibility when necessary. Recent versions of CORBA include the `#pragma version` interface allowing such numbers to be attached to RepositoryIDs. In a system like this, rather than creating `N` you might implement version 2.0 of `E`, assuming the implementation is one of those that allows access to multiple versions of the same interface simultaneously. Many practitioners feel the need for this type of feature is obvious. We disagree, and cite the following problems in the use of a single name for incompatible objects:

- It is a false economy. Incompatibility is a different relationship from upward compatibility, and the choice between incompatible things is almost always explicit. If the implementor must choose between `E` 1.0 and `E` 2.0 when writing client code, what has been gained by putting the two together?
- In the context of IDL, it is an illusion. IDL is a tool for specifying interfaces that will actually be implemented by and used in other languages, and none of the common languages has such version numbering features. To avoid an illegal namespace clash in the language, the version numbers are mangled into the derived symbol names, and either all symbols (including those that are not yet versioned) use this encoding or symbol names that mimic the chosen convention must be banned from IDL, leaving the versioning system doing little other than enforcing a naming scheme that could have been used by convention. Some other systems, such as the existing CORBA specification, do not do this sort of mangling but also don't provide access to multiple versions simultaneously.

This leads us to another principle, which might be obvious in retrospect:

Principle 2. *It is unwise to put incompatible things into the same point of a namespace.*

The inheritance-based solution to the aggregation problem is to define a new interface that inherits from both `E` and `N`, as shown in Fig. 4. The server can then implement the combined interface `C`. Objects of type `C` can be widened to and passed as either `E` or `N` as the situation requires, as suggested by the Liskov substitution principle. This design leaves `E` and `N` independent, so that in a subsequent release `E` *and* `C` can be dropped and the server can simply implement `N`. There are two basic problems with this approach.

```
interface C : E, N {
};
```

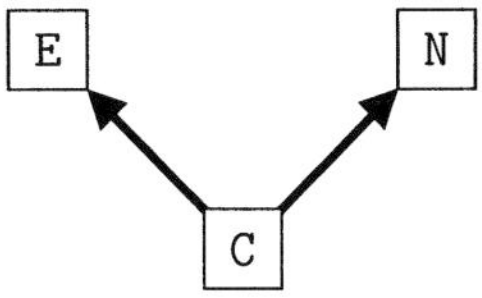

Fig. 4. Aggregation with inheritance

- When combined with `C`, `E` and `N` are left unlinked only as long as no client or intermediary actually uses `C`. This can be "enforced by convention," but if there is an accident and `C` is used it becomes more difficult to remove `E` later. In addition there is nothing intrinsic about `C` to indicate it should not be used directly. Terms like "aggregation" are hopelessly overloaded in the research literature, but we define it as a combination of interfaces on the server side that does not imply any combination on the client side.
- Nothing about `E` and `N` being distinct solves the problem of how to introduce `N` into the system. If references to objects implementing `E` are normally passed explicitly *as* `E`, the intuitive design would be to add new, corresponding methods to pass objects explicitly as `N`. But this creates a cascading change problem similar to that seen in the inheritance-based system for minor versioning.

```
#pragma server_only C;
interface C : E, N {
};
```

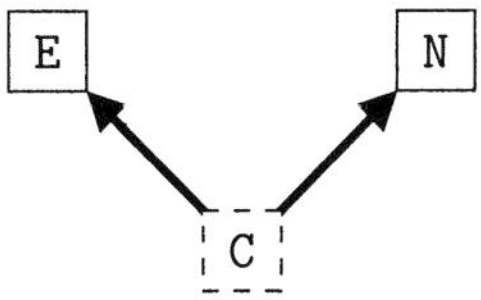

Fig. 5. Aggregation with a `server_only` interface

Our solution to the first problem takes the form of a new pragma named `server_only`. It is used to mark interfaces such as `C` for special treatment in the code derived from IDL files, as shown in Fig. 5. Interfaces marked `server_only` have these characteristics:

- Method definitions are illegal and result in an IDL compile-time error.
- Passing references to these interfaces or placing them in a constructed type (e.g., sequence, struct, union, typedef, array) is also illegal and results in an IDL compile-time error.
- The `_narrow` function always returns `nil`, regardless of the TypeCode associated with the reference.

These restrictions prevent any client-side use of a `server_only` interface, making them safe for their intended purpose of aggregation.

The second problem is much more significant than the first, but just as this problem is similar to the cascade problem of some of the minor versioning systems we rejected, it can be solved in an analogous way using our minor versioning features. In our example, there might be an object `Q` that, in the original version of the software, included a method that handed out references to `E` objects. In order to add `N` objects to the system, minor versioning can be used to add a new method to `Q` that distributes `N` references. The fact that the `E` and `N` references will point to `server_only C` objects is incidental. The ability to make incremental changes in the systems surrounding an incompatible change is the key to containing the impact of that change. In other words,

Principle 3. *An effective method of minor versioning is the most important feature of an effective system for major versioning.*

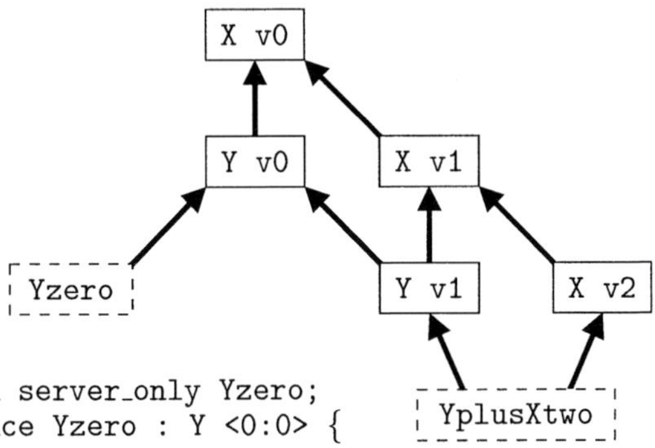


```
#pragma server_only Yzero;
interface Yzero : Y <0:0> {
};

#pragma server_only YplusXtwo;
interface YplusXtwo : Y <0:1>, X <0:2> {
};
```

Fig. 6. `server_only` objects and minor versioning

The `server_only` feature also helps address some limitations in the minor versioning system, as shown in the two examples in Fig. 6. Sometimes the version of an interface is increased to include additional functionality required by one development group when another group is not ready to implement the new version. `Yzero` is an example of how the older version of an interface, in this case `Y`, can be assigned a name, allowing the lagging group to continue to implement the older version.

In other instances, the development group that controls the definition of an interface is not ready to add an enhancement made in an ancestor interface into their own, but a third unrelated group needs the new functionality. For example, imagine you implement a server for `Y` but the interface of `Y` is supplied by a different development group, possibly even in a different company. `Y` inherits from `X`, but the version of `X` has been increased to 2 before the group that controls `Y` is prepared to add the inheritance of version 2. You need the functionality of `Y` but you also need the new functionality of `X`. In this case you can use an interface like `YplusXtwo` to combine `Y` with the new version of `X`.

The `server_only` pragma was the only feature we added specifically for major versioning, and, like our minor versioning system, it doesn't address the problem of versioning types that are not interfaces. We did not add any features for other types for the following reasons:

- We decided the only clear candidate for minor versioning among the other CORBA entities was the enumeration. Our thoughts on enums are discussed in Sect. 6. Other types that could be changed, such as structures, did not appear to have any inherent compatibility relationship.
- Major versioning for noninterface types made no sense in light of our namespace principle. Any desired change could be made by making a copy of the original element with a new name and making the desired changes. In fact, other than methods and interfaces, most names in IDL do not have a "network identity"; they are a convenience for specifying types passed in method invocations. This can be seen by examining the specification for the encoding of CORBA TypeCodes, which indicates that the names of types are considered local and optional [6].

2.3 A Quick Note on Syntactic Sugar

Our paper is focused on describing changes to the semantics of CORBA that provide interface versioning, and we have consciously avoided lengthy descriptions of convenience routines and other forms of syntactic sugar. However, two specific issues come up in discussion often enough that we will address them here.

The first is that when one interface inherits from another through a long succession of versions the default notation is cumbersome. For instance, if versions 0 through 4 of `K` inherit versions 0 through 3 and 5 of `J` the IDL notation for this pattern of inheritance would be the following:

```
interface  K : J, J <1:1>, J <2:2>, J <3:3>, J <4:5> {
```

There are many ways this notation could be compressed. Our favorite (but unimplemented) candidate is allowing multiple comma-separated inheritances in a single set of braces and providing the option of specifying ranges of equal size on either side of each colon, which would allow the `K` inheritances to be expressed this way:

```
interface  K : J <0-3:0-3,4:5> {
```

The high range number on the right side of colon could, of course, be optional.

The second issue is that when an interface has evolved for a long period of time its minimum version from a practical standpoint might be greater than zero, and servers that do not support this minimum should be considered obsolete. This semantic is available with the functions already described. For example, if the lowest version of L that should be considered valid is 2, the following code can be used:

```
L_ref = CORBA::nil;
if (L::_version(Obj_ref) >= 2) {
  L_ref = L::_narrow(Obj_ref);
  assert(!CORBA::is_nil(L_ref));
}
```

If this kind of check becomes commonplace, the IDL compiler could be enhanced to add a new static method to each derived interface definition combining the functionality of `_narrow` and `_version` and taking both an object reference and a minimum version as arguments. This would reduce the code for our example to one line:

```
L_ref = L::_version_narrow(Obj_ref, 2);
```

3 Life-Cycle Methodology

We now present an example to illustrate how these features work together and fit into the life-cycle of a product spanning multiple releases. We also point out where additional versioning features at other levels of the product are needed to overcome the limitations of what can be addressed at the level of IDL interfaces.

```
interface T {
  void T_i ();
};

interface F {
  T get_T (int);
};
```

Fig. 7. Original product interfaces

An existing product contains interfaces F and T, as shown in Fig. 7. Clients obtain a reference to F from the nameserver and then use it to obtain references to T objects. There are multiple, independent T servers, each of which corresponds to an integer passed into the get_T method on F. A client retains a T object for some period of time, making multiple invocations on it, but eventually releases its reference.

The group that maintains object T has decided that there is a better semantic for operations currently performed with T and have encoded it in object U. The mapping of integer to server has not changed, so for each T there is exactly one corresponding U. Because the servers and clients are part of a distributed system, the transition from the use of T to the use of U will include a period of time when both are in use simultaneously.

```
interface U {
  void U_i ();
};

interface F {
  T get_T (int);
  U get_U <1> (int);
}

#pragma server_only TandU;
interface TandU : T, U {
};
```

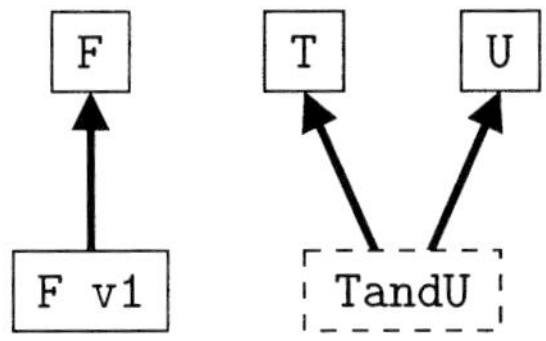

Fig. 8. Versioned product interfaces

In this case, U is introduced by versioning F to include a method called get_U with arguments corresponding to get_T. Then a server_only interface TandU is created, and the server that originally implemented T is modified to implement TandU. These changes are illustrated in Fig. 8.

The code in new clients is written to try get_U first, but if that method returns a VERSION exception additional code is included to use T objects. Because major versioning has been chosen to introduce the U semantic, the client must keep track of T and U objects with separate pointers.

If the system containing these objects is very loosely coupled, it may never be safe to eliminate support for T because it would be impossible to determine when all older clients have been removed from the system. However, most systems are more tightly coupled than this. Our own product has a version manager operating at the component level and accessed through our CORBA infrastructure. One of the features of the version manager is the ability to specify what product versions are allowed to interact. After each node in a cluster has been upgraded, the administrator runs a command that "commits" to the current level of functionality; after that point any node with lower-versioned subsystems will be prohibited from joining the cluster. With guarantees such as these, it is possible to remove support for T, first at the implementation level and then later at the interface level.

At the point when T will no longer be used, the implementation can be removed simply by throwing away any internal data structures associated with T in servers implementing F and U. The methods associated with T will still exist in the type system but, in the ideal, none will be invoked. This design by itself is sufficient for very tightly controlled architectures, but there will be other systems with a looser organization, in which support for T objects might be dropped but some clients might still try to retrieve them. The explicitly throwable form of the VERSION exception is provided for use in these cases. Implementations of get_T can start to throw VERSION so that errant clients will see a clean failure condition.[4]

Once the use of T has been officially disallowed in a release, the interface itself can be removed in the next release. In our example, both interfaces T and TandU are removed and the server simply implements U. The get_T method on F still exists but does nothing but throw the VERSION exception. In the long term, obsolete methods such as get_T that accumulate through minor versioning can be removed in clean-up projects that use major versioning to replace crufty, many-versioned interfaces with cleaned-up equivalents, but such efforts are more of a virtue than a requirement.

Before moving on, we would like to illustrate some of the limitations of server_only objects by making a slight change to our example. The interface TandU made sense because there was a one-to-one mapping between instantiations of T and U. If the semantic had changed differently so that the *granularity of instantiations* had changed, linking the two at the interface level would not have made sense. For instance, the problem with T might have been that it was not necessary to have separate T objects and the overhead of object creation lowered the performance of the system unacceptably. To solve that problem, U might simply be a copy of T with the integer added as an argument to each method, and the implementation would only ever instantiate one U server. To roll in this change, T and U would be implemented as separate objects with instantiations that cooperated at the implementation level (e.g., T could hold a reference to the single U). There are other cases in which the granularity of objects does not change but it is useful to have T and U reference-counted separately. As we said previously, the scope of major change is unlimited, and the key to making it tractable is limiting the area that needs to be changed with minor versioning.

4 Implementation

One of the reasons we based the new versioning functionality on inheritance was because much of the implementation could be achieved by rearranging mechanisms that already existed in our ORB, and although we did not make it clear in the discussion above, ease of implementation played a substantial role in determining the design of these features. Support for both major and minor versioning has been added to the ORB that ships in the Sun Cluster 3.1 product. A number of groups in our project have used the new functionality in the implementations of their own new features, and many of these are "feature complete" and can

[4] The only clients likely to catch explicitly thrown VERSION exceptions are those already aware that a method has become obsolete, and failure to catch one is an indication that the server and client are conceptually out of synchronization. In our ORB we distinguish the two flavors of the exception with different minor exception numbers, which are distinct from interface version numbers and are already part of the CORBA specification. This allows both the client and the infrastructure to handle the cases differently when desired. It would also be possible to give this exception a different name.

be successfully rolled into an existing cluster. The rest of this section discusses aspects of our implementation and how they might apply to other ORB implementations.

We believe that both minor versioning and `server_only` interfaces could be added to other ORBs in a way that is upwardly compatible with existing implementations. However, a few issues are not yet worked out because our ORB has some limitations, such as binding only with C++ and not supporting dynamic type discovery. The ORB does include some advanced features such as support for direct casting of CORBA objects in the same C++ domain. We do not know of any "deal-breakers" that would prevent our features from being used with other languages or with dynamic discovery, but without a complete prototype we cannot rule out the existence of this sort of problem.

4.1 Minor Versioning

We mentioned that one of the advantages of our minor versioning system is that it avoids an explosion in the number of interfaces, but here we need to be more specific. Because any interface could support multiple versions, the distributed type system must somehow communicate to clients what version level of each interface is supported. One way to do this is to examine everywhere in the ORB where a RepositoryID is used and attach an integer to it that represents the highest supported version. This provides each client with enough information, but it would also require changing the existing protocols.

We decided to add the version numbers into the RepositoryIDs and generate an internal type for each version of every interface. Each ID has an associated TypeCode that encodes only those methods and inheritances directly on that version of the interface and explicitly includes the inheritance of the previous version. So, although minor versioning does not create an interface explosion, it does create a RepositoryID explosion, but this is not a problem because the IDs are hidden in the implementation and there are hashing strategies for optimizing searches and matches. The versioned RepositoryIDs and TypeCodes are used exactly as the corresponding IDs and codes of the inheritance-based solution would have been.[5]

At first glance it might appear that the easiest way to adapt the C++ type hierarchy for interfaces is to place each version of an interface into a separate C++ class and duplicate the full version-level inheritance patterns. We did this in our early prototypes, using a private symbol naming scheme for the versioned types and then assigning the highest version of each interface the proper name with a `#typedef`. But this design does not work. Look at the type hierarchy

[5] Our ORB did not have version numbers associated with each RepositoryID before we started the project, so we added them. The current CORBA specification includes a two-level versioning scheme in which the lower number is supposed to indicate upward compatibility. The interface for these numbers isn't compatible with the semantic described here, so the numbers have to be encoded differently if minor versioning is added to a standards-compliant ORB.

```
interface D {
  void D_i ();
};

interface A : D <1:0> {
  void A_i ();
  void A_ii <1> ();
};

interface B : A <0:0> {
  void B_i ();
};
```

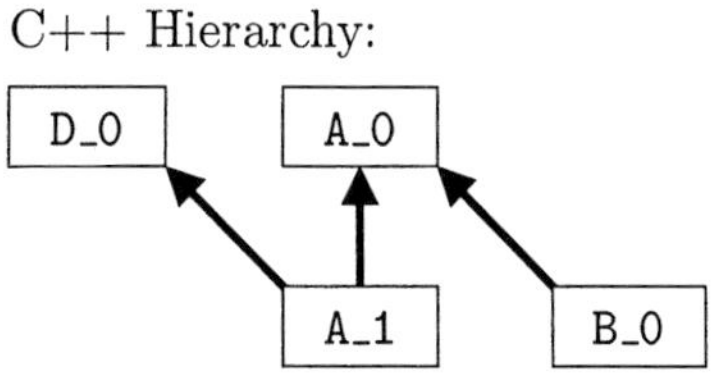

Fig. 9. Unworkable C++ type encoding

shown in Fig. 9. B version 0 inherits from A version 0, but there is also an A version 1 that inherits from D version 0. In the derived C++ there would be A_0, A_1, B_0, and D_0, with A mapping to A_1, B mapping to B_0, and D mapping to D_0. Logically, B inherits from A, so if you have a pointer to a B object you should be able to do a C++ widen to A. But you can't widen B_0 to A_1 safely. Also, you should be able to widen A to D, but if an object implementing B_0 is cast to A, widening it to D_0 would not be safe.

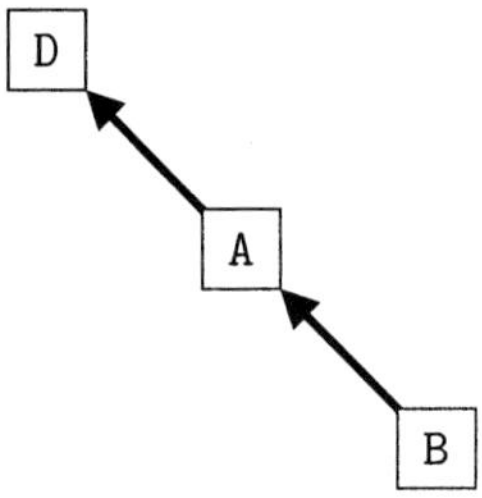

Fig. 10. Better C++ type encoding

Fixing this problem while keeping some kind of expanded hierarchy might be possible, but we did not see why it would be desirable. Instead, we chose a design that collapsed the hierarchy so there was one C++ object for each interface. The inheritance pattern between these objects is just the inheritance pattern that would result if the versions were removed, as shown in Fig. 10. This system is type-safe at the C++ level and supports every widen that caused a problem in the other encoding. There are some side effects, such as the fact that casting a B directly to D will be permitted, but these make sense in the context of the encoding and cause no harm.

Of course, a server implementing B should not be made to implement D just because this mapping has been chosen, so each object adapter should predefine dummy functions to implement any methods not in the object's true inheritance path. In our example, all methods on `A` version 1 and `D` version 0 would be implemented in the adapters output by the IDL compiler for objects of type `B`. If the ORB supports direct casting like ours, the implementation of these methods would simply throw the `VERSION` exception so that versioning semantics are preserved within the domain.

Another consequence of this design is that you cannot compile a portion of code against higher-versioned IDL interfaces and mix it with older code in the same ORB domain. All the code in a given domain needs to be compiled against the same interface definitions. ORBs that do not support local casting and always use the ORB infrastructure to manage invocations would not have this problem; the version differences can be sorted out by the invocation logic. We have also considered the possibility of creating separate subdomains for separate collections of interface versions, in which direct casting is supported for objects in the same subdomain but proxies are used for references that cross subdomains. These proxies would be optimized for handling different object versions, and full argument marshaling would not be required. This kind of design introduces the interesting possibility of using CORBA IDL as a framework for managing different versions of C++ objects in the same address space.

Thus, our implementation collapses the versions in the C++ classes but retains each interface version individually in the CORBA type system. The existing mechanisms governing inheritance already operate on the RepositoryIDs and TypeCodes, and because our minor versioning semantic is mapped onto the logic of inheritance, most of the implementation simply falls out of our rearrangement of the type system. The majority of the programming work went into modifying the IDL compiler to support version tags and output the correct patterns of C++ classes and RepositoryIDs. The ORB implementation itself only requires minor changes for things like the change in the semantics of `_narrow` and the new `_version` function.

4.2 Major Versioning

The implementation of `server_only` objects is trivial and is almost entirely confined to the IDL compiler, which is changed to keep track of interfaces marked with the `#pragma` and enforces the associated rules. We think it is a good idea to put these interfaces into a separate type space, which can be done by automatically adding another prefix to the RepositoryID of each `server_only` interface. This is done to ensure that using a name in the `server_only` space never interferes with using that name again in the normal space.

4.3 General Considerations

Both the minor versioning system and `server_only` objects retain important aspects of the CORBA type system. Each version of each interface inherits a precise list of versioned interfaces and implements a precise list of methods, and for a specific version both of these lists are immutable. This means that the TypeCode corresponding to a given RepositoryID never changes. And each server implements exactly one version of one interface, which defines all of the capabilities of the server. The capabilities of each object can continue to be represented by a single RepositoryID, and each domain needs to query for the schema of a given RepositoryID only once.

More recent versions of the CORBA GIOP specification state that the failure to narrow a reference to a given type at one time does not mean that the same narrow will not succeed later [6]. Our minor versioning system introduces situations in which an object can be narrowed to a type that has methods associated with versions the object does not support. In our ORB, the type associated with a given reference is immutable, so we are able to generate the appropriate `VERSION` exceptions in client stub code without ever contacting the server. In an ORB in which reference types are not final, it would be necessary to contact a server's ORB whenever a client invokes an unsupported method or the `_version` function is called.

Because new versions are added to an existing interface by editing the interface itself, we were very concerned about preventing accidental changes to the definitions of existing versions. We decided to add a new file to our build environment that contains a mapping of each interface RepositoryID we have included in our product to an ASCII encoding of its corresponding TypeCode, which is similar to a mangled C++ symbol name. We also added a flag to our IDL compiler to produce the same mapping for whatever interfaces are compiled, and a script compares the two mappings to verify that none of the existing product interfaces has been associated with a different TypeCode. Whenever a new product is released, the mapping file will be updated to include the new interface versions shipped to customers.

5 Related Work

Much of the research on object versioning has been done in relation to the semantics of specific programming languages and does not separate issues of interface inheritance with those of implementation inheritance. Also, the code compiled from these languages is generally started and stopped as a unit, so many of the problems commonly faced in distributed systems are not a factor. There are existing, if imperfect, engineering practices for these situations [7]. CORBA supports interface inheritance in all contexts but delegates implementation inheritance to the languages bound to it, and we believe it is best to think of CORBA as a system that has no intrinsic relationship to implementation inheritance. Therefore, only a small amount of object research applies to the versioning of CORBA interfaces in distributed systems.

The CORBA specification [6] allows version numbers to be attached to elements in the IDL namespace but does not define a formal relationship between elements with the same name but different versions. There is also no defined method of accessing two different versions of the same element simultaneously. The system includes both major and minor numbers and specifies that increasingly minor-numbered interfaces should maintain backward compatibility, but it doesn't seem that this compatibility necessarily confers substitutability.

A whitepaper written in 1993 suggested a similar system in which version numbers would be attached to all elements but access would be provided to all of them simultaneously by mangling the numbers into the IDL-derived symbol names [8]. Three alternate bindings were suggested, but all of them had the disadvantages associated with violating Principle 2.

Roush designed a system [9] in which IDL interfaces could have "translators" for other interfaces associated with them. This is effectively another form of aggregation. Because there is no type relationship between the main interface and the translated interfaces, information for each interface, roughly equivalent to its RepositoryID, must be included in and passed with the object reference. This system keeps the implementations of each object separate, which means that if `G` is a translator for `H` and both interfaces implement a method called `foo` with identical arguments it is possible to determine, when `foo` is invoked, whether the object had been cast to `G` or `H`. Our solution for aggregation avoids the need to pass extra type information, but it does not solve the problem of differentiating between identical methods on different interfaces. However, because it is not possible to narrow to a `server_only` object, the client-side ORB implementation knows unambiguously which method was invoked and passes the appropriate method and interface ids to the server, meaning this problem can be solved entirely on the server-side. The IDL compiler could, for instance, be enhanced to give one of the duplicate methods a different name in the POA binding.

The Component Object Model supports versioning through the aggregation of separate, immutable interfaces [10]. It has been argued that this is superior to the inheritance model, which is considered too complicated and brittle and interferes with the ability to remove old interfaces (that is, to support major versioning) [11]. We find this interpretation strange because interface aggregation is completely supported in the inheritance model; it can be achieved simply by not having clients directly use the interface that implements the aggregation. The `server_only` pragma helps enforce this inheritance pattern, but it has always been available for use as a convention.

It is more interesting to compare our new features against the COM model. The DCOM manual says [10]:

> The initial component exposes a core set of features as COM interfaces, on which every client can count. As the component acquires new features, most (often even all) of these existing interfaces will still be necessary; and new functions and properties appear in additional interfaces without changing the original interfaces at all. Old clients still access the core set of interfaces as if nothing had changed. New clients can test for the presence of the new interfaces and use them when available, or they can degrade gracefully to the old interfaces.

The problem with systems that support aggregation alone is that the lack of ability to impose any structure leads to an interface "soup." Aggregation is relatively safe when it is used to allow a single server to provide different interfaces *to different clients*, each of which will use only one of the interfaces. When individual clients are regularly using multiple interfaces on the same object and those interfaces have no relationship to one another, it quickly becomes difficult to characterize client behavior. If a client expects to be able to take an object with type `V` and also use it as a `W` through re-narrowing, the two types have been linked by the client regardless of the intention of the server's author, and such links will have to be accommodated when altering the system. After enough aggregations over many releases, determining the potential behavior of a client can require an exhaustive analysis of its code. Our model uses strong typing and inheritance (including the modified inheritance provided by minor versioning) to define the desired interfaces and limits the use of aggregation to their deployment, and this retains the benefits of an object methodology even in the presence of versioning.

The DCOM manual continues:

> With conventional object models, even a slight change to a method fundamentally changes the contract between the client and the component. In some models, it is possible to add new methods to the end of the list of methods, but there is no way to safely test for the new methods on old components. From the network's perspective, things become even more complicated: Encoding and wire-representation typically depend on the order of the methods and parameters. Adding or changing methods and parameters also changes the network protocol significantly.

By making use of the mechanisms already provided to support inheritance, our features allow interfaces to be versioned while not increasing the complexity of the wire protocols, and they provide clear semantics a client can use to test for the existence of new functionality in a server.

As of version 3.0, CORBA also includes explicit aggregation support in the Components specification [12]. Components are, in effect, a combination of functionality and conventions layered on top of CORBA that provide a number of added benefits. Unfortunately, the model appears to encourage flexibility through the use of a soupiness similar to that of DCOM, although it does not have to be used that way. We have examined the specification (which was not complete until after our implementation was largely finished) and do not feel it includes a model that simultaneously allows effective versioning and accurate characterization of (through effective limits on) client-side behavior. The specifications for both DCOM and CORBA Components seem to imply that combining distributed systems and true object-oriented programming with inheritance is too complex, and substituting flat interfaces with loose aggregation is "good enough." We continue to believe that the basic OO approach is sound and, with the addition of explicit versioning support, superior to these looser models in practice.

6 Future Work

As mentioned in Sect. 2.2, we did not implement support specific to versioning for any IDL types other than interfaces, but our initial experiences with creating new interfaces that interact with existing systems has revealed a painful omission: the lack of support for versioned enumerations. An enum places the names of the constant identifiers defined for it into the namespace of its parent, not its own namespace. This means that you can't version an enum by simply copying it because you also have to change all of the constant names. But when you must change all existing constants every time you need to add a new one, the code in both servers *and* clients suffers the death of a thousand `OR`s.

We would have liked to extend enumerations to allow version numbers to be attached to the names of the identifiers. These would be used to add new values in a way similar the way new methods are added to existing interfaces. Unfortunately, this design leads to complex run-time bounds-checking scenarios. If your client knows about version 3 of an enum but the server can only accept version 2 values, you have to produce a `VERSION` exception if the wrong value is used. In ORBs that support direct C++ casting within a domain, there is no interception point for this check. Even worse, if the enum is an `out` parameter, there is nothing to prevent a server from trying to *return* an inappropriate value. In addition to these problems, the language bindings generally associate IDL enumerations with built-in enum types, and unless one is willing to abandon these types for different, constructed types, very little can be done to provide a versioning semantic. We have not yet arrived at a design for versioned enumerations that satisfies us.

Acknowledgments. We would like to thank Ken Shirriff for his help reviewing earlier drafts of this paper, and Andy Hisgen for design guidance and asking good questions like "RPC can do this, why can't CORBA?"

References

1. Sun Microsystems Santa Clara, CA: ONC+ Developer's Guide. (2002) 816-1435-10.
2. Mitchell, J., etc.: An Overview of the Spring System. In: IEEE COMPCOM '94. (1994)
3. Liskov, B.: Data Abstraction and Hierarchy. In: OOPSLA '87 – Object Oriented Programming Systems, Languages and Applications (Addendum), Orlando, FL (1987) 17–34
4. Hamilton, G., Radia, S.: Using Interface Inheritance to Address Problems in System Software Evolution. Technical Report TR-93-21, Sun Microsystems (1993)
5. Schmidt, D.C., Vinoski, S.: CORBA and XML, Part 1: Versioning. C/C++ Users Journal C++ Experts Forum (2001)
6. Object Management Group: Common Object Request Broker Architecture (CORBA/IIOP). 3.0.2 edn. (2002)

7. Casais, E.: Managing Class Evolution in Object Oriented Systems. In Nierstrasz, O., Tsichritzis, D., eds.: Object Oriented Software Composition. Prentice-Hall (1995) 201–244
8. Anonymous: Interface Versioning for IDL. Project-internal proposal (1993)
9. Roush, E.: Cluster Rolling Upgrade using Multiple Version Support. In: CLUSTER '01 – 3rd IEEE International Conference on Cluster Computing, Newport Beach, CA (2001) 63–72
10. Microsoft Corporation: DCOM Technical Overview. (1996)
11. Szyperski, C.: 24.7 Component Assembly: Component Evolution. In: Component Software – Beyond Object-Oriented Programming. Second edn. Addison-Wesley, New York (2002) 479–480
12. Object Management Group: CORBA Components. 3.0 edn. (2002)

A Middleware Framework for the Persistence and Querying of Java Objects

Mourad Alia[1,2], Sébastien Chassande-Barrioz[1], Pascal Déchamboux[1], Catherine Hamon[1], and Alexandre Lefebvre[1]

[1] France Télécom R&D, DTL/ASR, 28 chemin du Vieux Chêne, B.P. 98, 38243 Meylan CEDEX, France

[2] LSR, B.P. 72, 38402 Saint-Martin-d'Hères CEDEX, France

{alia.mourad, sebastien.chassandebarrioz, pascal.dechamboux, catherine.hamon, alexandre.lefebvre}@rd.francetelecom.com

Abstract. This paper presents the adaptable and flexible architecture of a middleware framework for the persistence and querying of Java objects. The framework is composed of two sub-frameworks, each responsible for one aspect: persistence and queries. The persistence framework considers two kinds of objects: Memory instances (MI), which represent Java objects holding the data to be made persistent, and Data Store instances (DSI), which represent data items stored within data stores. It thus concentrates on the binding chain between a DSI and an MI, providing the management of the structural projection of persistent objects to a particular data store when performing I/Os. The query framework makes it possible to express, optimize and evaluate queries over heterogeneous data stores and in particular over the persistence framework objects. Query expression is independent of any query language and can be mapped to several standards. The middleware presented in this paper has been integrated in several contexts, thus validating its adaptability and flexibility.

1 Introduction

The problem of object persistence has been the subject of much research and industrial work over the last few years. The literature distinguishes two degrees of object persistence: *transparency* and *orthogonality*. Transparent persistence [2] makes a minor distinction between transient and persistent objects. This means that the programmer has some degree of persistence control, such as opening/closing transaction boundaries. *Orthogonal* persistence [1] [2] [3] supposes that the persistence property is independent of the object type: the programmer does not specify the objects that will be persistent and all objects are potentially persistent, as in the object model of ODMG [6]. Further details about approaches for adding persistence are detailed in [17] in the case of the Java programming language.

Implementing orthogonal persistence has been identified as a difficult task, even though it has been done. Transparent persistence is implemented and used primarily

M. Odersky (Ed.): ECOOP 2004, LNCS 3086, pp. 291-315, 2004.

in the industry. This trend is strongly driven by the fact that most enterprise data are stored in relational databases. The use of complex underlying object-to-relational mapping techniques leads to a layered application server design. In this context, transparent persistence is more appropriate. Several standards for transparent persistence have been developed, such as CORBA Persistent State Service (COS PSS) [7], Java Data Objects (JDO) [32] and EJB-CMP Entity Beans [31], for accessing persistent objects.

We address the problem of building persistence solutions for applications which manipulate persistent objects, whether these applications follow the transparent persistence or the orthogonal persistence approach. Programming such applications implies managing *storage instances* (e.g. database tuples) and *memory instances* (i.e. real-world Java objects). Programmers are then faced with managing both kinds of instances, that is, organizing transfers between the associated memory levels, accommodating formats and types which usually differ between these levels, and also translating references.

Storage instances may be stored in databases, file systems, ERP systems or mainframe transaction processing systems. These data stores are all referred to as Data Stores (DS) which can also support transactions and can potentially be federated (objects within one DS can refer to objects within another DS). The object persistence standards, such as those cited above, are referred to as Memory Instance Managers (MIM). Applications which manage persistent objects are considered to lie on an MIM. Another common requirement is that of querying the persistent objects, that is, providing associative access to these objects (usually by expressing a query), as opposed to direct access starting from a reference.

In this paper, we propose a middleware solution for tackling this problem independently of existing standards (MIMs) and persistent approaches, with the aim of ensuring that such a framework nevertheless be usable in the context of these standards and approaches. Thus, the middleware must be *adaptable* and *flexible* in order to allow pluggable implementations of DSs into MIMs: from the DS point of view, it must be possible to extend the middleware to incorporate different types of DSs (downward adaptability); from the MIM point of view, the interface exposed by the middleware must allow the implementation of different MIMs persistence approaches (upward adaptability). In particular, the proposed middleware framework makes it possible to implement both transparent persistence and orthogonal persistence.

These properties are transposed into the following goals for the middleware presented in this paper:

- Independence from the data store type (RDBMS, OODBMS, directories, flat files, etc).
- Independence from the memory object life cycle.
- Openness to other non-functional aspects, such as concurrency control, caching support and consistency control.
- Openness to DS federation and distribution.
- Independence from the query language.

We adopt the framework approach for designing the architecture of the middleware. A framework is defined as *"a reusable conception of one or part of one system that is represented by a set of abstract classes and the way their instances interact"* [16]. In order to be usable in the context of standards, the framework must be extended into so-called "personalities". In our case, the framework approach results in the definition of APIs for the persistence of objects in a DS, the retrieval of objects from a DS, interactions with the MIM layer, or the expression and evaluation of queries. Typical personalities include the above-cited standards (CORBA PSS, EJB CMP and JDO). An expected benefit of the framework approach is that of software reusability: the persistence and query frameworks can be re-used to implement different standards, as we have done with EJB [21] and JDO [24], thus reducing redundant code production.

This article presents the architecture of the persistence and query middleware framework. The architectural concepts are in the line of the ISO Reference Model of Open Distributed Processing [13] [14]. The paper is organized as follows. Section 2 positions our work with regard to related work. The overall architecture and principles are presented in Section 3. Sections 4 and 5 detail the persistence and query frameworks, respectively. Section 6 presents the implementation and usage of the framework, validating our approach. Section 7 concludes and presents future work.

2 Related Works

This work can be positioned with regard to many other works in two research domains: object persistence and data integration systems.

2.1 Object Persistence

Object persistence has been the focus of much work representing different approaches and viewpoints. The Pjava project [4] proposes *orthogonal* Java object persistence without changing the Java syntax. Data, metadata (classes) and code (methods) are made persistent by modifying the Java virtual machine.

Other approaches involve the definition of standard interfaces for the *transparent* persistence of objects into data stores. The CORBA Persistent State Service [7] interposes a CORBA-based abstraction layer between a server and its persistent storage. The persistent information is represented as *objects* stored in *storage homes*. Conceptually, a data store is a set of typed storage home objects. PSS users have to define objects and storage homes either using PSDL (Persistent State Description Language), which describes the persistent data, or directly in a programmatic way. In the case of PSDL, a compiler generates code in a target programming language, and in particular Java. JDO, Java Data Objects [32], is another example of transparent persistence for Java objects by *reachability*[1]. It consists of a simple set of interfaces

[1] Persistence by reachability is defined as follows: a given object that can be reached by following references starting from a persistent object becomes itself persistent.

which enable persistence capability for applicative objects. JDO instances are accessible via a Persistence Manager which represents a session with a data store. A simple method *makePersistent(obj)* of a Persistence Manager allows object *obj* to become persistent. JDO also provides a simple query language, JDOQL, for selecting instances of persistent objects. In the J2EE platform [31], Container-Managed Persistence (CMP) is responsible for handling the persistence of the entity bean states (their fields) and their interrogation at run-time. In the entity beans deployment descriptor, the user describes the abstract schema[2] which defines the beans persistent fields and relationships. The associated query language, EJB QL, is a SQL92-like query language with navigational expressions over the abstract schema. All these standards impose a way of managing the object's life cycle and are considered as Memory Instance Managers (see Section 3).

As a comparison, our framework is a lower-level middleware interface allowing the implementation of all these standards.

In the same spirit as the work presented here, many products and tools support the mapping of Java objects to persistent storage, and especially to relational database systems. Amongst the most representative of them are TopLink [19], originally from the Object People, PowerTier [27] from Persistence Software and the open source project OJB [26]. They are usually provided as autonomous systems and cover a wide range of functions (e.g. cache management or concurrency policies). However, such systems follow the black-box principle, hiding most of their internals. As a result, extending such systems for handling new functionalities such as distribution (distributed references between persistent objects) or handling new data store models is usually very difficult. These limitations motivate the downward adaptability and the flexibility of our framework.

The PerDiS project [9] treats the problem of distributed and shared persistent objects for distributed collaborative engineering applications with shared memory, caching and security management. Objects are inter-referenced by pointers and are nested into clusters within memories. Unlike the framework presented here, PerDiS imposes persistence by reachability and a particular object life cycle: objects reachable from persistent roots are made persistent and others are automatically garbage-3collected. For a transactional access to data stores, applications use the SDAI standard interface (Standard Data Access Interface) [15], which is at the same level as JDBC or ODBC gateways.

2.2 Data Integration Systems

The goal of the data integration systems is to provide uniform access (querying) over heterogeneous data sources. Most of these systems [10] [12] [28] follow the mediators/wrappers architecture [33]. The mediator interacts with several exported data

---

[2] An abstract schema is a virtual schema which is independent of the physical data store schema.

data store schema. It uses wrappers to interact with related data stores. There exist simple relational wrappers (such as JDBC or ODBC), but also object wrappers that hold and manage schemas (fat wrappers).

Compared with this architecture, our framework is more generic and can be used to generate wrappers for object mediation systems, as in [29]. The query framework can then be used by mediators to retrieve data from multiple data sources, accessed through the generated wrappers.

As the middleware needs to process queries, we reuse the results of research in query processing (query optimization and evaluation), whether in a centralized environment or in a distributed environment over multiple data sources [10] [11] [28].

3 Model and Principles

Our approach is to provide a middleware layer by "opening the black box" and following the separation of concerns principle. The middleware is composed of two subframeworks: the persistence framework and the query framework. It is these frameworks which make the middleware flexible and adaptable. In practice, it is also possible to use these two frameworks separately.

The persistence framework focuses on the I/O between the data store and the memory objects by identifying the persistent items using persistent object identifiers. This is achieved by interposing mediation objects, or *binding objects*[3], which represent Data Store Instances (DSI).

In addition to accesses through identifiers, the query framework is responsible for associative access. It thus manipulates collections of persistent objects and makes it possible to express and process MIM queries in their related query languages.

Figure 1 illustrates the interactions between the middleware layer and both the data stores and applicative layers. Persistent data of memory objects are projected into binding objects managed by the middleware, which are further mapped to data within data stores according to meta information. Persistent data of memory objects are typically attributes (fields) of a class. Objects managed by the persistence framework, typically binding objects, follow an object model presented in Section 4.2. This makes it possible to adapt the persistence object model to the MIM object model.

The interaction between binding objects and memory objects is achieved through objects called Memory Instances (MI), which hold the persistent fields. In order to access data stores, gateways such as JDBC or ODBC are used.

In the following, we present more explicit definitions of the general concepts related to each layer which will guide us in the presentation of the framework.

[3] A *binding object* is a computational object which holds a binding between other computational objects. Binding objects are subject to special provisions (RM ODP) [14].

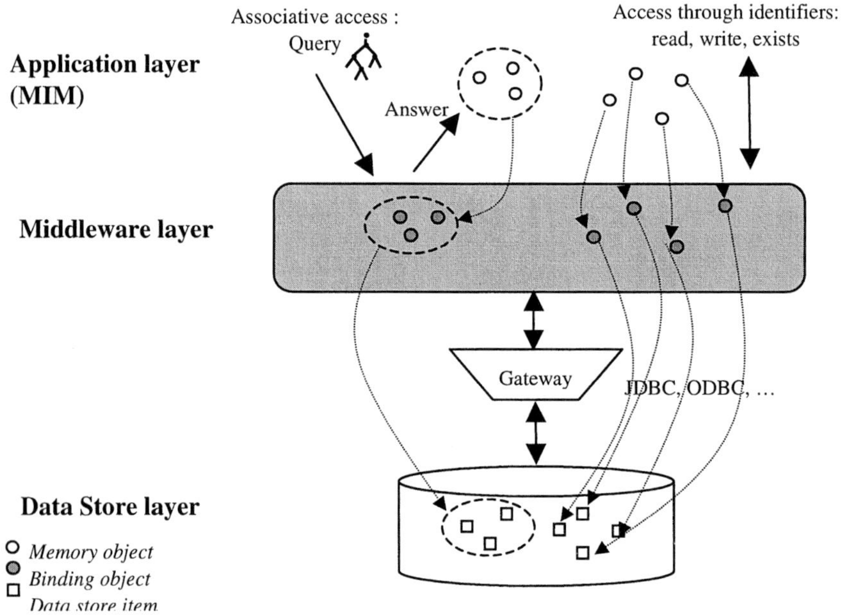

Fig. 1. The persistence and query middleware – the "big picture".

Data Store (DS). A DS provides the infrastructure for storing persistent information. A DS displays an interface which allows a client to manipulate its persistent data locally or remotely. Examples of DS include file systems, relational database systems, object database systems or directories.

Data Store Instance (DSI). A DSI is a data item stored within a DS. Such an item is identified by a persistent name within the middleware (see Section 4.3). A data item could be, e.g. a row of a relational database table, an object within an object database class or a file.

Memory Instance (MI). An MI is an object which holds the variables of the memory object to be made persistent. It can cooperate with a binding object in order to load/store its variables from/to the DS. From the persistence framework point of view, the MI is an Accessor (see Section 4.1). It could, for example, be the *PersistenceCapable* object in a JDO implementation of an MIM.

Memory Instance Manager (MIM). An MIM is the software (application) layer which manages the memory instances corresponding to the data store instances. This layer usually provides a high level of transparency with respect to the management of this projection (e.g. it hides load/store actions). It also defines the life cycle of an MI. Examples of MIMs include JDO, Corba PSS or CMP EJB implementations.

The separation between the MIs and the binding objects offers a freedom of choice for implementing various object life cycles, and allows several implementations. This is the key point which differentiates our approach from the related work mentioned in Section 2. In order to use the persistence framework, the user simply implements the MI and links it to the binding object managed by the framework, as explained in the next section.

4 Persistence Framework

4.1 Bindings and Accessors for Storage Synchronization

The basic architecture principle that governs the persistence framework consists in interposing *binding objects* between an MI and its associated DSI. They provide typed synchronizations (i.e. I/Os) between the MI and the DSI. There are two main synchronization actions: *read* and *write*. They are typed, as they support a particular structure for each persistent object class to be stored, as well as the way to map this structure to the associated DSI. Thus, a binding object is the Java object where the mapping occurs when performing I/O operations.

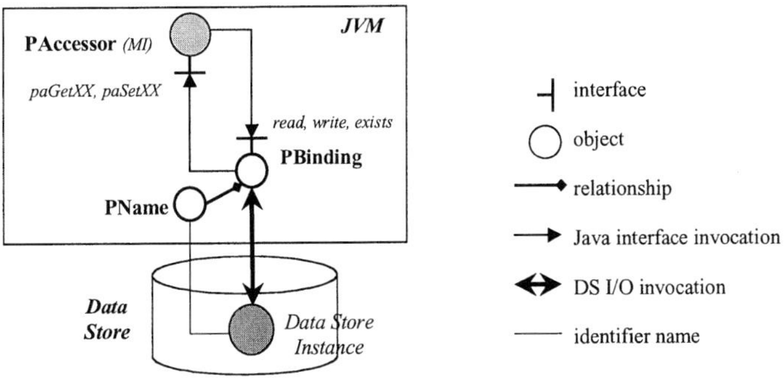

Fig. 2. Binding mediation for storing Java persistent objects.

Figure 2 illustrates the persistence chain between the DSI and the MI through three interfaces: *PBinding*, *PAccessor* and *PName*. Before being able to perform synchronizations, a binding object, represented by *PBinding* interface, must be assigned a persistent identifier, represented by the *PName* interface (see Section 4.3). This identifier is a Java object which designates the DSI to which the binding object is bound. Symmetrically, the binding object must also be assigned an accessor object, represented by the *PAccessor* interface, in order to have access to the state variables (or fields) of the MI to which it is bound. Once both assignments are done, the persistence chain is fully functional.

To make an object persistent, the *write* method is called on the *PBinding* object; the *PAccessor* object is used to read from the memory the values to be stored into the data store, by calling *paGetXXX* methods. Inversely, to read a persistent object from the data store, the *read* method is called on the *PBinding* object; the *PAccessor* object is used to write into memory the values obtained from the data store, by calling *paSetXXX* methods.

The user of the persistence framework is responsible for providing the implementation of the *PAccessor* interface, since the management of objects in memory is outside the scope of the persistence framework itself. The *PAccessor* interface is composed of field-specific setter and getter methods (i.e. *paSetXXX* and *paGetXXX* for the field named *XXX*). The *paGetXXX* method returns the value of field named xxx. The translation table between the middleware object model types and their Java counterparts determines the type of this value. For example, it can return a Java *int* value. The *paSetXXX* method performs the symmetrical action by assigning a truly typed value to the xxx field.

Analysis. These architecture principles satisfy the upward (MIM) and downward (DS) adaptability requirements:

1. The persistence chain is open to different MIM strategies. Synchronization points may occur when demarcating transaction boundaries, which can be done at the MIM level or in upper layers: the MIM layer decides when to call the read and write methods, and in which transactional contexts (the *read* and *write* methods of the *PBinding* offer an argument for propagating the connection). Thus the framework is independent of the transactional behaviour.
2. The binding objects support a unique *PBinding* interface, independent of the type of data store. Thus, this abstract interface provides adaptability and portability. While supporting this interface, a binding object hides the means to access the DS. For relational databases, it can use SQL statements, submitted through JDBC, in order to read/write Java persistent fields.

Moreover, the use of the object interposition approach does not require modifications to the Java Virtual Machine in order to support the persistence of objects.

In terms of implementation, the framework does not impose a way of composing the *PBinding*, *PAccessor* and memory objects. The only constraint is that the *PBinding* object must have a link to an object implementing the *PAccessor* interface. As a result, the user can freely compose the objects. By way of example, there is a single instance if the memory instance class directly implements *PAccessor* and the *PBinding* class extends this class. Thus, the framework offers great flexibility in terms of memory object architecture, as illustrated in Section 6.

Example. This example shows the binding and accessor objects in the case of a simple *Product* class with persistent fields *name* and *price*. Class *ProductAccessor* implements the getter and setter methods. Class *ProductBinding* implements the *read* and *write* methods.

```
public interface ProductAccessor extends PAccessor {

  //Accessors to the name field
  public void paSetName(String val) throws PException;
  public String paGetName() throws PException;

  //Accessors to the price field
  public void paSetPrice(float val) throws PException;
  public float paGetPrice() throws PException;
  ...
}

public abstract class ProductBinding implements PBinding {
  //Writes an object into the data store - uses the PAccessor
  //paGetXXX methods to get the memory values to be stored
  public void write(Object conn, PAccessor pa) {
  ...
  }
  //Reads an object from the data store - uses the PAccessor
  //psSetXXX methods to put the obtained values into memory
  public void read(Object conn, PAccessor pa)
          ...
  }
  ...
}
```

4.2 Internal Object Model

The basic principle of the persistence framework is to use binding objects between data stores and memory instances. Bindings perform the relevant mapping of Java structures to persistent structures which are specific to a particular DS, as illustrated in Figure 3. In order to do so, the persistence framework must be aware of the type of objects that are stored and also adaptable to MIM object models.

For this purpose, the persistence framework uses an object model to specify the types of entities it can store. This object model has been designed to be as close as possible to the Java object model and represents the structural part of objects. All entities described by this model are objects of persistent classes, composed of fields. There are three kinds of persistent classes: abstract classes, classes and generic classes[4]. There is no notion of value, dependent object, or second-class object in the model (this should be provided by a higher-level layer such as the MIM).

---

[4] The term "generic class" used in this article is not to be confused with the generic parametric classes of object languages.

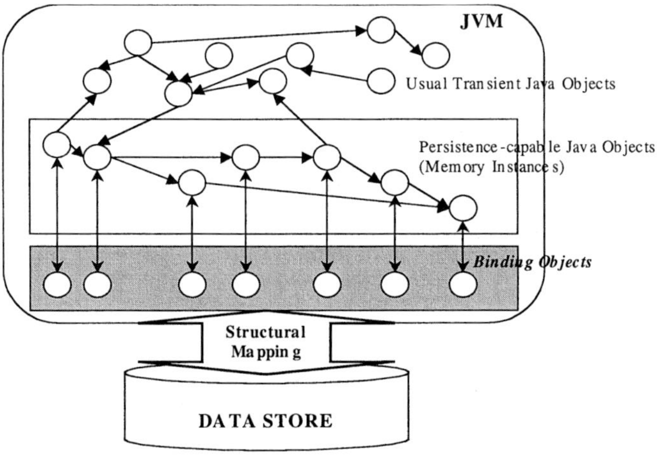

Fig. 3. Structural mapping performed by bindings (representing persistent objects of the framework model).

Classes and Fields. A persistent class defines a persistent object. It is composed of a set of fields described by a *field name* and a *field type*.

A field type belongs to one of the following three kinds:

- A *primitive type*, which is essentially one of those defined by Java.
- A *persistent class*, which means that the value of the field is a persistent name (representing the persistent identifier – see Section 4.3) that references a persistent object.
- A *persistent generic class*, which means that the value of the field is a persistent name that references a collection object (see below).

As in Java, a persistent class may be abstract, in which case no DSI can be created for this class. Abstract classes are used to factorize definitions between different non-abstract classes.

A class is always declared as belonging to a package, which is equivalent to the package concept in Java.

Persistent objects are always created within a persistent class, be it generic or not.

A class may inherit from other classes. Multiple-inheritance is supported among abstract classes, as well as between a non-abstract class and abstract classes (i.e. a class may derive several abstract classes). Only single-inheritance is supported among non-abstract classes (i.e. a class may be derived from at most one other class).

Collections and Generic Classes. A collection object is defined by a *generic class*. Generic classes have been designed to support different types of collections (e.g. lists, trees, maps).

Thus, a collection object is composed of a set of *indexed elements*. An indexed element has a value, which is the value of the element, and possibly several indexes, usually depending on the structure represented by that collection

As for the fields of a class, a generic class defines the type of its elements. The type of index values is restricted to scalar types (byte, char, short, int, or long) or the String type.

Persistent Names for Object Identification. Objects of non-abstract classes and generic classes are identified by a persistent name (see Section 4.3 for more details). The storage structure of the persistent name is declared in the class definition.

Such names can be managed by the underlying DS (e.g. an OODBMS usually associates persistent names to objects transparently), or by the framework users independently of the underlying DS. In this latter case, names are part of the object structure and must be defined as such (e.g. a primary key within an RDBMS). In the case of a DS managed name, a name may be defined as a value of an abstract type. Otherwise, a name may be defined as a basic type (byte, char, short, int, long, or string), or as a composite name. A composite name is a list of fields whose type is either one of the basic ones presented above, or is linked to one of the persistent object fields.

Analysis. The persistent object model is independent of any persistence model. Possible persistence models include "persistence by reachability" (objects are made persistent as soon as they are reachable from a "root" persistent object), "class-attached persistence" (all objects of a particular class are persistent), or "explicit per object persistence" (objects are explicitly made persistent using a dedicated command, such as "makePersist"). Our framework can support all these models, although it is the role of the upper layers using the framework to implement them. Conversely, the framework must be as neutral as possible with respect to the model supported by the underlying DS.

Example. The example below shows the XML descriptor of the object model for the class *Product* with two fields, *name* and *price*. The persistent name of the class *Product* is composed of one field, *name*.

```
<persistence>
  <package>invoice</package>
  <class abstract="FALSE" name="Product">
    <field name="name">
      <primitive-type type="string"/>
    </field>
    <field name="price">
      <primitive-type type="float"/>
    </field>
    ...
    <name-def name="">
      <field-ref field-name="name"/>
    </name-def>
  </class>
</persistence>
```

4.3 Persistent Object Identifiers and References Management

The persistence framework has to manage persistent object identifiers, assuming that each DSI representing a memory persistent object (i.e. an MI) has at least one persistent identifier, i.e. an object allowing its identification within its DS. Also, according to the object model, the persistence framework must deal with references between objects. In order to manage these, two naming concepts are used: *names* and *naming contexts*, borrowed from RM ODP [13].

Names and Naming Contexts. A *name* is an object that identifies a persistent object within a particular naming context (i.e. the name is valid in a particular naming context). A *naming context* is an object that associates an entity to each name it manages. A *name* is strongly dependent on the underlying DS. It may be composed of application-related information, such as primary keys in RDBMS. It may be a system-managed identifier (independent of user data), such as in OODBMS. The objective of the framework is not to make any assumption about the way names are managed. This means that the framework can support any kind of name.

Conceptually, these two concepts allow us to organize Data Store Instances into sets (i.e. naming contexts). These sets can also share Data Store Instances through their names. A naming context can, for example, represent instances of a given class or generic class, or tuples of a related data store. In naming concepts [ISO ODP part2], a name represents both an object identifier and a reference to this object.

The example of Figure 4 describes a complex situation where DSIs are stored within two Data Stores, *DS1* and *DS2* (a DSI always belongs to only one DS). It also shows fives naming contexts, *PNC1* to *PNC5*. A given DSI may have names valid in several naming contexts. For example, the DSIs of *PNC3* also have names within *PNC5*. Furthermore, a DSI may have names that are valid beyond its DS. This is the case for the DSIs of *PNC2* that also have names within *PNC4*, which federates the DSIs of two DSs.

Naming management essentially consists in three operations on naming contexts:

1. *export*: on a given naming context, this operation creates an association between an entity and a name within this naming context; the entity is either a persistent object or another name valid in another naming context. The entity is a parameter of this operation that yields the name designating it within this naming context. Performing the export operation again, by exporting the yielded name to another naming context, creates a so-called naming chain[5]. The behaviour of this operation depends on the naming context semantics. For example, it can look up an existing association involving this entity; then it yields the existing associated name or creates a new one, if no association exist. Or it can systematically create a new name, having the entity designated through different names within this

[5] A naming chain is also called a naming graph in RM ODP [13]. It is defined as a directed graph where each vertex denotes a naming context, and where each edge denotes an association between a name appearing in the source naming context and the target naming context.

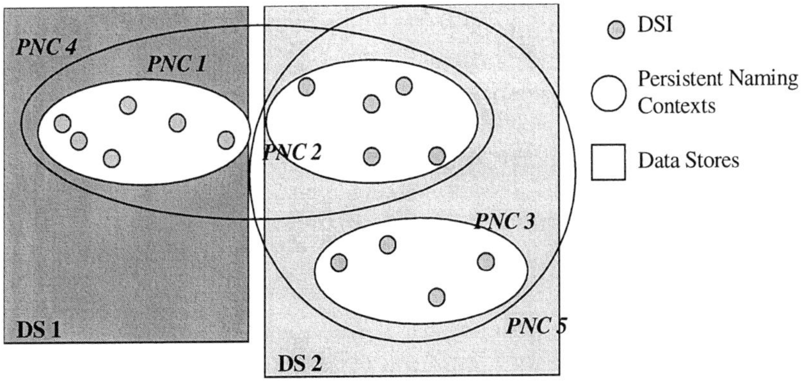

Fig. 4. Data stores (DS), Data Store Instances (DSI) and Persistent Naming Contexts.

naming context. In either case, name creation always occurs when calling `export`.

2. *resolve*: this operation is the reverse operation to export. It retrieves the entity that has been previously exported. It is used to look up the entity designated by a particular name within this naming context. The name is a parameter of this operation which yields the associated entity, if any exists. If this name is part of a naming chain, the operation yields the preceding name to the one passed as parameter.
3. *unexport*: this operation is used to remove an association within the current naming context. It takes a name as parameter and removes the association with the entity it designates within this naming context, if any exists.

In our framework, an entity represents a *PBinding* object (which represents a DSI) and a name represents a *PName* object. Naming context objects implement the *PNamingContext* interface. In order to manage binding objects and *PName* objects, two other kinds of objects are introduced: *binders* and *class mappings*.

In order to allow their storage in the DS, another important functionality is the encoding/decoding of names.

Binders and Class Mappings. The association between *PBinding* objects and *PName* objects is maintained by a *binder* object which implements the *PBinder* interface. Within a binder, there is always a unique persistent name that gives access to its associated DSI. Thus, a binder is a particular kind of naming context (the *PBinder* interface inherits from the *PNamingContext* interface).

Class mappings perform the creation of bindings. Each class has a class mapping associated to it. This is a factory producing binding objects (implementing *PBinding*). The management of *PNames* is delegated to a binder, also associated to the class. A class mapping object implements the *PClassMapping* interface and can be seen as the starting point for the management of the object instances of a related persistent class (*PBinding* and *PName* objects).

There are two cases when a class mapping creates a binding:

- A DSI already exists and a binding is requested by an MI in order to synchronise its values with it. This corresponds to a *bind* operation which associates a name to this binding, the binding being thus activated.
- No DSI exists. In this case, a binding is requested in order to create a new DSI. This corresponds to an *export* operation on this binding which creates a new name.

Example (continued). In addition to the class *Product* of the previous example, consider an additional class *InvoiceItem* representing the purchase of a given quantity of a product. This class has a field, which is a reference to a *Product* object. Figure 5 shows the corresponding naming chain managing the reference between an *InvoiceItem* object and the associated *Product* object. *pn1* is the persistent name of a *Product* object, managed by the binder associated to the *Product* class, *nc1*. Name *pn2* is the persistent name of the *Product* referenced from the *InvoiceItem*. Resolving *pn1* within *nc1* would yield *pn1* again, since *nc1* is the binder, and we are at the end of the naming chain. The following relationships hold:

```
pn2 = nc2.export(pn1)
pn1 = nc2.resolve(pn2)
```

The binding object corresponding to the *Product* object is obtained by calling `nc1.bind(pn1)`.

Analysis. Since the binder maintains the association between bindings and persistent name objects, it is always the end of a naming chain. This is why resolving a name within a binder always yields the final name related to its binding object. Thus, a binder can also be seen as the correct entry point to introduce caching mechanisms.

The use of names and naming contexts allows the introduction of any kind of reference semantics between DSIs, be they stored into co-located or into distributed DSs, activating MIs of referrer and referee into the same process or into distributed ones. In the case of distribution, this approach is the same as the one used in the Jonathan framework [8] used to implement open and flexible Object Request Brokers. The scope of a reference can be larger than a simple persistent class. It may cover several persistent classes within a DS: this is the case when naming contexts are used to deal with polymorphism. It may also cover several persistent classes within several DSs: this is the case when using naming contexts to federate DSs, such as *PN4* in Figure 4. As the framework argues for openness with respect to the federation of DSs, naming contexts are the feature which guarantees this openness. Indeed, users of the framework can assign (specialised) naming contexts to each reference field of a particular persistent class.

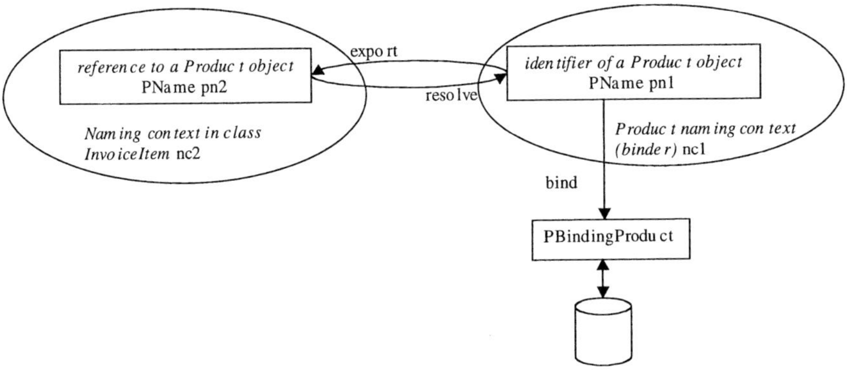

Fig. 5. Naming chain.

4.4 The Persistence Framework at Work: Mappers

The *mapper* is the root object which gives access to persistence functions. It is usually tied to one DS for which it manages synchronization between MIs and DSIs. Several mappers can coexist simultaneously within a JVM. A mapper gives access to binders which manage bindings. One binder is attached to each persistent class defined within the persistence framework.

The mapper also manages meta information for mapping the object schema to the corresponding DS. The mapping meta information describes the structural projection of objects in the object model onto the DS model. Associated to each class, and for each kind of data store within which the persistent object are stored, the mapping meta information contains *mapping definitions*. Such mapping definitions are similar to the ones described in [5]. The mapping information depends heavily on the type of data store. The architecture of the framework ensures that it can be extended to take into account new types of data store.

As an example, for relational database mapping, several mapping rules can be used in order to allow legacy database integration to be supported. A given class is mapped to a main table. If a class is projected onto more than one table, several external tables are possible, reachable through join conditions. Moreover, in the case of class references, it is possible to store the reference either in the class table, or as backward references in the table of the referenced class (in this latter case, the table is "collocated"). Finally, there are several possibilities for defining the mapping of generic classes, with or without an additional join table.

4.5 Type Management

Persistent objects are defined by persistent classes, which are composed of typed fields (see Section 4.2 for more details about the object model). When assigning a reference to a persistent object as the value of a field of another persistent object, type verification may occur. Even if Java enforces some kind of static typing, there are many situations where typing is poor and the relation between the Java typing mechanism and persistence typing is not always straightforward. This is especially true when dealing with generic classes. Furthermore, in the case of the federation of DSs, typing should be enforced in a larger context, potentially involving distributed JVMs.

In order to be able to perform type checking, typing information must be carried along with persistent names. Type verification can then occur when names are assigned as references, that is when a binding is going to store them. It is verified against the type associated to the field of the corresponding class: the type of the reference must satisfy the "isa" relationship which is enforced for the type of this field.

Types are closely related to names and are organized around type spaces. One type space is associated to each mapper. As naming contexts do not always share type spaces, when a name is exported into another naming context of another mapper, its type must be present in the type space of this destination naming context. If it is not present, it must be defined within this space, which means that its complete definition must be imported from the type space of the original naming context into the destination naming context. An object type in the framework is fully defined by a class name and the super classes of this class, recursively.

A type space can be combined with the object model containing the descriptions of all classes, as it defines a sub-part of the object model.

5 Query Framework

As objects are made persistent within data stores, the query framework must be able to interrogate such data stores. Thus, the problematic of the query framework is similar to that of query management in data integration systems [10] [12] [28]. In such systems, a global query expressed on an integrated schema is decomposed into subqueries corresponding to the underlying data stores.

In our case, the query framework must be able to fulfil the two following objectives. First, it must be possible to express queries directly on a DS. In this case, the framework must be aware of the schema exported by the DS. Second, it must be possible to express queries on the persistent object schema of the persistence framework. The expression of such queries is independent of the underlying DS onto which persistent data projected. This ensures that a given query remains valid even when data is migrated from one DS to another DS, provided that the object schema remains the same: only the mapping meta information is required to change. This second case is closer to the data integration systems: the persistent object schema can be seen as the integrated schema.

If queries are expressed directly on the DS, only values are returned as results. This is the case when querying directly relational databases. In the second case, the interaction of the query framework with the persistence framework makes it possible to obtain object references as query results, since the persistence framework manages persistent object names.

The purpose of queries is to select persistent data based on semantic criteria (e.g. products in the 100 to 200 price range, invoices for a given customer in a given time frame). The query framework makes it possible to express, optimize and evaluate queries over persistent data.

In the following sections, we detail each component of the query framework.

5.1 Query Expression

Rather than imposing yet another query language, the query framework offers a programmatic way to express queries. This approach guarantees adaptability to MIM query languages. This has been validated by the integration of the query framework in several systems (see Section 6). A query is expressed by the programmatic construction of an algebraic tree. This tree can be seen as an internal pivot representation of the corresponding initial MIM query.

As the query framework deals with objects, the algebra supports at least the algebraic operations described in [28] [30], which, in addition to the relational algebra (join, selection, projection), include collection manipulation operators, such as grouping (nesting), ungrouping (unnesting) or flattening on collections of tuples.

The algebraic tree is called a *query tree*, implementing the *QueryTree* interface. To each *QueryTree* object is attached a tuple structure, described as a list of typed named *fields* (the equivalent of the SELECT clause in SQL). For the root of the query tree, the tuple structure represents the type of the query results.

In a query tree, a *query node* represents an operation of the query algebra. The *QueryNode* interface inherits from the *QueryTree* interface. Several classes implement *QueryNode*, such as *Join*, *Selection*, *Nest*, *Unnest* or *Union*.

Data sources are represented as *query leaves* of the query tree. The *QueryLeaf* interface inherits from the *QueryTree* interface. The query framework contains, for each type of data store, query leaves corresponding to data of the data store. For example, a relational database query leaf can represent a relational table or a SQL query and its fields correspond to the SELECT part of the SQL query; an object database query leaf typically represents all instances of a given class. Other query leaves include persistent class extents (see below).

Fields of a query node can be defined in three ways.

1. A field can be *propagated* from another query tree: the latter query tree becomes a child of the current query node.
2. A field can be *calculated* from an expression applied to fields of other query nodes (see below for a detailed description of expressions).
3. A field can be the result of a nesting (grouping) operation: in this case, the nested field is a collection of tuples. The algebraic operation of the corresponding query node must be a *Nest*.

For a given query node, the set of query trees reachable through propagated or calculated fields constitutes the children of the current query node (the equivalent of the FROM clause in SQL).

A query node can also be attached a *query filter* (the equivalent of the WHERE clause in SQL). The query filter makes it possible to select data from the children query trees. The query filter is expressed as a well-formed Boolean and/or arithmetic *expression* over operands and operators. Operands of expressions can be constants, parameters, field operands on fields propagated from children nodes, or other expressions. Operators can be arithmetic operators (plus, minus, etc), logical operators (and, or) or string manipulation operators (concat, etc). As query trees, query filters are constructed programmatically. Query filters are trees where nodes are operators and leaves are operands. This enables extensibility of the query framework in order to introduce easily new types of operators.

Integration with the Persistence Framework. Integration with the persistence framework is first done through *extent* query leaves (the *ClassExtent* interfaces inherits from the *QueryLeaf* interface): an extent conceptually represent all objects of a given persistent class, independently of its mapping to a particular DS. The tuple structure associated to an extent contains one field for each field of the persistent class, plus the persistent name (*PName*) of the persistent class. The persistent name of a class can be manipulated as any other field (e.g. it can be projected or it can be part of a query filter).

Another important integration aspect concerns the support of path expressions. Navigation through the reference fields of persistent classes is done using the navigator operator. It makes it possible to construct a field operand for a field reached by a path expression (e.g. *invoiceItem.product.price*).

Query Expression on the Example. Consider that the example contains the additional class *Supplier*, with the field *supplierName* mapped onto the table *SE_SUPPLIER* with the column *SNAME.* Consider that the class *Products* has the additional field *supplier* of type reference to a *Supplier*. Consider the query *"Retrieve the product object identifiers (its PName) for products in the 100-200 price range supplied by "MySupplier"*.

The corresponding query tree is illustrated in Figure 6 below.

The code expressing this query looks like:

```
//creation of the two query leaves on Product and Supplier
ClassExtent pExtent = new ClassExtent("invoice.Product");
ClassExtent sExtent = new ClassExtent("invoice.Supplier");
//creation of the query tree root
QueryNode myQuery = new JoinProject();
//projection of PName(Product) into the result: pExtent becomes
a
//child of myQuery
myQuery.addPropagatedField(pExtent.getField("PName");
//query filter
Expression filter = new And(
```

```
  new And(
    new Greater(new FieldOperand(pExtent.getField("price")),
        new VariableOperand(100)),
    new Lower(new FieldOperand(pExtent.getField("price")),
        new VariableOperand(200))
    ),
  new And(
    new Equal(new FieldOperand(sExtent.getField("supplierName"),
      new VariableOperand("mySupplier")),
    new Equal(new FieldOperand(sExtent.getField("PName"),
      new FieldOperand(pExtent.getField("supplier"))
  )
);
//assigning the filter to myQuery - sExtent becomes another
child
myQuery.setFilter(filter);
```

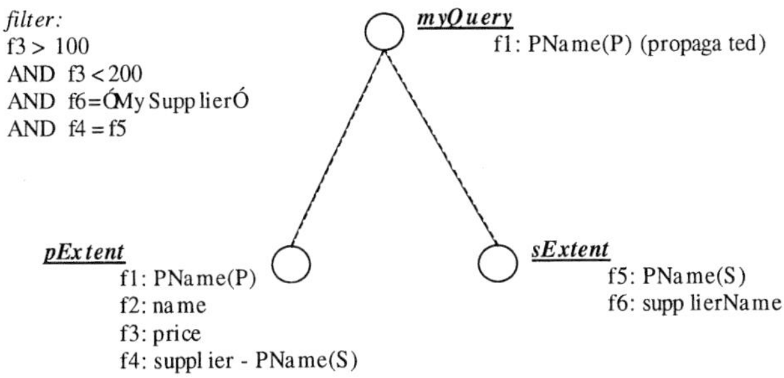

Fig. 6. Query expression: example of a query tree.

5.2 Query Optimization

Query optimization is an important step in query processing and is classical in database systems [11]. The approach used in the optimizer of the query framework is to use rewrite rules which transform a query tree in another query tree.

The three main tasks of the query optimizer are:

1. If appropriate, delegate query evaluation to the DS.
   a. The query optimizer first rewrites extents into the corresponding data store query leaves using mapping meta information. An important aspect is the management of persistent names: when rewriting an extent into a DS query leaf, the persistent name, which is a field of the extent, is transformed into a calculated field on the corresponding fields of the DS query leaves (e.g. the primary key in the case of a relational database mapping). For example, in the case of mapping to a relational database, the query leaves of class extents are rewritten into relational database query leaves. The query framework typically contains one such rewrite rule per data store type.

b. Then, depending on the data store evaluation capabilities, query leaves corresponding to the same data store are moved within the query tree so that they can be close to each other. A first generic rewrite rule is responsible for this task: *GroupSameDBRule*. Then, the query optimizer collapses these query leaves into a single query leaf in order to delegate the evaluation to the underlying DS. Currently, the framework contains one such rewrite rule per DS type. For more information about optimization depending on data store evaluation capabilities, see the work done in [10] [28].

For example, in the relational DS case, several query leaves on the same database can be grouped into one single relational database query leaf, with a single SQL query. On the other hand, in the case of simple file storage (one object per file), the file system does not have the capacity to evaluate queries, and the corresponding query leaves cannot be collapsed.

The DS query generated by the optimizer depends on the DS type. Even within the same DS type, various adaptors may be necessary to accommodate language differences (for example in the SQL case).

2. Apply "classical" optimization rules on the resulting query tree. This involves optimizations such as pushing selections down, removing useless projection nodes, which do not contain any filter.
3. Finally, the query optimizer produces the final query execution plan by choosing the appropriate join evaluation algorithms (hash join, nested join, etc). This can be done using statistical data on the data store (selectivity factors, histograms, etc).

The query optimization module contains a set of rewrite rules, each rule taking a query tree as input and producing a query tree as output. Configuring the query optimizer consists in choosing the rules to apply and the order in which they should be applied.

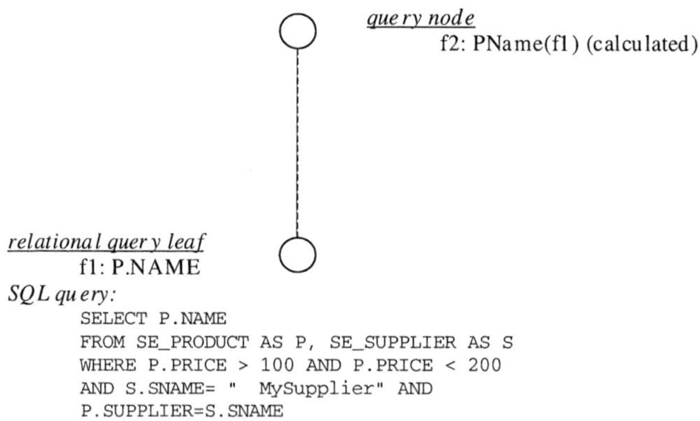

Fig. 7. Example of an optimized query.

Query Optimization on the Example. If both tables reside on the same DS, the query tree of Figure 6 is collapsed into a query tree containing a single relational query leaf, and a query node for constructing the *Product* persistent name, as illustrated in Figure 7 below. The optimizer performs tasks 1.a and 1.b above to produce this optimized query tree.

5.3 Query Evaluation

The query tree resulting from the optimization stage can now be evaluated. The evaluation process iterates over the collection of tuples issued from the query leaves. It works as a pipelined evaluation, with data flowing between query nodes.

For a given query tree, a global query evaluator first parses the optimized query tree and:

1. compiles the query filters of each query node by constructing typed buffer structures. This process avoids creating new objects when evaluating filters.
2. assigns a local query evaluator to each query node;
3. creates intermediate data structures for storing the tuple collections corresponding to each query node evaluation;
4. links each query leaf with its appropriate data store gateway;
5. coordinates the evaluation on the local query node evaluators. Each query node evaluator evaluates the corresponding compiled query filter over data coming from its children query node evaluators.

Prefetching. The persistence and query middleware contains an important optimization function. It consists of *prefetching* object fields at query evaluation time. A typical usage of the persistence and query framework is that the user first submits a query, asking for a set of persistent names of objects answering a given condition; later, the user interacts with the persistence framework to load the corresponding objects one by one into memory.

A naïve sequence of execution consists in performing a first access to the DS during query evaluation, in order to retrieve the persistent names, and then as many accesses to the DS as there are objects to be loaded in order to retrieve the field values.

The prefetching optimization gathers enough data from the DS at query evaluation time (i.e. the field data of the objects, and not just their persistent name) in order to be able to load the complete MI when requested without any further access to the DS.

5.4 Analysis

The adoption of a programmatic approach to express queries, together with the separation of the query optimizer and the query evaluator, ensure the high adaptability of the query framework at several levels:

1. Extensions of the optimizer. Given the rule-based structure of the optimizer, its extension is simply done by adding new rewrite rules.
2. Support of a new data store type. This is possible by adding the query leaves corresponding to this new DS type, and adding the rewrite rules responsible for transforming extents into the corresponding query leaves. Moreover, if the DS has some query evaluation capacity, the corresponding rewrite rule responsible for collapsing query leaves must be added.
3. Algebra and evaluation algorithms. The query framework has been designed to make it possible to introduce easily new algebraic operators (we have experienced it with aggregation), and new join evaluation algorithms (new query node evaluators).
4. Finally, new operators for expressions can also be added easily.

6 Implementation and Validation

The persistence and query middleware framework has been fully implemented in Java in the context of the ObjectWeb open source middleware consortium [25], respectively as the JORM [22] and MEDOR [23] projects.

In terms of mapping, legacy relational databases are supported with complex mapping rules. A simple mapping to files as well as a prototype mapping to a simple object database have also been implemented.

The implementation of mappings to several data store types has validated the extensibility of the framework. This includes the support of mapping definitions, generation of bindings for persistence and query management (rewrite rules and query leaves).

The middleware framework presented in this article has also been coupled with other middleware components related to persistence in order to integrate caching, concurrency and transaction management. This integration has shown that the persistence and query framework is indeed adaptable with regard to these other technical features.

The persistence and query framework has been used to implement transparent persistence in the JOnAS J2EE server [21] and the Speedo JDO implementation [24]. Both systems generate the object model and mapping meta information from their respective descriptors. In both cases, the corresponding binding classes are generated. Flexibility in terms of MIM is illustrated by the two following different approaches for integrating the generated binding classes:

1. In the case of JOnAS, the integration is done at the code generation level with inheritance: the generated binding class extends the JOnAS context switch. A container object implements the *PAccessor* interface.
2. In the case of Speedo, an additional proxy class is generated for each user class. This proxy class implements the necessary JDO interfaces imposed by the specification, as well as the *PAccessor* interface, and extends the generated binding class. Finally, the original user class is enhanced using byte code manipulation and is merged with the binding and proxy classes.

Regarding queries, the initial JDOQL or EJB QL query is transformed into the corresponding query tree. The query framework optimizes and runs the query, and the query results are loaded into the corresponding application server objects.

These two experiments have proved the re-usability of our persistence and query framework in different contexts, with different object life cycle management policies, and different implementation solutions.

Performance tests are under way in order to compare the persistence and query framework with other commercial products in the contexts of J2EE (JOnAS) and JDO (Speedo).

7 Conclusion and Future Work

This paper has presented an adaptable and flexible middleware framework for the persistence and querying of Java objects. The framework's downward and upward adaptability and its independence from other persistence aspects, such as caching and transactions, have clearly been demonstrated throughout this paper. The framework has been fully implemented and has been used in several contexts (JDO, EJB), thus validating its re-usability, as well as our initial objectives.

Regarding its extension to other data stores (new mappers), the possibility of the Lightweight Directory Access Protocol LDAP [37] as a data store is currently being investigated. Another extension (or personality) concerns the implementation of the Universal Description, Discovery and Integration protocol, UDDI [18], which is being carried out as an internal France Telecom project.

We are currently working on the integration of the persistence and query framework with other middleware aspects, such as distributed caching.

The persistence and query framework will be reengineered using the Fractal component model, and more precisely its Julia reference implementation [20]. Using Fractal should improve the integration and extensibility of the framework, simplify the configuration of the naming facilities, and provide a better structure for the rule-based query optimizer.

Acknowledgements. The authors would like to thank the anonymous referees for their many constructive and encouraging comments.

References

1. M.P. Atkinson, P.J. Bailey, K. Chisholm, W.P. Cockshott, R. Morrison: "An Approach to Persistent Programming". Computing Journal 26(4): 360-365, 1983.
2. M.P. Atkinson and R. Morrison. "Orthogonal persistent object systems". VLDB Journal, 4(3), 1995.
3. M. Atkinson, M. Jordan. "Providing Orthogonal Persistence for Java". Lecture Notes in Computer Science, Vol 1445, 1998.

4. M.P. Atkinson, M.J. Jordan, S. Spence. " Design Issues for Persistent Java: a type-safe object-oriented orthogonally". In Proceedings of the 7th Workshop on Persistent Object Systems, Cape May (NJ), USA, 1996.
5. M. Baldonado, C.-C.K Chang, L. Gravano, A. Paepcke, "The Stanford Digital Library Metadata Architecture". Int. J. Digit. Libr. 1 (1997) 108–121.
6. R.G.G. Cattell, D.K. Barry, M. Berler, J. Eastman, D. Jordan, C. Russel, O. Shadow, T. Stanienda, and F. Velez. The Object Data Standard: ODMG 3.0. Morgan Kaufmann Publishers, 2000.
7. The CORBA Persistence State Service Specification. http://www.omg.org/
8. B. Dumant, F. Horn, F. D. Tran, J.-B. Stefani. "Jonathan: an Open Distributed Processing Environment in Java". IFIP International Conference on Distributed Systems Platforms and Open Distributed Processing, The Lake District, U.K., September 1998.
9. P. Ferreira, M. Shapiro, X. Blondel, O. Fambon, J. Garcia, S. Kloosterman, N. Richer, M. Roberts, F. Sandakly, G. Coulouris, J. Dollimore, P. Guedes, D. Hagimont, S. Krakowiak. "PerDiS: design, implementation, and use of a PERsistent Distributed Store". Technical report, QMW TR 752, CSTB ILC/98-1392, INRIA RR 3525, INESC RT/5/98, October 1998.
10. H. Garcia-Molina, Y. Papakanstantinou, Q. Quass, A. Rajaraman, Y. Sagiv, J. Ullman, V. Vassalos, J. Widom "The TSIMIS Approach to Mediation: Data Models and Languages". Journal of the intelligent Information Systems (JIIS). 1997.
11. L.M. Haas, J.C. Freytag, G.M. Lohman, and H. Pirahesh. "Extensible Query Processing in Starburst". In Proceedings of ACM SIGMOD International Conference on Management of Data, pages 377--388, Portland, Oregon, May 1989.
12. L.M. Haas, R.J. Miller, B. Niswonger, M. Tork Roth, P.M Schwarz, E. L. Wimmers. "Transforming Heterogeneous Data with Database Middleware: Beyond Integration". IEEE Data Engineering Bulletin, vol 22, number 1, pages 31-36, 1999.
13. ISO. ITU/ISO Reference Model of Open Distributed Processing – Part 2. Foundations, International Standard ISO/IEC 10746-2, ITU-T Recommendation X.902, 1995.
14. ISO. ITU/ISO Reference Model of Open Distributed Processing – Part 2. Architecture, International Standard ISO/IEC 10746-3, ITU-T Recommendation X.903, 1995.
15. ISO 10303-22; Industrial automation system and integration – Product data representation and exchange – Part 22. Implementation methods: Standard Data Access Interface specification. 1996.
16. R. E. Johnson. "Framework = (components + patterns): How framework compare to other object-oriented reuse techniques". Communications of the ACM, 40(10):39-42, October 1997.
17. J.E.B. Moss, A.L. Hosking, "Approaches to Adding Persistence to Java", in First international Workshop on Persistence and Java, Drymen, Scotland, September 1996.
18. Oasis, The Universal Description, Discovery and Integration (UDDI), http://www.uddi.org/
19. The Object People. TopLink: Java object-to-relational persistence architecture. http://www.objectpeople.com/
20. ObjectWeb Consortium. The Fractal component model and framework, http://fractal.objectweb.org
21. ObjectWeb Consortium. JOnAS: Java Open Application Server, http://jonas.objectweb.org
22. ObjectWeb Consortium. JORM: Java Object Repository Mapping, http://jorm.objectweb.org

23. ObjectWeb Consortium. MEDOR: Middleware Enabling Distributed Object Requests, http://medor.objectweb.org
24. ObjectWeb Consortium. Speedo: JDO implementation. http://speedo.objectweb.org
25. Objectweb: Consortium for the promotion and the development of open source middleware. http://www.objectweb.org
26. OJB: Object Relational Bridge http://db.apache.org/ojb/
27. Persistence Software. Persistence PowerTier for J2EE http://www.persistence.com/products/powertier/index.php
28. A. Tomasic, L. Rashid, and P. Valduriez. "Scaling Heterogeneous Databases and the Design of DISCO". In Proc. 16th ICDCS Conf., Hong Kong, 1996.
29. M.T. Roth, P. Schwarz. "Don't Scrap It, Wrap It! A Wrapper Architecture fur Legacy Data Sources". In Proc. of the 23rd VLDB Conference, Athens, Greece, 1997.
30. G. M. Shaw, S. B. Zdonik A Query Algebra for Object-Oriented Databases. In Proceedings of the Sixth International Conference on Data Engineering, February 5-9, 1990, Los Angeles, California, USA; pp 154-162.
31. Sun Microsystems. Java 2 Enterprise Edition Specification. http://java.sun.com/j2ee
32. Sun Microsystems. Java Data Objects Specification. http://java.sun.com/products/jdo
33. G. Wiederhold, "Mediators in the Architecture of Future Information Systems", IEEE Computer, pp. 38-49, March 1992.

Sequential Object Monitors

Denis Caromel[1], Luis Mateu[1,2], and Eric Tanter[2,3]

[1] OASIS project, Université de Nice – CNRS – INRIA
2004, Rt. des Lucioles, Sophia Antipolis, France
denis.caromel@sophia.inria.fr

[2] University of Chile, Computer Science Dept.
Avenida Blanco Encalada 2120, Santiago, Chile
{lmateu,etanter}@dcc.uchile.cl

[3] OBASCO project, École des Mines de Nantes – INRIA
4, rue Alfred Kastler, Nantes, France
etanter@emn.fr

Abstract. Programming with Java monitors is recognized to be difficult, and potentially inefficient due to many useless context switches induced by the `notifyAll` primitive. This paper presents SOM, *Sequential Object Monitors*, as an alternative to programming with Java monitors. Reifying monitor method calls as requests, and providing full access to the pending request queue, gives rise to fully sequential monitors: the SOM programmer gets away from any code interleaving. Moreover, useless context switches are avoided. Finally, from a software engineering point of view, SOM promotes separation of concerns, by untangling the synchronization concern from the application logic.

This paper illustrates SOM expressiveness with several classical concurrency problems, and high-level abstractions like *guards* and *chords*. Benchmarks of the implementation confirm the expected efficiency.

1 Introduction

Programming with Java monitors is hard because the semantics of the operations `wait/notifyAll` is difficult to understand for most programmers, and, even when understood, getting the correct expected behavior can be cumbersome. Moreover, the resulting programs are inefficient because `notifyAll` awakes all waiting threads, triggering lots of thread context switches which are expensive in terms of execution time. Finally, from a software engineering point of view, using Java monitors enforces a *tangling* of the synchronization concern with the application logic.

In this paper we introduce a new concurrency abstraction called SOM, *Sequential Object Monitor*, as an alternative to Java monitors. We developed a 100% pure Java library providing powerful and efficient sequential object monitors. A SOM is a *sequential* monitor in the sense that the execution of a method cannot be interleaved with that of another method: once a method starts executing, it is guaranteed to complete before starting the execution of another method. We show that SOMs are *(i)* powerful because other high-level synchronization

M. Odersky (Ed.): ECOOP 2004, LNCS 3086, pp. 316–340, 2004.

abstractions (e.g., guards, chords) are easily expressed with SOMs, *(ii)* easier to understand and use due to their sequential nature and finally, *(iii)* efficient because they require less thread context switches than standard Java monitors. Performance measurements are provided to support our proposal. Finally, since it is based on a reflective infrastructure, SOM makes it possible to completely separate synchronization specification from application logic, thus achieving a clean separation of concerns [12], promoting reuse of both synchronization and application code.

Section 2 discusses related work in the area of concurrency and establishes the main motivation of our proposal. Section 3 presents SOM, through its main principles, API, and some canonical examples. Section 4 exposes how concurrency abstractions such as guards [6,13,17] and chords [4] can be expressed in SOM. Section 5 explores implementation issues, such as the SOM reflective infrastructure, how efficient scheduling is obtained, and finally some benchmarks validating our approach. Section 6 concludes with future work.

2 Related Work and Motivation

Two threads accessing simultaneously a shared data structure can lead the data structure to an inconsistent state. Such a programming error is called a *data race*. To avoid data races, programmers must *synchronize* the access to the shared data structure. In this section we describe the different mechanisms that have been proposed to allow programmers to write thread-safe programs (i.e., programs where data races do not occur).

2.1 Classical Synchronization Mechanisms

Monitors. A monitor is a language-level construct similar to a class declaration. In a monitor, private variables and public operations are declared. The semantics of the monitor ensures that concurrent invocations of operations are executed in mutual exclusion, hence avoiding data races. Monitors were invented by Brinch Hansen [7] and Hoare [16]. These monitors avoid thread context switches by introducing condition variables (thread queues) to explicitly resume only one thread instead of all threads. However, Brinch Hansen states in [8] that such monitors are *baroque and lack the elegance that comes from utter simplicity only.*

Guards. Guards are a simple concept, easy to understand and reason about. The idea of associating a boolean expression to indicate when a given operation may be executed was first introduced for the critical region construct [6]. These boolean expressions evolved to become the guarded commands of [13] and [17]. The main problem with guards is to implement them efficiently, that is, without requiring lots of thread context switches.

Schedulers. The scheduler approach relies on having an entity, called a *scheduler*, that is responsible for determining the order in which concurrent requests to a shared object are performed, similarly to the way an operating system scheduler manages the access to the CPU by concurrent processes. The scheduler approach relates to the *actor* and *active object* models[1], which focus on the separation of coordination and computation (see for instance [1,15,3]). They introduce the concept of a *body*: *"a distinguished centralized operation, which explicitly describes the types and the sequence of requests that the object might accept during its activity"* [9]. Such an approach originated in Simula-67 [5], and has been used in several distributed object systems like POOL [2], Eiffel// [10] and, in Java, ProActive [11].

Such approaches are usually in the framework of active entities which implies at least an extra thread for synchronization and extra context switches: a scheduler runs in its own thread of control in an infinite loop. The cost of context switches is not really an issue for systems aiming at parallel programming of distributed memory systems, since the overhead of thread context switches is hidden by network latency. On the other hand such an overhead is a concern for concurrent programming of shared memory multiprocessors.

2.2 Java Monitors

Java is one of the first massively-used languages that includes multi-threaded programming as an integral part of the language. For synchronization, Java offers a flavor of monitors which we will refer to as *Java monitors*. They are inspired from the *critical region* concept invented by Brinch Hansen [6]. The main idea behind the original critical regions is to support the *guard* programming pattern: each operation has an associated guard, a boolean expression which must be true before executing the operation. If the guard is false, the critical region transparently delays the operation until the guard becomes true.

Java monitors are somehow lower level than critical regions because the programmer must *explicitly* test the guard condition before each operation, and must *explicitly* notify waiting threads when guards must be evaluated. Fig. 1 shows the typical code of a guard-like implementation of the `get` method of a bounded buffer.

In Java, a monitor is a normal class definition that includes methods declared with the `synchronized` modifier (1). Concurrent invocations of synchronized methods are executed in mutual exclusion. Conversely, a guard does not have a special syntax construct in Java. It is implemented by a `while` statement where the boolean expression is the (negated) guard condition (2). The programmer must *explicitly* call `wait` (3) to suspend a thread until `notifyAll` is invoked by another thread (5).

This simple example clearly highlights the main disadvantages of the standard Java synchronization mechanism:

[1] The actor model is in a functional setting, while the active object model is rather in imperative object languages.

```
(1) public synchronized Object get()
        throws InterruptedException {
(2)     while (!bufarray.size() > 0)
(3)       wait();
(4)     Object o = bufarray.get();
(5)     notifyAll();
(6)     return o;
    }
```

Fig. 1. Guard-like code for a bounded buffer in Java.

- Java monitors are a low-level abstraction and therefore, programmers are prone to introduce many bugs in their programs: e.g., forgetting to specify the `synchronized` modifier, using an `if` statement instead of a `while` for evaluating guards, wrongly using `notify` instead of `notifyAll`[2] or not invoking `notifyAll` when needed, etc.
- The application functional code (4-6) is tangled with the synchronization concern (1-2-3-5). Tangling non-functional concerns with application code is a violation of the Separation of Concerns (SOC) principle [12], and leads to less understandable, reusable and maintainable code.
- From an efficiency point of view, calling `notifyAll` is inefficient because it awakes all waiting threads. When many threads are waiting on the same lock, this entails a lot of useless, expensive, thread context switches. For instance, in the bounded buffer problem, if many consumers are waiting for an item to be produced, putting a single item in the buffer will awake *all* consumers, although only one of them can get the item (see Sect. 5.5 for benchmarks).
- Programmers frequently disregard multi-threading when defining classes. This entails that there are plenty of useful libraries with classes which are not thread-safe. Making such classes thread-safe, if at all possible, is hard and error prone.

2.3 Recent Proposals

We now review two recent proposals in the area of concurrency, chords [4] and the Java Specification Request 166 [21].

Chords were first introduced in Polyphonic $C^\sharp$, an extension of the $C^\sharp$ language. Chords are join patterns inspired by the join calculus [14]. Functional Nets [22] is another example of join-inspired calculus. The vision of Functional Nets as a combination of Functional and Petri-Nets explains well the intrinsic nature of a join pattern: function applications conditioned by the presence of several inputs. Developed in a functional setting, the absence of state is some-

[2] Recall that `notify` only awakes a single thread, but using it is not recommended because in most cases it introduces subtle race conditions which are very hard to track down.

how hidden away by the memorization of tokens (function application) within pending continuations.

Within Polyphonic C$^\sharp$, a chord consists of a header and a body. The header is a set of method declarations, which may include at most one synchronous method name. All other method declarations are asynchronous events. The chord body is executed only when the chord has been *enabled*. A chord is enabled once all the methods in its header have been called. Method calls are implicitly queued up until they are matched up.

Chords do not address the mutual exclusion problem per se: multiple enabled chords are triggered simultaneously. Although mutual exclusion can be achieved with chords, it must be implemented explicitly and is error-prone. Indeed, to implement mutual exclusion of chord bodies, the programmer must include an additional asynchronous event to represent the idle state, adding it to the header of each chord requiring mutual exclusion and calling it at the end of constructors and chord bodies. Furthermore, there are some classical problems which are difficult to solve with chords, such as implementing a buffer which ensures servicing of get requests in order of arrival.

The Java Specification Request 166 [21] is a proposal for new standard Java abstractions for concurrency. It basically standardizes medium-level constructions, such as synchronizers and concurrent collections, and adds a few native lower-level constructions, such as locks and conditions. The aim behind the JSR 166 is to provide a wide set of constructions so that people can use the appropriate abstractions for a given problem, and hence does not promote any concurrent paradigm in particular. The basic synchronization facility are Hoare's style monitors. These monitors can be more fragile than current Java monitors, because programmers are responsible of explicitly asking and releasing monitors. In fact, the JSR 166 favors flexibility and efficiency at the expense of increased verbosity, with a risk of fragility.

2.4 Motivation

Overall, this paper proposes an alternative for programming concurrency which aims at solving the problems mentioned above:

- **easy**: it should be a high-level and easy-to-use concurrency mechanism, ensuring thread safety;
- **powerful**: it should be expressive enough to support any concurrency abstraction;
- **efficient**: it should avoid useless threads and useless thread context switches;
- **modular**: synchronization code should be specified separately from application code, in order to achieve a clean separation of concerns, and making it easy to "plug" synchronization onto existing, not thread-safe, classes;
- **portable**: the system should be a standard Java library, not requiring a specific virtual machine.

3 Sequential Object Monitors

Sequential Object Monitors, SOMs, are a high-level abstraction inspired by the scheduler approach (Sect. 2.1), intended as an alternative to Java monitors at the programming level. We do not modify the Java language, but instead provide an optional library, so that one can use the right abstraction depending on the problem to tackle and the actual programmer skills.

3.1 Main Ideas

A sequential object monitor, SOM, is a standard object to which a low-cost, thread-less, *scheduler* is attached (Fig. 2a). A SOM does not have its own thread of control, i.e. it is a *passive object*. The functional code of a SOM is a standard Java class in which synchronization does not need to be considered at all. The synchronization code is localized in a separate entity, a scheduler, which implements a *scheduling method* responsible for specifying how concurrent requests should be scheduled. A SOM system makes it possible to define schedulers and to specify which schedulers should be attached to which objects in an application.

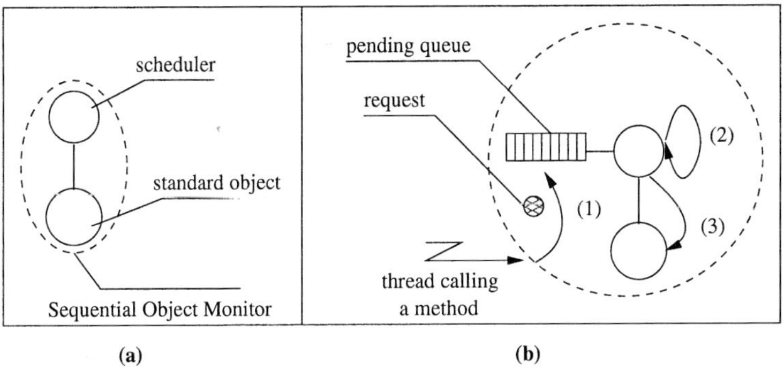

Fig. 2. Structure and operational sketch of a Sequential Object Monitor.

When a thread invokes a method on a monitor, this invocation is reified and turned into a *request* object (Fig. 2b(1)). Requests are then queued in a *pending queue* until they get scheduled by the scheduling method (Fig. 2b(2)). The scheduling method can mark several requests for scheduling. A scheduled request is safely executed (Fig. 2b(3)), in mutual exclusion with other scheduled requests (and the scheduling method).

A scheduling method simply states how requests should be scheduled. Fig. 3 is an example, in pseudo-code, of a scheduling method specifying a classic strategy for a bounded buffer.

A SOM is a *sequential* monitor since considering thread interleaving is not necessary when writing the functional code; a method body is always executed

```
schedule method:
  if buffer empty then schedule oldest put
  elseif buffer full then schedule oldest get
  else schedule oldest
```

Fig. 3. Pseudo-code of a fair scheduling strategy for a bounded buffer. (The equivalent code in SOM is shown later, in Fig. 8)

atomically from begin to end with regards to other invocations. Conversely, in a *quasi-parallel* monitor [18,9] (e.g., Hoare's, Java monitors) although only one thread can be active at a time, several method activations may coexist. It can make it complex to reason about the program. Fig. 4 summarizes the main principles of SOM.

1. *Any method invocation on a SOM is reified as a* request *and delayed in a pending queue until scheduled.*
2. *The scheduling method is guaranteed to be executed if a request may be scheduled.*
3. *A request is executed atomically with respect to other requests.*

Fig. 4. Main SOM principles.

SOM provides certain guarantees, as listed in Fig. 5. Some of these guarantees are functional, like monitor reentrancy and execution order of scheduled requests. Others have more to do with the thread management strategy of SOM, presented in detail in section 5.3. Recall that it aims at avoiding useless thread context switches.

The SOM model is indeed close to the active object model. The fundamental difference is that a sequential object monitor is a *passive object*, meaning it has no autonomous behavior, no additional scheduling thread: a SOM is much more lightweight than an active object. Nevertheless, the synchronization mechanism of both entities are similar. Compared to existing work carried out in the context of actors and active objects, the specific contribution of SOM rather relates to two specific original points: the sequential nature of synchronizations, for simplicity, and the absence of a synchronization thread, for efficiency.

3.2 Main Entities and API

We now present some elements concerning the entities and the API of the SOM library, in order to go through concrete examples afterwards. In SOM, a scheduler is defined in a class extending from the base abstract class `Scheduler` (Fig. 6). A scheduler must simply define the no-arg `schedule()` method. In this method,

1. *A SOM is reentrant, meaning that any self send on a monitor is executed immediately, without calling the scheduling method.*
2. *Given that the scheduling method can schedule several requests at a time:*
   - *After execution of the scheduling method, the scheduled requests are executed by their calling thread, in the scheduling order.*
   - *The scheduling method will not be called again before* all *scheduled requests complete.*
3. *There is no infinite busy execution of the scheduling method.*
4. *The scheduling method is executed by caller threads, in mutual exclusion. The exact thread executing this method is unspecified.*
5. *After a caller thread has executed its request, it is guaranteed to return at most after one execution of the scheduling method.*
6. *Whenever a SOM is free, if a request arrives and is scheduled by the scheduling method, the request is executed without any context switch.*

Fig. 5. Main SOM guarantees.

the scheduling strategy is defined. The basic idea is that a scheduler can *mark for execution* one or more pending requests, stored in a pending queue. This is called *scheduling (a) request(s)*. Such scheduling decision may be based on requests characteristics as well as the state of the associated base object (passed to the scheduler as a constructor parameter) or any other external criteria.

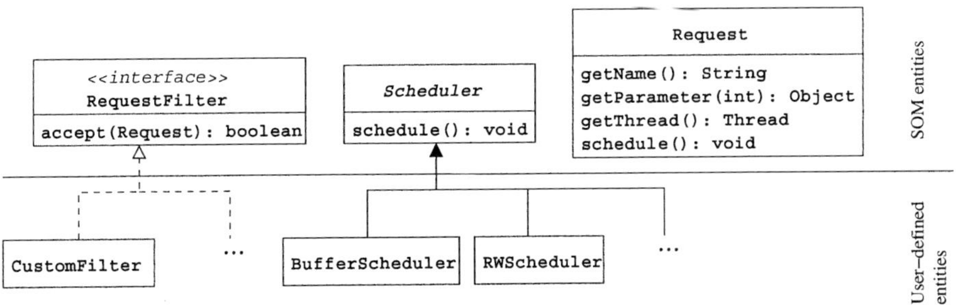

Fig. 6. Main entities provided by SOM, and some potential user-defined extensions.

Various methods are provided for the scheduler to express its scheduling strategies (Fig. 7). For instance, `scheduleOldest("put")` schedules the oldest pending request on method `put`, if any (otherwise it does nothing). Requests that are not scheduled remain in the queue to be scheduled later, on a future invocation of `schedule`. Requests are represented as `Request` objects. A scheduler can obtain an iterator on the pending queue using the `iterator()` method, and can then introspect request objects, in arrival order, to determine which

scheduling	queue management
void schedule(Request)	Iterator iterator()
void scheduleAll[1]	boolean hasRequest[1]
void scheduleOldest[1]	int requestCount[1]
void scheduleYoungest[1]	
void scheduleOlderThan[2]	
void scheduleAllOlderThan[2]	
void scheduleYoungerThan[2]	
void scheduleAllYoungerThan[2]	

- [1] Method available in various overloaded versions:
  - `()`: apply to all requests in the queue
  - `(String)/(String[])`: apply to request(s) with given name(s)
  - `(RequestFilter)`: apply to request(s) accepted by filter
- [2] Method available in 2 overloaded versions, taking either two `String` or two `RequestFilter` parameters.

Fig. 7. Scheduler API for scheduling and queue management.

one(s) to schedule. Once a request is scheduled, it is removed from the pending queue. Request objects encapsulate the name of the requested method, its actual parameters, and a reference to the calling thread (Fig. 6).

To express elaborated selection scheme, most scheduling methods accept *filters* as an alternative to simple request names. A request filter implements the `RequestFilter` interface (Fig. 6), defining the `accept()` method. For instance, `scheduleAll(rf)` will schedule *all* requests in the queue that are accepted by the `rf` filter, while `scheduleOldest(rf)` will only schedule *one* request, the oldest accepted by `rf` (if any).

Recall that scheduled requests are executed in the scheduling order. To execute requests in the original arriving order, they should simply be scheduled in that order. For instance, ensuring FIFO mutual exclusion with SOM is trivial: it is enough to attach a scheduler whose scheduling method simply calls `scheduleAll()`.

3.3 Canonical Examples

We now briefly present SOM solutions to some classical concurrency problems: bounded buffer, readers and writers, and dining philosophers.

Bounded buffer. Fig. 8 presents the implementation in SOM of a scheduler for the bounded buffer example. It is a straightforward mapping of the pseudo-code shown previously in Fig. 3. Class `Buffer` is a trivial, unsynchronized, implementation of a buffer (not presented). In this implementation, when the buffer is neither full nor empty, the oldest request is scheduled (`scheduleOldest`). Now, imagine we use the following schedule method instead:

```
public class BufferScheduler extends Scheduler {
  Buffer buffer;
  public BufferScheduler(Buffer b) {
    super(b);
    buffer = b;
  }
  public void schedule() {
    if (buffer.isEmpty()) scheduleOldest("put");
    else if (buffer.isFull()) scheduleOldest("get");
    else scheduleOldest();
} }
```

Fig. 8. Scheduler for the bounded buffer example.

```
public void schedule() {
  if (!buffer.isEmpty()) scheduleOldest("get");
  if (!buffer.isFull())  scheduleOldest("put");
}
```

In this case, when the buffer is neither full nor empty, it alternates serving `get` and `put` requests, not respecting the order. This calls for several first comments. The SOM abstraction provides the user with the ability to finely control and tune the synchronization if needed. Of course, higher-level abstractions, potentially with good non-determinism, are also needed. They will be expressed on top of the basic SOM primitives (see Section 4 for guards and chords).

Readers and writers. The readers and writers is another classical problem of concurrent programming. Readers are threads that query a given data structure and writers are threads that modify it. A coordinator object `c` is responsible for granting access to the data structure. Readers request access by calling `c.enterRead()` and notify when they stop accessing data with `c.exitRead()`, while writers use `c.enterWrite()` and `c.exitWrite()` respectively. This problem is easily solved by making the coordinator a sequential object monitor. The code of the solution is presented in Fig. 9. The functional part is the coordinator implementation, which is self-explaining. The code of the scheduler specifies the following strategy. First, `exitRead` and `exitWrite` requests are scheduled immediately and unconditionally, because they are just notifications, not requests for access – similarly for `getReaders` and `isWriting` requests.

If a writer is currently modifying the data structure, the scheduler does not grant other permissions for access. If there are readers accessing the data structure, it grants permission to another `enterRead`, if any. Finally, if there is currently no writer nor reader accessing the data structure, it schedules the oldest request.

```
public class RWCoordinator {
  int readers = 0;
  boolean write = false;

  void enterRead(){readers++;}
  void exitRead(){readers--;}

  void enterWrite(){write = true;}
  void exitWrite(){write = false;}

  int getReaders(){return readers;}
  boolean isWriting(){return write;}
}
```

```
public FairRWScheduler
       extends Scheduler {
  RWCoordinator c;
  // initialized in constructor

  public void schedule() {
    scheduleAll(new String[]{
       "exitRead", "exitWrite",
       "getReaders", "isWriting"});

    if(!c.isWriting()) {
      if(c.getReaders() > 0)
        scheduleOlderThan(
          "enterRead","enterWrite");
      else scheduleOldest();
} } }
```

Fig. 9. The coordinator and its associated scheduler.

Note that readers are scheduled by calling `scheduleOlderThan`, not `scheduleOldest`. This is to ensure that writers may not starve: an `enterRead` request is scheduled *only if it is older* than the first `enterWrite` in the pending queue.

Also, `schedule` only schedules one pending `enterRead` at a time (call to `scheduleOlderThan`). This does not mean that two or more readers cannot work in parallel. Indeed, when finishing the execution of `enterRead`, `schedule` will be reinvoked and another `enterRead` may be scheduled for execution, even if current readers have not called `exitRead`.

Dining philosophers. In this problem, several philosophers (concurrent threads) spend their time thinking and eating. To eat, they first need to get two forks. Fig. 10 shows the code of a philosopher.

A table monitor is used for granting access to two consecutive forks. The solution presented here is fair, meaning no philosopher may starve. Moreover, this solution ensures that forks are granted to philosophers in the same order as they request them. To avoid deadlocks, the table provides a method to atomically request two forks simultaneously (Fig. 11)

The table scheduler (Fig. 12) schedules all non `pick` requests, and all `pick` requests for which both requested forks are free and *none* have been *previously requested* by another philosopher. In the scheduling method, the local variable array `reservedFork`, created every time an iteration over the request queue begins, is used for ensuring that forks are granted in the desired order. When a fork is requested and cannot be granted because it is still busy, it is tagged as "reserved". A request including a previously reserved fork is rejected immediately

```
public class Philosopher implements Runnable {
  int id1; Table table;
  public void run(){
    int id2 = (id1+1)%5;
    for(;;){
      think();
      table.pick(id1, id2); eat(id1, id2); table.drop(id1, id2);
  } }
  void think(){...}  void eat(int id1, int id2){...}
}
```

Fig. 10. The philosopher class.

```
public class Table {
  boolean[] forks = new boolean[5];
  public void pick(int id1, int id2) { forks[id1] = forks[id2] = true; }
  public void drop(int id1, int id2) { forks[id1] = forks[id2] = false; }
  boolean mayEat(int id1, int id2) { return !forks[id1] && !forks[id2]; }
}
```

Fig. 11. The table.

```
public class TableScheduler extends Scheduler {
  Table table; // initialized in constructor

  public void schedule() {
    boolean[] reservedFork = new boolean[5]; // all start false
    Iterator it = iterator();
    while (it.hasNext()) {
      Request req = (Request) it.next();
      if (!req.is("pick")) req.schedule();
      else {
        int id1 = req.getIntParameter(0);
        int id2 = req.getIntParameter(1);
        if (!reservedFork[id1] && !reservedFork[id2] &&
            table.mayEat(id1, id2))
          req.schedule();
        reservedFork[id1] = reservedFork[id2] = true;
} } } }
```

Fig. 12. The table scheduler.

in the current scan, even if such a fork is free, because the fork must first be granted to the philosopher that first requested it. Of course, less fair strategies can also be easily expressed.

3.4 Modularity and Reuse of Synchronization Policies

SOM makes it easy to define various synchronization policies, thanks to the full access given in the scheduling method to the queue of pending requests. For instance, in the case of the readers and writers problem, several fairness policies can be devised. We already exposed (Fig. 9) a fair policy, where both writers and readers are ensured not to starve. Alternative policies can easily be provided, for instance giving priority to readers or writers (Fig. 13).

```
public WriterPriorityRWScheduler
       extends Scheduler {
  RWCoordinator c;
  // initialized in constructor

  public void schedule() {
    // schedule all notifications

    if(!c.isWriting()) {
     if(hasRequest("enterWrite")){
      if(c.getReaders() == 0)
       scheduleOldest("enterWrite");
     }
     else scheduleAll();
} } }
```

```
public ReaderPriorityRWScheduler
       extends Scheduler {
  RWCoordinator c;
  // initialized in constructor

  public void schedule() {
    // schedule all notifications

    if(!c.isWriting()) {
     if(hasRequest("enterRead"))
       scheduleAll("enterRead");
     else if(c.getReaders()==0)
       scheduleOldest();
} } }
```

Fig. 13. Alternative fairness policies for the readers and writers problem.

Reuse of synchronization policies in different contexts depends on their genericity. As of now, the schedulers we have exposed all depend on string names (e.g., `"put"`). A scheduler class can be made independent from actual method names through configuration. For instance, considering buffer-like containers, reusable policies just need to be configured in order to know which methods are to be considered *put* methods and which ones are *get* methods. Then, the `schedule` method can be made independent of method names, for instance (`putMethod` is an instance variable configured to hold the name of the *put* method):

```
void schedule() { if (buffer.isEmpty()) scheduleOldest(putMethod); ... }
```

Determining emptiness and fullness of the synchronized data structure can also be made generic: the reflection API can be used to invoke emptiness and fullness methods according to configuration. Apart from being reusable, generic synchronization classes are more robust with regards to changes.

```
public class GuardedBufferScheduler extends GuardScheduler {
  public GuardedBufferScheduler(final GuardedBuffer buf) {
    super(buf);
    addGuard("get",
      new RequestFilter() { public boolean accept(Request req) {
          return !buf.isEmpty();
      }});
    addGuard("put",
      new RequestFilter() { public boolean accept(Request req) {
          return !buf.isFull();
      }});
} }
```

Fig. 14. Code of a guard scheduler for the bounded buffer example.

4 Concurrency Abstractions with SOM

SOM is equivalent in expressiveness to the classic synchronization mechanisms like locks, semaphores, Hoare's monitors, Java monitors, guards, etc. This means that if a synchronization problem can be solved with the classic mechanisms it can also be solved with SOM and vice versa. To prove it, it is enough to show an implementation of a classic mechanism in terms of SOM and vice versa, because all classic mechanisms are equivalent. This proof is trivial as SOM is implemented in terms of Java monitors and implementing a lock with SOM is easy:

```
class Lock {
  boolean busy = false;
  void ask() {
    busy = true;
  }
  void release() {
    busy = false;
  }
}
```

```
class LockScheduler extends Scheduler {
  Lock lock;
  // initialized in constructor

  void schedule() {
    scheduleAll("release");
    if (!lock.busy)
      scheduleOldest("ask");
} }
```

However, such an equivalence is not enough. It is also important to show that solutions that are easily expressed with other synchronization mechanisms are also easily expressed with SOM. Although effectively proving this property is hard, a good approximation consists in showing how other synchronization mechanisms are easily expressed with SOM. In this section, we have chosen to present the concise implementation of two synchronization mechanisms with SOM: guards and chords.

```
public abstract class GuardScheduler extends Scheduler {
  HashMap guardMap = new HashMap();

  public GuardScheduler(Object o){ super(o); }
  public void addGuard(String name, RequestFilter guard){
    guardMap.put(name, guard);
  }

  public void schedule(){
    Iterator it = iterator();
    while (it.hasNext()){
      Request req = (Request) it.next();
      RequestFilter guard = (RequestFilter) guardMap.get(req.getName());
      if (guard == null || guard.accept(req)){ req.schedule(); break; }
    }
} }
```

Fig. 15. The (non-optimized) guard scheduler implemented with SOM.

4.1 Guards

In SOM Guards, a guard scheduler contains method guards and is responsible for scheduling concurrent requests. We provide an abstract class for guard schedulers, `GuardScheduler`, with a method for registering method guards, `addGuard`. A guard is defined by attaching a request filter, that indicates when a method fulfills the conditions to be executed, to a method name. It is worthwhile to highlight that the guard system presented here avoids unnecessary context switches (see Section 5.3 for an explanation of the efficient scheduling strategy of SOM). Fig. 14 illustrates an implementation of the bounded buffer based on SOM Guards. This code simply associates a request filter for `get` and one for `put`.

The expressiveness of SOM is illustrated by the simplicity of the base class `GuardScheduler` (Fig. 15), that completely implements the guard system. The scheduler simply iterates over the request queue and schedules the oldest request whose associated guard evaluates to true. Note that this scheduler is not optimized: the actual implementation of the guard scheduler avoids evaluating all guards upon each invocation of the scheduling method. If an invocation of `schedule` does not schedule any request, the scheduler will not re-evaluate the corresponding guards until a new request arrives *and* is scheduled.

4.2 Chords

Chords were first introduced in Polyphonic C♯ [4], a C♯ dialect offering dedicated syntax to define join patterns (see section 2.3).

Fig. 16 shows the implementation of a multiple-reader, single-writer lock with chords as exposed in [4]. It consists of just five chords and illustrates pretty well

```
class ReaderWriter {
(1)  public void shared() & async idle() { sharedRead(1); }
(2)  public void shared() & async sharedRead(int n) { sharedRead(n+1); }
(3)  public void releaseShared() & async sharedRead(int n) {
       if(n == 1) idle(); else sharedRead(n-1);
     }
(4)  public void exclusive() & async idle() {}
(5)  public void releaseExclusive() { idle(); }
}
```

Fig. 16. Solution to the readers and writers problem with chords (Polyphonic C♯ code).

the kind of concise definition enabled by chords. The chords 1 and 2 are *alternative chords*, meaning that the actual **shared** chord being executed depends on the previous asynchronous events that were fired. Chords 3 and 4 are *simple chords*, i.e. made of a synchronous method that only appears in one chord, and of some asynchronous events (in this case just one), while chord 5 is a standard synchronous method (*trivial chord*).

We implemented a chord system for Java based on SOM, presenting the same semantics as the chords of Polyphonic C♯. However, SOM Chords are implemented as a library, not as a language extension. Implications of this fact are discussed at the end of this section. The aim of this section is to show how SOM can be simply used to implement other synchronization mechanisms, thereby illustrating its expressiveness.

The main principle of SOM Chords is that an instance of a class declaring chords is associated to a *chord manager* (Fig. 17). A chord manager, instance of `ChordManager`, *is* a sequential object monitor (scheduled by a `ChordScheduler`), whereas the object using it *is not* (recall that mutual exclusion of chord bodies is not guaranteed in chords as formulated in [4]).

There are three types of chords in SOM Chords: *asynchronous events* (class `AsyncEvent`); *chords*, which are enabled when a set of asynchronous events is

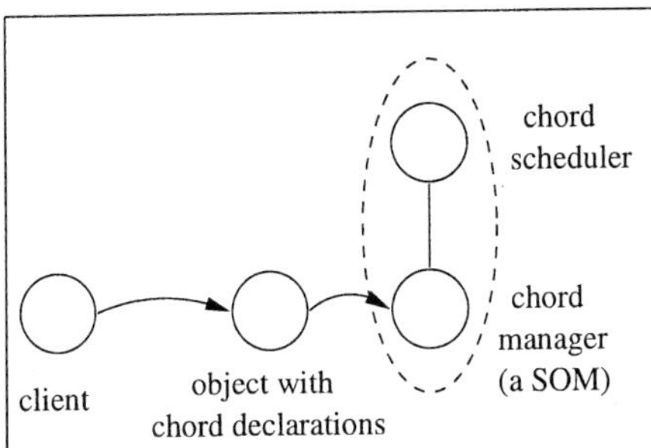


```
class ChordManager {
  AsyncEvent defineEvent();
  Chord defineChord(..);
  ChordSet defineChordSet(..);

  void trigger(AsyncEvent e, ..);
  void await(ChordSet c);
  boolean isEnabled(ChordSet c);
}
```

Fig. 17. Operational sketch of SOM Chords and public interface of the chord manager.

```
class ReaderWriter {
  ChordManager mgr = new ChordManager();
  AsyncEvent idle = mgr.defineEvent();
  AsyncEvent sharedRead = mgr.defineEvent();
  ChordSet idleOrSharedRead = mgr.defineChordSet(idle, sharedRead);

  // public void shared() & async idle() { sharedRead(1); }
  // public void shared() & async sharedRead(int n) { sharedRead(n+1); }
  public void shared() {
    EnabledChord ch = mgr.await(idleOrSharedRead);
    if(ch.is(idle)) mgr.trigger(sharedRead, new Integer(1));
    else {
      int n = ch.getIntParameter(sharedRead);
      mgr.trigger(sharedRead, new Integer(n+1));
  } }

  // public void releaseShared() & async sharedRead(int n) {
  //     if(n == 1) idle(); else sharedRead(n-1); }
  public void releaseShared() {
    EnabledChord ch = mgr.await(sharedRead);
    int n = ch.getIntParameter(sharedRead);
    if(n == 1) mgr.trigger(idle);
    else mgr.trigger(sharedRead, new Integer(n-1));
  }

  // public void exclusive() & async idle() {}
  public void exclusive() { mgr.await(idle); }

  // public void releaseExclusive() { idle(); }
  public void releaseExclusive() { mgr.trigger(idle); }
}
```

Fig. 18. Solution to the readers and writers problem with SOM Chords (Polyphonic C♯ code is given in commentaries).

matched up (class `Chord`); and *chord sets*, which are an alternative set of chords, enabled whenever one chord in the set is enabled (class `ChordSet`). Since a chord is indeed a chord set made of a single chord, and similarly an asynchronous event is a chord made of a single event, `AsyncEvent` is a subclass of `Chord` which is a subclass of `ChordSet`.

The chord manager makes it possible to define asynchronous events and chords (Fig. 17). The methods `await` and `trigger` make it possible to respectively wait for a chord to be enabled, and to trigger an asynchronous event. The method `isEnabled` checks if a given chord (or chord set) is enabled.

Fig. 18 shows the `ReaderWriter` class implemented with SOM Chords. First of all, a chord manager is associated with each instance. Asynchronous events,

```
public class ChordScheduler extends Scheduler {
  ChordManager mgr;
  public ChordScheduler(ChordManager mgr) {
    super(mgr); this.mgr= mgr;
  }
  public void schedule() {
    scheduleOldest(new RequestFilter(){
      public boolean accept(Request req){
        // schedule non await methods
        if (!req.is("await")) return true;

        // the chord specified as parameter in the await call
        ChordSet c = (ChordSet) req.getParameter(0);

        // true if all required events have been triggered
        return mgr.isEnabled(c);
      }
    });
} }
```

Fig. 19. The chord scheduler implemented with SOM.

chords and chord sets are declared as instance variables, in order to be able to refer to them. Then, a simple chord (i.e., whose synchronous method appears only once in all chords, such as `exclusive`) is expressed as a standard synchronous method that starts by waiting for the set of events to be matched up (`mgr.await(..)`). An alternative set of chords (i.e., that share the same synchronous method, such as `shared-idle` and `shared-sharedRead`) is expressed as one synchronous method that first waits for one of the chords to be enabled. Then, depending on which chord was actually enabled, the appropriate body is executed. An `EnabledChord` object represents an enabled chord instance, and stores the parameters associated with each event of the chord. Finally, method bodies are changed so that they trigger asynchronous events on the manager (e.g., `idle()` is replaced by `mgr.trigger(idle)`).

Fig. 19 shows the straightforward implementation of the chord scheduler controlling the chord manager. The scheduler uses a filter that accepts non-`await` requests, and accepts `await` requests only if all required events have been previously triggered. To this end, the chord manager uses bit masks to determine if a chord is ready to be processed (`isEnabled`), just as explained in [4].

A major benefit of Polyphonic C$^\sharp$ is that it is a *language extension*, not a simple API. This brings a number of benefits, in particular compact syntax and compiler support. Also, providing chords as a language extension results in clearer, more manageable code. In this regard, our claim here is that the underlying system supporting chords is concisely expressed with SOM, as validated by the code of the chord scheduler shown in Fig. 19. Obviously, the advantages of a language extension are not met by the SOM Chords library: however the set of transformations from a chord syntax to calls to the library is straightforward and linear. In other words, code of Fig. 18 can preferably be seen as code generated by a chords compiler using the SOM Chords library as its back end, rather than as hand-written code.

5 Implementation

5.1 Reifying and Synchronizing Method Calls

In order to remain portable while being able to transparently reify method calls as requests, the SOM library is based on a reflective infrastructure operating at load time. Using computational reflection also brings a clean separation of concerns between the application logic (at the base level) and the synchronization concern (at the metalevel). The SOM metaobject protocol (MOP) is defined within Reflex, an open behavioral reflective extension of Java [24]. When creating a sequential object monitor, the reflective infrastructure ensures interception of its method invocations. Doing so, a controller metaobject will be invoked *(a)* before requesting a method, and *(b)* just after returning from the method. The controller metaobject, provided by the SOM system, ensures scheduling and mutual exclusion of concurrent requests.

5.2 Initialization and Configuration

There are several alternatives to obtain sequential object monitors. Especially, there is a need for a means to specify the association between *standard objects* and *schedulers*.

First of all, at instantiation time, one can use:

```
Buffer b = (Buffer) SOM.newMonitor(Buffer.class, aScheduler);
```

This runtime approach however suffers from some limitations with `final` classes and methods, due to the fact that it is based on dynamic generation of implicit subclasses, and requires explicit use by programmers in client code (replacing standard `new` calls).

A transparent approach is also available. One can specify in a configuration file the desired associations $baseClass \rightarrow schedulerClass$, e.g.:

```
schedule: Buffer with: BufferScheduler
```

The SOM system offers two means to apply configuration files to an application: load time and compile time. Class `SOMGenerator` is provided as a compile-time utility to generate modified class files:

```
% java SOMGenerator <configuration-file> <target-directory>
```

will generate transformed class files for all classes which have to be scheduled, as specified by the given configuration file. Load-time transformation is also available, thanks to the `SOMRun` class:

```
% java SOMRun <configuration-file> <application>
```

will run the application by applying, at load time, the configuration specified in the configuration file.

5.3 Efficient Scheduling

This section explains the inner working of SOM thread management that makes it possible to avoid unnecessary context switches.

The controller mentioned in the section above handles two queues:

- The *wait queue* holds pending requests that have not been scheduled for execution by the scheduler.
- The *ready queue* keeps pending requests that have just been scheduled (during the last execution of the scheduling method), but have not been executed yet because the monitor is busy, either still executing the scheduling method, or executing another request.

A sequential object monitor M works as follows. Let T be a thread that has begun the execution of a request R on a method of M. Suppose the ready queue already contains requests made by other threads. T is said to *own* M and the other threads *wait*. M is in a *busy* state. When T finishes the execution of the method, the controller takes control and extracts the oldest request R' in the ready queue. Thread T thereby passes the ownership of M directly to thread T', the thread requesting R'. Finally, T wakes T' up and returns to the caller of M. T' starts the execution of its own request, R'.

When the ready queue is empty, the controller makes thread T automatically invoke the `schedule` method of the user-provided scheduler. Recall that this method will schedule one or several requests; these requests will be transferred from the wait queue to the ready queue. Making T invoke the scheduling method implies that T spends some time scheduling requests for other threads. Thus programmers should preferably write simple scheduling methods. If after invoking the scheduling method, the ready queue is still empty, the sequential object monitor is said to be *free*.

Let us now consider a thread T requesting a method of M. First, the request is put in the wait queue. If M is busy, T is blocked, provoking a context switch. If M is free, the controller makes T invoke the scheduling method. If the request is scheduled, T takes ownership of M and executes the method immediately, i.e. no context switch occurs. If the request is not scheduled, M remains free and T is blocked.

5.4 Limitations

The current implementation of SOM presents some limitations. In particular, constructors of classes that are to be scheduled should never expose a reference to `this` to another thread, otherwise the thread-safety guarantee will be broken.

Furthermore, a SOM is *sequential* and hence potentially entails a loss of parallelism. However, it must be clear that the sequential constraint relates to the synchronization code: the overall program indeed remains parallel. This constraint makes it possible to simplify the task of writing, maintaining and reasoning about concurrent programs, thanks to a clear semantics and high expressiveness. Furthermore, our conjecture is that there are no problems that cannot be solved with this constraint. One could indeed compare this constraint to the absence of a `goto` statement in modern programming languages. In cases where the loss of parallelism is a critical issue, an approach similar to the one we took for SOM Chords should be adopted: the considered class (e.g., the class with chord declarations) is not converted to a SOM, but rather uses an auxiliary class (e.g., the chord manager), converted to a SOM, that is responsible of the coordination and synchronization.

5.5 Micro-Benchmarks

We argued at the beginning of the paper that the main inefficiency of Java monitors comes from the fact that `notifyAll` wakes up all waiting threads.

This section presents measurements of the execution time of five different buffer implementations; the typical solution using legacy Java monitors, as advised in the Sun Java tutorial [23], a "smart" solution using condition variables and mutexes as presented in [19], and three SOM-based solution: the direct solution using SOM (as in Fig. 8), the solution using SOM Guards (as in Fig. 14), and a solution with SOM Chords.

The measurements are given for a buffer of one slot, with one producer, and with different number of consumers. As the interest is measuring the cost of the synchronization, the time to produce and consume items in the tests is marginal. The results (Tables 1 and 2) were obtained by performing five measurements – each of which consists in the production of 100,000 items– discarding the best and worst cases and taking the average of the remaining three measurements. The benchmarks were executed on a single processor Athlon XP 2600+ machine with 512 MB of memory, with Java 1.4.2 with native threads. We allocated a large heap size to the JVM in order to limit the number of garbage collections. We run the benchmarks under Windows 2000 (Table 1) and Linux, kernel 2.4 (Table 2).

The case with one consumer is a best case for the Java monitors solution, because when the producer puts an item in the buffer, `notifyAll` always wakes up one thread only, and this thread will get the item. Hence no useless context switches occur. SOM solutions, as well as the solution based on condition variables, are slower in this case because they are implemented with multiple Java monitors, and therefore there is an associated overhead.

Increasing the number of consumers while keeping a single producer is greatly disadvantageous for the Java monitors solution, because when the producer puts an item in the buffer, several consumers must be waken up, although only one will get the item. The others will be put to wait again. Each failed wake up is a useless context switch, which is expensive in terms of execution time. We can

Table 1. Benchmark results under Windows 2000 with JDK 1.4.2 (time in ms).

number of consumers	*Java monitors*	*Condition Variables*	*SOM*	*SOM Guards*	*SOM Chords*
1	390	1057	796	802	1203
2	510	1088	864	885	1229
4	771	1114	942	948	1265
8	1416	1120	1010	1026	1317
16	2823	1213	1166	1208	1541
32	7317	1375	1604	1593	1958
64	23479	2010	2322	2270	2708
128	80422	3234	3604	3442	4083

Table 2. Benchmark results under Linux 2.4 with JDK 1.4.2 (time in ms).

number of consumers	*Java monitors*	*Condition Variables*	*SOM*	*SOM Guards*	*SOM Chords*
1	1006	1905	1656	1642	1954
2	1225	2018	1708	1690	2029
4	1918	2276	1891	1839	2148
8	5723	2412	2125	1982	2276
16	16005	2451	2435	2199	2488
32	49767	2659	3156	2766	3123
64	133612	2946	4407	3771	4196
128	358218	3049	6653	5259	5934

easily see that SOM solutions scale much better with regards to the number of consumers, because *(i)* only one thread is waken up, and *(ii)* the evaluation of which thread to wake up is done by the thread leaving the monitor: no useless context switches occur.

The solution based on condition variables scales similarly well, and performs slightly better. With SOM, increasing the number of consumers lowers performance because the evaluation of the scheduling method depends on the size of the pending request queue (due to iterations over the queue). In contrast, the condition variables implementation is independent from the number of consumers, but still its performance slightly decreases because context switches seem to cost more when more threads are running.

An interesting point is that a straightforward implementation of the buffer with SOM (recall the simplicity of Fig. 8) brings better performance than the standard Java monitors solution, and comparable performance to the one with condition variables, which is more complex to correctly design and program.

The micro-benchmarks presented here do not take into account the cost of program transformation for SOM: classes were transformed statically before the benchmarks. If SOM was supported at the virtual machine level, no transfor-

Table 3. Benchmark results under Linux 2.6 with JDK 1.5 beta (time in ms).

number of consumers	*Java monitors*	*Condition Variables*	*SOM*	*SOM Guards*	*SOM Chords*	*Cond. Vars JDK1.5*
1	531	1279	1199	1157	1425	537
2	732	1234	1225	1196	1518	586
4	1131	1293	1333	1309	1573	556
8	2195	1281	1495	1378	1660	581
16	4312	1276	1851	1549	1916	592
32	9714	1350	2543	1969	2371	645
64	31637	1587	4305	2885	3601	850
128	95391	1762	7331	4414	5683	1062

mation cost would be incurred. We could also expect SOM to be at least as efficient as Java monitors even in the worst case. Hence, the micro-benchmarks presented here validate the interest of the SOM approach: although SOM implies an overhead at start, it scales very well. An efficient, VM-based, implementation of SOM would further reduce that overhead and make the approach even more competitive.

Finally, we have run the same benchmarks under Linux with the new 2.6 kernel, and with the beta version of JDK 1.5 (Table 3). Clearly, the results show that Linux is more competitive with the new optimized kernel. Furthermore, we have included another implementation: that of condition variables as included in the JDK 1.5, coming from the JSR 166 library [21]. Recall that normal condition variables are implemented with standard Java monitors, while condition variables of the JDK 1.5 are implemented with very efficient locks. The results, which are globally better than with JDK 1.4.2, confirm the previous analysis, and open new optimization perspective for SOM. Improvements similar to those that can be observed for condition variables should be obtainable in a new version of SOM implemented over the efficient locks of JDK 1.5.

6 Conclusion and Future Work

We have presented Sequential Object Monitors as an alternative to programming directly with standard Java monitors. Due to its sequential nature, a SOM is easier to reason about and maintain. We have illustrated the expressiveness of SOM through several examples, in particular through the implementation of high-level abstractions like guards and chords. Furthermore, SOM promotes good modularization properties by untangling the synchronization concern from the application logic. Programmers can concentrate on programming functional code without worrying too much about concurrency. SOM provides a means to turn sequential classes into thread-safe classes without modifying them. Finally, SOM seems more efficient and scalable than the standard Java monitors due to its explicit control over which thread is woken up and its efficient scheduling strategy, as opposed to the untargeted and context-switch expensive `notifyAll` primitive. SOM can be characterized by the use of *run-to-completion* methods. It also relies on the packaging of small closures (reified method calls) as the building blocks of practical concurrent programming constructions, in the line of Lea's Java fork/join framework [20].

As future work, it would be interesting to reengineer an existing, non-trivial, concurrent application with SOM in order to study the benefits of our approach on large-scale software. Future work also includes studying the possibility to provide alternative scheduler base classes, such as a non-systematically reentrant scheduler in which some self sends can also reified as requests to be scheduled, upon user choice. Other alternatives include a scheduler able to dispatch in parallel a set of requests (e.g., all read requests for the readers and writers problem). With these features, we then plan to study several alternatives of join patterns with SOM.

Acknowledgements. We would like to thank Jacques Noyé and the anonymous ECOOP reviewers for their constructive comments.

This work was partially funded by the CONICYT-INRIA project ProXiMoS, and the Millenium Nucleous Center for Web Research, Grant P01-029-F, Mideplan, Chile.

References

1. Gul Agha. *ACTORS: a model of concurrent computation in distributed systems.* The MIT Press: Cambridge, MA, 1986.
2. P. H. M. America and F. Van Der Linden. A parallel object-oriented language with inheritance and subtyping. In N. Meyrowitz, editor, *Proceedings of the OOPSLA/ECOOP'90 Conference on Object-Oriented Programming Systems, Languages and Applications.* ACM Press, October 1990. ACM SIGPLAN Notices, 25(10).
3. Colin Atkinson, Andrea Di Maio, and Rami Bayan. Dragoon: An object-oriented notation supporting the reuse and distribution of ada software. In *International Workshop on Real-Time Ada Issues*, 1990.
4. Nick Benton, Luca Cardelli, and Cédric Fournet. Modern concurrency abstractions for C♯. In B. Magnusson, editor, *ECOOP 2002 - Object-Oriented Programming: 16th European Conference*, volume 2374, Málaga, Spain, June 2002. Springer-Verlag.
5. G. M. Birtwistle, O.-J. Dahl, B. Myhrhaug, and K. Nygaard. *Simula Begin.* Petrocelli Charter, 1973.
6. Per Brinch Hansen. Structured multiprogramming. *Communications of the ACM*, 15(7):574–578, July 1972.
7. Per Brinch Hansen. A programming methodology for operating system design. In *Proceedings of the IFIP Congress 74*, pages 394–397, Amsterdam, Holland, August 1974. North-Holland.
8. Per Brinch Hansen. Monitors and concurrent pascal, a personal history. *ACM SIGPLAN Notices*, 28(3):1–35, March 1993.

9. Jean-Pierre Briot, Rachid Guerraoui, and Klaus-Peter Löhr. Concurrency and distribution in object-oriented programming. *ACM Computing Surveys*, 30(3):291–329, September 1998.
10. Denis Caromel. Towards a method of object-oriented concurrent programming. *Communications of the ACM*, 36(9):90–102, 1993.
11. Denis Caromel, Wilfried Klauser, and Julien Vayssière. Towards seamless computing and metacomputing in Java. *Concurrency Practice and Experience*, 10(11-13):1043–1061, September 1998.
12. Edsger W. Dijkstra. The structure of *THE* - multiprogramming system. *Communications of the ACM*, 11(5):341–346, May 1968.
13. Edsger W. Dijkstra. Guarded commands, nondeterminacy and formal derivation of programs. *Communications of the ACM*, 18(8):453–457, August 1975.
14. Cédric Fournet and Georges Gonthier. The reflexive chemical abstract machine and the join-calculus. In *Proceedings of POPL'96*, pages 372–385. ACM, January 1996.
15. Svend Frolund and Gul Agha. A language framework for multi-object coordination. In O. Nierstrasz, editor, *Proceedings of the 7th European Conference on Object-Oriented Programming (ECOOP'93)*, volume 952 of *Lecture Notes in Computer Science*, pages 346–360, Kaiserslautern, Germany, July 1993. Springer-Verlag.
16. Charles A. R. Hoare. Monitors: An operating system structuring concept. *Communications of the ACM*, 17(10):549–577, October 1974.
17. Charles A. R. Hoare. Communicating sequential processes. *Communications of the ACM*, 21(8):666–677, August 1978.
18. W.H. Kaubisch, R.H. Perrott, and C.A.R. Hoare. Quasi-parallel programming. *Software: Practice and Experience*, 6(3):341–356, 1976.
19. Doug Lea. *Concurrent Programming in Java, Design Principles and Patterns.* Addison Wesley, Reading, Massachusetts, 1997.
20. Doug Lea. A Java fork/join framework. In *Proceedings of the ACM 2000 Conference on Java Grande*, pages 36–43, San Francisco, California, USA, 2000.
21. Doug Lea. Java Specification Request 166: Concurrency utilities, 2003. `www.jcp.org/en/jsr/detail?id=166`.
22. Martin Odersky. Functional nets. In Gert Smolka, editor, *ESOP*, volume 1782 of *Lecture Notes in Computer Science*, pages 1–25. Springer, 2000.
23. Sun Microsystems, Inc. The producer/consumer example, from Java tutorials, 2003. `java.sun.com/docs/books/tutorial/essential/threads`.
24. Eric Tanter, Jacques Noyé, Denis Caromel, and Pierre Cointe. Partial behavioral reflection: Spatial and temporal selection of reification. In *Proceedings of the 18th International Conference on Object-Oriented Programming Systems, Languages and Applications (OOPSLA 2003)*, pages 27–64, Anaheim, CA, USA, October 2003. ACM Press. ACM SIGPLAN Notices, 38(11).

Increasing Concurrency in Databases Using Program Analysis

Roman Vitenberg, Kristian Kvilekval, and Ambuj K. Singh

Computer Science Department, UCSB, Santa Barbara, CA 93106, USA
{romanv,kris,ambuj}@cs.ucsb.edu
http://www.cs.ucsb.edu/{~romanv,~kris,~ambuj}

Abstract. Programmers have come to expect better integration between databases and the programming languages they use. While this trend continues unabated, database concurrency scheduling has remained blind to the programs. We propose that the database client programs provide a large untapped information resource for increasing database throughput.

Given this increase in expressive power between programmers and databases, we investigate how program analysis can increase database concurrency. In this paper, we demonstrate a predictive locking scheduler for object databases. In particular we examine the possibility to predict the client's use of locks. Given accurate predictions, we can increase concurrency through early lock release, perform deadlock detection and prevention, and determine whether locks should be granted before or during a transaction. Furthermore, we demonstrate our techniques on the OO7 and other benchmarks.

1 Introduction

The problem of transaction and lock scheduling is the most fundamental problem in concurrency control in databases. Finding the optimal schedule is known to be an NP-hard even for the offline version of the problem when all events (i.e., transactions) in the system are known in advance [16]. Furthermore, there is no general-case online algorithm that would approximate the optimal offline solution within some small bound. Yet, in many specific cases of the systems that exist in practice, it is possible to design a scheduler that takes advantage of the information about future transactions, producing a more efficient (even though non-optimal) schedule.

Knowledge of the future is the key to efficient scheduling of resources. This knowledge of future events can come from diverse sources, but has been traditionally in the form of programmer annotations. Programmer annotations, though used, are in general difficult for the programmers to construct and are likely to be error prone. Therefore, most systems have adopted an overly conservative view and assume no knowledge of future requests.

However, the knowledge of future access patterns is present in the client programs that use the database system. In recent years, there has been an increasing interest in object database languages with the acceptance of object-oriented and object-relational database systems. These systems already reduce the "impedance-mismatch" between the program code and data storage often experienced in traditional SQL environments.

M. Odersky (Ed.): ECOOP 2004, LNCS 3086, pp. 341–363, 2004.

With the emergence of complex database interface languages such as JDO [13], OQL [15], and the use of complex types in databases that bridge the gap between programming languages and data modelling languages, we explore the benefits that this tighter integration brings. Our work takes a new approach combining program analysis and object databases in order to extract information that will be useful to the database system. In this paper, we present new techniques for scheduling transactions in object-oriented database (OODB) management systems. The technique is also applicable to Object-Relational databases provided that the query language is rich enough to warrant analysis.

This paper's main contributions are: deadlock handling methods based on the types manipulated by the program, a technique that allows early lock release in order to increase concurrency, and a method to determine whether transaction locks should be preclaimed, e.g., before the transaction begins, or taken gradually during the transaction.

In detail, we investigate the use of program analysis to extract interesting properties of programs that can be used by a database system. Our technique is based on shape analysis, a whole-program analysis that has previously used in the compiler research community to determine certain static program properties. The output of shape analysis is a set of graphs representing the way a portion of a program navigates and manipulates its data structures. These structures allow the database system to determine what the client will do as it continues to execute thereby capturing future knowledge of the client's object use.

In order to test our ideas, we constructed a benchmark testbed and ran experiments with the standard OO7 benchmark set and with the prototype of a car reservation system that we have developed. The paper shows the gain obtained from using each proposed scheduling enhancement in terms of the average execution time of a transaction and its standard deviation.

2 Related Work

There has been a tremendous amount of work dealing with transaction concurrency and scheduling [3,19]. However, schedulers in most database systems that exist in practice do not attempt to predict. The main reason for this is twofold: a) Eliciting and collecting information about future transactions is a non-trivial task, and b) Such predictive schedulers would be highly specialized and tailored to a particular application.

Some database systems that attempt to predict based on the history of previous executions, which is collected with profiling. In particular, this technique is commonly used for query optimization in relational databases. However, history-based prediction is different from prediction that relies on program analysis: while the former predicts solely based on past workloads, the latter gives more precise information about the future execution of the currently running transactions.

Many predictors have been demonstrated in practice. Most of these are based on simplifying assumptions about how a program will access data. For example, programs often perform sequential reads from the disk. i.e. while reading a very large array. For this reason, many disk drives automatically perform k-block read-ahead. However, when data is complex and accessed in a scattered way, sequential lookahead not be appropriate behavior as we may read many unused pages.

Object-oriented programs can and usually do have complex object structures. These pointer-based structures make it especially difficult to predict what object(s) the system will be using in the future. Though an important problem, little work has been carried out for predicting access patterns in complex pointer-based structures. Knafla [10] demonstrates prefetching for OODBs using history-based techniques. Cahoon and McKinly [5] have examined a dataflow analysis for prefetching object structures in Java. In contrast, our approach constructs a succinct representation of the program's access pattern and uses it to drive the prediction process. Combining the program representation with real data allows the predictive scheduler to infer the most likely objects to be used by the program in the future.

3 Model

Our model encompasses the design of most existing middleware systems for object management. Clients may send requests to a server which may act over a set of objects that reside solely on the servers. An object server holds multiple objects and the database on a server consists of a set of root objects such that all other objects accessible from these root objects.

Multiple clients are allowed to access the server concurrently invoking server-side transactions. During each transaction, the client may reference multiple objects on the server. The database at the server includes a scheduler module which is responsible for maintaining the consistency of the transactions and the objects. In this work, we consider both pessimistic and optimistic concurrency control models.

4 Predicting Object Accesses and Execution Times Based on Shape Graphs

4.1 Background

Shape analysis is a program analysis technique based on an abstract interpretation of a program to determine the "shape" of possible runtime data structures. Shape analysis produces a *shape graph* for a program point, representing the way the program traverses program data structures from that particular point. A shape graph is a directed graph with nodes representing symbolic abstract runtime program values and edges representing program field references from those values. The shape graph is generated by symbolically executing the program code and adding edges for each access.

In order to provide intuition, we present a typical program fragment of integrated databases in Figure 1. The shape graph shown on the right of the figure is derived from the code lines on the left.[1]

[1] The code is taken from the OO7 database [6]; it navigates the database of machine parts in order to weigh the elements. However, the code semantics are not important for this example.

```
class Connector{
  Part partA, PartB; ... }
class Part {
  Connector left, right, up, down;
  Material material;
  Supplier supplier;
  Cost     cost;
  ...
  int volume (); }

weight = 0
while (part != null)
  weight += part.material.density
            * part.volume();
  connector = part.right;
  part = null;
  if (connector != null)
    part = connector.partB;
```

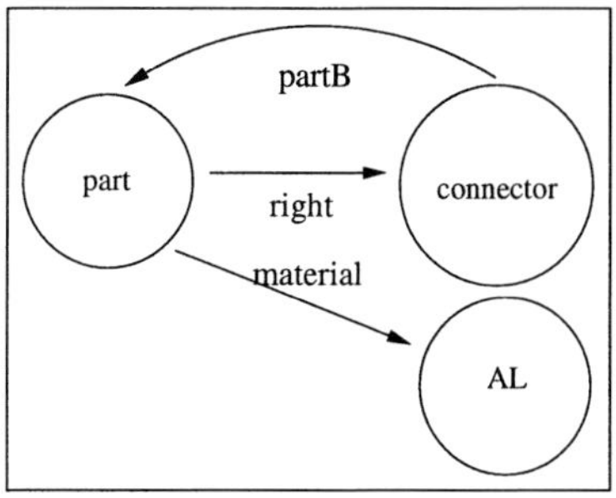

Fig. 1. Code fragment and its shape graph: only items used in the code (`part` and `material`) are in the graph.

The example code uses only the `material` and `right` fields of each `part` in the database ignoring the `cost` and `supplier` among other fields. This is quite typical for database programs: while the database may be large and have a very rich object structure, many programs may use only part of that structure. The access pattern is also revealed in the fact that the code fragment iterates through a list of `part` using the `right` field. In the graph, the node (`part`) is used to represent the values of the variable `part` which access `connector` through the field `right`. The runtime value `part.material` is shown in the shape graph as `AL`. The cycle `part` through the field `right` to `connector` through `partB` and back to `part` contains the needed loop information from the original code. Note that the `volume` function may access additional objects that are not presented in the shape graph.

Shape graphs have previously been used to determine static properties of programs and for many compile time optimizations including removing synchronization primitives [4,17], parallelization of codes [8], and type safety. Other uses include null analysis, pointer aliasing, cyclicity detection, reachability, and typing [9,14,20]. Use of shape graphs for prefetching has been explored in our previous work [11]. This work adopts the shape graph structure and its construction algorithm that are similar to the existing implementations. Yet, this is the first time to the best of our knowledge that shape graphs are exploited for improving lock schedulers in integrated database systems.

4.2 Overview of the Approach

Our lock scheduling techniques that we introduce later in Section 5 rely on the estimation of a) the set of objects to be accessed by a transaction and the order of those accesses,

b) whether the access is read or write, and c) the execution time of a transaction during which a given object is accessed. In this section, we describe how this information is obtained by using shape analysis.

Shape graphs that capture the way in which the program's code accesses data, allow us to follow the same datapaths that the original program would take in order to access the data effectively predicting its future access pattern. We cannot follow the exact path, as the code surely has data-dependent branches. However, we capture a unified view of all program paths in the program's shape graph. While this results in a necessarily conservative estimation (a superset which may be several times larger than the actual set of accessed objects), it is incomparably smaller than the entire database, which can be exploited to devise efficient lock schedulers.

Our implementation of shape analysis consists of two components: compile-time construction of a shape graph and runtime prediction, which uses the program's access pattern represented by the shape graph and the actual object graph contained in the OODB to generate the estimated set of future accesses and other required information. It is important to emphasize that deployment of these components does not require rewriting the existing database programs: the construction process can be coupled with the standard compilation process whereas the runtime predictor can be integrated with the scheduler of existing OODB systems in a way that is transparent for the application. Since shape graphs are small even for large programs, their storage does not require a lot of resources and their runtime traversal is computationally effective. Sections 4.3 and 4.4 provide further information about the shape analysis implementation.

In this paper, we also define the type–shape graph which is the reduction of the shape graph to track the types and the access order of the types that are manipulated by the program. The type–shape graph is used to determine static type properties of a transaction. The type–shape graph reduction is one-way in that given a shape-graph, we can construct a type–shape graph.

4.3 Compile-Time Construction

The variant of shape analysis we are using is a whole-program, flow-insensitive, context sensitive data flow analysis and is similar in design to those presented in [4,17,11]. Previously shape analysis has been used to determine static properties of programs that manipulate heap data structures. In this paper, we take a novel approach examining how the results of program analysis can be combined with an active runtime to increase runtime efficiency.

Shape graphs are created and extended by simulating the actions of the program through abstract interpretation, which creates and connects abstract heap tuples. Simple program actions, such as a field access instruction, create heap tuples. When two variables are determined to point to the same abstract location, we unify their heap representations. Unification is a recursive operation that begins with unifying the abstract locations and continues by unifying the compatible heap tuples that stem from the originally unified location. Heap tuples are compatible when two abstract locations have similarly labelled incoming shape edges. Given two abstract locations, that are to be unified, we first unify their abstract locations and then recursively unify their compatible tuples in the heap

The construction of the shape graph in Figure 1 begins as follows. The reference to the `part` in line 2 creates an abstract variable in the symbolic interpretation of the program. Line 3 creates the link from the `part` abstract location to some unspecified location (AL) when the field `material` is accessed. Similarly, line 5 creates both the abstract location `connector` and the edge `right` between them when interpreted. Finally, in line 7 the edge `partB` is created due to the field access and the resulting abstract location is unified to the original `part` because of the assignment. Line 4 contains a call to a sub-method. The analysis of the sub-method would be similar to the one described above. After both methods have been analyzed, the local parameters passed to the method are unified with the formal parameters by the process described below. Program actions causing unification are summarized in Table 1.

Method calls are combined in a bottom-to-top fashion. The static call-graph is used to drive the entire interprocedural analysis. The call-graph is partitioned into strongly connected components (SCC), then topologically sorted. The method contexts (locals, globals, return value, and exceptions) for each method are propagated bottom-up through all possible call sites. The shape graphs are propagated from callee to caller during this phase through the unification of shape graphs. This allows the analysis to be context-sensitive as the caller's shape information is not mixed into callee. We lose this sensitivity for methods belonging to the same SCC (mutually recursive methods) as all methods will share a single shape context [17]. In many cases the actual method receiver cannot be determined at compile time and this is a cause of uncertainty in the graph. Rapid Type Analysis [2] is applied to each call site in order to reduce the number of possible targets for each call site. For each target, the actual parameters are unified with a copy of callee method context in the caller's method context. As an example, the method call `part.volume()` in line 4 of Figure 1 generates a sub-shape graph based on the type of `part` at runtime. This sub-shape graph is merged into the caller's context at the call point. Since we cannot determine at compile time which runtime type `part` will have, we must unify all shape graphs from the target set.

Table 1. Statements causing unification of shape graphs and their effect. The fields *array*, *formal* and *return* are special fields for array reference, method local and return values respectively.

Statement	Abstract Location	Description
`x = y`	unify$(AL(x), AL(y))$	Assignment
`x.`*field*`=y, y=x.`*field*	unify$(AL(x)$.*field*, $AL(y))$	Field assignment
`x = a[i], a[i] = x`	unify$(AL(x), AL(a)$.array)	Array assignment
`return x`	unify$(AL(x), AL(m)$.return)	Function return
`v = f(`$a_1, \ldots, a_n$`)`	$\forall_{t \in \texttt{target}(f)}$unify$(AL(a_i), AL(t)$.formal$(i))$ $\forall_{t \in \texttt{target}(f)}$unify$(AL(v), AL(t)$.return)	Invocation
`x = new T`	$AL(x) = \emptyset$	Allocation

During shape analysis, we decorate the shape graph with attributes depending upon how the shape graph will be used. For example, a simple extension to the basic shape analysis described above labels each edge with `r/w` value depending if the resulting abstract location is the result a field read or field write operation respectively. During unification, a read operation unified with a write results in a write otherwise the attribute remains the same. This information can be used to statically determine whether the element could ever be the target of a write operation.

We also label each shape edge with the count of the first and last access instruction. This value is calculated by examining the basic blocks of the transaction and finding the minimum/maximum number of the instructions over all paths needed to access some abstract location. This value will be used to determine the object access order and assist in determining the expected execution time as explained in the following section.

Type-shape graphs are constructed by merging edges of a shape graph. Edges on which the end points have compatible types may be merged. During the analysis, abstract location (shape edge endpoints) are labelled with the set of types that they refer to in the actual program source. Compatible abstract locations are those that have a common super type in the class hierarchy.

The analysis must create shape graphs for the entire program as described above. However, we need to store only those shapes that will be useful at runtime. At a minimum, we must store an entire graph for each top-level variable in the transaction, in which case the predictor will run once before the beginning of the transaction. Further graphs may be stored depending on how often the predictive process will be used during the transaction. Each additional run will refine the prediction results but impose certain runtime overhead.

The shape graphs themselves may be stored either on the client or on the database server. The shape graphs are quite small (usually no more than several hundred nodes per transaction) and need to be communicated at most once during the entire client session.

4.4 Runtime Use

The runtime system can be triggered in a variety of ways to perform the actual prediction: either through programmer annotations or through automatic identification and instrumentation of transaction routines.

Upon entrance, the runtime interprets the shape graph over the actual program data generating the set of objects used by program. The runtime algorithm produces the future accessed objects based on the shapes extracted from the program. Along with each object to be accessed it also produces whether the object can be the target of a write operation, the expected order in which the objects will be accessed and finally the time the algorithm needs to compute while accessing the objects.

Before a transaction starts, we can follow the associated shape graph to generate an unordered set of the possibly accessed objects in the database. Given a transaction root object and the program point's associated shape graph, we generate all actual objects that *might* be accessed during the transaction. Each shape graph represents how the transaction will manipulate structures referred to in the future by its visible references (the object, arguments, globals) in the transaction body.

In our system, the database is responsible for interpreting the shape graphs of the client. Upon receiving a transaction request, the server will walk the shape graph with a real object database object. This effectively simulates all possible program paths taken during the transaction over the database.

```
// Input:  An initial object o
//         A shape graph sg)
// Return: A set of accessed objects
List DetermineObjects(Object o, ShapeGraph sg)
 Queue search  // Tuples of form (object, abstract node)
 Set   objects  // Set of objects found
 Set   seen    // Tuples (object, abstract node) already visited
 push (o, root (sg)) on search;
 while not empty search
   (o, rv) = pop search;
   if (o, rv) not in seen
     seen = seen ∪ (o, rv);
     for each edge e in adjacent edges of rv
       next = read field e.toNode of object o;
       push (next, rv.e.toNode) on search;
       objects = objects ∪ next;
 return objects;
```

Fig. 2. Algorithm to determine objects using shape graph and object graph

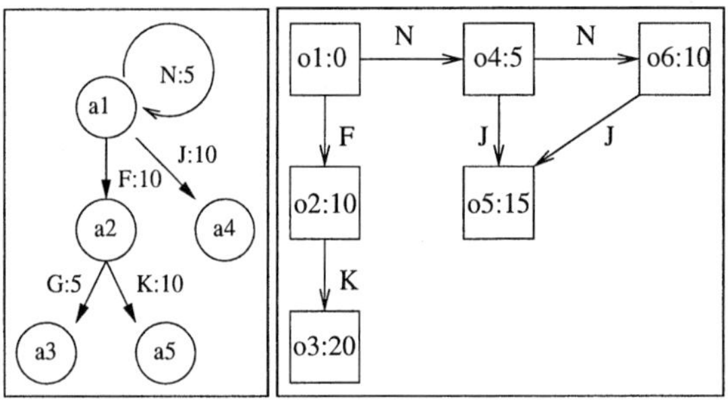

Fig. 3. Shape graph and object graph: Objects are linked through fields and have been labelled with expected access time using shape graph.

Our pseudo-code for walking the object graph is shown in Figure 2. The algorithm traverses the object graph based on program's field accesses represented by the shape graph. We search through the object graph in a breadth-first manner based on earliest expected access through the field. Thus, the runtime cost of prediction equals the cost of interpreting the shape graph over the input object graph.

The prediction walk is usually only done at the beginning of the transaction. However, the runtime system is capable of re-running the walk if further precision is desired and the associated shape graphs are available as discussed in Section 4.3.

The basic algorithm outlined above returns a unordered set of possibly accessed objects. We have extended the above algorithm in several ways to:

Determine R/W attributes. As described in the Section 4.3, a read/write attribute was added to each shape edge depending on whether the edge was created by a read/write operation in the source text. The runtime algorithm was modified to track these edges and return whether, during the transaction, an object *might* incur a write.

While visiting a shape node-object pair, the algorithm is allowed to visit all outgoing shape edges. If any edge had a write attribute, then the object was the target of a possible write and was labelled as such.

Determine access order. We modified the basic shape graph construction algorithm to label each shape edge with a minimum number of basic instructions passed through while reaching the shape node. During unification, we found the minimum of instructions over all paths before reaching a particular node.

While collecting the accessed objects at runtime, we maintain the number of instructions the code would take to reach the object. Each edge taken increases the total number of instructions needed to reach the object. The runtime algorithm was also modified to use a priority queue in order to maintain a sorted list of objects in expected access order.

For example, Figure 3 has a shape graph with each abstract location node labelled with the count of the earliest access instruction. On the right, we show a database object graph. The database objects (`o1`..`o6`) have been labelled with their expected first access time. In the example, Object `o5` was reachable both through `NNJ` with an instruction count of 20, or simply `NJ` with a count of 15. Note that it is possible that two objects may have the same first access time. This occurs when a data dependent branch in the program code is merged together in the shape graph.

Determine expected execution time. We measure the instructions contained in the basic-blocks creating the longest path between field accesses. By estimating the instruction time for these instruction sequences, we can arrive at an expected time of computation between accesses.

The object finding algorithm is modified again to keep track of the maximum number of instructions to be executed during the navigation of the data structure. After visiting the data structure guided by the shape graph, we estimate the number of instructions to completely execute the transaction. This technique gives a conservative measure of the total time needed to execute the transaction by summing over all program paths. Currently we model only execution time and do not take into account I/O costs. We believe this is not too strict a limitation, as in this case our target platform will have gathered the expected objects into local memory.

In each case the graph generated at compile time will be used during the runtime *on the actual data* to providing the runtime with knowledge of how the program will act in the future. The shape graph was annotated with aspects of the analyzed program which would be useful to the runtime system. In our next section we discuss these methods in detail.

5 Predictive Schedulers

The problem of transaction and lock scheduling is the most fundamental problem in concurrency control in databases that attracted a vast amount of research [3,16,19].

Yet, little work has been done on predictive schedulers. This is mainly due to the fact that eliciting and collecting information about future transactions is a non-trivial task, especially if this has to be done in a generic way that is not tailored to any specific application.

Shape analysis is of great aid here as it can provide information about the future execution and needs of the currently running transactions. Yet, exploiting this information is far from trivial. This is because finding the optimal schedule is known to be NP-hard even for the offline version of the problem when all events (i.e., transactions) in the system are known in advance [16]. Additionally, there is no general-case online algorithm that would approximate the optimal offline solution within some constant bound.

In this paper, we seek not to devise a completely new scheduler but rather to enhance commonly used schedulers, such as 2PL [3] by taking advantage of the partial future information that is provided by the shape analysis. Our approach is to augment existing OODBs with the prediction mechanisms of Section 4 and the scheduler extensions presented below. Specifically, we propose three separate enhancements of the the 2PL scheduler: deadlock handling, early lock release, and adaptive preclaiming. It is important to emphasize that while presented separately in this paper for the sake of clarity, in practice they are integrated into the same scheduler.

These techniques are particularly effective when locks are coarse-grain because for fine-grain locking, the runtime overhead of bookkeeping is high and only a small fraction of the database is locked, problems such as data contention are rare, which does not leave much to improve upon. However, fine-grain locks are unusual in practice because most object-oriented database systems group objects into pages and assign locks on per-page rather than per-object basis. In the presentation, we assume for the sake of clarity that each object has an associated lock. Yet, all the techniques that we discuss at the level of individual objects can be applied at the level of object pages.

5.1 Interaction between the Program, Scheduler, and Shape Analysis

Transparency is an important goal in the design of integrated database systems as the programmer would rather avoid learning a new programming model and rewriting existing database programs. In the method we propose the programmer only has to annotate the program with statements indicating the beginning and end of each transaction. Typically, such statements already exist in an OODB program so that no programmer's effort is required at all. This information is used by both the shape analysis, as described in Section 4.3, and the scheduler.

All other information about the objects, transactions, and locks can be derived from the program automatically. In particular, there is no special program interface for releasing locks. This is important because database systems that are enforcing some level of transaction isolation, do not trust applications to release locks. Yet, some additional annotations may turn useful, e.g., to indicate that there is no need to acquire a lock for a particular object and to account for this object in shape analysis. Since such (possibly useful) optimizations are not essential for the methodology we have developed, we do not consider them in this paper.

The interaction between the scheduler and shape analysis is somewhat more complicated even though this complexity is hidden from the programmer. To start with, they need to agree about unique identifiers for transactions and transaction types. Essentially, the runtime shape analysis has to convey the information about future object accesses of a transaction to the scheduler. This is done by invoking the FUTUREACCESSES method provided by the scheduler's API at least once for each transaction, when the transaction begins. It is possible that as the transaction proceeds, the shape analysis will have more precise information about future accesses and it will notify the scheduler by invoking the FUTUREACCESSES method again. The number of such invocations depends on the granularity of shape analysis as discussed in Section 4.3.

5.2 Deadlock Handling

In two-phase locking and other similar locking protocols, transactions need to wait when requested locks cannot be granted immediately. Thus, a set of transactions, each holding some locks and requesting an additional one, may end up being mutually blocked. Such cyclic wait situations are commonly known as *deadlocks*. There are several extensions of the basic two-phase locking protocol for handling deadlocks; those can be broadly divided into two categories: deadlock detection and deadlock prevention techniques. We now briefly describe the techniques and show how program analysis can be used to enhance them.

Deadlock detection approaches attempt to detect the deadlock situation if it occurs and then to break the cycle by aborting one or more transactions. The detection algorithms are generally based on the notion of a *waits-for graph* (WFG), which is a graph $G = (V, E)$ whose nodes are the active transactions, and in which an edge of the form (t_i, t_j) indicates that t_i waits for t_j to release a lock that it needs. There is a deadlock in the execution if and only if there is a cycle in WFG.

Maintaining WFG throughout the execution is considered expensive, which was the motivation for alternative deadlock prevention methods. These methods do not explicitly maintain WFG but rather detect "dangerous" situations that can possibly lead to a future deadlock and abort at least one of the conflicting transactions based on some heuristics, such as *wait-die* or *wound-wait*. Situations are identified as dangerous in an efficient but simple-minded way: for example, if there is a conflict between a pair of transactions and one transaction has a smaller identifier than the second one. Such deadlock prevention strategies impose a smaller overhead of additional testing operations compared with deadlock detection but may cause significantly more transaction aborts, many of which are in states that do not lead to deadlock.

If all locks that are needed for a transaction are known in advance when the transaction starts, it is possible to achieve almost "perfect deadlock prevention" that avoids aborts altogether without sacrificing concurrency. One such method is based on the notion of *resource-allocation* graph, in which both currently executing transactions and currently assigned locks are vertices. A directed edge from transaction T_i to lock L_i implies that either T_i waits for L_i or T_i will request L_i in the future. A directed edge from lock L_i to transaction T_i implies that L_i is being held by T_i. The lock scheduler maintains this graph and uses it as follows: a transaction T_i that requests L_i waits as long as granting L_i to T_i would create a cycle in the resource-allocation graph.

It should be noted that while this method is considered important from theoretical point of view, it is never used in practice, mainly because it is difficult to elicit information about the locks that a given transaction is going to request in the future. Another reason is that resource-allocation graph can have several times as many nodes as WFG and significantly more edges due to accounting for future lock requests. Thus, maintaining this graph and detecting cycles in it is considered too expensive.

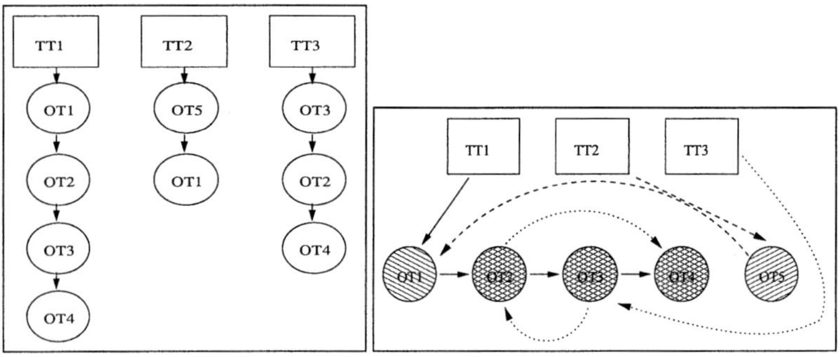

Fig. 4. Transaction object lock order and type graph.

Information obtained from program analysis as described in Section 4, can be used to facilitate deadlock handling in several ways. First of all, when constructing WFG, we can efficiently identify and prune dependencies that cannot be part of the deadlock cycle based on the type information. In this way, we reduce the size of WFG and make cycle detection faster, thereby eliminating the major deficiency of deadlock detection approaches. To illustrate how our technique works, let us consider the following example: transaction of type TT_1 first locks an object of type OT_1, then an object of type OT_2, an object of type OT_3 and finally an object of type OT_4. Transaction of type TT_2 locks objects of type OT_5 and OT_1 in this order. Transaction of type TT_3 locks objects of type OT_3, OT_2, and OT_4 (see Fig. 4). Observe that a cycle in WFG can be created only by transactions of types TT_1 and TT_3, and only due to waits on objects of types OT_2 and OT_3. Thus, transactions of type TT_2 and dependencies between transactions of TT_1 and TT_3 due to objects of type OT_4 do not need to be inserted into WFG.

To capture this intuition, we make use of the type shape graphs described in Section 4.2. Section 4.3 explains how to construct a type shape graph for each transaction type. In order to facilitate deadlock detection, graphs from different transaction types are merged into a single graph in the following way: all nodes in the graphs that correspond to the same object type are combined into a single node. For example, Figure 4 shows the merged graph for the example above.

Our methodology for pruning WFG nodes and edges is based on the following theorem:

Theorem 1. *If transactions $T_1, T_2, \dots, T_n$ create a cycle in WFG at runtime, then the static object types that belong to the type shape graphs of transaction types $Type(T_1)$, $Type(T_2), \dots, Type(T_n)$ create a cycle in the merged type shape graph. Furthermore, every edge that is part in the WFG cycle is due to wait on the object whose type is a node in the type shape graph cycle.*

It should be emphasized that while this technique is very general, it is inherently conservative due to being based on purely static compile-time program analysis. In other words, more scrupulous and dynamic analysis could prune more parts of WFG. We can lose precision at several stages: when the function that represents the transaction has many branches (as explained in Section 4.3) and when reducing an object shape graph to a type shape graph. Yet, this methodology can significantly decrease the size of WFG in many existing applications because most transactions traverse objects in the same order of types. For example, in the OO7 application described in Section 6, a transaction never accesses a low level construct called atomic part before accessing a higher level composite part which contains the same atomic part. Yet, we improve this methodology further by complementing it with runtime analysis that takes into account the dynamic information about the execution.

Program analysis not only facilitates deadlock detection but it also makes perfect deadlock prevention feasible. Specifically, having the information about future object accesses as described in Section 4.4 allows us to set up the edges in the resource-allocation graph that represent future lock requests. Admittedly, this method may sometimes yield a conservative estimate because shape analysis can deduce only a superset of the actual objects to be accessed. However, once created at the beginning of a transaction, future request edges can be incrementally removed as transaction proceeds and more precise knowledge about transaction execution is gained. The interaction between the lock scheduler and shape analysis as described in Section 5.1, allows such incremental updates.

Program analysis can also make algorithms based on the resource-allocation graph more efficient: similarly to WFG, we can reduce the size of the resource-allocation graph by using the information extracted from type shape graphs. Finally, we can use hybrid deadlock detection-prevention schemes. For example, we can use deadlock detection as long as the deadlock rate is low and switch to deadlock prevention if the deadlock rate exceeds a predefined threshold.

5.3 Early Lock Release

All of the existing variations of the classical two-phase commit protocol can be classified as strict or non-strict. In strict protocols, all locks are held until the end of transaction, while in non-strict protocols, locks can be released if the transaction no longer needs to access the object [3]. It is generally considered that an early release of a write lock may pose a problem because other transactions may obtain such a lock and read the new object value that has not been committed yet and may never be committed in the case of an aborted or failed transaction. However, early release of a read lock is highly desirable as it makes the object accessible to other transactions and improves the concurrency of the execution.

Yet, most practical systems are using strict protocols because implementing an early release of read locks is far from straightforward. The main reason for this is the challenge in detecting that the transaction has finished accessing the object. In order to perform such a detection without requiring the programmer to add annotations, the scheduler has to predict future object accesses by the transaction. Note that this is exactly where the shape analysis proves useful as we discussed in Section 4.4.

Another problem may arise if a transaction T_1 unlocks an object O_1 and then acquires a lock for another object O_2: if another transaction acquires write locks for both O_1 and O_2 and commits between the two operations of T_1, the two transactions cannot be serialized. To address this issue, the classical non-strict two-phase locking acquires all locks that the transaction requires prior to releasing the locks that are no longer needed. Again, this might require the scheduler to predict the future accesses of a transaction. Furthermore, preclaiming of locks (i.e., acquiring all the locks up front at the beginning of a transaction) can hurt the concurrency, especially if the transaction is long (see Section 5.4 for a discussion of preclaiming).

To eliminate the need of preclaiming, *altruistic locking* has been proposed [18]. Informally speaking, the general idea behind altruistic locking is that if a transaction T_1 releases a lock for O_1, then any other transaction T_2 that acquires a lock for O_1 before T_1 terminates, can acquire only locks released by T_1.[2] The rationale here is to prevent T_2 from accessing an object that may be required by T_1 in the future. However, altruistic locking is still conservative because an access of T_2 to an object that has not been released by T_1 does not necessarily lead to a problem.

It may appear that simply disallowing T_2 to access any object that may be required by T_1 in the future will solve the problem. Unfortunately, this is not the case: if T_2 modifies O_2 and then another transaction T_3 accesses first O_2 and then another object that is required by T_1 in the future, the execution is not serializable.

In this work, we propose a solution based on the notion of *causal dependency* [12]: transaction T_1 causally precedes transaction T_2 (denoted as $T_1 \stackrel{hb}{\rightarrow} T_2$ if either a) T_2 is initiated after T_1 by the same client, or b) T_2 acquires a lock that T_1 has released, or c) there is another transaction T_3 such that $T_1 \stackrel{hb}{\rightarrow} T_2$. Our *causality-aware* scheduler is the standard non-strict two-phase locking with the following extension: it precludes the situation when there are two transactions T_1 and T_2 such that $T_1 \stackrel{hb}{\rightarrow} T_2$ and T_2 holds a lock for O_1 that may be requested by T_1 in the future. If a transaction requests a lock and granting the lock may lead to such a situation, the request is blocked until T_1 acquires a lock on O_1 or terminates.

Theorem 2. *Causality-aware scheduler generates only executions that are one-copy serializable.*

Techniques for tracking causality, such as assigning increasing logical timestamps to transactions, are well known and have been extensively studied through the literature. However, the application of the knowledge of causal dependencies for locking schedulers appears to be new. Furthermore, by using type shape graphs we can exclude from our consideration some transaction types like we did for deadlock handling as presented in Section 5.2. We discuss the performance of the proposed scheme in Section 6.2.

[2] More precisely, altruistic locking extends the scheduler interface by adding a "donate" operation. This operation signifies that the transaction does not need the object any longer while the actual unlocking is done at the end of the transaction.

5.4 Adaptive Lock Preclaiming

While the standard two-phase locking protocol acquires a lock when the object is accessed for the first time, there is a group of schedulers called *conservative* two-phase locking [3,19] that *preclaim* all potentially required locks up front when the execution of a transaction begins. [3] explores the tradeoff between the two approaches. In summary, gradual lock acquisition works better when data contention is low and transactions are long whereas preclaiming is more suitable for the applications with high data contention and short transactions.

Note that preclaiming requires the knowledge of future accesses which can be obtained only by programmer annotations or tools like shape analysis. Furthermore, advanced knowledge of future accesses allows us to devise adaptive hybrid schemes. By using shape analysis we can estimate the future data contention level across the transactions that have already started and decide whether to use conservative or standard two-phase locking. Furthermore, predicting execution times makes it possible to preclaim locks for short transactions but assign locks gradually to longer ones.

Finally, by using shape analysis combined with the information about the execution history, we can sort objects by their popularity, i.e., the degree of concurrency in accessing the object. Observe that popular objects are typically accessed for a shorter time. This provides the rationale for preclaiming: If a transaction first accesses a popular object O_1, and then a less popular object O_2, it will be more efficient to acquire locks on the both objects simultaneously. The full algorithm is presented in Figure 5.

```
Upon starting a transaction
  S = set of all objects that will be locked with probability > α
  sort S by object popularity in the ascending order

Upon requesting a lock for object S[i]
  verify that preclaiming will not create a possibility for an induced deadlock
  acquire locks for all objects S[1], ..., S[i] that have not been acquired yet

Upon raising the probability of a lock L not in S
  recalculate S and acquire L if necessary and does not create a possibility for a deadlock
```

Fig. 5. Adaptive lock preclaiming based on object popularities

6 Experiments

We have developed a simulation test-bed in order to test the performance of the techniques described in Section 5 and their effect on data contention. Using the same simulation technique, we ran experiments with two different applications: a prototype of a car reservation system that we developed, and the standard OO7 benchmark [6] for object-oriented databases. In order to perform tests for varying data contention conditions, we have designed a synthetic workload generator that produces a sequence of operations to be invoked at certain times along with the parameters to be passed to those operations. We have also implemented an artificial client that replays a previously generated sequence of operations. The main venue of our experiments was to compare the predictive lock scheduler with the standard schedulers. To this end, we have implemented a strict two-phase locking (S2PL) and optimistic schedulers. The overall test-bed architecture is depicted in Figure 6.

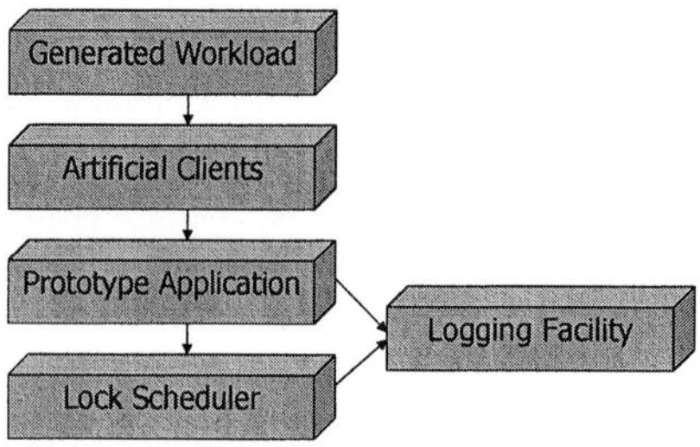

Fig. 6. The testbed implementation

6.1 Prototype of a Car Reservation System

Consider a database system for online car reservations that can be placed through Web requests. For the sake of an example, assume that the database contains three different parts: a large partition of reservations (A), a large partition of available cars (B), and the rest of data that contains, e.g., rental rules and terms (C). There are three different types of transactions: Frequent user transactions update already existing individual reservations and place new ones. To this end, they need to lock A. There are also infrequent traversing and maintenance transactions. A maintenance transaction updates the maintenance information for the fleet of cars owned by the company, thereby locking B for a very long time. A traversing transaction computes a tentative assignment of available cars to existing reservations. This transaction locks C, then A, and finally B. The following problem can occur if the scheduler incrementally assigns locks by only looking at the currently granted ones: A traversing transaction obtains locks for C and A. Then a maintenance transaction starts and it is granted a lock for B. The traversing transaction now cannot obtain a lock for B and it has to wait until the maintenance transaction terminates. Meanwhile, many user transactions are blocked because they cannot access A. If the scheduler knew to take future events into account, it would delay the maintenance transaction access to B in order to let the traversing transaction finish and release the lock it holds on A.

We defined three different sets of parameters for the purpose of testing. These parameters determine the frequency and the duration of locks for each transaction. The values of these parameters for each of the configurations are given in Table 2.

We repeatedly ran a simulation of our prototype 100 times for each configuration. Tables 3 and 4 summarize the results of our experiments. Table 3 shows execution

Table 2. Parameters used in different experiments

	Configuration 1	Configuration 2	Configuration 3
User transaction rate	*300/sec*	*30/sec*	*30/sec*
User transaction duration	*30ms*	*30ms*	*30ms*
Mainten. transaction duration	*60000ms*	*2000ms*	*2000ms*
Traversing transaction in A	*30ms*	*30ms*	*200ms*
Traversing transaction in B	*30ms*	*30ms*	*500ms*
Traversing transaction in C	*500ms*	*500ms*	*500ms*
Traversing transaction period	*1min*	*1min*	*1min*
Mainten. transaction period	*6min*	*2min*	*2min*

times in milliseconds for the S2PL, predictive, and optimistic schedulers as well as the proper execution time of the transactions. The predictive scheduler significantly outperforms the S2PL scheduler for the first configuration while being slightly better for the second and third configuration. This improvement is solely due to the adaptive preclaiming technique described in Section 5.4 because no lock can be released early in this application. The optimistic scheduler did not perform well in our experiments because of the high number of conflicts. For all configurations, the traversing transaction was either completely starved or took a very long time to complete. Furthermore, the abort rate was high for the optimistic scheduler as shown in Table 4.

Table 3. Comparison of transaction execution times in various configurations and for different schedulers

	Configuration 1			Configuration 2			Configuration 3		
	Traversal	User	Mainten.	Traversal	User	Mainten.	Traversal	User	Mainten.
Execution	560	30	60000	560	30	2000	1200	30	2000
S2PL	7577	3423	60024	860	43	2010	1241	43	2010
Predictive	6829	43	60024	876	40	2010	1242	43	2010
Optimistic	starved	54	60024	4327	40	2010	starved	40	2010

Table 4. Comparison of transaction abort rates in various configurations and for different schedulers

	Configuration 1			Configuration 2			Configuration 3		
	Traversal	User	Mainten.	Traversal	User	Mainten.	Traversal	User	Mainten.
Optimistic	many	15	0	6.33	0.07	0	many	0.07	0

6.2 The OO7 Benchmarks

Several standard benchmark sets for object-oriented databases, such as OO1 [7], and OO7 [6], have been designed to facilitate the testing of experimental database design techniques in realistic settings. We opted to conduct our experiments with the OO7 benchmark since it is the most complex in terms of the database structure and supported operation set. Additionally, the OO7 benchmark exhibits a rich object structure that lends itself well to program shape analysis. Since the original OO7 benchmark were written in C++ while our shape analysis implementation works for Java, we extended a Java port of the OO7 benchmarks [1].

The OO7 Database. In this section, we summarize those details of the OO7 database description in [6] that are relevant to our experiments. The benchmark models a database for CAD/CAM/CASE applications. A key component of the database is a set of *composite parts*. Each composite part corresponds to a design primitive such as a register cell in a VLSI CAD application.

At a lower level, each composite part has an associated graph of *atomic parts*. Intuitively, the atomic parts within a composite part are the units out of which the composite part is constructed. For example, if a composite part corresponds to a procedure in a CASE application, each of the atomic parts in its associated graph might correspond to a variable, statement, or expression in the procedure. One atomic part in each composite part's graph is designated as the "root part."

Composite parts are grouped into *base assemblies*.[3] For example, in a VLSI CAD application, an assembly might correspond to the design for a register file or an ALU. Base assemblies are further grouped into *complex assemblies*, which can be part of upper level complex assemblies. Cycles between assemblies are not allowed. Therefore, the overall organization can be visualized as a set of assembly hierarchies, each hierarchy being called a *module*.

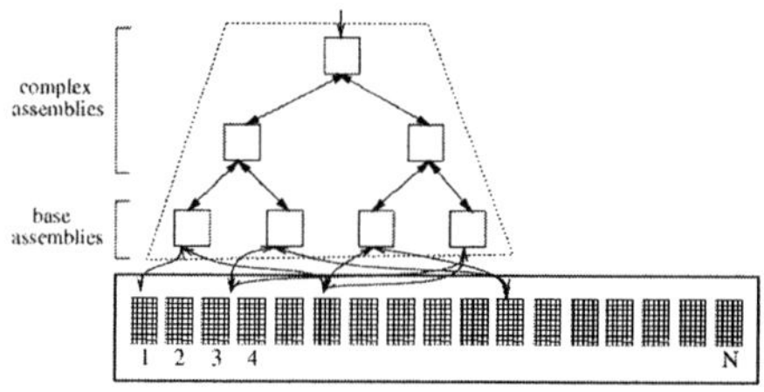

Fig. 7. OO7 module structure

Figure 7 depicts the full structure of an OO7 module. The hierarchy scale is configurable with respect to several parameters. In our experiments, we worked with a single module because all operations provided by the benchmarks act on a single module so that having multiple modules does not create any interesting concurrency issues. Other relevant parameters are the number of composite parts per module, the number of composite parts per base assembly, the number of levels in the assembly hierarchy, and the number

[3] Some parts may be shared across multiple assemblies while other parts may belong to a single assembly. This is unlike atomic parts that are never shared by multiple composite parts.

of child assemblies per complex assembly. Since the number of children nodes (child assemblies or composite parts) per assembly has a great impact on the degree of data contention, we varied it in our experiments while the other two parameters were fixed. Table 5 summarizes the values of these parameters that were used in the experiments.

Table 5. OO7 database configuration

# composite parts per module	500
# composite parts per base assembly	3–27
# levels in the hierarchy	3
# assemblies per complex assembly	1–5

Each object in the database has a number of attributes, including the integer attributes `id` and `buildDate`. `id` is a distinct identifier assigned to each entity to distinguish it from other entities while `buildDate` specifies the last time when this part or assembly was modified.

Benchmark Operations and Their Concurrency Patterns. The designers of the OO7 benchmarks provided a rich set of operations to manipulate the database. However, many of these operations are equivalent as far as concurrency goes. For example, a search for a composite part by any of two different attributes takes about the same time and requires the same locks. In fact, concurrency was not the focus of the OO7 design: each operation as a whole was considered a separate transaction while all lock assignments were handled by the underlying OODBMS. On the contrary, we need to consider the details of lock assignment by the concurrency manager, even if it is transparent for the application. In our experiments, we used the following three operations that represent different operation classes from concurrency standpoint:

- Querying an arbitrary composite part:

  The operation selects a random base assembly and a random composite part which is contained in this assembly. Thus, it needs to acquire a read lock for the base assembly and then a read lock for the part. If the base assembly is accessed directly using some index structure, then no other locks are required. Another way to reach the assembly is to traverse the assembly hierarchy from the root choosing a child assembly at each node by some arbitrary criteria. In this case, the operation also requires read locks for all assemblies on the path from the root to the base assembly of interest.
- Reorganizing an arbitrary composite part:

  Like the previous operation, this operation selects a random base assembly and a random composite part which is contained in this assembly. Then, it obtains a write lock for the part and performs a long update which involves recreation and reorganization of all atomic parts within this composite part.

  Updating an attribute of several related objects:

As a typical representative of this class, we took an operation that updates the `buildDate` of a composite part and its parent base assembly. The operation starts with obtaining a read lock for an arbitrary assembly, chooses an arbitrary part of this assembly, obtains a write lock for the assembly and updates it, and finally acquires a write lock for the part and performs an update on it.

The submission rate for the query, reorganization, and update transactions was 10, 600, and 3 transactions per minute, respectively. The execution times were 2ms, 2000ms, and 2ms as shown in Table 6.

Table 6. Comparison of transaction execution times for different schedulers

	Time	S2PL	Early release	Adaptive preclaiming	Both preclaiming and early release
`buildDate` update	2ms	92	48	116	58
Query composite part	2ms	15	9	5	5
Reorganization	2000ms	2041	2018	2010	2010

Performance of Locking Schedulers. In Table 6 we compare the average transaction time in milliseconds for strict 2-phase locking (S2PL) and our predictive scheduler. Furthermore, in order to understand the contribution of each individual mechanism, we ran the predictor with only early release activated, adaptive preclaiming activated, and both. As it can be seen, early release of read locks improved the average times of all transactions. In contrast, adaptive preclaiming significantly reduced the times for the query transaction but slightly increased the times for the `buildDate` update transaction which required two locks. This tradeoff is desirable for the OO7 application because short queries are more common than longer updates and the difference in their times is immediately perceived by the user.

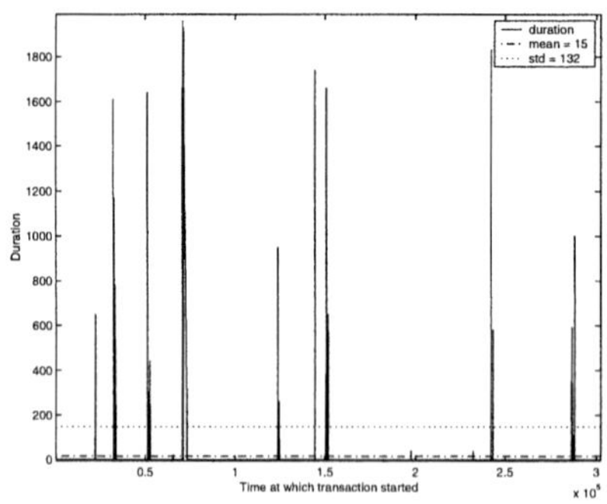

Fig. 8. A typical execution section for the S2PL scheduler

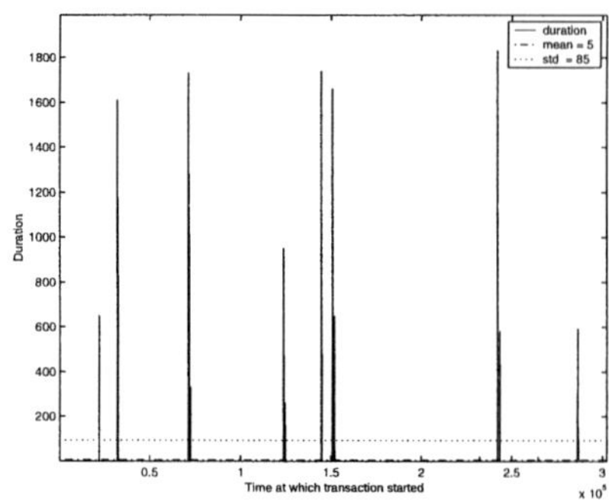

Fig. 9. A typical execution section for the predictive scheduler

Perhaps even more important than the difference in average times is the difference in the standard deviation. Figure 8 shows the times for the short query transaction in a section of a typical execution using a pessimistic strict 2 phase-lock scheduler. We can clearly see sharp peaks when the reorganization transaction blocked the `buildDate` update transaction, which in turn blocked the query transaction. Figure 9 presents execution times of the predictive scheduler for the same section in the same workload. Not only has the overall mean transaction time been significantly reduced but there are also fewer peaks and those peaks are not as high.

Execution Time Prediction. In Section 4.4 we outlined our method for determining the expected execution time of a transaction. The precision of estimation is important for the adaptive preclaiming mechanism used in the experiments that we described above. However, the standard OO7 benchmark does not create sufficient diversity in the duration of transactions of the same type. To create a better diversity, we modified the OO7 benchmark to create randomly sized composite parts having between 20 and 1000 atomic parts. We then executed 2187 random search and traversal queries on the database.[4] The traversal query transaction visited a section of the database in order to perform maintenance on a set of atomic parts.

In this experiment, we compared the accuracy of our predicted times to the actual runtime of the transaction. As the predicted times were dependent on the actual hardware used, we were mostly interested in the relationship between the predicted values and the actual execution times.

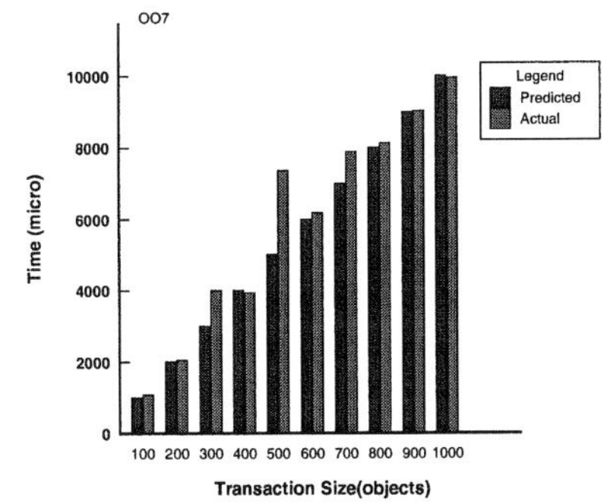

Fig. 10. Predicted time compared to actual execution times

Figure 10 shows our results for the OO7 traversal transaction. The results were sorted by transaction size and the overall times were averaged over 3 runs. In almost all cases the predicted time matches the actual time very closely. However, in two circumstances (300, 500) the times diverged. On closer inspection, several transactions took over 10

[4] Based on the number of Base Assemblies in the benchmark tiny configuration.

times the median. We believe this to be due to outside operating system issues and beyond our control.

Table 7 summarizes our results. We found a relatively strong correlation (0.64) between the predicted times and the actual run times. This will be true whenever the runtime of the transaction is dependent on navigation cost of the data structure. Again it should be noted that the transaction cost will usually be tied to the number of the objects used by the transaction code and not the number of objects in the database.

Table 7. Predicted time compared to actual execution times

Source	Sample Size	mean	median
Predicted	2187	4945	4800
Actual	2187	5214	4677

Our initial results show this technique to be promising. However, two caveats must be pointed out. First, since the shape graph contains all paths that a program may take, the analysis maybe overly conservative in estimating the total expected time. Secondly, if the majority of the transaction's total work is navigating the structure, the prediction time will be on the order of the execution time. Since our predictor effectively visits the data structure elements in a similar way to the original transaction.

7 Conclusions

We have presented several novel techniques for automatically increasing concurrency in object oriented database systems. In this paper, we have proposed using shape analysis for database programs. Using program analysis we can provide a succinct representation of the future accesses of a program fragment even across dispatched method calls in object oriented programs. Knowledge of the future accesses permits the simpler algorithms for early-lock release, data contention, and deadlock avoidance/detection. We demonstrated our technique using our own car-reservation simulation and the OO7 benchmark adapted to use multiple clients in order exercise the currency scheduler. Our techniques increased concurrency and have lowered the mean time to complete the workloads.

While we showed that our predictive scheduler is beneficial for the above applications, the power of prediction is bound to be inherently limited. Identifying individual cases when performance can be hurt because of the poor prediction accuracy is part of our future research. In particular, it would be desirable to devise a heuristics that would determine online whether the predictive scheduler mechanisms should be used.

In the future, we plan to investigate execution time prediction and lease scheduling. As the gap between traditional programming languages and database programming languages continues to diminish, applying program analysis to database problems will be a fruitful area of research.

Acknowledgments. The research was partially supported by the National Science Foundation under grants EIA-0080134, ANI-0123985, and IIS-9817432.

References

1. Ozone oodb. Technical report, www.ozone-db.org, 2001.
2. D. Bacon and P. Sweeney. Fast static analysis of C++ virtual function calls. In *OOPSLA Object-Oriented Programming Systems, Languages, and Applications*, San Jose, California, Oct 1996. ACM.
3. P. Bernstein, V. Hadzilacos, and H. Goodman. *Concurrency Control and Recovery in Database Systems*. Addison-Wesley, Reading, MA, 1987.
4. Jeff Bogda and Urs Hölzle. Removing unnecessary synchronization in Java. In *OOPSLA*, pages 35–465, Denver, CO, Nov 1999. ACM.
5. Cahoon and McKinley. Data flow analysis for software prefetching linked data structures in java. In *International Conference on Parallel Architectures and Compilation Techniques*, Barcelona, Spain, Sep 2001. ACM.
6. Michael J. Carey, David J. DeWitt, and Jeffrey F. Naughton. The OO7 benchmark. *SIGMOD Record (ACM Special Interest Group on Management of Data)*, 22(2):12–21, 1993.
7. R. G. G. Cattell and J. Skeen. Object operations benchmark. *TODS*, 17(1):1–31, 1992.
8. F. Corbera, Rafael Asenjo, and Emilio L. Zapata. New shape analysis techniques for automatic parallelization of C codes. In *International Conference on Supercomputing*, pages 220–227, Rhodes, Greece, Jun 1999. ACM.
9. Rakesh Ghiya and Laurie J. Hendren. Is it a tree, a dag, or a cyclic graph? A shape analysis for heap-directed pointers in C. In *Symposium on Principles of Programming Languages POPL*, pages 1–15, St. Petersburg, Florida, Jan 1996. ACM.
10. Nils Knafla. *Prefetching Techniques for Client/Server, Object-Oriented Database Systems*. PhD thesis, University of Edinburgh, 1999.
11. Kristian Kvilekval and Ambuj Singh. Prefetching for mobile computers using shape graphs. In *LCR 2002*, Washington DC, Mar 2002. ACM.
12. L. Lamport. Time, Clocks and the Ordering of Event in a DistributedSystem. *Communications of the ACM*, 21(7):558–565, July 1978.
13. Sun Microsystems. *Java Data Objects*, 2003.
14. Dor Nurit, Rodeh Michael, and Sagiv Mooly. Detecting memory errors via static pointer analysis. In *Workshop on Program Analysis for Software Tools and Engineering (PASTE'98)*, pages 27–34, New York, NY, Jun 1998. ACM.
15. ODMG. *Object Query Language*, 2003.
16. C. Papadimitriou. *The Theory of Concurrency Control*. Computer Science Press, Rockville, MD, 1986.
17. Erik Ruf. Effective synchronization removal for Java. In *SIGPLAN Conference on Programming Language Design and Implementation (PLDI2000)*, Vancouver, British Columbia, Jun 2000. ACM.
18. K. Salem, H. Garcia-Molina, and J. Shands. Atruistic locking. In *Transactions on Database Systems*. ACM, 1994.
19. Gottfried Vossen, Gerhard Weikum, and Jim Gray (Editor). *Transactional Information Systems: Theory, Algorithms, and Practice of Concurrency Control and Recovery*. Morgan Kaufmann, 2001.
20. R. Wilhelm, M. Sagiv, and T. Reps. Shape analysis. In *Proc. of CC 2000: 9th Int. Conf. on Compiler Construction*, Berlin, Germany, Mar 2000. Springer-Verlag.

Semantic Casts: Contracts and Structural Subtyping in a Nominal World

Robert Bruce Findler [1], Matthew Flatt [2], and Matthias Felleisen [3]

[1] University of Chicago; Chicago, IL, USA; robby@cs.uchicago.edu
[2] University of Utah; Salt Lake City, UT, USA; mflatt@cs.utah.edu
[3] Northeastern University; Boston, MA, USA; matthias@ccs.neu.edu

Abstract. Nominal subtyping forces programmers to explicitly state all of the subtyping relationships in the program. This limits component reuse, because programmers cannot anticipate all of the contexts in which a particular class might be used. In contrast, structural subtyping implicitly allows any type with appropriate structure to be used in a given context. Languagues with contracts exacerbate the problem. Since contracts are typically expressed as refinements of types, contracts in nominally typed languages introduce additional obstacles to reuse.
To overcome this problem we show how to extend a nominally typed language with semantic casts that introduce a limited form of structural subtyping. The new language must dynamically monitor contracts, as new subtyping relationships are exploited via semantic casts. In addition, it must also track the casts to properly assign blame in case interface contract are violated.

1 Enriching Nominal Subtypes with Semantic Casts

Conventional class-based object-oriented languages like C++ [45], C# [34], Eiffel [33], and Java [18] come with nominal typing systems. In such systems, a programmer explicitly names the superclass(es) and the implemented interfaces of a class. Thus, the declared type of any instance of a class must be one of the explicitly named interfaces or classes.

Language designers choose nominal type systems because they are easy to understand and easy to implement. A programmer doesn't need to investigate the structure of an interface I to find out whether an instance o of a class C can have type I; it suffices to check whether the definition of C mentions I as an implemented interface (or whether the superclasses and superinterfaces mention I). A compiler writer, in turn, can build a class graph and an interface graph and type check expressions and statements by comparing points in a graph.

Nominal typing, however, is also a known obstacle to software reuse. In particular, a programmer can only compose two objects if the creators of the two respective classes used the same (nominal) types. Unfortunately, in a world of software components where third-party programmers compose existing pieces of software, the implementor of a class cannot possibly anticipate all possible types for an object. Hence, programmers resort to casts and have invented adapter patterns to bridge the gap between third-party components.

M. Odersky (Ed.): ECOOP 2004, LNCS 3086, pp. 364–388, 2004.

One way to overcome this problem is to switch to a structural type system. The research community has long recognized this shortcoming of nominal subtype systems and that structural subtype systems do not suffer from this flaw. Some modern research languages like LOOM [3], OCaml [29], OML [40], PolyTOIL [4], and Moby [13] adopt structural subtype systems. Their designs demonstrate how their structural subtype systems empower their user communities to reuse classes in unanticipated situations.

Changing a language's subtype system from a nominal to a structural perspective is a drastic step. We therefore propose an alternative, smaller change to conventional languages that also overcomes the reuse problem. Specifically, our proposal is to introduce a "semantic cast" mechanism. The cast allows programmers to change the type of an object according to a structural subtype criteria. Thus, if an existing class *C* satisfies the needs of some interface *I* but doesn't explicitly implement it, a programmer can, even retroactively, specify that an instance of *C* is of type *I*.

Naturally, the programmer should only take such an action if the semantics of the class is that of the interface. We therefore allow the programmer to describe an executable approximation of the interface's semantics—called *contracts* here—and use that semantics to monitor the validity of the cast. If the cast object behaves according to the contracts, the execution proceeds as normal. Otherwise, the monitoring system raises an exception and attributes the misbehavior to a specific component, *i.e.*, either the object's use-context, the object itself, or the cast.

In this paper, we explain the need for these contract-based casts, their design, their implementation, and our experience with the contract system. We present the ideas in a Java-like setting to show how they can be adapted to conventional languages. Indeed, we only present the internal form of the new construct, rather than a surface syntax. Section 2 describes a common situation where nominal subtyping fails to support reuse effectively. Section 3 presents our semantic cast construct and reformulates the example from section 2 with this construct. Section 4 precisely specifies the new contract checker with a calculus. Section 5 discusses our implementation. The last three sections discuss related work, future work, and present our conclusions.

2 Contracts and Component Reuse

In this section, we introduce object-oriented contracts and illustrate how languages with contracts that augment a nominal subtyping hierarchy inhibit reuse.

Consider the canonical queue implementation in figure 1 (in Java syntax, using JML [27] notation for contracts). The queue supports three operations: *enq* to add an element to the queue, *deq* to remove an element from the queue, and *empty* to test if the queue contains any elements. The post-condition contract on *enq* guarantees that the queue is not empty after an element is added and the pre-condition contract on *deq* requires that there is an element in the queue to remove.

Enforcing pre- and post-conditions such as these is straightforward. When the *enq* method returns, the post-condition code is run and if it produces **false**, evaluation terminates and *enq* is blamed for breaking its contract. Similarly, when *deq* is called, the pre-condition code is run and if it produces **false**, evaluation terminates and *deq*'s caller is blamed for breaking *deq*'s contract. Although these contracts do not ensure that the

```
interface IQueue {
  void enq(int x);
  // @post !empty()

  void deq(int x);
  // @pre !empty()

  boolean empty();
}
```

```
class Q implements IQueue {
  void enq(int x) { ... }
  int deq() { ... }
  boolean empty() { ... }
}
```

Fig. 1. Queues

queue implementation is correct, experience has shown that such weak contracts provide a good balance between correctness and run-time overhead [41].

Object-oriented languages allow much more complex forms of interaction than those between the queue and its client. Since objects may be passed as arguments or returned as results from methods, the call structure of the program can depend on the flow of values in the program. Put differently, invoking an object's methods may trigger nested callbacks (a.k.a upcalls) between components [46].

```
class Q implements IQueue {
  IObserver o;
  void enq(int x) {
    ...
    if (o != null) o.onEnq(this, x);
  }
  int deq() {
    int hd = ...;
    if (o != null) o.onDeq(this, hd);
    ...
    return hd;
  }
  boolean empty() { ... }
  void registerObs(IObserver _o) {o=_o;}
}
```

```
interface IObserver {
  void onEnq(Queue q, int x);
  // @post !q.empty()

  void onDeq(Queue q, int x);
  // @pre !q.empty()
}
```

Fig. 2. Queues with Observers

Consider the revised queue class in figure 2; this variant of the class supports an observer. The additional method *registerObs* accepts an observer object. This observer object is saved in a field of the queue and its methods are invoked when an element is enqueued or dequeued from the queue.

Although this addition may seem innocuous at first, consider the misbehaved observer in figure 3. Instances of this observer immediately dequeue any objects added to the queue. Imagine that an instance of this observer were registered with an instance of the *Q* class. The first time the *enq* method is invoked, it adds an integer to the queue and then invokes the observer. Then the observer removes the integer, before the *enq* method returns. Due to the *onEnq* post-condition in the *IObserver* interface, however, *BadO* is immediately indicted, ensuring the *Q* class can always meet its contracts.

```
class BadO implements IObserver {
  ...
  onEnq(Queue q, int x) {
   q.deq(); }}
```

Fig. 3. Bad Observer

Programming language designers (including the authors of this paper) have historically been satisfied with contracts in interfaces and abstract classes [2, 8, 12, 17, 22–25, 32, 33]. Unfortunately, this design decision exacerbates the problems with software reuse in a nominally typed world. Independent producers of components cannot possibly foresee the precise contracts that some component should satisfy. Indeed, if they aim to produce software components that are as flexible as possible they must have the least constraining interface contracts (that are still safe). Accordingly, contract checkers must allow component programmers to refine a component's contracts. These refinements, in turn, allow programmers to rely on different extensions of a component's contracts when using it in different contexts.

Concretely, consider the interface *IPosQueue* and static method *ProcessManager* in figure 4. The interface limits the queue to contain only positive integers by adding a pre-condition to *enq* guaranteeing that its input is bigger than zero and a post-condition to *deq* promising that the result is bigger than zero. The static method *ProcessManager* accepts instances of *IPosQueue*. Clearly, the *Q* class satisfies the *IPosQueue* interface. Regardless, since interfaces must be declared when the class is declared, the code in figure 4 cannot be combined with the independently produced code in figure 2.

Programmers can work around this mismatch with several techniques, especially the adapter pattern. In this particular example, the programmer could derive a class from *Q* that inherits all the methods and superimposes the new, stronger contract interface. In general, however, the programmer that wishes to impose additional contracts to an object is not the programmer that originally created the object. In these other cases, a programmer may create an entirely new class that bridges the gap between the two components that are to be composed. No matter which solution the programmer chooses, however, the requirement to build and manually maintain an adapter, including error checking that catches and flags errors inside the adapter, is an obstacle to controlled composition of software. Worse, a programmer-produced mechanism for as-

```
interface IPosQueue {                    class QueueClient {
  void enq(int x);                         static void ProcessManager(IPosQueue q) {
  // @pre x > 0                              ...
  // @post !empty()                        }
                                         }
  int deq();
  // @pre !empty()
  // @post deq > 0

  boolean empty();
}
```

Fig. 4. Positive Queues, in a Separate Component

signing blame is ad-hoc and therefore less trustworthy than a mechanism designed into the programming language.

3 Contract Checking for Semantic Casts

The problem is that allowing contracts only in interfaces and classes means that each object supports only a fixed, pre-determined set of contracts, which prevents the direct use of a Q object as an *IPosQueue* object. To overcome this problem, we propose **semanticCast**, a new construct that allows programmers to cast an object to a structurally equivalent type.[1]

The shape of a **semanticCast** expression is:

[1] For the purposes of this paper, we treat **semanticCast** as a regular member of the programming language, to be written in programs at the programmer's whim. In fully integrated system, however, **semanticCast** expressions should only appear at component boundaries. For example, if Java's package system or some other form of module system were used to organize a program, **semanticCast** expressions should be inserted around each variable reference between modules. Abstractly, imagine that a module A refers to an export of module B, say $B.x$. The context of the variable reference expects it to match interface I but the actual type of the variable is a compatible, but different interface I'. The variable reference would be replaced by **semanticCast**($B.x$: I', I, "B", "A") allowing the user of the exported variable to refine the contracts in I' to I, while still ensuring that blame is properly assigned.

In a component model similar to Corba [36], components explicitly establish connections to each other via a function call protocol. To add contracts to this style of component system, **semanticCast** expressions would be added by the calls that establish the connections between the components.

Although each component system synthesizes **semanticCast** expressions in a different manner, all component systems can use some form of **semanticCast** expression. In essence, our intention is that a **semanticCast** expression *defines* the component boundaries, as far as our model is concerned. Accordinly, to understand its essence, we treat it as a feature in the programming language directly, with the understanding that it is only truly available to the programmer who implements the component mechanism.

semanticCast(*obj* : *t*, *Intf*, *in_str*, *out_str*)

It consists of four subexpressions: an object (annotated with its type), an interface, and two strings. The expression constructs an object that behaves like *obj*, except with type *Intf* (including the contracts in *Intf*). The typing rules guarantee that the type of *obj* has the same methods names and types as *Intf*, but does not require that *obj*'s class implements *Intf*, allowing *obj* to take on the contracts in *Intf*. In fact, the typing rules synthesize the type of *obj* from the context, but we include it explicitly here, for clarity. The string *in_str* represents the guilty party if *obj* is not treated as an *Intf* by the context, and the string *out_str* represents the guilty party if *o* itself does not behave according to the contracts in *Intf*. As a first approximation, *in_str* is blamed if a pre-condition in *Intf* is violated and *out_str* is blamed if a post-condition of *Intf* is violated.

Using **semanticCast**, we can now combine the code from figure 4 with the original *Q* class:

```
public static void Main(String argv[]) {
  Q q = new Q();
  IQueue iq = semanticCast(q : Q, IQueue, "Main", "Q");
  IPosQueue ipq = semanticCast(iq : IQueue, IPosQueue, "QueueClient", "Main");
  QueueClient.ProcessManager(ipq);
}
```

In the first line of its body, *Main* creates a *Q* object. In the second line, the **semanticCast** expression states that the new instance must behave according to the contracts in *IQueue*.[2] The third argument to **semanticCast** indicates that *Main* is responsible for any violations of *IQueue*'s pre-conditions. The fourth argument indicates that *Q* is responsible for any violations of *IQueue*'s post-conditions. The result of the first **semanticCast** is bound to *iq*.

In the third line, *Main* uses a **semanticCast** expression to add the contracts of *IPosQueue* to *iq*. The third argument to **semanticCast** indicates that *QueueClient* is responsible for pre-condition violations of the contracts in *IPosQueue*. The fourth argument to **semanticCast** indicates that *Main* is responsible for post-condition violations. The result of the second **semanticCast** expression is bound to *ipq*. Finally, in the fourth line, *ipq* is passed to *QueueClient.ProcessManager*.

Intuitively, the queue object itself is like the core of an onion, and each **semanticCast** expression corresponds to a layer of that onion. When a method is invoked, each layer of the onion is peeled back, and the corresponding pre-condition checked, to reveal the core. Upon reaching the core, the actual method is invoked. Once the method returns, the layers of the onion are restored as the post-condition checking occurs.

For instance, imagine that *QueueClient.ProcessManager* invokes its argument's *enq* method, with a positive number. First, the pre-condition on *enq* in *IPosQueue* is checked, since the last **semanticCast** expression added *IPosQueue*'s contracts to the

[2] Of course, the *Q* class declares that it implements the *IQueue* class and the contracts could have been compiled directly into its methods. Since we are focusing on semantic casts here, we assume that contracts are only checked with explicitly specified **semanticCast** expressions.

queue. The input is positive, so it passes. If it had failed, the blame would lie with the queue client. Next, that outer layer is peeled back to reveal an object that must meet *IQueue*'s contracts. Accordingly, the *enq* pre-condition in *IQueue* is checked. This pre-condition is empty, and thus trivially true. After removing this layer we reach the core, so the *enq* method in the *Q* class is invoked.

Once the *enq* method returns, its post-conditions are checked. First, the *enq* post-condition in *IQueue* is checked. If it fails, the blame lies with *Q*, since "Q" is the last argument to the innermost **semanticCast**. Assuming it succeeds, the post-condition on *enq* in *IPosQueue* is checked. If it fails, the blame lies with *Main*, since "Main" is the last argument to the outer **semanticCast** expression.

3.1 Supporting Positive Queues with Positive Observers

The code in figure 5 shows observers added to *IPosQueue*, mirroring the extension of the *IQueue* interface in figure 2. In addition to the *onEnq* and *onDeq* contracts from *IObserver*, the integer argument to both *onEnq* and *onDeq* is guaranteed to be positive.

```
interface IPosObserver {
  void onEnq(IPosQueue q, int x);
  // @pre x > 0
  // @post !q.empty()

  void onDeq(IPosQueue q, int x);
  // @pre x > 0
  // @pre !q.empty()
}
```

```
interface IPosQueue {
  ⋮
  void registerObs(IPosObserver o);
}
```

Fig. 5. Positive Queue with Observer

Imagine that the body of the *QueueClient.ProcessManager* static method creates an instance of some class that implements the *IPosObserver* interface and passes that object to the *registerObs* method of its argument:

```
class QueueClient {
  ⋮
  static void ProcessManager(IPosQueue ipq) {
    IPosObserver po = new ProcessObserver();
    ipq.registerObs(po);
    ipq.enq(5);
  }
}
```

Adding observers to the positive queue triggers additional, indirect contract obligations on the code that casts the queue object to a positive queue. To understand how the indirect contracts are induced and who should be blamed if they fail, let us examine the sequence of steps that occur when *ipq.enq* is invoked in the body of *ProcessManager*. There are five key steps:

(1) *ipq.enq(5)*

⋮

(2) test *IPosQueue* pre-condition, blame *QueueClient* if failure

⋮

(3) *q.enq(5)*

⋮

(4) *po.onEnq(q,5)*

⋮

(5) test *IPosObserver* pre-condition, blame *Main* if failure.

In the first step, *ipq.enq* is invoked, with *5* as an argument. This immediately triggers a check of the *IPosQueue* pre-condition, according to the contract added in *Main*. The contract check succeeds because *5* is a positive number. If, however, the check had failed, blame would lie with *QueueClient* because *QueueClient* supplied the argument to *ipq*.

Next, in step three, the original *IQueue* object's *enq* method is invoked, which performs the actual work of enqueing the object into the queue. As part of this work, it calls the observer (recall figure 2). In this case, *QueueClient* registered the object *po* with the queue, so *po.onEnq* is invoked with the queue and with the integer that was just enqueued.

Since the observer is an *IPosObserver* object, its pre-condition must be established, namely the argument must be a positive number. Because the *Q* class's *enq* method supplies its input to *onEnq*, we know that the contract succeeds at this point. The interesting question, however, is who should be blamed if *Q* had negated the number and passed it to the observer, forcing the *onEnq* contract to fail.

Clearly, *Q* must not be blamed for a failure to establish this pre-condition, since *Q* did not declare that it meets the contracts in the *IPosQueue* interface and, in fact, *IPosQueue* was defined after *Q*. Additionally, *QueueClient* must not be blamed. It only agreed to enqueue positive integers into the queue; if the queue object mis-manages the positive integers before they arrive at the observer, this cannot be *QueueClient*'s fault.

That leaves *Main*. In fact, *Main* should be blamed if the *IPosObserver* object does not receive a positive integer, since *Main* declared that instances of *Q* behave like *IPosQueue* objects knowing that these objects must respect *IPosObserver*'s contracts. Put another way, if the *Q* class had declared it implemented the *IPosQueue* interface, it would have been responsible for the pre-conditions of *IPosQueue*. Accordingly, by casting an instance of *Q* to *IPosQueue*, *Main* is promising that *Q* does indeed live up to the contracts in *IPosQueue*, so *Main* must be blamed if *Q* fails to do so.

More generally, since objects have higher-order behavior, the third and fourth arguments to **semanticCast** do not merely represent who to blame for pre- and post-condition violations of the object with the contract. Instead, the last argument to a **semanticCast** expression indicates who is to blame for any contract that is violated as a value flows *out* of the object with the contract, whether the value flows out as a result of a method or flows out by calling a method of an object passed into the original object. Conversely, the third argument to a **semanticCast** expression indicates who is to blame for any contract that is violated as a value flows *in* to the object, no matter if the bad value flows in by calling a method, or via a callback that returns the bad value.

This suggests that the casted objects must propagate contracts to method arguments and method results, when those arguments or results are themselves objects. The following equation roughly governs how **semanticCast** expressions propagate (assuming that the immediate pre and post-conditions are satisfied):

semanticCast(*o*: *I*, *J*, *in_str*, *out_str*).*m*(*x*)
=
semanticCast(*o*.*m*(**semanticCast**(*x* : *C*, *D*, *out_str*, *in_str*)) : *B*,
C,
in_str,
out_str)

if *I* and *J* have these shapes:

```
interface I {          interface J {
  B m(D x);              C m(C x);
}                      }
```

and *B* is a subtype of *C*, which is a subtype of *D*.

Informally, the equation says that when a method *m* of an objected casted to *I* is invoked, the cast is distributed to *m*'s argument and *m*'s result. Further, the distribution is based on *m*'s signature in *I*.

Notice that the blame strings are reversed in the cast around the argument object and stay in the same order in the cast around the result. This captures the difference between values that flow into and out of the object. That is, if a value flows into the argument object, it is flowing out of the original object and if a value flows out of the argument object, it is flowing into the original object. In contrast, when the context invokes methods on the result (assuming it is an object), the sense of the blame is like the original. The reversal corresponds to the standard notion of contra-variance for method or function arguments.

4 Calculus

This section presents a calculus for a core sequential Java (without reflection), enriched with **semanticCast** expressions, and it gives meaning to the semantic cast expressions via a translation to the calculus without them.

For familiarity, this paper builds on our model of Java [10, 16], but the core ideas carry over to any class-based object-oriented language, including C++, C#, Eiffel, or even MzScheme's class-based object system.

```
      P ::= defn* e

   defn ::= class c extends c
                implements i*
              { fld* mth* }
            | interface i extends i*
              { imth* }

    fld ::= t fd
    mth ::= t md ( arg* ) { body }
   imth ::= t md ( arg* )
            @pre { e }
            @post { e }
    arg ::= t var
   body ::= e | abstract

      e ::= new c | var | null
            | e.fd | e.fd = e
            | e.md (e*)
            | super.md (e*)
            | view t e
            | e instanceof i
            | let { binding* } in e
            | if ( e ) e else e
            | true | false
            | e == e
            | e || e | ! e
            | { e ; e }
            | str
            | semanticCast(e, i, e, e)
binding ::= var = e
    var ::= a variable name or this
      c ::= a class name or Object
      i ::= interface name or Empty
     fd ::= a field name
     md ::= a method name
    str ::= "a" | "ab" | ...
      t ::= i | boolean | String
```

(a) Surface Syntax

```
      P ::= defn* e

   defn ::= class c extends c
                implements i*
              { fld* mth* }
            | interface i extends i*
              { imth* }

    fld ::= t fd
    mth ::= t md ( arg* ) { body }
   imth ::= t md ( arg* )
            @pre { e }
            @post { e }
    arg ::= t var
   body ::= e | abstract

      e ::= new c | var | null
            | e : c .fd | e : c .fd = e
            | e.md (e*)
            | super≡this:c.md (e* )
            | view t e
            | e instanceof i
            | let { binding* } in e
            | if ( e ) e else e
            | true | false
            | e == e
            | e || e | ! e
            | { e ; e }
            | str
            | semanticCast
              (e : i, i, e, e)
binding ::= var = e
    var ::= a variable name or this
      c ::= a class name or Object
      i ::= interface name or Empty
     fd ::= a field name
     md ::= a method name
    str ::= "a" | "ab" | ...
      t ::= i | boolean | String
```

(b) Typed Contract Syntax

```
      P ::= defn* e

   defn ::= class c extends c
                implements i*
              { fld* mth* }
            | interface i extends i*
              { imth* }

    fld ::= t fd
    mth ::= t md ( arg* ) { body }
   imth ::= t md ( arg* )

    arg ::= t var
   body ::= e | abstract

      e ::= new c | var | null
            | e : c .fd | e : c .fd = e
            | e.md (e*)
            | super≡this:c.md (e* )
            | view t e
            | e instanceof i
            | let { binding* } in e
            | if ( e ) e else e
            | true | false
            | e == e
            | e || e | ! e
            | { e ; e }
            | str
            | blame(e)
binding ::= var = e
    var ::= a variable name or this
      c ::= a class name or Object
      i ::= interface name or Empty
     fd ::= a field name
     md ::= a method name
    str ::= "a" | "ab" | ...
      t ::= i | boolean | String
```

(c) Core Syntax

Fig. 6. Syntax; before and after contracts are compiled away

4.1 Syntax

Figure 6 contains the syntax for our enriched Java. The syntax is divided into three parts. Programmers use syntax (a) to write their programs. The type checker elaborates syntax (a) to syntax (b), which contains type annotations for use by the evaluator. The contract compiler elaborates syntax (b) to syntax (c). It elaborates the pre- and post-conditions and **semanticCast** expressions into monitoring code; the result is accepted by the evaluator for plain Java.

A program P is a sequence of class and interface definitions followed by an expression that represents the body of the *main* method. Each class definition consists of a sequence of field declarations followed by a sequence of method declarations. An interface consists of method specifications and their contracts. The contracts are arbitrary Java expressions that have type **boolean**. To simplify the model, we do not allow classes as types. This is not a true restriction to Java, however, since each class can be viewed as (implicitly) defining a interface based on its method signatures. This interface can be used everywhere the class was used as a type.

A method body in a class can be **abstract**, indicating that the method must be overridden in a subclass before the class is instantiated. Unlike in Java, the body of a method is just an expression whose result is the result of the method. Like in Java, classes are instantiated with the **new** operator, but there are no class constructors; instance variables are initialized to **null**. The **view** form represents Java's casting expressions and **instanceof** tests if an object has membership in a particular type. The **let** forms represent the capability for binding variables locally. The **if** expressions test the value of the first expression, if it is **true** the **if** expression results in the value of the second subexpression and if it is **false** the **if** expression results in the value of the third subexpression.[3] The == operator compares objects by their location in the heap. The || and ! operators are the boolean operations disjunction and negation, respectively. Expressions of the form { e ; e } are used for sequencing. The first expression is executed for its effect and the result of the entire expression is the result of the second expression. Finally, *str* stands for the string literals.

The expressions following **@pre** and **@post** in a method interface declaration are the pre- and post-conditions for that method, respectively. The method's argument variables are bound in both the expressions and the name of the method is bound to the result of calling the method, but only in the post-condition expression.

In the code fragments presented in this paper, we use several shorthands. We omit the **extends** and **implements** clauses when nothing would appear after them. We write sequencing expressions such as { e_1 ; e_2 ; e_3 ; ... } to stand for { e_1 ; {e_2 ; {e_3 ; ... }}} and sometimes add extra {} to indicate grouping. For field declarations, we write $t\ fd_1, fd_2$ to stand for $t\ fd_1$; $t\ fd_2$.

The type checker translates syntax (a) to syntax (b). It inserts additional information (underlined in the figure) to be used by the evaluator. In particular, field update and field reference are annotated with the class containing the field, and calls to **super** are annotated with the class.

The contract compiler produces syntax (c) and the evaluator accepts it. The **@pre** and **@post** conditions are removed from interfaces, and inserted into wrapper classes. Syntax (c) also adds the **blame** construct to the language, which is used to signal contract violations. This construct is only available to the programmer indirectly via the compilation process, to preserve the integrity of blame assignment (assuming correct synthesis of blame strings for **semanticCast**).

4.2 Relations and Predicates

A valid program satisfies a number of simple predicates and relations; these are described in figures 7 and 8. The sets of names for variables, classes, interfaces, fields, and methods are assumed to be mutually distinct. The meta-variable T is used for method signatures ($t \ldots \longrightarrow t$), V for variable lists ($var\ldots$), and Γ for environments mapping variables to types. Ellipses on the baseline (...) indicate a repeated pattern or contin-

[3] The **if** in our calculus matches e ? e : e expressions in Java, rather than Java's **if** statements.

$\prec^c_P$ Class is declared as an immediate subclass

$$c \prec^c_P c' \Leftrightarrow \textbf{class } c \textbf{ extends } c' \cdots \{ \cdots \} \text{ is in } P$$

$\leq^c_P$ Class is a subclass

$$\leq^c_P \equiv \text{the transitive, reflexive closure of } \prec^c_P$$

$\in^c_P$ Method is declared in class

$$\langle md, (t_1 \ldots t_n \longrightarrow t), (var_1 \ldots var_n), e\rangle \in^c_P c$$
$$\Leftrightarrow \textbf{class } c \cdots \{ \cdots t\ md\ (t_1\ var_1 \ldots t_n\ var_n)\ \{e\} \cdots \} \text{ is in } P$$

$\in^c_P$ Method is contained in a class

$$\langle md, T, V, e\rangle \in^c_P c$$
$$\Leftrightarrow (\langle md, T, V, e\rangle \in^c_P c' \text{ and } c' = \min\{c'' \mid c \leq^c_P c'' \text{ and } \exists e', V' \text{ s.t. } \langle md, T, V', e'\rangle \in^c_P c''\})$$

$\in^c_P$ Field is declared in a class

$$\langle c.fd, t\rangle \in^c_P c \Leftrightarrow \textbf{class } c \cdots \{ \cdots t\ fd \cdots \} \text{ is in } P$$

$\in^c_P$ Field is contained in a class

$$\langle c'.fd, t\rangle \in^c_P c$$
$$\Leftrightarrow \langle c'.fd, t\rangle \in^c_P c' \text{ and } c' = \min\{c'' \mid c \leq^c_P c'' \text{ and } \exists t' \text{ s.t. } \langle c''.fd, t'\rangle \in^c_P c''\}$$

$\prec_P$ Interface is declared as an immediate subinterface

$$i \prec_P i' \Leftrightarrow \textbf{interface } i \textbf{ extends} \cdots i' \cdots \{ \cdots \} \text{ is in } P$$

$\leq_P$ Interface is a subinterface

$$\leq_P \equiv \text{the transitive, reflexive closure of } \prec_P$$

$\in^i_P$ Method is declared in an interface

$$\langle md, (t_1 \ldots t_n \longrightarrow t), (var_1 \ldots var_n), e_b, e_a\rangle \in^i_P i$$
$$\Leftrightarrow \textbf{interface } i \cdots \{ \cdots t\ md(t_1\ var_1, \ldots t_n\ var_n)\ \textbf{@pre}\ \{ e_b \}\ \textbf{@post}\ \{ e_a \} \cdots \} \text{ is in } P$$

$\in^i_P$ Method is contained in an interface

$$\langle md, T, V, e_b, e_a\rangle \in^i_P i \Leftrightarrow \exists i' \text{ s.t. } i \leq_P i' \text{ and } \langle md, T, V, e_b, e_a\rangle \in^i_P i'$$

$\in_P$ Field or Method is in a type (method/interface)

$$\langle md, T\rangle \in_P i \Leftrightarrow \exists V, e_b, e_a \text{ s.t.} \langle md, T, V, e_b, e_a\rangle \in^i_P i$$

$\in_P$ Field or Method is in a type (field/type)

$$\langle c.fd, t\rangle \in_P c \Leftrightarrow \langle c.fd, t\rangle \in^c_P c$$

$\prec^c_P$ Class declares implementation of an interface

$$c \prec^c_P i \Leftrightarrow \textbf{class } c \cdots \textbf{implements} \cdots i \cdots \{ \cdots \} \text{ is in } P$$

$\ll^c_P$ Class implements an interface

$$c \ll^c_P i \Leftrightarrow \exists c', i' \text{ s.t. } c \leq^c_P c' \text{ and } i' \leq_P i \text{ and } c' \prec^c_P i'$$

$\otimes_P$ Structural subtyping for interfaces

$$i \otimes_P i' \Leftrightarrow$$
$$\forall \langle md, T, V, e_b, e_a\rangle \in^i_P i', \exists \langle md, T', V', e'_b, e'_a\rangle \in^i_P i, \text{ such that } T \circledast_P T'$$

$\otimes_P$ Structural subtyping for other types

$$\textbf{String} \otimes_P \textbf{String} \qquad \textbf{boolean} \otimes_P \textbf{boolean}$$

$\circledast_P$ Structural subtyping for method type specifications

$$t_1 \ldots t_n \longrightarrow t \circledast_P t'_1 \ldots t'_n \longrightarrow t' \Leftrightarrow t'_1 \otimes_P t_1, \ldots, t'_n \otimes_P t_n, t \otimes_P t'$$

Fig. 7. Relations on enriched Java programs

ued sequence, while centered ellipses ($\cdots$) indicate arbitrary missing program text (not spanning a class or interface definition).

Figure 7 is separated into four groups: relations for classes, relations for interfaces, relations that relate classes and interfaces, and finally the structural subtyping relations. As an example relation, the ClassesOnce(P) predicate states that each class name is defined at most once in the program P. The relation $\prec^c_P$ associates each class name in P to the class it extends, and the (overloaded) $\in^c_P$ relations capture the field and method declarations of the classes in P.

The syntax-summarizing relations induce a second set of relations and predicates that summarize the class structure of a program. The first of these is the subclass relation $\leq^c_P$, which is a partial order if the CompleteClasses(P) predicate holds and the WellFoundedClasses(P) predicate holds. In this case, the classes declared in P form a tree that has **Object** at its root.

ClassesOnce(P) — Each class name is declared only once

$$\textbf{class } c \cdots \textbf{class } c' \cdots \text{ is in } P \Longrightarrow c \neq c'$$

FieldOncePerClass(P) — Field names in each class declaration are unique

$$\textbf{class} \cdots \{ \cdots fd \cdots fd' \cdots \} \text{ is in } P \Longrightarrow fd \neq fd'$$

MethodOncePerClass(P) — Method names in each class declaration are unique

$$\textbf{class} \cdots \{ \cdots md\,(\cdots)\,\{ \cdots \} \cdots md'\,(\cdots)\,\{ \cdots \} \cdots \} \text{ is in } P \Longrightarrow md \neq md'$$

InterfacesOnce(P) — Each interface name is declared only once

$$\textbf{interface } i \cdots \textbf{interface } i' \cdots \text{ is in } P \Longrightarrow i \neq i'$$

MethodArgsDistinct(P) — Each method argment name is unique

$$md\,(t_1\ var_1 \ldots t_n\ var_n)\,\{ \cdots \} \text{ is in } P \Longrightarrow var_1, \ldots var_n, \text{ and } \mathit{this} \text{ are distinct}$$

CompleteClasses(P) — Classes that are extended are defined

$$\mathrm{rng}(\prec^c_P) \subseteq \mathrm{dom}(\prec^c_P) \cup \{\textbf{Object}\}$$

WellFoundedClasses(P) — Class hierarchy is an order

$$\leq^c_P \text{ is antisymmetric}$$

ClassMethodsOK(P) — Method overriding preserves the type

$$(\langle md, T, V, e\rangle \in^c_P c \text{ and } \langle md, T', V', e'\rangle \in^c_P c') \Longrightarrow (T = T' \text{ or } c \nleq^c_P c')$$

CompleteInterfaces(P) — Extended/implemented interfaces are defined

$$\mathrm{rng}(\prec_P) \cup \mathrm{rng}(\lessdot^c_P) \subseteq \mathrm{dom}(\prec_P) \cup \{\textbf{Empty}\}$$

WellFoundedInterfaces(P) — Interface hierarchy is an order

$$\leq_P \text{ is antisymmetric}$$

InterfaceMethodsOK(P) — Interface inheritance or redeclaration of methods is consistent

$$\langle md, T, V, e_b, e_a\rangle \in^i_P i \text{ and } \langle md, T', V', e'_b, e'_a\rangle \in^i_P i' \Longrightarrow (T = T' \text{ or } \forall i''(i'' \nleq_P i \text{ or } i'' \nleq_P i'))$$

ClassesImplementAll(P) — Classes supply methods to implement interfaces

$$c \lessdot^c_P i \Longrightarrow (\forall md, T\ \langle md, T, V, e_b, e_a\rangle \in^i_P i \Longrightarrow \exists e, V' \text{ s.t. } \langle md, T, V', e\rangle \in^c_P c)$$

Fig. 8. Predicates on enriched Java programs

If the program describes a tree of classes, we can associate each class in the tree with the collection of fields and methods that it accumulates from local declarations and inheritance. The source declaration of any field or method in a class can be computed by finding the *minimum* superclass (*i.e.*, farthest from the root) that declares the field or method. This algorithm is described precisely by the $\in^c_P$ relations. The $\in^c_P$ relation retains information about the source class of each field, but it does not retain the source class for a method. This reflects the property of Java classes that fields cannot be overridden (so instances of a subclass always contain the field), while methods can be overridden (and may become inaccessible).

Interfaces have a similar set of relations. The subinterface declaration relation $\prec_P$ induces a subinterface relation $\leq_P$. Unlike classes, a single interface can have multiple proper superinterfaces, so the subinterface order forms a DAG instead of a tree. The set of methods of an interface, as described by $\in^i_P$, is the union of the interface's declared methods and the methods of its superinterfaces. Classes and interfaces are related by **implements** declarations, as captured in the $\lessdot^c_P$ relation.

The structural subtyping predicate $\circledcirc_P$ relates types in a structural manner. The base types **boolean** and **String** are only related to themselves. Two interface types are related if one has a subset of the methods of the other and the corresponding method arguments and result are related. Note that the relation is contra-variant for method arguments and co-variant for method results.

The type system uses $\circledcirc_P$ to ensure that **semanticCast** expressions are well-formed.

4.3 Types

Type elaboration is defined by the following judgments:

$\vdash_{\mathsf{p}} P \Rightarrow P' : t$	P elaborates to P' with type t
$P \vdash_{\mathsf{d}} \mathit{defn} \Rightarrow \mathit{defn}'$	*defn* elaborates to *defn′*
$P, c \vdash_{\mathsf{m}} \mathit{mth} \Rightarrow \mathit{mth}'$	*mth* in c elaborates to *mth′*
$P, i \vdash_{\mathsf{i}} \mathit{imth} \Rightarrow \mathit{imth}'$	*imth* in i elaborates to *imth′*
$P, \Gamma \vdash_{\mathsf{e}} e \Rightarrow e' : t$	e elaborates to e' with type t in Γ
$P, \Gamma \vdash_{\mathsf{s}} e \Rightarrow e' : t$	e elaborates to e' with type t in Γ, using subsumption
$P \vdash_{\mathsf{t}} t$	t is a well-formed type in P

Type elaboration for complete programs ensures that the properties described in the previous section hold for the complete program and ensures that each subexpression in the program is properly typed. Type checking for classes and interface definitions merely ensures that each expression mentioned in each method is properly typed and that the types written in the method specifications are well-formed and that the method specifications match up with the bodies of the methods.

For each form of expression, the intended use dictates the types of its constituents. For example, the arguments to || and ! must be booleans. Similarly, the type of the first subexpression of **if** must be a boolean and the types of the two branches must match. There are four places where subsumption is allowed: at field assignment, method invocations (for the arguments), super calls, and, of course, **view** expressions. These correspond to the places where implicit or explicit casts occur. These rules are the same as in our prior work [16] and many are omitted here.

The typing rule for interface methods ensures that pre- and post-conditions use appropriate variables and have type boolean. The typing rule for **semanticCast** ensures that the last two arguments are both strings and that the first argument is an object. Further, the static type of the object must have the same structure as the type in the second argument, as determined by the $\otimes_P$ relation.

4.4 Contract Compilation

The contract compiler eliminates **semanticCast** expressions from the program and inserts **blame** expressions. The **blame** expression is a primitive mechanism that, when evaluated, aborts the program and assigns blame to a specific **semanticCast** for a contract violation.

The contract compiler, $C[\![\cdot]\!]$, is defined by the following judgments:

$C[\![P]\!] = P'$ if $\vdash_{\mathsf{p}} P \rightharpoonup P'$

$\vdash_{\mathsf{p}} P \rightharpoonup P'$	P elaborates to P'
$\vdash_{\mathsf{d}} \mathit{defn}, \mathit{defs} \rightharpoonup \mathit{defn}', \mathit{defs}'$	*defn* elaborates to *defn′* extending *defs* to *defs′*
$\vdash_{\mathsf{b}} \mathit{body}, \mathit{defs} \rightharpoonup \mathit{body}', \mathit{defs}'$	*body* elaborates to *body′* extending *defs* to *defs′*
$\vdash_{\mathsf{e}} e, \mathit{defs} \rightharpoonup e', \mathit{defs}'$	e elaborates to e' extending *defs* to *defs′*

The $\vdash_{\mathsf{p}}$ judgment rewrites a complete program from the second syntax in figure 6 to the third syntax. The other three judgments rewrite definitions, bodies, and expressions,

$\vdash_p$

$$\frac{\mathrm{ClassesOnce}(P)\ \ \mathrm{InterfacesOnce}(P)\ \ \mathrm{MethodOncePerClass}(P)\ \ \mathrm{FieldOncePerClass}(P)\ \ \mathrm{CompleteClasses}(P)\ \ \mathrm{WellFoundedClasses}(P)\ \ \mathrm{CompleteInterfaces}(P)\ \ \mathrm{WellFoundedInterfaces}(P)\ \ \mathrm{InterfaceMethodsOK}(P)\ \ \mathrm{MethodArgsDistinct}(P)\ \ \mathrm{ClassesImplementAll}(P)\ \ P \vdash_d defn_j \Rightarrow defn'_j \text{ for } j \in [1,n]\ \ P,[\,] \vdash_e e \Rightarrow e' : t \ \ \text{where } P = defn_1 \ldots defn_n\ e}{\vdash_p defn_1 \ldots defn_n\ e \Rightarrow defn'_1 \ldots defn'_n\ e' : t}$$

$\vdash_d$

$$\frac{P \vdash_t t_j \text{ for } j \in [1,n] \qquad P, c \vdash_m mth_k \Rightarrow mth'_k \text{ for } k \in [1,p]}{P \vdash_d \textbf{class}\ c \cdots \{\ t_1\ fd_1 \ldots t_n\ fd_n\ mth_1 \ldots mth_p\ \} \Rightarrow \textbf{class}\ c \cdots \{\ t_1\ fd_1 \ldots t_n\ fd_n\ mth'_1 \ldots mth'_p\ \}}$$

$$\frac{P \vdash_i imth_j \Rightarrow imth_j \text{ for } j \in [1,p]}{P, i \vdash_d \textbf{interface}\ i \cdots \{\ imth_1 \ldots imth_p\ \} \Rightarrow \textbf{interface}\ i \cdots \{\ imth_1 \ldots imth_p\ \}}$$

$\vdash_m$

$$\frac{P \vdash_t t \qquad P \vdash_t t_j \text{ for } j \in [1,n] \qquad P,[this : t_o, var_1 : t_1, \ldots var_n : t_n] \vdash_s e \Rightarrow e' : t}{P, t_o \vdash_m t\ md\ (t_1\ var_1 \ldots t_n\ var_n)\ \{\ e\ \} \Rightarrow t\ md\ (t_1\ var_1 \ldots t_n\ var_n)\ \{\ e'\ \}}$$

$$\frac{P \vdash_t t \qquad P \vdash_t t_j \text{ for } j \in [1,n]}{P, t_o \vdash_m t\ md\ (t_1\ var_1 \ldots t_n\ var_n)\ \{\ \textbf{abstract}\ \} \Rightarrow t\ md\ (t_1\ var_1 \ldots t_n\ var_n)\ \{\ \textbf{abstract}\ \}}$$

$\vdash_i$

$$\frac{\begin{array}{ll} P \vdash_t t & P,[this : i, var_1 : t_1, \ldots var_n : t_n] \vdash_e e_b \Rightarrow e'_b : \textbf{boolean} \\ P \vdash_t t_j \text{ for } j \in [1,n] & P,[this : i, md : t, var_1 : t_1, \ldots var_n : t_n] \vdash_e e_a \Rightarrow e'_a : \textbf{boolean} \end{array}}{\begin{array}{ll} P, i \vdash_i t\ md\ (t_1\ arg_1 \ldots t_n\ arg_n) & \Rightarrow t\ md\ (t_1\ arg_1 \ldots t_n\ arg_n) \\ \quad \textbf{@pre}\ \{\ e_b\ \} & \quad \textbf{@pre}\ \{\ e'_b\ \} \\ \quad \textbf{@post}\ \{\ e_a\ \} & \quad \textbf{@post}\ \{\ e'_a\ \} \end{array}}$$

$\vdash_e$

$$\frac{P,\Gamma \vdash_s e \Rightarrow e' : t}{P,\Gamma \vdash_e \textbf{view}\ t\ e \Rightarrow e' : t} \qquad \frac{P,\Gamma \vdash_e e \Rightarrow e' : t' \qquad t \in \mathrm{dom}(<_P) \cup \{\textbf{Empty}\}}{P,\Gamma \vdash_e \textbf{view}\ t\ e \Rightarrow \textbf{view}\ t\ e' : t}$$

$$\frac{P,\Gamma \vdash_s e \Rightarrow e' : t}{P,\Gamma \vdash_e e\ \textbf{instanceof}\ t \Rightarrow \{e'\ ;\ \textbf{true}\} : \textbf{boolean}} \qquad \frac{P,\Gamma \vdash_e e \Rightarrow e' : t' \qquad t \in \mathrm{dom}(<_P) \cup \{\textbf{Empty}\}}{P,\Gamma \vdash_e e\ \textbf{instanceof}\ t \Rightarrow e'\ \textbf{instanceof}\ t : \textbf{boolean}}$$

$$\frac{P,\Gamma \vdash_e pos \Rightarrow pos' : \textbf{String} \qquad P,\Gamma \vdash_e neg \Rightarrow neg' : \textbf{String} \qquad P,\Gamma \vdash_e e \Rightarrow e' : t' \qquad t' \circledless_P t}{P,\Gamma \vdash_e \textbf{semanticCast}(e, t, pos, neg) \Rightarrow \textbf{semanticCast}(e' : t', t, pos', neg') : t}$$

$\vdash_s, \vdash_t$

$$\frac{P,\Gamma \vdash_s e \Rightarrow e' : t' \qquad t' \leq_P t}{P,\Gamma \vdash_e e \Rightarrow e' : t} \qquad \frac{t \in \mathrm{dom}(<_P) \cup \{\textbf{Empty}, \textbf{boolean}, \textbf{String}\}}{P \vdash_t t}$$

Fig. 9. Context-sensitive checks and type elaboration rules

respectively. Each accepts a term and a set of definitions and produces the rewritten term and a new set of definitions.

The rules for the judgements are given in figures 10 and 11. The rule for $\vdash_p$ rewrites the definitions and expressions in the program, threading the sets of definitions through the rewriting of the subterms. Its result is the rewritten definitions and expressions, combined with the final set of threaded definitions. With the exception of the rule for **semanticCast**, all of the other rules produces the same term they accept, carrying forward the definitions sets from their subexpressions.

The **semanticCast** rule for booleans and strings merely removes the semantic cast. For interfaces, however, it adds the elaborated definition for the class *Cast_i'_i* to the

$\vdash_p$

$$\frac{\vdash_e e, \emptyset \rightharpoonup e', defs_0 \qquad \vdash_d defn_j, defs_{j-1} \rightharpoonup defn'_j, defs_j \text{ for } j \in [1,n]}{P \vdash_d defn_1 \ldots defn_n\ e \rightharpoonup defs_n\ defn'_1 \ldots defn'_n\ e'}$$

$\vdash_d$

$$\vdash_b e_j, defs_{j-1} \rightharpoonup e'_j, defs_j \text{ for } j \in [1,n]$$

```
P ⊢d class c ··· {                                    , defs0 ⇀ class c ··· {                                        , defsn
       fld ...                                                   fld ...
       t md(t11 x11 ... t1j x1j) { e1 } ...                      t md(t11 x11 ... t1j x1j) { e'1 } ...
       t md(tn1 xn1 ... tnj xnj) { en }                          t md(tn1 xn1 ... tnj xnj) { e'n }
     }                                                         }
```

```
⊢d interface i extends i' ··· {                  , defs ⇀ interface i extends i' ··· { , defs
      t md(t1 x1 ... tn xn)                                  t md(t1 x1 ... tn xn) ...
          @pre { e_b } @post { e_a } ...                   }
   }
```

$\vdash_b$

$$\frac{}{\vdash_b \textbf{abstract}, defs \rightharpoonup \textbf{abstract}, defs} \qquad \frac{\vdash_e e, defs \rightharpoonup e', defs'}{\vdash_b e, defs \rightharpoonup e', defs'}$$

Fig. 10. Contract Elaboration, part 1

set of definitions it produces (without duplication), and replaces the semantic cast with code that creates and initializes an instance of *Cast_i'_i*.

Figure 12 shows the full definition of the *Cast_i'_i* classes, where the interfaces *i'* and *i* match the interface schemas shown. The class contains all of the methods of *i*, plus three instance variables. Two instance variables are strings representing the classes that are to be blamed for values flowing in to and out of the object, respectively. The other instance variable holds the unwrapped object. Whenever a method is called through the wrapper object, the following tasks are performed:

- The pre-condition contract is checked and *inBlame* is blamed if it fails.
- All of the arguments are wrapped, according to their types.
- The method of the unwrapped object is invoked with the newly wrapped arguments and the result is stored in a variable with the same name as the method.
- The post-condition contract is checked and *outBlame* is blamed if it fails.
- The result of the unwrapped call is wrapped according to the result type of the method and the new wrapper object is the result of the method.

Note that the wrapper classes contain **semanticCast** expressions. Thus, compiling these expressions generates new classes. This means that an implementation of the contract compiler must not generate new classes for each occurrence of **semanticCast** it encounters, or it would not terminate. Instead, it is must only generate one *Cast_i'_i* class for each unique pair of interfaces, *i'* and *i*.

4.5 Operational Semantics

The operational semantics is defined as a contextual rewriting system on pairs of expressions and stores [16, 47]. Each evaluation rule has this shape:

$\vdash_{e}$

$$\frac{}{\vdash_{e} \textbf{new}\ c,\ \mathit{defs} \rightharpoonup \textbf{new}\ c,\ \mathit{defs}} \qquad \frac{}{\vdash_{e} \mathit{var},\ \mathit{defs} \rightharpoonup \mathit{var},\ \mathit{defs}} \qquad \frac{}{\vdash_{e} \textbf{null},\ \mathit{defs} \rightharpoonup \textbf{null},\ \mathit{defs}}$$

$$\frac{\vdash_{e} e,\ \mathit{defs} \rightharpoonup e',\ \mathit{defs}'}{\vdash_{e} e : c\ .\mathit{fd},\ \mathit{defs} \rightharpoonup e' : c\ .\mathit{fd},\ \mathit{defs}'} \qquad \frac{\vdash_{e} e,\ \mathit{defs} \rightharpoonup e',\ \mathit{defs}' \qquad \vdash_{e} e_v,\ \mathit{defs}' \rightharpoonup e'_v,\ \mathit{defs}''}{\vdash_{e} e : c\ .\mathit{fd} = e_v,\ \mathit{defs} \rightharpoonup e' : c\ .\mathit{fd} = e'_v,\ \mathit{defs}''}$$

$$\frac{\vdash_{e} e,\ \mathit{defs} \rightharpoonup e',\ \mathit{defs}_0 \qquad \vdash_{e} e_j,\ \mathit{defs}_{j-1} \rightharpoonup e'_j,\ \mathit{defs}_j \text{ for } j \in [1,n]}{\vdash_{e} e : c\ .\mathit{md}\ (e_1 \ldots e_n),\ \mathit{defs} \rightharpoonup e' : c\ .\mathit{md}\ (e'_1 \ldots e'_n),\ \mathit{defs}_n}$$

$$\frac{\vdash_{e} e_j,\ \mathit{defs}_{j-1} \rightharpoonup e'_j,\ \mathit{defs}_j \text{ for } j \in [1,n]}{\vdash_{e} \textbf{super}{\equiv}\mathit{this}{:}c.\mathit{md}(e_1 \ldots e_n),\ t \rightharpoonup \mathit{defs}_0,\ \textbf{super}{\equiv}\mathit{this}{:}c.\mathit{md}(e'_1 \ldots e'_n)\ \mathit{defs}_n}$$

$$\frac{\vdash_{e} e,\ \mathit{defs} \rightharpoonup e',\ \mathit{defs}'}{\vdash_{e} \textbf{view}\ t\ e,\ \mathit{defs} \rightharpoonup \textbf{view}\ t\ e',\ \mathit{defs}'} \qquad \frac{\vdash_{e} e,\ \mathit{defs} \rightharpoonup e',\ \mathit{defs}'}{\vdash_{e} e\ \textbf{instanceof}\ t,\ \mathit{defs} \rightharpoonup e'\ \textbf{instanceof}\ t,\ \mathit{defs}'}$$

$$\frac{\vdash_{e} e_1,\ \mathit{defs} \rightharpoonup e'_1,\ \mathit{defs}' \qquad \vdash_{e} e_2,\ \mathit{defs}' \rightharpoonup e'_2,\ \mathit{defs}''}{\vdash_{e} e_1 == e_2,\ \mathit{defs} \rightharpoonup e'_1 == e'_2,\ \mathit{defs}''}$$

$$\frac{\vdash_{e} e,\ \mathit{defs} \rightharpoonup e',\ \mathit{defs}_0 \qquad \vdash_{e} e_j,\ \mathit{defs}_{j-1} \rightharpoonup e'_j,\ \mathit{defs}_j \text{ for } j \in [1,n]}{\vdash_{e} \textbf{let}\ \{\ \mathit{var}_1 = e_1 \ldots \mathit{var}_n = e_n\ \}\ \textbf{in}\ e,\ \mathit{defs} \rightharpoonup \textbf{let}\ \{\ \mathit{var}_1 = e'_1 \ldots \mathit{var}_n = e'_n\ \}\ \textbf{in}\ e',\ \mathit{defs}_n}$$

$$\frac{}{\vdash_{e} \textbf{true},\ \mathit{defs} \rightharpoonup \textbf{true},\ \mathit{defs}} \qquad \frac{}{\vdash_{e} \textbf{false},\ \mathit{defs} \rightharpoonup \textbf{false},\ \mathit{defs}} \qquad \frac{}{\vdash_{e} \mathit{str},\ \mathit{defs} \rightharpoonup \mathit{str},\ \mathit{defs}}$$

$$\frac{\vdash_{e} e_1,\ \mathit{defs} \rightharpoonup e'_1,\ \mathit{defs}' \qquad \vdash_{e} e_2,\ \mathit{defs}' \rightharpoonup e'_2,\ \mathit{defs}'' \qquad \vdash_{e} e_3,\ \mathit{defs}'' \rightharpoonup e'_3,\ \mathit{defs}'''}{\vdash_{e} \textbf{if}\ (e_1)\ e_2\ \textbf{else}\ e_3,\ \mathit{defs} \rightharpoonup \textbf{if}\ (e'_1)\ e'_2\ \textbf{else}\ e'_3,\ \mathit{defs}'''}$$

$$\frac{\vdash_{e} e_1,\ \mathit{defs} \rightharpoonup e'_1,\ \mathit{defs}' \qquad \vdash_{e} e_2,\ \mathit{defs}' \rightharpoonup e'_2,\ \mathit{defs}''}{\vdash_{e} \{\ e_1\ ;\ e_2\ \},\ \mathit{defs} \rightharpoonup \{\ e'_1\ ;\ e'_2\ \},\ \mathit{defs}''}$$

$$\frac{\vdash_{e} e_1,\ \mathit{defs} \rightharpoonup e'_1,\ \mathit{defs}'}{\vdash_{e}\ !\ e,\ \mathit{defs} \rightharpoonup\ !\ e',\ \mathit{defs}'} \qquad \frac{\vdash_{e} e_1,\ \mathit{defs} \rightharpoonup e'_1,\ \mathit{defs}' \qquad \vdash_{e} e_2,\ \mathit{defs}' \rightharpoonup e'_2,\ \mathit{defs}''}{\vdash_{e} e_1 \parallel e_2,\ \mathit{defs} \rightharpoonup e'_1 \parallel e'_2\ ,\ \mathit{defs}''}$$

$$\frac{\begin{array}{l}\vdash_{e} e_1,\ \mathit{defs} \rightharpoonup e'_1,\ \mathit{defs}' \qquad \vdash_{e} e_2,\ \mathit{defs}' \rightharpoonup e'_2,\ \mathit{defs}'' \qquad \vdash_{e} e_3,\ \mathit{defs}'' \rightharpoonup e'_3,\ \mathit{defs}''' \\ \text{t is } \textbf{boolean} \text{ or } \textbf{String} \text{ and } x \text{ not free in } e'_2 \text{ or } e'_3\end{array}}{\vdash_{e} \textbf{semanticCast}(e_1 : t,\ t,\ e_2,\ e_3),\ \mathit{defs} \rightharpoonup \textbf{let}\ \{x = e'_1\}\ \textbf{in}\ \{\ e'_2\ ;\ e'_3\ ;x\ \},\ \mathit{defs}'''}$$

$$\frac{\vdash_{e} e_1,\ \mathit{defs} \rightharpoonup e'_1,\ \mathit{defs}' \quad \vdash_{e} e_2,\ \mathit{defs}' \rightharpoonup e'_2,\ \mathit{defs}'' \quad \vdash_{e} e_3,\ \mathit{defs}'' \rightharpoonup e'_3,\ \mathit{defs}''' \quad \vdash_{d} \textbf{class}\ \mathit{Cast\_i'\_i} \ldots,\ \mathit{defs}''' \rightharpoonup \mathit{defn},\ \mathit{defs}''''}{\begin{array}{ll}\vdash_{e} \textbf{semanticCast}(e_1 : i',\ i,\ e_2,\ e_3),\ \mathit{defs} \rightharpoonup \textbf{let}\ \{\ x = e'_1\ \ i = e'_2\ \ o = e'_3 & ,\ \mathit{defn} \uplus \mathit{defs}'''' \\ \qquad\qquad\qquad w = \textbf{new}\ \mathit{Cast\_i'\_i}()\ \} & \\ \qquad\qquad \textbf{in}\ \{\ w : \mathit{Cast\_i'\_i}\ .\mathit{unwrapped} = x; & \\ \qquad\qquad\qquad w : \mathit{Cast\_i'\_i}\ .\mathit{inBlame} = i; & \\ \qquad\qquad\qquad w : \mathit{Cast\_i'\_i}\ .\mathit{outBlame} = o; & \\ \qquad\qquad\qquad w\} & \end{array}}$$

Fig. 11. Contract Elaboration, part 2

$$P \vdash \langle e, \mathcal{S}\rangle \hookrightarrow \langle e, \mathcal{S}\rangle\ \textbf{[reduction rule name]}$$

A store ($\mathcal{S}$) is a mapping from *object*s (a set of identifiers distinct from the program variables) to class-tagged field records. A field record ($\mathcal{F}$) is a mapping from field names to values. We consider configurations of expressions and stores equivalent up to

```
class Cast_i'_i implements i {
  String inBlame, outBlame;
  i' unwrapped;
  t md(t1 x1 ... tn xn) {
    if (eb) {
      let {md = unwrapped.md(semanticCast(x1 : t1, t'1, outBlame, inBlame) ...
                             semanticCast(xn : tn, t'n, outBlame, inBlame))}
      in { if (ea) {
             semanticCast(md : t', t, inBlame, outBlame);
           } else { blame(outBlame); }}
    } else { blame(inBlame); }}
  ...
}

where i and i' match:

interface i extends ... { t md(t1 x1 ... tn xn) @pre { eb } @post { ea } ...}
interface i' extends ... { t' md(t'1 x1 ... t'n xn) ... }
```

Fig. 12. Compiler-generated Wrapper Classes

```
e = ... | object
v = object | null
  | true | false
  | str

E = [] | E : c .fd | E : c .fd = e | v : c .fd = E
  | E .md(e ...) | v.md(v ... E e ...)
  | super≡v:c.md(v ... E e ...)
  | view t E | let var = v ... var = E var = e ... in e
  | if ( E ) e else e | E instanceof i | E == e | v == E
  | E || e | ! E | { E ; e } | blame(E)
```

Fig. 13. Expressions, values, and contexts

α-renaming; the variables in the store bind the free variables in the expression. Each e is an expression and P is a program, as defined in figure 6. Figure 13 shows the contexts where reductions can occur.

The complete evaluation rules are in Figure 14. For example, the **call** rule models a method call by replacing the call expression with the body of the invoked method and syntactically replacing the formal parameters with the actual parameters. The dynamic aspect of method calls is implemented by selecting the method based on the run-time type of the object (in the store). In contrast, the *super* reduction performs **super** method selection using the class annotation that is statically determined by the type-checker.

The **blame** expressions terminate the program by throwing away the context and reducing to a configuration containing just an error, just like mis-use of **null** or a bad cast.

4.6 Soundness

A naïve soundness theorem for a contract compiler would guarantee that the additional code that the contract compiler adds to the program changes the behavior of the program only by signaling contract errors. Put positively, if no contract violations are signaled,

$$P \vdash \langle \mathsf{E}[object : t.md(v_1, \ldots, v_n)], \mathcal{S}\rangle \hookrightarrow \langle \mathsf{E}[e[object/this, v_1/var_1, \ldots v_n/var_n]], \mathcal{S}\rangle \quad \textbf{[call]}$$
$$\text{where } \mathcal{S}(object) = \langle c, \mathcal{F}\rangle \text{ and } \langle md, (t_1 \ldots t_n \longrightarrow t), (var_1 \ldots var_n), e\rangle \in^{c}_{P} c$$

$$P \vdash \langle \mathsf{E}[\textbf{super}\underline{\equiv object}{:}c.md(v_1, \ldots, v_n)], \mathcal{S}\rangle \quad \textbf{[super]}$$
$$\hookrightarrow \langle \mathsf{E}[e[object/this, v_1/var_1, \ldots v_n/var_n]], \mathcal{S}\rangle$$
$$\text{where } \langle md, (t_1 \ldots t_n \longrightarrow t), (var_1 \ldots var_n), e\rangle \in^{c}_{P} c$$

$$P \vdash \langle \mathsf{E}[\textbf{new } c], \mathcal{S}\rangle \hookrightarrow \langle \mathsf{E}[object], \mathcal{S}[object \mapsto \langle c, \mathcal{F}\rangle]\rangle \quad \textbf{[new]}$$
$$\text{where } object \notin \mathrm{dom}(\mathcal{S})$$
$$\text{and } \mathcal{F} = \{c'.fd \mapsto \textbf{null} \mid c \leq^{c}_{P} c' \text{ and } \exists t \text{ s.t. } \langle c'.fd, t\rangle \in^{c}_{P} c'\}$$

$$P \vdash \langle \mathsf{E}[object\underline{\,:\,c'\,}.fd], \mathcal{S}\rangle \hookrightarrow \langle \mathsf{E}[v], \mathcal{S}\rangle \quad \textbf{[get]}$$
$$\text{where } \mathcal{S}(object) = \langle c, \mathcal{F}\rangle \text{ and } \mathcal{F}(c'.fd) = v$$

$$P \vdash \langle \mathsf{E}[object\underline{\,:\,c'\,}.fd = v], \mathcal{S}\rangle \hookrightarrow \langle \mathsf{E}[v], \mathcal{S}[object \mapsto \langle c, \mathcal{F}[c'.fd \mapsto v]\rangle]\rangle \quad \textbf{[set]}$$
$$\text{where } \mathcal{S}(object) = \langle c, \mathcal{F}\rangle$$

$$P \vdash \langle \mathsf{E}[\textbf{view } t' \ object], \mathcal{S}\rangle \hookrightarrow \langle \mathsf{E}[object], \mathcal{S}\rangle \quad \textbf{[cast]}$$
$$\text{where } \mathcal{S}(object) = \langle c, \mathcal{F}\rangle \text{ and } c \ll^{c}_{P} t'$$

$$P \vdash \langle \mathsf{E}[object \textbf{ instanceof } t'], \mathcal{S}\rangle \hookrightarrow \langle \mathsf{E}[\textbf{true}], \mathcal{S}\rangle \quad \textbf{[ipass]}$$
$$\text{where } \mathcal{S}(object) = \langle c, \mathcal{F}\rangle \text{ and } c \ll^{c}_{P} t'$$

$$P \vdash \langle \mathsf{E}[object \textbf{ instanceof } t'], \mathcal{S}\rangle \hookrightarrow \langle \mathsf{E}[\textbf{false}], \mathcal{S}\rangle \quad \textbf{[ifail]}$$
$$\text{where } \mathcal{S}(object) = \langle c, \mathcal{F}\rangle \text{ and } c \not\ll^{c}_{P} t'$$

$$P \vdash \langle \mathsf{E}[bool == bool'], \mathcal{S}\rangle \hookrightarrow \langle \mathsf{E}[\textbf{if } (bool)\ bool' \textbf{ else } !\ bool'], \mathcal{S}\rangle \quad \textbf{[==b]}$$
$$P \vdash \langle \mathsf{E}[\textbf{let } var_1 = v_1 \ldots var_n = v_n \textbf{ in } e], \mathcal{S}\rangle \hookrightarrow \langle \mathsf{E}[e[v_1/var_1 \ldots v_n/var_n]], \mathcal{S}\rangle \quad \textbf{[let]}$$
$$P \vdash \langle \mathsf{E}[\textbf{if (true) } e_1 \textbf{ else } e_2], \mathcal{S}\rangle \hookrightarrow \langle \mathsf{E}[e_1], \mathcal{S}\rangle \quad \textbf{[iftrue]}$$
$$P \vdash \langle \mathsf{E}[\textbf{if (false) } e_1 \textbf{ else } e_2], \mathcal{S}\rangle \hookrightarrow \langle \mathsf{E}[e_2], \mathcal{S}\rangle \quad \textbf{[iffalse]}$$
$$P \vdash \langle \mathsf{E}[\textbf{true} \parallel e], \mathcal{S}\rangle \hookrightarrow \langle \mathsf{E}[\textbf{true}], \mathcal{S}\rangle \quad \textbf{[ortrue]}$$
$$P \vdash \langle \mathsf{E}[\textbf{false} \parallel e], \mathcal{S}\rangle \hookrightarrow \langle \mathsf{E}[e], \mathcal{S}\rangle \quad \textbf{[orfalse]}$$
$$P \vdash \langle \mathsf{E}[!\ \textbf{true}], \mathcal{S}\rangle \hookrightarrow \langle \mathsf{E}[\textbf{false}], \mathcal{S}\rangle \quad \textbf{[nottrue]}$$
$$P \vdash \langle \mathsf{E}[!\ \textbf{false}], \mathcal{S}\rangle \hookrightarrow \langle \mathsf{E}[\textbf{true}], \mathcal{S}\rangle \quad \textbf{[notfalse]}$$
$$P \vdash \langle \mathsf{E}[\{\ v\ ;\ e\ \}], \mathcal{S}\rangle \hookrightarrow \langle \mathsf{E}[e], \mathcal{S}\rangle \quad \textbf{[seq]}$$

$$P \vdash \langle \mathsf{E}[\textbf{blame}(s)], \mathcal{S}\rangle \hookrightarrow \langle \mathsf{error}{:}\ s \text{ violated contract}, \mathcal{S}\rangle \quad \textbf{[blame]}$$
$$P \vdash \langle \mathsf{E}[\textbf{view } t' \ object], \mathcal{S}\rangle \hookrightarrow \langle \mathsf{error}{:} \text{ bad cast}, \mathcal{S}\rangle \quad \textbf{[xcast]}$$
$$\text{where } \mathcal{S}(object) = \langle c, \mathcal{F}\rangle \text{ and } c \not\ll^{c}_{P} t'$$

$$P \vdash \langle \mathsf{E}[\textbf{view } t' \textbf{ null}], \mathcal{S}\rangle \hookrightarrow \langle \mathsf{error}{:} \text{ bad cast}, \mathcal{S}\rangle \quad \textbf{[ncast]}$$
$$P \vdash \langle \mathsf{E}[\textbf{null}\underline{\,:\,c\,}.fd], \mathcal{S}\rangle \hookrightarrow \langle \mathsf{error}{:} \text{ dereferenced null}, \mathcal{S}\rangle \quad \textbf{[nget]}$$
$$P \vdash \langle \mathsf{E}[\textbf{null}\underline{\,:\,c\,}.fd = v], \mathcal{S}\rangle \hookrightarrow \langle \mathsf{error}{:} \text{ dereferenced null}, \mathcal{S}\rangle \quad \textbf{[nset]}$$
$$P \vdash \langle \mathsf{E}[\textbf{null}.md(v_1, \ldots, v_n)], \mathcal{S}\rangle \hookrightarrow \langle \mathsf{error}{:} \text{ dereferenced null}, \mathcal{S}\rangle \quad \textbf{[ncall]}$$
$$P \vdash \langle \mathsf{E}[\textbf{null instanceof } i], \mathcal{S}\rangle \hookrightarrow \langle \mathsf{error}{:} \text{ dereferenced null}, \mathcal{S}\rangle \quad \textbf{[nisa]}$$
$$P \vdash \langle \mathsf{E}[\textbf{null} == v], \mathcal{S}\rangle \hookrightarrow \langle \mathsf{error}{:} \text{ dereferenced null}, \mathcal{S}\rangle \quad \textbf{[n==l]}$$
$$P \vdash \langle \mathsf{E}[v == \textbf{null}], \mathcal{S}\rangle \hookrightarrow \langle \mathsf{error}{:} \text{ dereferenced null}, \mathcal{S}\rangle \quad \textbf{[n==r]}$$

Fig. 14. Operational semantics

---

the original program with the contracts erased and the contract compiled program must behave identically.

Unfortunately, that theorem is too strong, for two reasons. First, the contract expressions themselves may change the behavior of the program (via side-effects or non-termination). So, we only consider a class of contracts that do not affect the behavior of the program, captured by this definition:

Definition 1 (Effect Free). *An expression e is said to be* effect free *if, for any store $\mathcal{S}$ and program P (that bind the free variables in e),*

$$P \vdash \langle e, \mathcal{S}\rangle \hookrightarrow^{*} \langle v, \mathcal{S}\rangle$$

for some value, v.

Second, because semantic casts allow structural subtyping, simply removing them would yield a type-incorrect Java program. Accordingly, we must replace semantic casts with wrapper classes that perform the type adaptation, but do not check contracts.

Definition 2 (Erasure).
The function $\mathcal{E}[\![\cdot]\!]$ *behaves just like the contract compiler, except for* **semanticCast** *expressions, where it instantiates adapter classes instead of the wrapper classes, according to this rule:*

$$\frac{\vdash_{\mathsf{e}} e_1, \mathit{defs} \rightharpoonup e'_1, \mathit{defs}' \qquad \vdash_{\mathsf{e}} e_2, \mathit{defs}' \rightharpoonup e'_2, \mathit{defs}'' \qquad \vdash_{\mathsf{e}} e_3, \mathit{defs}'' \rightharpoonup e'_3, \mathit{defs}''' \qquad \vdash_{\mathsf{d}} \textbf{class}\ \mathit{Adapt\_i'\_i} \ldots, \mathit{defs}''' \rightharpoonup \mathit{defn}, \mathit{defs}''''}{\begin{array}{l}\vdash_{\mathsf{e}} \textbf{semanticCast}(e_1 : i', i, e_2, e_3), \mathit{defs} \rightharpoonup \textbf{let}\ \{\ x = e'_1\ \ i = e'_2\ \ o = e'_3 \\ \qquad\qquad\qquad w = \textbf{new}\ \mathit{Adapt\_i'\_i}()\ \} \\ \qquad\quad \textbf{in}\ \{\ w : \mathit{Adapt\_i'\_i}\ .\mathit{unwrapped} = x; \\ \qquad\qquad w\} \qquad , \mathit{defn} \uplus \mathit{defs}''''\end{array}}$$

```
class Adapt_i'_i implements i {
  i' unwrapped;
  t md(t1 x1 ... tn xn) {
    let {md = unwrapped.md(semanticCast(x1 : t1, t'1, "", "") ...
                           semanticCast(xn : tn, t'n, "", ""))}
    in { semanticCast(md : t', t, "", ""); }} ...
}
```

Since the adapter classes never signal contract violations, the third and fourth arguments to **semanticCast** are ignored by the replacement $\vdash_{\mathsf{e}}$ rule. Similarly, the adapter class can safely use bogus string arguments to the nested **semanticCast** expressions.

In order to meaningfully state a soundness result, we must also ensure that the contract compiler and the erasure procedure both preserve the typing structure of programs.

Lemma 1. *For any program P = defn ... e that type checks:*

$$\vdash_{\mathsf{p}} P \Rightarrow P' : t$$

the erased and compiled versions of P must also type check and have the same type:

$$\vdash_{\mathsf{p}} C[\![P]\!] \Rightarrow P'' : t \qquad\qquad \vdash_{\mathsf{p}} \mathcal{E}_p[\![P]\!] \Rightarrow P''' : t$$

Proof (sketch). Both the erasure and contract compilation leave all expressions intact, except for **semanticCast** expressions. Inspection of the compiler and erasure definitions shows that they produce well-typed expressions and the typing rule for **semanticCast** gives the same types that erasure and the compiler give. □

With that background, we can now formulate a soundness theorem for our contract checker.

Theorem 1. *Let* $P = \mathit{defn} \ldots e$ *be a program such where all the contract expressions are effect free. Let* $C[\![P]\!] = P_c = \mathit{defn}_c \ldots e_c$ *and let* $\mathcal{E}[\![P]\!] = P_e = \mathit{defn}_e \ldots e_e$. *One of the following situation occurs:*

- $P_c \vdash \langle e_c, \emptyset\rangle \hookrightarrow^* \langle \textbf{blame}(s), \mathcal{S}\rangle$
- $P_c \vdash \langle e_c, \emptyset\rangle \hookrightarrow^* \langle \mathsf{error}\!: \mathit{str}, \mathcal{S}\rangle$ *and* $P_e \vdash \langle e_e, \emptyset\rangle \hookrightarrow^* \langle \mathsf{error}\!: \mathit{str}, \mathcal{S}\rangle$

- $P_c \vdash \langle e_c, \emptyset \rangle \hookrightarrow^* \langle v, \mathcal{S} \rangle$ *and* $P_e \vdash \langle e_e, \emptyset \rangle \hookrightarrow^* \langle v', \mathcal{S} \rangle$ *where either* $v = v'$ *and* v *is not an object, or both* v *and* v' *are objects.*
- *For each* e' *such that* $P_c \vdash \langle e_c, \emptyset \rangle \hookrightarrow^* \langle e', \mathcal{S} \rangle$ *there exists an* e'' *such that* $P_c \vdash \langle e', \mathcal{S} \rangle \hookrightarrow \langle e'', \mathcal{S} \rangle$ *and for each* e' *such that* $P_e \vdash \langle e_e, \emptyset \rangle \hookrightarrow^* \langle e', \mathcal{S} \rangle$ *there exists an* e'' *such that* $P_e \vdash \langle e', \mathcal{S} \rangle \hookrightarrow \langle e'', \mathcal{S} \rangle$

The formal statement of the theorem is divided into four cases, based on the behavior of the contract compiled program. If the contract compiled program produces a blame error, the theorem does not say anything about the erased program. If, however, the contract compiled program produces a value, a safety error, or does not terminate, the original program and the contract-free program must behave in the same manner. Note that if the contract compiled program produces an object, the erased program only has to produce an object, not necessarily the same object. If the contract compiled program results in a boolean or a string, the erased program must produce the same boolean or string.

Proof (sketch). The proof operates by relating the reduction sequences of the original program to the compiled program. Clearly, if there are no **semanticCast** expressions in the program, the new program contains extra definitions, but they are unused. Accordingly, the two programs reduce in lockstep until the first **semanticCast** expression. At that point, the erased program produces the adapter object and the compiled program produces a wrapper object. If the wrapper object ever signals a contract violation, we know that the theorem holds. If it does not, we can see from the definition of the wrapper objects that they behave identically to the adapter object when a method is invoked, because the contract expressions are effect free, by assumption. □

5 Implementation Status

We have implemented this contract checker as part of DrScheme [9], a 200,000 line MzScheme [15] program. Although the class system of MzScheme is not statically typed, its design is otherwise similar to the design of Java's class system. That is, the safety properties that Java's type system guarantees, *e.g.*, each method call has a receiver, are all also guaranteed, but the enforcement is entirely dynamic and implemented in terms of runtime checks. Accordingly, MzScheme benefits from contracts just as we have described in this paper.

Although the contract system described in this paper (with extensions to support all of the details of MzScheme's class system) has been implemented and is part of the current pre-release of DrScheme, the contract checker for the object sub-language is not widely used yet. In addition to contracts on objects, however, DrScheme also has a contract checker for higher-order functions. As far as contracts are concerned, a function is essentially an object with a single method.

We have studied the performance impact of contracts in DrScheme. An instrumented version of DrScheme counts the number of functions and function contracts. After starting up DrScheme and opening a few windows and Help Desk, there are 27962 reachable functions and only 507 wrappers, *i.e.*, slightly less than 2% of the functions are wrapped. With a different accounting annotation, DrScheme can also determine the number of function calls and calls to contract functions; for basically the same start-up action, the program performs 2,142,000 calls to user-defined functions, of which 1425 are calls to contract wrappers. That is, 0.06% of the calls to user-defined functions are calls to wrappers. Unfortunately, it is difficult to generalize these experiments, because it is a major undertaking to write contracts for a large system of components. Still, the experiment with DrScheme suggests that well-chosen contracts have little performance impact on a large program. Based on our experience, the number of contracts in a component rarely exceeds 10% of the number of functions proper. Yet, even if our system were to contain that many wrapper functions, our experiments suggest that only .3% of the function calls would be calls to wrapper functions. In short, we don't expect semantic casts to affect the overall system performance in a noticeable manner.

6 Related Work

Contracts have a long history. In 1972, Parnas [37] first suggested equipping module interfaces with contracts. His objective was to state the purpose of his proposed units of reuse in a formal manner. Soon thereafter, contracts appeared in a range of programming languages, including ADA [31], Euclid [26], and Turing [21]. In the 1980s, the designers of OO programming languages began to incorporate contracts [33] and OO researchers investigated the meaning of contracts in an OO context [1, 30]. By now, a fair number of OO languages support contracts either directly or as add-on packages [2, 5, 6, 8, 17, 22–25, 32, 33, 38, 39].

Over the past three years, we have investigated the theory and practice of contract and contract checking. Thus far, our theoretical research has focused on the soundness of contract checking in class hierarchies and in the presence of higher-order functions [10–12]. Our practical efforts have led to the implementation of a contract checking system for our Scheme class and mixin system. Experience with contracts in our DrScheme product suggested the proposal for a semantic cast in this paper.

Beyond contract checking systems, researchers are also investigating notations, theorem provers, and other tools for supporting contracts. For example, JML [27] is a notation for stating and reasoning about contracts. We use it in this paper to notate our contracts. JML is also used for many tools that go well beyond mere dynamically checked behavioral contracts. For example, ESC/Java [7, 14] is a theorem-prover that can validate theorems about JML contracts. In addition to ESC/Java, EML [42, 43] and Larch [19] are systems that statically verify contracts. Although our work focuses on dynamic validation, we believe that a static validation of such contracts is feasible and useful. Specifically, we hope that existing extended static checking efforts, like those of Flanagan et al [14], can be modified to account for semantic casts.

ML's module and signature language [35, 28] has been a different source of inspiration. It has long supported *signature ascription*, the ability to refine an existing ML structure's interface with the rest of the program. Our work can be seen as an extension of signature ascription to dynamically checked contracts.

The implementation of **semanticCast** with wrapper objects is suggestive of creating a denotational retract [41]. Although this intuition does not carry over directly, it suggested certain directions for our investigations. Also, our wrapper classes are reminiscent of the coercions that Henglein considers in his work [20].

7 Future Work

So far, we have only explored semantic up casts, that is, casts from a subtype to a supertype. It may, however, be useful to permit some form of semantic down casts. In particular, if an object were first cast to a super type, it is often useful to be able to cast it back to its original type. For example, when using container classes, the type of the container is some supertype of all of the objects that may ever be stored in the container. Accordingly, when retrieving objects from the container, it may be sensible to down cast them to a type with more information.

Clearly, one simple way to support semantic down casts is to remove layers of wrapping from the downcast object. Unfortunately, this would circumvent the contract checking. In general, components depend on contracts being enforced on the objects that play a role in their communication with other components. That is, if a downcast were to remove the contract checking code from some object, one component's contract violation may not be detected, leading to another component being blamed for a subsequent contract violation, or perhaps even erroneous output.

We have not yet found a consistent, simple extension to a nominally typed language design that manages to both support semantic down casts and preserves contract checking.

8 Conclusion

This paper introduces semantic casts, a modest extension to languages with nominal subtype systems. A semantic cast enables programmers to reuse classes and interfaces that match structurally but not nominally. Our calculus validates that doing so is compatible with conventional languages such as C++ [45], C# [34], Eiffel [33], and Java [18]. In the future, we plan to continue our investigations of how contracts can overcome the limitations of conventional type systems in a safe manner.

Acknowledgments. Thanks to Adam Wick for instrumenting his garbage collector so we could collect wrapper and function counts. Thanks also to the anonymous ECOOP reviewers for their comments.
This research is partially supported by the National Science Foundation.

References

1. America, P. Designing an object-oriented programming language with behavioural subtyping. In *Proceedings of Foundations of Object-Oriented Languages*, volume 489 of *Lecture Notes in Computer Science*, pages 60–90. Springer-Verlag, 1991.

2. Bartetzko, D., C. Fischer, M. Moller and H. Wehrheim. Jass - Java with assertions. In *Workshop on Runtime Verification*, 2001. Held in conjunction with the 13th Conference on Computer Aided Verification, CAV'01.
3. Bruce, K. B., A. Fiech and L. Petersen. Subtyping is not a good "match" for object-oriented languages. In *Proceedings of European Conference on Object-Oriented Programming*, pages 104–127, 1997.
4. Bruce, K. B., A. Schuett and R. van Gent. PolyTOIL: A type-safe polymorphic object-oriented language. *Lecture Notes in Computer Science*, 952:27–51, 1995.
5. Carrillo-Castellon, M., J. Garcia-Molina, E. Pimentel and I. Repiso. Design by contract in smalltalk. *Journal of Object-Oriented Programming*, 7(9):23–28, 1996.
6. Cheon, Y. A runtime assertion checker for the Java Modelling Language. Technical Report 03-09, Iowa State University Computer Science Department, April 2003.
7. Detlefs, D. L., K. Rustan, M. Leino, G. Nelson and J. B. Saxe. Extended static checking. Technical Report 158, Compaq SRC Research Report, 1998.
8. Duncan, A. and U. Hölzle. Adding contracts to Java with handshake. Technical Report TRCS98-32, The University of California at Santa Barbara, December 1998.
9. Findler, R. B., J. Clements, C. Flanagan, M. Flatt, S. Krishnamurthi, P. Steckler and M. Felleisen. DrScheme: A programming environment for Scheme. *Journal of Functional Programming*, 12(2):159–182, March 2002. A preliminary version of this paper appeared in PLILP 1997, LNCS volume 1292, pages 369–388.
10. Findler, R. B. and M. Felleisen. Contract soundness for object-oriented languages. In *Object-Oriented Programming, Systems, Languages, and Applications*, 2001.
11. Findler, R. B. and M. Felleisen. Contracts for higher-order functions. In *Proceedings of ACM SIGPLAN International Conference on Functional Programming*, 2002.
12. Findler, R. B., M. Latendresse and M. Felleisen. Behavioral contracts and behavioral subtyping. In *Proceedings of ACM Conference Foundations of Software Engineering*, 2001.
13. Fisher, K. and J. H. Reppy. The design of a class mechanism for Moby. In *Proceedings of ACM SIGPLAN Conference on Programming Language Design and Implementation*, 1999.
14. Flanagan, C., K. R. M. Leino, M. Lillibridge, G. Nelson, J. B. Saxe and R. Stata. Extended static checking for Java. In *Proceedings of ACM SIGPLAN Conference on Programming Language Design and Implementation*, pages 234–245, 2002.
15. Flatt, M. PLT MzScheme: Language manual. Technical Report TR97-280, Rice University, 1997. http://www.mzscheme.org/.
16. Flatt, M., S. Krishnamurthi and M. Felleisen. Classes and mixins. In *Proceedings of the ACM Conference Principles of Programming Languages*, pages 171–183, Janurary 1998.
17. Gomes, B., D. Stoutamire, B. Vaysman and H. Klawitter. *A Language Manual for Sather 1.1*, August 1996.
18. Gosling, J., B. Joy and J. Guy Steele. *The Java(tm) Language Specification*. Addison-Wesley, 1996.
19. Guttag, J. V. and J. J. Horning. *Larch: Languages and Tools for Formal Specification*. Springer-Verlag, 1993.
20. Henglein, F. Dynamic typing: Syntax and proof theory. *Science of Computer Programming*, 22(3):197–230, 1994.
21. Holt, R. C. and J. R. Cordy. The Turing programming language. In *Communications of the ACM*, volume 31, pages 1310–1423, December 1988.
22. Karaorman, M., U. Hölzle and J. Bruno. jContractor: A reflective Java library to support design by contract. In *Proceedings of Meta-Level Architectures and Reflection*, volume 1616 of *lncs*, July 1999.
23. Kizub, M. Kiev language specification. http://www.forestro.com/kiev/, 1998.
24. Kölling, M. and J. Rosenberg. *Blue: Language Specification, version 0.94*, 1997

25. Kramer, R. iContract: The Java design by contract tool. In *Technology of Object-Oriented Languages and Systems*, 1998.
26. Lampson, B. W., J. J. Horning, R. L. London, J. G. Mitchell and G. J. Popek. Report on the programming language Euclid. *ACM Sigplan Notices*, 12(2), Feburary 1977.
27. Leavens, G. T., K. R. M. Leino, E. Poll, C. Ruby and B. Jacobs. JML: notations and tools supporting detailed design in Java. In *Object-Oriented Programming, Systems, Languages, and Applications Companion*, pages 105–106, 2000. Also Department of Computer Science, Iowa State University, TR 00-15, August 2000.
28. Leroy, X. Applicative functors and fully transparent higher-order modules. In *Proceedings of the ACM Conference Principles of Programming Languages*, pages 142–153. ACM Press, 1995.
29. Leroy, X. *The Objective Caml system, Documentation and User's guide*, 1997.
30. Liskov, B. H. and J. Wing. Behavioral subtyping using invariants and constraints. Technical Report CMU CS-99-156, School of Computer Science, Carnegie Mellon University, July 1999.
31. Luckham, D. C. and F. von Henke. An overview of Anna, a specification language for Ada. In *IEEE Software*, volume 2, pages 9–23, March 1985.
32. Man Machine Systems. Design by contract for Java using JMSAssert. http://www.mmsindia.com/DBCForJava.html, 2000.
33. Meyer, B. *Eiffel: The Language*. Prentice Hall, 1992.
34. Microsoft Corporation. *Microsoft C# Language Specifications*. Microsoft Press, 2001.
35. Milner, R., M. Tofte and R. Harper. *The Definition of Standard ML*. MIT Press, 1990.
36. Object Management Group. The object management architecture guide, 1997. http://www.omg.org/.
37. Parnas, D. L. A technique for software module specification with examples. *Communications of the ACM*, 15(5):330–336, May 1972.
38. Plösch, R. Design by contract for Python. In *IEEE Proceedings of the Joint Asia Pacific Software Engineering Conference*, 1997. http://citeseer.nj.nec.com/257710.html.
39. Plösch, R. and J. Pichler. Contracts: From analysis to C++ implementation. In *Technology of Object-Oriented Languages and Systems*, pages 248–257, 1999.
40. Rémy, D. and J. Vouillon. Objective ML: A simple object-oriented extension of ML. In *Proceedings of the ACM Conference Principles of Programming Languages*, pages 40–53, January 1997.
41. Rosenblum, D. S. A practical approach to programming with assertions. *IEEE Transactions on Software Engineering*, 21(1):19–31, Janurary 1995.
42. Sannella, D. Formal program development in Extended ML for the working programmer. In *Proc. 3rd BCS/FACS Workshop on Refinement; Springer Workshops in Computing*, pages 99–130, 1991.
43. Sannella, D. and A. Tarlecki. Essential concepts of algebraic specification and program development. *Formal Aspects of Computing*, 9:229–269, 1997. http://www.dcs.ed.ac.uk/home/dts/eml/.
44. Scott, D. S. Data types as lattices. *Society of Industrial and Applied Mathematics (SIAM) Journal of Computing*, 5(3):522–586, 1976.
45. Stroustrup, B. *The C++ Programming Language*. Addison-Wesley, 1997.
46. Szyperski, C. *Component Software*. Addison-Wesley, second edition, 1998.
47. Wright, A. and M. Felleisen. A syntactic approach to type soundness. *Information and Computation*, pages 38–94, 1994. First appeared as Technical Report TR160, Rice University, 1991.

LOOJ: Weaving LOOM into Java*

Kim B. Bruce[1] and J. Nathan Foster[2]

[1] Department of Computer Science
Williams College
Williamstown, MA USA 01267
kim@cs.williams.edu

[2] Department of Computer & Information Science
University of Pennsylvania
Philadelphia, PA USA 19104
jnfoster@cis.upenn.edu

Abstract. LOOJ is an extension of Java obtained by adding bounded parametric polymorphism and new type expressions `ThisClass` and `ThisType`, which are similar to *MyType* in LOOM. Through examples we demonstrate the utility of this language even over very expressive extensions such as GJ. The LOOJ compiler generates standard JVML code and supports `instanceof` and casts for all types including type variables and the other new type expressions. The core of the LOOJ type system is sound, as demonstrated by a soundness proof for an extension of Featherweight GJ. This paper also highlights difficulties that arise from the use of both classes and interfaces as types in Java.

Keywords: Object-oriented language design, static type systems, *MyType*, `ThisClass`, `ThisType`, formal semantics.

1 Introduction

Modularity and reusability are two core concepts in object-oriented programming systems. Unfortunately, too often the type systems of object-oriented languages make it difficult to write modular, reusable code because they lack expressive power. Java's type system is often criticized because it does not allow explicit type abstractions and applications, making it impossible to write generic data structures within the static type system. The many proposals for adding parametric polymorphism to Java [AFM97,OW97,CS98,MBL97], including GJ [BOSW98], aim to overcome this deficiency.[1] However another limitation – the lack of a precise type for `this` – makes it difficult to write many useful programs. In this paper, we extend Java to a language LOOJ that includes two constructs analogous to *MyType*, as well as bounded polymorphism and support for weak reflection constructs.

* This work was partially supported by the National Science Foundation under grants CCR-0306486 and CCR-9988210.

[1] Parametric polymorphism based on GJ will be included in Java 1.5.

M. Odersky (Ed.): ECOOP 2004, LNCS 3086, pp. 389–413, 2004.

Contributions

We demonstrate that *MyType* can be added cleanly to an extension of Java alongside bounded parametric polymorphism, producing a very expressive type system. First, we introduce `ThisClass`, which closely captures the class type of `this`. We also introduce *exact types*, which are needed to ensure that uses of `ThisClass` are type safe. Second, we give a brief description of the LOOJ compiler that implements the language in a homogeneous, type-passing compilation style. Our implementation supports the use of `instanceof` and type casts for all type expressions including type variables. Third, we describe an extension to Featherweight GJ [IPW99], which models a core subset of LOOJ, and its type soundness proof. Fourth, we discuss some problems that result when `ThisClass` is used in combination with interfaces and introduce `ThisType` to stand for the interface type of `this`.

In the remainder of this section, we show some examples where the expressiveness of GJ falls short.

1.1 Motivation

We will present a formal definition of a binary method later; for now, consider a binary method to be a method that has a parameter whose type is intended to be the same as the type of the object it is used with. In what follows, we will write all examples using a Java-like syntax, though we write method types using → notation instead of the syntax of methods in Java interfaces.

As our first example of a binary method, consider the `setNext` method in a `Node` which represents singly-linked list elements with type:

```
setNext: Node → void
```

As the parameter has type `Node`, `setNext` meets our definition of binary method.

However, suppose we try to define a subclass `DoubleNode` of `Node` to represent doubly-linked nodes. Then the inherited version of `setNext` still takes a parameter with type `Node`, even though its parameter should have type `DoubleNode` if it is intended to remain a binary method in the subclass. The poor support for binary methods in Java's static type system allows programs to link singly-linked nodes as the next field of a doubly-linked node. Clearly this behavior is not what the programmer wants. She would be better off if she could specify that `setNext` should only ever be applied to an argument whose type is the *same* as the object that it is invoked on.

A similar problem arises in programs that create an object of the same type as the currently executing object. Java's standard library includes an interface `Cloneable` that is implemented by classes which may be cloned.[2] The `clone` method has the type:

```
clone: () → Object
```

[2] That classes which implement `Cloneable` can be safely cloned is enforced at runtime; the interface itself is empty.

which is not precise enough to describe the high-level behavior that programmers want of `clone`. The method's return type, `Object`, gives no information about the type of the object that it returns. As a result, if a programmer clones an object with type `C`, she must cast the result of the `clone` method to `C` before using it. Part of this problem could be fixed by allowing covariant changes in the return types of methods.[3] However, adding this flexibility does not solve a more fundamental problem. Even if class `C`'s `clone` method is defined with return type `C`, there is nothing to guarantee that each subclass will override the method with a definition whose return type is its own type. If the programmer neglects to override the method for a particular subclass, `D`, then she can invoke its `clone` method and get an object whose type is `C`, not `D`. Again, the type system is unable to express that a particular type, here the return type, is the same as the type of the object that it is used with.

2 Introducing `ThisClass` and Exact Types

The two examples above share a common trait: the lack of a name for the type of `this` in Java's type system makes it very difficult to express important properties about programs. In the example involving `setNext` and linked-list nodes, the desired property is that singly-linked nodes are only ever linked in to a list containing other singly-linked nodes. In the `clone` example, it is that `clone` always returns an object with the same type as the object that it is invoked on. Adding a primitive type for `this`, similar to the *MyType* construct in LOOM [BFP97,Bru02], gives the flexibility needed to solve both of these problems and others.

The `ThisClass` type in LOOJ is directly inspired by *MyType* in LOOM (LOOJ also has a type `ThisType`, described in Section 5). However, because the type system of LOOM differs from Java's in two key ways, adding a construct like *MyType* to Java requires some care. First, LOOM has structural type relations whereas Java's type relations are nominal. Second, in LOOM, classes and object types are distinct. In Java, the two are conflated and a class is commonly used both as the generator of an object and as its type. As a result of these differences, finding a clean way of adapting LOOM's *MyType* to Java so that the extended type system is a natural fit with existing programming styles and idioms is not immediately obvious.

We begin by introducing the type `ThisClass`, which stands for the class type of `this`. If a class `C` defines a method `m`, then when `m` is used with an object whose runtime type is `C`, any occurrences of `ThisClass` in the method's type signature may be safely assumed to be `C`. The power of `ThisClass` becomes apparent when `m` is inherited in a subclass, `D`. In this case, occurrences of `ThisClass` in the same method type are assumed to have all the features of `D`, *not* just those of `C`. This

[3] Java's type system does not allow changes to method signatures in subclasses; however, a covariant change in return type would be safe and is supported by the JVM; it is allowed in GJ and will be allowed in Java 1.5 [BCK+01].

behavior – that ThisClass corresponds to the type of the runtime object that it is actually used with – is the hallmark behavior of *MyType*.

In order to ensure that methods type checked in superclasses are type safe when used in subclasses, the type checker analyzes all fields and methods of a class in a type context which includes the assumption that ThisClass extends the class type that is currently being checked. When it checks an individual method invocation, it substitutes the static class type of the object that the method is being invoked on for all occurrences of ThisClass in the method's type signature. As an example, suppose that d is an expression of type D, and that binMeth is a method defined in D with static type

```
binMeth: ThisClass → void
```

When the type checker analyzes the method invocation d.binMeth(o), it treats the type signature of binMeth just like a method with type0

```
d.binMeth: D → void
```

That is, it checks that the static type of o extends D. Formal rules for type checking ThisClass in a core calculus are given in the appendix.

Henceforth, we use the term *binary method* to refer to methods where ThisClass appears in a negative (value consuming) position in its type signature.[4] In particular, every method where ThisClass appears in the type of one of its parameters is a binary method. In order to ensure that a binary method invocation is safe, we need to be able to determine the precise class type that the receiver will have at run-time. To see why this property is needed, consider the following declarations:

```
class C { public void binMeth(ThisClass tc) { ... } }
class D extends C {
    public void newMeth() {...};
    public void binMeth(ThisClass tc) { ... tc.newMeth() ... }
}

void problem(C c1, C c2) {
  c1.binMeth(c2);
}

problem(new D(), new C());    // error!
```

Note that method newMeth() does not occur in C, but is used in the redefinition of binMeth in D.

If the line labelled "error" were legal in the LOOJ type system, then the evaluation of binMeth in the body of problem would send the message newMeth to an object of type C, which has no such method.

[4] Later we extend this definition to include methods with parameter types involving ThisType.

To avoid this problem, we introduce *exact types* to LOOJ. Normally a Java expression with type `C` might at runtime contain an object with type `C` or any extension of `C`. For an exact type, denoted with the `@` symbol, we rule out this second case; an expression whose static type is `@C` always refers to an object with runtime type `C`. One can think of exact types as ruling uses of subsumption for specific expressions.

With exact types, we can design a sound type system by requiring that the receiver of each binary method invocation must have an exact type. This restriction eliminates problems such as the one above where a binary method call on a receiver whose type is not known exactly can lead to a hole in the static type system. We cannot write the `problem` method, because `c1` is used as the call site for a binary method but `c1`'s type is not exact. If we change the type of the first parameter of `problem` to `@C`, then the method body type checks, but the type checker will rule out the invocation of `problem` with a first parameter whose type is `D`.

We can summarize the typing properties of programs that use `ThisClass` as follows. When type checking methods in a class `C` we assume that:

- `this` has type `@ThisClass`,
- `ThisClass` extends `C`.[5]

When type-checking message sends,

- The receiver of a binary method invocation must have an exact type.
- The type of a binary method invocation is obtained from the method's type signature by substituting the receiver's static type for each occurrences of `ThisClass`.
- The type of a (non-binary) method invocation where `ThisClass` appears in the method's type signature, but the receiver is not exact, is safe if `ThisClass` appears only in positive (value producing) positions. We calculate the type of such a method call from the method's type signature by substituting the receiver's static type first for each occurrence of `@ThisClass` and then for each remaining occurrence of `ThisClass`.

Exact types have uses beyond type checking binary methods in LOOJ. They are also useful for writing *homogeneous* data structures. In general, exact type expressions can be used to more precisely describe the shape of program computations. They do so, of course, at the cost of flexibility and extensibility at each use because exact types prohibit uses of subtype polymorphism for particular expressions. In certain programs, this tradeoff between increased precision and flexibility of reuse may lean towards precision and away from flexibility – exact types provide a primitive for specifying exact typing constraints.

---

[5] To correctly model the semantics of the `private` access modifier, some care is required. Note that `this` and other expressions of type `ThisClass` have access to private instance variables and methods of `C`, while expressions whose type is just known to be an extension of `C` do not.

Java programs also use interfaces as types and we have also introduced a construct, `ThisType`, that stands for the interface of `this`. As there are some subtle negative interactions between interfaces and `ThisClass`, we postpone all discussion of interfaces and `ThisType` for now. We will address these issues in detail in Section 5. Meanwhile, we restrict our attention to Java programs that do not use interfaces.

3 Motivating Examples Revisited

Our two motivating examples which caused problems in GJ's type system are easily solved in LOOJ using `ThisClass`. For example, we can write `Node`'s `setNext` method as:

```
setNext: @ThisClass → void
```

In this program, the static type system ensures that `setNext` is only ever passed arguments whose type is the same as the object that the method is invoked on. In particular, we cannot link a `Node` into a list consisting of elements of type `DoubleNode`, as desired.

The example involving cloning also has a simple solution with `ThisClass`. Instead of declaring the return type of the `clone` method as `Object`, we can write it as `@ThisClass`. This declaration ensures that `clone` always returns an object whose type is the same as the object that it was invoked upon, even when it is used in a subclass. Note that with this type declaration, if `clone` is called on a receiver with type `@C` then the result will have static type `@C`, while if it is called on a receiver with type `C`, then the result will has static type `C`. This last point illustrates that `ThisClass` may safely appear positively in a method's type signature even when the method is invoked with an unexact receiver.

However, it is not immediately obvious what we can write in the body of `clone` in order to manufacture an object whose type is `@ThisClass`. We need an expression whose type is `C` when the method is used with a `C`, and `D` when used with a subclass `D`. We cannot simply call `C`'s constructor because an object with type `@C` is not a subtype of `@ThisClass`. However, using a Factory pattern [GRJV94], we can produce a new object with the correct type. Suppose that the interface of a factory is:

```
interface Factory<T> {
  @T create();
}
```

Then if `C` contains an instance variable `thisClassFactory` with type `Factory<ThisClass>`, we can write

```
thisClassFactory.create();
```

as the body of `clone`. We can then add a new parameter to the constructors of `C` to initialize the factory object:

```
public C(..., Factory<ThisClass> cfact) {
    ...
    thisClassFactory = cfact;
}
```

When we create an instance of `C`, we can initialize `cfact` by passing the constructor an argument with type `Factory<C>`.[6]

We can use factory classes to code up many useful expressions. For example, the expression `new X()` where `X` is a type variable, can be simulated by sending a `create` message to an object with type `Factory<X>`. A previous version of LOOJ supported special syntax for distinguished `This` constructors (an idea originally due to Bill Joy). These were just factories that returned an object with type `@ThisClass`. We have found that in practice, constructing the factories and passing them to standard constructors explicitly is not prohibitively burdensome, and so the current version of LOOJ does not support special `This` constructor syntax. It remains simple to write expressions that have the same behavior as `This` constructors in LOOJ using the Factory pattern with `ThisClass`.

4 Type Safety in LOOJ and an Implementation

LOOJ is more than a mere design; we have implemented a compiler and developed a proof of static type safety for the language.

In previous work we provided both translational semantics [Bru02] and high-level operational semantics [BFSvG03,BFP97] for object-oriented languages with a *MyType* construct. For LOOJ we have proved soundness for a subset of the language using the techniques introduced in Featherweight Java [IPW99]. Due to space constraints we do not include the full proof in this paper. Instead, we give the syntax, type-checking rules, and evaluation rules in the appendix, along with a proof sketch of type soundness. An extended version of this paper that contains the full type system and soundness proof is available as a companion technical report [?].

The LOOJ compiler supports the additional type `ThisClass` and exact types (as well as the new type `ThisType` to be discussed later). Moreover, unlike current versions of GJ,[7] our compiler supports `instanceof` expressions and type casts for all types, including those involving type variables and `ThisClass`.

All legal Java programs are legal programs of LOOJ and produce the same results. GJ and LOOJ differ on some minor points. In LOOJ, all instantiations of type variables must be written explicitly, as opposed to, GJ where instantiations of type abstractions private to methods are inferred. Our compiler does not

[6] The static type of the "receiver" of a `new` expression is just the exact type of the class type being created; hence, when we type check `new C(...)`, it is safe to substitute `C` for `ThisClass` in the constructor's type signature. Calls of `super` constructors in subclasses also use the subclass as the receiver type.

[7] Future implementations of GJ, along the lines of NextGen [CS98], will address these current limitations.

perform type reconstruction for invocations of polymorphic methods, as we prefer explicit instantiations of type variables. More substantially, the compiler differs in the translation style used to compile programs to Java bytecodes. Rather than using pure erasure, the LOOJ compiler uses a homogeneous translation originally proposed by Burstein [Bur98] that is based on erasure, but that also annotates classes with private instance variables representing the runtime values of type variables.

In our type-passing implementation, the private variables are initialized in constructors by passing representations of class types obtained from Java's reflection utilities. With this information, each object can determine the values of its type variables at runtime. This is useful for performing lightweight introspective operations such as dynamically-checked type casts and `instanceof` type tests. We believe that providing these operations for all types including generics, `ThisClass`, and exact types is a closer fit with Java's existing semantics. As an example, consider this simple class:

```
class C<T> {
  T myT;
  public C() { }
}
```

A compiler that uses pure erasure to implement generics translates this fragment to bytecodes equivalent to:

```
class C {
  Object myT;
  public C() { }
}
```

whereas the LOOJ compiler translates it to:

```
class C {
  Object myT;
  private PolyClass T$$class;
  public C(PolyClass T$$class) {
    this.T$$class = T$$class;
  }
  public boolean instanceOfC(PolyClass otherT$$class) {
    return T$$class.equals(otherT$$class);
  }
}
```

Here, `PolyClass` objects explicitly hold information about polymorphic types in the same way that `Class` objects in Java hold information about Java types. The LOOJ compiler uses these objects to implement operations that require runtime type information, such as `instanceof` expressions, and type casts. The translations of these expressions have the correct runtime semantics for most types.[8]

For example, the expression

```
obj instanceof C<T>
```

is not allowed in GJ, because its erased version would be true whenever `obj` is a `C`. It is translated in LOOJ to

```
((obj != null)
  && (obj instanceof C)
  && (((C)obj).instanceOfC(T$$class)))
```

It is easy to see that this expression is only true if `obj` is an instance of `C<T>`. Similar translations are used to implement these and many similar expressions:

```
obj instanceof @ThisClass
((C<T>)obj)...
```

Unfortunately, the same technique cannot be extended to array types as there is no uniform location where we can transparently hold the runtime representations of instantiations of type variables for array types. We provide a wrapper class for arrays with polymorphic element types that can be used to simulate the correct semantics for these operations if needed. Additionally, because the runtime type representations of type variables are available, expressions such as

```
new T[n];
new ThisClass[n];
```

can be translated to expressions using Java's reflection facilities to create an array of the correct base type at runtime. GJ statically translates the first expression (with a warning that the translation is unchecked) to a `new` array expression of T's bound.

More details about the LOOJ compiler are available in honors theses by Burstein [Bur98] and Foster [Fos01].

5 Interfaces, `ThisClass`, and `ThisType`

Thus far, we have described how LOOM's *MyType* can be mapped onto class types in Java's type system in `ThisClass`. However, we have carefully avoided mentioning how `ThisClass` interacts with Java interfaces. In this section we discuss some of the problems that result when `ThisClass` is used together with interface types. We conclude that `ThisClass` should not appear in interfaces and introduce the new type expression `ThisType`, to represent the *interface* of `this`. Later we show how `ThisType` can be used to solve problems that arise when programs using the the Visitor pattern are extended.

---

[8] Runtime operations involving array types are not currently supported, as discussed below.

5.1 ThisClass in Interfaces

As a first attempt at expressing binary methods in interfaces, we might try to write ThisClass directly in an interface. Unfortunately, it is not clear what such a use of ThisClass would mean. Consider these source fragments:

```
interface I {
  void binMeth(ThisClass tc);
}
class C implements @I {
  // instance variable declarations
  void binMeth(ThisClass tc) { ... }
}
class D implements @I {
  // instance variable declarations
  public void binMeth(ThisClass tc) { ... }
}

@I i1 = new D();
@I i2 = new C();
i1.binMeth(i2);
```

Notice that the class declarations state that both C and D implement @I. In LOOJ, a class implements an interface exactly if its public methods are *exactly* the methods in the interface. A class declaration may only declare a single exact interface type (this restriction is a consequence of Java's nominal type relations: multiple exact interfaces would be structurally identical, but their names would be distinct and hence, the two would be unrelated in the type system). As in Java, classes may also implement as many non-exact interfaces as are desired. The annotation of the classes with an exact interface informs the type checker that objects from classes C and D can be used in contexts expecting objects of type @I. As a result, the assignments above to i1 and i2 are legal.

In the example above, C and D are unrelated in Java's by name inheritance hierarchy except that they both implement I:

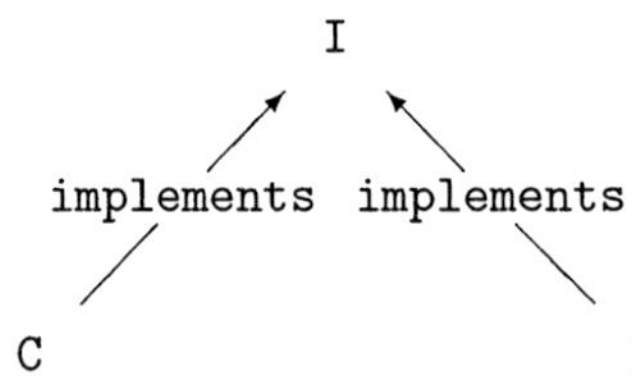

The code for the implementations of binMeth in C and D may access their respective (and different) instance variables. Hence, it is not safe to invoke the binMeth method of one on an object of the other type. But we cannot determine from its type, @I, if i1 is a C or a D. We reluctantly conclude that we cannot reliably identify the class type of the receiver of a binary method call at compile time if the static type of the receiver is an interface. As a result, the last line of code above is not legal in the LOOJ type system.[9]

It is often useful, however, to be able to write interfaces that include declarations of binary methods. To facilitate this, we introduce a second version of *MyType*, `ThisType`, which stands for the *public interface type* of the definition where it occurs.

We can rewrite the above example, replacing `ThisClass` with `ThisType`:

```
interface I {
  void binMeth(ThisType tc);
}
class C implements @I {
  void binMeth(ThisType tc) { ... }
}
class D implements @I {
  public void binMeth(ThisType tc) { ... }
}
@I i1, i2;
i1.binMeth(i2);
```

Now the message send in the last line is safe because the parameter of `binMeth` is an interface type, `ThisType`. As such, the method bodies of `binMeth` in `C` and `D` may not access instance variables or non-public methods. They may, however, invoke methods that are included in their exact interface from inside `binMeth`.

As with `ThisClass`, when type checking a method call involving `ThisType` on an object `obj`, each occurrence of `ThisType` in the signature is replaced by the *interface type* of the receiver. If the type of the receiver is a class, then the exact interface associated with that class is used in the substitution.[10] Note that if `I` is extended by an interface `J`, then the meaning of `ThisType` within inherited methods changes, just as the meaning of `ThisClass` changes when it is used in subclasses.

The typing properties of programs provided earlier can be extended to a type system with `ThisType` as follows. When type checking methods in a class `C` with exact interface `I`, we are allowed to assume that:

- `this` has type `@ThisClass`,
- `ThisClass` extends `C`.
- `ThisType` extends `I`,

[9] It would be type safe to allow `ThisClass` in parameter positions of methods in interfaces if we also required that the receiver of any invocation of that method must be an exact *class* type. In LOOJ, we use a conceptually simpler rule that forbids the use of `ThisClass` in interfaces and instead will provide `ThisType` as a *MyType* construct for interface types.

[10] In our implementation, the compiler synthesizes the public interface of a class if `ThisType` is used with the class, but an exact interface is not declared by the programmer.

- ThisClass implements @ThisType, and
- C implements @I.

A consequence of the last two items is that a value with type @C can be used in a context expecting a value of type @I and a value with type @ThisClass can be used in a context expecting a value of type @ThisType.

5.2 Visitors and ThisType

The addition of ThisType provides a natural way to write programs containing both binary methods and interfaces. We illustrate this point by showing an example where using ThisType and interfaces solves a challenging problem.

Suppose that we wish to write a statically type-safe, extensible interpreter for integer expressions in a GJ-like language. By extensible, we mean that when we extend the language with some new syntactic forms, the new interpreter can reuse all of the existing code for interpreting the initial language without modification. This example is adapted from [Bru03]; a survey of various solutions to the problem can be found in Torgersen's recent paper [?].

The initial language we interpret is a very simple language of integer constants and negations. We use the Visitor pattern [GRJV94] to implement our interpreter and each visitor returns values of type int. The classes ConstForm and NegForm, representing constants and negations, respectively, both implement the interface

```
interface Form {
   int visit(Visitor v);
}
```

A visitor is an interface that has methods for processing each of the forms in the language, producing an integer value as its result:[11]

```
interface Visitor {
  int constCase(ConstForm cf);
  int negCase(NegForm nf);
}
```

The visit method in each formula class sends a message to the corresponding method of the visitor. For example, the code for visit method in NegForm is

```
public int visit(Visitor v) {
  return v.negCase(this);
}
```

When a visit message is sent to a formula, dynamic dispatch results in a message being sent to the appropriate case in the visitor.

The advantage of separating the syntax from the visitors that implement particular high level operations (e.g., evaluation, type checking, pretty printing)

[11] More generally, the Visitor interface would be parameterized by the return type.

is that it is very easy to add new operations on syntax trees by adding new visitors. However, it is difficult to extend the syntax with new forms without modifying the original definitions. For example, if we want to add a new form `PlusForm`, representing abstractly the concrete syntax $e_1 + e_2$, we cannot reuse our existing visitor. To see why it is hard, first consider how we might write the new form and extended visitor to process it:

```
class PlusForm implements @Form {
  @Form lhs, rhs;
  public int visit(ExtVisitor ev) {
    ev.plusCase(this);
  }
}
interface ExtVisitor extends Visitor {
  int plusCase(PlusForm pf);
}
```

Unfortunately as written, this code will not pass the GJ type checker because the interface of all syntactic forms, `Form`, requires each class that implements it to define a method named `visit` with type

```
visit: Visitor → int
```

and the `visit` method of `PlusForm` has a different type. But if we write the `visit` method for `PlusForm` with the required type, then we cannot invoke `plusCase` from the visitor on it because the `Visitor` interface does not include it!

A natural next step is to introduce type variables to abstract the type of the visitor that is used to process each syntactic element. Following this approach, we might rewrite the definitions of visitors and syntactic forms like this:

```
interface Visitor {
  ...
  int negCase(NegForm<Visitor> nf);
}
interface Form<V extends Visitor> {
  int visit(V v);
}
class NegForm<V extends Visitor> implements @Form<V> {
  @Form exp;
  public int visit(V v) {
    v.negCase(this);  // error!
  }
}
```

However when we try to type-check this code, we get an error because of GJ's invariant subtyping rule for parameterized class types. The visitor has a method `negCase` with type:

```
negCase: NegForm<Visitor> → int
```

and the occurrence of `this` in the expression

```
v.negCase(this)
```

has type `NegForm<V>`,[12] and `NegForm<V>` is not a subtype of `NegForm<Visitor>`.

Thus introducing a type variable to stand for the type of the visitor does not lead to a natural solution to the extensible interpreter problem.[13]

Though the problem does not obviously contain binary methods, it can be solved by using `ThisType` as the instantiation of the type variable `V` in the definitions of visitors. We can revise the definition of the visitor class to the following:

```
interface Visitor {
  int constCase(ConstForm<ThisType> cf);
  int negCase(NegForm<ThisType> nf);
}
```

Now the `visit` methods for each of the syntactic forms in the language can be written as follows (we give the case for `NegForm<V>` only, the others are similar):

```
class NegForm<V extends Visitor> implements @Form<V> {
  ...
  public int visit(@V v) { return v.negCase(this); }
}
```

The problematic expression from above, `v.negCase(this)`, no longer leads to a type error as witnessed by the following reasoning steps:

- The method `negCase` has type

  ```
  negCase: NegForm<ThisType> → int
  ```

- As `v` has type `@V`,[14] where `V` is a type variable with bound `Visitor`, when we type check the message send to `v`, we replace `ThisType` with `V`:

  ```
  [V/ThisType](NegForm<ThisType> → int) = NegForm<V> → int
  ```

- Recall that the class `NegForm<V>` is type checked under the assumptions that `this` has type `@ThisClass` and `ThisClass` extends `NegForm<V>`. Thus `this` can be used as the parameter to `v.negCase` in the `visit` method, as desired.

---

[12] More accurately, `this` has some type that extends `NegForm<V>`.

[13] A more subtle error arises if `Visitor` takes a type parameter and `Form` uses F-bounded polymorphism. See [Bru03] for more on various attempts at type-checking this example.

[14] We declare v's type exactly because it is used as the call site for a binary method.

Extending the interpreter to handle `PlusForm` is now straightforward:

```
interface ExtVisitor extends Visitor {
  int plusCase(PlusForm<ThisType> pf);
}
```

The definition of `PlusForm<V>` also follows naturally:

```
class PlusForm<V extends ExtVisitor> implements @Form<V> {
  ...
  public int visit(@V v) { return v.plusCase(this); }
}
```

This class can be type checked using similar derivation steps as described above.

The interpreters are written as classes which implement the appropriate visitor interface. An interpreter for the smaller language looks like this:

```
class Interp implements @Visitor {
  public int constCase(ConstForm<ThisType> cf) {
    return cf.value;
  }
  public int negCase(NegForm<ThisType> nf) {
    return (0 - nf.exp.visit(this));
  }
}
```

`ThisType` is used in the instantiations of the classes representing syntactic forms in the methods so that the extended interpreter can reuse the code for interpreting all of the old forms. This satisfies the extensibility requirement that was set out in the beginning. The extended interpreter is also easy to write:

```
class ExtInterp extends Interp implements @ExtVisitor {
  public int plusCase(PlusForm<ThisType> pf) {
    int lval = pf.lhs.visit(this);
    int rval = pf.rhs.visit(this);
    return lval + rval;
  }
}
```

In fact, the solution to the visitor problem with `ThisType` is not yet ideal, as we would also like to be able to parameterize visitors by their return type in order to write other visitors (e.g., type checkers, pretty printers, etc.). A more detailed discussion of this problem along with a suggested solution using a generalization of *MyType* to mutually recursive types is given in [Bru03].

5.3 Bounded Polymorphism and `ThisType`

In GJ, one can declare type variables with bounds that restrict the types that can be used to instantiate them. GJ's rules for bounded type variable instantiation state that if the bound is a class, then any class that extends that class may instantiate its variable. If the bound is an interface, then any interface that extends the type, or any class that implements the interface type may instantiate it. In GJ, a type variable such as `V` in the `Form` class might be instantiated with an interface type or a class type at runtime.

This convenient conflating of the notions of an interface extending another and a class implementing an interface runs into difficulties in the presence of `ThisType`. As a result, in LOOJ, if `I` is an interface and a class or interface declares a type variable `T` extending `I`, then only interfaces can be used to instantiate `T`. For example, with the `Form` interface, we may instantiate `V` with `Visitor` or `ExtVisitor`, but *not* with a class `C`.

The following example illustrates why this restriction is needed:

```
interface Iter {
  @ThisType getNext();
  void setNext(@ThisType newNext);
}
class C implements @Iter { ... }
class D implements @Iter { ... }
class E<X extends Iter> {
  @X x;
  public void setX(@X newX) { this.x = newX; }
  public @X getX() { return x; }
  public @X peekAhead() {
    return x.getNext();
  }
}
```

This code is excerpted from a program that iterates across some values; similar examples come up in many different data structures.

The body of method `peekAhead` is clearly type safe: as `x` has type `@X`, `x.getNext()` also has type `@X` (as always, we replace occurrences of `ThisType` by the interface type of the receiver, `X`). However, this leads to problems if we attempt to instantiate type variable `X` of class `E` with a class type. Consider the following program fragment:

```
void hole(@E<C> e) {
   @C c;
   @D d;
   c.setNext(d);        // (1)
   e.setX(c);           // (2)
   c = e.peekAhead(); // (3)
}
```

The line marked `(1)` type checks because `setNext`, when invoked on an object with type `@C`, has type

```
c.setNext: @I → void
```

and d has type @D, and hence @I. The line marked (2) is unproblematic because setX has the following type when used with an @E<C>:

```
e.setX: @C → void
```

and c has type @C. The line marked (3) also type checks, because

```
e.peekAhead: void → @C
```

and c has type @C. But note that here, peekAhead actually returns an object with type @D! Thus, this code allows us to assign a D to a C – a hole.

To avoid this problem we must modify the rules from GJ for instantiating type variables. Unlike GJ's more flexible rule, which allows type variables that are bounded by interface types to be instantiated with either classes or interfaces, in LOOJ such a type variable may only be instantiated with an interface type.[15]

We believe that the loss in expressiveness at the level of bounded polymorphism is not prohibitively great, while the gains from making the restriction on instantiation, which allows us to use ThisType with receivers that are type variables, are significant. In practice, we have found that a natural programming style is to use either ThisClass or ThisType to describe the type of this, but rarely to mix both types in programs. The first style rarely uses interfaces, as is common with many Java programs; the second only uses classes to generate objects and rarely uses them as types, emulating the programming style of a language like LOOM. Instead all classes are declared with the exact interfaces that they define and interfaces are used as types in the program.

6 Summary and Related Work

In this paper we have described an extension to Java, LOOJ, that supports bounded polymorphism, exact types and new type expressions ThisClass and ThisType to represent, respectively, the class and interface of this. The language and type system is an extension of that of GJ except that parameterized methods must be instantiated with a parameter (they are not inferred as in GJ) and, if a type parameter is declared with a bound that is an interface, then it may only be instantiated with interfaces. Unlike GJ, LOOJ supports the use of instanceof and type casts with types that involve type variables. Our LOOJ compiler generates standard bytecodes that can be run on any standard JVM. We also include a sketch of the proof of soundness of Featherweight LOOJ, an extension of Featherweight Java that includes ThisClass and exact types.

This extension was directly inspired by our earlier work on the languages LOOM [BFP97] and PolyTOIL [BSvG95], which both support a *MyType* construct. (See also [Bru02] for more on *MyType*). Because Java allows both classes

[15] There are several additional points in the design space; in particular, we could make a distinction between class and interface types in the bound declaration syntax. For example, we considered introducing the syntax C<T implements I>. However, in LOOJ we chose the simplest design and instead require that type variables bounded by an interface type are only ever instantiated with interface types.

and interfaces to be used as types, we added both `ThisClass` and `ThisType` to the language. The use of both classes and interfaces as types added complications to LOOJ that did not arise in the design of LOOM or PolyTOIL. In particular, occurrences of `ThisClass` in the parameter types of methods in interfaces are difficult to make sense of. Another complication that did not arise in LOOM stems from the useful notational ambiguity of GJ that allows programs to instantiate type variables whose bound is an interface type with a class type. Both of these complications are a result of allowing both classes and interfaces to be used as types. We would prefer that only interfaces be used as types, but we realize that many programmers like the convenience of using classes as types.

There have been many proposals for extensions of Java involving bounded polymorphism. including GJ [BOSW98], Pizza [OW97], NextGen [CS98], and PolyJ [MBL97], however none of these has included constructs similar to `ThisClass` or `ThisType`. Our use of instance variables to hold `PolyClass` objects for each type variable in order to support `instanceof` and type casts was originally proposed in Burstein [Bur98], and further refined in Foster [Fos01]. Viroli and Natali [VN00] independently proposed a similar scheme. Their scheme provided optimizations that could be adopted in our implementation to improve efficiency. NextGen, and it more recent offspring, MixGen [ABC03], both support `instanceof` and type casts using a relatively efficient heterogeneous translation that results in a different (though compact) class being generated for each instantiation of a parameterized class.

We have also designed languages with a generalized *MyType* construct for groups of mutually recursive classes. An early version is reported in [BV99], while a more powerful version is sketched in [Bru03], which also includes much more detail on solutions to typing visitors (the so-called "Expression problem").

In related work, Gonzalez [Gon03] has designed and implemented a verifier for the JVM that accepts annotated bytecode generated by a variant of the LOOJ compiler. After verifying the bytecode, all type information is stripped away and standard JVML bytecode is executed. As the type variable information is available to the verifier, we can eliminate many of the casts inserted by the GJ compiler that the type system guarantees will succeed. While we have not yet run careful benchmarks, we expect that this change will result in increased performance over the GJ compiler. An advantage of this approach is that the efficiency of existing high performance JVML JITs can be improved by replacing their existing verifiers with verifiers that are aware of the extended type system.

Acknowledgements. We wish to thank the anonymous ECOOP reviewers, Stephen Freund, and Alan Schmitt for very helpful comments on an earlier draft.

References

[ABC03] Eric Allen, Jonathan Bannet, and Robert Cartwright. A first-class approach to genericity. In *Proceedings of the 18th ACM SIGPLAN conference on Object-oriented programing, systems, languages, and applications*, pages 96–114. ACM Press, 2003.

[AFM97] Ole Agesen, Stephen N. Freund, and John C. Mitchell. Adding type parameterization to the java language. In *Proceedings of the 12th ACM SIGPLAN conference on Object-oriented programming, systems, languages, and applications*, pages 49–65. ACM Press, 1997.

[BCK+01] Gilad Bracha, Norman Cohen, Christian Kemper, Steve Marx, Martin Odersky, Sven-Eric Panitz, David Stoutamire, Kresten Thorup, and Philip Wadler. Adding generics to the Java programming language. URL: `http://jcp.org/aboutJava/communityprocess/review/jsr014/index.html`, 2001.

[BFP97] Kim B. Bruce, Adrian Fiech, and Leaf Petersen. Subtyping is not a good "match" for object-oriented languages. In *ECOOP '97*, pages 104–127. LNCS 1241, Springer-Verlag, 1997.

[BFSvG03] Kim B. Bruce, Adrien Fiech, Angela Schuett, and Robert van Gent. PolyTOIL: A type-safe polymorphic object-oriented language. *ACM TOPLAS*, 25(2):225–290, 2003.

[BOSW98] Gilad Bracha, Martin Odersky, David Stoutamire, and Philip Wadler. Making the future safe for the past: Adding genericity to the Java programming language. In *Object-Oriented Programming: Systems, Languages, Applications (OOPSLA)*, Vancouver, October 1998. ACM.

[Bru02] Kim B. Bruce. *Foundations of Object-Oriented Languages: Types and Semantics.* MIT Press, Cambridge, MA, 2002.

[Bru03] Kim B. Bruce. Some challenging typing issues in object-oriented languages. In *Electronic notes in Theoretical Computer Science*, volume 82 (no. 8), 2003. URL: `http://www.elsevier.nl/gej-ng/31/29/23/133/51/show/Products/notes/index.htt`, 29 pages.

[BSvG95] Kim B. Bruce, Angela Schuett, and Robert van Gent. PolyTOIL: A type-safe polymorphic object-oriented language, extended abstract. In *ECOOP '95*, pages 27–51. LNCS 952, Springer-Verlag, 1995.

[Bur98] Jon Burstein. *Rupiah: An extension to Java supporting match-bounded parametric polymorphism, ThisType, and exact typing.* Williams College Senior Honors Thesis, 1998.

[BV99] Kim B. Bruce and Joseph C. Vanderwaart. Semantics-driven language design: Statically type-safe virtual types in object-oriented languages. In *Electronic notes in Theoretical Computer Science*, volume 20, 1999. URL: `http://www.elsevier.nl/locate/entcs/volume20.html`, 26 pages.

[CS98] R. Cartwright and G. Steele, Jr. Compatible genericity with run-time types for the Java programming language, 1998.

[Fos01] John N. Foster. *Rupiah: Towards an Expressive Static Type System for Java.* Williams College Senior Honors Thesis, 2001.

[Gon03] Robert Gonzalez. *In the World of Type Checking, Smarter Is Faster.* Williams College Senior Honors Thesis, 2003.

[GRJV94] E. Gamma, R.Helm, R. Johnson, and J. Vlissides. *Design Patterns: Abstraction and reuse of object-oriented designs.* Addison-Wesley, 1994.

[IPW99] Atshushi Igarashi, Benjamin Pierce, and Philip Wadler. Featherweight Java: A minimal core calculus for Java and GJ. In Loren Meissner, editor, *Proceedings of the 1999 ACM SIGPLAN Conference on Object-Oriented Programming, Systems, Languages & Applications (OOPSLA'99)*, volume 34(10), pages 132–146, N. Y., 1999.

[MBL97] Andrew C. Myers, Joseph A. Bank, and Barbara Liskov. Parameterized types for Java. In *ACM Symposium on the Principles of Programming Languages*, pages 132–145. ACM, 1997.

[OW97] Martin Odersky and Philip Wadler. Pizza into Java: Translating theory into practice. In *24th ACM Symp. on the Principles of Programming Languages*, pages 146–159. ACM, 1997.

[VN00] Mirko Viroli and Antonio Natali. Parametric polymorphism in Java: an approach to translation based on reflective features. In *Object-Oriented Programming: Systems, Languages, Applications (OOPSLA)*, Minneapolis, October 2000. ACM.

Featherweight LOOJ

The formal language Featherweight Java only models a small subset of Java – notably it does not include imperative features or interfaces – but has a correspondingly simple dynamic semantics and soundness proof. Its main virtue is that it is easy to extend. In their original paper, its designers extend it immediately by modelling the core features of GJ in the Featherweight GJ (FGJ) calculus.

In this section, we describe an extension to FGJ with `ThisClass` and exact types. The extended calculus, Featherweight LOOJ (FLJ), formalizes the core of the LOOJ type system. Much of what follows is similar to and assumes familiarity with FGJ. That FLJ is such a modest extension to FGJ is, we claim, a virtue, and suggests that `ThisClass` would be easy to add to many Java-like languages. To keep the presentation compact, we highlight the important differences while eliding some of the less interesting details that are the same in both calculi. As noted earlier, the full system and soundness proof is available in an accompanying technical report [?].

The essential difference between GJ and LOOJ is that the latter includes `ThisClass`. Accordingly, the most substantial differences in the core calculi FGJ and FLJ appear in the parts of the type system that deal with fields and methods whose type involves `ThisClass`. As we have described in earlier sections, uses of `ThisClass` are type checked statically by substituting the type of the receiver of a message send (or field access) for occurrences of `ThisClass`. Hence, in the calculi, the key differences arise in the auxiliary definitions that define the operations for looking up the fields (*fields*), method type and method body (*mtype* and *mbody*) of members of a class. Other major differences have to do with tracking exact types in the type system. In particular we do not wish to allow instantiation of type variables by exact types, or to allow doubly-exact types. Ensuring these well-formedness constraints induces some notational complexity. Most of the rest of the complexity of FLJ is directly inherited from FGJ.

The syntax of FLJ is shown in Figure 1. Following the syntactic conventions of FJ, we abbreviate `extends` with $\triangleleft$, and `return` with $\uparrow$; $\overline{\mathtt{T}}$ is used as shorthand for $\mathtt{T}_1, ...\mathtt{T}_n$, $\overline{\mathtt{T}}\ \overline{\mathtt{f}}$ abbreviates $\mathtt{T}_1\mathtt{f}_1, ...\mathtt{T}_n\mathtt{f}_n$, etc. Term contexts Γ are partial functions from variables to types; similarly, type contexts Δ map type variables and `ThisClass` to their bounds. The class table CT is assumed to be fixed, and maps class names to their definitions.

We adopt the syntactic convention introduced in FJ that `x` ranges over the set of variable names and the special variable `this`. Similarly, `X` ranges over the

Syntax

$$
\begin{array}{lrl}
\textit{Classes} & \mathsf{CL} ::= & \mathtt{class}\ \mathtt{C}\langle\overline{\mathtt{Z}} \triangleleft \overline{\mathtt{N}}\rangle \triangleleft \mathtt{D}\langle\overline{\mathtt{N}}\rangle\ \{\ \overline{\mathtt{T}}\ \overline{\mathtt{f}};\ \mathtt{K}\ \overline{\mathtt{M}}\ \} \\
\textit{Constructors} & \mathsf{K} ::= & \mathtt{C}(\overline{\mathtt{S}}\ \overline{\mathtt{g}}, \overline{\mathtt{T}}\ \overline{\mathtt{f}})\ \{\ \mathtt{super}(\overline{\mathtt{g}});\ \mathtt{this}.\overline{\mathtt{f}} = \overline{\mathtt{f}};\ \} \\
\textit{Methods} & \mathsf{M} ::= & \langle\overline{\mathtt{Z}} \triangleleft \overline{\mathtt{N}}\rangle\ \mathtt{T}\ \mathtt{m}(\overline{\mathtt{T}}\ \overline{\mathtt{x}})\ \{\ \uparrow \mathtt{e};\ \} \\
\textit{Expressions} & \mathsf{e} ::= & \mathtt{x} \mid \mathtt{e.f} \mid \mathtt{x.m}\langle\overline{\mathtt{H}}\rangle(\overline{\mathtt{e}}) \mid \mathtt{new}\ \mathtt{C}\langle\overline{\mathtt{H}}\rangle(\overline{\mathtt{e}}) \mid (\mathtt{T})\mathtt{e} \\
\textit{Types} & \mathsf{T} ::= & \mathtt{H} \mid @\mathtt{H} \\
\textit{Hash Types} & \mathsf{H} ::= & \mathtt{X} \mid \mathtt{C}\langle\overline{\mathtt{H}}\rangle \\
\textit{Bound Types} & \mathsf{N} ::= & \mathtt{C}\langle\overline{\mathtt{Z}}\rangle \mid \mathtt{C}\langle\overline{\mathtt{N}}\rangle
\end{array}
$$

Field Lookup

$$\textit{fields}(\mathtt{Object}, \_) = \emptyset \qquad \text{(F-OBJ)}$$

$$\frac{\mathsf{CT}(\mathtt{C}) = \mathtt{class}\ \mathtt{C}\langle\overline{\mathtt{Z}} \triangleleft \overline{\mathtt{N}}\rangle \triangleleft \mathtt{D}\langle\overline{\mathtt{U}}\rangle\ \{\ \overline{\mathtt{S}}\ \overline{\mathtt{f}};\ \ldots\ \} \qquad \textit{fields}(\mathtt{D}\langle\overline{\mathtt{U}}\rangle, @\mathtt{ThisClass}) = \overline{\mathtt{Y}}\ \overline{\mathtt{g}}}{\textit{fields}(\mathtt{C}\langle\overline{\mathtt{T}}\rangle, @\mathtt{R}) = [\overline{\mathtt{T}}/\overline{\mathtt{Z}}][\mathtt{R}/\mathtt{ThisClass}](\overline{\mathtt{Y}}\ \overline{\mathtt{g}}, \overline{\mathtt{S}}\ \overline{\mathtt{f}})}\ \text{(F-@CL)}$$

$$\frac{\begin{array}{c}\mathtt{R}\ \text{not exact} \qquad \mathsf{CT}(\mathtt{C}) = \mathtt{class}\ \mathtt{C}\langle\overline{\mathtt{Z}} \triangleleft \overline{\mathtt{N}}\rangle \triangleleft \mathtt{D}\langle\overline{\mathtt{U}}\rangle\ \{\ \overline{\mathtt{S}}\ \overline{\mathtt{f}};\ \ldots\ \} \\ \textit{fields}(\mathtt{D}\langle\overline{\mathtt{U}}\rangle, @\mathtt{ThisClass}) = \overline{\mathtt{Y}}\ \overline{\mathtt{g}} \qquad \textit{pos}(\overline{\mathtt{Y}}\ \overline{\mathtt{S}})\end{array}}{\textit{fields}(\mathtt{C}\langle\overline{\mathtt{T}}\rangle, \mathtt{R}) = [\overline{\mathtt{T}}/\overline{\mathtt{Z}}][\mathtt{R}/@\mathtt{ThisClass}, \mathtt{ThisClass}](\overline{\mathtt{Y}}\ \overline{\mathtt{g}}, \overline{\mathtt{S}}\ \overline{\mathtt{f}})}\ \text{(F-CL)}$$

Method Type Lookup

$$\frac{\mathsf{CT}(\mathtt{C}) = \mathtt{class}\ \mathtt{C}\langle\overline{\mathtt{Z}} \triangleleft \overline{\mathtt{N}}\rangle \triangleleft \mathtt{D}\langle\overline{\mathtt{U}}\rangle\ \{\ \ldots\ \overline{\mathtt{M}}\ \} \qquad \langle\overline{\mathtt{Y}} \triangleleft \overline{\mathtt{O}}\rangle\mathtt{V}\ \mathtt{m}(\overline{\mathtt{V}}\ \overline{\mathtt{x}})\{\uparrow \mathtt{e};\} \in \overline{\mathtt{M}}}{\textit{mtype}(\mathtt{m}, \mathtt{C}\langle\overline{\mathtt{T}}\rangle, @\mathtt{R}) = [\overline{\mathtt{T}}/\overline{\mathtt{Z}}][\mathtt{R}/\mathtt{ThisClass}](\langle\overline{\mathtt{Y}} \triangleleft \overline{\mathtt{O}}\rangle\overline{\mathtt{V}} \to \mathtt{V})}\ \text{(MT-@CL)}$$

$$\frac{\begin{array}{c}\mathsf{CT}(\mathtt{C}) = \mathtt{class}\ \mathtt{C}\langle\overline{\mathtt{Z}} \triangleleft \overline{\mathtt{N}}\rangle \triangleleft \mathtt{D}\langle\overline{\mathtt{U}}\rangle\ \{\ \ldots\ \overline{\mathtt{M}}\ \} \qquad \langle\overline{\mathtt{Y}} \triangleleft \overline{\mathtt{O}}\rangle\mathtt{V}\ \mathtt{m}(\overline{\mathtt{V}}\ \overline{\mathtt{x}})\{\uparrow \mathtt{e};\} \in \overline{\mathtt{M}} \\ \mathtt{R}\ \text{not exact} \qquad \mathtt{ThisClass}\ \text{does not appear in}\ \overline{\mathtt{V}} \qquad \textit{pos}(\mathtt{V})\end{array}}{\textit{mtype}(\mathtt{m}, \mathtt{C}\langle\overline{\mathtt{T}}\rangle, \mathtt{R}) = [\overline{\mathtt{T}}/\overline{\mathtt{Z}}][\mathtt{R}/@\mathtt{ThisClass}, \mathtt{ThisClass}](\langle\overline{\mathtt{Y}} \triangleleft \overline{\mathtt{O}}\rangle\overline{\mathtt{V}} \to \mathtt{V})}\ \text{(MT-CL)}$$

$$\frac{\mathsf{CT}(\mathtt{C}) = \mathtt{class}\ \mathtt{C}\langle\overline{\mathtt{Z}} \triangleleft \overline{\mathtt{N}}\rangle \triangleleft \mathtt{D}\langle\overline{\mathtt{U}}\rangle\ \{\ \ldots\ \overline{\mathtt{M}}\ \} \qquad \langle\overline{\mathtt{Y}} \triangleleft \overline{\mathtt{O}}\rangle\mathtt{V}\ \mathtt{m}(\overline{\mathtt{V}}\ \overline{\mathtt{x}})\{\uparrow \mathtt{e};\} \notin \overline{\mathtt{M}}}{\textit{mtype}(\mathtt{m}, \mathtt{C}\langle\overline{\mathtt{T}}\rangle, @\mathtt{R}) = [\overline{\mathtt{T}}/\overline{\mathtt{Z}}][\mathtt{R}/\mathtt{ThisClass}](\textit{mtype}(\mathtt{m}, \mathtt{D}\langle\overline{\mathtt{U}}\rangle, @\mathtt{ThisClass}))}\ \text{(MT-@SUP)}$$

$$\frac{\begin{array}{c}\mathsf{CT}(\mathtt{C}) = \mathtt{class}\ \mathtt{C}\langle\overline{\mathtt{Z}} \triangleleft \overline{\mathtt{N}}\rangle \triangleleft \mathtt{D}\langle\overline{\mathtt{U}}\rangle\ \{\ \ldots\ \overline{\mathtt{M}}\ \} \\ \langle\overline{\mathtt{Y}} \triangleleft \overline{\mathtt{O}}\rangle\mathtt{V}\ \mathtt{m}(\overline{\mathtt{V}}\ \overline{\mathtt{x}})\{\uparrow \mathtt{e};\} \notin \overline{\mathtt{M}} \qquad \textit{mtype}(\mathtt{m}, \mathtt{D}\langle\overline{\mathtt{U}}\rangle, @\mathtt{ThisClass}) = \langle\overline{\mathtt{Y}} \triangleleft \overline{\mathtt{O}}\rangle\overline{\mathtt{V}} \to \mathtt{V} \\ \mathtt{R}\ \text{not exact} \qquad \mathtt{ThisClass}\ \text{does not appear in}\ \overline{\mathtt{V}} \qquad \textit{pos}(\mathtt{V})\end{array}}{\textit{mtype}(\mathtt{m}, \mathtt{C}\langle\overline{\mathtt{T}}\rangle, \mathtt{R}) = [\overline{\mathtt{T}}/\overline{\mathtt{Z}}][\mathtt{R}/@\mathtt{ThisClass}, \mathtt{ThisClass}]\langle\overline{\mathtt{Y}} \triangleleft \overline{\mathtt{O}}\rangle\overline{\mathtt{V}} \to \mathtt{V}}\ \text{(MT-SUP)}$$

Positive Occurrences of ThisClass

$$\textit{pos}(\mathtt{Object}) \qquad \textit{pos}(\mathtt{X}) \qquad \frac{\textit{pos}(\mathtt{T})}{\textit{pos}(@\mathtt{T})} \qquad \frac{\mathtt{ThisClass}\ \text{does not appear in}\ \overline{\mathtt{T}}}{\textit{pos}(\mathtt{C}\langle\overline{\mathtt{T}}\rangle)}$$

Fig. 1. FLJ Syntax and Auxiliary Definitions

set of type variables and the special type `ThisClass`. The metavariables `Y` and `Z`, however, only range over type variable names. For example, the declared type variables of a class, $\overline{\mathtt{Z}}$, may not include `ThisClass`. The syntax also enforces the following restriction: the bound of a type variable declaration may not contain `ThisClass`, `ThisType` or an exact type. Otherwise the syntax is a straightforward extension of FGJ.

The auxiliary definitions *fields* and *mtype* define the fields of a class and the type of a method respectively. Note that some of the definitions make use of a non-standard substitution operation. When we write the substitution expression:

$$[\mathtt{R}/@\mathtt{ThisClass}, \mathtt{ThisClass}]\mathtt{T}$$

we mean the operation that substitutes `R` for each occurrence of `@ThisClass` in `T` and `R` for each *remaining* `ThisClass` in `T`.[16]

The definitions of *mbody*, which looks up the body of a method, bound_Δ, which looks up the bound of a type in Δ, and *override*, which ensures that a class correctly overrides a method, are very similar to their versions in FGJ and are elided here. Figure 1 shows the definitions of *fields*, *mtype*, and *pos*. The definition *mtype* takes three arguments: the method's name, the class where we start searching for its definition, and the type of the receiver of the method invocation and returns the method's type. The definition of *fields* is similar; it takes the type of the class and the type of the receiver of the field access and returns the types and names of the fields. In each of these definitions, occurrences of `ThisClass` in the signature are replaced by the type of the the receiver. Finally, *pos* asserts that `ThisClass` only appears positively in a type. In particular *pos*(`ThisClass`) and *pos*(`@ThisClass`) are defined but *pos*(`C⟨ThisClass⟩`) is not, because `C⟨Z⟩` might have a method that takes a parameter of type `Z` and thus, use `ThisClass` negatively.[17]

Note that when used with an unexact receiver, *mtype* and *fields* can be undefined if, for example, `ThisClass` appears in a negative position in the type signature.

The evaluation relation for FLJ is given in Figure 2. Note the minor change from FGJ that a cast expression reduces if the object's type (which at runtime is known exactly) is a subtype of the specified type, `T`, in an empty type context.[18] We elide the congruence rules EC-Field, EC-Invk-Recv, EC-Invk-Arg, and EC-New-Arg, which are all similar to the versions given in FGJ.

---

[16] This is not quite the same as sequential or simultaneous substitution. In the compiler, this special substitution operation is realized by first renaming occurrences of `ThisClass` in `R` to a fresh name, performing the two substitutions simultaneously, and then renaming the occurrences in `R` back to `ThisClass`.

[17] A more complicated definition of *pos* could allow *pos*(`C⟨ThisClass⟩`) by examining the definition of `C⟨Z⟩` and ensuring that `Z` is only used positively in `C`. We use the simpler but more restrictive rule.

[18] To retain consistency with FJ, we use the word "subtype" and symbol <: to stand for the transitive closure of the extension operator in Java. However, the actual relation defined is more similar to matching (see [Bru02,BFP97]) than subtype.

Evaluation

$$\frac{\mathsf{CT(C)} = \texttt{class C}\langle\overline{\texttt{Z}} \triangleleft \overline{\texttt{N}}\rangle \triangleleft \texttt{D}\langle\overline{\texttt{U}}\rangle\ \{\ \ldots\ \} \qquad \mathit{fields}(\texttt{C}\langle\overline{\texttt{T}}\rangle, @\texttt{C}\langle\overline{\texttt{T}}\rangle) = \overline{\texttt{Q}}\ \overline{\texttt{f}}}{\texttt{new C}\langle\overline{\texttt{T}}\rangle(\overline{\texttt{e}}).\texttt{f}_\texttt{i} \rightarrow \texttt{e}_\texttt{i}} \quad \text{(E-FIELD)}$$

$$\frac{\mathsf{CT(C)} = \texttt{class C}\langle\overline{\texttt{Z}} \triangleleft \overline{\texttt{N}}\rangle \triangleleft \texttt{D}\langle\overline{\texttt{U}}\rangle\ \{\ \ldots\ \} \qquad \mathit{mbody}(\texttt{m}\langle\overline{\texttt{Y}}\rangle, \texttt{C}\langle\overline{\texttt{T}}\rangle, @\texttt{C}\langle\overline{\texttt{T}}\rangle) = (\overline{\texttt{x}}, \texttt{e}_0)}{\texttt{new C}\langle\overline{\texttt{T}}\rangle(\overline{\texttt{e}}).\texttt{m}\langle\overline{\texttt{Y}}\rangle(\overline{\texttt{d}}) \rightarrow [\overline{\texttt{d}}/\overline{\texttt{x}}, \texttt{new C}\langle\overline{\texttt{T}}\rangle(\overline{\texttt{e}})/\texttt{this}]\texttt{e}_0} \quad \text{(E-INVK)}$$

$$\frac{\emptyset \vdash @\texttt{C}\langle\overline{\texttt{T}}\rangle <: \texttt{T}}{(\texttt{T})\texttt{new C}\langle\overline{\texttt{T}}\rangle(\overline{\texttt{e}}) \rightarrow \texttt{new C}\langle\overline{\texttt{T}}\rangle(\overline{\texttt{e}})} \quad \text{(E-CAST)}$$

Well-Formed Types

$$\Delta \vdash \texttt{Object}\ \mathit{ok} \quad \text{(WF-OBJ)} \qquad \frac{\texttt{X} \in \mathit{dom}(\Delta)}{\Delta \vdash \texttt{X}\ \mathit{ok}} \quad \text{(WF-VAR)}$$

$$\frac{\Delta \vdash \texttt{T}\ \mathit{ok} \qquad \texttt{T}\ \text{not exact}}{\Delta \vdash @\texttt{T}\ \mathit{ok}} \quad \text{(WF-@)}$$

$$\frac{\begin{array}{c}\mathsf{CT(C)} = \texttt{class C}\langle\overline{\texttt{Z}} \triangleleft \overline{\texttt{N}}\rangle \triangleleft \texttt{D}\langle\overline{\texttt{U}}\rangle\ \{\ \ldots\ \} \\ \Delta \vdash \overline{\texttt{T}}\ \mathit{ok} \qquad \Delta \vdash \overline{\texttt{T}} <: [\overline{\texttt{T}}/\overline{\texttt{Z}}]\overline{\texttt{N}} \qquad \text{None of } \overline{\texttt{T}} \text{ exact}\end{array}}{\Delta \vdash \texttt{C}\langle\overline{\texttt{T}}\rangle\ \mathit{ok}} \quad \text{(WF-CLASS)}$$

Subtyping

$$\Delta \vdash \texttt{T} <: \texttt{T} \quad \text{(S-REFL)} \qquad \Delta \vdash \texttt{X} <: \Delta(\texttt{X}) \quad \text{(S-VAR)} \qquad \Delta \vdash @\texttt{T} <: \texttt{T} \quad \text{(S-EXACT)}$$

$$\frac{\Delta \vdash \texttt{S} <: \texttt{T} \qquad \Delta \vdash \texttt{T} <: \texttt{U}}{\Delta \vdash \texttt{S} <: \texttt{U}} \quad \text{(S-TRANS)}$$

$$\frac{\mathsf{CT(C)} = \texttt{class C}\langle\overline{\texttt{Z}} \triangleleft \overline{\texttt{N}}\rangle \triangleleft \texttt{D}\langle\overline{\texttt{U}}\rangle\ \{\ \ldots\ \}}{\Delta \vdash \texttt{C}\langle\overline{\texttt{T}}\rangle <: [\overline{\texttt{T}}/\overline{\texttt{Z}}]\texttt{D}\langle\overline{\texttt{U}}\rangle} \quad \text{(S-SUPER)}$$

Method Typing

$$\frac{\begin{array}{c}\Delta = \overline{\texttt{Z}} <: \overline{\texttt{N}}, \overline{\texttt{Y}} <: \overline{\texttt{O}}, \texttt{ThisClass} <: \texttt{C}\langle\overline{\texttt{Z}}\rangle \\ \Delta \vdash \overline{\texttt{T}}, \texttt{T}, \overline{\texttt{O}}\ \mathit{ok} \qquad \Delta; \overline{\texttt{x}} : \overline{\texttt{T}}, \texttt{this} : @\texttt{ThisClass} \vdash \texttt{e}_0 : \texttt{S} \\ \Delta \vdash \texttt{S} <: \texttt{T} \qquad \mathsf{CT(C)} = \texttt{class C}\langle\overline{\texttt{Z}} \triangleleft \overline{\texttt{N}}\rangle \triangleleft \texttt{D}\langle\overline{\texttt{U}}\rangle\ \{\ \ldots\ \} \qquad \mathit{override}(\texttt{m}, \texttt{D}\langle\overline{\texttt{U}}\rangle, \langle\overline{\texttt{Y}} \triangleleft \overline{\texttt{O}}\rangle\overline{\texttt{T}} \rightarrow \texttt{T})\end{array}}{\langle\overline{\texttt{Y}} \triangleleft \overline{\texttt{O}}\rangle\ \texttt{T m}(\overline{\texttt{T}}\ \overline{\texttt{x}})\ \{\ \uparrow \texttt{e}_0;\ \}\ \text{OK in } \texttt{C}\langle\overline{\texttt{Z}} \triangleleft \overline{\texttt{N}}\rangle}$$

Class Typing

$$\frac{\begin{array}{c}\overline{\texttt{Z}} <: \overline{\texttt{N}} \vdash \overline{\texttt{N}}, \texttt{D}\langle\overline{\texttt{V}}\rangle, \overline{\texttt{T}}\ \mathit{ok} \qquad \mathit{fields}(\texttt{D}\langle\overline{\texttt{V}}\rangle, @\texttt{ThisClass}) = \overline{\texttt{U}}\ \overline{\texttt{g}} \\ \overline{\texttt{M}}\ \text{OK in } \texttt{C}\langle\overline{\texttt{Z}} \triangleleft \overline{\texttt{N}}\rangle \qquad \texttt{K} = \texttt{C}(\overline{\texttt{U}}\ \overline{\texttt{g}}, \overline{\texttt{T}}\ \overline{\texttt{f}})\ \{\ \texttt{super}(\overline{\texttt{g}});\ \texttt{this}.\overline{\texttt{f}} = \overline{\texttt{f}};\ \}\end{array}}{\texttt{class C}\langle\overline{\texttt{Z}} \triangleleft \overline{\texttt{N}}\rangle \triangleleft \texttt{D}\langle\overline{\texttt{V}}\rangle\ \{\ \overline{\texttt{T}}\ \overline{\texttt{f}};\ \texttt{K}\ \overline{\texttt{M}}\ \}\ \text{OK}}$$

Fig. 2. FLJ Semantics, Well-formedness, Subtyping, Class and Method Typing

Expression Typing

$$\Delta;\Gamma \vdash \mathtt{x} : \Gamma(\mathtt{x}) \qquad \text{(T-VAR)}$$

$$\frac{\Delta;\Gamma \vdash \mathtt{e_0} : \mathtt{T_0} \qquad \mathit{fields}(\mathrm{bound}_\Delta(\mathtt{T_0}),\mathtt{T_0}) = \overline{\mathtt{T}}\ \overline{\mathtt{f}}}{\Delta;\Gamma \vdash \mathtt{e_0.f_i} : \mathtt{T_i}} \ \text{(T-FIELD)}$$

$$\frac{\begin{array}{c}\Delta;\Gamma \vdash \mathtt{e_0} : \mathtt{T_0} \qquad \mathit{mtype}(m,\mathrm{bound}_\Delta(\mathtt{T_0}),\mathtt{T_0}) = \langle \overline{\mathtt{Y}} \triangleleft \overline{\mathtt{O}}\rangle\overline{\mathtt{U}} \rightarrow \mathtt{U} \\ \Delta \vdash \overline{\mathtt{V}}\ \mathit{ok} \qquad \Delta \vdash \overline{\mathtt{V}} <: [\overline{\mathtt{V}}/\overline{\mathtt{Y}}]\overline{\mathtt{O}} \qquad \Delta;\Gamma \vdash \overline{\mathtt{e}} : \overline{\mathtt{S}} \qquad \Delta \vdash \overline{\mathtt{S}} <: [\overline{\mathtt{V}}/\overline{\mathtt{Y}}]\overline{\mathtt{U}}\end{array}}{\Delta;\Gamma \vdash \mathtt{e_0.m}\langle\overline{\mathtt{V}}\rangle(\overline{\mathtt{e}}) : [\overline{\mathtt{V}}/\overline{\mathtt{Y}}]\mathtt{U}} \ \text{(T-INVK)}$$

$$\frac{\begin{array}{c}\mathtt{CT(C)} = \mathtt{class}\ \mathtt{C}\langle\overline{\mathtt{Z}} \triangleleft \overline{\mathtt{N}}\rangle \triangleleft \mathtt{D}\langle\overline{\mathtt{U}}\rangle\ \{\ ...\ \} \\ \Delta \vdash \mathtt{C}\langle\overline{\mathtt{T}}\rangle\ \mathit{ok} \qquad \Delta;\Gamma \vdash \overline{\mathtt{e}} : \overline{\mathtt{S}} \qquad \mathit{fields}(\mathtt{C}\langle\overline{\mathtt{T}}\rangle, @\mathtt{C}\langle\overline{\mathtt{T}}\rangle) = \overline{\mathtt{R}}\ \overline{\mathtt{f}} \qquad \Delta \vdash \overline{\mathtt{S}} <: \overline{\mathtt{R}}\end{array}}{\Delta;\Gamma \vdash \mathtt{new}\ \mathtt{C}\langle\overline{\mathtt{T}}\rangle(\overline{\mathtt{e}}) : @\mathtt{C}\langle\overline{\mathtt{T}}\rangle} \ \text{(T-NEW)}$$

$$\frac{\Delta \vdash \mathtt{T}\ \mathit{ok} \qquad \Delta;\Gamma \vdash \mathtt{e_0} : \mathtt{T_0} \qquad \Delta \vdash \mathtt{T_0} <: \mathtt{T}}{\Delta;\Gamma \vdash (\mathtt{T})\mathtt{e_0} : \mathtt{T}} \ \text{(T-UCAST)}$$

$$\frac{\Delta \vdash \mathtt{T}\ \mathit{ok} \qquad \Delta;\Gamma \vdash \mathtt{e_0} : \mathtt{T_0} \qquad \Delta \vdash \mathtt{T} <: \mathtt{T_0} \qquad \mathtt{T_0} \neq \mathtt{T}}{\Delta;\Gamma \vdash (\mathtt{T})\mathtt{e_0} : \mathtt{T}} \ \text{(T-DCAST)}$$

$$\frac{\Delta \vdash \mathtt{T}\ \mathit{ok} \qquad \Delta;\Gamma \vdash \mathtt{e_0} : \mathtt{T_0} \qquad \Delta \vdash \mathtt{T_0} \not<: \mathtt{T}, \mathtt{T} \not<: \mathtt{T_0} \qquad \mathit{stupid\ warning}}{\Delta;\Gamma \vdash (\mathtt{T})\mathtt{e_0} : \mathtt{T}} \ \text{(T-SCAST)}$$

Fig. 3. FLJ Expression Typing

Well-Formed Types. The rules for well-formed types are given in Figure 2. The interesting cases here involve exact types: rule WF-@ states that an exact type is well-formed if its non-exact version is well-formed and not an exact type (this prevents us from forming doubly-exact types such as `@@T`). Similarly, the types used to instantiate a class's type variables must not be exact, as specified by rule WF-CLASS.

The subtyping rules for FLJ are given in Figure 2. The only interesting difference here is the addition of S-EXACT. It says that an exact type is a subtype of its unexact version. Intuitively, this makes sense: we can use an object of type `@T` anywhere that we expected an object whose type was `T`.

The rule for typing classes and methods are given in Figure 2. Note that methods are type checked in a context where `ThisClass` extends the class that the method appears in, and where `this` is assumed to have type `@ThisClass`.

Figure 3 gives the rules for typing expressions. The most interesting cases are for field access and method invocation. Because they are similar, we explain only method invocation here. Recall that a binary method may only be invoked on a receiver whose type is known exactly. In rule T-INVK, the type of the receiver, `T_0`, of the method call is passed to *mtype*. If `T_0` is exact, then *mtype* substitutes it for `ThisClass` in the signature before returning the method type.

If T_0 is not exact and ThisClass appears in a negative position, then *mtype* is undefined. Otherwise it substitutes T_0 for @ThisClass and then substitutes T_0 for ThisClass. Finally, we check that the types of the actual parameters are subtypes of the types of the formal parameters. Typing for fields is similar. Rule T-NEW states that a new expression has the exact class type of the object created. The rule T-DCAST is more flexible than the GJ version because LOOJ is not implemented by erasure, so unlike GJ, we do not need to rule out casts that would fail at the source level but succeed in their compiled versions.

Featherweight LOOJ Properties. Because of space limitations, we only give the statements of the relevant lemmas and theorems.

Lemma 1 (Inversion).

1. If $\Delta \vdash \mathtt{S} <: @\mathtt{T}$ with no exact types appearing in Δ, then S is @T.
2. If *pos*(T) then either T is ThisClass or @ThisClass, or else ThisClass does not appear in T.

Lemma 2 (Fields Lookup). If $\Delta \vdash \mathtt{S} <: \mathtt{T}$ and $\mathit{fields}(\mathrm{bound}_\Delta(\mathtt{T}), \mathtt{T}) = \overline{\mathtt{C}}\ \overline{\mathtt{f}}$ then $\mathit{fields}(\mathrm{bound}_\Delta(\mathtt{S}), \mathtt{S}) = \overline{\mathtt{D}}\ \overline{\mathtt{g}}$ and $\forall i \leq \#(\overline{\mathtt{f}}), \Delta \vdash \mathtt{D_i} <: \mathtt{C_i}$ and $\mathtt{f_i} = \mathtt{g_i}$

Lemma 3 (MType Lookup). If $\Delta \vdash \mathtt{S} <: \mathtt{T}$ and $\mathit{mtype}(\mathtt{m}, \mathrm{bound}_\Delta(\mathtt{T}), \mathtt{T}) = \langle \overline{\mathtt{Y}} \lhd \overline{\mathtt{O}} \rangle \overline{\mathtt{C}} \rightarrow \mathtt{C}$ then $\mathit{mtype}(\mathtt{m}, \mathrm{bound}_\Delta(\mathtt{S}), \mathtt{S}) = \langle \overline{\mathtt{Y}} \lhd \overline{\mathtt{O}} \rangle \overline{\mathtt{C}} \rightarrow \mathtt{C}'$ and $\Delta, \overline{\mathtt{Y}} <: \overline{\mathtt{O}} \vdash \mathtt{C}' <: \mathtt{C}$

Lemma 4 (Substitution). If $\Delta_1, \overline{\mathtt{X}} <: \overline{\mathtt{N}}, \Delta_2 \vdash \mathtt{S} <: \mathtt{T}$ and $\Delta_1 \vdash \overline{\mathtt{U}} <: [\overline{\mathtt{U}}/\overline{\mathtt{X}}]\overline{\mathtt{N}}$ and $\Delta_1 \vdash \overline{\mathtt{U}}$ *ok* and none of $\overline{\mathtt{U}}$ exact and none of $\overline{\mathtt{X}} \in \Delta_1$ then

1. $\Delta_1, [\overline{\mathtt{U}}/\overline{\mathtt{X}}]\Delta_2 \vdash [\overline{\mathtt{U}}/\overline{\mathtt{X}}]\mathtt{S} <: [\overline{\mathtt{U}}/\overline{\mathtt{X}}]\mathtt{T}$
2. $\Delta_1, [\overline{\mathtt{U}}/\overline{\mathtt{X}}]\Delta_2 \vdash [\overline{\mathtt{U}}/\overline{\mathtt{X}}]\mathtt{T}\ \mathit{ok}$
3. Additionally, if $\Delta_1, \overline{\mathtt{X}} <: \overline{\mathtt{N}}, \Delta_2; \Gamma \vdash \mathtt{e} : \mathtt{T}$ then $\Delta_1, [\overline{\mathtt{U}}/\overline{\mathtt{X}}]\Delta_2; [\overline{\mathtt{U}}/\overline{\mathtt{X}}]\Gamma \vdash [\overline{\mathtt{U}}/\overline{\mathtt{X}}]\mathtt{e} : \mathtt{S}$ for some S such that $\Delta_1, [\overline{\mathtt{U}}/\overline{\mathtt{X}}]\Delta_2 \vdash \mathtt{S} <: [\overline{\mathtt{U}}/\overline{\mathtt{X}}]\mathtt{T}$
4. And if $\Delta; \Gamma, \overline{\mathtt{x}} : \overline{\mathtt{T}} \vdash \mathtt{e} : \mathtt{T}$ and $\Delta; \Gamma \vdash \overline{\mathtt{d}} : \overline{\mathtt{S}}$ and $\Delta \vdash \overline{\mathtt{S}} <: \overline{\mathtt{T}}$ then $\Delta; \Gamma \vdash [\overline{\mathtt{d}}/\overline{\mathtt{x}}]\mathtt{e} : \mathtt{S}$ for some S such that $\mathtt{S} <: \mathtt{T}$

Theorem 1 (Preservation). If $\Delta; \Gamma \vdash \mathtt{e} : \mathtt{T}$ and $\mathtt{e} \rightarrow \mathtt{e}'$ then $\Delta; \Gamma \vdash \mathtt{e}' : \mathtt{T}'$ and $\Delta \vdash \mathtt{T}' <: \mathtt{T}$.

Theorem 2 (Progress). Suppose that $\vdash \mathtt{e} : \mathtt{T}$

1. If the expression e contains $\mathtt{new}\ \mathtt{C}\langle\overline{\mathtt{T}}\rangle(\overline{\mathtt{e}}).\mathtt{f}$ as a sub-expression then $\mathit{fields}(\mathtt{C}\langle\overline{\mathtt{T}}\rangle, @\mathtt{C}\langle\overline{\mathtt{T}}\rangle) = \overline{\mathtt{T}}\ \overline{\mathtt{f}}$ and $\mathtt{f} \in \overline{\mathtt{f}}$.
2. If the expression e contains $\mathtt{new}\ \mathtt{C}\langle\overline{\mathtt{T}}\rangle(\overline{\mathtt{e}}).\mathtt{m}\langle\overline{\mathtt{V}}\rangle(\overline{\mathtt{d}})$ as a sub-expression then $\mathit{mbody}(\mathtt{m}\langle\overline{\mathtt{V}}\rangle, \mathtt{C}\langle\overline{\mathtt{T}}\rangle, @\mathtt{C}\langle\overline{\mathtt{T}}\rangle) = (\overline{\mathtt{x}}, \mathtt{e_0})$ and $\#(\overline{\mathtt{x}}) = \#(\overline{\mathtt{d}})$.

Theorem 3 (Type Soundness). If $\vdash \mathtt{e} : \mathtt{T}$ and $\mathtt{e} \rightarrow^* \mathtt{e}'$ and $\mathtt{e}'$ is a normal form, then either $\mathtt{e}'$ is a value, or it contains a failed cast.

While Featherweight LOOJ omits imperative features, typing problems with instance variables generally also arise with parameters, so we are confident that the addition of instance variables will add no new difficulties.

Modules with Interfaces for Dynamic Linking and Communication

Yu David Liu and Scott F. Smith

Department of Computer Science
The Johns Hopkins University
{yliu, scott}@cs.jhu.edu

Abstract. Module systems are well known as a means for giving clear interfaces for the static linking of code. This paper shows how adding explicit interfaces to modules for 1) dynamic linking and 2) cross-computation communication can increase the declarative, encapsulated nature of modules, and build a stronger foundation for language-based security and version control. We term these new modules *Assemblages.*

1 Introduction

Module systems traditionally excel in static linking. In typical module systems such as ML functors [Mac84], mixins [BC90,DS96,HL02], Units [FF98] and Jiazzi [MFH01], each module has a list of features (including functions, classes, types, submodules, *etc*) as exports, and a list of imported features. Applications can then be built by statically linking together a collection of modules. Definitions of imported features are unknown when the module is written, but all names must be resolved the moment the module is loaded and executed.

The rapid evolution of the Internet has changed the landscape of software design, and now it is more common that encapsulated code segments contain name references that can only be resolved *at runtime*. Applications of this nature can generally be placed into two distinct categories, which we term *dynamic plugins* and *reactive computations*, respectively.

Dynamic Plugins. A dynamic plugin is our term for dynamically linked code: a piece of code is dynamically plugged into an already running computation. Dynamic plugins are ubiquitous in modern large-scale software designs, from browser and operating system plugins, to incremental as-needed loading of application features, and for dynamic update of critical software systems demanding non-stop services. When the main application is loaded, future dynamic plugins may be completely unknown, and name references to them must be bound at runtime.

Reactive Computations. Reactive computations are the collection of autonomous coarse-grained computations that are reactive to requests in a distributed environment. A reactive computation has its own collection of objects;

M. Odersky (Ed.): ECOOP 2004, LNCS 3086, pp. 414–439, 2004.

so, a thread in a JVM is not a reactive computation, but a whole JVM is, as is an application domain in the Microsoft CLR. In the grid computing paradigm, each grid cell can be viewed as a reactive computation communicating with other cells. The communication between a Java applet and its loading virtual machine can also be viewed as one between two reactive computations. Compared to a dynamic plugin, reactive computations are much more loosely coupled since object references cannot be shared; this is because the computations are on different nodes or involve parties with limited trust in each other.

As with dynamic plugins, cross-computation invocation also requires name binding at runtime: when a computation is loaded, it cannot yet know about the existence of other computations it intends to communicate with.

Previous research on dynamic linking [Blo83,LB98,SPW03,DLE03] and software updating [HMN01,BHSS03] also focuses on the dynamic plugin problem, and numerous projects on remote invocation such as RPC and RMI have targeted reactive computations. In this paper we develop a new *module-centered* approach to these two forms of computation which offers advantages over the existing approaches by making interfaces more explicit, and increasing understanding and expressiveness of the code. In particular, we develop a new module theory that, along with a standard form of interface for static linking, also incorporates explicit interfaces for dynamic plugins and reactive computations.

2 Our Approach: Assemblages

In this paper, we present a type safe module calculus with a single notion of module that supports static linking, dynamic linking, and communication between reactive computations. Our modules are called *assemblages*. Assemblages are code blocks that can be statically linked with one another to form bigger assemblages. When an assemblage is loaded into memory, it becomes an *assemblage runtime* (or *runtime* for short), which serves as a reactive computation with an explicit interface for cross-computation communication and an explicit interface for dynamically plugging other assemblages into its current runtime. All interactions of a runtime should be through these interfaces alone, giving complete encapsulation.

2.1 Basic Model

Fig. 1 shows the three fundamental processes our calculus addresses. We now introduce them separately, together with concepts and terms we will use throughout the paper.

Static Linking. Our module calculus comes with a fairly standard notion of static linking. Fig. 1 (a) shows expression $A+A'$, which represents the static linking of assemblages A and A'. One somewhat unusual feature is that assemblages themselves are first-class values in our calculus, and static linking is also a first-class expression: linking can happen anywhere in a program. Each assemblage

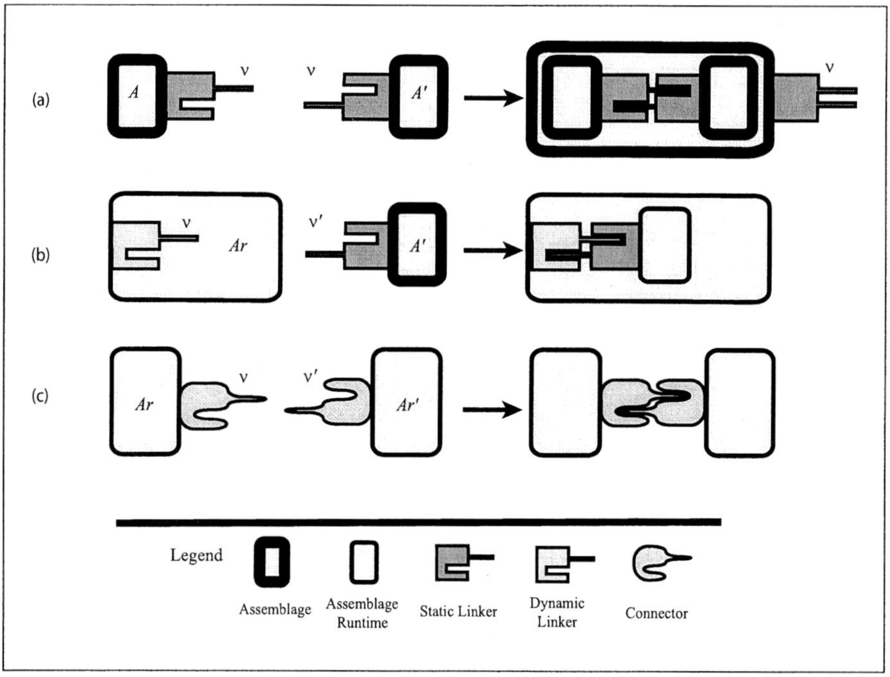

Fig. 1. Three Fundamental Processes (a) Static Linking (b) Dynamic Linking (c) Cross-computation Communication

is associated with a list of *static linkers*, each of which defines what features it imports and what ones it exports. In the static linking process, suppose A and A' each have a static linker of the name ν. The pair of static linkers are thus matched against each other, where imports of A are satisfied by exports of A' and *vice versa.* In the resulting assemblage, a new static linker with name ν will be created, which bears the exported features of both static linkers. Static linkers that are not matched will also be carried to the composed assemblage (suppose A has a static linker named ν' but A' does not). Notice that A and A' are stateless code entities. Units, mixin module systems, and various other calculi for the static linking of code fragments [Car97,DEW99,WV00,AZ02] all work in a related way, so this aspect of our theory is not particularly unique.

Dynamic Linking. Dynamic linking is illustrated in Fig. 1 (b); expression $\textbf{plugin}_{\nu\mapsto\nu'}\ A'$ in our calculus triggers a dynamic linking. Assemblage A' is loaded and linked into the current assemblage runtime Ar where the **plugin** expression is defined. The interesting thing here is not only that A' is an assemblage, but also Ar is an *assemblage* runtime. Thus, unlike some projects [Blo83, FF98,SPW03] which recognize dynamic plugins can be modelled as modules, we also recognize dynamic linking happens *between a module runtime and a mod-*

ule. By equipping Ar with interfaces describing its dynamic linking behaviors (which we call *dynamic linkers*), a successful dynamic linking process can thus be conceived as a *bi-directional* interface matching between the plugin initiator's codebase module and the module representing the dynamic plugin. We believe this is more precise and explicit than the unidirectional notion of dynamic linking found in other module systems, where the initiating computation has no explicit interface to the module being linked.

A *dynamic linker* is the dynamic linking interface of an assemblage. It specifies the dynamic linking behaviors after the assemblage is loaded to become an assemblage runtime. Specifically, it defines what type of dynamic plugins the assemblage expects. In Fig. 1 (b), the **plugin** initiating assemblage runtime has a dynamic linker named ν, and when expression $\mathbf{plugin}_{\nu \mapsto \nu'}\ A'$ is evaluated, dynamic linker ν of the initiating assemblage runtime is matched with the *static linker* ν' of A'. This may seem like a mismatch, linking a static linker and a dynamic linker, but the linking is in fact occurring across sorts: a runtime is being linked with a piece of code. The result of a **plugin** expression is for the runtime to be the original runtime plus the runtime form of the newly added plugin. Dynamic linking here does not increase the number of runtimes, because dynamic linking is a tightly-coupled interaction. A non-example is Java applets; they are not tightly coupled with the loading JVM, they are best *not* viewed as dynamically linked code. Individual applets are better modeled as distinct runtimes communicating with its inhabiting VM, which can be better modelled by the cross-computation communication we introduce next.

Cross-Computation Communication. Fig. 1 (c) demonstrates how expression $\mathbf{connect}_{\nu \mapsto \nu'}\ Ar'$ sets up a cross-computation connection between two assemblage runtimes, the runtime containing the **connect** expression (Ar) and the runtime Ar'. In a similar vein to dynamic linking, both the party *receiving* the cross-computation invocation and the party *initiating* the invocation must have explicit interfaces declaring the form of this interaction on their codebase assemblages, which we call *connectors*. A successful communication process is thus a *bi-directional* interface matching between the initiator module runtime and the receiver module runtime.

A *connector* specifies the cross-computation communication interface of an assemblage runtime. Specifically, it defines what type of assemblage runtimes the assemblage expects to communicate with. In Fig. 1 (c), the **connect**-initiating assemblage runtime has a connector named ν, and when its $\mathbf{connect}_{\nu \mapsto \nu'}\ Ar$ expression is evaluated, connector ν of the initiating assemblage runtime is matched with connector ν' of the assemblage runtime Ar. The **connect** expression will not lead to merging of runtimes, and since the runtimes must remain distinct, all parameters passed between the two must be passed by (deep) copy. These runtimes may also be on the same or different network nodes.

Before presenting further details of the system, we introduce a simple real-world example.

```
VolcanoMain = assemblage {
    static linker NetLib{
     ... statically linked some network library ...
    }
    dynamic linker DetectorPlugin{
        import detectMethod()
        export getEnv == ... get current environment snapshot ...
    }
    connector CodeUpdate{
        import getDetectCode();
        export check(condition) == ... check applicability of detect model ...
    }
    ⋮
    // local feature implementation
    updateDetector == λx.(let cb = connect_{CodeUpdate↦Code} x in
                          let code = cb ▷ getDetectCode ← () in
                          let comp = plugin_{DetectorPlugin↦Detect} code in
                          comp.detectMethod())
    ⋮
}
```

Fig. 2. A Sensor Network Example

2.2 A Real World Example

In this section, we introduce a simplified volcano sensor network example to demonstrate the basic ideas of assemblages. The example is in Fig. 2. For the purpose of improved readability, we here use sugared syntax slightly different from our calculus; type declarations are also omitted here for brevity. Initially we define an example with core features only, and will extend it below to illustrate more advanced features of our calculus.

In a typical sensor network [HSW+00] for a volcano sensing application, a number of smart tiny sensor nodes are scattered in the crater of a volcano, each of which functions as an independent computer. In addition to the parts for regular computation, each sensor node is also equipped with sensing device to collect environment information, such as temperature, electromagnetism, *etc.* Different sensor nodes can communicate with each other; at least some sensor node can communicate with base station situated out of the volcano to report data or receive control information.

One critical necessity in the design of such a system is that, once sensor nodes are physically deployed, they are not likely to be reclaimable for purposes such as software upgrade. In the example shown in Fig. 2, function updateDetector provides support to dynamically update the mathematical model of volcano detection used in the sensor: in reality, it is not uncommon for scientists to adjust the mathematical models after the sensors have been deployed.

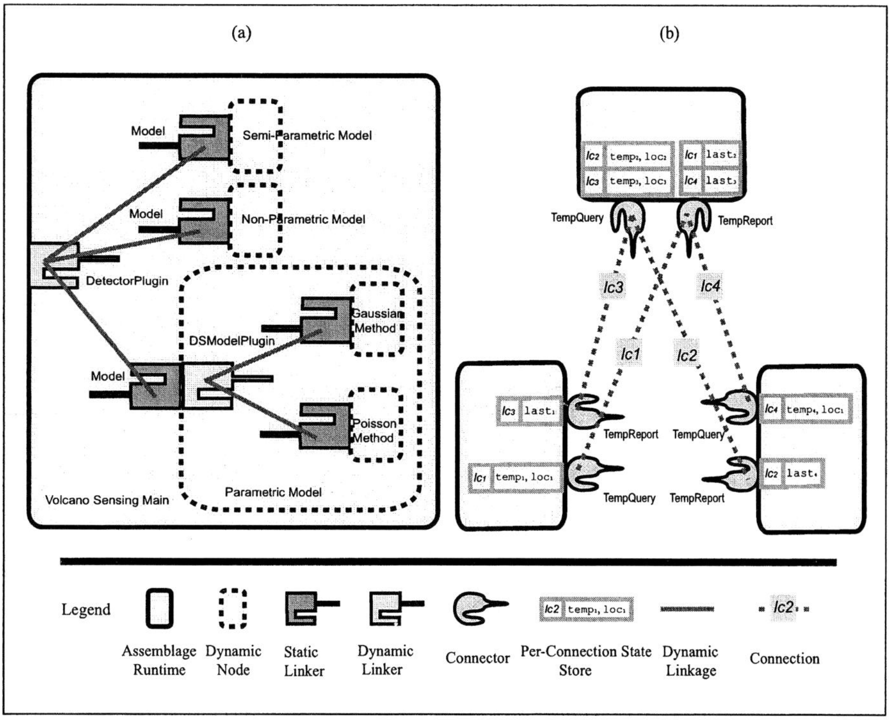

Fig. 3. An Example on (a) Rebindable Dynamic Linkers (b) Generative Stateful Connectors

Without getting into too much detail, the function works as follows: it first sets up a connection cb with base station represented by function argument x, via $\mathbf{connect}_{\mathsf{CodeUpdate}\mapsto\mathsf{Code}}\ x$. A new version of the detection model code is thus acquired by invoking $cb \triangleright \mathsf{getDetectCode} \leftarrow ()$; subsequently, it is dynamically plugged into the current runtime via $\mathbf{plugin}_{\mathsf{DetectorPlugin}\mapsto\mathsf{Detect}}\ code$. The up-to-date detection method may then be invoked via $comp.\mathsf{detectMethod}()$.

This example demonstrates some basic uses of dynamic linkers and connectors. Observe how the dynamic linker and connector are both bi-directional interfaces: they import some features and export others. Interface matching is a component of both dynamic linking and connection. The $\mathbf{connect}_{\mathsf{CodeUpdate}\mapsto\mathsf{Code}}\ x$ indicates the CodeUpdate connector of the current assemblage runtime is connected to the Code connector of x. A connection can be successfully established only if each party exports what the other party needs to import (extra exports can be present and are ignored). We also show a standard static linker NetLib, expecting some network libraries; this importer will need to be satisfied before the sensor program is up and running.

⟨⟨⟨ leave out bootstrapping; not version control -YL ⟩⟩⟩

2.3 More on Assemblages

With the basic model introduced and a simple example given, we now look at more advanced features of our calculus.

Rebindable Dynamic Linkers. In the basic model presented in Fig. 1, dynamic linking was presented as a one-to-one relation between the initiating assemblage runtime and the dynamic plugin. This is however an oversimplified view of the calculus, and does not completely coincide with reality. Consider the sensor example again. Scientists might prefer to run multiple detection models at the same time, and compare the results of different models. The current VolcanoMain assemblage however only has one dynamic linker. In a one-to-one dynamic linking model, plugging in one detection assemblage would lead to the invalidation of previous dynamic plugins on the same dynamic linker.

For this reason, dynamic linkers in our calculus are rebindable. This implies different assemblages may be plugged in to the same dynamic linker at the same time, and not interfere with each other. Fig. 3 (a) shows this one-to-N relation. Here the Volcano Sensing Main assemblage runtime is the runtime form of assemblage VolcanoMain after its static linker is satisfied; it is here dynamically linked to three different dynamic plugins representing three different detection mathematical models; interestingly, since dynamic plugins themselves can have dynamic linkers, it might plug in other assemblages as *its* plugins. In Fig. 3 (a), a dynamic plugin of the Volcano Sensing Main assemblage runtime, one representing say a parametric probabilistic detection approach, further plugs in different distribution models to its DSModelPlugin dynamic linker, such as a Gaussian distribution or Poisson distribution method.

The dynamic linking established by a **plugin** expression is called a *dynamic linkage*, and the expression returns a value we call a *dyanmic linkage handle*; programmers can use it to refer to the particular assemblage just plugged in.

(can we make an argument that our rebindable dynamic linkers are a more reasonable way to address the question of dynamic code update, in that you need to from the beginning create an interface whereby the code update can happen (and, code without such an interface cannot be updated)? My vague recollection of the existing systems is that they are total pile-o-shit hacks. – SS)

Generative Connectors. Our connectors are also more nuanced than as presented in Fig. 1: connectors also need to be rebound, as we just saw for dynamic linkers. As shown in Fig. 2.3 (b), a task such as temperature measurement in a typical volcano sensor network is achieved by the collaboration of a number of sensors; each one of them usually communicates with its neighbors to exchange data such as temperature information. Since the configuration of the network is not fixed until sensors are scattered in the crater, the program developer can not define an *a priori* list of connectors, each of which is assigned to one neighbor. Instead, each sensor must only be equipped with rebindable connectors like TempQuery and TempReport given in Fig. 3 (b), where at any moment the TempQuery connector of a sensor may be connected with multiple TempReport connectors of its neighbors, and *vice versa.*

Another important issue is that each connection will need to keep its per-connection data: sensors need to record collected temperature information from its neighbors, together with the location information on where the temperature is sampled. This kind of information varies from connection to connection; a global state of assemblage for this purpose is not enough. In Fig. 3 (b), each connector is associated with a *per-connection state store*, which records the private generative states associated with each connections. The index of the store is the connection ID generated when connection is established via a **connect** expression.

Our calculus supports generative connectors where per-connection states are supported. It implicitly also supports rebindability. Each successful **connect** expression creates a *connection*, and the expression returns a value that is a *connection handle*; with the handle, programmers can refer to different connections (and the private per-connection state) on the same connector in the same program. One additional advantage of using handles is there is no problem with programs trying to access features on a non-connected connector—there is no name by which to refer to the features on the connector until there is a handle. Since multiple handles can be active and each connection has a unique state, there is an analogy of a connection definition with a class, and each active connection with an object, with the connection handle being the reference to the object. These "objects" are something like facades in the facade design pattern—they are the external interface to the component.

Typed Calculus and Types as Features. Our calculus is typed, and the type system has several pleasant properties such as soundness and decidability of type checking. There is no runtime error associated with attempting to use a connector that is not connected to anything, because connectors are only accessed via handles which only exist because a connection was created. The only error possible is the handle could be stale because the connection has terminated. We have also explored the possibilities that types are themselves treated as features that are imported and exported across static linkers, dynamic linkers and connectors. In this presentation however, we do not focus on these aspects due to limited space. Interested readers can refer to [LS04] for details.

(could add something about polymorphism on the generative connectors. – SS)

2.4 Why Dynamic Linkers and Connectors?

Static linkers, dynamic linkers and connectors together form the interfaces of assemblages. Before proceeding to the formalization, we address an important question concerning the purpose of the paper: Why dynamic linkers and connectors?

First, *modules with fully declarative interfaces lead to a more complete program specification.* Assemblages are highly declarative; in fact, all of an assemblage's potential for interaction with outside the codebase can be read off of the interfaces. This is obviously a good thing for language design, leading to provable type safety without obscurity. The idea also has impact on paradigms of software development. Indeed, interfaces (static linkers, dynamic linkers and connectors) can be defined at the design phase, reflecting designer's intention of the assemblage to interact with other parties. A declaration of DetectorPlugin dynamic linker coincides with the designer's intention that VolcanoMain module will dynamically link to some detection model plugins; the CodeUpdate connector coincides with the designer's expectation that the module will communicate with some codebase. In a large-scale software development process, software design and software implementation are typically accomplished by different people. The module calculus' type system ensures the implementation will faithfully follow the intention of the designer. For instance, a compile-time type mismatch would occur if implementor of VolcanoMain desires to communicate with a codebase which does not provide a getDetectCode function.

Second, *these interfaces provide crucial support for extending the calculus to other important language features.* Since all of the external interactions are declared on the static linkers, dynamic linkers, and connectors, new modes of external interaction can easily be layered on top of these existing notions. Examples include security (on connectors), transaction management (on connectors), and version control (on dynamic linkers). For example, for security, since every cross-computation invocation will need to be directed through connectors, access control on connectors is enough to secure assemblage runtimes from unauthorized nonlocal access. We do not directly address these topics here, but the module theory is designed with them in mind.

Third, *dynamic linkers and connectors better model the complex interactions between different parties* than is possible in systems without them. A naive implementation for dynamic plugins can be achieved by direct dynamic loading, and invocations can thus be made on exported functions of the plugins. An obvious problem of this approach however is when there is a need for callback functions. For reactive computations, distributed protocols often involve message exchanges back and forth. If RMI or RPC is used, this interaction protocol will be completely submerged in the code in the various methods, and no single point in the program will indicate the protocol as a whole. In our example, the CodeUpdate connector specifies all the possible interactions between a code provider and a code client. The whole code updating protocol, although simple in this example, is captured by CodeUpdate connector, giving a clear protocol specification.

3 Syntax

The syntax of our calculus is shown in Fig. 4. It differs from the syntax used in Sec. 2, but in a trivial manner only: in the calculus syntax we remove the keywords (such as **assemblage**, **import** and **export**) used in the sugared syntax; otherwise the two forms of syntax are identical. Notation $\overline{m}$ is used to represent a sequence of entities $m_1, \ldots, m_n$, and we take the empty sequence as a special

A	$::=$	$\langle \overline{S}; \overline{D}; \overline{C}; \overline{L} \rangle$	*assemblage*
S, D	$::=$	$\nu \mapsto \langle \overline{I}; \overline{E} \rangle$	*static linker, dynamic linker*
C	$::=$	$\nu \mapsto \langle \overline{I}; \overline{E}; \overline{J} \rangle$	*connector*
I	$::=$	α	*imported feature*
E	$::=$	$\alpha == \lambda x.e$	*exported feature*
L	$::=$	$\alpha == F$	*local feature*
J	$::=$	$\alpha ==$ **ref** F	*per − connection state*
F	$::=$	$cst \mid A \mid \lambda x.e \mid$ **ref** F	*feature*
e	$::=$	$() \mid x \mid cst \mid$ **thisc** $\mid$ **thisd**	*null value, variable, const*
		$\mid A : \tau \mid e + e$	*first class assemblage, sum*
		$\mid$ **plugin**$_{\nu \mapsto \nu'}$ e $\mid$ **connect**$_{\nu \mapsto \nu'}$ e	*dynamic plugin, connect*
		$\mid \alpha$@`local` $\mid \alpha @ \nu \mid e.\alpha \mid e \rhd \alpha \mid e \rhd \alpha \leftarrow e$	*feature access*
		$\mid \lambda x.e : \tau \mid e\ e$	*first class function, app*
		$\mid$ **ref** $e \mid\ !\,e \mid e := e$	*state*
ν			*interface name*
α			*feature name*
τ			*type, defined in Fig.8*
cst			*integer constant*
x			*variable*

Fig. 4. Assemblage Language Syntax

value ϕ. The $\uplus$ operator denotes the concatenation of two sequences; for the empty sequence, $\overline{m} \uplus \phi = \phi \uplus \overline{m} = \overline{m}$ for any $\overline{m}$. Since in this presentation, each m_i can only take one of the three syntactical forms $a \mapsto b$, $a == b$ and $a : b$, we also view $\overline{m}$ as a mapping and call it well-formed if it is a function, *i.e.* there does not exist $a_1 = a_2$ but $b_1 \neq b_2$; in this case when no confusion arises, we also define $\overline{m}(a) = b$. $\overline{m}(a) = \bot$ iff $a \mapsto b$ (or $a == b$, or $a : b$) is not present for any b, or $\overline{m}$ is not well-formed. $\overline{m}\{a \mapsto b\}$ denotes a mapping update; it is a mapping the same as $\overline{m}$, except $\overline{m}\{a \mapsto b\}(a) = b$ while $\overline{m}(a)$ could be other values.

An assemblage (A) is composed of a well-formed sequence of static linkers ($\overline{S}$), dynamic linkers ($\overline{D}$), connectors ($\overline{C}$) and its local private code ($\overline{L}$). Each static linker or dynamic linker has a name (ν), a well-formed sequence of imported features ($\overline{I}$) and a well-formed sequence of exported features ($\overline{E}$); each connector, in addition, is associated with a well-formed sequence of per-connection states ($\overline{J}$). $\overline{I} \uplus \overline{E}$ (and in the connector case $\overline{I} \uplus \overline{E} \uplus \overline{J}$) also must be well-formed: we disallow the case where the same feature is imported and exported on the assemblage. Features are chosen from constants (cst), functions ($\lambda x.e$), references (**ref** F) and nested assemblages (A). This particular choice is made to preserve a balance between functional features and imperative features. With references and functions around, primitive classes and objects can also be modelled with widely known encoding techniques, and are left out of the calculus for simplicity. Features to be imported/exported on interfaces must be functions. This function-only restriction however does not restrict the expressiveness of the calculus:

importing/exporting references can be encoded as importing/exporting a pair of getter function and a setter function; importing/exporting assemblages can be encoded as importing/exporting a function taking a null value and returning the assemblage. Per-connection state (J) is defined via feature $\alpha ==$ **ref** F, which means the state is named α, and **ref** F will be its initial value.

Most of the expressions e have been explained in Sec. 2. Additionally, we use α@`local` to refer to a feature α defined in locally (in $\overline{L}$). $\alpha @ \nu$ refers to a feature α defined in static linker ν. **thisd** refers to the *current* dynamic linkage, and **thisc** refers to the *current* connection. The meaning of "current" depends on the dynamic linkage handle or connection handle which invokes the function **thisd**.α expression is situated in. Because of the rebindable nature of dynamic linking, we disallow a syntax like $\alpha @ \nu$ where ν is a dynamic linker name: it would be ambiguous which version of the dynamic linkages is referred to if there were more than one dynamic linkage created from the same dynamic linker, and would be undefined if none were present. This restriction on syntax also holds for connectors for similar reasons. $e.\alpha$ is used to refer to a feature α in dynamic linkage handle e. Syntax $e \triangleright \alpha$ refers to a per-connection state α in connection handle e. $e \triangleright \alpha \leftarrow e$ denotes an invocation of a function defined in a connection handle. This expression can potentially denote a cross-computation invocation, and has a different semantics from regular function application; we therefore use different syntax for the two cases. () is used to denote a null value of **unit** type, as in ML. **let** is encoded by function application.

4 Operational Semantics

In this section we present the dynamic semantics of our calculus. We first informally explain the big picture of how a typical application appears at run-time, and then we discuss formal details of the operational semantics.

4.1 The Big Picture

Sec. 2.3 gave an example of a temperature measurement application for sensor networks; the illustrations used in that section (Fig. 3), however, are only intended to target high-level concepts. In this section, the *precise* runtime snapshot of the same application is illustrated in Fig. 5. Here the whole network is composed of multiple sensor nodes in the form of Fig. 3 (b) to perform temperature measurement, while individual nodes are experimenting with different computational models in the form of Fig. 3 (a).

At runtime, the entire application space, with all reactive computations of concern, is called a *runtime global*; the whole temperature measurement network is a runtime global for instance. Inside it, independently deployed assemblage runtimes are running on potentially distributed locations. Each of them can be created by explicit **load** expressions, during which a static assemblage is loaded into memory. The first assemblage runtime in the runtime global is loaded via a *bootstrapping* process. At load time, each runtime is associated with an ID. In

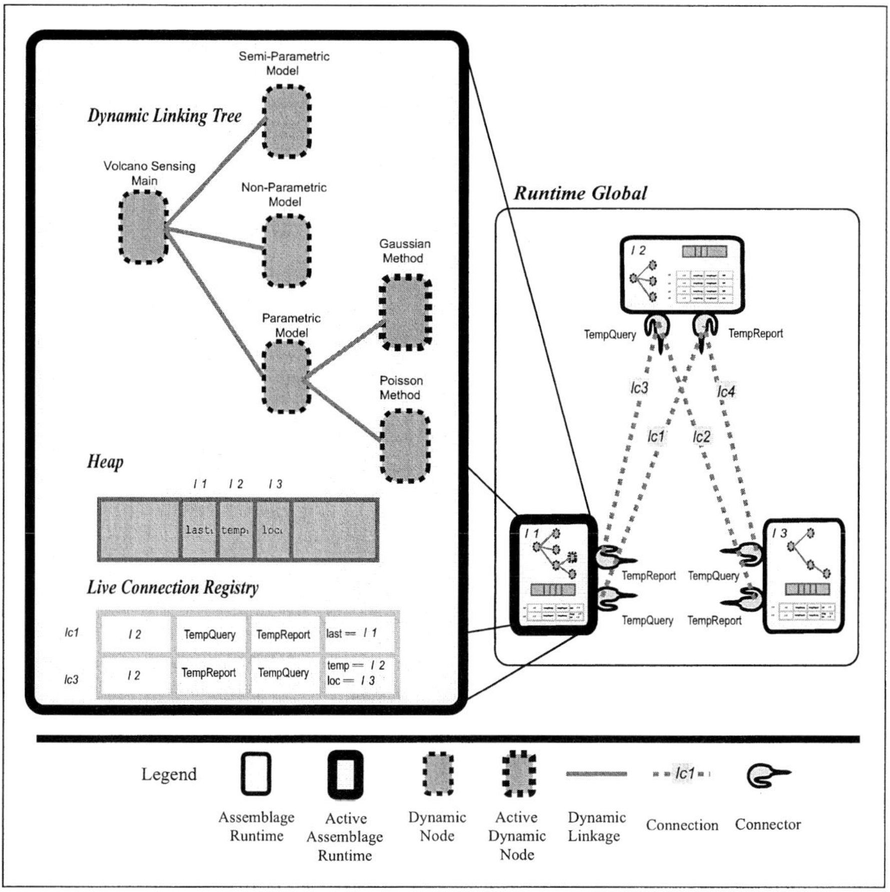

Fig. 5. The Big Picture

Fig. 5, we have three runtimes with IDs ιr_1, ιr_2 and ιr_3. Assemblage runtimes communicate with each other via connections over paired connectors, which also have connection ID's, their *connection handle*. In the figure, runtimes with ID's ιr_1 and ιr_2 are communicating via two connections; the connection with ID ιc_1 is between the connector TempQuery of ιr_1 and connector TempReport of ιr_2.

Internally, each runtime contains a *dynamic linking tree*, a *heap* and a *live connection registry*. The heap is standard and holds the multable data; it is defined as a sequence of stores, each of which is associated with a store ID. In Fig. 5, the heap of runtime ιr_1 currently has a store ιs_2 which holds a constant value $\mathtt{temp}_1$. A runtime's live connection registry holds the currently active connections. It is defined as a table indexed by connection IDs; each entry contains information such as what parties are involved in the connection (runtime IDs and connector names), and the per-connection state store. For instance, the first

$\iota r \quad \in \mathbb{R}$	*assemblage runtime ID*
$\iota s \quad \in \mathbb{S}$	*store ID*
$\iota n \quad \in \mathbb{N}$	*dynamic node ID*
$\iota d \quad \in \mathbb{D}$	*dynamic linkage ID*
$\iota c \quad \in \mathbb{C}$	*connection ID*
$G ::= \overline{R}$	*runtime global*
$R ::= \iota r \mapsto \langle T; H; Y \rangle$	*assemblage runtime*
$T ::= \langle \overline{N}; \overline{K} \rangle$	*dynamic linking tree*
$H ::= \overline{\iota s \mapsto v}$	*heap*
$Y ::= \overline{\iota c \mapsto \langle \iota r; \nu_1; \nu_2; \overline{Jr} \rangle}$	*live connection registry*
$N ::= \iota n \mapsto \langle \overline{Sr}; \overline{Dr}; \overline{Cr}; \overline{Lr} \rangle$	*dynamic node*
$K ::= \iota d \mapsto \langle \iota n_1; \nu_1; \iota n_2; \nu_2 \rangle$	*dynamic linkage*
$Jr ::= \alpha \mapsto \iota s$	*per − connection state*
$fv ::= cst \mid A \mid \mathbf{fun}(\iota r, \iota n, \lambda x.e) \mid \iota s$	*feature value*
$v ::= () \mid \iota r \mid \iota d \mid \iota c \mid fv$	*value*
$e ::= \cdots \mid v \mid \mathbf{inR}(\iota r, \iota n, e)$	*expression at runtime*
$\mathbf{E} ::= [\,] \mid \mathbf{plugin}_{\nu \mapsto \nu'}\ \mathbf{E} \mid \mathbf{connect}_{\nu \mapsto \nu'}\ \mathbf{E}$ $\mid \mathbf{E} + e \mid v + \mathbf{E}$ $\mid \mathbf{E}\ e \mid v\ \mathbf{E} \mid \mathbf{ref}\ \mathbf{E} \mid !\mathbf{E} \mid \mathbf{E} := e \mid v := \mathbf{E}$ $\mid \mathbf{E}.\alpha \mid \mathbf{E} \triangleright \alpha \mid \mathbf{E} \triangleright \alpha \leftarrow e \mid v \triangleright \alpha \leftarrow \mathbf{E} \mid \mathbf{load}\ \mathbf{E}$	*evaluation context*
$cst,\ A,\ \alpha,\ J$	*defined in Fig.* 4
$Sr,\ Dr,\ Cr\ , Lr$	*see Sec.* 4.2

Fig. 6. Operational Semantics Auxiliary Definitions

row of the live connection registry of runtime ιr_1 shown in Fig. 5 indicates it currently has a connection ιc_1 on its TempQuery connector, and that connection is to TempReport of runtime ιr_2. The last column indicates the per-connection field last has a reference value ιs_1: the value is a reference since per-connection states always contain mutable data, just as object fields in object-oriented languages are mutable. The meanings of connector-related expressions of our calculus, such as $\mathbf{connect}_{\nu \mapsto \nu'}\ e$, are related to operations on live connection registries. For instance, when a connection is established via a **connect** expression, both involved parties of the connection have one entry added to their live connection registry. Per-connection states are allocated and initialized at connection establishment time.

A dynamic linking tree is used to reflect the rebindable nature of dynamic linkers, as described informally in Sec. 2.3. Indeed, if rebindability were not supported, a **plugin** expression could just merge the codebase of the current assemblage runtime with the code of dynamic plugin, in the same manner as static linking $A_1 + A_2$. However due to rebindability, each dynamic linker of the current runtime can be associated with multiple independent dynamic plugins at the same time. The data structure is in general a tree: when the main assemblage is first loaded to memory, it creates a root node, with all application logic of the main assemblage defined inside. Each **plugin** expression executed in the root will result in the creation of a tree node representing the dynamic plugin (with all application logic of the dynamic plugin defined inside), and the newly created node becomes a child of the root. Since child nodes can themselves plug in code (the plugin of a plugin), the tree can in general have depth greater than two. The fact that the data structure is a tree other than a DAG or some random graph can be easily proved by the way it is constructed. In Fig. 5, the dynamic linking tree is the internal representation of the application whose high-level requirement is shown in Fig. 3 (a). A dynamic linking tree is composed of a series of *dynamic nodes* (the tree nodes) and *dynamic linkages* (the tree edges). Each dynamic linkage is referenced by its dynamic linkage ID ιd, which is the realization of the *dynamic linkage handle* of the previous section. The behaviors of dynamic linker-related expressions, such as $\mathbf{plugin}_{\nu \mapsto \nu'}\ e$, are operations on dynamic linking trees. For instance, when a plugin is assembled via a **plugin** expression, the dynamic plugin will becomes a dynamic node that is a leaf of the initiator runtime's dynamic linking tree.

Since concurrency is not the focus of this paper, our calculus assumes for simplicity that at any moment only one assemblage runtime is active, and only one dynamic node in this active runtime is performing the reduction. This fact is shown in Fig. 5, where distinct notation is used for active runtimes and active dynamic nodes.

4.2 A Formal Overview of Dynamic Semantics

Fig. 6 defines the relevant data structures that play a part in defining the dynamic semantics. Most of them have been explained with the example in Fig. 5. The rest is explained below.

Formal Details of the Dynamic Linking Tree. Each dynamic node is associated with an ID ιn. Given a static assemblage $A = \langle \overline{S}; \overline{D}; \overline{C}; \overline{L} \rangle$, its corresponding dynamic node form $N = \iota n \mapsto \langle \overline{Sr}; \overline{Dr}; \overline{Cr}; \overline{Lr} \rangle$ is almost identical to A, except that it has an ID ιn, and the features defined in $\overline{Sr}$, $\overline{Dr}$, $\overline{Cr}$, $\overline{Lr}$ are slightly different in form from its static counterparts due to function closure and mutable states, which will be made clear when we explain feature values shortly. A dynamic linkage is of the form $\iota d \mapsto \langle \iota n_1; \nu_1; \iota n_2; \nu_2 \rangle$, denoting a tree edge with an ID ιd linking dynamic linker ν_1 of dynamic node ιn_1 with static linker ν_2 of dynamic node ιn_2. We use $root(T)$ to denote the root node of the dynamic linking tree T.

Feature Values. At the source code level, our language supports four kinds of features; see Fig. 4. At runtime, not all of them are values; the possible feature values *fv* are defined in Fig. 6. **ref** F features are not values, since this indicates a heap allocation; the corresponding value is the store ID where the value is allocated on the heap. Function values are closures $\mathbf{fun}(\iota r, \iota n, \lambda x.e)$, where ιr and ιn are the IDs of the runtime and the dynamic node where the function is defined. The reason why $\lambda x.e$ is not a value is that the body e might refer to other features such as α@local. At runtime, if functions as first-class values are passed from one dynamic node to another, the meaning of α@local would not be preserved if the defining dynamic node were not recorded; passing around closures would make parameter passing of first-class functions have a consistent meaning universally. Our language does not allow functions to be passed from one runtime to another, so theoretically, the ιr information in function closures could be removed. We keep it here to show our language could easily support function passing across runtimes without technical difficulty, which also implies mechanisms like RMI could also be easily supported. The reason we do not support function passing across runtimes is that it gives an indirect access to a runtime that is not explicit in an interface; this topic is elaborated in Sec. 5.1.

Source-code level features are converted to feature values when assemblages are loaded either through bootstrapping process, or loaded via an explicit **load** expression, or added to the current runtime via a **plugin** expression.

Values and Expressions at Runtime. Values in our calculus can be feature values; assemblage runtime IDs ιr (which serve as handles to assemblage runtimes, returned from **load** expressions); dynamic linkage IDs ιd (which serve as handles to dynamic linkages, returned from **plugin** expressions); or, connection IDs ιc (which serve as handles to connections, returned from **connect** expressions).

We extend the expressions given in Fig. 4 with new syntax in Fig. 6 (see e definition) to aid in implementing the operational semantics. $\mathbf{inR}(\iota r, \iota n, e)$ is an auxillary expression defining a code context switch, meaning e is evaluated in runtime with ID ιr and dynamic node with ID ιn; the expression is particularly useful to model function invocations, during which the current execution point is switched.

4.3 A Guided Tour to Reduction Rules

Operational semantics of our language is given in Fig. 7. $G,\ e \xrightarrow{\iota r, \iota n} G', e'$ indicates a reduction of expression e in the presence of global runtime G, where the current active runtime has ID ιr, and the current active dynamic node in ιr has ID ιn. Evaluation contexts are defined in Fig. 6. Here we omit the rules for expressions **ref** e, $e{:=}e'$, $!e$, $\alpha @\nu$, α@local and $e.\alpha$; these rules are relatively straightforward. Also note that some of the rules might get stuck on certain combinations of G and e. We largely omit the specifications of the faulty cases here, but claim that the static type system introduced in Sec. 5 will ensure these faulty cases never appear when real reductions happen at dynamic time. Details on omitted reduction rules, specifications of these faulty expressions, and proof to back up the forementioned claim can be found in [LS04].

We use $e\{e'/x\}$ to denote capture-free substitution. If e is an assemblage, the substitution does nothing: assemblages do not contain free variables, and even all import feature names need to be explicitly declared on their static linkers, dynamic linkers or connectors.

$$\textbf{(mcnxt)} \quad \overline{R}, \mathbf{E}[\,e\,] \xrightarrow{\iota r_1, \iota n_1} \overline{R}', \mathbf{E}[\,e'\,] \qquad \text{if } \overline{R}, e \xrightarrow{\iota r_1, \iota n_1} \overline{R}', e'$$

$$\begin{array}{lll}\textbf{(plugin)} & \overline{R}, \mathbf{plugin}_{\nu_1 \mapsto \nu_2}\ A \xrightarrow{\iota r, \iota n} & \overline{R}\{\iota r \mapsto R'\}, \iota d \\ & & \text{if } \overline{R}(\iota r) = \langle T; H; B\rangle,\ T = \langle \overline{N}; \overline{K}\rangle \\ & & \quad start(A, \iota r, \iota n_2) = (N_2, H_2),\ \iota n_2, \iota d \text{ fresh} \\ & & \quad K_2 = (\iota d \mapsto \langle \iota n; \nu_1; \iota n_2; \nu_2\rangle) \\ & & \quad R' = \langle\langle \overline{N} \uplus N_2; \overline{K} \uplus K_2\rangle; H \uplus H_2; B\rangle \end{array}$$

$$\textbf{(fun)} \quad \overline{R}, \lambda x.e \xrightarrow{\iota r_1, \iota n_1} \overline{R}, \mathbf{fun}(\iota r_1, \iota n_1, \lambda x.e)$$

$$\textbf{(app)} \quad \overline{R}, \mathbf{fun}(\iota r_1, \iota n_2, \lambda x.e)\ v \xrightarrow{\iota r_1, \iota n_1} \overline{R}', \mathbf{inR}(\iota r_2, \iota n_2, e\{v/x\})$$

$$\begin{array}{lll}\textbf{(sum)} & \overline{R}, A_1 + A_2 \xrightarrow{\iota r, \iota n} & \overline{R}, \langle \overline{S}_1 \diamond \overline{S}_2; \overline{D}_1 \uplus \overline{D}_2; \overline{C}_1 \uplus \overline{C}_2; \overline{L}_1 \uplus \overline{L}_2\rangle \\ & & \text{if } A_i = \langle \overline{S}_i; \overline{D}_i; \overline{C}_i; \overline{L}_i\rangle, i = \{1, 2\} \end{array}$$

$$\begin{array}{lll}\textbf{(coninv)} & \overline{R}, \iota c \triangleright \alpha \leftarrow v \xrightarrow{\iota r_1, \iota n_1} & \begin{cases} \overline{R}\{\iota r_2 \mapsto R_2\}, \mathbf{inR}(\iota r_2, \iota n_2, \overline{E}_2(\alpha)\{\iota c/\mathbf{thisc}\}\ v') \\ \overline{R}, \mathbf{inR}(\iota r_1, \iota n_1, \overline{E}_1(\alpha)\{\iota c/\mathbf{thisc}\}\ v) \end{cases} \\ & & \text{if } \overline{R}(\iota r_i) = \langle T_i; H_i; Y_i\rangle \\ & & \quad root(T_i) = (\iota n_i \mapsto \langle \overline{Sr}_i; \overline{Dr}_i; \overline{Cr}_i; \overline{Lr}_i\rangle) \\ & & \quad \overline{Cr}_i(\nu_i) = \langle \overline{I}_i; \overline{E}_i; \overline{J}_i\rangle \text{ for } i \in \{1, 2\} \\ & & \quad Y_1(\iota c) = \langle \iota r_2, \nu_1, \nu_2, \overline{Jr}_1\rangle \\ & & \quad dcopy(v, H_1) = (v', H'),\ R_2 = \langle T_2; H_2 \uplus H'; Y_2\rangle \end{array}$$

$$\begin{array}{lll}\textbf{(cons)} & \overline{R}, \iota c \triangleright \alpha \xrightarrow{\iota r_1, \iota n_1} & \overline{R}, \overline{Jr}_1(\alpha) \\ & & \text{if } \overline{R}(\iota r_1) = \langle T_1; H_1; Y_1\rangle, Y_1(\iota c) = \langle \iota r_2, \nu_1, \nu_2, \overline{Jr}_1\rangle \end{array}$$

$$\begin{array}{lll}\textbf{(conn)} & \overline{R}, \mathbf{connect}_{\nu_1 \mapsto \nu_2}\ \iota r_2 \xrightarrow{\iota r_1, \iota n_1} & \overline{R}\{\iota r_1 \mapsto R_1'\}\{\iota r_2 \mapsto R_2'\}, \iota c \\ & & \text{if } \iota c \text{ fresh },\ \overline{R}(\iota r_i) = \langle T_i; H_i; Y_i\rangle \\ & & \quad initS(T_i, \nu_i, \iota r_i, \iota c) = (\overline{Jr}_i, H_i'),\ \text{for } i \in \{1, 2\} \\ & & \quad R_1' = \langle T_1; H_1 \uplus H_1'; Y_1 \uplus \{\iota c \mapsto \langle \iota r_2; \nu_1; \nu_2; \overline{Jr}_1\rangle\}\rangle \\ & & \quad R_2' = \langle T_2; H_2 \uplus H_2'; Y_2 \uplus \{\iota c \mapsto \langle \iota r_1; \nu_2; \nu_1; \overline{Jr}_2\rangle\}\rangle \end{array}$$

$$\begin{array}{lll}\textbf{(load)} & \overline{R}, \mathbf{load}\ A \xrightarrow{\iota r_1, \iota n_1} & \langle \overline{R} \uplus (\iota r_2 \mapsto \langle\langle N_2; \phi\rangle; H_2; \phi\rangle), \iota r_2 \\ & & \text{if } \iota n_2, \iota r_2 \text{ fresh}, start(A, \iota r_2, \iota n_2) = (N_2, H_2) \end{array}$$

$$\textbf{(inre)} \quad \overline{R}, \mathbf{inR}(\iota r_2, \iota n_2, e) \xrightarrow{\iota r_1, \iota n_1} \overline{R}', \mathbf{inR}(\iota r_2, \iota n_2, e') \qquad \text{if } \overline{R}, e \xrightarrow{\iota r_2, \iota n_2} \overline{R}', e'$$

$$\begin{array}{lll}\textbf{(inrv)} & \overline{R}, \mathbf{inR}(\iota r_2, \iota n_2, v) \xrightarrow{\iota r_1, \iota n_1} & \overline{R}\{\iota r_1 \mapsto R_1\}, v' \\ & & \text{if } \overline{R}(\iota r_1) = \langle T_1; H_1; Y_1\rangle, \overline{R}(\iota r_2) = \langle T_2; H_2; Y_2\rangle \\ & & \quad dcopy(v, H_2) = (v', H'),\ R_1 = \langle T_1; H_1 \uplus H'; Y_1\rangle \end{array}$$

Fig. 7. Selected Reduction Rules

Assemblage Loading and Bootstrapping. We now first explain how an assemblage runtime loads in another assemblage, and proceed to discuss the process of bootstrapping, where the first assemblage in runtime global is loaded.

The (**load**) rule in Fig. 7 shows how loading is simply the creation of a new assemblage runtime, and the result returned is a runtime handle, the ID of the new runtime. Function $start(A, \iota r, \iota n) = (N, H)$ prepares the initial dynamic node (N) out of a static assemblage (A), together with the initial heap (H). This function, whose formal definition is skipped here, is fairly straightforward according to the following rules:

- For every function feature in $\alpha == \lambda x.e$ form defined in A, its corresponding place in N is substituted with $\alpha == \mathbf{fun}(\iota r, \iota n, \lambda x.e)$.

- For every reference feature in $\alpha == \textbf{ref}\ F$ form defined in A, its corresponding place in N is substituted with $\alpha == \iota s$, where ιs is a fresh store ID, and at the same time $\iota s \mapsto fv$ is in H. Here fv is the feature value form of F. Since reference feature could be in the form like **ref ref** 0, this process could lead to multiple stores defined in H.
- A and N are otherwise identical.

The (**load**) rule doesn't perform any initialization, because an initializing load can easy be defined using this primitive one; for example, one method could be

$$\begin{aligned}\textbf{loadinit}\ A \ \stackrel{\text{def}}{=}\ & \textbf{let}\ x_1 = \textbf{load}\ A\ \textbf{in}\\ & \textbf{let}\ x_2 = \textbf{connect}_{\texttt{InitIn}\mapsto\texttt{InitOut}}\ x_1\ \textbf{in}\\ & x_2 \triangleright \texttt{Main} \leftarrow ()\end{aligned}$$

which assumes connectors `InitIn/InitOut` are present on loaders/loadees respectively, importing/exporting function `Main()`. Bootstrapping the first assemblage $A_{\text{boot}} = \langle \overline{S}; \overline{D}; \overline{C}; \overline{L} \rangle$ is accomplished by initiating execution in the state

$$\langle \iota r \mapsto \langle \langle N; \phi \rangle; H; \phi \rangle, \iota r \rangle,\quad \overline{C}(\texttt{InitOut})(\texttt{Main})()$$

where ιr, ιn are fresh, $start(A_{\text{boot}}, \iota r, \iota n) = (N, H)$.

Static Linking. The (**sum**) rule shows how static linking of two first-class assemblages happens. It merges their dynamic linkers, connectors and local definitions, with preconditions that these parts do not clash by name. The fact that clash of local feature names would lead to stuck computations might be counter-intuitive: in reality, local features are supposed to be invisible from the outside, and therefore static linking of two assemblages with some shared local feature names *should* be a valid operation. To avoid this dilemma, we stipulate assemblages are freely α-convertible with regard to local feature names.

Static linkers are matched by name, according to the $\diamond$ operator. Given two sequences of static linkers $\overline{S}_1$ and $\overline{S}_2$, $\overline{S}_1 \diamond \overline{S}_2$ is the shortest sequence satisfying all of the following conditions:

- If $\overline{S}_1$ has a static linker S by name ν but $\overline{S}_2$ does not, or *vice versa.*, S is a static linker in $\overline{S}_1 \diamond \overline{S}_2$.
- If $\overline{S}_1$ and $\overline{S}_2$ both have a static linker by name ν whose bodies are $\langle \overline{I}_1; \overline{E}_1 \rangle$ and $\langle \overline{I}_2; \overline{E}_2 \rangle$ respectively, then $\overline{S}_1 \diamond \overline{S}_2$ also has a static linker named ν and a body $\langle \overline{I}; \overline{E}_1 \uplus \overline{E}_2 \rangle$, where $\overline{I}$ exactly include imported features whose names are listed in $\overline{I}_1$ but not $\overline{E}_2$, or listed in $\overline{I}_2$ but not $\overline{E}_1$.

Dynamic Linking. The (**plugin**) rule dynamically links a new assemblage to the initiating runtime. A new dynamic node (N_2) is created out of the assemblage to be plugged in, via the *start*() function, and it is then added to the initiating assemblage runtime by adding the node and an edge with ID ιd to the runtime's dynamic linking tree. Note that in dynamic linking, no new runtime is created;

the plugin will eventually become *part of* the initiating assemblage runtime. This can be illustrated by the way the *start*() function is used: the initiating runtime's ID is passed to create the new dynamic node, not a fresh runtime ID. The return value of the **plugin** expression is the ID of the newly created edge; this is the dynamic linkage handle to the plugin, and conceptually represents the link created out of the dynamic linking process. With this, features exported from the plugin or from the initiating party can thus be accessed via an $e.\alpha$ expression.

Cross-Computation Communication. Connections are established by the (**conn**) rule, which adds an entry to the live connection registry (Y) of both connected parties. Per-connection states are also initialized at this point through a simple function *initS*(); since all per-connection states are mutable, this function predictably deals with initialization of reference features, which is detailed when we explained the *start*() function. Function features defined in connectors are invoked by expression $e \triangleright \alpha \leftarrow v$, and its semantics is defined by (**coninv**). Per-connection state can be referred to via expression $e \triangleright \alpha$; the related reduction rule is (**cons**).

In the (**coninv**) rule, $\iota c \triangleright \alpha \leftarrow v$ invokes a function named α on a previously established connection ιc, with v as the parameter. Since α could be defined by either of the two parties connection ιc connects, there are two possibilities: 1) α is exported in the assemblage runtime containing the expression; in this case, the invocation is an intra-runtime one. 2) α is imported in the assemblage runtime containing the expression; the invocation is thus an inter-runtime one. A deep copy of parameter v should be passed to the target runtime; specifically, when v is a store ID, the heap cells associated with v will be passed around, with store IDs refreshed. The underlying design principle for the copy semantics is object confinement: each assemblage runtime should have its own political boundaries and direct references across boundaries would cause many problems such as security. Function $dcopy(v, H) = (v', H')$ defines the value (v') and the heap cells (H') that need to be transferred if v under heap H needs to be passed across computations. v' is not always the same as v because stores are refreshed if v is a store ID. In both case 1) and case 2), substitution of ιc for **thisc** is needed to determine what the "current connection" means.

5 The Type System

In this section, we informally explain the type system of our calculus. We start with an overview which covers the major ideas behind the type system, then we explain the type-checking process in detail. Some properties of the type system are stated at the end. The complete formal type system with proofs of its properties can be found in a technical report [LS04].

τ	$::=$	$\textbf{unit} \mid \textbf{int} \mid \tau \rightarrow \tau \mid \tau\ \textbf{ref}$	*primitive types*
		$\mid \textbf{Asm}(\overline{\mathcal{S}}, \overline{\mathcal{D}}, \overline{\mathcal{C}}, \overline{\mathcal{L}})$	*assemblage type*
		$\mid \textbf{Rtm}(\overline{\mathcal{C}})$	*runtime type*
		$\mid \textbf{Dlnk}(\overline{\mathcal{E}})$	*dynamic linkage type*
		$\mid \textbf{Cnt}(\overline{\mathcal{E}}, \overline{\mathcal{J}})$	*connection type*
$\mathcal{S}, \mathcal{D}$	$::=$	$\nu \mapsto \langle \overline{\mathcal{I}}; \overline{\mathcal{E}} \rangle$	*static linker/dynamic linker type*
$\mathcal{C}$	$::=$	$\nu \mapsto \langle \overline{\mathcal{I}}; \overline{\mathcal{E}}; \overline{\mathcal{J}} \rangle$	*connector type*
$\mathcal{I}, \mathcal{E}, \mathcal{J}, \mathcal{L}$	$::=$	$\alpha : \tau$	*feature type declaration*

Fig. 8. Type Syntax

5.1 Overview

The Types. The types are defined in Fig. 8. The assemblage type $\textbf{Asm}(\overline{\mathcal{S}}, \overline{\mathcal{D}}, \overline{\mathcal{C}}, \overline{\mathcal{L}})$ contains type declarations of static linkers, dynamic linkers, connectors, and local features. It is used in two situations: top-level typechecking and typechecking of first-class assemblages. At the top level, each assemblage is a separate compilation unit in our type system and is given an assemblage type. In the second situation, first-class assemblages can appear anywhere as expressions, be passed as arguments, *etc.*

The runtime type $\textbf{Rtm}(\overline{\mathcal{C}})$ is the type of assemblage runtimes. When an assemblage runtime is viewed by other assemblage runtimes, the only thing other runtimes care about is how to communicate with the runtime. Thus, a runtime type only contains the list of connector types. The dynamic linkage type $\textbf{Dlnk}(\overline{\mathcal{E}})$ structurally is a sequence of type declarations for functions either exported from dynamic linking initiator's dynamic linker or the dynamic plugin's corresponding static linker. The connection type $\textbf{Cnt}(\overline{\mathcal{E}}, \overline{\mathcal{J}})$ is structurally a sequence of type declarations for functions either exported from connection initiator's connector or connection receiver's connector, and $\overline{\mathcal{J}}$ is type declaration of per-connection states.

Interface Matching. As introduced in Sec. 2, static linking, dynamic linking and connection establishment share one common trait: all three fundamental processes involve bi-directional interface matchings. This commonality is reflected in the typecheckings of three related expressions: $A_1 + A_2$, $\textbf{plugin}_{\nu_1 \mapsto \nu_2}\ e$ and $\textbf{connect}_{\nu_1 \mapsto \nu_2}\ e$; an *interface match* check is performed for all three typecheckings, between two static linkers in the first case, one dynamic linker and one static linker in the second case, and two connectors in the third case. By definition, each interface type, be it static linker type, dynamic linker type or connector type, is composed of a list of type declarations for imported features and a list for exported features. Two interface types, say i_1 and i_2, are considered a match iff

1. If i_1 exports a feature α of type τ, and if i_2 imports a feature α of type τ', then τ must be a subtype of τ'. The same should also hold if i_2 exports and i_1 imports.
2. i_1 and i_2 do not export features by the same name.
3. If i_1 and i_2 are both static linker types, they do not import features of the same name. If one of them is not a static linker type, then every imported feature in i_1 (or i_2) must match an exported feature of the same name in i_2 (or i_1).

Condition 1 is the most important one: features matched by name also match by type. The flexible part is that our type system does not demand exact matching of types; instead, it is acceptable if the export feature has a more precise type than what is expected from the import counterpart. Our subtyping relation is standard for primitive types; for types $\mathbf{Asm}(\overline{\mathcal{S}}, \overline{\mathcal{D}}, \overline{\mathcal{C}}, \overline{\mathcal{L}})$, $\mathbf{Rtm}(\overline{\mathcal{C}})$, $\mathbf{Dlnk}(\overline{\mathcal{E}})$, and $\mathbf{Cnt}(\overline{\mathcal{E}}, \overline{\mathcal{J}})$, subtyping is given the natural structural definition.

Condition 2 is used to avoid a feature name clash. For instance, if ιd is the result of $\mathbf{plugin}_{\nu \mapsto \nu'}\ e$, the meaning of expression $\iota d.\alpha$ would be ambiguous if both dynamic linker ν of the initiator and static linker ν' of the dynamic plugin exported the feature α. The restriction here might not correspond to reality: in real life, dynamic plugins might be developed independently, and such a name clash does have a chance to happen. However, such a clash can easily be avoided if the language supports either feature name renaming, or casting to remove some exported features. Our calculus currently does not include these operators, but they can easily be added without affecting the calculus core.

Condition 3 states that for dynamic linking and connection case, no dangling imports are allowed if interface match succeeds; for static linking, our calculus does allow some imports to not be satisfied, since the result (say A) of $A_1 + A_2$ can still be statically linked in the future, *e.g.*, by $A + A_3$.

Principle of Computation Encapsulation and Parameter Passing Across Computations. One of the design principles of our calculus is computation encapsulation: reactive computations should only communicate with each other via *explicit* interfaces, in our context, connectors. Parameter passing across reactive computations, if not handled properly, could however violate this principle. The three types of parameters that cause troubles are function closures, dynamic linkage handles, and connection handles; our type system disallows the passing of these three types of values.

We first consider the problematic case of passing connection handles. Suppose assemblage runtime with ID ιr_1 contains a $\mathbf{connect}_{\nu \mapsto \nu'}\ \iota r_2$ expression which returns a connection handle ιc. Had we allowed ιc to be passed as a parameter, runtime ιr_1 could pass it to some runtime ιr_3 via some previously existing connection. Now although runtime ιr_3 does not have a connector ν (or ν'), it would still be able to use features associated with connection ιc via $\iota c \triangleright \alpha \leftarrow e$ expressions, meaning it is accessing a feature not through an explicit interface on its runtime, ιr_3. Similarly, passing dynamic linkage handles could allow assemblage runtimes to gain direct access to dynamic plugins they do not have interfaces to plug in to.

The case for passing function closures across assemblage runtimes suffers from a similar problem, but it is less obvious. In Sec. 4, we have already mentioned how there is no technical difficulty in passing function closures across assemblage runtimes; indeed we could just pass function closures in a manner similar to how Java RMI passes object references. Now let us consider why a mechanism like this would violate our encapsulation principle. Suppose assemblage runtime with ID ιr_1 has a function closure $\mathbf{fun}(\iota r_1, \iota n_1, \lambda x.e)$ and e contains an expression $\alpha@\nu$ to use a feature α exported from static linker ν of ιr_1. Had we allow this closure to be passed to another runtime, it could, by several indirections (ιr_1 to ιr_2, and ιr_2 to ιr_3 for instance), eventually be received by some runtime ιr_3 that has no direct communication with ιr_1. But, by applying the function, this assemblage runtime ιr_3 would be able to access to feature α of static linker ν of ιr_1, through a channel not explicit in ιr_3's interface.

The legal parameters that can be passed across computations are primitive values such as integers, runtime handles, references and first-class assemblages. Passing runtime handles is an important means for a runtime to "advertise" itself to other runtimes. References are passed by deep copy (recall the reduction rule (**coninv**) in Sec. 4). The exclusion of function closures from passable parameters across computations might appear to disallow the possibility of any code passing in our calculus, but in fact not. If passing code is needed, users can encapsulate the code as an assemblage and pass the assemblage; assemblages are completely self-contained, without need for a closure, and so are nothing more than a kind of data.

To enforce the principle of computation encapsulation, our type system checks that for every imported function feature given in a connector type, its parameter and return value can not have the aforementioned types. This well-formedness property must hold for all connector types.

5.2 Details of Typechecking

We now explain how top-level typechecking is achieved, and how some important expressions are typechecked, in our type system.

Assemblage Typechecking. At top level, assemblage $\langle \overline{S}; \overline{D}; \overline{C}; \overline{L} \rangle$ as a separate compilation unit is well typed if all exported features defined in its static linkers $\overline{S}$, dynamic linkers $\overline{D}$ and connectors $\overline{C}$, and all locally defined features $\overline{L}$, are well-typed. Well-typed assemblages have an assemblage type $\mathbf{Asm}(\overline{\mathcal{S}}, \overline{\mathcal{D}}, \overline{\mathcal{C}}, \overline{\mathcal{L}})$, which structurally corresponds to $\langle \overline{S}; \overline{D}; \overline{C}; \overline{L} \rangle$ in an intuitive way.

To typecheck an assemblage appearing inside a program as a first-class value is the same as top-level typechecking, with the only exception that if the assemblage is annotated with assemblage type $\mathbf{Asm}(\overline{\mathcal{S}}, \overline{\mathcal{D}}, \overline{\mathcal{C}}, \overline{\mathcal{L}})$ and typechecks, the type we give to this assemblage expression is $\mathbf{Asm}(\overline{\mathcal{S}}, \overline{\mathcal{D}}, \overline{\mathcal{C}}, \phi)$. Assemblages are encapsulated entities and on the outside local features should be invisible, just as with private fields of objects.

Static Linking. To typecheck expression A_1+A_2, the following conditions have to be satisfied:

- A_1 and A_2 both need to be well-typed, with type $\mathbf{Asm}(\overline{\mathcal{S}}_1, \overline{\mathcal{D}}_1, \overline{\mathcal{C}}_1, \phi)$, and $\mathbf{Asm}(\overline{\mathcal{S}}_2, \overline{\mathcal{D}}_2, \overline{\mathcal{C}}_2, \phi)$ respectively.
- If $\overline{\mathcal{S}}_1$ includes a static linker named ν and $\overline{\mathcal{S}}_2$ includes a static linker with the same name, the two linkers must match according to Sec. 5.1.
- No dynamic linkers in $\overline{\mathcal{D}}_1$ and $\overline{\mathcal{D}}_2$ can share the same name.
- No connectors in $\overline{\mathcal{C}}_1$ and $\overline{\mathcal{C}}_2$ can share the same name.

Expression $A_1 + A_2$ has type $\mathbf{Asm}(\overline{\mathcal{S}}_1 \diamond_t \overline{\mathcal{S}}_2, \overline{\mathcal{D}}_1 \uplus \overline{\mathcal{D}}_2, \overline{\mathcal{C}}_1 \uplus \overline{\mathcal{C}}_2, \phi)$ if the above conditions are met. Here the $\diamond_t$ operator is the same as that of the $\diamond$ operator explained in Sec. 4.3, but changing $\overline{S}$, $\overline{I}$, $\overline{E}$ to $\overline{\mathcal{S}}$, $\overline{\mathcal{I}}$, $\overline{\mathcal{E}}$. Also notice that since first-class assemblages are given a type in which local feature types are set to ϕ, there can be no name clash checking on local features of A_1 and A_2. This is not a problem, however, since assemblages are α-convertible with respect to local feature names (see Sec. 4).

Dynamic Linking. Expression $\mathbf{plugin}_{\nu_1 \mapsto \nu_2}\ e$, when well-typed in our type system, has a dynamic linkage type $\mathbf{Dlnk}(\overline{\mathcal{E}})$; this corresponds to the fact that the return value of a **plugin** expression is a dynamic linkage handle. It typechecks iff

- It appears in an assemblage whose type is $\mathbf{Asm}(\overline{\mathcal{S}}_1, \overline{\mathcal{D}}_1, \overline{\mathcal{C}}_1, \overline{\mathcal{L}}_1)$.
- Expression e, which will evaluate to an assemblage, has a type $\mathbf{Asm}(\overline{\mathcal{S}}_2, \overline{\mathcal{D}}_2, \overline{\mathcal{C}}_2, \phi)$.
- $\overline{\mathcal{D}}_1$ includes a dynamic linker type $\nu_1 \mapsto \langle \overline{\mathcal{I}}_1; \overline{\mathcal{E}}_1 \rangle$, and $\overline{\mathcal{S}}_2$ includes a static linker type $\nu_2 \mapsto \langle \overline{\mathcal{I}}_2; \overline{\mathcal{E}}_2 \rangle$, and the two types match according to Sec. 5.1.
- $\overline{\mathcal{E}} = \overline{\mathcal{E}}_1 \uplus \overline{\mathcal{E}}_2$.
- $\overline{\mathcal{C}}_2$ must be ϕ.
- Static linker ν_2 is the only static linker in $\overline{\mathcal{S}}_2$ which has imported features.

The last two conditions merit some further explanation. $\overline{\mathcal{C}}_2$ must be ϕ because if dynamic plugins had extra connectors, the assemblage runtime, after being plugged in with dynamic plugins of this kind, would be faced with a dilemma: it either needs to dynamically change its type to reflect some connectors that are dynamically added, or these new connectors are not exposed to outsiders and are *de facto* useless. Our calculus does not tackle this dilemma to preserve simplicity. The last condition is necessary because otherwise, the imported features not satisfied by dynamic linking would become dangling unresolved name references.

Cross-Computation Communication. Expression $\mathbf{connect}_{\nu_1 \mapsto \nu_2}\ e$, when well-typed in our type system, has a connection type $\mathbf{Cnt}(\overline{\mathcal{E}}, \overline{\mathcal{J}}_1)$; this corresponds to the fact that the return value of a **connect** expression is a connection handle. It typechecks iff:

- It appears in an assemblage whose type is $\mathbf{Asm}(\overline{\mathcal{S}}_1, \overline{\mathcal{D}}_1, \overline{\mathcal{C}}_1, \overline{\mathcal{L}}_1)$.
- Expression e, which evaluates to an assemblage runtime handle, has a type $\mathbf{Rtm}(\overline{\mathcal{C}}_2)$.
- $\overline{\mathcal{C}}_1$ includes a connector type $\nu_1 \mapsto \langle \overline{\mathcal{I}}_1; \overline{\mathcal{E}}_1; \overline{\mathcal{J}}_1 \rangle$, and $\overline{\mathcal{C}}_2$ includes a connector type $\nu_2 \mapsto \langle \overline{\mathcal{I}}_2; \overline{\mathcal{E}}_2; \overline{\mathcal{J}}_2 \rangle$, and the two connector types match according to Sec. 5.1.
- $\overline{\mathcal{E}} = \overline{\mathcal{E}}_1 \uplus \overline{\mathcal{E}}_2$.

5.3 Properties of the Type System

We have proved soundness of our type system [LS04], in which we have shown the bootstrapping process preserves type, and the subject reduction property holds, *i.e.*, the $G,\ e \xrightarrow{\iota r, \iota n} G', e'$ reduction always preserves type. In addition, the typechecking process is decidable.

6 Related Work

In terms of static linking alone, our calculus is in the spirit of numerous module systems and calculi mentioned in Sec. 1 and Sec. 2. The calculus presented here supports first-class modules and static linking as first-class expressions, which some of the aforementioned projects, such as ML functors, do not support. In this presentation, we omitted how types can themselves be imported or exported as features, but type importing/exporting, including bounded parametric types and cross-module recursive types is covered in the long version [LS04]. Previous works in this category, with the exception of Units, do not consider dynamic linking or cross-computation communication. For instance, ML modules do not themselves constitute a runtime, and even though structures have explicit interfaces for runtime interaction via $S.x$, this is for tightly-coupled interaction within a single runtime, not cross-computation invocation.

Dynamic linking is supported in Java. Although it does not support source-level dynamic linking expressions, classes are loaded dynamically [LB98,DLE03]. The classloader mechanism provides a very powerful way to customize the dynamic linking process, but its maximum expressiveness, particularly classloader delegation, requires much of the typechecking work to happen at dynamic link time. In addition, we believe the granularity of modules provides a better layer for dynamic linking, because explicit dynamic linking interfaces can be specified without too much labor, and users can have more programmatic control over the dynamic linking process. Dynamic linking of modules is explored in Argus [Blo83], in the **invoke** expressions of Units [FF98], and in the `dynamic export` declarations of MJ [CBGM03]. These projects only take advantage of the fact that dynamic plugins are modules and so the interface is unidirectional only: the running program has no explicit interface to the plugged-in code.

There have been many effective protocols developed for reactive computations, including RMI, RPC, and component architectures such as COM+ and CORBA. These protocols generally define a one-way communication interface only; the receiver has an interface, but not the sender. The bidirectional connector as a concept has existed in the software engineering community for some time, *e.g.* in [AG97], but those closest to our are two programming language efforts: ArchJava [ASCN03], and Cells [RS02]. In ArchJava, connectors are more low-level than ours. Each connector may have a `typecheck` method which maximize flexibility of typechecking, something we do not support. Connectors in our calculus share the same notion as in Cells language, but connectors in Cells do not consider rebindability and per-connection states. These projects in general do not have module system as a priority, and it therefore do not address type imports and exports.

Research on software components [Szy98] is diverse. A number of industrial component systems (such as COM+, Javabeans) have been successful in modelling reactive computations, and some support both static linking and cross-computation communication, such as CORBA CCM. They are only loosely related to our project, as they do not consider dynamic linking issue and type issues.

7 Conclusions and Future Work

The major contribution of this paper is a novel module system where static linking, dynamic linking and cross-computation communication are all defined in a uniform framework by declaring explicit, bi-directional interfaces. Explicit interfaces for dynamic linking and cross-computation communication provide more declarative specifications of the interaction between parties, and also gives a stronger foundation for adding other critical language features such as security and version control. We have yet to see a fully bi-directional dynamic linking interface in the literature. Bi-directional communication interfaces are found for example in [ASCN03,RS02], but our work builds this feature into module systems. In the full version of this paper [LS04] we show how the calculus presented here can be extended to include types as features, and how they are useful for situations involving dynamic linking and cross-computation communication. Since every cross-computation communication must be directed through connectors in our calculus, access control on connectors is enough to ensure the network security of the assemblage. Assemblages provide a good granularity for encapsulation, and our type system and semantics of the calculus restricts the types of data that can be transfered across computations, which also coincides with a proper policy of confinement in security. A future topic is to define a complete security architecture based on this calculus.

It is our belief that rebindable dynamic linkers can provide a strong initial basis upon which a rigorous theory of code version control can be built. Since dynamic plugins can be rebound, each successive binding at runtime is a new version of the code. Rebindability also allows multiple versions to co-exist. We are interested in building a version control layer on top of our calculus.

Acknowledgements. We would like to acknowledge Ran Rinat for contributions at earlier stages of this project.

References

[AG97] Robert Allen and David Garlan. A formal basis for architectural connection. *ACM Transactions on Software Engineering and Methodology*, 6(3):213–249, 1997.

[ASCN03] Jonathan Aldrich, Vibha Sazawal, Craig Chambers, and David Notkin. Language support for connector abstractions. In *Proceedings of the Seventeenth European Conference on Object-Oriented Programming*, June 2003.

[AZ02] D. Ancona and E. Zucca. A calculus of module systems. *Journal of functional programming*, 11:91–132, 2002.

[BC90] Gilad Bracha and William Cook. Mixin-based inheritance. In Norman Meyrowitz, editor, *Proceedings of OOPSLA/ECOOP*, pages 303–311, Ottawa, Canada, 1990. ACM Press.

[BHSS03] G. Bierman, M. Hicks, P. Sewell, and G. Stoyle. Formalizing dynamic software updating, 2003.

[Blo83] Toby Bloom. Dynamic module replacement in a distributed programming system. Technical Report MIT/LCS/TR-303, 1983.

[Car97] Luca Cardelli. Program fragments, linking, and modularization. In *Conference Record of POPL'97: The 24th ACM SIGPLAN-SIGACT Symposium on Principles of Programming Languages*, pages 266–277, 1997.

[CBGM03] John Corwin, David F. Bacon, David Grove, and Chet Murthy. MJ: a rational module system for java and its applications. In *Proceedings of the 18th ACM SIGPLAN conference on Object-oriented programing, systems, languages, and applications*, pages 241–254, 2003.

[DEW99] Sophia Drossopoulou, Susan Eisenbach, and David Wragg. A fragment calculus towards a model of separate compilation, linking and binary compatibility. In *Logic in Computer Science*, pages 147–156, 1999.

[DLE03] Sophia Drossopoulou, Giovanni Lagorio, and Susan Eisenbach. Flexible models for dynamic linking. In *12th European Symposium on Programming*, 2003.

[DS96] Dominic Duggan and Constantinos Sourelis. Mixin modules. In *Proceedings of the ACM SIGPLAN International Conference on Functional Programming (ICFP '96)*, volume 31(6), pages 262–273, 1996.

[FF98] Matthew Flatt and Matthias Felleisen. Units: Cool modules for HOT languages. In *Proceedings of the ACM SIGPLAN '98 Conference on Programming Language Design and Implementation*, pages 236–248, 1998.

[HL02] Tom Hirschowitz and Xavier Leroy. Mixin modules in a call-by-value setting. In *European Symposium on Programming*, pages 6–20, 2002.

[HMN01] Michael W. Hicks, Jonathan T. Moore, and Scott Nettles. Dynamic software updating. In *SIGPLAN Conference on Programming Language Design and Implementation*, pages 13–23, 2001.

[HSW+00] Jason Hill, Robert Szewczyk, Alec Woo, Seth Hollar, David E. Culler, and Kristofer S. J. Pister. System architecture directions for networked sensors. In *Architectural Support for Programming Languages and Operating Systems*, pages 93–104, 2000.

[LB98] Sheng Liang and Gilad Bracha. Dynamic class loading in the Java virtual machine. In *Conference on Object-oriented programming, systems, languages, and applications (OOPSLA'98)*, pages 36–44, 1998.

[LS04] Yu David Liu and Scott F. Smith. Modules With Interfaces for Dynamic Linking and Communication (long version), `http://www.cs.jhu.edu/~scott/pll/assemblage/asm.pdf`. Technical report, Baltimore, Maryland, March 2004.

[Mac84] D. MacQueen. Modules for Standard ML. In *Proceedings of ACM Conference on Lisp and Functional Programming*, pages 409–423, 1984.

[MFH01] S. McDirmid, M. Flatt, and W. Hsieh. Jiazzi: New-age components for old-fashioned Java. In *Proc. of OOPSLA*, October 2001.

[RS02] Ran Rinat and Scott Smith. Modular internet programming with cells. In *Proceedings of the Sixteenth ECOOP*, June 2002.

[SPW03] Nigamanth Sridhar, Scott M. Pike, and Bruce W. Weide. Dynamic module replacement in distributed protocols. In *Proceedings of the 23rd International Conference on Distributed Computing Systems*, May 2003.

[Szy98] Clemens Szyperski. *Component Software: Beyond Object-Oriented Programming*. ACM Press and Addison-Wesley, New York, NY, 1998.

[WV00] J. B. Wells and René Vestergaard. Equational reasoning for linking with first-class primitive modules. In *Programming Languages and Systems, 9th European Symp. Programming*, volume 1782, 2000.

Early Identification of Incompatibilities in Multi-component Upgrades

Stephen McCamant and Michael D. Ernst

Massachusetts Institute of Technology
Computer Science and Artificial Intelligence Laboratory
32 Vassar Street, Cambridge MA USA
{smcc,mernst}@csail.mit.edu

Abstract. Previous work proposed a technique for predicting problems resulting from replacing one version of a software component by another. The technique reports, before performing the replacement or integrating the new component into a system, whether the upgrade might be problematic for that particular system. This paper extends the technique to make it more applicable to object-oriented systems and real-world upgrades. First, we extend the theoretical framework to handle more complex upgrades, including components with internal state, callbacks, and simultaneous upgrades of multiple components. The old model is a special case of our new one. Second, we show how to handle four real-world situations that were not addressed by previous work: non-local state, non-determinism, distinguishing old from new incompatibilities, and lack of test suites. Third, we present a case study in which we upgrade the Linux C library, for 48 Unix programs. Our implementation identified real incompatibilities among versions of the C library that affected some of the programs, and it approved the upgrades for other programs that were unaffected by the changes.

1 Introduction

A frequent cause of software failures is the use of software in unexpected or untested situations, in which it does not behave as intended or desired. Such problems are inevitable because it is impossible to foresee, much less to test, every possible situation in which software might be used. As one example, consider a software system that successfully uses a component. A supposedly compatible software upgrade may cause system failure or misbehavior if the system uses the new component in a manner for which it was not designed or tested. Even if the component developer conscientiously tests the component in many situations, the new component may not have been tested in an environment like the user's, or the developer may have inadvertently changed the behavior in the user's environment.

This paper builds on previous research [15] that seeks to identify unanticipated interactions among software components, before the components are actually integrated with one another. The approach is to compare the observed

M. Odersky (Ed.): ECOOP 2004, LNCS 3086, pp. 440–464, 2004.

behavior of an old component to the observed behavior of a new component, and permit the upgrade only if the behaviors are compatible, for the way that the component is used in an application. The method issues a warning when the behaviors of the new and old components are incompatible, but lack of such a warning is not a guarantee of correctness, nor is its presence a guarantee that the program's operation would be incorrect.

The two key techniques that underlie the method are formally capturing observed behaviors and a test that compares those behaviors via logical implication. The observed behavior is captured via dynamic detection of likely program invariants [9], which generalizes over program executions to produce an *operational abstraction*. An operational abstraction is a set of mathematical properties describing the observed behavior. An operational abstraction is syntactically identical to a formal specification — both describe program behavior via logical formulas over program variables — but an operational abstraction describes actual program behavior and can be generated automatically. In practice, formal specifications are rarely available, because they are tedious and difficult to write and verify, and when available they may fail to capture all of the properties on which program correctness depends.

The previous technique has a number of positive qualities. It is application-specific, so it can indicate that an upgrade is safe for one client but unsafe for a different client. It operates before integrating the new component into the system (perhaps even before deciding whether to purchase the new component!) or running system tests. It is automated and does not require writing or proving formal specifications. It issues warnings for errors made by either the component vendor or the component client, and it does not require the vendor to have any knowledge of client behavior. It does not require an oracle indicating correct behavior, and it does not require access to source code.

However, the previous technique suffers a number of shortcomings, which we address in this paper. Most seriously, the upgrade model is overly simplistic: it is more applicable to functional than to object-oriented programs. It assumes that the upgrade involves a single module being upgraded, that the system interacts with the module only by calling it, and that each such call is independent. No accommodation is made for simultaneous upgrades of multiple components, or for components that keep internal state or make callbacks, as is common in object-oriented frameworks. Furthermore, in applying the technique to a real-world component, we discovered four circumstances that arise in practice and that require extensions to the technique. The previous technique is too permissive (it issues too few warnings) when a component's behavior depends on non-local state. The previous technique is too restrictive (it issues too many warnings) when procedure results are non-deterministic (or depend on unavailable facts), when test suites are insufficient, and when pre-existing apparent incompatibilities are present that did not prevent correct system behavior in the past. This paper addresses all of these issues, so its technique covers the essence of objects. The paper also describes a case study in which we upgraded the Linux C library and observed the predicted and actual effects on 48 Unix programs.

The remainder of this paper is organized as follows. Section 2 outlines the technique for detecting incompatibilities, in the simplest case of upgrading a single component that is called by the rest of the system. Section 3 extends the framework to accommodate more sophisticated interactions between upgraded components and the system. Section 4 gives examples of the more sophisticated interactions and shows how our implementation handles them. Section 5 further extends the technique to handle non-local state, lack of test suites, non-determinism, and pre-existing incompatibilities. Section 6 describes our case studies with the C library and 48 Unix programs. Section 7 discusses related work, and Section 8 concludes.

2 Overview: Upgrading a Component

This section describes our upgrade-checking technique in outline. For simplicity of exposition, we describe the case of a single component. Suppose that there is a complete software system, the *application*, that includes a separately developed module, the *component*. The component may be a library of procedures, a collection of classes, or a formally packaged component in the sense of COM or CORBA; we assume only that it is used according to some procedure call interface. The application is observed to function properly with some version of the component, and we ask whether it will still function correctly if that component is replaced by a different version.

The method consists of four steps.

(1) Before an upgrade, when the application is running with the older version of a component, a tool automatically computes an operational abstraction from a representative subset (perhaps all) of its calls to the component. Our implementation computes this abstraction using the Daikon tool [9]. The result of this step is a formal mathematical description of those facets of the behavior of the old component that are used by the system. This abstraction depends on both the implementation of the component and the way it is used by the application.

(2) Before distributing a new version of a component, the component vendor computes the operational abstraction of the new component's behavior as exercised by the vendor's test suite. This abstraction can be created as a routine part of the testing process. The result of this step is a mathematical description of the successfully tested aspects of the component's behavior.

(3) The vendor supplies the new component's operational abstraction (with respect to its test suite) to the customer.

(4) The customer's system automatically compares the two operational abstractions, to test whether the new component's abstraction is stronger than the old component's abstraction. The test determines whether the new component has been verified (via testing) to perform correctly (i.e., as the old component did) for at least as many situations as the old component was ever exposed to. The specific test is described formally in Sect. 3. Our implementation performs this checking using the Simplify automatic theorem prover [5]. (Additional implementation details appear in a technical report [16].) Success of the test suggests that the new component will work correctly wherever the system used the old component.

If the test does not succeed, the system might behave differently with the new component, and it should not be installed without further investigation. The tool reports the incompatibility in terms of specific procedure preconditions and postconditions. Further analysis could be performed (perhaps with human help) to decide whether to install the new component. In some cases, analysis will reveal that a serious error was avoided by not installing the new component. In other cases, the changed behavior might be acceptable:

- The change in component behavior might not affect the correct operation of the application.
- It might be possible to work around the changed behavior by modifying the application.
- The changed behavior might be a desirable bug fix or enhancement.
- The component might work correctly, but the vendor's testing might have insufficiently exercised the component, thus producing an operational abstraction that was too weak to indicate that the upgrade would perform compatibly.

3 Upgrades Involving Many Modules

The comparison technique described in [15] is appropriate for upgrades of a single component, containing a single procedure that is called from the rest of a system. It can easily be generalized to a component with several independent procedures (by checking the safety of an upgrade to each procedure independently), or an upgrade to several cooperating components that are called by the rest of a system (by treating the components as a single entity for the purposes of an upgrade). More complicated situations that arise in object-oriented systems, such as components with state, components that make callbacks, or a simultaneous upgrade to two components that communicate via the rest of a system, require a more sophisticated approach. This section describes a model that generalizes the formulation and consistency condition for a single component as used by a single application. We consider systems to be divided into *modules* grouping together code that interacts closely and is developed as a unit. Such modules need not match the grouping imposed by language-level features such as classes or Java packages, but we assume that any upgrade affects one or more complete modules.

Our approach to upgrade safety verification takes advantage of the modular structure: we attempt to understand the behavior of each module on its own. Unlike many specification-based methods, however, the approach is not merely compositional, starting from the behavior of the smallest structures and combining information about them to predict or verify the behavior of the entire system. For our purpose of searching for differences in behavior, we examine each module of a running system to understand its workings in the context of the system, but conversely we also summarize the behavior of the rest of the system, as it was observed by that module. By combining these forms of information, we can predict problems that occur either when a module's behavior changes, or when the behavior that the system requires of a module goes beyond what the module has demonstrated via testing.

3.1 Relations inside and among Modules

Given a decomposition of a system into modules, we model its behavior with three types of relations. *Call and return relations* represent how modules are connected by procedure calls and returns. *Internal data-flow relations* represent the behavior of individual modules, in context: that is, the way in which each output of the module potentially depends on the module's inputs. *External summary relations* represent a module's observations of the behavior of the rest of the system: how each input to the module might depend on the behavior of the rest of the system and any previous outputs of the module.

Call and return relations. Roughly speaking, each module is modeled as a black box, with certain inputs and outputs. When module A calls procedure `f` in module B, the arguments to `f` are outputs of A and inputs to B, while the return value and any side effects on the arguments are outputs from B and inputs to A. In the module containing a procedure `f`, we use the symbol f to refer to the input consisting of the values of the procedure's parameters on entrance, and f' to refer to the output consisting of the return value and possibly-modified reference parameters. We use f_c and f_r for the call to and return from a procedure in the calling module. Collectively, we call these moments of execution *program points*. All non-trivial computation occurs within modules: calls and returns simply represent the transfer of information unchanged from one module to another. Each tuple of values at an f_c is identical to some tuple at f, and likewise for f' and f_r.

Internal data-flow relations. Internal data-flow relations connect each output of a module to all the inputs to that module that might affect the output value. In a module M, $M(v|u_1, \ldots, u_k)$ is the data-flow relation from inputs u_1 through u_k to an output v. As a degenerate case, an *independent output* $M(v)$ is one whose value is not affected by any input to the module. A constant-valued output would be independent. An independent output might also be influenced by interactions not captured by our model: it might be the output of a pseudo-random number generator, or it might come from a file.

Conceptually, this relation is a set of tuples of values at the relevant inputs and at the output, having the property that on some execution of the output point, the output values might be those in the tuple, if the most recent values at all the inputs have their given values. Because each variable might have a large or infinite domain, it would be impractical or impossible to represent this relation by a table. Instead, our approach summarizes it by a set of logical formulas that are

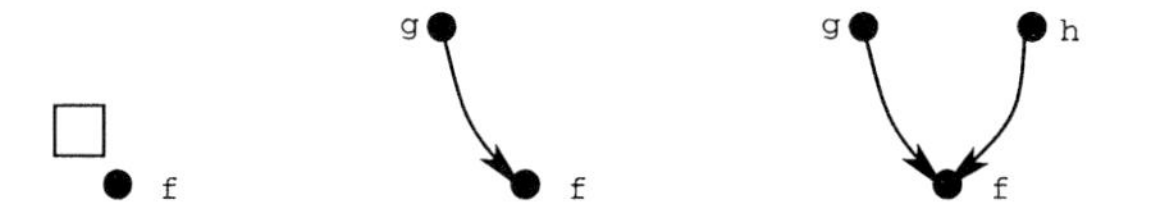

$f.x$ is even $\quad f.x > g.a \quad f.x = 2 \cdot g.a + h.c$

$f.y \leq 42 \quad g.b = 2 \cdot f.y \quad g.b < f.y < h.d$

Fig. 1. Examples of data-flow relations over one, two, and three program points.

(observed to be) always true over the input and output variables. The values that satisfy these formulas are a superset of those that occurred in a particular run. This representation is *not* merely an implementation convenience. Generalization allows our technique to declare an upgrade compatible when its testing has been close enough to its use, without demanding that it be tested for every possible input.

The technique must be extended slightly to capture the fact that data-flow relationships may hold only after certain executions of the input points. A flow edge from an input u to an output v does not imply that every execution of u is followed by some execution of v: for instance, u might be the entry point of a procedure that calls another procedure at v under some circumstances but not others. (Object-oriented dispatch is an example of such a situation; also see Sect. 4.3.) To keep track of when u might be followed by v, our technique computes a property ϕ that held on executions of u that were followed by executions of v, but did not hold on executions of u that were followed by another execution of u without an intervening v. Such a property is used to guard the statements describing a relationship between u and v; in other words, we write those properties as implications with ϕ as the antecedent.

External summary relations. External summary relations are in many ways dual to internal data-flow relations. Summary relations connect each input of a module to all of the module outputs that might feed back to that input via the rest of the system. In a module M, we refer to the summary relation from outputs u_1 through u_k to an input v as $\overline{M}(v|u_1, \ldots, u_k)$. As a degenerate case, an *independent input* $\overline{M}(v)$ is one not affected by any outputs. The line over the M is meant to suggest that while this relation is calculated with respect to the interface of M, it is really a fact about the complement of M—that is, all the other modules in the system.

Graphical representation. In explaining which conditions must be checked to assess the safety of an upgrade, it is helpful to represent the relational description of modules as a directed graph, in which nodes correspond to program points (module inputs and outputs). Each relation corresponds to zero or more edges, from each input to the output for a data-flow relation, and from each output to the input for a summary relation. We call the edges so created data-flow edges and summary edges, respectively. If an input or output is independent, then the relation is associated directly with the relevant node. Also, procedure calls and returns are represented by edges in the direction of control flow. Figure 1 shows our representation of relations. For examples of this graphical model, see Figs. 2, 6, and 10.

3.2 Considering an Upgrade

So far, we have described a model of the behavior of a modular system. For each module, its external summary relations represent assumptions about how the module has been used, and subject to those assumptions, its internal data-flow relations describe its behavior. Now, suppose that one or more modules in the system are replaced with new versions. We presume that each new module has been tested, and that in the context of this test suite new sets of data-flow and summary relations have been created. Under what circumstances do we expect that the system will continue to operate as it used to, using the new components in place of their previous versions? We replace the models of old components with models created during testing, and must check that this upgraded model is consistent. The key is obeying the summary relations.

In short, we must check that the assumptions embodied in each external summary relation are preserved: both those in the new component (so we know that the component will only be used in ways that exercise tested behavior) and those in the other modules (so we know that the rest of the system will continue to behave as expected). Each summary relation summarizes the relationship between zero or more outputs and an input, which might be mediated by the interaction of many other relations in the system. The summary relation will be obeyed if every tuple of values consistent with the rest of the relations in the system is allowed by the summary; in other words, if its abstraction as a formula is a logical consequence of the combination of all the other relevant relation formulas. The system as a whole will behave as expected if all of the summary relations can be simultaneously satisfied given all the data-flow relations. For each summary relation, we construct a logical combination of the relevant data-flow relations, describing the states in which the data flow relations could simultaneously be satisfied. If this combination logically entails the summary relation, we can be confident that the summary relation will hold in the upgraded program.

Our algorithm for computing a consistency condition has two purposes. First, it determines how to connect data-flow relations to model a system's control flow. One might expect control flow modeling to be straightforward: for instance, sequential execution of code simply corresponds to conjunction of the corresponding flow relations. However, control flow join points (which occur at procedure entrances) require disjunction, or equivalently in our approach, the distribution of checking obligations over multiple paths. This construction of a consistency condition is similar in effect to the construction of verification conditions to check whether a program satisfies properties based on its implementation, as by weakest precondition / strongest postcondition predicates [7,10] or symbolic evaluation [19]. However, we operate at the granularity of modules rather than of statements.

Second, the consistency condition includes only data-flow relations that might play a role in checking a summary relation, when deciding which assumptions to supply to a theorem prover. This is just an optimization, but it is an important one because automatic theorem provers are generally not effective at ignoring irrelevant hypotheses. This aspect of our technique resembles a backward slice [26]; our use of a functional representation that combines control flow with data dependence is reminiscent of the slicing algorithm of [8].

Feasible subgraphs. To describe which relations must be checked to verify that a summary relation holds, we define the concept of a *feasible subgraph* for a given summary relation. Roughly, a feasible subgraph captures a subset of system execution over which a summary relation should hold. A summary relation may have many corresponding feasible subgraphs. An upgrade is safe if it allows each summary relation to hold over every corresponding feasible subgraph.

To obtain a single feasible subgraph for a given summary relation, use the following backward marking algorithm on the graph describing the relations of a system. (This algorithm, similar to a form of context-free language graph reachability [22], is given merely to clarify the concept. It could be extended into a search algorithm that produces all feasible subgraphs, but below we discuss techniques for more efficient implementation.)

Starting with no nodes marked and no relations in the subgraph, mark the input of the given summary relation. Then, until no more nodes can be marked, repeat the following:

(a) If the output of a data-flow relation is marked, mark all the corresponding input nodes, and add the relation to the feasible subgraph.
(b) If the return value input node of a procedure return edge is marked, mark the exit point output node.
(c) If a procedure entry input node is marked, and a return node connected to the same procedure's exit output node is marked, then mark the procedure call output node for that procedure in the module with the return node.
(d) If a procedure entry input node is marked, and none of the corresponding call nodes or any of the return nodes connected to the same procedure's exit output node are marked, then choose one procedure call node connected to the entry and mark it.

The above algorithm describes a feasible subgraph as consisting only of data-flow relations (including independent outputs). One might also imagine including call and return edges, but we will adopt the convention that the identity between formal parameters and actual arguments entailed by the call edges, and the similar identity for return values, are represented implicitly by giving the same names to both sets of variables.

For a summary relation to be satisfied in an upgraded system, it must be guaranteed by each possible corresponding feasible subgraph. Representing each relation as a logical formula that must hold over certain variables, we can express this consistency condition for a summary relation $\overline{M}_0(v_0|u_1,\ldots,u_k)$ as

$$\bigwedge_{\substack{\text{feasible } G \\ \text{for } \overline{M}_0(v_0|u_1,\ldots,u_k)}} \left[\left(\bigwedge_{M_i(v_i|\ldots)\in G} M_i(v_i|\ldots) \right) \Rightarrow \overline{M}_0(v_0|u_1,\ldots,u_k) \right] \tag{1}$$

In other words, for each feasible subgraph, the conjunction of the formulas representing data-flow relations in the subgraph must imply the formula for the summary relation.

A direct evaluation of the consistency condition for an upgrade, as described in the previous paragraph, would be potentially inefficient, performing unnecessary logical comparisons. In the worst case, there may be exponentially many feasible subgraphs, but it is not necessary to evaluate each one individually. Three techniques can be used to evaluate an upgrade's safety more efficiently. First, if all of the relations that should be checked to verify a summary relation are unchanged since the previous version of the system, they do not need to be rechecked. Second, if the subgraph to be checked has a smaller subgraph that corresponds to a summary relation that has already been checked, an implementation can substitute that summary relation for the conjunction of those subgraph relations, since it has already been verified to be a consequence of them. If this implication is verified, then the summary relation is satisfied. If this implication fails, an implementation should fall back to using the conjunction of the data-flow relations, since they may be logically stronger than the summary. Such double checking should be rare in practice. Third, the feasible subgraphs for a summary relation may share some data-flow relations. Rather than evaluate each subgraph separately, the conjunctions for subgraphs that share relations can be combined into a single formula by eliminating repeated conjuncts and combining the remaining conjuncts as disjuncts, according to the identity

$$(A \wedge C \Rightarrow D) \wedge (B \wedge C \Rightarrow D) \iff ((A \vee B) \wedge C \Rightarrow D) .$$

This merging of feasible subgraphs is an important optimization to reduce the total number of graphs that must be evaluated.

The relation model as described is context-insensitive. A single relation includes information about all the inputs that might influence an output, even if some of them are mutually exclusive, as the different call sites of a procedure are: any particular time a procedure is invoked, its results depend upon the values at only one of its call sites. If there really is a difference in the behavior in different contexts, such context sensitivity can still be represented internally to the relation by using logical formulas that are conditional. For instance, when properties are discovered using the Daikon dynamic invariant detection tool, Daikon can search separately for properties that hold on the subsets of input values corresponding to distinct call sites, and express those differences as properties that are conditional on the values of the inputs.

A related imprecision of this model is that a single feasible subgraph cannot separately represent distinct traversals of a data-flow edge. If a procedure is used in different ways by two distinct modules within a single feasible subgraph, or if two procedures in different modules are mutually recursive, the consistency condition may contain a contradiction. A partial solution would be to duplicate a module to separate distinct uses, but duplication can potentially be expensive, it is inapplicable in the case of recursion, and simple duplication will be incorrect if multiple using modules interact via state in the duplicated module.

3.3 Special Case: Upgrading a Functional Procedure

The upgrade condition for a system of two modules and a single procedure in one module called from the other [15] is a special case of the more general framework described in this section.

Consider a system with two modules, U and C, where C is a third-party component that defines a procedure `f`, and U calls `f`. Further, suppose that each call to `f` is independent. In our model, C would have an independent input $\overline{C}(f)$ describing the preconditions of `f`, and a data-flow relation $C(f'|f)$ describing the postconditions of `f`, both based on the vendor's testing of C. Conversely, U has an independent output $U(f)$ of preconditions describing how it calls `f`, and a summary relation $\overline{U}(f'|f)$ describing the postconditions it expects from the call.

Our technique claims that the new component may be safely substituted for the old one in the application if and only if

$$U(f) \Rightarrow \overline{C}(f) \qquad \text{and} \qquad (U(f) \wedge C(f'|f)) \Rightarrow \overline{U}(f'|f) \ .$$

Our original reasons for choosing this formula, and its relation to alternative formulas, are explained in [15]; it is also the result given by the algorithm of Sect. 3.2. Chen and Cheng [4] prove formally, using a relational semantics, that this condition is the weakest (most general) condition on a component that is guaranteed to preserve application behavior. This formula is similar to, but more general than, the classic substitutability condition of behavioral subtyping [1, 14], used to check that objects of a subtype are a safe replacement for supertype objects. In our notation, the condition that behavioral subtyping imposes on a single functional method is that

$$U(f) \Rightarrow \overline{C}(f) \qquad \text{and} \qquad C(f'|f) \Rightarrow \overline{U}(f'|f) \ .$$

4 Examples of Upgrades

The framework for upgrade safety checks described in Sect. 3 generalizes that of [15] to be applicable to more complex software systems, including object-oriented systems. The new framework is more general in three aspects: it can model modules with state and multiple interacting procedures, it can model interactions between modules in which procedure calls are made in both directions, and it applies to systems with more than two modules. The following subsections illustrate these capabilities with simple concrete examples of each of these new possibilities. In each case, the determination of which relationships to check was made automatically using a implementation of the unoptimized algorithm described in Sect. 3.2; an abstraction including the properties shown was discovered by the Daikon tool; and the verification of all of the required properties, including ones not shown, was performed by the Simplify automatic theorem prover. The verification, requiring the proof of hundreds of properties, took a total of less than one second for each example. For brevity, we show shortened operational abstractions with a representative fraction of the actual properties. We also do not show the complete code, nor do we show the necessary test suites for the applications or the new modules.

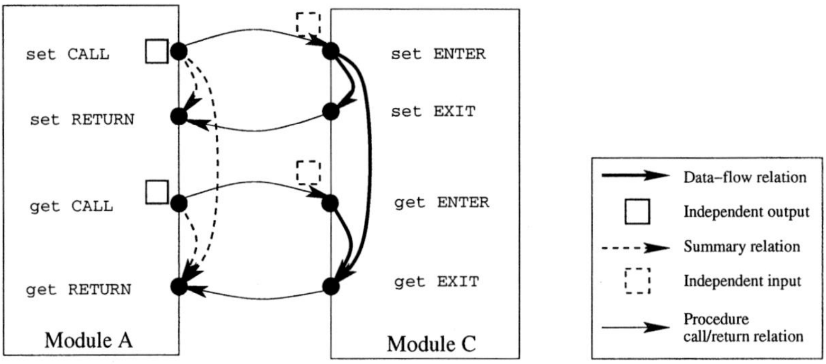

Fig. 2. A system with a module C whose procedures share state.

$$\begin{aligned} A(s_c) &\Rightarrow \overline{C}(s) \\ A(s_c) \wedge C(s'|s) &\Rightarrow \overline{A}(s_r|s_c) \\ A(g_c) &\Rightarrow \overline{C}(g) \\ A(s_c) \wedge A(g_c) \wedge C(g'|s,g) &\Rightarrow \overline{A}(g_r|s_c,g_c) \end{aligned}$$

Fig. 3. Consistency conditions, derived from equation 1 of Sect. 3.2, for the system shown in Fig. 2; s and g represent the `set` and `get` procedures.

4.1 Modules with Internal State

Figures 2 and 4 show a system in which one module, C, provides two procedures whose behavior is interdependent: the result of `get` depends on the previous call to `set`. Such dependencies often arise when methods share state in an object instance, but our approach is independent of how the state is recorded. To model

```
public class C {
  private int private_x;

  int set(int x) {                    int get() {
    private_x = x;                      return private_x + 1;
    return 0; // success              }
  }
}
```

Fig. 4. Source code for a module with the structure of C from Fig. 2.

$$\begin{aligned} A(s_c)&: s.x \text{ is even} \\ \overline{A}(s_r|s_c)&: s'.\mathit{return} = 0 \\ A(g_c)&: \mathit{true} \\ \overline{A}(g_r|s_c, g_c)&: g'.\mathit{return} = s.x + 1 \\ & \quad g'.\mathit{return} \text{ is odd} \end{aligned} \qquad \begin{aligned} \overline{C}(s)&: s.x \text{ is an integer} \\ C(s'|s)&: s'.\mathit{return} = 0 \\ \overline{C}(g)&: \mathit{true} \\ C(g'|s, g)&: g'.\mathit{return} = s.x + 1 \end{aligned}$$

Fig. 5. Operational abstractions for A and C as in Fig. 2. Variables are prefixed according to the procedure they belong to. For instance, $s'.\mathit{return}$ is the return value of `set`, while $g'.\mathit{return}$ is the return value of `get`.

this dependency, a data-flow edge connects the entrance of the `set` procedure to the exit of the `get` procedure; symmetrically, we presume that module A expects this relationship, as indicated by the summary edge connecting the call of `set` and the return of `get`. For the upgrade of module C to be behavior preserving, the four implications shown in Fig. 3 must hold. For instance, consider a behavior-preserving upgrade to C, which has been well-tested on its own, but suppose that module A happens to only call `set` with even integers. The operational abstractions shown in Figure 5 describe this situation, and it can be seen that the conditions in Fig. 3 do hold. For instance, consider the last condition: if $s.x$ is even, and $g'.\mathit{return} = s.x + 1$, then $g'.\mathit{return}$ will be odd.

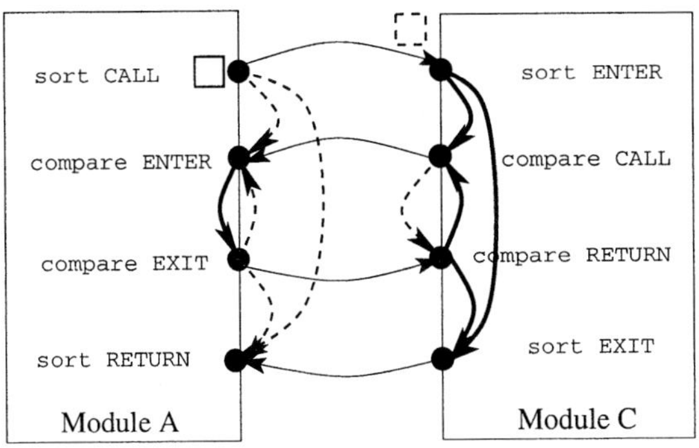

Fig. 6. A system with a module C that calls back to the using module A.

$$A(s_c) \Rightarrow \overline{C}(s)$$
$$A(s_c) \wedge C(c_c|s, c_r) \wedge A(c'|c) \Rightarrow \overline{A}(c|s_c, c')$$
$$A(s_c) \wedge C(c_c|s, c_r) \wedge A(c'|c) \Rightarrow \overline{C}(c_r|c_c)$$
$$A(s_c) \wedge C(c_c|s, c_r) \wedge A(c'|c) \wedge C(s'|s, c_r) \Rightarrow \overline{A}(s_r|s_c, c')$$

Fig. 7. Consistency conditions, derived from equation 1 of Sect. 3.2, for the system shown in Fig. 6; s and c represent the `sort` and `compare` procedures.

```
public class A {
  private static class MyCompare
      implements Compare {
    public int compare(int x, int y) {
      return (x > y) ? 1 : (x < y) ? -1 : 0;
    }
  }
  ...
    obj.sort(employee_ids, new MyCompare());
  ...
}
```

```
public class C {
  void sort(int[] a, Compare comp) {
    for (int i = a.length - 1; i > 0; i--)
      for (int j = 0; j < i; j++)
        if (comp.compare(a[j], a[j+1]) > 0) {
          int temp = a[i];
          a[i] = a[j];
          a[j] = temp;
        }
  }
}
```

Fig. 8. Source code for a module C and part of a module A with the structure shown in Fig. 6.

4.2 Modules with Callbacks

Figure 8 shows source code from a system in which A calls C's `sort` procedure, which calls back to the `compare` procedure defined in A. Figure 6 models this system conservatively with respect to changes in C, by including each possible data-flow edge in C and corresponding summary edge in A: the arguments passed to `compare` might depend on the results of the previous call, as well as the arguments to `sort`, and the results of `sort` potentially depend not only on its arguments but also on the results of the most recent call to `compare`. Here the callback is encapsulated in an object, but the same model could describe a callback passed by a function pointer. A change to this system is behavior-preserving only if the implications shown in Fig. 7 hold. For instance, the left-hand column of Fig. 9 gives an operational abstraction for A, which sorts only four-digit employee identification numbers. The right-hand column gives an operational abstraction for a well-tested behavior-preserving upgrade to C — for

$A(s_c)$: $\forall i \in s.a: i \geq 1000$	$\overline{C}(s)$: $\forall i \in s.a: i \geq -2^{31}$
$\overline{A}(c\|s_c, c')$: $c.x, c.y \in s.a$ $c.x, c, y \geq 1000$	$C(c_c\|s, c_r)$: $c.x, c.y \in s.a$
$A(c'\|c)$: $c'.return \in \{-1, 0, 1\}$ $c'.return < c.x, c.y$	$\overline{C}(c_r\|c_c)$: $c'.return \in \{-1, 0, 1\}$
$\overline{A}(s_r\|s_c, c')$: $\forall i \in s'.a: i \in s.a$ $\forall i \in s.a: i \in s'.a$ $\forall i \in s'.a: i \geq 1000$	$C(s'\|s, c_r)$: $\forall i \in s'.a: i \in s.a$ $\forall i \in s.a: i \in s'.a$

Fig. 9. Operational abstractions for A and C as in Fig. 6.

instance, a change to the sorting algorithm. Note that not all of the possible relations corresponding to edges in Fig. 6 were observed: for instance, calls to `compare` were not inter-dependent. Again, we can easily see that conditions of Fig. 7 hold. Considering the last line, if every element of $s.a$ is at least 1000, and every element of $s'.a$ is also a member of $s.a$, then every element of $s'.a$ is also at least 1000.

4.3 More than Two Modules

Figure 12 shows an excerpt of pseudocode from a client-server system for performing simple arithmetic. Modules R and M each perform two calculations in response to requests dispatched by module D. These services are used by two modules U and P, making a system of five modules with the structure shown in Fig. 10. In this example, the dispatch is performed explicitly, but a similar model could be used for dynamic dispatch as in an object-oriented language, given the sets of potential method targets. The conditions needed to verify the behavioral compatibility of a change to this system are shown in Fig. 11 (each condition containing a disjunction was formed by combining the conditions for two feasible subgraphs). Now, suppose that we wish to upgrade module U, and the new version U_2 requires a new version R_2 of module R, in which the behavior of the rounding operation has changed to round negative values toward negative infinity rather than toward zero. Because the change to R is incompatible, both modules must be replaced simultaneously. A similar simultaneous upgrade would be needed whenever two components, say a producer and a consumer of data, change the format they use without a change to the module mediating between them.

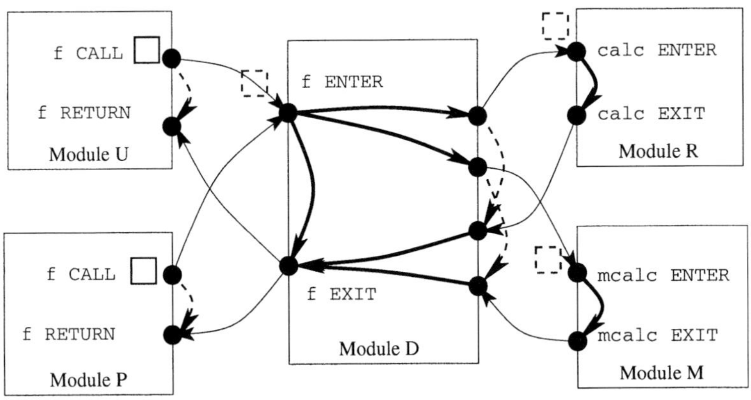

Fig. 10. A system consisting of five modules.

By checking the conditions of Fig. 11 using the operational abstractions shown in Fig. 13 (with the new R_2 and U_2), we can see that such an upgrade

$$
\begin{aligned}
(U(f_c) \vee P(f_c)) &\Rightarrow \overline{D}(f) \\
(U(f_c) \vee P(f_c)) \wedge D(c_c|f) &\Rightarrow \overline{R}(c) \\
(U(f_c) \vee P(f_c)) \wedge D(M_c|f) &\Rightarrow \overline{M}(m) \\
(U(f_c) \vee P(f_c)) \wedge D(c_c|f) \wedge R(c'|c) &\Rightarrow \overline{D}(c_r|c_c) \\
(U(f_c) \vee P(f_c)) \wedge D(m_c|f) \wedge M(m'|m) &\Rightarrow \overline{D}(m_r|m_c) \\
U(f_c) \wedge D(c_c|f) \wedge R(c'|c) \wedge D(m_c|f) \wedge M(m'|m) \wedge D(f'|f, c_r, m_r) &\Rightarrow \overline{U}(f_r|f_c) \\
P(f_c) \wedge D(c_c|f) \wedge R(c'|c) \wedge D(m_c|f) \wedge M(m'|m) \wedge D(f'|f, c_r, m_r) &\Rightarrow \overline{P}(f_r|f_c)
\end{aligned}
$$

Fig. 11. Consistency conditions, derived from equation 1 of Sect. 3.2, for the system shown in Fig. 10. f, c, and m represent the `f`, `calc`, and `mcalc` procedures respectively.

```
public class D {  // Dispatches to M or R
  static int f(String op, int input) {
    if (op.equals("double")
        || op.equals("triple"))
      return M.mcalc(op, input);
    else if (op.equals("increment")
             || op.equals("round"))
      return R.calc(op, input);
  }
}
```

```
public class R {  // Rounds or increments
  static int calc(String op, int input) {
    if (op.equals("round"))
      // In version 2, changed to:
      // return 10 * Math.floor(input / 10.0);
      return 10 * (input / 10);
    else if (op.equals("increment"))
      return input + 1;
  }
}
public class M {  // Multiplies by 2 or 3
  static int mcalc(String op, int input) {
    if (op.equals("double"))
      return 2 * input;
    else if (op.equals("triple"))
      return 3 * input;
  }
}
```

Fig. 12. Java-like pseudocode for modules D, R, and M as in Fig. 10.

$U(f_c)$:	$f.o \in \{\mathtt{d}, \mathtt{i}, \mathtt{r}\}$	$\overline{D}(f)$:	$f.o \in \{\mathtt{d}, \mathtt{i}, \mathtt{r}, \mathtt{t}\}$
$P(f_c)$:	$f.i \geq 0, f.o \in \{\mathtt{i}, \mathtt{r}, \mathtt{t}\}$		
$D(c_c\|f)$:	$f.o \in \{\mathtt{i}, \mathtt{r}\} \Rightarrow (f.o = c.o, f.i = c.i)$	$\overline{R}(c)$:	$c.o \in \{\mathtt{i}, \mathtt{r}\}$
$D(m_c\|f)$:	$f.o \in \{\mathtt{d}, \mathtt{t}\} \Rightarrow (f.o = m.o, f.i = m.i)$	$\overline{M}(m)$:	$m.o \in \{\mathtt{d}, \mathtt{t}\}$
$R(c'\|c)$:	$c.o = \mathtt{r} \Rightarrow c'.return \equiv 0 \pmod{10}$	$\overline{D}(c_r\|c_c)$:	$c.o = \mathtt{r} \Rightarrow c'.return \equiv 0 \pmod{10}$
	$c.o = \mathtt{i} \Rightarrow c'.return = c.i + 1$		$c.o = \mathtt{i} \Rightarrow c'.return = c.i + 1$
	$c.i \geq 0 \Rightarrow c'.return \geq 0$		
$M(m'\|m)$:	$m.o = \mathtt{d} \Rightarrow m'.return = 2 \cdot m.i$	$\overline{D}(m_r\|m_c)$:	$m.o = \mathtt{d} \Rightarrow m'.return = 2 \cdot m.i$
	$m.o = \mathtt{t} \Rightarrow m'.return = 3 \cdot m.i$		$m.o = \mathtt{t} \Rightarrow m'.return = 3 \cdot m.i$
$D(f'\|f, c_r, m_r)$:	$f.o \in \{\mathtt{i}, \mathtt{r}\} \Rightarrow f'.return = c'.return$	$\overline{U}(f_r\|f_c)$:	$f.o = \mathtt{d} \Rightarrow f'.return = 2 \cdot f.i$
	$f.o \in \{\mathtt{d}, \mathtt{t}\} \Rightarrow f'.return = m'.return$		$f.o = \mathtt{i} \Rightarrow f'.return = f.i + 1$
			$f.o = \mathtt{r} \Rightarrow f'.return \equiv 0 \pmod{10}$
		$\overline{P}(f_r, f_c)$:	$f.o = \mathtt{i} \Rightarrow f'.return = f.i + 1$
			$f.o = \mathtt{r} \Rightarrow f'.return \equiv 0 \pmod{10}$
			$f.o = \mathtt{t} \Rightarrow f'.return = 3 \cdot f.i$
			$f'.return \geq 0$

$U_2(f_c)$:	$f.o \in \{\mathtt{d}, \mathtt{i}, \mathtt{r}\}$	$\overline{R_2}(c)$:	$c.o \in \{\mathtt{i}, \mathtt{r}\}$
$R_2(c'\|c)$:	$c.o = \mathtt{r} \Rightarrow c'.return \equiv 0 \pmod{10}$	$\overline{U_2}(f_r\|f_c)$:	$f.o = \mathtt{d} \Rightarrow f'.return = 2 \cdot f.i$
	$c.o = \mathtt{r} \Rightarrow c'.return \leq c.i$		$f.o = \mathtt{i} \Rightarrow f'.return = f.i + 1$
	$c.o = \mathtt{i} \Rightarrow c'.return = c.i + 1$		$f.o = \mathtt{r} \Rightarrow f'.return \equiv 0 \pmod{10}$
	$c.i \geq 0 \Rightarrow c'.return \geq 0$		$f.o = \mathtt{r} \Rightarrow f'.return \leq f.i$

Fig. 13. Operational abstractions for modules in Fig. 10. The arguments `op` and `input` are abbreviated o and i, and the values `double`, `increment`, `round`, and `triple` are abbreviated to their initial letters. The abstractions labeled U_2 and R_2 represent potential upgrades to the U and R modules respectively.

will be behavior preserving. U_2 will function correctly because R_2 provides the functionality it requires, and P will function correctly because the functionality it uses (on non-negative integers only) was unchanged. The data-flow edges in D from f to c_c and m_c show an application of the guarding technique described in Sect. 3: observe that the corresponding properties in Fig. 13 are implications whose antecedents are properties over a variable of f.

5 Enhancements to the Upgrade Technique

We have developed several additional enhancements that make the upgrade technique more effective in validating upgrades to complex software systems. These techniques are general solutions to specific problems that we encountered while running our tools to evaluate upgrades of the C library (Sect. 6). This section describes four improvements: a change to make more information about a program's behavior available to our system, which improves its accuracy; two techniques that indicate which detected behavioral differences are most relevant to upgrade safety; and a technique to avoid the need for a large test suite.

5.1 Including Non-local State Information

In order to conclude that an upgraded module will still produce the desired outputs, our technique must capture, on at least a superficial level, how those outputs are a function of inputs. Sometimes, the inputs that determine a subroutine's behavior are not all supplied as parameters or as object fields. For instance, in the Unix system-call interface, functions like `open` and `close` create and destroy stateful 'file descriptor' objects that are actually small integer indices into a table that exists only in the kernel.

This sort of extra information can be thought of as residing in virtual fields. The program's own (pure) accessor methods are one source of contents for such fields. Additionally, we used annotations to indicate values that should be virtual fields, for instance associating the file-descriptor pseudo-datatype with `fstat`, a function that returns a variety of information about a file.

5.2 Distinguishing Non-deterministic Differences

Section 5.1 describes how our technique can work on software whose behavior is determined by information elsewhere in the programming system. In some cases, however, a program's behavior may depend on information that is completely inaccessible. For example, such non-determinism is often associated with errors.

Suppose that a return value, thrown exception, or side effect representing an error occurred during testing but never in an application's use. Then our technique would reject an upgrade, unless it could demonstrate that the application could never induce the erroneous behavior (as the application never had while using the old component). It is reasonable to establish this for a divide-by-zero error – say, if the application never passes in a zero value. However, other faults are effectively non-deterministic. It is not reasonable to predict a 'disk full' error by considering the hard disk's previous state as an input to every 'write file' operation. Failures that result from a physical fault like a broken cable or dust on a floppy disk are completely unpredictable.

For such effectively non-deterministic failures, we assume that if they never occurred with the old component, they will never occur with the new component either. This is unsound, but effective in practice. Our technique determines what results represent such failures by examining language features such as exceptions and error codes, possibly augmented by annotations.

5.3 Highlighting Cross-Version Incompatibilities

When our technique issues a warning, the warning might be an indication of a behavioral difference (or use of undefined functionality) between the two versions of the component. On the other hand, the upgrade may be a valid, behavior-preserving upgrade, but the warning results from insufficient testing, an inadequate grammar of the operational abstraction, or a theorem proving weakness.

This section proposes a post-processing technique that aims to distinguish between cases where our technique does not have enough information to verify that an upgrade is safe, and when it has some particular information that implies an upgrade might be unsafe. Classifying warnings permits users or tools to focus on those that are most likely to result from a behavioral difference.

The postprocessing step first considers a *self-upgrade* from the old module to itself. Such an 'upgrade' is always behavior-preserving, but our technique might still fail to verify the upgrade's safety. Any warning is a false alarm, and is likely to also be issued for the real upgrade. By contrast, a warning that occurs only with the new module, but not the old, certainly represents a behavioral difference, a *cross-version* incompatibility. Our technique highlights these cross-version warnings for the user's immediate consideration. (An earlier version of this idea was mentioned in [15], under the name 'meta-comparison', but not developed, implemented, or evaluated.)

This postprocessing is effective no matter whether the abstractions describing the old component version are derived from the old or new versions of the component test suite. The operational abstraction most likely to be available for the old module is one based on the test suite current at the time of its release; in our scenario, it would have been supplied along with the old module. If the test suite has changed, however, better results can be obtained by testing the old module version with the new version's test suite. Using the new test suite with the old module allows the technique to better compensate for deficiencies existing only in the new test suite, or common to the application and the old test suite.

5.4 Using Other Applications as a Test Suite

Extensive testing is an important part of software engineering, but not all software has a large formal test suite, nor are operational abstractions from those formal test suites necessarily available to users considering an upgrade. When an organized test suite is unavailable, the role of the 'test suite' in our technique can instead be played by other applications. For each application, we use as the 'test suite' all uses of the new component by all of the other available applications. Analogous to the 'late adopter' practice of letting one's colleagues use a new software version first, this is effective if the other uses of the component are both sufficiently extensive and sufficiently similar to the uses of the application in question. In addition to being useful to users, this technique lets us run experiments even in the absence of formal test suites. However, the testing achieved in this way is still less comprehensive than the results of formal testing, so the technique of Sect. 5.3 should also be used, to reduce the number of warnings that indicate only insufficient testing.

6 Case Studies

In order to test our techniques, we performed case studies of upgrading a large software component, the Linux C library. On Unix systems a single library, traditionally named `libc`, provides the C standard library functions, wrappers around the low-level system calls, and miscellaneous utility functions. Most Linux systems use version 2 of the GNU C library [11], which provides a large shared library that is dynamically linked with virtually every system executable.

The authors of the GNU C library attempt to maintain compatibility, especially backward compatibility, between releases. Each procedure or global variable in the library is marked with the earliest library version it is compatible with, the library contains multiple versions of some procedures, and the static and dynamic linkers enforce that appropriate versions are used. This mechanism assists with maintaining compatibility and avoiding incompatibility, but it is insufficient. We subverted this check, and added a small number of stubs to our instrumentation library to simulate functions missing from older versions. Our experiments demonstrate that libraries marked as incompatible can be used without error by most applications, but also that in some cases differences between procedures marked with the same version can cause errors.

Our experiments use unmodified binary versions of applications and the library. We capture an application's use of the library via dynamic interposition: a stub library wraps each function call (approximately 1000 in all), and records the arguments to and results from each invocation.

6.1 A Compatible C Library Upgrade

The Linux C library implements a stable API and attempts to maintain compatibility between versions. To see how well our technique validates large, but relatively safe upgrades, we compared versions 2.1.3 and 2.3.2 of the C library, as they were used by 48 programs from version 7.3 of the standard Red Hat Linux distribution.

We chose a suite of 48 commonplace applications, including many of the applications that the authors use in everyday work. These include a number of large graphical applications such as text editors and a web browser, games, interface accessories, text-based application programs, and utility programs. Application usage is represented by 20 minutes of scripted and recorded human usage, which exercises the programs in a fashion typical of daily use. The programs performed correctly, in all visible respects, with both library versions.

Because the (largely volunteer) authors of the GNU C library have provided only a limited formal test suite, the role of the 'test suite' in our case studies is instead played by the other applications, as described in Sect. 5.4. The subject programs called 199 instrumented library procedures. Because our technique requires procedures to be tested by several clients, we restricted our attention to the 76 procedures that were used by 4 or more of the subject programs.

For the 76 procedures, our tool correctly warns of behavior differences in 10 of them and correctly approves 57 upgrades as having unchanged behavior. For 9 procedures, the tool warns (incorrectly, we believe) that the behavior differs for at least one application.

Our comparison technique discovers 10 genuine behavioral differences between the library versions; for the application programs that we examined, these differences appear to be innocuous. For example, the `dirent` structure returned by `readdir` holds information about an entry in a directory and contains a field named `d_type`. In version 2.1.3, this field was always zero, while in version 2.3.2 it took on a variety of values between 0 and 12. Our tool also reports a number of behavioral differences arising from the members of the `FILE` structure used by standard IO routines such as `fopen` and `fclose`. Because the definition of this structure is visible to user-written code, examining its members is conservative, but the differences our technique finds are not relevant to programs that correctly treat the structure as opaque.

The 9 false positive incompatibility warnings are summarized in on the left in Fig. 14. The two tallest bars correspond to `tcgetattr` and `select`. When `tcgetattr` is applied to a file descriptor that is not a terminal, it copies over a returned structure from uninitialized memory, causing spurious properties to be detected over these values. For `select`, two expected properties fail to hold: one bounding a return value indicating the number of microseconds left to wait when the procedure returns, and one concerning a field that our tools treats as an integer, though in fact it is part of a bit vector in which some bits are meaningless. On average, a user of our tool checking this C library upgrade for one of these applications would need to examine 2.69 failing procedures; of these reports, 0.75 would be spurious, and the remaining 1.94 would represent real differences, which upon examination do not affect the application in question. The distribution of numbers of procedures flagged for different programs is shown on the right in Fig. 14. As would be expected, larger applications have more potential for incompatibility: the two programs with the most warnings were Netscape Communicator and GNU Emacs.

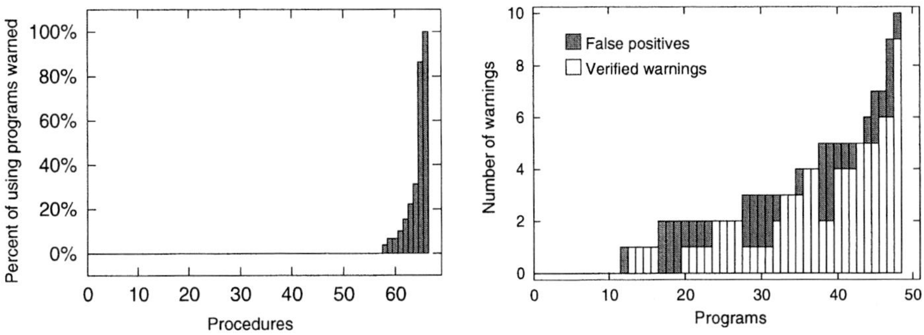

Fig. 14. Reported incompatibilities between C library versions 2.1.3 and 2.3.2. On the left, for 66 procedures whose behavior did not change, the percentage of the programs that used that procedure for which a behavioral difference warning was reported (false positives). On the right, the number of warnings produced per program. Unshaded bars show incompatibilities that we have verified by hand. Shaded bars show warnings that are probably false positives.

6.2 C Library Incompatibilities

We used our technique to examine two incompatible changes made by the authors of the GNU C library. Coincidentally, both relate to procedures that operate on representations of time; of course, our technique is not limited to such procedures. These procedures were not considered in the experiment described in Sect. 6.1 because they were used by too few of those programs, though one of the differences exists between the versions considered there.

The `mktime` procedure. The `mktime` procedure converts date and time values specified with separate components (year through seconds) into a single value of type `time_t`, which is traditionally a signed integer counting seconds since the 1970 'epoch'. If the time cannot be so represented, `mktime` returns −1. Before April 2002, the GNU `mktime` converted dates between 1901 and 1970 into negative `time_t` values. In April of 2002, the C library maintainers concluded that this behavior was in conflict with the Single Unix Specification [25] (the successor to POSIX), and changed `mktime` to instead return −1 for any time before the epoch. (Though this change was not incorporated into version 2.2.5 of the library as released by the GNU maintainers, it was adopted by Red Hat in the version of the library distributed with Red Hat 7.3, which is also labeled as version 2.2.5. This incompatibility, between two versions with the same label, underscores the dangers of relying on developers to label incompatibilities by hand.)

To see how our technique observed this change, we compared the behavior of the `mktime` procedure in the version of the C library on a Red Hat 7.3 workstation (Red Hat version 2.2.5-43), and in a freshly compiled version of 2.2.5 as released by its maintainers. Our subject programs were `date`, `emacs`, `gawk`, `pax`, `pdfinfo`, tar, touch, and wget; for each program, the library was considered to be tested by the remaining programs, as described in Sect. 5.4.

Our tool reports that this upgrade to mktime would not be safe for any of the programs we examined. Though the correct behavior of mktime is too complex to be described in the grammar of our operational abstraction generation tool, our technique does discover differences between the old and new behaviors of mktime. Specifically, when mktime completes successfully, it updates several fields of the supplied time structure, but when it returns an error, these fields remain uninitialized. The new version of mktime gives these uninitialized values for pre-1969 dates when the old version did not. Because of this phenomenon, our tool reports that a number of properties involving these fields will not hold using the upgraded version of mktime. In the applications we tested, the change to mktime's functionality does cause user-visible functionality to be reduced. For instance, date with the new library refuses to operate on dates between 1901 and 1970 which would be accepted when running with the old library. This error has the same underlying cause as one discovered in a previous case study of Perl modules [15]; however, this manifestation is completely different and its effects were discovered in a different way and in different programs.

The utimes procedure. The C library's utimes procedure updates the last-modification and last-access timestamps on a file. The interface of utimes allows these times to specified by a two integers counting seconds and microseconds. Our version of the Linux kernel stores file timestamps with one-second granularity, so the C library must convert the times to a whole number of seconds. During the summer of 2003, this time conversion was changed from truncation to rounding. This change was incompatible with other Unix programs: for instance, rounding up caused the touch command to give files a timestamp in the future, which in turn caused make to exit with an error message. After wide distribution of this library, including in the Debian Linux development distribution, the change was reverted in response to user complaints.

Our technique recognized this change. We compared the behavior of the system 2.2.5 version of the C library with that of a version from the development CVS repository as of September 1st, 2003. Our subject programs were the standard utilities cp, emacs, mail, pax, and touch; for cp, mail, and touch, we used more recent versions (from the Debian development distribution). We wrote a short script to exercise each program's use of utimes; for each program, we used the other four as the test suite.

Our tool reports that an upgrade to the C library version with the round-to-nearest behavior would be unsafe for all five of the applications we considered. For each application, it reports that the new library fails to guarantee a property that the old one did, namely that the last-access timestamp of the affected file in seconds, after the call to utimes, should equal the seconds part of the new access timestamp passed to utimes. Note that the timestamps of the file are not arguments to utimes; they are found using the stat procedure as a virtual field of the filename, as discussed in Sect. 5.1.

7 Related Work

Our technique builds on previous work that formalized the notion of component compatibility, and complements other techniques that attempt to verify the correctness of multi-component systems. Our work differs in that it characterizes a system based on its observed behavior, rather than a user-written specification, and it is applicable in more situations.

7.1 Subtyping and Behavioral Subtyping

Strongly typed object-oriented programming languages, such as Java, use subtyping to indicate when component replacement is permitted [23,2,3]. If type-checking succeeds and a variable has declared type T, then it is permissible to supply a run-time value of any type T' such that $T' \sqsubseteq T$: that is, T' is either T or a subtype of T. However, type-checking is insufficient, because an incorrect result can still have the correct type.

One approach to verifying the preservation of semantic properties across an upgrade is for the programmer to express those properties in a formal specification. This is the principle of behavioral subtyping [1,14]: type T' is a behavioral subtype of type T if for every property $\phi(t)$ provable about objects t of type T, $\phi(t')$ is provable about objects t' of type T'.

In practice, the requirement of behavioral subtyping is both too strong and too weak for use in validating a software upgrade. Like any condition that pertains only to a component and not the way it is used, the requirement is too strong for applications that use only a subset of the component's functionality. Formal specifications are also too weak because a system may inadvertently depend on a fact about the implementation of a component version that is omitted (perhaps intentionally) from the specification.

7.2 Specification Matching

Zaremski and Wing generalize behavioral subtyping to consider several varieties of matching between specifications [28]. Such comparisons can be used for a number of purposes in which the question to be answered is, broadly, whether one component can be substituted for another. Most previous research, however, has focused on retrieving components from a database, to facilitate reuse [21, 24].

Though they considered a large number of possible comparison formulas, Zaremski and Wing omitted the one that we adopted for our single-component upgrade [15]. Formulas equivalent to the single-component formula have been used for reuse (sometimes called the "satisfies" match [21]) and in work building on behavioral subtyping [6]. Also, in the VDM tradition [12], proof obligations analogous to the condition (with the addition of a function mapping concrete instances to abstract ones) and called the "domain rule" and the "result rule" are used to demonstrate that a concrete specification correctly implements an abstract specification. To our knowledge, no previous work considers all the issues raised by the multi-module model introduced in this paper, or uses the same formula that it does.

Ours is also not the first attempt to automate the comparison of specifications with theorem proving technology. Zaremski and Wing use a proof assistant in manually verifying a few specification comparisons [28]. Schumann and Fischer use an automated theorem prover with some specialized preprocessing [24]. By comparison, the operational abstractions we automatically verify are significantly larger than the hand-written specifications used in previous work, though the individual statements in our abstractions are mostly simple.

7.3 Other Component-Based Techniques

The use of black-box components in systems construction increases the need for automatically checkable representations of component behavior. Technically, our approach is most closely related to techniques based on behavioral subtyping; their use in the component-based context is well summarized by [13]. A more common approach has been to abstract component behavior with finite state representations such as regular languages [20] or labeled transition systems [17]. Like our operational abstractions, such representations can be automatically checked to determine if one component can be substituted for another. The kinds of failure found by the different techniques are complementary, though. Finite-state techniques excel at checking properties that are simple, but global; for instance that a file must always be opened before being read. Our operational abstractions can capture a richer set of properties, including infinite state ones, but only as they are localized to the pre- or postconditions on a particular interface. Incorporating temporal properties into our framework might be a fruitful direction for future work.

7.4 Avoiding Specifications

Ideally, a technique like the one we describe could be used with hand-written specifications in the place of operational abstractions. However, not only would the component specification need to be proved to describe the component's actual behavior, the application would have to correctly specify the particular component behaviors it relied on. Creating and proving such comprehensive specifications would likely be too difficult and time-consuming for most software projects.

In the absence of specifications, one might also attempt to statically verify that two versions of a component produce the same output for any input. However, such checking is generally only possible when the versions are related by simple code transformations [27]. For instance, techniques based on symbolic evaluation can verify the correctness of changes made by an optimizing compiler, such as common subexpression elimination [18]. If a program change was subtle enough to require human expertise in its application, it is probably too subtle to be proved sound automatically.

8 Conclusion

We have provided a technique for predicting problems resulting from behavioral differences among purportedly compatible versions of software components. The technique runs before the new versions are integrated or system tests are run. It logically compares two subsets of behavior: tested behavior and behavior used by an application. The technique is based on a rich component model, capturing many situations common in object-oriented frameworks, such as multiple simultaneous upgrades, shared state, callbacks, and indirect communication through the system. The logical test generalizes that used by previous work, subsuming the previous test as a special case. We also extended the technique to situations that arise in real-world code: non-local state, apparent non-determinism, innocuous pre-existing incompatibilities, and lack of test suites. We have implemented all these enhancements, enabling us to perform a case study of upgrading the Linux C library in 48 Unix programs. Our tool approved upgrades of most parts of the library, indicated genuine behavioral differences, and had a low false positive rate. Furthermore, it also identified several differences that led to user-visible errors.

References

1. America, P., van der Linden, F.: A parallel object-oriented language with inheritance and subtyping. In: Conference on Object-Oriented Programming, Systems, Languages, and Applications and 4th European Conference on Object-Oriented Programming (OOPSLA/ECOOP '90), Ottawa, Canada (1990) 161–168
2. Black, A., Hutchinson, N., Jul, E., Levy, H., Carter, L.: Distributed and abstract types in Emerald. IEEE Transactions on Software Engineering **13** (1987) 65–76
3. Cardelli, L.: A semantics of multiple inheritance. Information and Computation **76** (1988) 138–164
4. Chen, Y., Cheng, B.H.C.: A semantic foundation for specification matching. In: Foundations of Component-Based Systems. Cambridge University Press, New York, NY (2000) 91–109
5. Detlefs, D., Nelson, G., Saxe, J.B.: Simplify: A theorem prover for program checking. Technical Report HPL-2003-148, HP Labs, Palo Alto, CA (2003)
6. Dhara, K.K., Leavens, G.T.: Forcing behavioral subtyping through specification inheritance. In: Proceedings of the 18th International Conference on Software Engineering, Berlin, Germany, IEEE Computer Society Press (1996) 258–267
7. Dijkstra, E.W.: Guarded commands, nondeterminacy and formal derivation of programs. Communications of the ACM **18** (1975) 453–457
8. Ernst, M.D.: Practical fine-grained static slicing of optimized code. Technical Report MSR-TR-94-14, Microsoft Research, Redmond, WA (1994)
9. Ernst, M.D., Cockrell, J., Griswold, W.G., Notkin, D.: Dynamically discovering likely program invariants to support program evolution. IEEE Transactions on Software Engineering **27** (2001) 1–25 A previous version appeared in *ICSE '99, Proceedings of the 21st International Conference on Software Engineering*, pages 213–224, Los Angeles, CA, USA, May 19–21, 1999.
10. Flanagan, C., Saxe, J.B.: Avoiding exponential explosion: Generating compact verification conditions. In: Proceedings of the 28th Annual ACM SIGPLAN-SIGACT Symposium on Principles of Programming Languages, London, UK (2001) 193–205

11. Free Software Foundation: GNU C library (2003) `http://www.gnu.org/software/libc/libc.html`.
12. Jones, C.B.: Systematic Software Development using VDM. Second edn. Prentice Hall (1990)
13. Leavens, G.T., Dhara, K.K.: Concepts of behavioral subtyping and a sketch of their extension to component-based systems. In: Foundations of Component-Based Systems. Cambridge University Press, New York, NY (2000) 113–135
14. Liskov, B.H., Wing, J.M.: A behavioral notion of subtyping. ACM Transactions on Programming Languages and Systems **16** (1994) 1811–1841
15. McCamant, S., Ernst, M.D.: Predicting problems caused by component upgrades. In: Proceedings of the 10th European Software Engineering Conference and the 11th ACM SIGSOFT Symposium on the Foundations of Software Engineering, Helsinki, Finland (2003) 287–296
16. McCamant, S., Ernst, M.D.: Predicting problems caused by component upgrades. Technical Report 941, MIT Laboratory for Computer Science, Cambridge, MA (2004) Revision of first author's Master's thesis.
17. Moisan, S., Ressouche, A., Rigault, J.P.: Behavioral substitutability in component frameworks: A formal approach. In: Proceedings of the 2003 Workshop of Specification and Verification of Component Based Systems, Helsinki, Finland. (2003)
18. Necula, G.C.: Translation validation for an optimizing compiler. In: Proceedings of the ACM SIGPLAN 2000 Conference on Programming Language Design and Implementation, Vancouver, BC, Canada (2000) 83–94
19. Necula, G.C., Lee, P.: The design and implementation of a certifying compiler. In: Proceedings of the ACM SIGPLAN'98 Conference on Programming Language Design and Implementation, Montreal, Canada (1998) 333–344
20. Nierstrasz, O.: Regular types for active objects. In: Proceedings of the Eighth Annual Conference on Object-Oriented Programming Systems, Languages, and Applications, ACM Press (1993) 1–15
21. Penix, J., Alexander, P.: Toward automated component adaptation. In: Proceedings of the 9th International Conference on Software Engineering and Knowledge Engineering (SEKE-97), Madrid, Spain, June 18-20, 1997. (1997)
22. Reps, T., Horwitz, S., Sagiv, M.: Precise interprocedural dataflow analysis via graph reachability. In: Proceedings of the 22nd Annual ACM SIGPLAN-SIGACT Symposium on Principles of Programming Languages, San Francisco, CA (1995) 49–61
23. Schaffert, C., Cooper, T., Bullis, B., Kilian, M., Wilpolt, C.: An introduction to Trellis/Owl. In: Conference on Object-Oriented Programming Systems, Languages and Applications, Portland, OR, USA (1986) 9–16
24. Schumann, J., Fischer, B.: NORA/HAMMR: Making deduction-based software component retrieval practical. In: Proceedings of the 1997 International Conference on Automated Software Engineering (ASE '97), Lake Tahoe, California. (1997) 246–254
25. The Open Group, ed.: The Single UNIX Specification, Version 3. The Open Group (2003) `http://www.unix.org/version3/`.
26. Tip, F.: A survey of program slicing techniques. Journal of Programming Languages **3** (1995) 121–189
27. Yang, W., Horwitz, S., Reps, T.: A program integration algorithm that accommodates semantics-preserving transformations. ACM Transactions on Software Engineering and Methodology **1** (1992) 310–354
28. Zaremski, A.M., Wing, J.M.: Specification matching of software components. ACM Transactions on Software Engineering and Methodology **6** (1997) 333–369

Typestates for Objects

Robert DeLine and Manuel Fähndrich

Microsoft Research
One Microsoft Way
Redmond, WA 98052-6399 USA
{rdeline,maf}@microsoft.com

Abstract. Today's mainstream object-oriented compilers and tools do not support declaring and statically checking simple pre- and postconditions on methods and invariants on object representations. The main technical problem preventing static verification is reasoning about the sharing relationships among objects as well as where object invariants should hold. We have developed a programming model of typestates for objects with a sound modular checking algorithm. The programming model handles typical aspects of object-oriented programs such as downcasting, virtual dispatch, direct calls, and subclassing. The model also permits subclasses to extend the interpretation of typestates and to introduce additional typestates. We handle aliasing by adapting our previous work on practical linear types developed in the context of the Vault system. We have implemented these ideas in a tool called Fugue for specifying and checking typestates on Microsoft .NET-based programs.

1 Introduction

Although mainstream object-oriented languages, like C$^\sharp$ and Java, automatically catch or prevent many programming errors through compile-time checks and automatic memory management, there remain two related sources of error that often manifest as runtime exceptions. First, a developer must obey the rules for properly calling an object's methods, including calling them in an allowed order and obeying the preconditions on the methods' arguments. Today, such rules are captured in the class's documentation, if at all. Second, a developer implementing a class must ensure that each public method upholds the class's representation invariant, including any invariants inherited from the superclass.

Types are the main mechanism through which programmers currently specify mechanically checked preconditions, postconditions and representation invariants. These mechanical checks are critical for spotting errors early in the development cycle, when they are cheapest to fix. Types, however, are a very limited specification tool, particularly in imperative programming languages, where objects change state over time. Using standard type systems, we cannot address the sources of errors described above. On the other hand, providing the programmer with a rich logic for writing preconditions, postconditions, and

M. Odersky (Ed.): ECOOP 2004, LNCS 3086, pp. 465–490, 2004.

object invariants quickly runs into decidability problems. For example, the ESC/Java system [1] supports rich specifications, but does not fully verify object invariants.

In this paper, we propose a statically checkable *typestate* system to declare and verify state transitions and invariants in imperative object-oriented programs. Typestates [2] specify extra properties of objects beyond the usual programming language types. As the name implies, typestates capture aspects of the state of an object. When an object's state changes, its typestate may change as well. Typestates provide an abstraction mechanism for predicates over object graphs, but retain some of the simplicity and feel of types. Typestates can be used to restrict valid parameters, return values, or field values, and thereby provide extra guarantees on internal object properties.

Previous research demonstrated the utility of typestates for capturing interface rules in non-object-oriented, imperative languages [2,3]. In this paper, we adapt and extend the programming methodology [3,4] that we developed for reasoning about non-object oriented imperative programs to the object-oriented setting. The technical contributions are the following:

Typestates are modular. A typestate is a description of the contents of all of an object's fields. However, at a given program point, a modular static checker only knows about those fields declared in an object's declared type or its superclasses. Hence, some of the object's state (introduced by subclasses) is unknown. Typestates are a good match for this problem, since typestates provide names for abstract predicates over field state. A modular static checker can know an object's state by name without knowing the exact invariant that an unknown subclass associates with that name. This approach allows a clean description of how subclasses can extend the interpretation of a typestate and the language features of upcasts, downcasts, and virtual method invocation. We also describe the limits of expressiveness of our typestate formulation.

Typestates generalize object invariants. Commonly, an object invariant (or representation invariant) is a predicate that is established during object construction that remains true throughout the object's lifetime. We believe in practice that this view is too limiting, since objects tend to satisfy different properties at different stages of their lifetimes. Instead, we view an object as having different typestates over its lifetime, where each typestate is a named predicate over the object's concrete state. By making the object typestate explicit at pre- and postconditions of all methods, we also avoid the problem of defining where object invariants must hold, which in the past has been approached using ad-hoc notions of "visible states" [5]. In our model, traditional object invariants are simply properties that are common to all typestates of the object.

Typestates support incremental object state changes. Any given method implementation only has a partial view of an object. Hence, describing how an object's state (including the statically unknown subclass state) changes is nontrivial. Furthermore, because an object's state change is neces-

(a)

```
[ TypeStates("Open", "Closed") ]
class WebPageFetcher {

  [ Post("Closed"), NotAliased ]
  WebPageFetcher([NotNull] string s)
  {
    this . site = s;
  }

  [ Pre("Closed"), Post("Open"), NotAliased ]
  virtual void Open()
  {
    this .cxn = new Socket();
    this .cxn.Bind(this . site );
    this .cxn.Connect();
  }

  [ Pre("Open"), Post("Closed"), NotAliased ]
  virtual void Close() {
    this .cxn.Close ();
    this .cxn = null;
  }

  [ Pre("Open") ]
  [ return: NotNull ]
  virtual string GetPage( [NotNull] string path) {
    return this .cxn.Receive ();
  }

  [ Pre("Closed") ]
  virtual void SetSite ([NotNull] string site ) {
    this .cxn = site;
  }

  [ NotNull(WhenEnclosingState="Open") ]
  [ NotAliased(WhenEnclosingState="Open") ]
  [ InState("Connected", WhenEnclosingState="Open") ]
  [ Null(WhenEnclosingState="Closed") ]
  private Socket cxn;

  [ NotNull ]
  private string site ;
}
```

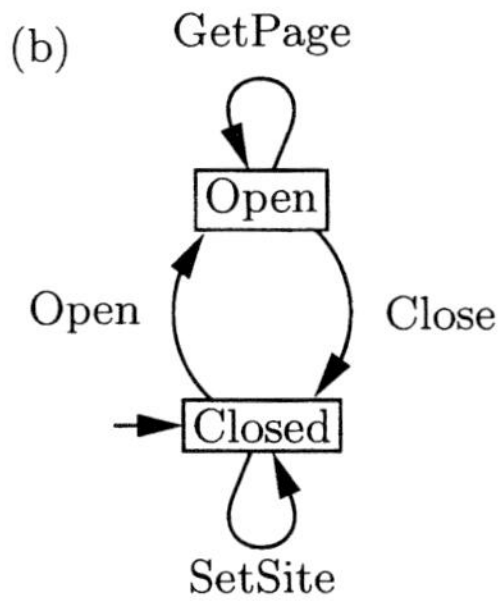

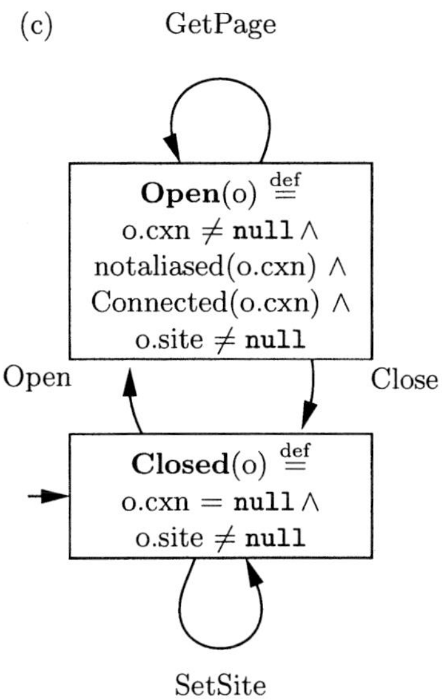

Fig. 1. Web page fetcher example

sarily implemented incrementally (by changing individual fields), typestates must be able to describe intermediate states, where different parts of an object have different states. We introduce *frame typestates* and *sliding method signatures* to address these issues.

2 Motivating Example

This section informally introduces typestates for objects and illustrates some of its expressive power, as well as technical aspects that we will further discuss

```
[ TypeStates("Raw", "Bound", "Connected", "Closed") ]
class Socket {

  [ Post("Raw"), NotAliased ]
  Socket();

  [ Pre("Raw"), Post("Bound"), NotAliased ]
  void Bind(string endpoint);

  [ Pre("Bound"), Post("Connected"), NotAliased ]
  void Connect();

  [ Pre("Connected") ]
  void Send(string data);

  [ Pre("Connected") ]
  string Receive();

  [ Pre("Connected"), Post("Closed"), NotAliased ]
  void Close();
}
```

Fig. 2. Simplified socket interface

in the rest of the paper. Our examples are in C$^\sharp$ syntax. We use attributes (in brackets) to record typestates, pre-, and postconditions. These correspond to how typestates are specified for our checking tool Fugue [6]. We use this syntax to make the examples more readable, but will only informally describe it. Later, in Section 6, we introduce a small formal language to make these examples precise. Fig. 1(a) contains the source of a simple class WebPageFetcher providing the functionality to open a particular web server, to fetch pages from the server, and to close the connection to the server. A WebPageFetcher object can be in one of two typestates, Open and Closed. The constructor produces an object in typestate Closed, the method Open changes the object's typestate from Closed to Open, and the method Close changes the typestate back from Open to Closed. Method GetPage can be called only when the object satisfies typestate Open, but does not change the typestate. Similarly, method SetSite can only be called when the object satisfies typestate Closed. These state changes can be pictured as the finite state machine in Fig. 1(b).

The Pre and Post annotations on methods restrict the order of operations that clients can invoke on the object. Such order restrictions are useful because a method's implementation makes assumptions about the object's state when it is invoked. For example, calling GetPage on a Closed object results in a null dereference exception because the method's code assumes that the field cxn is not null. In our approach, we make the relationship between typestate and object invariants explicit.

The annotations on the fields cxn and site define each typestate in terms of what properties of the object's concrete state hold in that typestate. If the object is in state Closed, the private Socket cxn to the web server is null. If the object is in state Open, then the private Socket cxn is non-null and in typestate Connected, which is a typestate of the Socket class, as shown in Fig. 2. The annotation NotNull on field site specifies a classic invariant, since it is not qualified by a particular typestate and therefore holds in all typestates.

In short, a typestate is a predicate over an object's field state. To a client, this predicate is an uninterpreted function to be matched by name; to an implementor, the predicate is defined in terms of predicates over the fields' values. Fig. 1(c) shows the same state machine as in (b), with each state enlarged to show the predicate that holds in that typestate. The state machine in (b) is the client's view of a WebPageFetcher object, while the state machine in (c) is the implementor's view.

Given these annotations, we can mechanically verify that every method implementation assumes only the stated precondition and guarantees the stated postcondition. Starting with the constructor, we observe that it sets field site to the non-null constructor argument s. That satisfies the invariant of field site in typestate Closed. However, field cxn is not assigned. In our approach, we assume that the implicit pre-state of objects in constructors is typestate Zeroed, in which all fields are initialized to their zero-equivalent value. In state Zeroed, field cxn contains null and therefore satisfies the necessary condition for typestate Closed. Since both of the WebPageFetcher's fields satisfy the conditions for typestate Closed at the end of the constructor, the constructor satisfies its postcondition.

Method Open is interesting in that it changes the typestate of the receiver from Closed to Open. It does so by initializing field cxn to a fresh socket. After the constructor call, the socket has typestate Raw (see Fig. 2). Thus, before satisfying the postcondition of method Open, the socket has to be put into the right typestate by calling methods Bind and Connect in that order, according to the Pre and Post annotations in class Socket. After calling Bind and Connect, the field cxn is in typestate Connected and the field site is unchanged (and therefore still non-null). Hence, the receiver is in typestate Open and, the method Open satisfies its postcondition.

So far, we have ignored two issues: 1) the annotations NotAliased appearing in the code, and 2) the fact that there could be subclasses of WebPageFetcher. The next two sections deal with object typestates and subclasses. Section 5 describes a programming model that allows static tracking of typestates in the presence of aliasing. Section 6 presents the formal language and typestate checking rules. Section 7 revisits our examples in the formal language, discusses limits of the approach and some extensions.

3 Object Typestate

Consider again the typestates of our WebPageFetcher example. We can view these in the form of the table in Figure 3. The table maps a class and typestate to a formula over the fields of an object of that class. The formula consists of atomic predicates such as value equalities, aliasing assumptions, as well as recursive typestate assumptions about the state of objects referenced through fields. In this paper we assume that formulae include at least equalities and disequalities

o	Closed(o)	Open(o)
WebPageFetcher	o.cxn = null ∧ o.site ≠ null	o.cxn ≠ null ∧ notaliased(o.cxn) ∧ Connected(o.cxn) ∧ o.site ≠ null

Fig. 3. Typestate interpretation

between variables and null. In practice, any richer theory for which there are decidable satisfiability checkers is suitable.

As we can see from this table, the typestates we have used so far in our examples were really not typestates of an entire object, but only *frame typestates*, *i.e.*, a typestate of a particular *class frame* of an object. A class frame of an object is the set of fields of the object declared in that particular class, not in any super- or sub classes. In our example so far, we used frame typestates expressing properties of the WebPageFetcher frame.

To obtain an *object typestate*, we must be able to describe properties of all frames of an object, leading to the following issues:

Modularity of the typestate definition. The meaning of an object typestate cannot be fully defined when the typestate is introduced, subclasses must be able to give new interpretations of typestates for their own fields. Nevertheless, a typestate should describe all parts of an object, even unknown subclasses. We address these issues in Section 3.1.

Non-uniformity of typestates. Because a change in typestate is implemented as individual field updates, an object's typestate changes only gradually. Hence, typestates must be able to describe intermediate states of objects, where part of the object is in state A, other parts in state B. Section 4 discusses this issue in more detail.

To accommodate the above problems we define an object typestate to be a collection of frame typestates, one per class frame of the object's allocated (dynamic) type. In other words, we use one frame typestate for the static type frame of a reference, one for each super class frame, and one for each potential subclass frame. Since we are interested in a modular system, we cannot statically know the subclasses of a particular type. Therefore, our object typestates require an abstraction that gives a *uniform* typestate to all unknown subclass frames. Formally, an object typestate takes the form σ_C:

$$\begin{array}{lll} \text{(object typestate)} & \sigma_C ::= \chi_C :: \mathbf{rest}@s \mid \chi_C :: \bullet & \\ \text{(frames)} & \chi_C ::= \chi_B :: C@s \text{ where } B = \mathsf{baseclass}(C) & \\ & \qquad \mid \mathsf{Object}@s \quad \text{where } C = \mathsf{Object} & \end{array}$$

An object typestate σ_C is a collection of frame typestates χ_C and either a rest typestate s (specifying that all possible subclass frames of C satisfy s), or no rest state indicating that the dynamic object type is exactly C (for example,

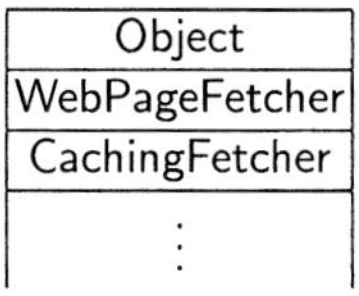

An object decomposed into class frames. The ellipsis reflects that the object's dynamic type may be more derived than its declared type.

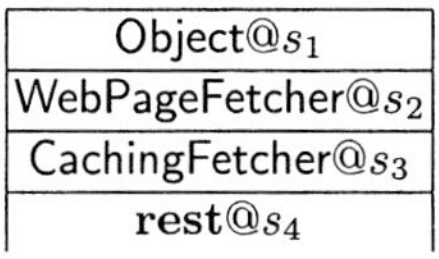

A frame typestate per frame ($s_1..s_3$) and one frame typestate (s_4) for statically unknown subclasses.

Fig. 4. Illustration of class frames and frame typestates

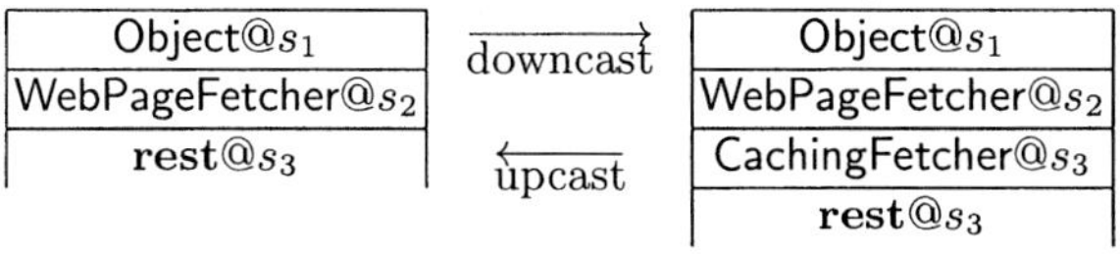

Fig. 5. Illustration of upcast and downcast with typestates

right after new, or because class C is restricted from having subclasses, as with sealed classes in C$^\sharp$). A collection of frame typestates χ_C consists of a frame typestate for frame C and each supertype of C. Class C in an object typestate σ_C corresponds to the traditional static type of an object.

To keep the presentation simple, our formulation assumes a single typestate per class frame whereas in principle, an object can satisfy multiple compatible typestates.

Fig. 4 graphically illustrates the idea of separate frame typestates in an object and the rest state for all subclasses. Our model contains the restriction that a frame typestate can only constrain fields in that frame, but not in any frames of superclasses. This restriction enables modular reasoning in that writing a field of a particular frame can only affect that frame's typestate, but none of the typestates of any subclass frames.

Fig. 5 illustrates how upcasts and downcasts work in the presence of typestates. To downcast to an immediate subclass, the newly materialized frame typestate is simply equal to the original rest typestate for the subclasses (s_3). For an upcast, the disappearing frame must have the same typestate as the rest state that absorbs the frame; otherwise, the upcast is illegal.

Typestate shorthands in examples. Explicitly specifying each frame typestate of an object in our examples is a nuisance. We use the following convention to specify entire object typestates. By default, a typestate specification applies to the class frame that introduces the typestate name (via the TypeStates annotation on the class) and to all subclass frames. Alternatively, each typestate annotation can be targeted at a particular frame C using the qualifier Type=C, or at the frames of all subclasses using the qualifier Type=Subclasses in Pre, Post, or InState annotations. The root class Object has a single typestate Default, which all classes inherit. Those frames for which no explicit typestate is given are assumed to be in typestate Default.

Given this description, we can now interpret the object typestates specified in class WebPageFetcher. Method WebPageFetcher::Open, for instance, specifies the receiver precondition object typestate Object@Default :: WebPageFetcher@Closed :: **rest**@Closed, and method WebPageFetcher.GetPage specifies the receiver precondition Object@Default :: WebPageFetcher@Open :: **rest**@Open.

3.1 Typestates and Subclasses

Let us now turn to the subclass CachingFetcher in Fig. 6 to see how typestates work in the presence of object extensions. The caching web page fetcher has a new cache field to hold a cache of already fetched pages. The natural invariants for this field are that it is null when the fetcher is Closed and non-null when the fetcher is Open. Since the subclass can provide it's own interpretation for typestates Open and Closed, adding this invariant is not a problem. The following table summarizes the frame typestates for a CachingFetcher object.

o	Default(o)	Closed(o)	Open(o)	CacheOnly(o)
Object	true	Default(o)	Default(o)	Default(o)
WebPageFetcher	o.cxn $\neq$ null$\wedge$ maybealiased(o.cxn)$\wedge$ Default(o.cxn)$\wedge$ o.site $\neq$ null	o.cxn $=$ null$\wedge$ o.site $\neq$ null	o.cxn $\neq$ null$\wedge$ notaliased(o.cxn) $\wedge$ Connected(o.cxn)$\wedge$ o.site $\neq$ null	Default(o)
CachingFetcher	o.cache $\neq$ null	o.cache $=$ null	o.cache $\neq$ null	o.cache $\neq$ null

This table illustrates the two ways in which a subclass can extend its superclasses' typestates: (1) by associating its own field invariants to a typestate defined in a superclass (e.g., the invariants on field cache); and (2) by adding new typestates (e.g., the typestate CacheOnly). Notice that when a typestate is not defined for a given frame, we use the typestate Default.

Looking at method override CachingFetcher.GetPage, we see how this method can take advantage of the object typestate precondition on the receiver. Since the parent method WebPageFetcher.GetPage specified frame typestate Open for all subclass frames (an abstract specification, since these typestate have not been defined at that point), the overriding method can rely on the extra properties provided by its frame typestate. If we had instead limited the typestate of subclasses to a known predicate (e.g., true), subclasses could not make any assumptions about their own fields in such overridden methods. In our example, CachingFetcher.GetPage assumes that field cache is not null.

4 Sliding Methods

Given the ideas presented so far, there is a problem with methods that purport to change the typestates of subclass frames, such as WebPageFetcher::Open. Its

```
[ TypeStates("CacheOnly") ]
class CachingFetcher : WebPageFetcher {

  [ Post("Closed"), NotAliased ]
  CachingFetcher(string site ) : base( site ) {}

  [ Pre("Closed"), Post("Open"), NotAliased ]
  override void Open()
  {
    base.Open();
    this.cache = new Hashtable();
  }

  [ Pre("Open"), Post("Closed"), NotAliased ]
  override void Close()
  {
    base.Close();
    this.cache = null;
  }

  [ Pre("Open") ]
  [ return: NotNull ]
  override string GetPage( [NotNull] string path)
  {
    string page = this.cache.GetValue(path);
    if (page == null) {
      page = base.GetPage(path);
      this.cache.Add(path, page);
    }
    return page;
  }

  [ Null(WhenEnclosingState="Closed"), NotNull(WhenEnclosingState="Open,CacheOnly") ]
  private Hashtable cache;

  [ Pre("Open"), Post("CacheOnly"), Post("Closed", Type=WebPageFetcher), NotAliased ]
  void CloseKeepCache()
  {
    base.Close();
  }

  [ Pre("CacheOnly"), Pre("Closed", Type=WebPageFetcher) ]
  [ return:MayBeNull ]
  string GetCachedPage(string path)
  {
    string page = this.cache.GetValue(path);
    return page;
  }

  [ Pre("CacheOnly"), Pre("Closed", Type=WebPageFetcher), Post("Closed"), NotAliased ]
  void DeleteCache() {
    this.cache = null;
  }

}
```

Fig. 6. Caching web page fetcher

Post specification states that all frames, including all unknown subclasses, will be in typestate Open at the end of the method body. As written, this specification is unfortunately not satisfied by the implementation. The method can assign only to fields that are visible through the static type and therefore cannot have any effect on fields of subclasses. Thus, on exit, the subclass typestates must still be Closed. This begs the question how a method can possibly change subclass states.

A method can only directly affect fields of its frame or the fields of superclasses. In order to change the typestate of subclasses, a virtual method call to a *sliding method* is required. The idea behind a sliding method is that each subclass implements a slightly stronger state change, namely each subclass changes the typestate of its frame and all frames of superclasses, but leaves the subclass typestates unchanged. As long as each subclass correctly implements such a sliding method, a virtual call to a sliding method is guaranteed to change the entire object typestate, since it dispatches to the dynamic type (the lowest class frame) and changes that frame as well as all super class frames.

We call such methods *sliding* because the typestate of the class introducing the method keeps sliding down the class hierarchy with each subtype, overriding the rest state. Graphically, we can illustrate this as follows:

	Object@Default		Object@Default
WebPageFetcher::Open	WebPageFetcher@Closed	⟶	WebPageFetcher@Open
	rest@Closed		**rest**@Closed

	Object@Default		Object@Default
	WebPageFetcher@Closed		WebPageFetcher@Open
CachingFetcher::Open	CachingFetcher@Closed	⟶	CachingFetcher@Open
	rest@Closed		**rest**@Closed

In the limit, i.e., the effect observed for a virtual call, the signature is simply:

	Object@Default		Object@Default
virtual call to Open	WebPageFetcher@Closed	⟶	WebPageFetcher@Open
	rest@Closed		**rest**@Open

We fix our example by relaxing the post typestate of subclasses to remain Closed in methods Open and Close, and by treating these methods as sliding methods. For method Open in both classes WebPageFetcher and CachingFetcher, the corrected annotations are:

```
[ Pre("Closed"), Post("Open"), Post("Closed", Type=Subclasses) ]
virtual void Open () { ... }
```

4.1 Sliding Signatures

In general, for each virtual method M, we thus have a family of related method signatures: the virtual signature $\mathsf{virtSig}_C$ (used at a virtual call site), and one implementation signature $\mathsf{implSig}_D$ per implementation of the method by class D. These signatures are derived from the implementation signature of M in class C which introduces virtual method M. The signature relations are illustrated in Figure 7 and formally defined in Figure 15. We assume that class C introduces

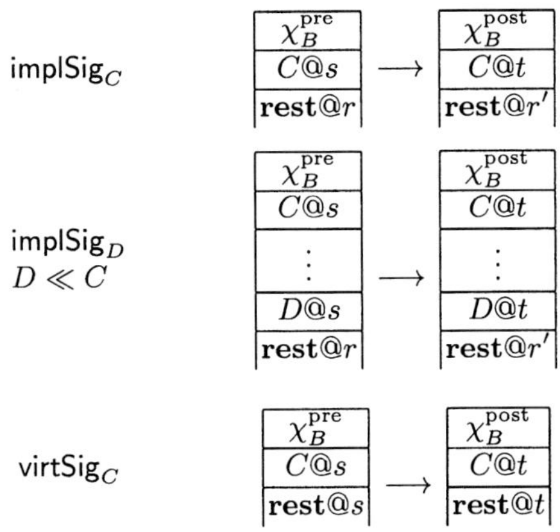

Fig. 7. Relation between typestates of this in signatures of sliding method implementations and the virtual call signature

---

sliding method M, and D is some subclass of C (notation $D \ll C$). The pre and post states of base classes of C are χ_B^{pre} and χ_B^{post}.

Note that the rest states r and r' used in the implementation method signatures can be arbitrary (they need not be related to the pre-state s or the post-state t). It is instructive to study the different possible scenarios and what they imply for implementations.

For method Open, we have $C =$ WebPageFetcher, $D =$ CachingFetcher, $s =$ Closed, $t =$ Open, and $r = r' =$ Closed. This specification requires that the implementation of CachingFetcher::Open calls the base-class Open method *before* changing its own frame state, for otherwise, the pre-condition at the base-class call is not satisfied for its frame. An alternative is to pick $r = r' =$ Open, which forces implementations of Open to first change their own frame to state Open before calling the base-class method. Finally, if $r = r'$ is yet a third state, then implementations must first change their own frame to r, then call the base-class method, then change their own frame from r to Open.

In most signatures, rest states r and r' are equal. However, there are useful cases where that is not the case. Consider for instance a wrapper method containing a virtual call to Open. It would have $s =$ Closed, $r =$ Closed, $t =$ Open, and $r' =$ Open.

Given these definitions, we can now illustrate how to prove that method CachingFetcher::Open implements its signature correctly. Note how CachingFetcher::Open calls the base class Open method before changing its own frame. This base call is non-virtual, and therefore the method signature implSig$_{\text{WebPageFetcher}}$ applies (rather than the virtual signature). We thus have the progression of the receiver object through the following typestates:

- on entry (implSig$_{\text{CachingFetcher}}$)
  Object@Default :: WebPageFetcher@Closed :: CachingFetcher@Closed :: **rest**@Closed
- upcast for direct base-call to WebPageFetcher::Open
  Object@Default :: WebPageFetcher@Closed :: **rest**@Closed
- direct base-call to WebPageFetcher::Open (implSig$_{\text{WebPageFetcher}}$)
  Object@Default :: WebPageFetcher@Open :: **rest**@Closed
- safe down-cast to CachingFetcher
  Object@Default :: WebPageFetcher@Open :: CachingFetcher@Closed :: **rest**@Closed
- after update to field cache and post of implSig$_{\text{CachingFetcher}}$
  Object@Default :: WebPageFetcher@Open :: CachingFetcher@Open :: **rest**@Closed

We now illustrate the situation at a virtual call site.

- Assume x has typestate
  Object@Default :: WebPageFetcher@Closed :: CachingFetcher@Closed :: **rest**@Closed
- upcast for virtual call to Open
  Object@Default :: WebPageFetcher@Closed :: **rest**@Closed
- virtual call to Open (virtSig$_{\text{WebPageFetcher}}$)
  Object@Default :: WebPageFetcher@Open :: **rest**@Open
- after safe down-cast to CachingFetcher
  Object@Default :: WebPageFetcher@Open :: CachingFetcher@Open :: **rest**@Open

The virtual call to Open changes all frames to typestate Open, since, dynamically, every frame of the object is changed.

5 Alias Confinement

Any sound static checker of object invariants must be aware of all the references to an object in order not to miss any of the object's state transitions. We use a version of the adoption and focus model [4] for dealing with aliasing. We distinguish two modes for each object and statically track this mode for all pointers to objects. An object is either NotAliased, meaning that we statically know perfect aliasing information for this object (all must-aliases and no may-aliases). Otherwise, the object is MayBeAliased, in which case there can be arbitrary may-aliasing to the object among pointers tracked as MayBeAliased.

At allocation, an object is not-aliased. Objects can undergo arbitrary state changes when not-aliased, since we can statically track their state. Explicit deallocation of NotAliased objects is safe, but in this paper we don't discuss it further.

A NotAliased parameter guarantees to a method that it can access the object only through the given parameter or copies of the pointer that it makes, but the method cannot reach this object through any other access paths. At the same time, NotAliased guarantees to the caller that, upon return, the method will not have produced more aliases to the object. On fields, NotAliased specifies that the object with that field holds the only pointer to the referenced object. NotAliased objects can be transferred in and out of fields at any point. NotAliased objects can be returned from methods, guaranteeing to the caller that no other aliases are still alive.

A NotAliased object can also *leak*, *i.e.*, transition to the MayBeAliased mode.[1] When an object leaks, all references to the object are considered MayBeAliased and may be copied arbitrarily. References to a MayBeAliased object are typestate-invariant; the object's typestate can no longer change. Thus, the moment an object leaks, its typestate is essentially frozen to the current typestate. We make this simplifying assumption to make the system tractable. A *focus* operation [4] can be used for temporarily changing the typestate of maybe-aliased objects, but for simplicity we ignore *focus* in this paper.

Since we allow a not-aliased object to leak, we must choose the rules for accessing the leaked object's not-aliased fields. There are three reasonable options:

Recursively leak. Treat NotAliased fields of MayBeAliased objects as MayBe-Aliased. This approach is simple, works in the presence of concurrency, and allows both reading and writing of the field, but does not preserve the not-aliased status of sub-structures.

Leave not-aliased. Allow access only via an atomic field-variable swap operation. This approach retains not-aliased status of such objects and also works in the presence of concurrency.

Disallow access to such fields. Require a focus scope on the containing object to access such fields [4]. This approach requires extra locking in the presence of concurrency.

The formalism in the next section uses the first option.

6 Formal Language

To formalize our approach, we present a small imperative, object-oriented language with a static typestate system. This language and type system form the kernel of a tool, called Fugue [6], which is a typestate checker for programming languages that compile to the .NET Intermediate Language, like C♯, Visual Basic, and Managed C++.

Besides the typestate aspects, the language is a standard object-oriented language, with classes, fields and methods. Each class has a single base class, unless it is the predefined class Object. The subclass relation ($\ll$) is the reflexive, transitive closure of the baseclass relation.[2] A class consists of virtual method

[1] Leak corresponds to adoption in [4]. Here, we do not distinguish multiple adopters, but simply assume a single implicit adopter, namely the garbage collector.

[2] We assume the baseclass relation is non-cyclic, but the static semantics does not enforce it.

(program)	$P ::= class_1 \mathinner{..} class_n\ \mathtt{in}\, b$
(class)	$class ::= \mathtt{class}\, C : D\ \{\overline{d}\}$
(declaration)	$d ::= \mathtt{virt}\, M : \psi \mid \mathtt{impl}\, M\{\overline{b}\} \mid \mathtt{field}\, f \mid \mathtt{state}\, s : \tau$
(method sig)	$\psi ::= \forall[\Delta](\rho_1 \mathinner{..} \rho_n); \Theta; \varphi \to \exists\rho.(\Theta'; \varphi')$
(code block)	$b ::= \psi\, \ell = \lambda(x_1 \mathinner{..} x_n).stmt$
(statement)	$stmt ::= \mathtt{let}\, x = e\ \mathtt{in}\ stmt$
	$\mid \mathtt{set}\, x.f = y\ \mathtt{in}\ stmt$
	$\mid \mathtt{pack}[C@s]\ x\ \mathtt{in}\ stmt$
	$\mid \mathtt{unpack}[C]\ x\ \mathtt{in}\ stmt$
	$\mid \mathtt{leak}\ x\ \mathtt{in}\ stmt$
	$\mid \mathtt{goto}\ tt$
(expression)	$e ::= x \mid c \mid y.f \mid \mathtt{new}\, C \mid y.[C::]M(y_1 \mathinner{..} y_n)$
(targets)	$tt ::= \bullet \mid \ell[\rho_1 \mathinner{..} \rho_m](y_1 \mathinner{..} y_n)\ \mathtt{when}\, A,\ tt \mid \mathtt{return}\, x\ \mathtt{when}\, A,\ tt$
(condition)	$A ::= \mathtt{true} \mid x = c \mid x = y \mid x \neq c \mid x \neq y \mid A \wedge A \mid A \vee A$
	$\mid \mathsf{hastype}(x, C)$
(constant)	$c ::= 0, 1, \ldots$
(binding)	$\delta ::= x : \rho \mid \ell : \psi \mid C@s : \tau \mid M : (\psi, C) \mid C::M : \psi \mid f : C$
(type env)	$\Gamma ::= \bullet \mid \delta, \Gamma$
(name env)	$\Delta ::= \bullet \mid \rho, \Delta$
(heap)	$\Theta ::= \bullet \mid \rho \mapsto (a, \sigma_C), \Theta$
(aliasing)	$a ::= 1 \mid + \mid \bot$
(object typestate)	$\sigma_C ::= \chi_C :: \mathbf{rest}@s \mid \chi_C :: \bullet$
(frames)	$\chi_C ::= \chi_{\mathsf{baseclass}(C)} :: F_C$
	$\chi_{\mathsf{Object}} ::= F_{\mathsf{Object}}$
(frame)	$F_C ::= C@s \mid C\{f_1 : \rho_1 \mathinner{..} f_n : \rho_n\}@s$
(frame typestate)	$\tau ::= \exists\{f_1 : \rho_1 \mathinner{..} f_n : \rho_n\}.(\Theta; \varphi)$
(value formula)	$\varphi ::= \mathtt{true} \mid \rho = c \mid \rho = \rho' \mid \rho \neq c \mid \rho \neq \rho' \mid \varphi \wedge \varphi \mid \varphi \vee \varphi$
	$\mid \mathsf{hastype}(\rho, C)$
(value name)	ρ
(typestate name)	s
(block label)	ℓ
(variable name)	x, y
(class name)	C
(field name)	f
(method name)	M

Fig. 8. Syntax of the language

declarations (`new`), method implementations (`impl`), fields, and typestates. To simplify the presentation, we assume all methods are virtual, sliding, and have distinct names.

The syntax of the formal language makes the checker's assumptions about the heap and values fully explicit in the form of pre- and postconditions at every basic block in the method body. This allows us to separate checking from inference. In order to be practical, a system like Fugue infers the intermediate states inside a method, but inference is beyond the scope of this paper.

Fig. 8 contains the syntax of the language. A program is a set of classes and a single code block. Each class consists of virtual method declarations, method implementations, fields, and typestate interpretations τ. A typestate interpretation τ is an existentially closed predicate over the fields of a class frame. A method is a named set of labeled code blocks, where execution begins at the first block. Each code block is a closed function. Signatures ψ of methods and code blocks have the form

$$\forall[\Delta](\rho_1 \mathinner{..} \rho_n); \Theta; \varphi \to \exists\rho.(\Theta'; \varphi')$$

where $\Theta; \varphi$ are the constraints on the heap and values on entry to the method or block, ρ names the result, and $\Theta'; \varphi'$ are the constraints on the heap and values (including the result) on exit of the method. The signature of a method is the signature of the first block in its body. The receiver is always the first parameter of a method. As usual, type equivalence is syntactic modulo renaming of bound variables.

There are no local variables. Data is passed between blocks through explicit parameters (think registers). Each code block ends in a set of control transfers to other code blocks or in a return, where each transfer is guarded by a condition A. When control reaches the end of the block, control follows an edge (chosen nondeterministically) whose condition is true at that point. The $\mathsf{hastype}(x, C)$ condition is an explicit type test that succeeds if x's dynamic type is C or a subclass of C. In conjunction with the rules in Figure 14, it allows for dynamic downcasts as well as recovering the static type after an upcast.

There are two kinds of method calls: virtual calls $y.M(...)$; and non-virtual calls $y.C{::}M(...)$ directly to the method M implemented in class C. We model object construction as a new expression followed by a non-virtual call to a constructor method.

The expressions leak, pack and unpack are non-standard constructs. A leak expression changes the mode of an object from not-aliased to maybe-aliased. The pack and unpack operations are used on not-aliased objects to coerce between the abstract typestate view and the concrete field view of a class frame of a particular object. In order to access (read or write) a field of a not-aliased object, the frame containing the field must be unpacked. Thus pack and unpack operations are required such that all accesses to fields are performed on unpacked frames. Packed frames are typically required at method boundaries. Aliased objects are never packed or unpacked.

Our type system assigns each value a symbolic name ρ, a form of singleton type. These names are used for pointers and scalars alike. Heaps Θ are mappings from pointer names ρ to an aliasing assumption a and the object's typestate σ_C. Formulae φ provide pure value constraints on ρ's. The typestate σ_C also specifies the static class type C of ρ. Alias assumptions take the forms 1 for not-aliased, + for maybe-aliased, and $\bot$ for alias-polymorphic parameters. A heap mapping $\rho \mapsto (a, \sigma_C)$ is interpreted as a conditional mapping, predicated on $\rho \neq \mathsf{null}$.

There are implicit well-formedness conditions on heaps Θ regarding duplicates. If Θ contains duplicate mappings $\rho \mapsto (a_1, \sigma_1)$ and $\rho \mapsto (a_2, \sigma_2)$, then $a_1 = a_2 = +$ and $\sigma_1 = \sigma_2$, otherwise we consider the heap predicate unsatisfiable.

6.1 Static Semantics

The static semantics enforces type and typestate safety. Figure 13 shows the rules for programs, classes and class members. Type environment Γ contains method signatures (both virtual and particular implementations), as well as frame typestate interpretations, and fields. In methods, Γ also contains local variables. Rules [**virt**] and [**impl**] enforce the relationship between virtual and implementation signatures of sliding methods described in Section 4. To simplify the class rules, we force classes to implement all virtual methods that could be invoked on them. An implementation can of course just call the base class method. The auxiliary function fn denotes the free names (ρ) of Γ, ψ, or τ.
Figure 9 contains the rules for statements and expressions. Judgment $\Delta; \Gamma; \Theta; \varphi \vdash \mathit{stmt} : \exists\rho.(\Theta'; \varphi')$ states that *stmt* is well formed in environment $\Delta; \Gamma; \Theta; \varphi$ and produces result ρ, in heap Θ' and value constraints φ'.

The judgments use a few notational shortcuts. The syntax $\sigma_C@s$ denotes the uniform object typestate $\mathsf{Object}@s :: ... :: C@s :: \bullet$. The syntax $F_C :: \sigma$ is a convenient pattern match to extract frame F_C from an object typestate.

Operation $\Theta|_\rho$ restricts the memory predicate Θ to the domain ρ (or the empty heap if not present). Similarly, $\varphi|_{\rho_j}$ restricts the value constraint to a conjunction of predicates on ρ_j only. Operation $\overline{\Theta}^a$ changes the aliasing of all not-aliased locations in Θ to a. It is used when accessing aliased or alias-polymorphic objects in order to adjust the aliasing of not-aliased fields. Accessing a not-aliased field of an alias-polymorphic parameter yields itself an alias-polymorphic object, thereby preventing it from changing, leaking, or escaping.

The judgment $\Theta; \varphi \vdash \Theta'; \varphi'$ is implication of heaps and value constraints. Heaps must be equivalent up to duplication of aliased locations and implication of formulae and typestates. Fig. 14 contains the implication rules.

The side condition σ_C packed in rule [**leak**] states that all frames of σ_C must be packed before the object can transition to an aliased mode.

Our decision on how to deal with aliased objects is visible in rule [**read**], governing access to fields of aliased objects. We re-instantiate the typestate predicate for the frame containing the field, since we assume that between any instruction, the field could change (this is conservative even in the presence of thread shared objects). Similarly, updating a field of an aliased object (rule [**set**]) requires that we prove the typestate predicates after substituting the new value name for the old, thereby guaranteeing that the update retains all invariants of the affected object.

This treatment makes explicit that field correlations cannot be observed of aliased objects, unless we extend the system with read-only fields or explicit focus scopes in which the object fields are not changed by the environment [4].

6.2 Soundness

Although we have no formal proof, we believe the system to be sound. We leave a study of its meta-theory for future work.

$$\frac{\varphi' = \varphi \wedge \rho = c}{\Delta; \Gamma; \Theta; \varphi \vdash c : \rho; \Delta, \rho; \Theta; \varphi'}\ \textbf{const}$$

$$\frac{\begin{array}{l}\Theta(\rho) = (1, C\{f_1{:}\,\rho_1 \mathinner{..} f_n{:}\,\rho_n\}@s :: \sigma) \\ \varphi \Rightarrow \rho \neq \mathtt{null}\end{array}}{\Delta; \Gamma, y{:}\,\rho; \Theta; \varphi \vdash y.f_j : \rho_j; \Delta; \Theta; \varphi}\ \textbf{read1}$$

$$\frac{\Gamma(y) = \rho}{\Delta; \Gamma; \Theta; \varphi \vdash y : \rho; \Delta; \Theta; \varphi}\ \textbf{var}$$

$$\frac{\begin{array}{l}\Theta(\rho) = (a, C@s :: \sigma) \quad a = + \vee a = \bot \\ \Gamma(C@s) = \exists\{f_1{:}\,\rho_1 \mathinner{..} f_n{:}\,\rho_n\}.(\Theta_2; \varphi_2) \\ \Theta' = \Theta, \overline{\Theta_2|_{\rho_j}}^{a} \quad \varphi \wedge \varphi_2|_{\rho_j} \quad \varphi \Rightarrow \rho \neq \mathtt{null}\end{array}}{\Delta; \Gamma, y{:}\,\rho; \Theta; \varphi \vdash y.f_j : \rho_j; \Delta, \rho_j; \Theta'; \varphi'}\ \textbf{read}$$

$$\frac{\begin{array}{l}\Theta' = \Theta, \rho \mapsto (1, \sigma_C@\mathsf{Zeroed}) \\ \varphi' = \varphi \wedge \rho \neq 0\end{array}}{\Delta; \Gamma; \Theta; \varphi \vdash \mathtt{new}\, C : \rho; \Delta, \rho; \Theta'; \varphi'}\ \textbf{new}$$

$$\frac{\Delta; \Gamma; \Theta; \varphi \vdash tt : \exists\rho'.(\Theta'; \varphi')}{\Delta; \Gamma; \Theta; \varphi \vdash \mathtt{goto}\, tt : \exists\rho'.(\Theta'; \varphi')}\ \textbf{goto}$$

$$\frac{\begin{array}{l}\Gamma(y_i) = \rho_i \qquad i = 0..n \\ \Gamma([C{::}]M) = \forall[\Delta''](\rho_1..\rho_n); \Theta_0; \varphi_0 \to \exists\rho'.(\Theta_1; \varphi_1) \\ \Theta; \varphi \vdash \Theta_0, \Theta_2; \varphi_0\end{array}}{\Delta; \Gamma; \Theta; \varphi \vdash y_0.[C{::}]M(y_1..y_n) : \rho'; \Delta, \rho'; \Theta_1, \Theta_2; \varphi \wedge \varphi_1}\ \textbf{call}$$

$$\frac{\begin{array}{l}\Delta; \Gamma; \Theta; \varphi \vdash e : \rho; \Delta'; \Theta'; \varphi' \\ \Delta'; \Gamma, x{:}\,\rho; \Theta'; \varphi' \vdash \mathit{stmt} : \exists\rho'.(\Theta'; \varphi')\end{array}}{\Delta; \Gamma; \Theta; \varphi \vdash \mathtt{let}\, x = e\, \mathtt{in}\, \mathit{stmt} : \exists\rho'.(\Theta'; \varphi')}\ \textbf{let}$$

$$\frac{\begin{array}{l}\Theta \ \ = \rho_x \mapsto (1, C\{f_1{:}\,\rho_1 \mathinner{..} f_j{:}\,\rho_j \mathinner{..} f_n{:}\,\rho_n\}@s :: \sigma), \Theta_1 \qquad \varphi \Rightarrow \rho_x \neq \mathtt{null} \\ \Theta_2 = \rho_x \mapsto (1, C\{f_1{:}\,\rho_1 \mathinner{..} f_j{:}\,\rho_y \mathinner{..} f_n{:}\,\rho_n\}@s :: \sigma), \Theta_1 \\ \Delta; \Gamma, x{:}\,\rho_x, y{:}\,\rho_y; \Theta_2; \varphi \vdash e : \exists\rho'.(\Theta'; \varphi')\end{array}}{\Delta; \Gamma, x{:}\,\rho_x, y{:}\,\rho_y; \Theta; \varphi \vdash \mathtt{set}\, x.f_j = y\, \mathtt{in}\, e : \exists\rho'.(\Theta'; \varphi')}\ \textbf{set1}$$

$$\frac{\begin{array}{l}\Theta(\rho_x) = (a, C@s :: \sigma) \qquad a = + \vee a = \bot \qquad \Theta(\rho_y) \neq (\bot, \_) \\ \Gamma(C@s) = \exists\{f_1{:}\,\rho_1 \mathinner{..} f_n{:}\,\rho_n\}.(\Theta_2; \varphi_2) \qquad \varphi \Rightarrow \rho_x \neq \mathtt{null} \\ \Theta, \overline{\Theta_2}^{a}; \varphi \wedge \varphi_2 \vdash \Theta, \overline{\Theta_2}^{a}[\rho_y/\rho_j]; \varphi_2[\rho_y/\rho_j] \\ \Delta; \Gamma, x{:}\,\rho_x, y{:}\,\rho_y; \Theta; \varphi \vdash e : \exists\rho'.(\Theta'; \varphi')\end{array}}{\Delta; \Gamma, x{:}\,\rho_x, y{:}\,\rho_y; \Theta; \varphi \vdash \mathtt{set}\, x.f_j = y\, \mathtt{in}\, e : \exists\rho'.(\Theta'; \varphi')}\ \textbf{set}$$

$$\frac{\begin{array}{l}\Theta \ \ = \rho \mapsto (1, \sigma_C), \Theta_1 \qquad \sigma_C \text{ packed} \\ \Theta_2 = \rho \mapsto (+, \sigma_C), \Theta_1 \\ \Delta; \Gamma, x{:}\,\rho; \Theta_2; \varphi \vdash e : \exists\rho'.(\Theta'; \varphi')\end{array}}{\Delta; \Gamma, x{:}\,\rho; \Theta; \varphi \vdash \mathtt{leak}\ x\, \mathtt{in}\, e : \exists\rho'.(\Theta'; \varphi')}\ \textbf{leak}$$

$$\frac{\begin{array}{l}\Theta = \rho \mapsto (1, C\{f_1{:}\,\rho_1 \mathinner{..} f_n{:}\,\rho_n\}@s' :: \sigma), \Theta_1 \\ \Gamma(C@s) = \exists\{f_1{:}\,\rho_1 \mathinner{..} f_n{:}\,\rho_n\}.(\Theta_0; \varphi_0) \\ \Theta_1; \varphi \vdash \Theta_2, \Theta_0; \varphi_0 \\ \Delta; \Gamma, x{:}\,\rho; \rho \mapsto (1, C@s :: \sigma), \Theta_2; \varphi \vdash e : \exists\rho'.(\Theta'; \varphi')\end{array}}{\Delta; \Gamma, x{:}\,\rho; \Theta; \varphi \vdash \mathtt{pack}[C@s]\ x\, \mathtt{in}\, e : \exists\rho'.(\Theta'; \varphi')}\ \textbf{pack}$$

$$\frac{\begin{array}{l}\Theta = \rho \mapsto (1, C@s :: \sigma), \Theta_1 \\ \Gamma(C@s) = \exists\{f_1{:}\,\rho_1 \mathinner{..} f_n{:}\,\rho_n\}.(\Theta_0; \varphi_0) \\ \Theta_2 = \rho \mapsto (1, C\{f_1{:}\,\rho_1 \mathinner{..} f_n{:}\,\rho_n\}@s :: \sigma), \Theta_1, \Theta_0 \\ \Delta, \rho_1..\rho_n; \Gamma, x{:}\,\rho; \Theta_2; \varphi \wedge \varphi_0 \vdash e : \exists\rho'.(\Theta'; \varphi')\end{array}}{\Delta; \Gamma, x{:}\,\rho; \Theta; \varphi \vdash \mathtt{unpack}[C]\ x\, \mathtt{in}\, e : \exists\rho'.(\Theta'; \varphi')}\ \textbf{unpack}$$

Fig. 9. Static semantics of statements and expressions

7 Discussion

Having given a formal definition for the language and its type system, we now discuss how it catches common programming errors, limits of the approach, and some extensions.

7.1 Example and Errors That Can Be Caught

Fig. 10 shows the methods CachingFetcher.Open and CachingFetcher.GetPage in the formal language. For brevity, we abbreviate *CachingFetcher* as *CF* and *WebPageFetcher* as *WPF* and drop all occurrences of • at the end of lists. These two methods represent common cases: Open changes the receiver's typestate and therefore its field invariants; GetPage assumes the field invariants of typestate Open and leaves the receiver in the same typestate.

We illustrate two kinds of programming errors that are common in mutator methods such as Open. First, the programmer of CachingFetcher::Open may forget to call the overridden method in the superclass, thereby not changing the typestate of the superclasses. In this case, at the method return point, the heap Θ would contain the entry

$$\rho_{\text{this}} \mapsto (1, \text{Object@Default} :: \text{WPF@Closed} :: \text{CF@Open} :: \mathbf{rest}\text{@Closed})$$

which does not match that post clause, since frame WPF is Closed rather than Open.

Second, the programmer may fail to establish the object properties associated with the post-typestate Open of frame CachingFetcher, which is

$$\text{CF@Open} \equiv \exists\{\text{cache}: \rho_1\}.(\ \rho_1 \mapsto (+, \text{Object@Default} :: \text{Hashtable@Default})\ ;\ \rho_1 \neq \texttt{null})$$

Assuming the programmer sets field cache to null rather than a newly allocated Hashtable, an error manifests when applying rule [**pack**] to expression pack[CF@Open] of method CF::Open with the following bindings

$$\begin{aligned}
&\Delta \equiv \rho_{\text{this}}, \bullet\\
&\Gamma \equiv \text{this} : \rho_{\text{this}}, \bullet\\
&\Theta \equiv \rho_{\text{this}} \mapsto (1, \text{Object@Default} :: \text{WPF@Open} :: \text{CF}\{\text{cache} : \rho_1\}\text{@Closed} :: \mathbf{rest}\text{@Closed}), \bullet\\
&\varphi \equiv \rho_{\text{this}} \neq \texttt{null} \wedge \rho_1 = \texttt{null}
\end{aligned}$$

The critical premise in the [**pack**] rule is the implication

$$\Theta_1; \varphi \vdash \Theta_2, \Theta_0; \varphi_0$$

Given the current heap Θ_1 (minus the object being packed) and current value facts φ, we need to satisfy the heap Θ_0 and value invariants φ_0 associated with the typestate to which we are packing. (Θ_2 represents the unused portion of the heap.) In our hypothetical example, we have

$$\begin{aligned}
&\Theta_1 \equiv \bullet\ ;\ \varphi \equiv (\rho_{\text{this}} \neq \texttt{null} \wedge \rho_1 = \texttt{null}) \qquad \Theta_2 \equiv \bullet\\
&\Theta_0 \equiv \rho_1 \mapsto (+, \text{Object@Default} :: \text{Hashtable@Default})\ ;\ \varphi_0 \equiv (\rho_1 \neq \texttt{null})
\end{aligned}$$

which is not satisfiable, since ρ_1 is null.

```
CF::Open {
  start : λ[ρ_this](this : ρ_this)
    pre  ρ_this ↦(1, Object@Default :: WPF@Closed :: CF@Closed :: rest@Closed);
         ρ_this ≠ null
    post ∃ρ'.(ρ_this ↦(1, Object@Default :: WPF@Open :: CF@Open :: rest@Closed);
           true)
      let _ = WPF::Open(this) in
      let h = new Hashtable in
      let _ = Hashtable::ctor(h) in
      unpack[CF] this in
      set this.cache = h in
      pack[CF@Open] this in
      goto return null when true
}

CF.GetPage {
  start: λ[ρ_this, ρ_path](this : ρ_this, path : ρ_path)
    pre  ρ_this ↦(⊥, Object@Default :: WPF@Open :: CF@Open :: rest@Open),
         ρ_path ↦(+, Object@Default :: String@Default);
         ρ_this ≠ null ∧ ρ_path ≠ null
    post ∃ρ'.(ρ_this ↦(⊥, Object@Default :: WPF@Open :: CF@Open :: rest@Open),
           ρ' ↦(+, Object@Default :: String@Default); ρ' ≠ null)
      let c = this.cache in
      let page = Hashtable::GetItem(c, path) in
      goto   missing[ρ_this, ρ_path, ρ_cache](this,path,c) when page = null,
             return page when page ≠ null

  missing: λ[ρ_this, ρ_path, ρ_cache](this : ρ_this, path : ρ_path, c : ρ_cache)
    pre  ρ_this ↦(⊥, Object@Default :: WPF@Open :: CF@Open :: rest@Open),
         ρ_path ↦(+, Object@Default :: String@Default),
         ρ_cache ↦(+, Object@Default :: Hashtable@Default);
         ρ_this ≠ null ∧ ρ_path ≠ null ∧ ρ_cache ≠ null
    post ∃ρ'.(ρ_this ↦(⊥, Object@Default :: WPF@Open :: CF@Open :: rest@Open),
           ρ' ↦(+, Object@Default :: String@Default); ρ' ≠ null)
      let page = WPF.GetPage(this, path) in
      let _ = Hashtable::Add(c, path, page) in
      goto return page when true
}
```

Fig. 10. Two CachingFetcher methods. We abbreviate CachingFetcher as *CF* and WebPageFetcher as *WPF* and reformat block heads for improved readability.

The code for method GetPage is more complicated because it has two basic blocks. There are two parts of the mechanics of checking this method that are worth pointing out. First, the code's correctness relies on the field invariants of typestate Open. GetPage treats the this parameter as alias-polymorphic rather than NotAliased (to make the method more widely callable). Hence, the method can assume the typestate's field invariants, but cannot `unpack` the object and thereby change the field state. (The second premise of [**unpack**] requires that the object to unpack have alias mode 1.) The first block reads the field cache and binds it to the name c. This expression is checked with [**read**], rather than [**read1**], since this is possibly aliased. The conclusion of [**read**] yields a heap and value facts that are supplemented with the heap and value invariants of the field we are reading (namely, $\Theta, \overline{\Theta_2|_{\rho_j}}^a; \varphi \wedge \varphi_2|_{\rho_j}$). Here, we have $\rho_j \equiv \rho_{\text{cache}}$, $\Theta_2 \equiv \rho_{\text{cache}} \mapsto (+, \text{Object@Default} :: \text{Hashtable@Default})$ and $\varphi_2 \equiv \rho_{\text{cache}} \neq \texttt{null}$. The fact that $\rho_{\text{cache}} \neq \texttt{null}$ is needed to show the correctness of the next expression, the call to Hashtable::GetItem, which requires that its first argument not be null. The same proof-obligation exists in the second block at the call to Hashtable::Add.

Second, proving the correctness of this method relies on refining the value facts on conditional branches. The object ρ_{page} is the result of the call to Hashtable::GetItem, whose postcondition does *not* ensure that $\rho_{\text{page}} \neq \texttt{null}$. Hence, the legality of the return in start relies on the branch condition given in the `when` clause (in this case, page $\neq$ `null`). The use of conditions is explicit in the third premise of rule [**return**], where $\varphi \wedge \varphi_A$ is used to show the postcondition, and φ_A is the formula corresponding to condition A.

Finally, after discussing how the typing rules can be used to prove the correctness of method implementations, we look at how they catch such client errors as calling methods in the wrong order. Consider the following code sequence in which the programmer has forgotten to call Open before calling GetPage:

```
let f = new CachingFetcher in
let _ = CachingFetcher::ctor(f) in
let p = GetPage(f, "http://...") in ...
```

The critical premise of [**call**] is the implication $\Theta; \varphi \vdash \Theta_0, \Theta_2; \varphi_0$, requiring that the current heap Θ and value facts φ imply the heap Θ_0 and value precondition φ_0 of the called method (Θ_2 is the part of the heap unused by the method). The relevant facts here are $\Theta(\rho_{\text{f}})$ = Object@Default::WPF@Closed::CF@Closed :: **rest**@Closed, but the method expects $\Theta_0(\rho_{\text{f}})$ = Object@Default::WPF@Open :: CF@Open :: **rest**@Open. All typestates below the Object frame are thus in the wrong state.

7.2 Expressive Power

This section examines the limits on the constraints that can be placed on object graphs using the object typestates formulated so far.

One can constrain any part of the object graph to form a tree using the not-aliased pointer predicates. Any field can be constrained to any unary predicate in the predicate language, including typestate predicates. Field values within the same class frame can be constrained arbitrarily using relational predicates (e.g., $x.f = x.g$, where f and g are within the same class frame.

Besides the restricted form of sharing constraints, the limitation of the object typestates described so far is that relations between fields of different frames or different objects in the graph cannot be expressed, (e.g., $x.f = x.g.h$). The reason for this is that the only way to constrain the contents of an object referenced through a field is to specify its typestate. One cannot directly refer to $x.g.h$ in any formula. Typestates therefore fully abstract what can be observed about an object. Our formalization makes this explicit by modeling frame typestates with existential bindings for all fields:

$$C@s : \exists\{f_1{:}\,\rho_1..f_n{:}\,\rho_n\}.(\Theta, \varphi)$$

This states that the contents of frame C with typestate s is the set of field values ρ_i (one per field f_i), constrained by heap Θ and formula φ. The existential binding restricts the context to know nothing about the field values beyond the constraints φ.

Existentially abstracting only the field values implies that all frames referred to in Θ are packed (because the entire formula must not contain free value names). This choice is not fundamental and our framework can easily be extended to accommodate unpacked frames by allowing arbitrary existential abstraction of the form

$$C@s : \exists[\Delta].(\{f_1{:}\,\rho_1..f_n{:}\,\rho_n\}; \Theta, \varphi)$$

In such a formulation, constraints between different objects such as $x.f = x.g.h$ can be expressed, as long as the frame containing field h in object $x.g$ is unpacked in the typestate containing this constraint. Constraints between frames of the same object however remain outside this framework.

The typestates described so far are suited only to finite-state abstractions. For instance, typestates can enforce that Pop be called on a Stack object only after a call to Push or a non-emptiness test, but cannot enforce that Push be called at least as many times as Pop. Parameterized typestates (or dependent typestates) could support such counting abstractions similarly to the way they are enforced in ESC/Java using an integer ghost field.

7.3 Client and Implementation Views of Typestates

There is a freedom in our formalization that we probably do not want. In this formulation, any code that has a not-aliased reference to an object may unpack and repack the object and thereby potentially change its typestate. In particular, this allows client code to change an object's typestate by directly accessing its fields rather than by calling its methods. If the programmer has made the object's representation private, this problem cannot arise, since the field assignments would be illegal. However, to promote programming hygiene, it is preferable to restrict client code to packing to the same typestate they unpacked. Only methods declared in the class whose frame is being packed (or one of its subclasses) are allowed to pack to different typestates.

```
[ TypeStates("InBounds ", " OutOfBounds") ]
interface IEnumerator
{
  [ Pre("InBounds") ]
  object Current { get; }

  [ Post("InBounds", WhenReturnValue=true),
    Post("OutOfBounds", WhenReturnValue=false) ]
  bool MoveNext ();

  [ Post("OutOfBounds") ]
  void Reset ();
}
```

Fig. 11. Using correlated return values to specify the IEnumerator class.

7.4 Correlating Typestate and Return Values

In the typestate system presented so far, a method can specify only a single post-typestate for every parameter. This limitation prevents us from describing protocols in which a method can change a parameter to one of several post-typestates, correlated to the value of a returned status code. Fig. 11 shows a typestate specification for the popular .NET interface IEnumerator. To use an IEnumerator object, a program repeatedly calls MoveNext until it returns false and can call Current only when the latest call to MoveNext returned true. To capture this protocol, we need to correlate the object's typestate to the return value from MoveNext, using an extended feature WhenReturnValue=*constant*.

To support this feature in our formalism, we need to introduce typestate variables and allow quantification and constraints to range over such variables.

8 Related Work

Our work draws from several lines of research. Our aliasing approach has been heavily influenced by the work on alias types [7,8], and region type systems [9,10], in particular, the use of linear permissions and dependent types in some of these systems to control access to memory and to allow strong updates. This formulation allows for a natural imperative programming style, without the drawback of singly threading values as in traditional linear type systems.

Alias-polymorphic functions are closely related to the idea of let! by Wadler [11] and Boyland's alias burying [12]. See [4] for a detailed discussion of let! in the presence of imperative updates.

Our formulation of typestates for objects is novel. Previous work on typestates [2,3] does not provide an interpretation of typestates as predicates over objects, nor did it consider the complications of subclasses. Role analysis [13] captures some referencing relations of structures and is similar to a typestate system, but does not address issues of subtyping and inheritance.

The Fugue project shares the general goal of the extended static checker ESC [14], namely to provide automatic checking of specifications for OO programs [15]. However, the two approaches differ in the following ways. Fugue focuses on a simple, sound programming model and a natural way to express object properties via typestates. ESC allows rich specifications, since it is based on FOL and general theorem proving. However, the expressiveness comes at a price. ESC does not aim for sound checking, nor the efficiency expected from a type checker. In order to reason about a program, ESC requires similar aliasing restrictions in the form of injective pivot fields, but ESC lacks the ability to freeze typestates (object properties) as provided by leak statements.

The interaction of typestates and subclasses generally follows the notion of behavioral subtypes of Liskov et.al. [16]. Our formalism however does not support history constraints. On the other hand, unlike in Liskov's approach, our pre- and post-conditions are abstract predicates that allow subclasses to rely on strong properties not anticipated by the author of a supertype.

The use of a **rest** state in our object typestates is at first glance similar to the use of row-polymorphism to encode class types in Objective ML [17]. However, object typestates have a very different purpose in that the **rest** state restricts the typestates of all possible extensions, whereas row-polymorphism does not restrict the types of fields in extensions. Furthermore, our type system is based on name-based subclassing, not structural, where row-polymorphism is most useful.

9 Conclusion

We have attempted to strike a balance between expressiveness and practicality for specifying and checking object properties. Our approach supports the extension mechanism of class based programs in that it both allows subclasses to refine the interpretation of object typestates defined in superclasses, as well as to introduce entirely new typestates. Further work is required to capture history and other program properties that are not object centric, such as those arising in event-based OO programs.

Acknowledgments. We thank the anonymous reviewers for their helpful comments and suggestions.

References

1. Flanagan, C., Leino, K.R.M., Lillibridge, M., Nelson, G., Saxe, J.B., Stata, R.: Extended static checking for Java. In: [18]
2. Strom, R.E., Yemini, S.: Typestate: A programming language concept for enhancing software reliability. IEEE TSE **12** (1986) 157–171
3. DeLine, R., Fähndrich, M.: Enforcing high-level protocols in low-level software. In: Proceedings of the 2001 ACM SIGPLAN Conference on Programming Language Design and Implementation. (2001) 59–69
4. Fähndrich, M., DeLine, R.: Adoption and focus: Practical linear types for imperative programming. In: [18] 13–24

5. Guttag, J.V., Horning, J.J.: Larch: Languages and Tools for Formal Specification. Texts and Monographs in Computer Science. Springer-Verlag (1993)
6. DeLine, R., Fähndrich, M.: The Fugue protocol checker: Is your software Baroque? Technical Report MSR-TR-2004-07, Microsoft Research (2004) URL: http://research.microsoft.com/~maf/fugue.
7. Smith, F., Walker, D., Morrisett, J.G.: Alias types. In: European Symposium on Programming. (2000) 366–381
8. Walker, D., Morrisett, G.: Alias types for recursive data structures. In: Proceedings of the 4th Workshop on Types in Compilation. (2000)
9. Tofte, M., Talpin, J.P.: Implementation of the typed call-by-value λ-calculus using a stack of regions. In: Conference Record of the 21st Annual ACM Symposium on Principles of Programming Languages. (1994) 188–201
10. Crary, K., Walker, D., Morrisett, G.: Typed memory management in a calculus of capabilities. In: Conference Record of the 26th Annual ACM SIGPLAN-SIGACT Symposium on Principles of Programming Languages, ACM Press (1999)
11. Wadler, P.: Linear types can change the world! In Broy, M., Jones, C., eds.: Programming Concepts and Methods. (1990) IFIP TC 2 Working Conference.
12. Boyland, J.: Alias burying: Unique variables without destructive reads. Software—Practice and Experience **31** (2001) 533–553
13. Kuncak, V., Lam, P., Rinard, M.: Role analysis. In: Conference Record of the 29th Annual ACM Symposium on Principles of Programming Languages. (2002)
14. Detlefs, D.L., Leino, K.R.M., Nelson, G., Saxe, J.B.: Extended static checking. Research Report 159, Compaq Systems Research Center (1998)
15. Leino, K.R.M., Stata, R.: Checking object invariants. Technical Report #1997-007, DEC SRC, Palo Alto, USA (1997)
16. Liskov, B.H., Wing, J.M.: A behavioral notion of subtyping. ACM Transactions on Programming Languages and Systems **16** (1994) 1811–1841
17. Rémy, D., Vouillon, J.: Objective ML: an effective object-oriented extension to ML. Theory and Practice of Object Systems **4** (1998) 27–50
18. Proceedings of the 2002 ACM SIGPLAN Conference on Programming Language Design and Implementation. (2002)

Appendix

$$\boxed{\Gamma;\Theta \vdash A : \varphi}$$

$$\frac{\Gamma(x) = \rho \qquad \Theta(\rho) = (a, \sigma)}{\Gamma;\Theta \vdash \mathsf{hastype}(x, C) : \mathsf{hastype}(\rho, C)} \qquad \frac{A \in \mathtt{true}, =, \neq}{\Gamma;\Theta \vdash A : \Gamma(A)}$$

$$\frac{\Gamma;\Theta \vdash A_1 : \varphi_1 \qquad \Gamma;\Theta \vdash A_2 : \varphi_2}{\Gamma;\Theta \vdash A_1 \vee A_2 : \varphi_1 \vee \varphi_2} \qquad \frac{\Gamma;\Theta \vdash A_1 : \varphi_1 \qquad \Gamma;\Theta \vdash A_2 : \varphi_2}{\Gamma;\Theta \vdash A_1 \wedge A_2 : \varphi_1 \wedge \varphi_2}$$

Fig. 12. Static rules for conditions

$$\frac{\begin{array}{c} P = class_1..class_n \ \mathtt{in}\, b \\ \Gamma \vdash class_i \quad i = 1..n \\ \Gamma \vdash b \\ \mathsf{fn}(\Gamma) = \emptyset \end{array}}{\Gamma \vdash P}\ \textbf{program} \qquad \frac{\begin{array}{c} \Gamma(M) = (\psi, C) \\ \Gamma(C{::}M) = \psi' \\ \mathsf{virtSig}_C(\psi') = \psi \end{array}}{\Gamma, C \vdash \mathtt{virt}\ M : \psi}\ \textbf{virt}$$

$$\frac{\begin{array}{c} \forall M.\Gamma(M) = (\psi, B) \wedge C \ll B \implies \mathtt{impl}\, M\{\overline{b}\} \in \overline{d} \\ \Gamma, C \vdash \overline{d} \end{array}}{\Gamma \vdash \mathtt{class}\, C : D\{\overline{d}\}}\ \textbf{class}$$

$$\frac{\begin{array}{c} b_i = \psi_i\, \ell_i \ldots \quad i = 1..n \\ \Gamma(C{::}M) = \psi_1 \quad \Gamma(M) = (\_, B) \quad \Gamma(B.M) = \psi' \quad \psi_1 = \mathsf{implSig}_C(\psi') \\ \mathsf{fn}(\psi_i) = \emptyset \quad i = 1..n \\ \Gamma, \ell_1 : \psi_1, .., \ell_n : \psi_n \vdash b_i \quad i = 1..n \end{array}}{\Gamma, C \vdash \mathtt{impl}\, M\{b_1..b_n\}}\ \textbf{impl}$$

$$\frac{\Gamma(f) = C}{\Gamma, C \vdash \mathtt{field}\, f}\ \textbf{field} \qquad \frac{\begin{array}{c} \Gamma(C@s) = \tau \quad \mathsf{fn}(\tau) = \emptyset \quad \Theta \not\vdash \bot \\ \tau = \exists\{f_1{:}\rho_1 \,..\, f_n{:}\rho_n\}.(\Theta; \varphi) \\ \Gamma(f_i) = C \quad i = 1..n \end{array}}{\Gamma, C \vdash \mathtt{state}\, s : \tau}\ \textbf{state}$$

$$\frac{\begin{array}{c} \psi = \forall[\Delta](\rho_1..\rho_n); \Theta; \varphi \to \exists\rho.(\Theta'; \varphi') \\ \Delta; \Gamma, x_1{:}\rho_1..x_n{:}\rho_n; \Theta; \varphi \vdash e : \exists\rho.(\Theta'; \varphi') \end{array}}{\Gamma \vdash \psi\, \ell = \lambda(x_1..x_n).e}\ \textbf{block}$$

$$\boxed{\Delta; \Gamma; \Theta; \varphi \vdash tt : \exists\rho'.(\Theta'; \varphi')}$$

$$\frac{\begin{array}{l} \Gamma(\ell) = \forall[\overline{\rho}'](\rho_1..\rho_m); \Theta_0; \varphi_0 \to \exists\rho_r.(\Theta_1; \varphi_1) \qquad \Gamma; \Theta \vdash A : \varphi_A \\ \Gamma(y_i) = \rho_i[\overline{\rho}/\overline{\rho}'] \quad i = 1..m \\ \Theta; \varphi \wedge \varphi_A \vdash \Theta_0[\overline{\rho}/\overline{\rho}']; \varphi_0[\overline{\rho}/\overline{\rho}'] \\ \Theta_1[\overline{\rho}/\overline{\rho}']; \varphi_1[\overline{\rho}/\overline{\rho}'] \vdash \Theta'; \varphi' \\ \Delta; \Gamma; \Theta; \varphi \vdash tt : \exists\rho_r.(\Theta'; \varphi') \end{array}}{\Delta; \Gamma; \Theta; \varphi \vdash \ell[\overline{\rho}](y_1..y_m)\ \mathtt{when}\, A,\ tt : \exists\rho_r.(\Theta'; \varphi')}\ \textbf{label}$$

$$\frac{\begin{array}{l} \Gamma(x) = \rho' \quad \Gamma; \Theta \vdash A : \varphi_A \quad \Theta; \varphi \wedge \varphi_A \vdash \Theta'; \varphi' \\ \Delta; \Gamma; \Theta; \varphi \vdash tt : \exists\rho'.(\Theta'; \varphi') \end{array}}{\Delta; \Gamma; \Theta; \varphi \vdash \mathtt{return}\, x\, \mathtt{when}\, A,\ tt : \exists\rho'.(\Theta'; \varphi')}\ \textbf{return}$$

$$\frac{}{\Delta; \Gamma; \Theta; \varphi \vdash \bullet : \exists\rho'.(\Theta'; \varphi')}$$

Fig. 13. Well-formedness of programs, classes, methods, blocks, and goto targets

$$\boxed{\Theta;\varphi \vdash \Theta';\varphi'}$$

$$\frac{\varphi;\sigma \vdash \varphi';\sigma'}{\rho\mapsto(a,\sigma),\Theta;\varphi \vdash \rho\mapsto(a,\sigma'),\Theta;\varphi'} \qquad \frac{}{\bullet;\varphi \vdash \bullet;\varphi}$$

$$\frac{\varphi \Rightarrow \rho_1 = \rho_2}{\rho_1\mapsto(+,\sigma),\rho_2\mapsto(+,\sigma),\Theta;\varphi \vdash \rho_1\mapsto(+,\sigma),\Theta;\varphi} \qquad \frac{\varphi \Rightarrow \rho = \mathtt{null}}{\rho\mapsto(a,\sigma),\Theta;\varphi \vdash \Theta;\varphi}$$

$$\frac{}{\rho\mapsto(+,\sigma),\Theta;\varphi \vdash \rho\mapsto(+,\sigma),\rho\mapsto(+,\sigma),\Theta;\varphi} \qquad \frac{\varphi \Rightarrow \rho = \mathtt{null}}{\Theta;\varphi \vdash \rho\mapsto(a,\sigma),\Theta;\varphi}$$

$$\frac{}{\rho\mapsto(+,\sigma),\Theta;\varphi \vdash \Theta;\varphi} \qquad \frac{\Theta;\varphi \vdash \Theta';\varphi' \qquad \varphi' \Rightarrow \varphi''}{\Theta;\varphi \vdash \Theta';\varphi''}$$

$$\boxed{\varphi;\rho;\sigma \vdash \varphi';\sigma'}$$

$$\frac{\begin{array}{l}\varphi' = \varphi \wedge \mathsf{hastype}(\rho, C)\\ \varphi';\rho;\chi_B :: \mathbf{rest}@s \vdash \varphi'';\sigma_D\end{array}}{\varphi;\rho;\chi_B :: C@s :: \mathbf{rest}@s \vdash \varphi'';\sigma_D}\ \mathbf{upcast} \qquad \frac{\varphi;\chi_C \vdash \chi'_C}{\varphi;\rho;\chi_C :: \bullet \vdash \varphi;\ \chi'_C :: \mathbf{rest}@s}$$

$$\frac{\begin{array}{l}\varphi;\rho;\sigma_D \vdash \varphi';\chi_B :: \mathbf{rest}@s\\ \varphi' \Rightarrow \mathsf{hastype}(\rho, C)\\ \mathsf{baseclass}(C) = B\end{array}}{\varphi;\rho;\sigma_D \vdash \varphi';\ \chi_B :: C@s :: \mathbf{rest}@s}\ \mathbf{downcast} \qquad \frac{\varphi;\chi_C \vdash \chi'_C}{\varphi;\rho;\chi_C :: r \vdash \varphi;\ \chi'_C :: r}$$

$$\boxed{\varphi;\chi_C \vdash \chi'_C}$$

$$\frac{\varphi;\chi_B \vdash \chi'_B}{\varphi;\chi_B :: C@s \vdash \chi'_B :: C@s} \qquad \frac{}{\varphi;\bullet \vdash \bullet}$$

$$\frac{\varphi;\chi_B \vdash \chi'_B \qquad \varphi \Rightarrow \rho_i = \rho'_i}{\varphi;\chi_B :: C\{f_1{:}\,\rho_1..f_n{:}\,\rho_n\}@s \vdash \chi'_B :: C\{f_1{:}\,\rho'_1..f_n{:}\,\rho'_n\}@s}$$

Fig. 14. Implication rules

$$\begin{aligned}&\mathsf{implSig}_C(\forall[\Delta](\rho_1..\rho_n);\Theta;\varphi \to \exists\rho.(\Theta';\varphi')) =\\ &\qquad \forall[\Delta](\rho_1..\rho_n);\mathsf{implSig}_C(\rho_1,\Theta);\varphi \to \exists\rho.(\mathsf{implSig}_C(\rho_1,\Theta');\varphi')\end{aligned}$$

$$\begin{aligned}&\mathsf{virtSig}_C(\forall[\Delta](\rho_1..\rho_n);\Theta;\varphi \to \exists\rho.(\Theta';\varphi')) =\\ &\qquad \forall[\Delta](\rho_1..\rho_n);\mathsf{virtSig}_C(\rho_1,\Theta);\varphi \to \exists\rho.(\mathsf{virtSig}_C(\rho_1,\Theta');\varphi')\end{aligned}$$

$$\mathsf{implSig}_C(\rho,(\rho\mapsto(a,\sigma),\Theta)) = \rho\mapsto(a,\mathsf{implSig}_C(\sigma)),\Theta$$

$$\mathsf{virtSig}_C(\rho,(\rho\mapsto(a,\sigma),\Theta)) = \rho\mapsto(a,\mathsf{virtSig}_C(\sigma)),\Theta$$

$$\begin{array}{ll}\mathsf{implSig}_C(\chi_B :: C@s :: \mathbf{rest}@r) = \chi_B :: C@s :: \mathbf{rest}@r & \\ \mathsf{implSig}_D(\chi_B :: C@s :: \mathbf{rest}@r) = \chi_B :: C@s :: \cdots :: D@s :: \mathbf{rest}@r & D \ll C\\ \mathsf{virtSig}_C(\chi_B :: C@s :: \mathbf{rest}@r) = \chi_B :: C@s :: \mathbf{rest}@s & \end{array}$$

Fig. 15. Definitions of implSig and virtSig for sliding methods

---

Object Invariants in Dynamic Contexts

K. Rustan M. Leino[1] and Peter Müller[2]

[1] Microsoft Research, Redmond, WA, USA
leino@microsoft.com
[2] ETH Zurich, Switzerland
peter.mueller@inf.ethz.ch

Abstract. Object invariants describe the consistency of object-oriented data structures and are central to reasoning about the correctness of object-oriented software. Yet, reasoning about object invariants in the presence of object references, methods, and subclassing is difficult. This paper describes a methodology for specifying and verifying object-oriented programs, using object invariants to specify the consistency of data and using ownership to organize objects into contexts. The novelty is that contexts can be dynamic: there is no bound on the number of objects in a context and objects can be transferred between contexts. The invariant of an object is allowed to depend on the fields of the object, on the fields of all objects in transitively-owned contexts, and on fields of objects reachable via given sequences of fields. With these invariants, one can describe a large variety of properties, including properties of cyclic data structures. Object invariants can be declared in or near the classes whose fields they depend on, not necessarily in the class of an owning object. The methodology is designed to allow modular reasoning, even in the presence of subclasses, and is proved sound.

1 Introduction

The design and correctness of computer programs rely on *invariants*, consistency conditions on the program's data that are to be maintained throughout the execution of the program. In object-oriented programs, which permit a flexible and extensible organization of data and control, the invariants are dominated by *object invariants*, which relate the data fields of objects. Fig. 1 illustrates the use of an object invariant in a simple class, whose correctness relies on the object invariant to hold on entry to the method m. In this paper, we consider the specification and verification of object-oriented programs with object invariants.

The dynamic nature of object-oriented programs makes it difficult to construct a systematic technique for reasoning modularly about object invariants. Such a technique would allow one to verify the correctness of a class, or a set of classes, independently of possible subclasses and other parts of the program. A central problem is that an object invariant may temporarily be violated during the update of an object's data, and any method call performed by the update code during this time may potentially cause control to re-enter the object's public interface where the object invariant is expected to hold. For example, in Fig. 1, $a = b$ may hold at the time P is called, a temporary violation of the object invariant which results in a division-by-zero error if P calls back

M. Odersky (Ed.): ECOOP 2004, LNCS 3086, pp. 491–516, 2004.

```
class T {
  int a, b ;
  invariant 0 ⩽ a < b ;
  public T() { a := 0 ; b := 3 ; }
  public void m(...) {
    int k := 100/(b − a) ;
    a := a + 3 ; P(...) ; b := (k + 4) ∗ b ;
  }
}
```

Fig. 1. A simple class illustrating the use of an object invariant. The invariant is to be established by the constructor and maintained by the method m. Upon entry to m, the invariant implies the absence of a division-by-zero error. The fact that the invariant may not hold at the time m calls procedure P is a central problem in reasoning: if P calls back into m, then m may erroneously divide by 0.

into m. Recently, some progress has been made in tackling this problem (*e.g.*, [2,30]), but more progress is required to handle more programs.

To make reasoning easier, various restrictions on the dynamism of programs have been considered, including *alias confinement* techniques which impose restrictions on a program's object references. A promising alias confinement approach is based on *ownership* (*e.g.*, [9,4,31,5]), where an object is considered to *own* the objects that form parts of its data representation, its *constituent objects*. The methodology we present in this paper uses ownership to organize objects into a hierarchy of *contexts*, where the objects in each context have a common owner. In our methodology, an owner is a pair consisting of an object reference and a class name. Other than ownership, we do not restrict object references; an object may have non-owning references to other objects. Our methodology allows *ownership transfer*, whereby the owner of an object is changed during program execution, that is, whereby an object changes contexts.

An important consideration in a methodology for object invariants is what object fields an invariant is allowed to depend on. We allow object invariants to depend on three sorts of object fields. First, the invariant declared for an object X in a class T is allowed to depend on the fields of X declared in any superclass of T (here and throughout, we use "superclass" and "subclass", unless further qualified, to include the class itself). Second, the invariant is allowed to depend on the fields of any object transitively owned by $[X, S]$ for any superclass S of T. We allow an invariant to quantify over these owned objects, which means that the invariant can depend on the fields of an unbounded number of objects. Moreover, because we allow such quantifications, X's invariant can depend on the fields of owned objects even for owned objects that are not reachable from X in the heap. Third, our methodology allows the invariant of X to depend on the fields of any specified object $X.f_1.\cdots.f_n$ $(n \geqslant 1)$—that is, an object reachable from X by a fixed sequence of field dereferences—provided certain visibility requirements are met. Altogether, this set of permissible object invariants is larger than those allowed by previous work. The invariants can, for example, describe properties of cyclic data structures and they can be declared in or near the classes whose fields they depend on.

In the next section, we summarize the previous work that forms a basis for our approach. In Section 3, we describe our ownership model and show how object invariants are checked. Section 4 describes visibility-based invariants and shows how these can be

class C **extends** B { **int** w ; **invariant** $w < 100$; ... }
class B **extends** A { **int** z ; **invariant** $y < z$; ... }
class A **extends** **object** { **int** x, y ; **invariant** $x < y$; ... }

C:	$w = 43$
B:	$z = 6$
A:	$x = 5 \quad y = 7$
object:	$inv = A \quad \ldots$

Fig. 2. Given the declarations of classes A, B, and C, which include field and invariant declarations, the object of allocated type C depicted to the right is in a possible state. In particular, since $inv = A$, the invariant declared in class A is known to hold, whereas the other invariants may or may not hold.

declared and checked within local portions of a context. In Section 5, we give the technical encoding of our methodology and prove a soundness theorem. Section 6 discusses usability aspects of our methodology, and the paper ends with related work, conclusions, and future work.

2 Approach

Our approach combines two previous techniques, summarized in this section, to produce a methodology for specifying and verifying object invariants that is more flexible than any previous sound, modular technique. In this paper, we consider a Java-like object-oriented language, but omit treatment of static fields (global variables) and concurrency.

2.1 Explicit Representation of Which Parts of Object Invariants Are Known to Hold

One of the previous methodologies on which we build ours is that of Barnett *et al.* [2]. In that methodology, whether or not an object invariant is known to hold is explicitly represented in the program's state and an ownership model is enforced through a set of constrained assignments to two special object fields (inv and $committed$, described next). Here, we summarize this previous methodology; for a full description of its rationale, see the other paper [2].

Declarations of object invariants can appear in every class. The invariants that pertain to an object o are those declared in the classes between **object**—the root of the single-inheritance hierarchy—and $\mathbf{type}(o)$—the allocated type of o. Each object o has a special field inv, whose value names a class in the range from **object** to $\mathbf{type}(o)$, and which represents the most refined subclass whose invariant can be relied upon for this object. More precisely, for any object o and class T and in any execution state of the program, if $o.inv$ is a subclass of T, which we denote by $o.inv \leqslant T$, then all object invariants declared in class T are known to hold for o. The object invariants declared in other classes may or may not hold for o, so they cannot be relied upon. For example, Fig. 2 shows a possible state of an object of allocated type C. If $o.inv$ equals $\mathbf{type}(o)$, then we say the object is *consistent*. Thus, all invariants hold of consistent objects. For example, the object depicted in Fig. 2 is not consistent.

As part of the ownership model of the methodology, each object also has a special boolean field $committed$, representing whether or not the object is owned. Moreover, the program's field declarations can be tagged with the modifier **rep**. An object o is the owning object of p, that is, object p is owned by o, if and only if p is committed and there is a rep field f declared in a class T such that $o.inv \leqslant T$ and $o.f = p$. Only consistent objects can be committed (that is, $p.committed$ implies $p.inv = \mathbf{type}(p)$), and a committed object has exactly one owning object.

The special fields *inv* and *committed* can be mentioned in routine specifications, but cannot be mentioned in object invariants and cannot directly be read or updated by the code of the program. Instead, two program statements, **pack** and **unpack**, are introduced for the purpose of changing the values of the two special fields. For any class T with immediate superclass S and any object expression o of type T, these statements are defined as

$$
\begin{array}{l}
\mathbf{pack}\ o\ \mathbf{as}\ T \ \equiv \\
\quad \mathbf{assert}\ o \neq \mathbf{null} \wedge o.inv = S\ ; \\
\quad \mathbf{assert}\ Inv_T(o)\ ; \\
\quad \mathbf{foreach}\ p \in Constit_T(o)\ \{\ \mathbf{assert}\ p.inv = \mathbf{type}(p) \wedge \neg p.committed\ \} \\
\quad \mathbf{foreach}\ p \in Constit_T(o)\ \{\ p.committed := true\ \} \\
\quad o.inv := T \\
\mathbf{unpack}\ o\ \mathbf{from}\ T \ \equiv \\
\quad \mathbf{assert}\ o \neq \mathbf{null} \wedge o.inv = T \wedge \neg o.committed\ ; \\
\quad o.inv := S\ ; \\
\quad \mathbf{foreach}\ p \in Constit_T(o)\ \{\ p.committed := false\ \}
\end{array}
$$

where the **assert** statements give the conditions under which the **pack** and **unpack** statements are legal, the assignment statements describe the effects of the **pack** and **unpack** statements, $Inv_T(X)$ is the condition that says an object X satisfies the object invariant declared in class T, $Constit_T(X)$ is the set of expressions $X.f$ for all rep fields f declared in T, and the **foreach** statements, like all quantifications over object references in this paper, range over allocated non-null objects. In words, the **pack** statement checks that o's T-invariant holds, that the objects referenced by o's rep fields in T are consistent and uncommitted, marks o's T-constituent object as being committed, and records the fact that now o's T-invariant is known to hold. The **unpack** statement records the fact that o is now in a state where its T-invariant may be violated and decommits o's T-constituent objects.

The methodology ensures that the following two conditions are *program invariants*—that is, they hold in every reachable program state—for every class T:

$$
\begin{array}{l}
(\forall o \bullet\ o.inv \leqslant T \Rightarrow Inv_T(o) \wedge (\forall p \in Constit_T(o) \bullet\ p.committed\ )) \\
(\forall p \bullet\ p.committed \ \Rightarrow p.inv = \mathbf{type}(p)\ )
\end{array}
$$

Three more things are needed to guarantee that these conditions are program invariants. First, the methodology prescribes the **object** constructor to have the postcondition $inv = \mathbf{object} \wedge \neg committed$. Second, for any field f declared in a class T, a field update statement $o.f := e$ is legal only if $T < o.inv$. If the class T is understood from context, then we may refer to the condition "$T < o.inv$" as "*o is sufficiently unpacked*". That is, a precondition for updating $o.f$ is that o is sufficiently unpacked. Third, an invariant is admissible only if all of the field-access expressions it mentions have the form $\mathbf{this}.g_1.\cdots.g_n.f$, where **this** denotes the object whose invariant is being described, $n \geqslant 0$, and the fields $g_1, \ldots, g_n$ are all rep fields. (And, of course, all statements and expressions are subject to ordinary typechecking.) Like in Java, the prefix "**this.**" can be omitted.

Note that this methodology permits an object invariant to depend on fields declared in superclasses and on fields of transitively-owned objects. However, because an object is an owned object only if it is referenced by a rep field, there is a static limit on the number of owned objects an owning object can have. In particular, the number of objects with owner $[X, T]$ is bounded by the number of rep fields declared in class T. Our methodology in this paper removes this limitation.

Note also that the encoding of the methodology records only which objects are committed, not the owning objects to which they are committed. In this paper, we extend the encoding also to record the owner.

Finally, note that this methodology allows ownership transfer. For example, the following code sequence, where f is a rep field declared in a class T and r and o are distinct non-null objects of type T, transfers from o to r the ownership of the object initially referenced by $o.f$:

> **unpack** o **from** T ; **unpack** r **from** T ;
> $r.f := o.f$; **pack** r **as** T ;
> $o.f :=$ **null** ; **pack** o **as** T

2.2 Universe Types

The other of the previous methodologies on which we build ours is that in Müller's thesis [30,32,31]. In that methodology, an ownership type system organizes objects into contexts, called *universes*, and object invariants are specified as the representation of special boolean *abstract fields*, which are often-underspecified functions of actual object fields. The state of a universe is *encapsulated*, that is, the fields of the universe's objects can be modified only when control is in a method applied to an object within the universe.

A universe can have several owner objects, all of which belong to the enclosing universe. The invariant of an object o is allowed to depend on the fields of all objects in o's universe and in all nested universes. In particular, the invariant may depend on fields of objects that are not transitively owned by o. Such invariants are enabled by imposing a *visibility requirement* [24,30] that essentially requires that an invariant be visible in every method that might violate the invariant of an object in the universe in which the method executes. This requirement allows one to use the declaration of the invariant to show that invariants are preserved.

In this paper, we too allow invariants to depend on non-owned fields (unlike the methodology by Barnett *et al.*), provided an appropriate visibility requirement is met. Because we don't have (or need) the encapsulation provided by universes, we force certain declarations to be mutually visible by making sure they refer to each other (using a **dependent** clause, as we shall see later).

A limitation with this previous methodology is that objects cannot be partially unpacked, to use the parlance of the previous subsection. That is, an object is either in a state where all its invariants (which may be declared in several subclasses) are known to hold or in a state where all of these invariants are allowed to be violated, but never anything in between. Therefore, it is not possible to reason separately about the object invariants declared in different subclasses. In this paper, we overcome this limitation by following the methodology by Barnett *et al.*

Another limitation with this previous methodology is that call-backs from a nested universe to an enclosing universe are disallowed, except for calling so-called *pure* methods, which are not allowed to rely on the object invariant and are not allowed to modify the program's state. This limitation comes about because a nested universe has no way of knowing whether or not the invariants in an enclosing universe hold. In this paper, we overcome this limitation by explicitly representing when an object's invariants hold.

A third limitation with this previous methodology is that the type system that tracks ownership does not allow ownership transfer. As we shall see in this paper, visibility-based invariants also complicate the situation with ownership transfer, but we are able to overcome the limitation.

3 Ownership

In this section, we explain the basics of our methodology.

Following Barnett *et al.*, our methodology uses an explicit representation, namely the special fields inv and $committed$, of when object invariants are known to hold. In addition, we explicitly encode the ownership relation itself, using a special field $owner$. The value of $owner$ is a pair $[\mathbf{object}\ obj, \mathbf{type}\ typ]$, representing by obj the owning object and by typ the class of the owning object that induces the ownership. If $p.owner = [o, T]$ for a non-null o, then committing p means committing it to o at class T. More precisely, if $p.owner = [o, T]$, then $p.committed$ if and only if $o.inv \leqslant T$. We also allow $p.owner.obj$ to be **null**, in which case p has no owning object and the value of $p.owner.typ$ is not used.

The $owner$ field can be mentioned in routine specifications and object invariants, but it cannot directly be read or updated by the code of the program. The $owner$ field is initialized by the **object** constructor, which takes an owner as a parameter:

$$
\begin{array}{l}
\mathbf{class\ object}\ \{ \\
\quad \mathbf{object}(\mathbf{pair}[\mathbf{object}, \mathbf{type}]\ ow) \\
\qquad \mathbf{requires}\ ow.obj \neq \mathbf{null} \Rightarrow \mathbf{type}(ow.obj) \leqslant ow.typ < ow.obj.inv\ ; \\
\qquad \mathbf{ensures}\ owner = ow \wedge inv = \mathbf{object} \wedge \neg committed\ ;
\end{array}
$$

We use **requires** clauses to declare preconditions and **ensures** clauses to declare postconditions. Note that the owning object is required to be sufficiently unpacked, that is, the invariants declared in the owning class must not be assumed to hold for the owning object. The $owner$ field can be updated only by the ownership transfer statement, described below.

Since our methodology includes the field $owner$, we replace the definitions of **pack** and **unpack** from Section 2.1 as follows. In our methodology, the statement **pack** o **as** T commits every object that claims $[o, T]$ as its owner, that is, every object whose *owner* field equals $[o, T]$. Formally, for any class T with immediate superclass S and any object expression o of type T, our methodology defines the **pack** and **unpack** statements as follows (note that we don't need the somewhat awkward $Constit_T$ construction from Section 2.1):

$$
\begin{array}{l}
\textbf{pack } o \textbf{ as } T \;\; \equiv \\
\quad \textbf{assert } o \neq \textbf{null} \wedge o.inv = S \; ; \\
\quad \textbf{assert } Inv_T(o) \; ; \\
\quad \textbf{assert } (\forall \textbf{object } p \mid p.owner = [o, T] \bullet p.inv = \textbf{type}(p)) \; ; \\
\quad \textbf{foreach object } p \mid p.owner = [o, T] \; \{ \; p.committed := true \; \} \\
\quad o.inv := T \\
\textbf{unpack } o \textbf{ from } T \;\; \equiv \\
\quad \textbf{assert } o \neq \textbf{null} \wedge o.inv = T \wedge \neg o.committed \; ; \\
\quad o.inv := S \; ; \\
\quad \textbf{foreach object } p \mid p.owner = [o, T] \; \{ \; p.committed := false \; \}
\end{array}
$$

The owner of an object o can be changed to $[p, T]$ by the ownership transfer statement, defined as follows:

$$
\begin{array}{l}
\textbf{transfer } o \textbf{ to } [p, T] \;\; \equiv \\
\quad \textbf{assert } o \neq \textbf{null} \wedge o.inv = \textbf{object} \; ; \\
\quad \textbf{assert } o.owner.obj \neq \textbf{null} \Rightarrow o.owner.typ < o.owner.obj.inv \; ; \\
\quad \textbf{assert } p \neq \textbf{null} \Rightarrow T < p.inv \; ; \\
\quad o.owner := [p, T]
\end{array}
$$

Note that both the old and new owning objects are required to be sufficiently unpacked. We define the transfer statement to typecheck only if T is a superclass of the type of the expression p. Moreover, we require that the type of the expression o be a class tagged with the modifier **transferable**. For now, one can think of this modifier as giving programmers more control, in a way similar to Java's *Cloneable* and *Serializable* interfaces; later, we shall find a more prominent use of the **transferable** modifier. The **transferable** modifier is inherited, that is, subclasses of a transferable class are transferable as well. The predefined class **object** is not transferable.

The invariant of an object o in a class T is allowed to depend on the fields of o declared in any superclass of T and on the fields of any objects transitively owned by $[o, S]$ for any superclass S of T.

We allow fields to be tagged with the **rep** modifier. The declaration of a rep field f in a class T gives rise to an implicit object invariant in class T:

$$\textbf{invariant this}.f \neq \textbf{null} \Rightarrow \textbf{this}.f.owner = [\textbf{this}, T] \; ;$$

Later in the paper, we will also use the **rep** modifiers to formulate a syntactic restriction for policing admissible invariants.

3.1 Example: Invariants of a Doubly-Linked List

Let us give an example that exhibits the expressiveness of the invariants allowed by our methodology. Fig. 3 shows a class *List* that represents lists of integers. Each list

```
class List {
  rep Node head ;
  invariant head ≠ null ∧ head.prev = null ;
  invariant (∀ Node n | n.owner = [this, List] • wf(n) ) ;
  void Insert(int x)
    requires ¬committed ∧ inv = List ;
    ensures (∀object x | ¬old(x.alloc) • x.inv = type(x) ) ;
    {
      unpack this from List ;
      head.Insert(x) ;
      pack this as List ;
    }
  /* Constructors and other methods are omitted */
}

final class Node {
  int val ;
  Node prev ;
  Node next ;
  invariant next ≠ this ∧ prev ≠ this ;
  void Insert(int x)
    requires ¬committed ;
    requires (∀ Node n | n.owner = this.owner • wf(n) ∧ n.inv = Node ) ;
    modifies {X.prev, X.next | X.owner = this.owner} ;
    ensures (∀ Node n | n.owner = this.owner • wf(n) ∧ n.inv = Node ) ;
    ensures (∀ Node n | n.owner = this.owner •
                 old(n.alloc) ∧ old(n.prev) = null ⇒ n.prev = null ) ;
    ensures (∀object x | ¬old(x.alloc) • x.inv = type(x) ) ;
    {...}
  Node(int x, Node n, pair[object, type] ow)
    requires n ≠ null ⇒
      ¬n.committed ∧ n.inv = Node ∧ n.next ≠ n ∧ n.owner = ow ;
    requires ow.typ < ow.obj.inv ;
    modifies n.prev ;
    ensures prev = null ∧ next = n ∧ ¬committed ∧ owner = ow ∧ wf(this) ;
    ensures n ≠ null ⇒ n.prev = this ∧ wf(n) ;
    ensures (∀object x | ¬old(x.alloc) • x.inv = type(x) ) ;
    {...}
}
```

Fig. 3. An example of ownership-based invariants. *List* objects are represented by doubly-linked *Node* objects. The object invariant in *List* specifies which *Node* objects the list owns and specifies properties about those *Node* objects. Class *Node* illustrates that, without visibility-based invariants, *Node* methods need very strong specifications to enable one to verify that the calling *List* methods preserve the *List* invariant.

is represented by a doubly-linked set of $Node$ objects. To simplify the implementation, the $head$ field of a list references a dummy node, where $head.next$ is the first actual element of the list and $head.prev$ is **null**.

All of the $Node$ objects that are part of the representation of a $List$ object are owned by the $List$ object. This is specified by the **rep** modifier on the field $head$ and by (part of) the quantification in the $List$ invariant, where we have used the following abbreviation:

$$\begin{aligned} wf(n) \equiv\ & (n.next \neq \mathbf{null} \Rightarrow n.next.owner = n.owner \wedge n.next.prev = n) \wedge \\ & (n.prev \neq \mathbf{null} \Rightarrow n.prev.owner = n.owner \wedge n.prev.next = n) \end{aligned}$$

The invariant also specifies that the $next$ and $prev$ fields of adjacent nodes correspond.

The implementation of $List.Insert$ simply unpacks the list and then calls $Node.Insert$ on the dummy node. When $List.Insert$ then re-packs the list, it needs to know that the $List$ invariant holds, a fact that follows from the rather complicated postcondition of $Node.Insert$.

The postcondition of $List.Insert$ says that all objects allocated from the time the method is entered are, upon exit, consistent. We use the special field $alloc$ to indicate whether or not an object has been allocated. This is useful in postconditions, where $\mathbf{old}(E)$ gives the value of expression E in the method's pre-state. Recall that quantifications over object references range over allocated non-null objects.

In addition to **requires** and **ensures** clauses, a routine specification can include **modifies** clauses. The set of given **modifies** clauses contributes to the postcondition of the routine, constraining what can be modified. We follow Barnett *et al.* to say that a routine is allowed to modify those object fields explicitly indicated by a **modifies** clause, the fields of newly allocated objects, and the fields of objects that are committed in the routine's pre-state (see [2] for the rationale behind this design). That's why, for example, $List.Insert$ has an empty set of **modifies** clauses. The **modifies** clause of $Node.Insert$ uses a set comprehension where X is the bound variable.

Summarizing the example, our methodology allows an object's invariant to depend on the fields of all objects that it owns. Since a list's context is dynamic, this example is not handled by the encoding of Barnett *et al.* where owners are not explicated. However, in what we've presented so far, a problem is that the specifications of routines that are executed while the owning object is unpacked can be rather complicated. Another problem is that there are subtle issues in formally determining whether or not the invariant in $List$ is admissible (to define which $Node$ objects are owned by a list, the $List$ invariant has to depend on the $owner$ field of the object it says it owns). The visibility-based invariants that we introduce in the next section overcome the first of these problems by allowing specifications to be stated more locally. To overcome the second problem, we later introduce a modifier **peer**, which, analogously to the modifier **rep**, gives an indirect way of specifying the ownership part of $List$'s invariant (in fact, our syntactic rules for admissible invariants will then disallow the explicit definition of ownership in the Fig. 3 $List$ invariant).

$$
\begin{array}{l}
\textbf{transferable class } \mathit{Possession}\ \{\ldots\} \\
\textbf{class } \mathit{Person}\ \{ \\
\quad \textbf{rep } \mathit{Possession}\ \mathit{possn}\ ; \\
\quad \textbf{void } \mathit{donateTo}(\mathit{Person}\ p) \\
\quad\quad \textbf{requires } \neg \mathit{committed} \wedge \mathit{inv} = \mathit{Person}\ ; \\
\quad\quad \textbf{requires } \mathit{possn} \neq \textbf{null} \wedge\ \wedge \textbf{type}(\mathit{possn}) = \mathit{Possession}\ ; \\
\quad\quad \textbf{requires } p \neq \textbf{null} \wedge p \neq \textbf{this} \wedge \neg p.\mathit{committed} \wedge p.\mathit{inv} = \mathit{Person}\ ; \\
\quad\quad \textbf{modifies } \mathit{possn}, p.\mathit{possn}\ ; \\
\quad\quad \{ \\
\quad\quad\quad \textbf{unpack this from } \mathit{Person}\ ; \quad \textbf{unpack } p \textbf{ from } \mathit{Person}\ ; \\
\quad\quad\quad \textbf{unpack } \mathit{possn} \textbf{ from } \mathit{Possession}\ ; \\
\quad\quad\quad \textbf{transfer } \mathit{possn} \textbf{ to } [p, \mathit{Person}]\ ; \\
\quad\quad\quad \textbf{pack } \mathit{possn} \textbf{ as } \mathit{Possession}\ ; \\
\quad\quad\quad p.\mathit{possn} := \mathit{possn}\ ; \quad \textbf{pack } p \textbf{ as } \mathit{Person}\ ; \\
\quad\quad\quad \mathit{possn} := \textbf{null}\ ; \quad \textbf{pack this as } \mathit{Person}\ ; \\
\quad\quad \} \\
\quad \ldots \\
\}
\end{array}
$$

Fig. 4. The *donateTo* method shows that objects can be transferred from one owner to another, provided the old and new owners are sufficiently unpacked. The class *Possession* is tagged with the modifier **transferable**, indicating that its objects may undergo ownership transfers.

3.2 Example: Ownership Transfer

Fig. 4 shows a method that transfers the ownership of a *Possession* object. Type checking requires the *Possession* class to be declared as **transferable**. To be able to unpack *possn* by a single unpack operation, we require it to be an instance of class *Possession*. To allow arbitrary subclass objects, one would have to unpack *possn* by a dynamically-bound method that is overridden for each subclass of *Possession* and unpacks the object step by step. (For more information about such issues with subclasses and specification support thereof, see [2].)

The transfer statement requires both the old owner and the new owner to be sufficiently unpacked. The *possn* field of **this** is set to **null** to re-establish the implicit invariant (induced by the **rep** modifier on *possn*) that the object referenced by **this**.*possn* is owned by **this**, which is not the case immediately following the transfer.

Note that our methodology deems the code at the end of Section 2.1 to be incorrect, because without using a **transfer** statement, $r.f.owner$ would still be $[o, T]$, not the required $[r, T]$, before the packing of r.

4 Visibility-Based Invariants

In this section, we generalize the ownership-based methodology of the previous section to allow object invariants to express properties of the state of objects in arbitrary contexts, including peer objects—objects with the same owner. Soundness is achieved by imposing a syntactic visibility requirement as well as stronger proof obligations for field updates and ownership transfers.

4.1 Limitations of Ownership-Based Invariants

The ownership-based invariants of the previous section allow object invariants to express properties of owned objects, such as the nodes in the doubly-linked list example. Such specifications are typical if the class of the owned objects (*e.g.*, *Node*) comes from a library and does not provide invariants that are strong enough for the context in which the class is reused. Additional invariants can then only be specified in the next abstraction layer, that is, in the class of the owner object (*List*).

However, insisting that all invariants about the owned objects be expressed in the owner has several shortcomings. We illustrate them by comparing the ownership-based solution for the doubly-linked list (Fig. 3) with an alternative implementation where invariants are specified locally in class *Node* (Fig. 5).

The **peer** modifier in the declarations of the $next$ and $prev$ fields expresses that the *Node* objects X, $X.next$, and $X.prev$ are *peers*, that is, they have the the same owner. Analogously to **rep** modifiers, **peer** declarations lead to implicit invariants like the following for class *Node*:

$$\textbf{invariant this}.next \neq \textbf{null} \Rightarrow \textbf{this}.owner = \textbf{this}.next.owner \; ;$$
$$\textbf{invariant this}.prev \neq \textbf{null} \Rightarrow \textbf{this}.owner = \textbf{this}.prev.owner \; ;$$

Such invariants cannot be handled by the methodology described so far (note that the invariant depends on fields of $\textbf{this}.next$ but $\textbf{this}.next$ is not owned by $[\textbf{this}, Node]$), but are handled by the generalization presented in this section.

With ownership-based invariants, verification of *List* methods involves reasoning about properties of the underlying node structure. That is, the modifications of *Node* objects are not reasoned about locally in the *Node* class. This lack of locality blurs the interface between different layers of abstraction, which leads to two problems:

1. *Complicated method specifications:* Method specifications of class *Node* must be strong enough to enable one to show that the calling *List* methods preserve the invariant. As illustrated by method *Node.Insert* in Fig. 3, one essentially has to repeat the well-formedness property of *Node* objects in every pre- and postcondition, which is not necessary in the alternative implementation.
2. *Bulky reasoning:* In order to verify that *List* methods preserve the ownership-based invariant, one has to consider *all* nodes owned by the list. With the local invariant of the alternative *Node* implementation, modification of one node can affect only the invariants of its predecessor and successor nodes. That is, showing that invariants are preserved does not involve universal quantifications but only properties of directly referenced objects, which can simplify reasoning.

In the rest of this section, we explain how we extend the methodology of the previous section to support invariants like in the alternative *Node* implementation.

4.2 Example: Invariants over Peer Objects

A field update may cause an invariant to be violated. In the presence of just ownership-based invariants, we ensure that no invariant is violated at an inappropriate time by making sure the updated object is sufficiently unpacked, which implies that all transitive

```
class List {
  rep Node head ;
  invariant head ≠ null ∧ head.prev = null ;
  ...
}

final class Node {
  int val ;
  peer Node prev dependent Node ;
  peer Node next dependent Node ;
  invariant (next ≠ null ⇒ next.prev = this) ∧ next ≠ this ;
  invariant (prev ≠ null ⇒ prev.next = this) ∧ prev ≠ this ;
  void Insert(int x)
    requires ¬committed ;
    requires (∀ Node n | n.owner = this.owner • n.inv = Node ) ;
    modifies {X.prev, X.next | X.owner = this.owner} ;
    ensures (∀ Node n | n.owner = this.owner •
      old(n.alloc) ∧ old(n.prev) = null ⇒ n.prev = null ) ;
    ensures (∀ object x | ¬old(x.alloc) • x.inv = type(x) ) ;
    {
      if (next ≠ null ∧ ...)  { next.Insert(x) ; }
      else {
          unpack this from Node ;
          next := new Node(x, next, this.owner) ;
          unpack next from Node ; next.prev := this ; pack next as Node ;
          pack this as Node ;
        }
    }
  Node(int x, Node n, pair[object, type] ow)
    requires n ≠ null ⇒
      ¬n.committed ∧ n.inv = Node ∧ n.prev.inv = object ∧ n.owner = ow ;
    requires ow.typ < ow.obj.inv ;
    modifies n.prev ;
    ensures prev = null ∧ next = n ∧ (n ≠ null ⇒ n.prev = this) ;
    ensures ¬committed ∧ inv = Node ∧ owner = ow ;
    ensures (∀ object x | ¬old(x.alloc) • x.inv = type(x) ) ;
    {
      super(ow) ; val := x ; prev := null ; next := n ;
      if (n ≠ null)
        { unpack n from Node ; n.prev := this ; pack n as Node ; }
      pack this as Node ;
    }
}
```

Fig. 5. The alternative specification of class *List* has a simpler invariant, since the well-formedness of the list nodes is specified locally in class *Node*. The alternative implementation of class *Node* uses **peer** declarations to express that predecessor and successor nodes belong to the same owner as **this**. The **dependent** declarations are necessary to allow invariants of peer objects to depend on fields of **this**.

owner objects are unpacked. However, to allow invariants to refer to objects in arbitrary contexts, not just transitively owned contexts, we need additional requirements to ensure that *all* objects whose invariants might be affected by the modification are sufficiently unpacked, not only the updated object and its owner objects.

To illustrate these requirements, we revisit the *Person* example and add a *spouse* field as well as a *marry* method (see Fig. 6). The invariant states that the spouse of a *Person* object's spouse is the object itself. This invariant is very similar to the well-formedness of nodes, but is easier to verify.

```
class Person {
  rep Possession possn ;
  peer Person spouse dependent Person ;
  owner-dependent Person ;
  invariant this.spouse ≠ null ⇒ this.spouse.spouse = this ;
  ...
  void marry(Person p)
    requires p ≠ this ∧ ¬committed ∧ inv = Person ∧ spouse = null ;
    requires p ≠ null ∧ ¬p.committed ∧ p.inv = Person ∧ p.spouse = null ;
    modifies spouse, p.spouse ;
    {
      unpack this from Person ;  unpack p from Person ;
      this.spouse := p ;  p.spouse := this ;
      pack p as Person ;  pack this as Person ;
    }
}
```

Fig. 6. Method *Person.marry* requires that neither person already has a spouse, which guarantees that the assignments to the *spouse* fields do not break invariants of other *Person* objects.

Field updates. *Person* contains an invariant that refers to **this**.*spouse*.*spouse*, which is a field of a peer object of **this**. The assignment **this**.*spouse* := *p* in method *marry* might violate the invariant of **this** and of all *Person* objects t where $t.spouse = \mathbf{this}$. Therefore, we impose the following precondition for the field update:

$$\textbf{assert}\ (\forall\, Person\ t \mid t.spouse = \mathbf{this} \bullet Person < t.inv\ ) ;$$

This condition ensures that all potentially affected object invariants are allowed to be violated. Meeting this quantified precondition is easy for a class like *Person*: For any t for which the *Person* invariants are known to hold, we have $t.spouse.spouse = t$, and so if $t.spouse = \mathbf{this}$, then $\mathbf{this}.spouse = t$. From this observation and the fact that t ranges of non-null references, the *marry* precondition $\mathbf{this}.spouse = \mathbf{null}$ suffices to establish the quantified precondition for the field update.

Transfer. As explained in Section 3, a transfer is essentially an assignment to the *owner* field of the transferred object. Therefore, the generalized invariants also lead to stronger proof obligations for transfer statements, as illustrated by the following class:

```
class Thief { peer Possession haul ; ... }
```

Since $haul$ is declared as peer, the class has the implicit invariant

$$\mathbf{invariant}\ haul \neq \mathbf{null}\ \Rightarrow\ haul.owner = owner\ ;$$

which is violated if the object referenced by $haul$ is transferred to another owner. Consequently, such a transfer statement needs an additional precondition that ensures that possibly affected $Thief$ objects are sufficiently unpacked before a $Possession$ object is transferred.

4.3 Visibility

The above example shows that in the presence of invariants over objects in arbitrary contexts, field updates and transfers have to be guarded by preconditions that assert that all objects that might be affected by the update are sufficiently unpacked. However, such preconditions can be imposed only if the invariants that depend on the updated field are visible in the method that performs the update or transfer. In this subsection, we present the visibility requirements that are necessary to generate the appropriate assertions.

Visibility requirement for declared fields. An invariant is called a *visibility-based invariant* if it refers to a field f of an object that is different from **this** and that might not be transitively owned by **this**. Throughout the next few paragraphs, we assume that f is not the $owner$ field; the treatment of $owner$ is discussed below. To guarantee that a visibility-based invariant is visible in every method that might assign to f, we introduce **dependent** clauses for field declarations.

If the invariant of a class T contains a field-access expression of the form $\mathbf{this}.g_1.\cdots.g_n.f\ (n \geqslant 1)$, where the object $\mathbf{this}.g_1.\cdots.g_n$ might not be (transitively) owned by **this**, then T must be declared a dependent of f. In our example, $Person$ is declared a dependent of $spouse$, because its invariant refers to $\mathbf{this}.spouse.spouse$, and $spouse$ is not a rep field:

$$\mathbf{peer}\ Person\ spouse\ \mathbf{dependent}\ Person\ ;$$

The dependent-clause allows us to impose the precondition for updates of the $spouse$ field that was presented in the example above.

By the visibility requirement, we can allow more invariants than before. An invariant declared in class T is admissible if for each of its field-access expressions of the form $\mathbf{this}.g_1.\cdots.g_n.f\ \ (n \geqslant 1)$, either g_1 is a rep field and each of the other g_i is a rep or peer field, or T is a dependent of f. Whether an invariant is admissible can be checked syntactically by referring to the **rep** and **peer** modifiers as well as the **dependent** clauses of the involved fields.

As illustrated by the invariants of $Person$ and $Node$ (Fig. 5), visibility-based invariants allow us, for instance, to specify properties of recursive data structures as long as the class that contains the invariant is visible in the classes that declare the fields the invariant depends on. This visibility requirement can easily be met if all involved classes are developed together (in our examples, only one class is involved). However, if a class T comes from a class library, for instance, then the visibility requirement is in general not met; moreover, assuming the library cannot be modified, dependent classes cannot be added to the **dependent** clauses of the field declarations in T. In such cases, ownership-based invariants have to be used. That is, if a class S declares a field f of type T and declares an invariant that mentions the fields of f, then f has to be declared with **rep**. Having to use ownership in this situation does not seem needlessly limiting, but realistic: S implements a new layer on top of class T. Forcing clients to access (especially modify) the state of lower layers by invoking methods of higher layers is a common design practice.

Visibility requirement for the $owner$ **field.** Ownership transfer is essentially an assignment to the $owner$ field of the transferred object. However, the visibility requirement for ordinary fields is too strong to be useful for $owner$: since $owner$ is a predefined field of class **object**, the implementor of a class T cannot mention T in the dependent-clause of $owner$. Nevertheless, visibility-based invariants that refer to $owner$ fields are often useful, for instance as implicit invariants for peer fields.

To be able to determine all classes that contain invariants that might be violated by a transfer, we use the **transferable** modifier introduced in Section 3 and ensure that all dependent classes are visible in the transferable class. Consequently, the dependent classes are visible in any method that contains a **transfer** statement, which allows us to impose an appropriate precondition. We describe this solution in the following.

If the invariant of a class T contains a field-access expression of the form $\mathbf{this}.g_1.\cdots.g_n.owner$ $(n \geqslant 1)$, where the object $\mathbf{this}.g_1.\cdots.g_n$ might not be owned by **this**, then T must be declared an *owner-dependent* of the static type of g_n. That is, we use the same concept as for dependent-clauses, but instead of listing a dependent class in the field declaration, we specify it in the class of the static type of the field on which $owner$ is accessed. For instance, the implicit invariant for the peer field *spouse* in class $Person$ refers to $\mathbf{this}.spouse.owner$. Consequently, we have to mention the class that declares the invariant, $Person$, in the owner-dependent declaration of the static type of $\mathbf{this}.spouse$, which also is $Person$. Thus, $Person$ has to contain the declaration **owner-dependent** *Person*;.

Owner-dependent declarations may be specified only for non-transferable classes (*e.g.*, $Person$) and for transferable classes with non-transferable direct superclasses (*e.g.*, $Possession$). That is, transferable classes with transferable superclasses never have any owner-dependent declarations. This restriction allows us to determine all invariants that might be affected by a transfer of the form **transfer** x **to** $[q, U]$. The classes that declare such invariants are declared owner-dependents of the static type of x, say T, or T's superclasses. Like T and T's superclasses, these owner-dependents are visible in the method that contains the transfer statement. Proper subclasses of T, which might not be visible in this method, are transferable and have a transferable superclass. Therefore, they must not contain owner-dependent declarations and invariants of clients may, in general, not refer to $g.owner$ if the static type of g is a proper subclass of T.

4.4 Proof Obligations

The visibility requirement allows us to generalize the proof obligations for field updates and transfers to support both ownership-based and visibility-based invariants.

Precondition for field updates. Besides the invariants of x and the invariants of x's transitive owner objects, an update of the field $x.f$ may affect invariants of objects of the classes in the dependent-clause of f. Therefore, we have to impose the following proof obligation in addition to the assertions described in Section 2.1:

> If a class T is mentioned in the **dependent** clause of field f and an invariant of T refers to f such that a T object t depends on $x.f$, then t must be sufficiently unpacked ($T < t.inv$).

This requirement guarantees that visibility-based invariants of an object can be violated only when the object is in a state in which it is known that the invariants may not hold. We formalize this proof obligation in Section 5.

For example, we determine the precondition of the field update $\mathbf{this}.spouse := p$ in method $marry$ (Fig. 6) as follows. The field $spouse$ mentions class $Person$ in its dependent-clause, so we look at the object invariants of $Person$ to determine which invariants may be affected by the $spouse$ assignment. Among the $Person$ invariants, there is one access expression of the form $E.spouse$ where E might not be owned, namely for E being $\mathbf{this}.spouse$. In other words, any $Person$ object t satisfying $t.spouse = \mathbf{this}$ may be affected by the assignment to $\mathbf{this}.spouse$ in $marry$. Thus, our methodology prescribes the following precondition for the field update:

$$\mathbf{assert}\ (\forall\, Person\ t \mid t.spouse = \mathbf{this} \bullet\ Person < t.inv\ ) ;$$

Precondition of transfer. The rules for **transferable** modifiers and owner-dependent declarations guarantee that, besides the old and new owning objects of x, a transfer of the form **transfer** x **to** $[q, U]$ can only affect invariants of classes that are mentioned in the owner-dependent declarations of x's static type or of their superclasses. Therefore, we impose a proof obligation that objects of these classes are sufficiently unpacked before the transfer. That is, the following condition has to hold in the pre-state of a transfer of the above form in addition to the requirements presented in Section 3:

> If a class T is mentioned in the owner-dependent declaration in any superclass of x's static type, and the (implicit or explicit) invariant of T refers to $owner$ such that a T object t depends on $x.owner$, then t must be sufficiently unpacked ($T < t.inv$).

* * *

This completes the informal presentation of our methodology. By the visibility requirement, we can allow the invariant of X to refer to objects that are not owned by X without sacrificing modular reasoning. Visibility-based invariants allow one to express properties of data structures locally in a representation class such as $Node$, which simplifies specification and verification of both representation classes and owners. In particular, one can express invariants of object structures even if the owner of the objects is not known. This flexibility is necessary for data structures such as singly-linked lists, where designated owner objects are rather artificial.

5 Technical Treatment

In this section, we present the technical treatment of our methodology. That is, we define precisely which invariants are admissible, formalize the assertions for the relevant statements, and prove a soundness theorem.

5.1 Admissible Invariants

The invariant of a class C may depend on fields of **this** and of objects transitively owned by **this**, on fields that contain C in their dependent-clause, and on *owner* fields if C is mentioned in owner-dependent declarations of the static type of the field on which *owner* is accessed:

Definition 1 (Admissible invariant). *An invariant declaration in class C is admissible if its subexpressions typecheck according to the rules of the programming language and if each of its field-access expressions has one of the following forms:*

1. $\mathbf{this}.g_1.\cdots.g_n.f$, *where either* $n = 0$, *or* g_1 *is a rep field and each of the fields* $g_2, \ldots, g_n$ *is either a rep or a peer field.*
2. $\mathbf{this}.g_1.\cdots.g_n.f$, *where* $n \geqslant 1$, f *is different from* $owner$, *and* C *is mentioned in the dependent-clause of* f.
3. $\mathbf{this}.g_1.\cdots.g_n.owner$, *where* $n \geqslant 1$ *and* C *is mentioned in an owner-dependent declaration of the type of* g_n.
4. $x.f$, *where* x *is bound by a universal quantification of the form*

$$(\forall\, T\ x \mid x.owner = [\mathbf{this}, B] \bullet\ P(x)\ )$$

and B *is a superclass of* C. $P(x)$ *may refer to the identity and the state of* x, *but not to the states of objects referenced by* x.

The field f *must not be one of the predefined fields* inv *and* $committed$.

The access expression $\mathbf{this}.f$ is a special case of kind 1. Access expressions of kinds 1 and 4 are, for instance, used in the *List* class shown in Fig. 3. Field-access expressions of kinds 2 and 3 enable visibility-based invariants.

5.2 Proof Rules

The methodology presented in this paper does not assume a particular programming logic to reason about programs and specifications. Special rules are required only for those statements that deal with the fields *inv* and *committed* (**pack**, **unpack**, and field update) as well as *owner* (object creation and **transfer**). The rules for pack and unpack statements as well as the specification of **object**'s constructor are presented in Section 3. We describe the rules for the remaining statements in the following.

Field updates. The rule for field updates was explained in Section 4.4. More formally, a field update of the form $x.f := e$ is guarded by the following preconditions:

1. **assert** $x \neq$ **null** $\wedge$ $F < x.inv$;
   where F is the class in which f is declared.
2. For each class T mentioned in the dependent-clause of f, and for each access expression $\mathtt{this}.g_1.\cdots.g_n.f$ of kind 2 (and not of kind 1) in an invariant declared in T: **assert** $(\forall\, T\ t \mid t.g_1.\cdots.g_n = x \bullet\ T < t.inv\ )$;.

The first precondition is identical to the methodology with ownership-based invariants only. It guarantees that x's transitive owner objects are sufficiently unpacked. Preconditions of the second kind are necessary to handle invariants with field-access expressions of kind 2 in Def. 1.

Transfer. The rule for ownership transfer is analogous to field updates, but refers to owner-dependent declarations instead of dependent-clauses: A transfer statement of the form $\mathbf{transfer}\ x\ \mathbf{to}\ [q, U]$ is guarded by the following preconditions:

1. **assert** $x \neq$ **null** $\wedge\ x.inv =$ **object** ;
2. **assert** $x.owner.obj \neq$ **null** $\Rightarrow\ x.owner.typ < x.owner.obj.inv$;
3. **assert** $q \neq$ **null** $\Rightarrow\ U < q.inv$;
4. For each class T mentioned in an owner-dependent declaration in any superclass of x's static type, and for each access expression $\mathtt{this}.g_1.\cdots.g_n.owner$ of kind 3 (and not of kind 1) in an invariant declared in T:

   assert $(\forall\, T\ t \mid t.g_1.\cdots.g_n = x \bullet\ T < t.inv\ )$;

The first three preconditions were also part of the methodology with ownership-based invariants only. They ensure that both x's old and new owner objects are sufficiently unpacked. Preconditions of the last kind are necessary to handle invariants with field-access expressions of kind 3 (Def. 1), which occur for instance in the implicit invariants for peer fields.

5.3 Soundness

For our methodology, soundness means that the inv field of an object x correctly reflects which invariants of x can be assumed to hold. In this subsection, we formalize and prove this property for well-formed programs. A program **P** is well-formed if **P** is syntactically correct, type correct, and **P**'s invariants are admissible (see Def. 1).

Theorem 1 (Soundness theorem). *In each reachable execution state of a well-formed program, the following program invariant holds:*

$$(\forall\, x, T \bullet\ x.inv \leqslant T \Rightarrow Inv_T(x)\ )$$

where $Inv_T(x)$ expresses that x satisfies all (explicit and implicit) invariants declared in class T.

Soundness proof. Because of limited space, we present the proof of a simplified theorem here that assumes that all field-access expressions of admissible invariants (Def. 1) refer to fields of **this** or a bound variable, or to fields of objects directly referenced by **this**. That is, for field-access expressions of kinds 1 to 3, we assume $n \leqslant 1$. A generalization of the proof is straightforward, but requires several auxiliary lemmas about transitive ownership we cannot present here.

The proof runs by induction over the sequence of states of a program **P**. The induction base is trivial. For the induction step, only the statements that create objects or manipulate fields of objects are interesting. We omit all trivial cases for brevity.

Object creation. Creation of a new object x does not change the values of fields of existing objects. Since a precondition of the operation is that any given owning object of x is sufficiently unpacked, we only have to show that the property holds for x itself, which is a direct consequence of the fact that $x.inv = \textbf{object}$ and class **object** does not have invariants.

Pack. A pack statement changes the inv field of the packed object as well as the $committed$ fields of objects directly owned by that object, but nothing else. Since invariants must not refer to inv or $committed$ fields (see Def. 1), the value of $Inv_T(x)$ cannot be changed by a pack statement. The value of $x.inv \leqslant T$ is only changed by the statement **pack** x **as** T. However, the precondition of the pack statement checks that $Inv_T(x)$ holds. Therefore both sides of the implication yield $true$ after the statement.

Unpack. Like pack statements, unpack statements only change inv and $committed$ fields, which implies that $Inv_T(x)$ is not affected by any unpack statement. The value of $x.inv$ after the statement is a direct superclass of the value before the statement. Thus, the value of $x.inv \leqslant T$ might only be changed from $true$ to $false$. That is, the implication still holds after the unpack statement.

Field update. Let f be a field declared in a class F and consider the effect of an update $y.f := e$ on $Inv_T(x)$ for some x and T. In particular, we show that if $Inv_T(x)$ contains an access expression that denotes $y.f$, then x is sufficiently unpacked: $T < x.inv$ (that is, the left side of the implication is $false$). For this proof, we only only need to consider access expressions in the invariants that end with dereferencing f. Access expressions that mention f somewhere in the middle contain as a subexpression an access expression that ends with f. Following (the simplified) Def. 1, we consider the following cases:

1a. An invariant of T refers to **this**.f and $x = y$: The precondition of the field update requires $F < x.inv$. Since T is a subclass of F (otherwise the expression $x.f$ would not typecheck), we get $T < x.inv$.
1b. An invariant of T refers to **this**.$g.f$, where g is a rep field declared in a superclass S of T, and $x.g = y$: From the precondition of the update of $y.f$, we know that y is not consistent. Since $x.g = y$ and g is a rep field, x must be unpacked beyond S: $S < x.inv$. (The definition of the unpack operation guarantees that an owner object x is unpacked beyond the owner type S before an object owned by $[x, S]$ can be unpacked. The pack operation guarantees that objects are packed in the reverse order.) Since T is a subclass of S, we have $T \leqslant S < x.inv$.

2. An invariant of T refers to $\mathbf{this}.g.f$, $x.g = y$, and T is mentioned in f's dependent-clause: The field update has the precondition

$$\textbf{assert } (\forall\, T\ t \mid t.g = y \bullet T < t.inv\ ) \ ;$$

   Instantiating t with x, we have $T < x.inv$.
3. An invariant of T refers to $\mathbf{this}.f.owner$ and $x = y$: Since we only have to consider access expressions that end with dereferencing f, there is nothing to be shown for this case. $\mathbf{this}.f.owner$ has $\mathbf{this}.f$ as a subexpression, which is handled in Case 1a.
4. An invariant of T refers to $o.f$, where o is a variable bound by quantification, $o = y$, $o.owner = [x, S]$, and $T \leqslant S$: Analogously to Case 1b, y is not consistent, and y's owner object, x, must be unpacked beyond the owner type, S: $S < x.inv$. Since T is a subclass of S, we have $T \leqslant S < x.inv$.

Transfer. Consider the statement **transfer** y **to** $[q, U]$. This transfer is essentially an update of $y.owner$. Therefore, the proof for a transfer is similar to the proof for field updates: Cases 1a, 1b, and 4 are analogous. Case 2 for transfers is analogous to Case 3 of field updates and vice versa. However, Case 3 for transfers has to refer to the owner-dependent declaration of the static type of $\mathbf{this}.g$ instead of the dependent-clause of f. Moreover, all cases have to consider both the old and the new owner of y. However, since both owner objects are sufficiently unpacked before the transfer, the arguments of the cases for field updates apply as well to the new owner object of the transferred object. □

6 Usability

In this section, we discuss the expressiveness and practicability of our methodology.

Expressiveness. The methodology presented here can express properties of many interesting implementations. Ownership-based invariants allow us to specify properties of the internal representation of an object structure in a modular way. By supporting quantifications over all objects owned by an object, we can handle complex object structures such as the union-find data structure, where not all constituent objects are reachable from the owning object. Visibility-based invariants enable one to declare invariants locally in classes of constituent objects, which simplifies specifications and proofs and, in particular, allow us to handle data structures that do not have an explicit owner.

Although we do not restrict aliasing, our methodology requires that modifications of objects always be initiated by their owner objects since the owner object has to be unpacked before the modification. Therefore, data structures like collections with iterators are difficult to handle with ownership-based invariants; essentially, an iterator needs to arrange to unpack the collection before it can modify the collection's state. In our *List* example, we could use visibility-based invariants for a class *Iterator* if *Node* and *Iterator* are mutually visible. But either the list or its owner would have to know all iterators of the list to be able to unpack them all before the list is modified. To provide better support for such patterns, one might consider generalizing our methodology to allow multiple owners for each object and adding support for packing and unpacking all owners of an object simultaneously.

In this paper, we omitted arrays for brevity. The treatment of arrays is analogous to other objects. In particular, arrays can have (implicit) invariants specifying the owner of their elements. So far, our methodology does not support static fields. However, static fields can be treated as fields of class objects, which allows visibility-based invariants to express properties of global state.

Specification support. Due to the semantics of **modifies** clauses, methods can allocate and modify new objects without explicitly specifying these modifications. However, if the caller has no knowledge about new objects and their consistency, it is in general not possible to reason about invariants that quantify over all objects owned by a certain owner. To deal with this problem, the specifications in our *List* example contain **ensures** clauses that state that all newly allocated objects are consistent upon termination of a routine (see Fig. 5). Instead of writing such **ensures** clauses, it would be helpful to provide a designated **expands** clause that specifies the owners of objects allocated by a routine. Analogous with the rule for **modifies** clauses, if the owning object is newly allocated or on entry is committed, then the **expands** clause would not need to mention the owner. For instance, the clause **expands** *ow* for *Node*'s constructor would say that the constructor does not create objects for owners other than *ow*, which would simplify the corresponding **ensures** clause.

In this paper, we use dependent-clauses to check the visibility requirement. Such clauses make potential dependencies explicit, but lead to additional specification overhead. For languages that provide modules with acyclic import, dependent-clauses are not necessary. A tool could infer the dependent-clauses within one module. Inter-module dependencies violate the visibility requirement and are, thus, forbidden. This approach is, for instance, taken in Müller's thesis [30].

Many of the specification constructs we've discussed are often used in certain stylized forms. For example, methods often require their parameters to be consistent and uncommitted, pack and unpack statements tend to occur in pairs in the bodies of public methods, and the owner parameter passed to constructors often mention **this** and the enclosing class. We'd like to experiment with useful defaults that reduce the number of explicit specifications are needed in a program.

Tool support. Although we consider our work a significant improvement in the treatment of object invariants, reasoning is still tedious and appropriate tool support is indispensable. One of the key considerations for the design of our methodology was to avoid reachability predicates in proof obligations since existing theorem provers can have trouble handling such recursive predicates automatically (*cf.* [19]). Specifications such as *all nodes reachable from* **this**.*head are owned by* [**this**, *List*] can be avoided by quantification in ownership-based invariants (see Fig. 3) or by visibility-based invariants (see Fig. 5).

We plan to implement our methodology as part of the .NET program checker Boogie at Microsoft Research and use this implementation for non trivial case studies. Applying the Extended Static Checker for Java [16] to a special encoding of the examples used in this paper lead to promising results: all proof obligations except those for **modifies** clauses, which are not checked by ESC/Java, were proved automatically.

7 Related Work

In this section, we discuss papers from the large literature on invariants that are directly related to invariants for object structures. A more detailed discussion of related work is found in Müller's thesis [30], and we gave a more detailed comparison with two previous methodologies in Section 2.

Classical proof systems for invariants such as Meyer's work [29,28] or the approach of Liskov, Wing, and Guttag [27,26] are not sound if invariants express properties of more than one object. They require exported methods to preserve the invariant only of the current object or of all objects of the enclosing class, neither of which is sufficient for general object structures with aliasing [32]. Especially, behavioral subtyping [22,13] is necessary but not sufficient to guarantee modular soundness for invariants over object structures. Other specification languages such as JML [21,20] or several Larch languages [17] permit invariants over object structures but do not provide a sound modular proof system.

Huizing and Kuiper [18] present a proof system that supports invariants for object structures. Invariants are analyzed syntactically to determine which methods of a program might violate which invariants. However, without appropriate restrictions, this analysis is not modular.

Banerjee and Naumann [1] consider what it means, formally, for the exported interface of a class to be independent of the implementation of the class, which may rely on object invariants. They use ideas from separation logic and permit the heap to be partitioned in a flexible way (for example, constituent objects need not be reached from the owner). Their semantic results are sound even in the presence of call-backs, but just how one goes about establishing the antecedents of their theorems is mostly left unaddressed.

The approach presented in our paper is based on recent work by Barnett *et al.* [2]. We replaced the static declaration of components by a dynamic encoding of ownership, which enables invariants over dynamically growing and shrinking object structures such as linked lists. In addition, our approach supports visibility-based invariants, which can simplify specifications and proofs, and which allow us to handle object structures that do not have explicit owner objects.

The treatment of visibility-based invariants was influenced by Müller's thesis [30]. Müller uses a visible state semantics for invariants that requires invariants of relevant objects to hold in pre- and postconditions of all exported methods, whereas our methodology allows invariants to be violated as long as such violations are made explicit by the inv field. This type-valued inv field especially provides a better handling of inheritance [2]. Müller's thesis supports invariants over so-called abstract fields in a sound way, which we consider future work for the methodology presented here. Müller's approach has been applied to more restricted invariants [32] and to the treatment of **modifies** clauses [33].

The programming model supported by Müller's universe type system corresponds to the restrictions used in this paper: Objects can be freely aliased, but modifications of objects have to be initiated by owners. Besides universes, several other type systems have been proposed to express ownership statically [4,5,6,7,8,9]. Some ownership type systems use ownership parameters to express ownership relations like the ones we specify with **rep** and **peer** tags. In contrast to our work, these type systems restrict aliasing of objects and do not support ownership transfer. Ownership type systems guarantee the ownership relation in all execution states, whereas the ownership relations specified by our object invariants (including the implicit object invariants for **rep** and **peer** fields) are conditions that need not always hold. This dynamic encoding simplifies transfer, but makes the soundness proof more difficult. Clarke and Wrigstad [10] combine ownership types with externally unique references to permit transfer. Fähndrich and DeLine [15] present a type system with linearity for checking interface protocols of objects. Their adoption and focus statements provide a controlled way of creating aliases and accessing aliased objects, loosening the rigid uniqueness requirements imposed by linear type systems.

Barnett and Naumann [3] extend the work presented in our paper. In their encoding, each object X maintains a (possibly abstract) set of objects whose visibility-based invariants depend on fields of X. This set can be used to establish the preconditions for updating X's fields more easily than in our approach. Another novelty of Barnett and Naumann's paper is update guards. An update guard abstracts the weakest precondition for a field update, to enable the update without unpacking potentially affected objects or exposing internal state in that precondition.

Like our methodology, the work by Leino *et al.* [23,24,11] imposes visibility requirements to enable a modular sound treatment of abstract fields. However, their work is not based on the notion of ownership, which leads to more complicated requirements for specifying properties over object structures and makes the soundness proof difficult. The Extended Static Checker for Modula-3 [12] uses the technique of Leino and Nelson [24] to reason about validity of object structures by defining a boolean abstract field $valid$ to represent validity. Usage of this field in specifications is similar to our inv field.

The Extended Static Checker for Java [16] uses heuristics to determine which object invariants to check for method invocations. Described in detail in the ESC/Java User's Manual [25], these heuristics are a compromise between flexibility and likelihood of errors and do not guarantee soundness.

Our technique requires programmers to specify invariants as well as rep and peer annotations explicitly. Tools such as Daikon [14] could be used to guess possible object invariants automatically and then check them by our methodology.

8 Conclusions

We presented a methodology for specifying and reasoning about object invariants. Our solution allows one to express properties of object structures without restricting aliasing. A combination of ownership- and visibility-based invariants provides enough expressiveness to handle non-trivial implementations such as (mutually) recursive data structures and re-entrant method calls. Inheritance is fully supported. The methodology is modular and proven to be sound.

As future work, we plan to generalize our methodology to allow objects to have multiple owners, which is, for instance, necessary for certain implementations of collections with iterators. Invariants over abstract fields are useful to describe properties of data structures without referring to their concrete implementation. We plan to adapt our previous work on abstract fields [30,23] to the methodology presented here.

Acknowledgments. We are grateful to Mike Barnett, John Boyland, Rob DeLine, Manuel Fähndrich, Bertrand Meyer, Dave Naumann, and Wolfram Schulte for helpful discussions on invariants and ownership. We especially thank Dave Naumann, who suggested we separate the concepts of peer fields and visibility-based invariants, which in a previous version had been entangled. We also thank the referees for helping improve the presentation.

References

1. Anindya Banerjee and David A. Naumann. Ownership confinement ensures representation independence for object-oriented programs. Manuscript available on `http://guinness.cs.stevens-tech.edu/~naumann/publications/`, December 2002.
2. Mike Barnett, Robert DeLine, Manuel Fähndrich, K. Rustan M. Leino, and Wolfram Schulte. Verification of object-oriented programs with invariants. *Journal of Object Technology*, 2004. To appear.
3. Mike Barnett and David Naumann. Friends need a bit more: Maintaining invariants over shared state. In *Mathematics of Program Construction*, Lecture Notes in Computer Science. Springer-Verlag, 2004. To appear.
4. Boris Bokowski and Jan Vitek. Confined types. In *Proceedings of the 1999 ACM SIGPLAN Conference on Object-Oriented Programming Systems, Languages and Applications (OOPSLA '99)*, volume 34, number 10 in *SIGPLAN Notices*, pages 82–96. ACM, October 1999.
5. Chandrasekhar Boyapati, Robert Lee, and Martin Rinard. Ownership types for safe programming: Preventing data races and deadlocks. In *Proceedings of the 2002 ACM SIGPLAN Conference on Object-Oriented Programming Systems, Languages and Applications, OOPSLA 2002*, volume 37, number 11 in *SIGPLAN Notices*, pages 211–230. ACM, November 2002.
6. Chandrasekhar Boyapati, Barbara Liskov, and Liuba Shrira. Ownership types for object encapsulation. In *Conference Record of POPL 2003: The 30th SIGPLAN-SIGACT Symposium on Principles of Programming Languages*, volume 38, number 1 in *SIGPLAN Notices*, pages 213–223. ACM, January 2003.
7. Dave Clarke. *Object Ownership and Containment*. PhD thesis, University of New South Wales, 2001.
8. Dave G. Clarke and Sophia Drossopoulou. Ownership, encapsulation and the disjointness of type and effect. In *Proceedings of the 2002 ACM SIGPLAN Conference on Object-Oriented Programming Systems, Languages and Applications, OOPSLA 2002*, volume 37, number 11 in *SIGPLAN Notices*, pages 292–310. ACM, November 2002.

9. Dave G. Clarke, John. M. Potter, and James Noble. Ownership types for flexible alias protection. In *Proceedings of the 1998 ACM SIGPLAN Conference on Object-Oriented Programming Systems, Languages and Applications (OOPSLA '98)*, volume 33, number 10 in *SIGPLAN Notices*, pages 48–64. ACM, October 1998.
10. Dave G. Clarke and Tobias Wrigstad. External uniqueness is unique enough. In Luca Cardelli, editor, *ECOOP 2003—Object-Oriented Programming, 17th European Conference*, volume 2743 of *Lecture Notes in Computer Science*, pages 176–200. Springer, 2003.
11. David L. Detlefs, K. Rustan M. Leino, and Greg Nelson. Wrestling with rep exposure. Research Report 156, Digital Equipment Corporation Systems Research Center, July 1998.
12. David L. Detlefs, K. Rustan M. Leino, Greg Nelson, and James B. Saxe. Extended static checking. Research Report 159, Compaq Systems Research Center, December 1998.
13. Krishna Kishore Dhara. Behavioral subtyping in object-oriented languages. Technical Report 97-09, Iowa State University, May 1997.
14. Michael D. Ernst, Jake Cockrell, William G. Griswold, and David Notkin. Dynamically discovering likely program invariants to support program evolution. *IEEE Transactions on Software Engineering*, 27(2):1–25, 2001.
15. Manuel Fähndrich and Robert DeLine. Adoption and focus: practical linear types for imperative programming. In *Proceedings of the 2002 ACM SIGPLAN Conference on Programming Language Design and Implementation (PLDI)*, volume 37, number 5 in *SIGPLAN Notices*, pages 13–24. ACM, May 2002.
16. Cormac Flanagan, K. Rustan M. Leino, Mark Lillibridge, Greg Nelson, James B. Saxe, and Raymie Stata. Extended static checking for Java. In *Proceedings of the 2002 ACM SIGPLAN Conference on Programming Language Design and Implementation (PLDI)*, volume 37, number 5 in *SIGPLAN Notices*, pages 234–245. ACM, May 2002.
17. John V. Guttag and James J. Horning, editors. *Larch: Languages and Tools for Formal Specification*. Texts and Monographs in Computer Science. Springer-Verlag, 1993. With Stephen J. Garland, Kevin D. Jones, Andrés Modet, and Jeannette M. Wing.
18. Kees Huizing and Ruurd Kuiper. Verification of object-oriented programs using class invariants. In Tom Maibaum, editor, *Fundamental Approaches to Software Engineering*, volume 1783 of *Lecture Notes in Computer Science*, pages 208–221. Springer-Verlag, 2000.
19. Rajeev Joshi. Extended static checking of programs with cyclic dependencies. In James Mason, editor, *1997 SRC Summer Intern Projects*, Technical Note 1997-028. Digital Equipment Corporation Systems Research Center, 1997.
20. Gary T. Leavens, Albert L. Baker, and Clyde Ruby. JML: A notation for detailed design. In Haim Kilov, Bernhard Rumpe, and Ian Simmonds, editors, *Behavioral Specifications of Businesses and Systems*, pages 175–188. Kluwer Academic Publishers, 1999.
21. Gary T. Leavens, Albert L. Baker, and Clyde Ruby. Preliminary design of JML: A behavioral interface specification language for Java. Technical Report 98-06v, Iowa State University, Department of Computer Science, May 2003. See `www.jmlspecs.org`.
22. Gary T. Leavens and Krishna Kishore Dhara. Concepts of behavioral subtyping and a sketch of their extension to component-based systems. In Gary T. Leavens and Murali Sitaraman, editors, *Foundations of Component-Based Systems*. Cambridge University Press, 2000.
23. K. Rustan M. Leino. *Toward Reliable Modular Programs*. PhD thesis, California Institute of Technology, 1995.
24. K. Rustan M. Leino and Greg Nelson. Data abstraction and information hiding. *ACM Transactions on Programming Languages and Systems*, 24(5):491–553, September 2002.
25. K. Rustan M. Leino, Greg Nelson, and James B. Saxe. ESC/Java user's manual. Technical Note 2000-002, Compaq Systems Research Center, October 2000.
26. Barbara Liskov and John Guttag. *Abstraction and Specification in Program Development*. MIT Electrical Engineering and Computer Science Series. MIT Press, 1986.

27. Barbara Liskov and Jeannette M. Wing. A behavioral notion of subtyping. *ACM Transactions on Programming Languages and Systems*, 16(6), 1994.
28. Bertrand Meyer. *Eiffel: The Language*. Prentice Hall, 1992.
29. Bertrand Meyer. *Object-Oriented Software Construction*. Prentice Hall, second edition edition, 1997.
30. Peter Müller. *Modular Specification and Verification of Object-Oriented Programs*, volume 2262 of *Lecture Notes in Computer Science*. Springer-Verlag, 2002. PhD thesis, FernUniversität Hagen.
31. Peter Müller and Arnd Poetzsch-Heffter. Universes: A type system for alias and dependency control. Technical Report 279, FernUniversität Hagen, 2001.
32. Peter Müller, Arnd Poetzsch-Heffter, and Gary T. Leavens. Modular invariants for layered object structures. Technical Report 424, Department of Computer Science, ETH Zurich, 2003.
33. Peter Müller, Arnd Poetzsch-Heffter, and Gary T. Leavens. Modular specification of frame properties in JML. *Concurrency and Computation: Practice and Experience*, 15:117–154, 2003.

Rich Interfaces for Software Modules

Thomas A. Henzinger

EPFL and University of California, Berkeley

Interfaces play a central role in the modular design of systems. Good interface design is based on two principles. First, an interface should expose enough information about a module so to make it possible to predict if two or more modules work together properly, by looking only at their interfaces. Second, an interface should not expose more information about a module than is required by the first principle. The technical realization of these two principles depends, of course, on the precise interpretation of what it means for two or more modules to "work together properly." A simple interpretation is offered by typed programming languages: a module that implements a function and a module that calls that function are compatible if the function definition and the function call agree on the number, order, and types of the parameters.

We present richer notions of interfaces, which expose in addition to type information, also temporal information about software modules. For example, the interface of a file server with the two methods `open_file` and `read_file` may stipulate that `read_file` must not be called before `open_file` has been called. Symmetrically, then, the interface of a client must specify the possible sequences of `open_file` and `read_file` calls during its execution, so that a compiler can check if the server and the client fit together. Such *behavioral interfaces*, which expose temporal information about a module and at the same time impose temporal requirements on the environment of the module, can be specified naturally using an automaton-based language [1,2]. In other situations, the appropriate notion of compatibility between software modules, as suggested by the first principle of interface design, is richer still and may require, for example, the exposure of assertional, real-time, and resource-use information. This leads, in turn, to *push-down*, *timed*, and *resource interfaces* [3,4,5]. For instance, resource interfaces can be used to ensure that no two modules simultaneously access a unique resource.

We formally capture the requirements on interfaces by axiomatizing *interface theories* [6]. For example, the axiom of "independent implementability" of interfaces guarantees that if A and B are compatible interfaces, and A' is a module that conforms to interface A, and B' is a module that conforms to interface B, then the composition $A'||B'$ of the two modules conforms to the composite interface $A||B$. For selected interface formalisms, such as behavioral, push-down, timed, and resource interfaces, we show that they satisfy the axioms of interface theories, and we discuss the following three algorithmic problems:

M. Odersky (Ed.): ECOOP 2004, LNCS 3086, pp. 517–518, 2004.

1. *Compatibility*: given two interfaces, are they compatible?
2. *Conformance*: given an interface and a software module, does the module conform to the interface?
3. *Interface extraction*: given an interface theory and a software module, what is the interface of the module with respect to the theory?

In particular, we show that the compatibility checking of interfaces amounts to solving a game in which the interfaces and the unknown environment represent players. Furthermore, we show that the conformance relationship between a module and its interface must be a contravariant one, which as in subtyping, treats inputs and outputs differently. This distinguishes interface conformance from many formal methods for stepwise refinement.

Acknowledgments. The work reported here is joint with Arindam Chakrabarti, Luca de Alfaro, Marcin Jurdziński, Freddy Mang, and Marielle Stoelinga.

References

1. E.A. Lee and Y. Xiong. System-level types for component-based design. In *EMSOFT 01: Embedded Software*, Lecture Notes in Computer Science 2211, pages 237–253. Springer-Verlag, 2001.
2. L. de Alfaro and T.A. Henzinger. Interface automata. In *Proceedings of the Ninth Annual Symposium on Foundations of Software Engineering*, pages 109–120. ACM Press, 2001.
3. A. Chakrabarti, L. de Alfaro, T.A. Henzinger, M. Jurdziński, and F.Y.C. Mang. Interface compatibility checking for software modules. In *CAV 02: Computer-Aided Verification*, Lecture Notes in Computer Science 2404, pages 428–441. Springer-Verlag, 2002.
4. L. de Alfaro, T.A. Henzinger, and M. Stoelinga. Timed interfaces. In *EMSOFT 02: Embedded Software*, Lecture Notes in Computer Science 2491, pages 108–122. Springer-Verlag, 2002.
5. A. Chakrabarti, L. de Alfaro, T.A. Henzinger, and M. Stoelinga. Resource interfaces. In *EMSOFT 03: Embedded Software*, Lecture Notes in Computer Science 2855, pages 117–133. Springer-Verlag, 2003.
6. L. de Alfaro and T.A. Henzinger. Interface theories for component-based design. In *EMSOFT 01: Embedded Software*, Lecture Notes in Computer Science 2211, pages 148–165. Springer-Verlag, 2001.

Transactional Monitors for Concurrent Objects

Adam Welc, Suresh Jagannathan, and Antony L. Hosking

Department of Computer Sciences
Purdue University
West Lafayette, IN 47906
{welc,suresh,hosking}@cs.purdue.edu

Abstract. *Transactional monitors* are proposed as an alternative to monitors based on mutual-exclusion synchronization for object-oriented programming languages. Transactional monitors have execution semantics similar to mutual-exclusion monitors but implement monitors as lightweight transactions that can be executed concurrently (or in parallel on multiprocessors). They alleviate many of the constraints that inhibit construction of transparently scalable and robust applications.

We undertake a detailed study of alternative implementation schemes for transactional monitors. These different schemes are tailored to different concurrent access patterns, and permit a given application to use potentially different implementations in different contexts.

We also examine the performance and scalability of these alternative approaches in the context of the Jikes Research Virtual Machine, a state-of-the-art Java implementation. We show that transactional monitors are competitive with mutual-exclusion synchronization and can outperform lock-based approaches up to five times on a wide range of workloads.

1 Introduction

Managing complexity is a major challenge in constructing robust large-scale server applications (such as database management systems, application servers, airline reservation sytems, *etc*). In a typical environment, large numbers of clients may access a server application concurrently. To provide satisfactory response time and throughput, the applications themselves are often made concurrent. Thus, object-oriented programming languages (*eg*, Smalltalk, C++, Modula-3, Java) provide mechanisms that enable concurrent programming via a thread abstraction, with threads being the smallest unit of concurrent execution.

A key mechanism offered by these languages is the notion of *guarded* code regions in which accesses to shared data performed by one thread are *isolated* from accesses performed by others, and all updates performed by a thread within a guarded region become visible to other threads *atomically*, once the executing thread exits the region.

Guarded regions are usually implemented using mutual-exclusion locks: a thread acquires a lock before it is allowed to enter the guarded region and blocks if the lock has already been acquired by another thread. Isolation results since threads must execute the guarded region serially: only one thread at a time can be active in the region, although this serial order is not necessarily deterministic. Atomicity of updates is also achieved with

M. Odersky (Ed.): ECOOP 2004, LNCS 3086, pp. 519–542, 2004.

respect to shared data accessed within the region; updates are visible to other threads only when the current thread releases the lock.

Unfortunately, enforcing isolation and atomicity using mutual-exclusion locks suffers from a number of potentially serious drawbacks. Most importantly, locks often serve as poor abstractions since they do not help to guarantee high-level properties of concurrent programs such as atomicity or isolation that are often implicitly assumed in the specification of these programs. In other words, locks do not obviate the programmer from the responsibility of (re)structuring programs to guarantee atomicity, consistency, or isolation invariants defined in a program's specification. The mismatch between the low-level semantics of locks, and the high-level reasoning programmers should apply to define concurrent applications leads to other well-known difficulties. For example, threads waiting to acquire locks held by other threads may form cycles, resulting in deadlock. Priority inversion may result if a high-priority thread must wait to enter a guarded region because a low-priority thread is already active in it. Finally, for improved performance, code must often be specially tailored to provide adequate concurrency. To manipulate a complex shared data structure like a tree or heap, applications must either impose a global locking scheme on the roots, or employ locks at lower-level nodes or leaves in the structure. The former strategy is simple, but reduces realizable concurrency and may induce false exclusion: threads wishing to access a distinct piece of the structure may nonetheless block while waiting for another thread that is accessing an unrelated piece of the structure. The latter approach permits multiple threads to access the structure simultaneously, but leads to implementation complexity, and requires more memory to hold the necessary lock state.

Recognition of these issues has prompted a number of research efforts aimed at higher-level abstract notions of concurrency that omit any definition based on mutual-exclusion locks [25,24,20,19]. In this paper, we propose *transactional monitors* as an alternative to mutual exclusion for object-oriented programming languages. Transactional monitors implement guarded regions as lightweight transactions that can be executed concurrently (or in parallel on multiprocessor platforms). Transactional monitors define the following data visibility property that preserves isolation and atomicity invariants on shared data protected by the monitor: all updates to objects guarded by a transactional monitor become visible to other threads only on successful completion of the monitor's transaction.[1]

Our work is distinguished from previous efforts in two major respects. First, we provide a semantics and detailed exploration of alternative implementation schemes for transactional monitors, all of which enforce desired isolation and atomicity properties. These different schemes are tailored to different concurrent access patterns, and permit a given application to use potentially different transactional monitor implementations in different contexts. We focus on two specific alternatives: an approach that works well when contention for shared data is low (*eg*, mostly read-only guarded regions), and a scheme better suited to handle highly concurrent accesses with a more uniform mix of

[1] A slightly weaker visibility property is present in Java for updates performed within a synchronized block (or method); these are guaranteed to be visible to other threads only upon exit from the block.

reads and updates. These alternatives reflect likely patterns of use in realistic concurrent programs.

Second, we examine the performance and scalability of these different approaches in the context of a state-of-the-art Java compiler and virtual machine, the Jikes Research Virtual Machine (RVM) [2] from IBM. Jikes RVM is an ideal platform in which to explore alternative implementations of transactional monitors, and to compare them with lock-based mutual exclusion, since Jikes already uses sophisticated strategies to minimize the overhead of traditional mutual-exclusion locks [4]. A detailed evaluation in this context provides an accurate depiction of the tradeoffs and benefits in using lightweight transactions as an alternative to lock-based mutual exclusion.

2 Overview

Unlike mutual-exclusion monitors (*eg*, synchronized blocks and methods in Java), which force threads to acquire a given monitor serially, transactional monitors require only that threads *appear* to acquire the monitor serially. Transactional monitors permit concurrent execution within the monitor so long as the effects of the resulting schedule are *serializable*. That is, the effects of concurrent execution of the monitor are equivalent to *some* serial schedule that would arise if no interleaving of different threads occurred within the guarded region. The executions are equivalent if they produce the same observable behavior; that is, all threads at any point during their execution observe the same state of the shared data. Thus, while transactional monitors and mutual-exclusion monitors have the same observable behavior, transactional monitors permit a higher degree of concurrency.

Transactional monitors maintain serializability by tracking accesses to shared data within a thread-specific *log*. When a thread attempts to release a monitor on exit from a guarded region, an attempt is made to *commit* the log. The commit operation has the effect of verifying the consistency of shared data with respect to the information recorded in the log, *atomically* performing all logged operations at once with respect to any other commit operation. If the shared data changes in such a way as to invalidate the log, the monitored code block is re-executed, and the commit retried. A log is invalidated if committing its changes would violate the serializability property of the monitored region.

For example, consider the code sample shown in Fig. 1 (using Java syntax). Thread T_1 computes the total balance of both checking and savings accounts. Thread T_2 transfers money between these accounts. Both account operations (balance and transfer) are guarded by the same `account_monitor` – the code region guarded by the monitor is delimited by curly braces following the `monitored` statement. If the account operations were unguarded, concurrent execution of these operations could potentially yield an incorrect result: the total balance computed after the withdrawal but before the deposit would not include the amount withdrawn from the checking account. If `account_monitor` were a traditional mutual-exclusion monitor, either thread T_1 or T_2 would win a race to acquire the monitor and would execute fully before releasing the monitor; regardless of the order in which they execute, the total balance computed by thread T_1 would be correct (it would in fact be the same in both cases).

T_1

```
monitored (account_monitor)
{
  balance1 = checking.getBalance();
  balance2 = savings.getBalance();
  print(balance1 + balance2);
}
```

T_2

```
monitored (account_monitor)
{
  checking.withdraw(amount);
  savings.deposit(amount);
}
```

Fig. 1. Bank account example

If `account_monitor` is a transactional monitor, two scenarios are possible, depending on the interleaving of the statements implementing the account operations. The interleaving presented in Fig. 2 results in both threads successfully committing their logs – it preserves serializability since T_2's withdrawal from the checking account does not compromise T_1's read from the savings account. This interleaving is equivalent to a serial execution in which T_1 executes before T_2.

The interleaving presented in Fig. 3 results in T_1's execution of the monitored code being aborted since T_1 reads an inconsistent state. Serializability is enforced by re-executing the guarded region of thread T_1.

	T_1	T_2
(1)	checking.getBalance	
(2)		checking.withdraw
(3)	savings.getBalance	
(4)		savings.deposit

Fig. 2. Serializable execution.

These examples illustrate several issues in formulating an implementation of transactional monitors. Threads executing within a transactional monitor must execute in *isolation*: their view of shared data on exit from the monitor must be *consistent* with their view upon entry. Isolation and consistency imply that shared state appears unchanged by other threads. A thread executing in a monitor cannot see the updates to shared state by other threads. Transactional monitor implementations must permit threads to detect state changes that violate isolation and to abort, roll-back, and restart their execution in response to such violations.

	T_1	T_2
(1)		checking.withdraw
(2)	checking.getBalance	
(3)	savings.getBalance	
(4)		savings.deposit

Fig. 3. Non-serializable execution.

In Fig. 3, the execution of thread T_1 is **not** isolated from the execution of thread T_2 since thread T_1 sees the effects of the withdrawal but does not see the effects of the deposit. Thus, T_1 is obliged to abort and re-execute its operations. In general, a thread may abort at any time within a transactional monitor. To ensure that partial results of a computation performed by a thread do not affect the execution of other threads, the execution of any monitored region must be *atomic*: either the effects of all operations performed within the monitor become visible to other threads upon successful commit or they are all discarded upon abort. The semantics of transactional monitors thus comprise the ACI (*atomicity*, *consistency*, and *isolation*) properties of a classical ACID transaction model, and their realization may be viewed as adapting optimistic concurrency control protocols [29] to concurrent object-oriented languages.

The properties of transactional monitors described here are enforced only between threads executing within the same monitor; no guarantees are provided for threads executing within different transactional monitors, nor for threads executing outside of any transactional monitor. These properties result in semantics similar to those of Java's mutual-exclusion monitors. Accesses to data shared by different threads are synchronized only if they acquire the same monitor.

3 Design

There are a number of important issues that arise in a formulating a semantics for transactional monitors:

1. *Transparency*: The degree of programmer control and visibility of internal transaction machinery influences the degree of flexibility provided by the abstraction, and the complexity of using it. For example, if a programmer is given control over how shared data accesses are tracked, objects known to be immutable need not be logged when accessed.
2. *Barrier Insertion*: A code fragment used within a guarded region to track accesses to shared data is called a *barrier*. Barriers can be inserted at the source-code level, injected into the code stream at compile time, or handled explicitly at runtime (in the case of interpreted languages).
3. *Serializability Violation Detection*: A thread executing within a guarded region may try to detect serializability violation whenever a barrier is executed, or may defer detecting such violation until a commit point (*eg*, monitor exit).
4. *Re-Execution Model*: When a region guarded by a transactional monitor aborts, the updates performed by the thread in that region must be discarded. An important

design decision is whether threads perform updates directly on shared data, reverting these updates on aborts (an undo model), or whether threads perform updates on a local journal, propagating them to the corresponding (original) shared objects upon successful commit (a redo model).

5. *Nesting*: Transaction models often permit transactions to nest freely [32], permitting division of any transaction into some number of sub-transactions. In the presence of nesting, a transactional monitor semantics must define rules on visibility of updates made by sub-transactions.

We motivate our design decisions with respect to the issues above. One of the most important principles underlying our design is transparency of the transactional monitors mechanism: an application programmer should not be concerned with how monitors are represented, nor with details of the logging mechanism, abort or commit operations. After marking a region of code at source level as guarded by a given transactional monitor, a programmer can simply rely on the underlying compiler and run-time system to ensure transactional execution of the region (satisfying the properties of atomicity, consistency, and isolation).

Our choice for the barrier placement is to have the compiler insert the barriers (rather than, for example, inserting them at the source-level). We plan to take advantage of existing compiler optimizations (*eg*, escape analysis) to be able to remove unnecessary barrier overhead automatically (*eg*, for thread-private or immutable objects).

The decision about *when* a thread should attempt to detect serializability violation is strongly dependent on the cost of detection and may vary from one implementation of transactional monitors to another. When choosing the most appropriate point for detecting serializability violations, we must consider the trade-off between reducing the overall cost of checking any serializability invariant (once if performed at the exit from the monitor, or potentially multiple times if performed in access barriers), and reducing the amount of computation performed by a thread that may eventually abort.

Our design assumes a *redo* semantics for aborts of guarded regions. Implementations must therefore provide thread-specific redo logs to enable re-execution of guarded regions. We chose a redo semantics because the space overheads related to maintaining logs is not excessive since a log (associated with a thread object) needs to be maintained only when a thread is executing within a transactional monitor, and can be discarded upon exit from the monitor. Our design requires all updates performed within a transactional monitor to be re-directed to the log, and atomically installed in the shared (globally-visible) heap upon successful commit (no action is taken upon abort).

An alternative design might consider the use of *undo* logs in which all updates are performed directly on shared data, and reverted using information from the log upon abort. However, using undo logs can lead to *cascading aborts*[2] which may severely impact overall performance, or require a global per-access locking protocol (*eg*, two-phase locking [21]) to prevent conflicting data accesses by different threads. Per-access locking also has the disadvantage of requiring deadlock detection or avoidance.

Modularity principles dictate that our design support nested transactional monitors. A given monitor region may contain a number of child monitors. Because monitors are

[2] All threads that have seen updates of a thread being aborted must be aborted as well.

released from the bottom up, child monitors must always release before their parent. Thus, a child monitor will re-execute (as needed) until it can be (successfully) released. The updates of child monitors are visible only within the scope of their parent (and, upon release of the outermost monitor, are propagated to the shared space). Updates performed by a parent monitor are always visible to the child.

4 Implementation

An implementation that directly reflects the concept behind transactional monitors would redirect all shared data accesses performed by a thread within a transactional monitor to a thread-local log. When an object is first accessed, the accessing thread records its current value in the log and refers to it for all subsequent operations. Serializability violation would be detected by traversing the log and comparing values of objects recorded in the log with those of the original. The effectiveness of this scheme depends on a number of different parameters all of which are influenced by the data access patterns that occur within the application:

- expected contention (or concurrency) at monitor entry points;
- the number of shared objects (both read and written) accessed per-thread;
- the percentage of operations that occur within a transactional monitor that are benign with respect to shared data accesses (method calls, local variable computation, type casts /etc)

Because the generic implementation is not biased towards any of these parameters, it is not clear how effectively it would perform under varying application conditions. Therefore, we consider implementations of transactional monitors optimized towards different shared data access patterns, informally described as low-contention and high-contention.

Both optimized implementations must provide a solution to logging, commit, and abort actions. These actions can be broadly classified under the following categories:

1. *Initialization*: When a transactional monitor is entered, actions to initialize logs, *etc*, may have to be taken by threads before they are allowed to enter the monitor.
2. *Read and Write Operations*: Barriers define the actions to be taken when a thread performs a read or write to an object when executing within a transactional monitor.
3. *Conflict Detection*: Conflict detection determines whether the execution of a region guarded by a given monitor is serializable with respect to the concurrent execution of other regions guarded by the same monitor and it is safe to commit changes to shared data made by a thread.
4. *Commitment*: If there are no conflicts, changes to the original objects must be committed atomically; otherwise guarded region must be re-executed.

Our current implementation does not yet include support for nested transactions.

4.1 Low-Contention Concurrency

Conceptually, transactional monitors use thread-local logs to record updates and install these updates into the original (shared) objects when a thread commits. However, if the contention on shared data accesses is low, the log is superfluous. If the number of objects concurrently written by different threads executing within the same monitor is small and the number of threads performing concurrent writes is also small [3], then reads and writes can operate directly over original data. To preserve correctness, the implementation must still prevent multiple non-serializable writes to objects and must disallow readers from seeing partial or inconsistent updates to the the objects performed by the writers.

To address these concerns, we define an implementation that stores the following information in the transactional monitor object:

- *writer*: uniquely identifies a thread currently executing within a given monitor that has performed writes to this object;
- *thread count*: number of threads concurrently operating within a given monitor.

Initialization: A thread attempting to enter the monitor must first check whether there are any active writers within the monitor. If there are no active writers, the thread can freely proceed. Otherwise, shared data is not guaranteed to be in a consistent state, and the entering thread must spin until there are no more active writers, thus achieving serializability of guarded execution.

Read and Write Barriers: Because there are no object copies or logs, there are no read barriers; threads read values from the original shared objects. Write barriers are necessary to record whether writes performed by other threads which have yet to exit the monitor have taken place. A write to a shared object can occur if one of the following conditions exist:

- The writer field in the monitor object is nil, indicating there are no active writers. In this case, the current thread atomically sets the writer field, increments the thread count, and executes the write.
- The writer field in the monitor points to the current thread. This implies that the current thread has previously written to this object within the same monitor. The current write can proceed.

If either condition fails, the thread must re-execute the monitor.

Conflict Detection: In order for the shared data operations of a thread exiting a monitor to be consistent and serializable with respect to other threads, there must be no other writers still active within this monitor besides the exiting thread. It is guaranteed (by the actions taken in the write barrier) that if the exiting thread performed any writes when executing within a monitor, it is the only active writer within this monitor. If the guarded region executed by the exiting thread was read-only and there is an active writer still executing within the monitor, it implies that the exiting thread might have seen an

[3] An example of the low-contention scenario could be multiple mostly read-only threads traversing a tree-like structure or accessing a hash-table

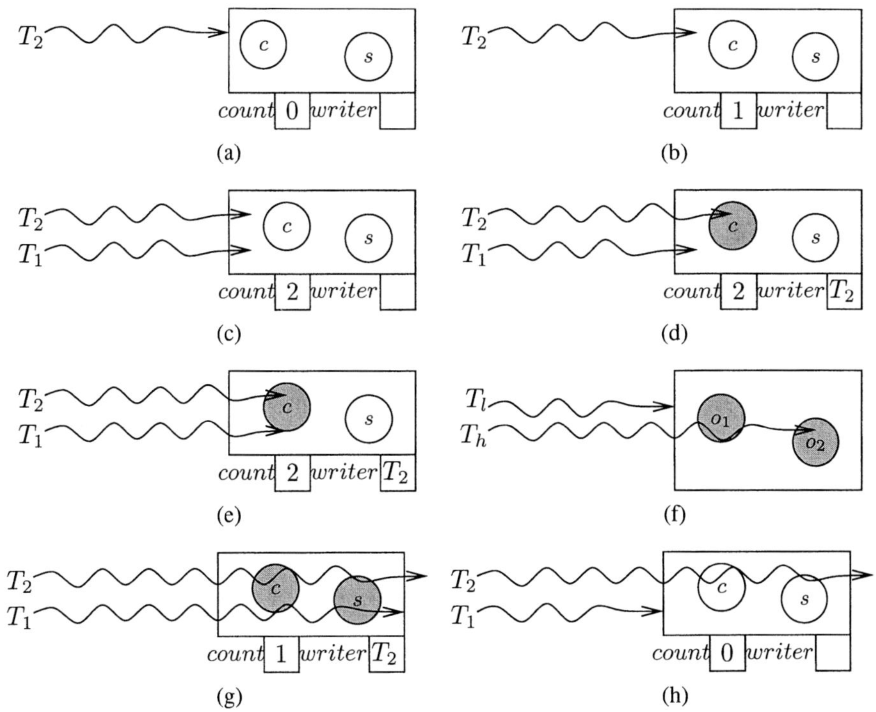

Fig. 4. Low contention scheme example

inconsistent state which leads to a conflict. If the execution was read-only and there are no active writers, it implies that any threads concurrently executing within the monitor have performed only reads and no conflicts were possible.

Monitor Exit: Any thread that exits a transactional monitor must atomically decrement the thread count. When a writer exits a monitor, it must first check whether the thread count is one. A number greater than one indicates that there are still other active threads executing within a monitor. To ensure that these threads are aware that writes have occurred when they perform conflict detection, the writer field cannot be reset. The last thread to exit the monitor as part of the monitor exit procedure will decrement the count to zero, and reset the writer field. Since there are no copies or logs, all updates are immediately visible in the original copy.

The actions performed in this scheme executing the account example from Fig. 3 is illustrated in Fig. 4, where wavy lines represent threads T_1 and T_2, circles represent objects c (checking account) and s (saving account), updated objects are marked gray. The large box represents the dynamic scope of a common transactional monitor *account_monitor* guarding code regions executed by the threads and small boxes represent additional information associated with the monitor: writer field (initially nil) and thread count (initially 0). In Fig. 4(a) thread T_2 is about to enter the monitor, which it does in Fig. 4(b) incrementing thread count. In Fig. 4(c) thread T_1 also enters the monitor and increments thread count. In Fig. 4(d) thread T_2 updates object c and sets the writer to itself. Subsequently thread T_1 reads object c (Fig. 4(e)), thread T_2 updates object s and exits the monitor (Fig. 4(f)) (no conflicts are detected since there were no intervening writes on behalf of other threads executing within the monitor). Thread count gets decremented but the writer cannot be reset since thread T_1 is still executing within the monitor. In Fig. 4(g) thread T_1 reads object s and attempts to exit the monitor, but the writer field still points to thread T_2 indicating a potential conflict[4] – guarded region of thread T_1 must be re-executed. Since thread T_1 is the last one to exit the monitor, in addition to decrementing thread count it also resets the writer field.

4.2 High-Contention Concurrency

When there is notable contention for shared data, the previous strategy is not likely to perform well because attempts to execute multiple writes even to distinct objects result in a conflict, and subsequent aborts of all but one writer executing within the same monitor. We can relax this restriction by allowing threads to manipulate *copies* of shared objects, committing their changes when it does not conflict with other shared data operations [5]. This implementation is closer to the conceptual idea underlying transactional monitors: updates and accesses performed by a thread are tracked within a log, and committed only when serializability of a guarded region's execution is not compromised. However, since applications tend to perform a lot more reads than writes, we decided to use a copy-on-write strategy [6] to reduce the cost of read operations (trading it for a potential loss of precision in detecting serializability violations).

In this scheme, the following information is stored in each monitor:

- *global write map*: identifies objects written by threads executing within the monitor. This map is implemented as a bitmap with a bit being set for every modified object. The mapping is conservative and multiple objects can potentially be hashed into the same bit;
- *thread count*: number of threads concurrently operating within a transactional monitor.

The monitor object also contains information about whether any thread executing within a monitor has already managed to install its updates. The global write map and thread count can be combined into one data structure with the thread count occupying the n lowest bits of the write map. In addition to the data stored in the monitor object, the header of every object is extended to hold the following information:

- *copies*: circular list of the object copies created by threads executing within transactional monitors (original object is the head of the list)
- *writer*: if the object is copy generated by a T within a transactional monitor, this field contains a reference to T.

---

[4] This example is based on the interleaving of operations where the conflict really exists (serializability property is violated)

[5] An example of the high-contention scenario could be multiple threads traversing disjoint subtrees of a tree-like structure or accessing different buckets in a hash-table

[6] Instead of creating copies on both reads and writes

There is also the following (local) information associated with every thread:

- *local writes*: list of object copies created by a given thread when executing within a transactional monitor;
- *local read map*: identifies objects read by a given thread when executing within a monitor (implemented in the same way as the global write map), and is used for conflict detection;
- *local write map*: identifies objects written by a given thread when executing within a monitor (implemented the same way as the global write map), and is used to optimize read and write barriers.

Initialization: The first thread attempting to enter a monitor must initialize the monitor by initializing the global write map and setting the thread counter to one. Any subsequent thread entering the monitor simply increments the thread counter and is immediately allowed to enter the monitor, provided that no thread has yet committed its updates. If the updates have already been installed, the remaining threads still executing within the monitor are allowed to continue their execution, but no more threads are allowed to enter the monitor (they spin) to allow for the global write map to be cleaned up (otherwise out-dated information about updates performed within the monitor could be retained for indefinite amount of time forcing entering threads to repeatedly abort). Each thread entering a monitor must also initialize its local data structures.

Read and Write Barriers: The barriers implement a copy-on-write semantics. The following actions are taken on writing an object:

- If the bit in the local write map representing the object is not set, *ie*, the current thread has not yet written to this object, a copy of the original object is created [7], the local write map is tagged, and the write is redirected to the copy.
- If the bit in the local write map representing the object is set, *ie*, the current thread has potentially (it is a conservative mapping because of our hash construction) written to this object, the copy is located by traversing the list of copies to find the one created by the current thread. Otherwise, a new copy is created and the write is redirected to the copy.

The following actions are taken on reading an object:

- If the bit in the local write map representing the object is not set, *ie*, the current thread has not yet written to this object, read from the original object, tag the local read map end exit the barrier.
- If the bit in the local write map representing the object is set, *ie*, the current thread has potentially written to this object, and a copy of the object created by this thread exists, the contents of this copy is read. If no such copy exists because the thread did not actually write to it, the contents of the original object is read.

[7] Creation of a copy also involves inserting this copy to the appropriate copy and local write lists.

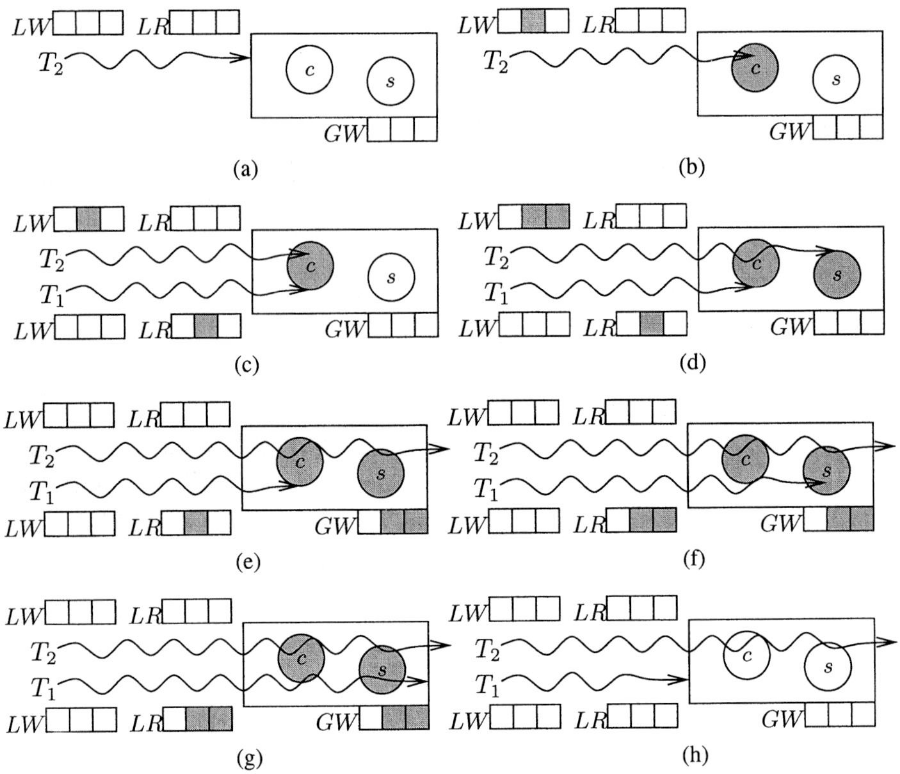

Fig. 5. High contention scheme example

Conflict Detection: When a thread exits the monitor, a conflict detection algorithm checks if the global write map associated with the monitor object is disjoint for the local read map associated with the thread. If so, it means that no reads of the current thread were interleaved with the committed writes of other threads executing within the same monitor; otherwise a potentially harmful interleaving could occur violating serializability – guarded region must be re-executed. (The global write map gets updated after a thread installs its local updates into the shared objects.)

Monitor Exit: If a thread is allowed to commit, all updates to copies (accessible from the local writes list) performed during monitored execution must be installed in the original objects and the local write map must be merged with the global write map to reflect writes performed by the current thread (both these operations must be performed atomically with respect to other threads potentially exiting the same monitor at the same time). Regardless of whether a thread is committing or aborting, all the lists containing copies created by this thread must be at this point updated. An exiting thread must also decrement the thread counter and free the monitor if the counter reaches zero (no active threads executing within the monitor).

The actions performed in this scheme executing the account example from Fig. 3 is illustrated in Fig. 5, where wavy lines represent threads T_1 and T_2, circles represent objects c (checking account) and s (saving account), updated objects are marked gray, and the box represents the dynamic scope of a common transactional monitor $account\_monitor$ guarding code regions executed by the threads. Both global write map (GW) associated with the monitor and local maps (local write map LW and local read map LR) associated with each thread have three slots. Local maps above the wavy line representing thread T_2 belong to T_2 and local maps below the wavy line representing thread T_1 belong to T_1. In Fig. 5(a) thread T_2 is about to enter the monitor, which it does in Fig. 5(b), modifying object c. Object c is shaded and information about the update gets reflected in the local write map of T_2 (we assume that object c hashes into the second slot of the map). In Fig. 5(c) thread T_1 enters the same monitor and reads object c (the read operation gets reflected in the local read map of T_1). In Fig. 5(d) thread T_2 modifies object s, object s gets shaded and the update also gets reflected in T_2's local write map (we assume that object s hashes into the third slot of the map). In Fig. 5(e) thread T_2 exits the monitor. Since no conflicts are detected (there were no intervening writes on behalf of other threads executing within the monitor), T_2 installs its updates, modifies the global write map to reflect updates performed within the guarded region and resets its local maps. Thread T_1 subsequently reads object s marking its local read map (Fig 5(f)) and attempts to exit the monitor (Fig. 5(g)). In the case of thread T_1 however its local read map and the global write map overlap indicating a potential conflict[8]; thus, the guarded region of thread T_1 must be re-executed (Fig. 5(h)). Since thread T_1 is the last thread to exit the monitor, in addition to reseting its local maps, it also frees the monitor by resetting the global write map.

5 Experimental Evaluation

We validate the effectiveness of transactional monitors in a prototype implementation for IBM's Jikes Research Virtual Machine (RVM) [2]. The Jikes RVM is a state-of-the-art Java virtual machine with performance comparable to many production virtual machines. It is itself written almost entirely in Java and is self-hosted (*ie*, it does not require another virtual machine to run). Java bytecodes in the Jikes RVM are compiled directly to machine code. The Jikes RVM's public distribution includes both a "baseline" and optimizing compiler. The "baseline" compiler performs a straightforward expansion of each individual bytecode into a corresponding sequence of assembly instructions. The optimizing compiler generates high quality code due in part to sophisticated optimizations implemented at various levels of intermediate representation, and because it uses adaptive compilation techniques [3] to selectively target code best suited for optimizations. Our transactional monitors prototype targets the Intel x86 architecture.

---

[8] This example is also based on the interleaving of operations where the conflict really exists and serializability invariants are violated)

5.1 Java-Specific Issues

Realizing transactional monitors for Java requires reconciling their implementation with Java-specific features such as native method calls, existing thread synchronization mechanisms (including the `wait`/`notify` primitives). We now briefly elaborate on these issues.

Native Methods: In general, the effects of executing a native method cannot be undone. Thus, we disallow execution of native methods within regions guarded by transactional monitors. However, it is possible to relax this restriction in certain cases. For example, if the effects of executing a native method do not escape the thread (*eg*, a call to obtain the current system time), it can safely execute within a guarded region. In the abstract, it may be possible to provide compensation code to be invoked when a transaction aborts that will revert the effects of the native method calls executed within the transaction. However, our current implementation does not provide such functionality. Instead, when a native method call occurs inside the dynamic context protected by a transactional monitor, a commit operation is attempted for the updates performed up to that point. If the commit fails, then the monitor re-executes, discarding all its updates. If the commit succeeds, the updates are retained, and execution reverts to mutual-exclusion semantics: a conventional mutual-exclusion lock is acquired for the remainder of the monitor. Any other thread that attempts to commit its changes while the lock is held must abort. Any thread that attempts to enter the monitor while the lock is held must wait.

Existing Synchronization Mechanisms: Double guarding a code fragment with both a transactional monitor and a mutual-exclusion monitor (expressed using `synchronized` methods or blocks) does not strengthen existing serializability guarantees. Indeed, code protected in such a manner will behave correctly. However, the visibility rule for mutual-exclusion monitors embedded within a transactional monitor will change with respect to the original Java memory model: all updates performed within a region guarded by a mutual-exclusion monitor become visible only upon commit of the transactional monitor guarding that region.

Wait-Notify: We allow invocation of `wait` and `notify` methods inside of a region guarded by a transactional monitor, provided that they are also guarded by a mutual-exclusion monitor (and invoked on the object representing that mutual-exclusion monitor [9]). Invoking `wait` releases the corresponding mutual-exclusion monitor and the current thread waits for notification, but updates performed so far do not become visible until the thread resumes and exits the transactional monitor. Invoking `notify` postpones the effects of notification until exit from the transactional monitor. [10]

[9] This requirement is identical to the original Java execution semantics – a thread invoking wait or notify must hold the corresponding monitor.

[10] Notification modifies the shared state of a program and is therefore subject to the same visibility rules as other shared updates.

5.2 Compiler Support

Transactional monitors are implemented in both optimizing and "baseline" compilers. This is necessary because Jikes RVM configured to use only the optimizing compiler may still have certain methods (*eg*, class initializers) compiled by the "baseline" compiler. The implementation for both compilers is analogous. For the sake of brevity, our description here is limited to modifications to the optimizing compiler.

Barriers: Read and write barriers conceptually consist of two parts: (1) a check to determine if the operation occurs inside the dynamic context of a transactional monitor, and (2) if so, the actions to be undertaken to support a specific implementation strategy as described earlier. An inlined static method first checks whether any special processing of the operation is required. If the current thread is executing inside of RVM code or transactional monitors are turned off (*eg*, during RVM startup), no further action is required. Code for read and write barriers is inserted at an early stage of compilation allowing the compiler to apply appropriate optimizations during subsequent compilation stages.

Re-execution of a Guarded Region: When a thread attempts to commit its updates within a region guarded by a transactional monitor, and a conflict is detected, the thread must abort its changes and re-execute the region. Our implementation adapts the Jikes RVM exception handling mechanism to return control to the beginning of the aborted region and uses bytecode rewriting[11] to save program state (values of local variables and method parameters) for restoration on re-execution. Each code region guarded by a transactional monitor is wrapped within an exception scope that catches an internal *rollback* exception. The rollback exception is thrown internally by the RVM, but the code to catch it (implementing re-execution) is injected into the bytecode stream. We also modify the compiler and run-time system to suppress generation (and invocation) of "default" exception handlers during a rollback operation. The "default" handlers include both `finally` blocks, and `catch` blocks for exceptions of type `Throwable`, of which all exceptions (including *rollback*) are instances. Running these intervening handlers would violate the requirement that an aborted synchronized block produce no side-effects.

5.3 Benchmark

To evaluate the performance of the prototype implementation, we chose a multi-threaded version of the OO7 object operations benchmark [14], originally developed in the database community. Our incarnation of OO7 benchmark uses modified traversal routines to allow parameterization of synchronization and concurrency behavior. We have selected this benchmark because it provides a great deal of flexibility in the choice of runtime parameters (*eg*, percentage of reads and writes to shared data performed by the application) and extended it to allow control over placement of synchronization primitives and the amount of contention on data access. When choosing OO7 for our

[11] We use the Bytecode Engineering Library (BCEL) from Apache for this purpose.

measurements, our goal was to accurately gauge various trade-offs inherent with different implementations of transactional monitors, rather than emulating workloads of selected potential applications. Thus, we believe the benchmark captures essential features of scalable concurrent programs that can be used to quantify the impact of the design decisions underlying a transactional monitor implementation.

The benchmark operates on a synthetic design database consisting of a set of composite parts (see Fig. 6). Each composite part consists of a graph of atomic parts and a document object. Composite parts are arranged in an assembly hierarchy, called a module. Each assembly contains either composite parts (base assemblies) or other assemblies (composite assemblies).

The multi-threaded workload consists of multiple threads running a set of parameterized traversals composed of primitive operations. A traversal chooses a single path through the assembly hierarchy and at the composite part level randomly chooses a fixed number of composite parts to visit. When the traversal reaches the composite part, it has two choices: (a) it may perform read-only traversal of a graph of atomic parts; or, (b) it may perform read-write traversal of a graph of atomic parts, swapping certain scalar fields in each atomic part visited. To foster some degree of interesting interleaving and contention, the benchmark defines a parameter that allows overhead to be added to read operations to increase the time spent performing traversals.

Our implementation of OO7 conforms to the standard OO7 database specification. Our traversals differ from the original OO7 traversals in allowing multiple composite parts to be visited during a single traversal rather than just one as in the original specification, and in allowing entry of monitors at various levels of the database hierarchy.

Component	Number
Modules	1
Assembly levels	7
Subassemblies per complex assembly	3
Composite parts per assembly	3
Composite parts per module	500
Atomic parts per composite part	20
Connections per atomic part	3
Document size (bytes)	2000
Manual size (bytes)	100000

Fig. 6. Component organization of the OO7 benchmark.

5.4 Measurements

Our measurements were taken on an eight-way 700MHz Intel Pentium III with 2GB of RAM running Linux kernel version 2.4.20-20.9 (RedHat 9.0) in single-user mode. We ran each benchmark configuration in its own invocation of RVM, repeating the benchmark six times in each invocation, and discarding the results of the first iteration,

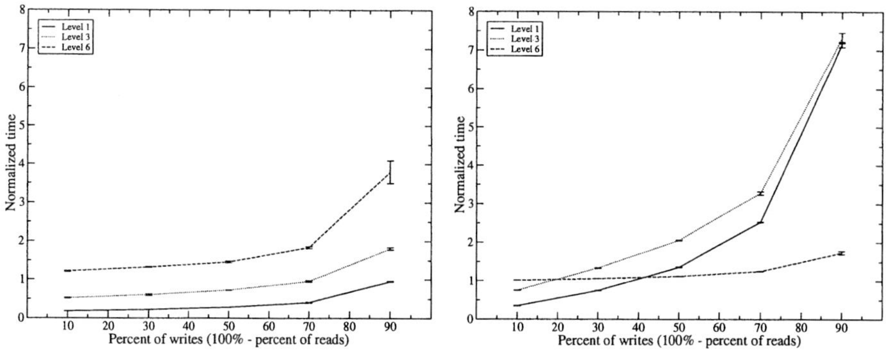

(a) high-contention (b) low-contention

Fig. 7. Normalized execution time for 64 threads running on 8 processors

in which the benchmark classes are loaded and compiled, to eliminate the overheads of compilation.

When running the benchmarks we varied the following parameters:

- number of threads competing for shared data access along with the number of processors executing the threads: we ran $P * 8$ threads (where P is the number of processors) for $P = 1, 2, 4, 8$.
- ratio of shared reads to shared writes: from 10% shared reads and 90% shared writes (mostly read-only guarded regions) to 90% shared reads and 10% shared writes (mostly write-only guarded regions)
- level of the benchmark database at which monitors were entered: level one (module level), level three (second layer of composite parts) and level six (fifth layer of composite parts)

Every thread performed 1000 traversals (entered 1000 guarded regions) and visited 2000k atomic parts during each iteration.

5.5 Results

The expected behavior for transactional monitor implementations optimized for low-contention applications is one in which performance is maximized when contention on guarded shared data accesses is low, for example, if most operations in guarded regions are reads. The expected behavior for transactional monitor implementations optimized for high-contention applications is one in which performance is maximized when contention on guarded shared data accesses is moderate, the operations protected by the monitor contain a mix of reads and writes, and concurrently executing threads do not often attempt concurrent updates of the *same* object. Potential performance improvements over a mutual-exclusion implementation arise from the improved scalability that should be observable when executing on multi-processor platforms.

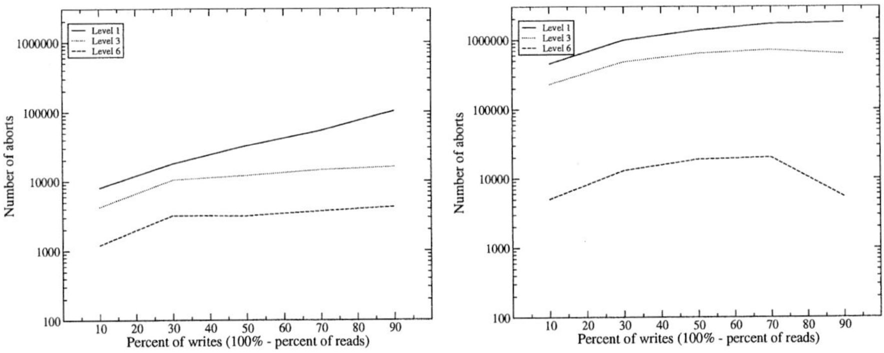

(a) high-contention (b) low-contention

Fig. 8. Total number of aborts for 64 threads running on 8 processors

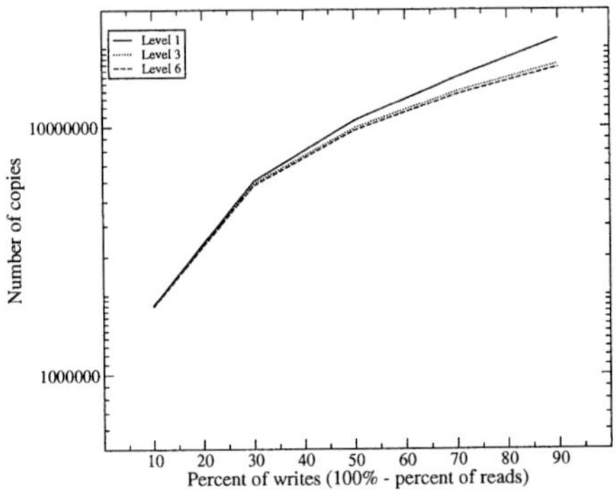

Fig. 9. Total number of copies created for 64 threads running on 8 processors

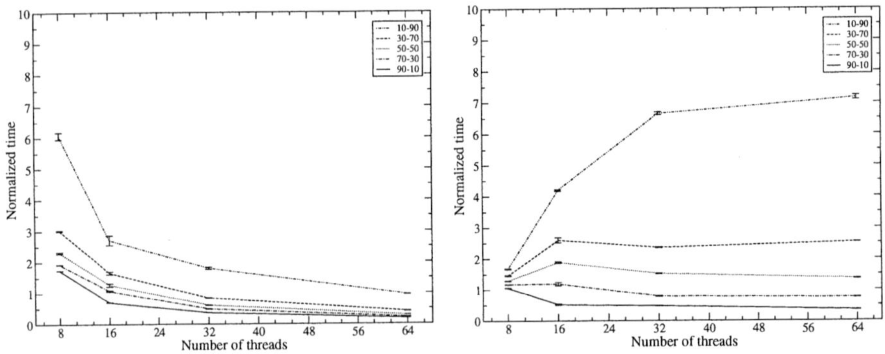

(a) high-contention (b) low-contention

Fig. 10. Normalized execution times – monitor entries at level 1

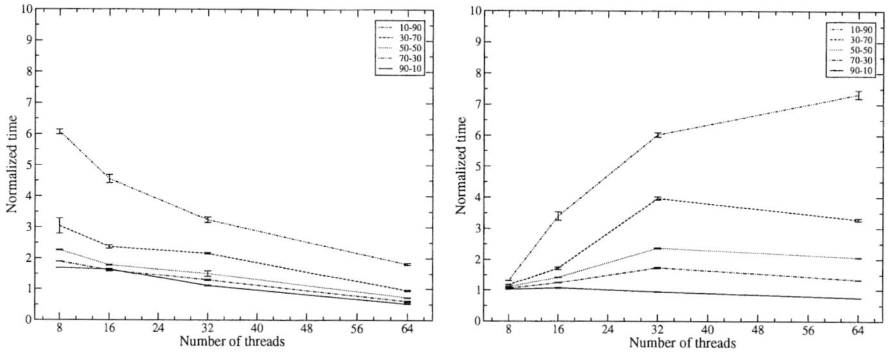

(a) high-contention (b) low-contention

Fig. 11. Normalized execution times – monitor entries at level 3

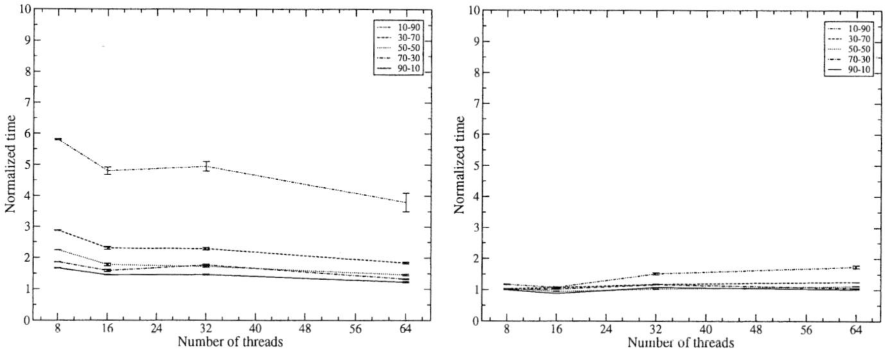

(a) high-contention (b) low-contention

Fig. 12. Normalized execution times – monitor entries at level 6

Our experimental results confirm these hypotheses. Contention on shared data accesses depends on the number of updates performed within guarded regions combined with the amount of contention on entering monitors [12]. Fig. 7 plots execution time for 64 threads running on 8 processors for the high-contention scheme (Fig. 7(a)) and low-contention scheme (Fig. 7(b)) normalized to the execution time for standard mutual-exclusion monitors [13], while varying the ratio of shared reads and writes and the level at which monitors are entered. It is important to note that only monitor entries at levels one and three creates any reasonable contention (and thus on shared data accesses) – at level six the probability of two threads concurrently entering the same monitor is very low (thus no performance benefit can be expected). In Fig. 7(a) we see the high-contention scheme outperforming mutual-exclusion monitors for *all* configurations when monitors

[12] Threads contend on entering a monitor only if they enter the *same* monitor

[13] To obtain results for the mutual-exclusion case we used an unmodified version of Jikes RVM (no compiler or run-time modifications). Figures reporting execution times show 90% confidence intervals in our results.

are entered at level one. When monitors are entered at level three, the high-contention scheme outperforms mutual-exclusion monitors for the configurations where write operations constitute 70% of all data operations. For larger write ratios, the number of aborts and the number of copies created during guarded execution overcome any potential benefit from increased concurrency.

The low-contention scheme's performance is illustrated in Fig. 7(b): it outperforms mutual-exclusion monitors for configurations where write operations constitute 30% of all data operations (low contention on shared data accesses). The total number of aborts across all iterations for both high-contention scheme and low-contention scheme appears in Fig. 8(a-b). The total number of copies created across all iterations for the high-contention scheme appears in Fig. 9. The remaining graphs illustrate the scalability of both schemes by plotting normalized execution times for the high-contention scheme (Figs. 10-12(a)) and low-contention scheme (Figs. 10-12(b)) when varying the number of threads (and processors) for monitor entries placed at levels one, three, and six (Figs. 10-12, respectively).

6 Related Work

Several recent efforts explore alternatives to lock-based concurrent programming. Harris *et al* [24] introduce a new synchronization construct to Java called *atomic* that is superficially similar to our transactional monitors. The idea behind the atomic construct is that logically only one thread appears to execute *any* atomic section at a time. However, it is unclear how to translate their abstract semantic definition into a practical implementation. For example, a complex data structure enclosed within *atomic* is subject to a costly *validation* check, even though operations on the structure may occur on separate disjoint parts. We regard our work as a significant extension and refinement of their approach, especially with respect to understanding implementation issues related to the effectiveness of new concurrency abstractions on realistic multi-threaded applications. Thus, we focus on a detailed quantitative study to measure the cost of logging, commits, aborts, *etc*; we regard such an exercise as critical to validate the utility of these higher-level abstractions on scalable platforms.

Lock-free data structures [35,28] and transactional memory [26,38] are also closely related to transactional monitors. Herlihy *et al* [25] present a solution closest in spirit to transactional monitors. They introduce an form of software transactional memory that allows for the implementation of *obstruction-free* (a weaker incarnation of lock-free) data structures. However, because shared data accesses performed in a transactional context are limited to statically pre-defined *transactional objects*, their solution is less general than the dynamic protection afforded by transactional monitors. Moreover, the overheads of their implementation are also unclear. They compare the performance of operations on an obstruction-free red-black tree only with respect to other lock-free implementations of the same data structure, disregarding potential competition from a carefully crafted implementation using mutual-exclusion locks. The notion of transactional lock removal proposed by Rajwar and Goodman [35] also shares similar goals with our work, but their implementation relies on hardware support.

Rinard [37] describes experimental results using low-level optimistic concurrency primitives in the context of an optimizing parallelizing compiler that generates parallel C++ programs from unannotated serial C++ source. Unlike a general transaction facility of the kind described here, his optimistic concurrency implementation does not ensure atomic commitment of multiple variables. Moreover in contrast to a low-level facility, the code protected by transactional monitors may span an arbitrary dynamic context.

There has been much recent interest in data race detection for Java. Some approaches [7,8] present new type systems using, for example, ownership types [17] to verify the absence of data races and deadlock. Recent work on generalizing type systems allows reasoning about higher-level atomicity properties of concurrent programs that subsumes data race detection [20,19]. Other techniques [41] employ static analyses such as escape analysis along with runtime instrumentation that meters accesses to synchronized data. Transactional monitors share similar goals with these efforts but differ in some important respects. In particular, our approach does not rely on global analysis, programmer annotations, or alternative type systems. While it replaces lock-based implementations of synchronization sections, the set of schedules it allows is not identical to that supported by lock-based schemes. Indeed, transactional monitors ensure preservation of atomicity and serializability properties in guarded regions without enforcing a rigid schedule that prohibits benign concurrent access to shared data. In this respect, they can be viewed as a starting point for an implementation that supports higher-level atomic operations.

Incorporating explicit concurrency abstractions within high-level languages has a long history [22,23,18,9,36], as does deriving parallelism from unannotated programs either through compiler analysis [31] or through explicit annotations and pragmas [39]. Our ideas differ from these efforts insofar as we are concerned with providing abstractions that simplify the complexity of locking and synchronization. Although we do not elaborate on this point in this paper, we believe transactional monitors can be generalized to serve as a building block upon which higher-level concurrency abstractions can be defined and implemented. We believe such an approach might profitably be used as part of a Java-centric operating system.

There have been several attempts to reduce locking overhead in Java. Agesen *et al* [1] and Bacon *et al* [4] describe locking implementations for Java that attempt to optimize lock acquisition overhead when there is no contention on a shared object. Transactional monitors obviate the need for a multi-tiered locking algorithm by allowing multiple threads to execute simultaneously within guarded regions provided that updates are serializable.

Finally, the formal specification of various flavors of transactions has received much attention [30,16,21]. Black *et al* [6] present a theory of transactions that specifies atomicity, isolation and durability properties in the form of an equivalence relation on processes. Choithia and Duggan [15] present the pik-calculus and pike-calculus as extensions of the pi-calculus that support abstractions for distributed transactions and optimistic concurrency. Their work is related to other efforts [10] that encode transaction-style semantics into the pi-calculus and its variants. The work of Busi, Gorrieri and Zavattaro [11] and Busi and Zavattaro [13] formalize the semantics of JavaSpaces, a transactional coordination language for Linda, and discuss the semantics of important extensions such as leasing [12]. Berger and Honda [5] examine extensions to the pi-calculus to handle various forms of distributed computation include aspects of transactional processing such as two-phase commit protocols for handling commit actions in the presence of node failures. We have recently applied the ideas presented here to define an optimistic concurrency (transaction-like) semantics for a Linda-like coordination language that addresses scalability limitations in these other approaches [27]. A formalization of a general transaction semantics for programming languages expressive enough to capture the behavior of transactional monitors is presented in [40].

References

1. Ole Agesen, David Detlefs, Alex Garthwaite, Ross Knippel, Y. S. Ramakrishna, and Derek White. An efficient meta-lock for implementing ubiquitous synchronization. In OOPSLA'99 [34], pages 207–222.
2. Bowen Alpern, C. R. Attanasio, John J. Barton, Anthony Cocchi, Susan Flynn Hummel, Derek Lieber, Ton Ngo, Mark Mergen, Janice C. Shepherd, and Stephen Smith. Implementing Jalapeño in Java. In OOPSLA'99 [34], pages 314–324.
3. Matthew Arnold, Stephen J. Fink, David Grove, Michael Hind, and Peter F. Sweeney. Adaptive optimization in the Jalapeño JVM. In *Proceedings of the ACM Conference on Object-Oriented Programming Systems, Languages, and Applications*, volume 35, pages 47–65, October 2000.
4. David Bacon, Ravi Konuru, Chet Murthy, and Mauricio Serrano. Thin locks: Featherweight synchronization for Java. In *Proceedings of the ACM Conference on Programming Language Design and Implementation*, volume 33, pages 258–268, May 1998.
5. Martin Berger and Kohei Honda. The Two-Phase Commitment Protocol in an Extended pi-Calculus. In Luca Aceto and Bjorn Victor, editors, *Electronic Notes in Theoretical Computer Science*, volume 39. Elsevier, 2003.
6. Andrew Black, Vincent Cremet, Rachid Guerraoui, and Martin Odersky. An equational theory for transactions. Technical Report CSE 03-007, Department of Computer Science, OGI School of Science and Engineering, 2003.
7. Chandrasekhar Boyapati, Robert Lee, and Martin C. Rinard. Ownership types for safe programming: preventing data races and deadlocks. In *Proceedings of the ACM Conference on Object-Oriented Programming Systems, Languages, and Applications*, volume 37, pages 211–230, November 2002.
8. Chandrasekhar Boyapati and Martin Rinard. A parameterized type system for race-free Java programs. In OOPSLA'01 [33], pages 56–69.
9. Silvia Breitinger, Rita Loogen, Yolanda Ortega-Mallén, and Ricardo Pena. The Eden coordination model for distributed memory systems. In *High-Level Parallel Programming Models and Supportive Environments (HIPS)*. IEEE Press, 1997.
10. R. Bruni, C. Laneve, and U. Montanari. Orchestrating transactions in the join calculus. In Lubos Brim, Mojmír Kretíský Petr Jancar, and Antonín Kucera, editors, *International Conferenec on Concurrency Theory*, volume 2421 of *Lecture Notes in Computer Science*, pages 321–337, 2002.
11. Nadia Busi, Roberto Gorrieri, and Gianluigi Zavattaro. On the Semantics of JavaSpaces. In *Formal Methods for Open Object-Based Distributed Systems IV*, volume 177. Kluwer, 2000.
12. Nadia Busi, Roberto Gorrieri, and Gianluigi Zavattaro. Temporary Data in Shared Dataspace Coordination Languages. In *FOSSACS'01*, pages 121–136. Springer-Verlag, 2001.
13. Nadia Busi and Gianluigi Zavattaro. On the serializability of transactions in JavaSpaces. In *Proc. of International Workshop on Concurrency and Coordination (CONCOORD'01)*. Electronic Notes in Theoretical Computer Science 54, Elsevier, 2001.

14. Michael J. Carey, David J. DeWitt, and Jeffrey F. Naughton. The OO7 benchmark. In *Proceedings of the ACM International Conference on Management of Data*, volume 22, pages 12–21, June 1993.
15. Tom Choithia and Dominic Duggan. Abstractions for fault-tolerant computing. Technical Report 2003-3, Department of Computer Science, Stevens Institute of Technology, 2003.
16. Panos Chrysanthis and Krithi Ramamritham. Synthesis of extended transaction models using ACTA. *ACM Transactions on Database Systems*, 19(3):450–491, 1994.
17. David G. Clarke, John M. Potter, and James Noble. Ownership types for flexible alias protection. In *Proceedings of the ACM Conference on Object-Oriented Programming Systems, Languages, and Applications*, volume 33, pages 48–64, October 1998.
18. Cormac Flanagan and Matthias Felleisen. The semantics of future and its use in program optimizations. In *Conference Record of the ACM Symposium on Principles of Programming Languages*, pages 209–220, 1995.
19. Cormac Flanagan and Stephen N. Freund. Type-based race detection for Java. In *Proceedings of the ACM Conference on Programming Language Design and Implementation*, volume 35, pages 219–232, June 2000.
20. Cormac Flanagan and Shaz Qadeer. Types for atomicity. In *Proceedings of the 2003 ACM SIGPLAN International Workshop on Types in Language Design and Implementation*, pages 1–12, 2003.
21. Jim Gray and Andreas Reuter. *Transaction Processing: Concepts and Techniques*. Data Management Systems. Morgan Kaufmann, 1993.
22. Robert H. Halstead, Jr. Multilisp: A language for concurrent symbolic computation. *ACM Transactions on Programming Languages and Systems*, 7(4):501–538, October 1985.
23. K. Hammond and G. Michaelson, editors. *Research Directions in Parallel Functional Programming*. Springer-Verlag, 1999.
24. Tim Harris and Keir Fraser. Language support for lightweight transactions. In *Proceedings of the ACM Conference on Object-Oriented Programming Systems, Languages, and Applications*, volume 38, pages 388–402, November 2003.
25. Maurice Herlihy, Victor Luchangco, Mark Moir, and William N. Scherer, III. Software transactional memory for dynamic-sized data structures. In *Proceedings of the Annual ACM Symposium on Principles of Distributed Computing*, pages 92–101, 2003.
26. Antony L. Hosking and J. Eliot B. Moss. Object fault handling for persistent programming languages: A performance evaluation. In *Proceedings of the ACM Conference on Object-Oriented Programming Systems, Languages, and Applications*, volume 28, pages 288–303, October 1993.
27. Suresh Jagannathan and Jan Vitek. Optimistic Concurrency Semantics for Transactions in Coordination Languages. In *Coordination Models and Languages*, volume 2949 of *Lecture Notes in Computer Science*, pages 183–198, 2004.
28. E. H. Jensen, G. W. Hagensen, and J. M. Broughton. A new approach to exclusive data access in shared memory multiprocessors. Technical report, Lawrence Livermore National Laboratories, 1987.
29. H. T. Kung and J. T. Robinson. On optimistic methods for concurrency control. *ACM Transactions on Database Systems*, 9(4):213–226, June 1981.
30. Nancy Lynch, Michael Merritt, William Weihl, and Alan Fekete. *Atomic Transactions*. Morgan Kaufmann, 1994.
31. G. Michaelson, N. Scaife, P. Bristow, and P. King. Nested algorithmic skeletons from higher order functions. *Parallel Algorithms and Applications*, 2000. Special issue on High Level Models and Languages for Parallel Processing.
32. J. Eliot B. Moss. *Nested Transactions: An Approach to Reliable Distributed Computing*. MIT Press, Cambridge, Massachusetts, 1985.

33. *Proceedings of the ACM Conference on Object-Oriented Programming Systems, Languages, and Applications*, volume 36, November 2001.
34. *Proceedings of the ACM Conference on Object-Oriented Programming Systems, Languages, and Applications*, volume 34, October 1999.
35. Ravi Rajwar and James R Goodman. Transactional lock-free execution of lock-based programs. In *Proceedings of the ACM International Conference on Architectural Support for Programming Languages and Operating Systems*, volume 37, pages 5–17, October 2002.
36. John Reppy. *Concurrent Programming in ML.* Cambridge University Press, 1999.
37. Martin Rinard. Effective fine-grained synchronization for automatically parallelized programs using optimistic synchronization primitives. *ACM Transactions on Computer Systems*, 17(4):337–371, November 1999.
38. Nir Shavit and Dan Touitou. Software transactional memory. In *Proceedings of the Annual ACM Symposium on Principles of Distributed Computing*, pages 204–213, 1995.
39. Philip W. Trinder, Kevin Hammond, Hans-Wolfgang Loidl, and Simon L. Peyton Jones. Algorithms + strategy = parallelism. *Journal of Functional Programming*, 8(1):23–60, 1998.
40. Jan Vitek, Suresh Jagannathan, Adam Welc, and Antony L. Hosking. A semantic framework for designer transactions. In David E. Schmidt, editor, *Proceedings of the European Symposium on Programming*, volume 2986 of *Lecture Notes in Computer Science*, pages 249–263, 2004.
41. Christoph von Praun and Thomas R. Gross. Object race detection. In OOPSLA'01 [33], pages 70–82.

Adaptive Tuning of Reserved Space in an Appel Collector

José Manuel Velasco, Katzalin Olcoz, and Francisco Tirado

Complutense University, Madrid. Spain.
mvelascc@fis.ucm.es
Katzalin@dacya.ucm.es
ptirado@dacya.ucm.es

Abstract. The use of automatic memory management in object-oriented languages like Java is becoming widely accepted because of its software engineering benefits, its reduction of programming time and its safety aspects. Nevertheless, the complexity of garbage collection results in an important time cost for the virtual machine's job. Until now, garbage collection strategies have focused on analyzing and adjusting regions in the heap based on different approaches and algorithms. Each strategy has its own distinct advantages over the others depending on the data behavior of a specific application, but none succeeds in taking advantage of all available resources for all application behaviors. In this paper, we present and evaluate two adaptive strategies based on data lifetime that reallocate at run time the reserved space in the nursery of generational Appel collectors. The adaptive tuning of reserved space produces a drastic reduction in the number of collections and the total collection time, and has a clear effect on the final execution time.

1 Introduction

The automatic recycling of used memory blocks is one of the most attractive characteristics of Java for both the programmer and the software engineer. This process, known as garbage collection (GC), makes the development of applications agile and facilitates the cohesion between independent modules. Nevertheless, due to its complexity, GC is a critical time consumer in the virtual machine.

There is no optimal collection policy for all types of programs, languages and restrictions of memory. Thus, the designers of each virtual machine have to decide on one strategy or another.

Generational collectors [1] with a copying policy in the nursery take advantage of the best qualities of copying collectors. The allocation of new objects is fast, they are relatively simple to implement and the copy of living objects eliminates most of the fragmentation problem. Nevertheless, the copying policy has two main weaknesses.

The first problem associated with the copying policy is that long lived data is copied several times. Generational collection avoids this problem by dividing memory into generations. The collector's effort is focused on the younger generations. After

M. Odersky (Ed.): ECOOP 2004, LNCS 3086, pp. 543-559, 2004.

surviving a specific number of collections, the objects are advanced into an older generation, which is collected less often.

The other important problem of copying policy is the extra space needed. The memory is divided into two halves. Allocation takes place in one half and the other half is reserved for copying the objects that survive a collection. Thus, we lose half of the available space.

This paper describes an adaptive strategy that reduces the reserved space for copying surviving data in the youngest generation within generational collection, specifically, within the Appel collection policy. The collector makes its decisions based on dynamic feedback gathered from the past collections.

The remainder of this paper is organized as follows: Section 2 gives an overview of our adaptive strategy. Section 3 describes our method of experimentation. Experiment results are analyzed in section 4. Section 5 describes the related work and finally we summarize our conclusions and discuss future work in section 6.

2 Adaptive Appel Collector

The generational Appel collector [3] divides the heap into two generations: nursery and mature. When an object is created, it is assigned to the youngest generation, the nursery space, in which all free space is contained. Figure 2a describes an Appel collector with a copying policy in the nursery. In mature space, it can use a copying policy or a mark&sweep strategy.

Since the collection policy for the nursery is semispace copying collection, available memory is divided into two halves. These halves, or semispaces, are known as tospace (reserved space) and fromspace (allocation space). Memory allocation is carried out in fromspace.

When the nursery is full, the collector copies all surviving objects to the mature space, and then reduces the nursery size by the same volume. It repeats this process until the nursery size falls below a certain threshold, at which point it performs a full heap collection. The collector returns the freed space to the nursery. In Jikes RVM, this threshold is fixed by default to 0.50 Mb. This strategy has been proven as the best performing for generational collectors [4].

2.1 Adaptive Tuning of the Reserved Space

As mentioned earlier, the traditional copying policy reserves half of the available memory for the copy of surviving data, just in case all allocated data is alive when the collection is done. As we show in our experiment results, the amount of copied data can be significantly smaller than the reserved space. In figure 1, we show the ratio between memory copied into the reserved space and assigned memory in the allocation space. This ratio gives us the percentage of data that survive a collection relative to the allocated memory. As we can see in figure 1a, for these benchmarks the ratio of copied memory is always under 20% (_202_jess and _228_jack) or under 50%

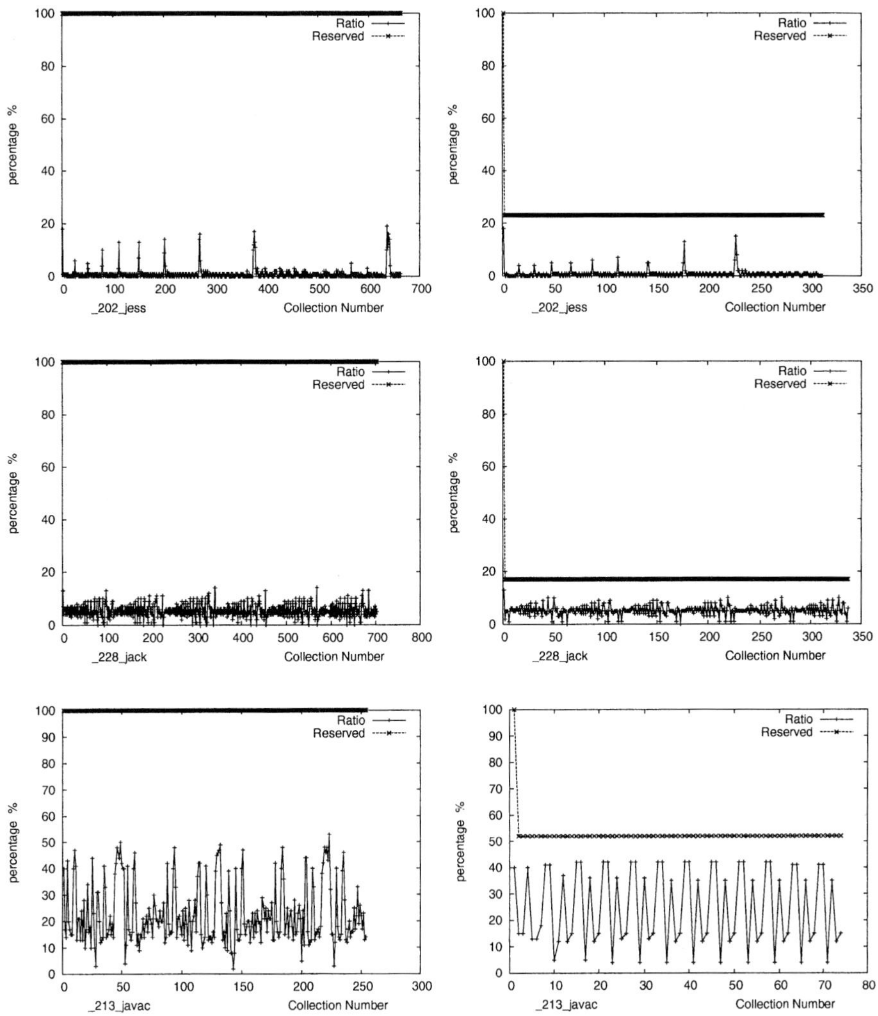

a) Appel Collector. b) Adaptive-Conservative.

Fig. 1. On the x axis we show the different collections during a long run. On the y axis, we represent: 1) the ratio between the copied memory into the reserved space and the allocated memory in the nursery for each collection, and 2) the percentage of reserved space relative to the allocation space (thick line at top). The Appel collector reserves the 100% of the allocating space. Our collector reduces this percentage close to 20% (_202_jess and _228_jack) or 50% (_213_javac).

(_213_javac) of the allocating space. Nevertheless, a traditional collector reserves 100% of allocating space. Therefore, in this example it is squandering at least 80% or 50%, respectively, of the reserved space. In the other benchmarks, we find similar behaviors.

We propose to modify the sizes of the semispaces so that the allocation space is bigger than the reserved space, figure 2b. We cannot change this parameter prior to the execution without risk, because we do not know the behavior of data until run-time. However, during execution the JVM can know the amount of copied memory from the last collections. This information allows the collector to readjust the reserved space in an optimal way, to respond to the real demand.

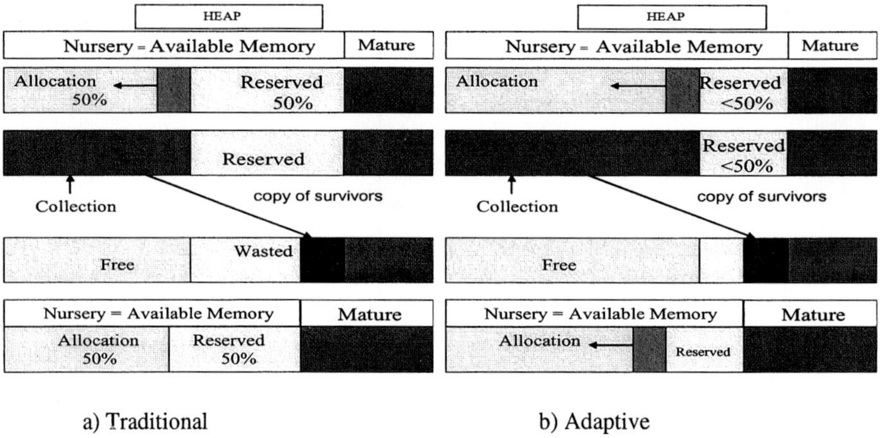

Fig. 2. a) A generational Appel Collector with copying policy in the nursery. b) Our Adaptive Appel Collector with copying policy in the nursery. The space reserved for copying the surviving data is readjusted on demand during the execution

If we reduce tospace, we get more memory for fromspace. We are also able to reduce the number of collections, and the amount of surviving data because a larger fromspace implies giving objects more time to die.

We have looked for very simple strategies that need as little profiling as possible. In figure 3, we show the pseucode of our strategies. When preparing a collection, we record the nursery and mature sizes that we will later use for calculating the ratio of copied memory. Just after finishing a collection, we get the new mature size and calculate the ratio of copied memory from the last collection. Once we have this information we are able to dynamically readjust the reserve space. In this paper, we have experimented with two different strategies:

1) Adaptive "Average" strategy. The first strategy calculates the average of the ratio between the memory copied into the reserved space and the assigned memory in the nursery for the last N collections. Then, it adds a certain security margin to this

```
globalPrepare
--------------------------------------------------------------------------
recordAllocationNurserySizeBeforeCollection
recordMatureSizeBeforeCollection
if (biggestAllocationNurserySize<AllocationNurserySizeBeforeCollection)
  { biggestAllocationNurserySize=AllocationNurserySizeBeforeCollection)}
--------------------------------------------------------------------------


globalRelease
--------------------------------------------------------------------------
recordMatureSizeAfterCollection
 lastRatio = copiedMemory / allocationNurserySize
if (strategy = = Conservative){
        if ( lastRatio > worstRatioRecorded) {
                worstRatioRecorded = lastRatio
                newSecurityMargin = newAverageRatio  *  marginC
                nurseryReserve= lastRatio + newSecurityMargin
                newNurseryThreshold =
                   biggestAllocationNurserySize * nurseryReserve /100
        }
}
else if (strategy = = average) {
        sumRatio += lastRatio
        profileCounter ++
        if  (profileCounter = = N) {
                profileCounter = 0
                newAverageRatio = sumRatio/ N
                if (newAverageRatio< minimumReserve)
                        {newAverageRatio = minimumReserve}
                newSecurityMargin = newAverageRatio  *  marginA
                nurseryReserve= newAverageRatio + newSecurityMargin
                newNurseryThreshold =
                      biggestAllocationNurserySize  *  nurseryReserve/100
        }
}
```

Fig. 3. Pseudocode for our two adaptive strategies. In the results of the experiments conducted for this paper, marginA is equal to 0.5 and marginC is equal to 0.3.

average to get the final percentage of reserve. We do not allow the percentage of reserve to fall below a certain minimum. This is the most aggressive policy and therefore has a higher probability of error.

2) Adaptive "Conservative" strategy. In the second strategy, the percentage of reserved space is equal to the worst ratio registered during the execution so far, plus an added margin of security. This is a more conservative policy, resulting in almost no mistakes.

2.2 Adaptive Tuning of the Threshold

As the collector copies surviving data to the mature space, the nursery size decreases. The time between consecutive collections also decreases, meaning the objects have less time to die. Therefore, the amount of surviving data can increase very quickly and the collector would not be able to respond to this behavior on time. To avoid this situation we have developed two ideas:

a) After a collection, the collector compares the reserved space with the amount of copied memory. If they are closer than a certain value, it increases the reserved space by this value.

b) Every time the collector readjusts the percentage of reserved space, it changes the nursery size threshold that triggers a full heap collection. The new threshold will be a percentage of the new allocation space. The percentage is the same as the current percentage of reserve space. It is important to note that a small reserved space means a larger allocation space. In figure 4a, we can see the evolution of the allocation space in a traditional Appel collector for the _228_jack benchmark with a global heap of 40 Mb. The biggest size for the nursery allocation space is 17 Mb and the threshold that triggers a full heap collection is 0.5 Mb (the default value in the Jikes RVM). This results in 4 full heap collections and over 500 nursery collections. In figure 4b, we show this evolution with our adaptive-average strategy. The reduced reserved space produces a new maximum size close to 30 Mb for the allocation space. The threshold changes to 1.5 Mb, and progresses to 2 Mb and 3.5 Mb. This way, our collector needs only 3 full heap collections and less than 200 nursery collections.

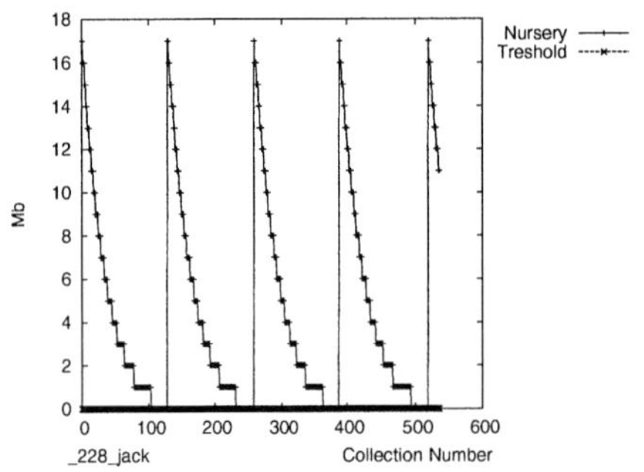

a) Appel Collector. Jack.

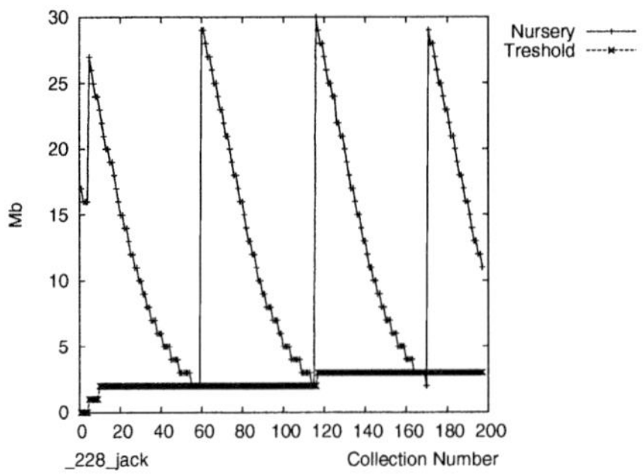

b) Adaptive Average. Jack

Fig. 4. On the X axis we show the different collections during an extended run. On the Y axis, we represent: 1) the amount of memory of the nursery allocation space in Mb, and 2) the threshold that triggers a full heap collection (thick line at bottom). In the Jikes' Appel collector, this threshold is 0.5 Mb, by default. In our strategy, the threshold changes to 1.5 Mb and progresses to 2 Mb and to 3.5 Mb.

2.3. Recovering from an Erroneous Prediction

Because we are making predictions, it is important that we have the ability to recover from those that are incorrect. The data behavior can change quickly and the collector can have too little memory to copy all surviving objects. In that case, our collector stops the nursery collection and frees space in the mature generation, and eliminates the data surviving due to "nepotism". "Nepotism" refers to data that survives a collection because they are referenced by dead objects in the mature space. These are the phases of a nursery collection:

- First, the collector computes all the roots and stores them in a queue.
- When processing this queue the collector finds gray objects (living objects whose offspring are not yet processed), which are also processed into a queue.
- Finally, it processes the locations stored in the remembered set. This phase can produce new gray objects that need to be processed.

If, during this process, our collector attempts to copy an object and sees it has too little reserved memory, it triggers a recovery phase:

- First, the collector saves the queues of roots and gray objects, and it dumps the remembered set.
- The nursery area is set as non moveable.
- The collector computes all roots again and begins a full heap collection but without copying the nursery objects.
- The references from mature objects to the nursery are saved in a new remembered set, thereby eliminating nepotism.
- When finishing the full heap collection the collector continues with the nursery collection using the old queues of roots and gray objects and the new remembered set.

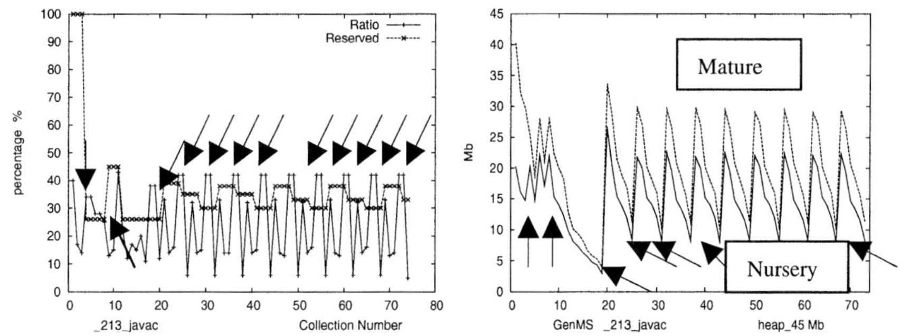

Fig. 5. Worst case scenario for adaptive-Average strategy and _213_javac benchmark. On the X axis we show the different collections during an extended run. In the left figure we show the reserved space and the actual ratio of surviving data, which produces 12 mispredictions, marked with an arrow. In the right figure, we show the fromspace size (solid line), the tospace size (dashed line) and the mature size. Therefore, we can see the amount of freed memory in the mature space during the recovering phase in the 12 mispredictions, marked with an arrow.

In our experiments, the amount of freed memory in the mature space is much bigger than the needed extra reserved space. In figure 5, we can see the worst scenario registered: the adaptive-Average strategy with _213_javac benchmark. Here our strategy incurs in 12 mispredictions, figure 5a. The amount of needed extra space is always under 2 Mb. On the contrary, the amount of freed memory in the mature is never smaller than 6 Mb, figure 5b. In Table 1, we show a summary of the extra memory needed in the reserved space and the freed memory in the mature for this worst-case scenario.

Table 1. Summary of extra memory needed in the reserved space and freed memory in the mature space for our adaptive-Average strategy and _213_javac benchmark.

Misprediction Number	1	2	3	4	5	6	7	8	9	10	11	12
Misprediction %	8	2	12	3	12	4	12	4	12	4	12	4
Needed Memory (Mb)	2	0.5	0.5	0.5	1	0.5	1	0.5	1	0.5	1	0.5
Freed Memory (Mb)	8	6	30	18	19	18	19	18	19	18	18	18

3 Experiment Setup

The tool used in our experiments is Jikes RVM (research virtual machine), initially called Jalapeño, from the Watson Research Center of IBM [5]. Jikes RVM is a Java virtual machine designed for research and has a performance comparable to modern Java virtual machines [6]. Jikes was designed as a modular system with the ability to choose between different compilers and collectors. We have used version 2.2.0 along with the recently developed memory manager JMTk (Java Memory management Toolkit), which replaces the UMass GC Toolkit of the previous versions. Jikes RVM can support different garbage collectors. The user chooses one when creating the image of the virtual machine [8].

We have modified the hybrid generational collector, genMS (which uses a copying policy in the nursery and a mark&sweep strategy in the mature space), to develop our strategy.

JMTK reserves a region of the heap for the objects bigger than a certain threshold. This is the Large Object Space (LOS). It also needs to reserve space for immortal data and meta data (used in buffers for the remembered set), figure 6.

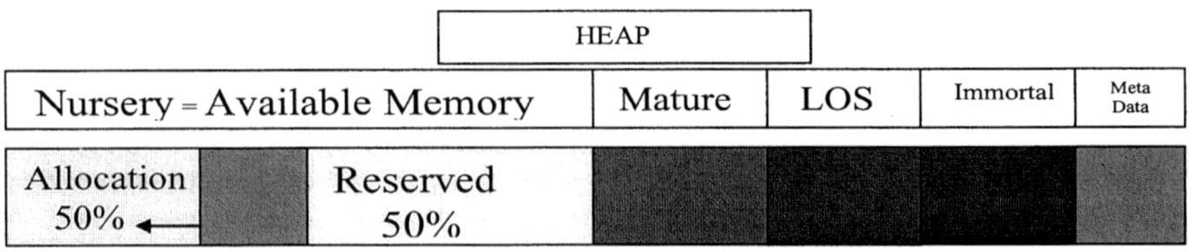

Fig. 6. Heap layout in JikesRVM with an Appel style collector.

We have experimented with the eight benchmarks included in SPECjvm98 [8]. The most significant of them in terms of allocated data are:

_228_jack is a parser based on the Purdue Compiler Construction Tool Set (PCCTS). A parser determines the syntactic structure of a chain of symbols received from the exit of the lexical analyzer.

_202_jess is the Java version of expert shell system using NASA CLIPS.

_228_mtrt is the version of 205.raytrace. It works in a graphical scene of a dinosaur. It has two threads, which make a rendering of the scene removed from a file of 340 KB.

_205_raytrace raytraces a scene into a memory buffer.

_213_javac is the java compiler.

The hardware platform is a Pentium III, 866MHz, 1024Mb with a Linux Red Hat 7.3.

3.1 Measurements

There are several factors to consider when measuring the behavior of a collection strategy:

- *Memory copied from nursery to mature.* This is the main time consumer in the copying collectors.
- *The number of collections.* The running of the application is paused during the garbage collection. After every execution thread stops in a safe point, the virtual machine must save and retrieve the program context for each. Therefore, there is an inherent minimum time to each collection that we can only avoid by reducing their frequency. It is also important to minimize the number of full heap collections because they have an even longer time span.
- *Global garbage collection time.* This is the sum of time used by every collection during a run. It is important to remember that this figure does not include the total time used by the memory management. It would be necessary to consider the memory allocation as well as the updates of references in the write-barriers. As they are interleaved with the code of the application, there is no way of measuring it directly, so we need to look into the execution time.
- *Total execution time.* This time includes the total time of collection, write-barriers and any interference or improvement in data locality.

Since the measurement of these factors introduces an added cost in time, we conducted independent experiments to avoid the overhead due to the instrumentation.

Each benchmark was executed a different number of times with the standard "autorun" option, so that we got an average of ten minutes of execution. This process was repeated 5 times to obtain a trustworthy average.

We varied the global heap size between 1.5 and 4.5 times the minimum heap size needed for executing the benchmark with the Appel collector. For larger heap sizes, the generational strategy performance decreases relative to the semispace copying policy, due to the time cost of write-barriers.

4 Experiment Results

In the "Average" strategy, the reserved space is readjusted according to the ratio of copied/ assigned memory in the last N collections. We have experimented with different values for N and there were no significant changes. For these results, N was equal to five.

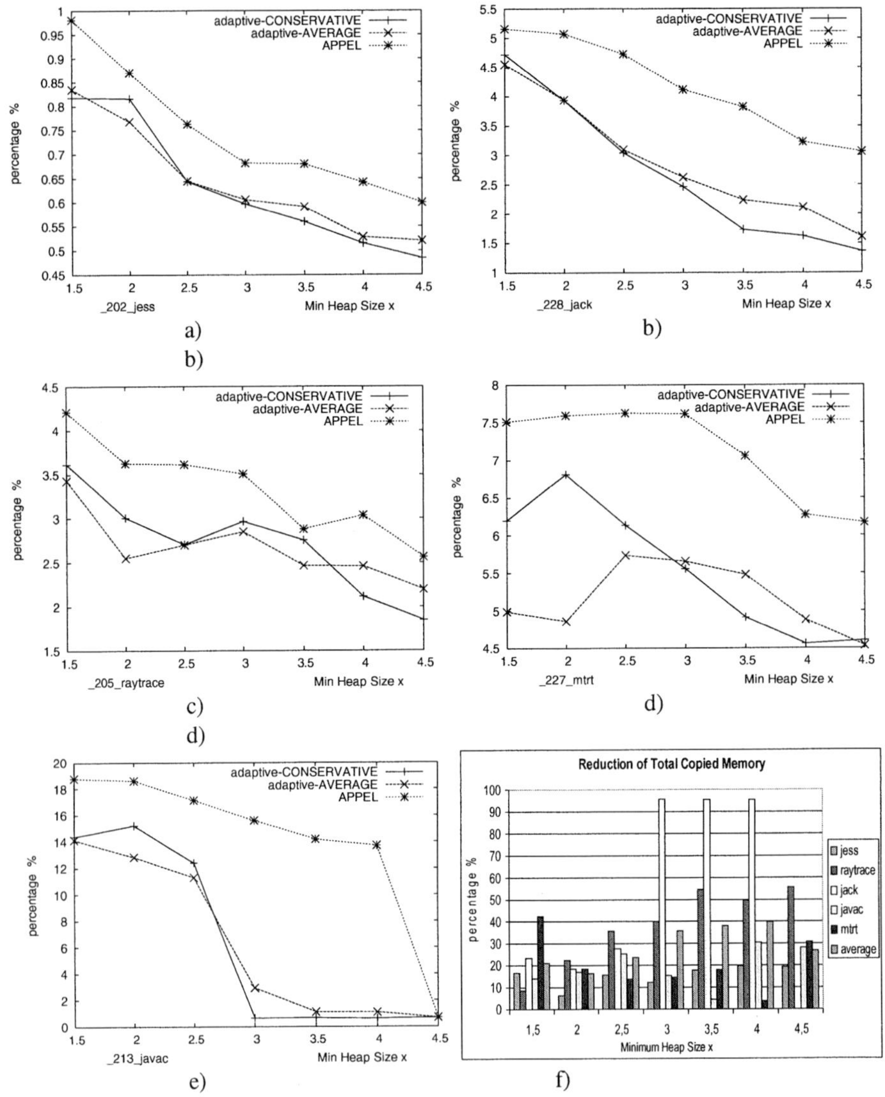

Fig. 7. Total percentage of copied memory to mature space relative to allocated memory in the nursery for traditional Appel and our two adaptive strategies. f) Summary of the reduction in the number of collections for "Conservative" strategy relative to Appel collector.

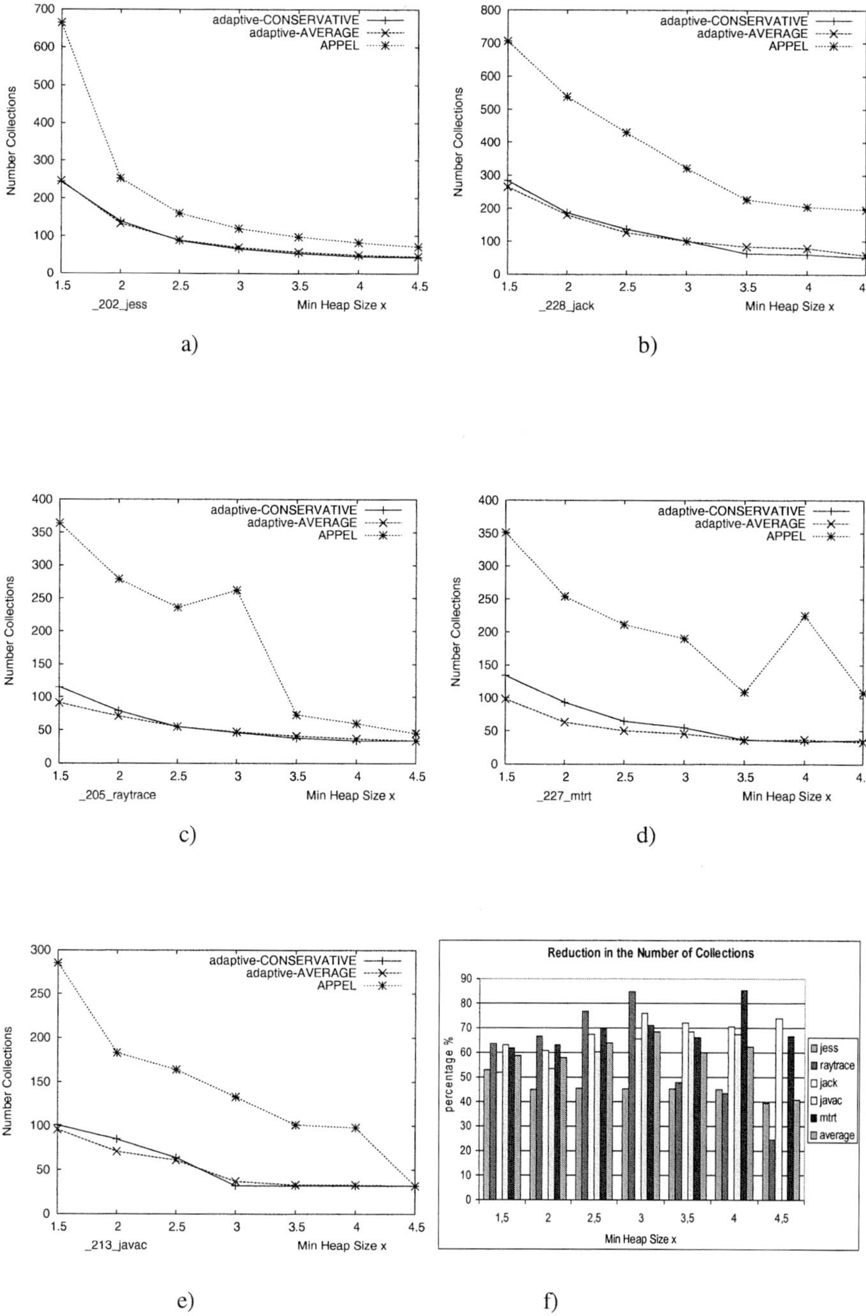

Fig. 8. The number of collections for Appel collector and our two adaptive strategies. f) Summary of the reduction in the number of collections for "Conservative" strategy relative to Appel collector.

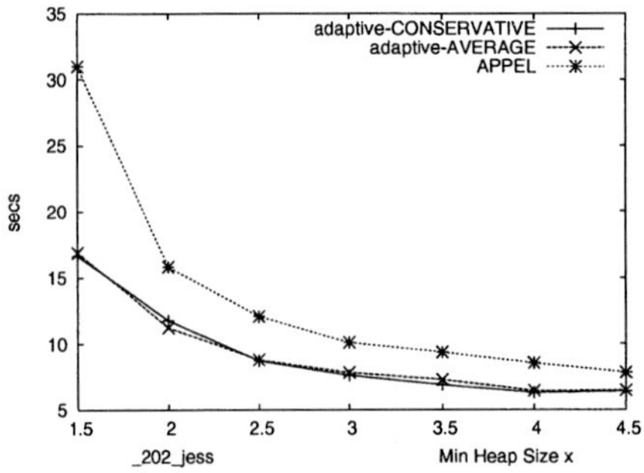

a)

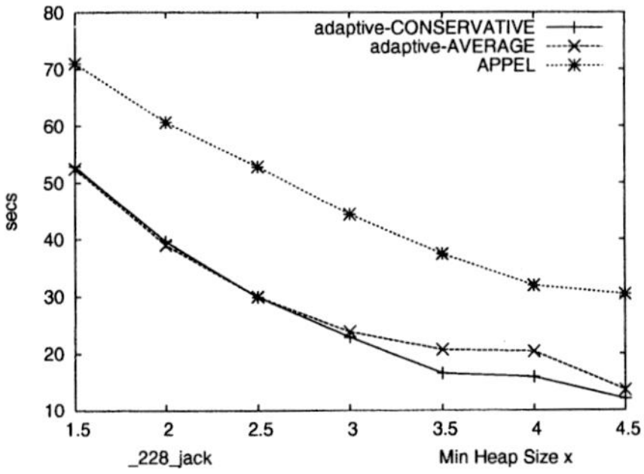

b)

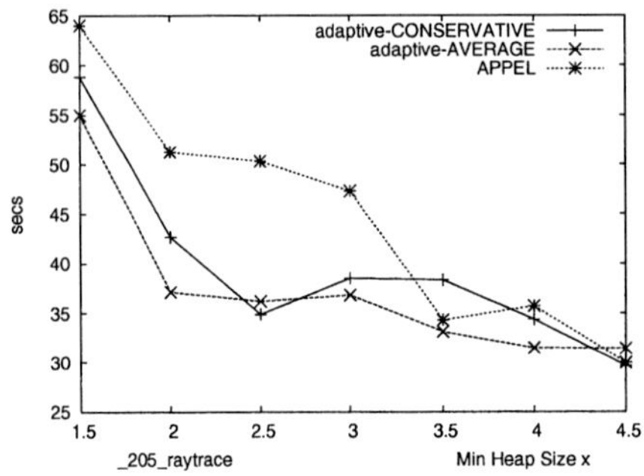

c)

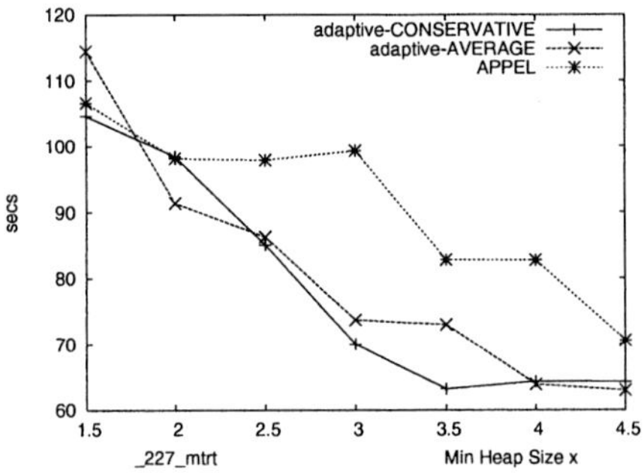

d)

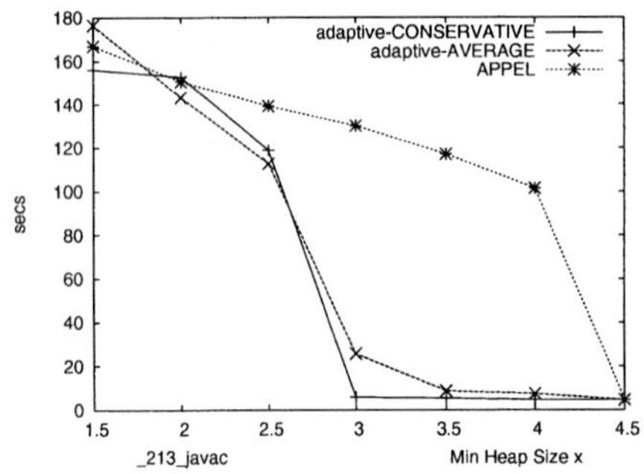

d)

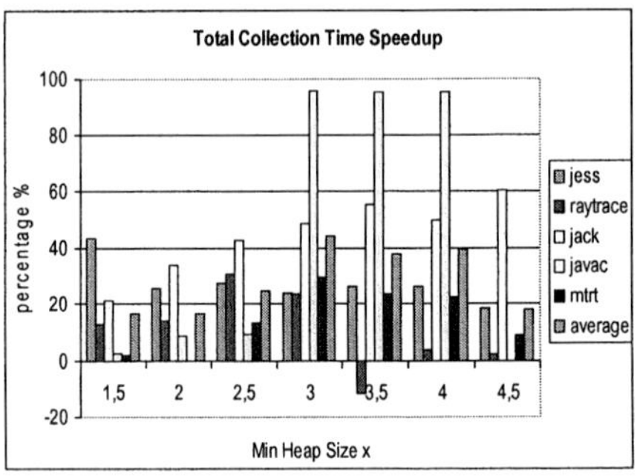

f)

Fig. 9. Total collection time for traditional Appel and our two adaptive strategies. f) Summary of the speedup in the global collection time for "Conservative" strategy relative to Appel collector.

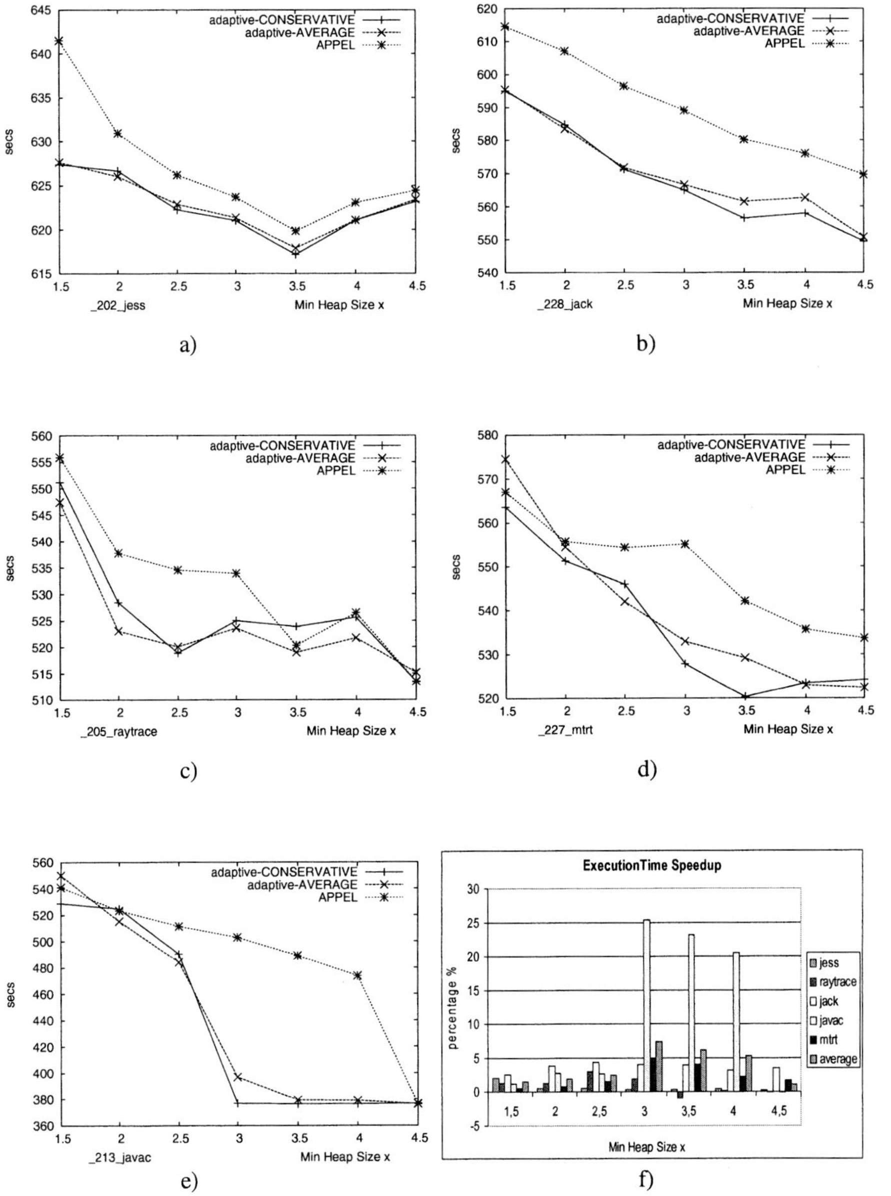

Fig. 10. Total collection time for traditional Appel and our two adaptive strategies. f) Summary of the speedup in the final execution time for "Conservative" strategy relative to Appel collector

We have also experimented with different values for the security margin and again there were no significant changes in the results. In these graphs, the margin was 50% for the "Average" strategy and 30% for the "Conservative" option.

In figure 7, we show the percentage of total copied memory in the mature space relative to the total allocated memory in the nursery. In figure 7f we can see that, on average, the reduction on this percentage varies from 19% to 40%.

In figure 8, we show the number of collections for each benchmark with the Appel collector and our two adaptive strategies. This number is the sum of the nursery and full heap collections. We can see that for every benchmark and all heap sizes, our adaptive strategies produce a clear reduction in this parameter. This reduction is larger for smaller heap sizes, which makes our approach optimal for systems with memory restrictions.

The Javac benchmark has a great number of garbage collections not due to resource exhaustion, but which are requested by the application. With the Appel collector and a heap size, which is 4.5 times larger than the minimum heap size, figure 8e, we reached a point in which all garbage collections are requested by the program. For our adaptive strategies, this point is reached with a heap size of 3 times the minimum. Thus, although this high number of collections requested by the application disturbs the statistics that our strategies need, we obtain an important reduction in this measure.

In the _205_raytrace and _228_mtrt graphs, abnormal peaks are detected for the Appel lines with none corresponding in the adaptive lines, figures 8c and 8d. These peaks are due to a high number of nursery collections when the nursery allocation size is slightly over the threshold size that triggers a full heap collection. This problem is avoided in our strategies because they are able to change this threshold on the fly, based on the nursery size and the reserved space percentage.

In figure 8f, we summarize the reduction in the number of collections for the "Conservative" strategy, with an average for each heap size. The reduction average is never under the 40% and at the middle point of our heap size range, the average is almost 70%.

In figure 9, we show the global collection time. This parameter is the sum of all collection times of both nursery and full heap collections.

Although the average pause time for nursery collections is longer in the adaptive strategies than in the traditional Appel collector (because they have a larger allocating space), we can see that the reduction in the number of collections is accompanied unequivocally by a shorter total collection time.

In the _205_raytrace graph, figure 9c, with a heap size of 3.5x min heap size, we reached a point in which the Appel collector is better than the "Conservative" strategy, idem for _228_mtrt with 1.5x min heap size and the "Average" strategy, figure 9d. This is due to an error in the estimation of reserved space, which results in a full heap collection in order to search for free memory in the mature space. In all other cases and for both adaptive strategies, our approach produces an interesting speedup. In this parameter, unlike the number of collections, we can observe differences between the two strategies. This is due to the number of full heap collections that each one produces.

In figure 9f, we summarize the speedup in collection time for the "Conservative" strategy, with an average for each heap size. Our collector obtains a speedup average of 16% at least, and at the middle point of our heap size range the average climbs over 40%.

We can also deduce from these results that less memory is needed to achieve a similar performance. Actually, when reducing the reserved space size, the collector runs as if it had more memory available.

In figure 10, we show the speedup in the execution time. As we said earlier, this final parameter is the result of global collection time, the number of collections (multiplied by the pause needed for synchronizing the threads before and after a GC), the write-barriers costs and the effects on the data locality. Thus, the adaptive tuning of reserved space for copying means an improvement in the final execution time. As before, at the middle point of figure 10f we got an average speedup of 7%.

5 Related Work

The parallel collector of HotSpot Virtual Machine [13] uses a generational collector with a fixed nursery size. Its strategy is similar to ours in the fact that it does not reserve all needed memory in the mature space to guarantee space for copying all live objects. If it does not find enough memory when attempting to copy an object, it compacts the nursery. It is also able to dynamically adjust its tunable parameters in response to the application's heap allocation behavior, although they do not describe the means by which this is achieved.

Like our collector, Sachindran and Moss´ collector [12] looks for the better usage of available memory. They use a generational collector with a copying policy for mature objects. Their strategy differs from ours in that it is focused on the mature space. The mature space is divided into windows and after marking all living objects, the data is copied through several passes, releasing one or more windows in each pass. Trying to combine these two techniques will make for interesting work in the future.

The Collector from Chives [14] has three generations. The first generation is very small and the second generation is included in order to avoid early tenuring. The third generation is collected either incrementally or concurrently (or both). Harris [9] offers a technique for pre-tenuring objects on the fly. A pre-tenured object is one that when created is allocated in a mature generation. Shuf [10] has offered an alternative to generational collection that avoids the use of the write-barriers. This strategy segregates the objects into different areas according to their types instead of their ages. We think that our dynamic approach would provide benefits when used with Shuf´s strategy.

Stefanovic´s policy [11] requires less reserved space than do traditional generational copying collectors. Its technique makes collections in windows, instead of complete spaces, and beginning with the oldest allocated objects. An implementation of this technique, using Jikes RVM, has been proven [4] successful. One problem associated with this strategy is that it will never reclaim circular or double linked lists with inter-windows references. The Beltway [2] is a generalization of possible combinations of copying generational and incremental copying collectors. An adaptive tuning of heap organization in Beltway will also be an interesting future work.

6 Conclusions

We have presented an adaptive technique that dynamically reorganizes the heap in a generational Appel collector. Our collector reduces the reserved space in the nursery for copying surviving data when possible and does so without taking risks. The collector's decisions are based on information obtained from the most recent collections. We have studied two different strategies for choosing the percentage of reserved space. A conservative one, based on the worst ratio of copied memory registered during execution, and a more aggressive one, based on the average ratio recorded during a certain number of collections.

Our measurements show that for both strategies, our collector achieves an important speedup in global collection time, while providing a clear reduction in the final execution time. Our conservative strategy obtains a global collection speedup, on average, of 16% at least, and the running time speedup varies by up to 7%. The reduction in the number of collections average is never under the 40%, and the reduction on the percentage of total copied memory varies from 19% to 40%.

In addition, the importance of our work resides in presenting an adaptive approach, which can be used along side other garbage collection strategies based on the copying policy.

Acknowledgments. We are grateful to Urs Hölzle for his many detailed comments that helped us strengthen the paper. We are also grateful to Antonio Ortiz for his contribution in the early stage of the work. We thank the anonymous reviewers for their suggestions for improving the paper.

This work is partially supported by the Spanish Government Research Grant TIC2002/0750.

References

[1] Paul R. Wilson. *Uniprocessor Garbage Collection Techniques.* IWMM 1992, International workshop on Memory Management.

[2] Stephen M. Blackburn, Richard Jones, Kathryn S. McKinley and J. Eliot B Moss. *Beltway: Getting around garbage collection gridlock.* Proceedings of Conference on Programming Languages Design and Implementation, PLDI 2002.

[3] Appel, A.W. *Simple generational garbage collection and fast allocation.* Software Practice and Experience. 1989

[4] Darko Stefanovic, Matthew Hertz, Stephen M. Blackburn, Kathryn S. McKinley and J. Eliot B Moss. *Older-first Garbage Collection in Practice: Evaluation in a Java Virtual Machine.* ACM SIGPLAN Workshop on Memory System Performance, Berlin, Germany, June, 2002.

[5] B. Alpern, C. R. Attanasio, J. J. Barton, M. G. Burke, P.Cheng, J.-D. Choi, A. Cocchi, S. J. Fink, D. Grove, M. Hind, S. F. Hummel, D. Lieber, V. Litvinov, M. F. Mergen, T. Ngo, J.R. Russell, V. Sarkar, M. J. Serrano, J. C. Shepherd, S. E. Smith, V. C. Sreedhar, H. Srinivasan, and J. Whaley. *The Jalapeño Virtual Machine.* IBM System Journal, Vol 39, No 1, February 2000.

[6] Matthew Arnold, Stephen Fink, David Grove, Michael Hind, and Peter F. Sweeney. *Adaptive Optimization in the Jalapeño JVM.* ACM SIGPLAN Conference on Object - Oriented Programming Systems, Languages, and Applications (OOPSLA 2000), Minnea polis, Mi.

[7] The Jikes™ Research Virtual Machine User's Guide 2.2.0. http://oss.software.ibm.com/developerworks/oss/jikesrvm/

[8] Standard Performance Evaluation Corporation. SPECjvm98 Documentation, release 1.03 d., March 1999.

[9] Timothy L Harris. *Dynamic Adaptive Pre-Tenuring.* Proceedings of the 2000 ACM International Symposium on Memory Management.

[10] Yefim Shuf, Manish Gupta, Rajesh Bordawekar, and Jaswinder Pal Singh. *Exploiting Prolific Types for Memory Management and Optimizations.* In proc. of POPL 2002 (Symposium on Principles of Programming Languages), Portland, OR, January 2002.

[11] Darko Stefanovic, J. Eliot B. Moss, and Kathryn S. McKinley. *Age-Based Garbage Collection.* Proceedings of the ACM Conference on Object-Oriented Programming Systems, Languages, and Applications, Denver, Colorado, November 1999)

[12] Naredran Sachindran and J. Eliot B. Moss. *Mark-Copy: Fast copying GC with less space verhead.* ACM SIGPLAN Conference on Object-Oriented Programming Systems, Languages, and Applications (OOPSLA 2003), Anaheim, California.

[13] The Java HotSpot Virtual Machine, v1.4.1. White Paper. http://java.sun.com/products/hotspot/docs/whitepaper/Java_Hotspot_v1.4.1

[14] Chives. Cooperative Highly Innovative Virtual Execution System http://chives.sunsite.dk/doc/garbage.html

Lock Reservation for Java Reconsidered

Tamiya Onodera, Kikyokuni Kawachiya, and Akira Koseki

IBM Research, Tokyo Research Laboratory
1623-14, Shimotsuruma, Yamato-shi, Kanagawa-ken 242-8502 Japan
{tonodera,kawatiya,akoseki}@jp.ibm.com

Abstract. *Lock reservation*, a powerful optimization for Java locks, is based on the observation that, in Java, each lock tends to be dominantly acquired and released by a specific thread. Reserving a lock for such a dominant thread allows the owner thread of the lock to acquire and release the lock without any atomic read-modify-write instructions.
A recently proposed algorithm has embodied this idea and significantly reduced the synchronization overhead on a reservation hit. However, on a reservation miss, the algorithm stops the owner thread in order to cancel the reservation, which incurs a significant performance penalty.
We propose a new algorithm for lock reservation for Java without such penalties. We derive the algorithm in two steps. First, we create a new, reservation-based algorithm for spin lock. Second, observing that the conventional spin lock is embedded in a widely-used Java lock, we attempt to replace it with our new spin lock.
We evaluated our algorithm in IBM's production virtual machine and JIT compiler. The results show that our algorithm attained comparable speedups in the SPECjvm98 benchmarks, and that it even improved the performance of two scientific programs which the previous algorithm actually degraded.

1 Introduction

The Java programming language [15] contains built-in support for multi-threaded programming. Putting locks into objects, the language provides two constructs, *synchronized methods and blocks.*

Primarily because class libraries are written as thread-safe, synchronization operations are extremely frequent. As a result, a tremendous effort has been devoted to optimizing Java locks. The optimization techniques proposed so far can be divided into two categories, runtime techniques and compile-time techniques. Runtime techniques attempt to lower the cost of lock operations [3,6,21,25], while compile-time techniques attempt to reduce the number of lock operations [4,7,8,9,29,32].

In principle, the runtime techniques improve performance by optimizing the common cases. In their seminal work, Bacon et al.[6] exploited the observation that Java locks are mostly not contended, and proposed an excellent optimization for Java locks, called *thin locks*, which allows a lock to be acquired and

M. Odersky (Ed.): ECOOP 2004, LNCS 3086, pp. 560–584, 2004.

released with a few machine instructions in the uncontended case. Other runtime techniques such as the Meta-Lock [3] have also been proposed to optimize the uncontended case.

While these techniques allow the instruction sequence of lock acquisition and release to become very short in the uncontended case, the sequence contains one (in thin locks) or more (in the Meta-Lock) atomic read-modify-write instructions such as compare-and-swap (CAS), which are becoming relatively more and more expensive in modern, shared-memory multiprocessor systems.

We recently proposed an interesting runtime optimization for Java locks, called *lock reservation*, which does not require any atomic read-modify-write instructions in a common case [21]. We observed that most Java locks exhibit *thread locality*. That is, each lock tends to be dominantly acquired and released by a specific thread. Attempting to exploit this observation, we *reserve* a lock for such a dominant thread, or let the dominant thread be the *owner* of the lock. The owner thread of a lock can acquire and release the lock without any atomic read-modify-write instructions, resulting in a significantly higher performance on a reservation hit.

However, when a non-owner thread attempts to acquire the lock, the algorithm requires the non-owner thread to *cancel* the reservation by stopping the owner thread, which incurs a significant performance penalty. Although few reservations were canceled in the benchmarks we measured, this makes the algorithm lack robustness and allows for pathological behaviors.

In this paper, we propose a new algorithm for lock reservation for Java which does not require a non-owner thread to stop the owner thread. We derive the algorithm in two steps. First, applying lock reservation to spin lock for the first time, we develop a new algorithm, called the *KKO lock* (after the authors' initials). Interestingly, this new algorithm is a hybridization of a CAS-based spin lock and a Dekker-style spin lock. Second, observing that the conventional spin lock is subsumed in a widely-used algorithm for Java locks, we attempt to replace the spin lock with the KKO lock. This results in a new reservation-based algorithm for Java lock which possesses the properties we desire: While the owner thread of a lock can acquire and release the lock with no atomic read-modify-write instruction, a non-owner thread does not have to cancel the reservation, thus avoiding the need to stop the owner thread.

We have evaluated our new algorithm in IBM's production Java virtual machine and JIT compiler. The results of micro-benchmarks show that the new algorithm achieves high performance close to our previous algorithm on a reservation hit, while it removes the anomalous behavior the previous algorithm exhibits on a reservation miss. For macro-benchmarks, while the new algorithm achieved comparable speedups in the SPECjvm98 benchmarks, it even improved the performance of two scientific programs for which the previous algorithm caused degradation.

Our contributions in this paper are as follows.

– *A new algorithm for spin lock.* We devised a novel optimization for spin lock based on lock reservation. The KKO lock allows the owner thread of a lock

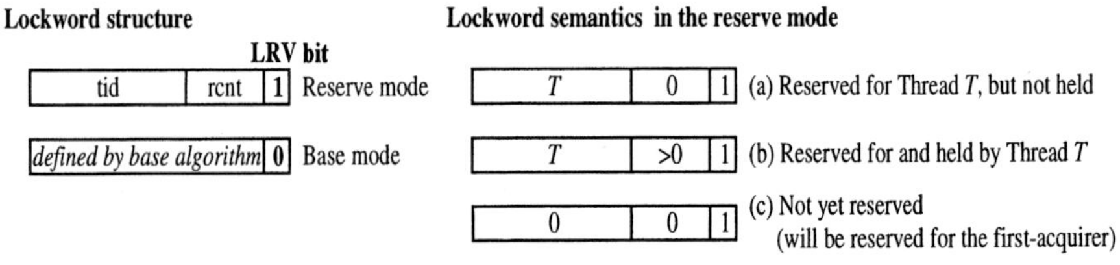

Fig. 1. Lockword structure and semantics of the stop-the-owner algorithm

to acquire and release the lock with a few read and write instructions, while it does not cause a non-owner thread to stop the owner thread.

– *A new algorithm of lock reservation for Java.* We developed a new algorithm for Java lock by embedding the KKO spin lock into a widely-used algorithm for Java lock. The resulting algorithm allows the owner thread of a lock to acquire and release the lock with a few read and write instructions, while it does not cause a non-owner thread to stop the owner thread.
– *Evaluation on a production virtual machine and JIT compiler.* We implemented our lock reservation algorithm on a production Java virtual machine and JIT compiler, and measured the performance on a multiprocessor system, using an industry-standard benchmark set and scientific programs.

The rest of the paper is organized as follows. Section 2 reviews the previous algorithm for lock reservation which stops the owner thread on a reservation miss. Section 3 describes the KKO lock, our new algorithm for spin lock. Section 4 constructs a new reservation-based algorithm for Java lock by embedding the KKO spin lock into a widely-used algorithm for Java lock. Section 5 presents experimental results, while Section 6 discusses related work. Finally, Section 7 offers conclusions.

2 Stop-the-Owner Algorithm for Lock Reservation

In this section, we review our previous algorithm [21]. We constructed that algorithm upon an existing algorithm. The requirements for the existing algorithm are that it uses a *lockword*[1], a word in the object header for synchronization, and that one bit could be made available there. The bit is used for representing the lock reservation status, and hence called the *LRV* bit. When the LRV bit is set, the lockword is in the *reserve* mode, and the structure is defined by our algorithm. When the bit is not set, the lockword is in the *base* mode, and the structure is defined by the existing base algorithm.

Figure 1 shows the details of the data structure. The lockword in the reserve mode is further divided into the thread identifier (`tid`) field and the recursion

[1] Actually, we do not necessarily require the full word and can do with a *lock field* rather than a lockword. For simplifying this explanation, we assume that the full word is available for synchronization.

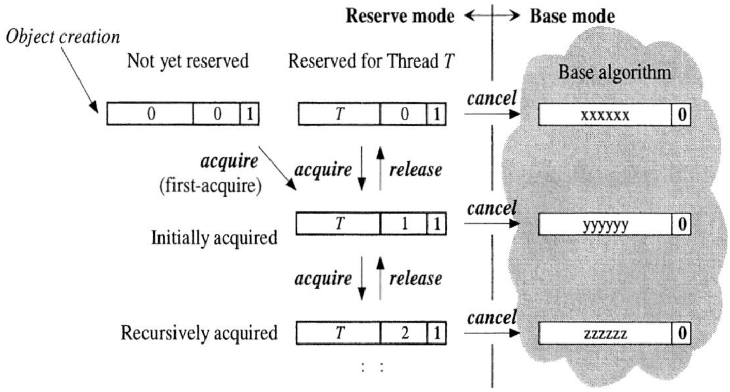

Fig. 2. Lock state transitions in the stop-the-owner algorithm

count (`rcnt`) field. The `tid` field contains the identifier of the owner thread, while the `rcnt` field keeps the lock recursion level. When the `rcnt` field is zero, the lock is reserved but not held by any thread (Figure 1(a)). When the field is non-zero, the lock is held by the owner thread (Figure 1(b)).

In general, when using lock reservation, a *reservation policy* must be defined to specify when and for which thread each lock is reserved. For example, when a thread is creating an object, the object's lock could be reserved for the creating thread. Alternatively, when a thread attempts to acquire an object's lock for the first time, the lock could be reserved for that thread. We adopted the second policy, called the *first-acquirer policy* [21].

According to this reservation policy, when an object is created, the lock state is initialized to be the *not-yet-reserved* state[2], meaning that the lockword is in the reserve mode but not reserved for (or held by) any thread (Figure 1(c)).

We now explain how the algorithm works by using a lock's state transitions as summarized in Figure 2. We only cover the important cases here, but refer to [21] for the full details. As mentioned earlier, the state of a lock is initialized to be the not-yet-reserved state. The first thread attempting to acquire the lock makes the state transition from the not-yet-reserved state to the state indicating that the lock is reserved for and held by the thread. It does so by using an atomic read-modify-write instruction, since more than one thread might simultaneously attempt to make the transition.

When the lock is reserved for a thread, the owner thread can acquire the lock by incrementing the `rcnt` field, and release the lock by decrementing the field. This is the case whether the owner thread does so initially or recursively. Thus, it only takes a few reads and writes to acquire and release a lock in the common cases, with no atomic read-modify-write instructions. This allows the algorithm to attain the higher performance in the synchronization-intensive Java programs we measured.

---

[2] We previously called the state *anonymously reserved* [21].

When the lock is reserved for a thread and a non-owner thread attempts to acquire the lock, the non-owner thread first cancels the reservation, and then falls back to the base algorithm. Canceling a reservation is the most crucial and trickiest part of the algorithm. In doing so, the non-owner thread stops the owner thread, replaces the lockword in the reserve mode with the equivalent state in the base mode, and allows the owner thread to resume execution.

When canceling the reservation, special care must be taken since the owner thread might be stopped in the middle of acquiring or releasing the lock. To avoid data race, the algorithm clearly defines *unsafe regions* in the acquisition code and release code, and carefully makes the unsafe regions restartable by preventing any side effects from occurring there. After having stopped the owner thread, the non-owner thread obtains the execution context of the owner thread to see whether the thread is in an unsafe region. If it is, the non-owner thread modifies the program counter of the owner thread so that the owner thread retries the unsafe region.

While few reservations were canceled in the benchmarks we measured, canceling a reservation requires expensive system calls and incurs a very large overhead. This makes the algorithm lack robustness and makes it subject to pathological behavior. As we will see later, we remedy these weaknesses by taking a completely different approach to lock reservation. More concretely, while the previous approach defines an extension layer to an existing algorithm, thus making it applicable for most of the existing algorithms, our new approach takes a particular class of the existing algorithms, and replaces the spin locks used in those algorithms with new, reservation-based spin locks.

Finally, we note that the stop-the-owner algorithm never re-reserves the lock. That is, once a lock's reservation has been canceled, the algorithm never restores the lock back to the reserve mode. The justification was that the algorithm supporting repeated reservations would become too complicated, while at the same time it might result in more cancellations and thus degrade performance.

3 Optimizing Spin Locks by Reservations

In this section, we attempt to apply lock reservation to spin locks. We first review two existing algorithms, a commonly-used CAS-based algorithm and a Dekker-style algorithm. We then present a new, reservation-based algorithm. We will see the new algorithm is an interesting hybridization of the CAS-based lock and the Dekker-style lock.

3.1 A CAS-Based Spin Lock

Modern processors provide atomic read-modify-write instructions such as test-and-set and compare-and-swap (CAS) in order to facilitate creating locks in software. Thus, spin locks are commonly implemented with such atomic instructions.

```
#define SUCCESS 1
#define FAILURE 0
typedef int thread_t;

void acquire(volatile thread_t *lock){
  while (try_acquire(lock)!=SUCCESS) continue;
}

int try_acquire(volatile thread_t *lock){
  return compare_and_swap(lock, 0, myself());
}

void release(volatile thread_t *lock){
  *lock=0;
}
```

Fig. 3. A CAS-based spin lock

Figure 3 presents one of the simplest of such spin locks. When some thread holds the lock, the lockword contains the thread's identifier. Otherwise, the value is zero. To acquire a lock, a thread atomically changes the value from zero to its identifier by using the CAS.[3]

The algorithm in Figure 3 usually has to be augmented for practical use. For instance, many algorithms in use in real world support recursive locking, and check in the `release` function to see whether or not the current thread is actually holding the lock. Furthermore, they typically incorporate optimizations such as spin-on-read and the exponential back-off [2] for scalability. We omit all of these extensions and optimizations for the sake of simplifying the explanation.

3.2 A Dekker-Style Spin Lock

It was of academic interest to design algorithms for spin locks using read and write instructions [11,12,22,28]. Figure 4 shows one example of such an algorithm which we obtained by simplifying Dekker's algorithm [12]. Notice that it is *two-thread algorithm.* The algorithm assumes that only two threads, whose identifiers are zero and one, are involved.

Each of the two threads attempts to acquire the lock by setting its own status element (Line 10), and then checking the other thread's status element (Line 11). If the other thread's element is not set, the thread has successfully acquired the lock. Otherwise, the thread has failed in acquisition, and resets its own status element (Line 14).

While the algorithm provides mutual exclusion and does not deadlock, it may livelock. That is, when the two threads simultaneously attempt to acquire the lock, they may continously execute Line 10, 11, 14, and 15. Although we omit the details in this paper, the complete version of Dekker's algorithm resolves the issue by introducing a field that indicates which of the two takes precedence on

[3] We assume a typical implementation of the CAS which takes three inputs, an address, an old value, and a new value. It first compares the contents at the address with the old value. If the two are equal, it stores the new value at the address and returns `SUCCESS`. Otherwise, it returns `FAILURE`.

```
struct {
  int status[2]; // initialized as {0,0}.
} DS_t;

void acquire(volatile DS_t *ds){
  while (try_acquire(ds)!=SUCCESS) continue;
}

int try_acquire(volatile DS_t *ds){
  ds->status[myself()]=1;
  if (ds->status[otherself()]==0)
     return SUCCESS;
  else {
     ds->status[myself()]=0;
     return FAILURE;
  }
}

void release(volatile DS_t *ds){
  ds->status[myself()] = 0;
}
```

Fig. 4. A Dekker-style spin lock

contention and by changing the value alternatively. It is hence named the `turn` field.

We can generalize the algorithm in Figure 4 for `N` threads. However, the number of memory operations required becomes proportional to the number of threads. Thus, as the number of threads increases, the performance becomes worse than the CAS-based spin lock in Section 3.1. As far as we know, all the algorithms composed from read and write instructions suffer from this issue, including those in [11,12,22,28].

3.3 Reservation-Based Spin Locks

We now construct a new algorithm for spin lock, called the KKO lock, by applying lock reservation to spin lock for the first time. The new algorithm issues no atomic read-modify-write instructions on a reservation hit.

The data structure for our reservation-based spin lock consists of three fields, `owner`, `other`, and `owner_status`. The lock is either in the *not-yet-reserved* state or the *reserved* state. When the lock is in the not-yet-reserved state, the `owner` field is zero. When it is in the reserved state, the field holds the identifier of the owner thread of the lock. When the lock is held by the owner, the `owner_status` field is set to one, and the `other` field is zero or will sooner or later be set to zero. When the spin lock is held by a non-owner thread, the `other` field contains the identifier of the thread, and the `owner_status` field is zero or will sooner or later be set to zero.

Figure 5 summarizes the state transitions of the KKO lock. Like the reservation-based algorithm for Java lock in Section 2, the KKO lock uses the first-acquirer reservation policy. Thus, the state of a lock is initialized to be the not-yet-reserved state, and is changed into the reserved state by the first thread which attempts to acquire the lock. In addition, we note that, once the lock has been reserved for a thread, the reservation is never switched to another thread, and it continues to be reserved for the same owner thread.

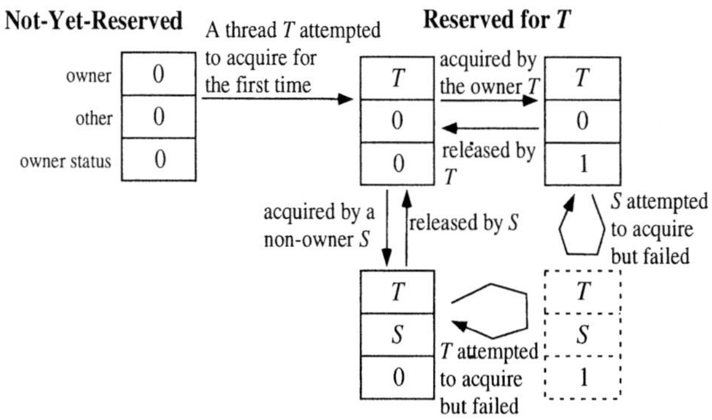

Fig. 5. State transitions of the KKO lock. The dotted box is a phantom state, and disappears sooner or later.

We now explain the algorithm in detail. The actual code depends on the layout of the three fields, since the different layouts require the underlying architecture to provide different sets of memory operations. We consider the following two embodiments.

- Three-word KKO. This allocates each field in a separate word[4], and assumes the CAS, the atomic write, and the atomic read which all act upon 32-bit data.
- One-word KKO. This packs the three fields into one word, and assumes the CAS is for 32-bit data, the atomic read is for 32-bit data, and the atomic writes are for 8-bit and 16-bit data.

The three-word KKO is simpler, and more clearly conveys the key ideas and the essential properties of the KKO lock, while the space efficiency of the one-word embodiment is necessary when we construct a Java lock from the KKO lock. Actually, we derive the Java lock from the one-word KKO in Section 4. We focus on the three-word KKO in this subsection, and consider the one-word KKO in the next subsection.

Figure 6 shows the code for the three-word KKO lock, where the `try_acquire` function does the essential task. Let us first consider the case when a thread attempts to acquire the lock in the not-yet-reserved state (Line 15 – Line 19). It performs the CAS in order to change the lock state from the initial state to the reserved state. If it does not succeed in the CAS, its attempt has failed, and some other thread must have succeeded in the state transition. Otherwise, the thread proceeds to the case for the owner thread.

It is important to observe that the KKO lock hybridizes the CAS-based lock in Figure 3 and the Dekker-style lock in Figure 4. The non-owner threads first compete with each other in the preliminary round and the winner advances to the final, while the owner thread is seeded to the final. The preliminary round

[4] Unless otherwise stated, we assume that a word is 32 bits long.

```
1 typedef struct {
2   thread_t owner;
3   thread_t other;
4   status_t owner_status;
5 } KKO_t;
6
7 void acquire(volatile KKO_t *kko){
8   while (try_acquire(kko)!=SUCCESS) continue;
9 }
10
11 int try_acquire(volatile KKO_t *kko){
12   thread_t owner = kko->owner;
13   thread_t myid = myself();
14
15   if (owner==0){ /* attempt in the initial state */
16     if (compare_and_swap(&kko->owner,0,myid)!=SUCCESS)
17       return FAILURE;
18     owner = myid;
19   }
20
21   if (owner==myid){ /* attempt by the owner */
22     kko->owner_status=1;
23     if (kko->other==0)
24       return SUCCESS;
25     else {
26       kko->owner_status=0;
27       return FAILURE;
28     }
29   }
30   else { /* attempt by a non-owner thread */
31     if (compare_and_swap(&kko->other,0,myid)!=SUCCESS)
32       return FAILURE;
33     if (kko->owner_status==0)
34       return SUCCESS;
35     else {
36       kko->other=0;
37       return FAILURE;
38     }
39   }
40 }
41
42 void release(volatile KKO_t *kko){
43   if (kko->owner==myself())
44     kko->owner_status=0;
45   else
46     kko->other=0;
47 }
```

Fig. 6. Algorithm of the three-word KKO lock

is performed through the CAS-based lock (Line 31). The final, involving exactly two threads, is done using the Dekker-style lock (Line 22 to 28 for the owner, and Lines 31 and 33 to 38 for the winner of the preliminary round).

The performance of the KKO lock in the absence of contention can be summarized as follows. The owner thread can acquire and release the lock with two writes and three reads, requiring no atomic read-modify-write instruction, while the non-owner thread can do so with one atomic read-modify-write instruction, one write, and three reads.

The KKO lock as presented in Figure 6 may livelock in exactly the same manner as the Dekker-style lock in Figure 4. However, again we can resolve the issue by introducing the `turn` field as in Dekker's algorithm. Also, we note that the one-word KKO we will soon present does not cause livelock.

The `owner_status` field is only modified by the owner thread, while the `other` field is only modified by the non-owner threads. Thus, the writes to these two fields must not interfere with each other. In addition, as in the CAS-based lock in Figure 3, we omit in Figure 6 such features as recursive locking and illegal state check in lock release. The prototype system we evaluate in Section 5 obviously supports these features.

In the remainder of the subsection, we discuss two important aspects of the KKO lock.

Multiprocessor Considerations. While our algorithm does not require any atomic read-modify-write instructions on a reservation hit, it does rely on the program order execution of reads and writes. More concretely, for instance, the write in Line 22 and the read in Line 23 must be executed in the program order.

Multiprocessor architectures with *relaxed memory consistency models* [1,10] do not necessarily guarantee the program order of memory operations, but provide hardware instructions to force the program order. Modern architectures include dedicated instructions called *memory barriers* or *fences*, while older architectures rely on atomic read-modify-write instructions to achieve the same effect.

Some architectures allow the program order to be preserved with *software techniques*, although the details significantly vary depending on processor architectures and even processor implementations. For instance, for the IBM 370, we can preserve the order of `write into X` and `read from Y` (`X` and `Y` are different memory locations) with the sequence of `write into X`, `read from X` and `read from Y` [1]. In general, software techniques are cheaper than hardware instructions.

Whether the program order is preserved with hardware instructions or software techniques, it must be noted that the KKO lock provides performance gains on those multiprocessor systems where the cost of the atomic read-modify-write instruction (which it removes) is higher than the cost of program-order enforcement (which it introduces).

Finally, we note that while enforcing the program order obviously affects some optimizations such as speculation, the atomic read-modify-write instruction also does so in the same manner.

Optimizations. If we have the CAS that can act upon both the `other` and `owner_status` fields, the execution path by a non-owner thread could become much simpler, since it allows the CAS on `other` at Line 31 and the check of `owner_status` at Line 33 to be combined. Similarly, if we have the CAS that can act upon both `owner` and `owner_status` fields, the execution path in the not-yet-reserved state could be made simpler, since a thread could directly change the lock state from the not-yet-reserved state to the state actually reserved for and acquired by the thread itself.

These optimizations do not necessarily require the underlying processor architecture to support *double compare-and-swap* [16]. We could achieve the same effect by co-locating multiple fields in a single memory region upon which the CAS could act. The technique is used in the one-word KKO we will describe below.

```
 1 #define OWNERMASK  0x0000fffe
 2 #define OTHERMASK  0x7fff0000
 3
 4 /*
 5  * The following definitions assume Little Endian addressing.
 6  */
 7 #define OWNER_STATUS_BYTE(word) (((char*)word)[0])
 8 #define OTHER_SHORT(word)       (((short*)word)[1])
 9
10 /*
11  * We assume that the special function myself() returns the thread identifier
12  * shifted to fit into the owner field. The following macro further shifts
13  * the value to fit into the other field.
14  */
15 #define SHIFT_OWNER_TO_OTHER(tid)  ((tid)<<15)
16
17 void acquire(volatile word_t *kko){
18   while (try_acquire(kko)!=SUCCESS) continue;
19 }
20
21 int try_acquire(volatile word_t *kko){
22   word_t word = *kko;
23   if ((word & OWNERMASK)==0){ /* attempt in the initial state */
24     word_t locked=(myself() | 0x01);
25     return compare_and_swap(kko,0,locked);
26   }
27   else if ((word & OWNERMASK)==myself()){ /* attempt by the owner */
28     OWNER_STATUS_BYTE(kko) = (word | 0x01);
29     if (((*kko) & OTHERMASK)==0)
30       return SUCCESS;
31     else {
32       OWNER_STATUS_BYTE(kko) = (word & ~0x01);
33       return FAILURE;
34     }
35   }
36   else { /*  attempt by a non-owner thread */
37     word_t unlocked= (word & OWNERMASK);
38     word_t locked=(unlocked | (SHIFT_OWNER_TO_OTHER(myself())));
39     return compare_and_swap(kko, unlocked, locked);
40   }
41 }
42
43 void release(volatile word_t *kko){
44   word_t word = *kko;
45   if ((word & OWNERMASK)==myself())
46     OWNER_STATUS_BYTE(kko) = (word & ~0x01);
47   else
48     OTHER_SHORT(kko) = 0;
49 }
```

Fig. 7. Algorithm of the one-word KKO lock

3.4 One-Word Embodiment

Assuming the CAS is for 32-bit data, the atomic read is for 32-bit data, and the atomic writes are for 8-bit and 16-bit data, the one-word KKO uses the following layout.

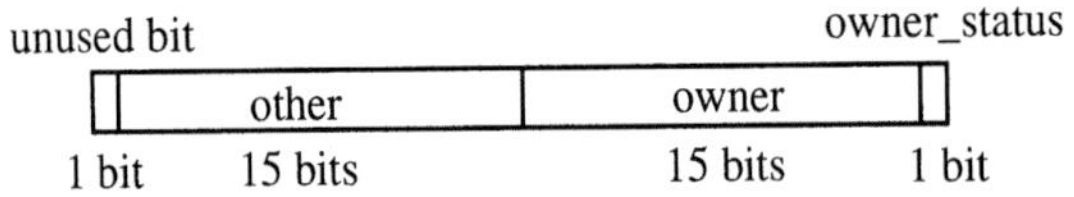

The data structure now includes an unused bit, since it does not make sense to have the `other` field longer than the `owner` field.

Figure 7 shows the algorithm for the one-word KKO. Note that we assume Little Endian addressing here. The algorithm applies the two optimizations of the last subsection at Line 39 and Line 25, using the CAS on 32-bit data. As we mentioned earlier, the writes to the the `owner_status` and `other` fields must not interfere with each other. Thus, the one-word KKO sets and resets the `owner_status` field with the 8-bit write, while it clears the `other` field using the 16-bit write in the `release` function. In addition, note that involving (the lower seven bits of) the `owner` field in the 8-bit write for the `owner_status` field does not cause any problem. This is because the value of the `owner` field is never changed once the KKO lock has been set to the reserved state.

The one-word KKO as presented in Figure 7 does not cause livelock. That is, the owner and a non-owner thread never continuously fail. If the owner thread takes the path to return `FAILURE` at Line 33, it implies that the non-owner thread has succeeded in the CAS at Line 39, meaning that the non-owner thread has succeeded in the acquisition of the lock.

The upper limit of the number of threads that can simultaneously exist is smaller in the one-word embodiment. However, the layout shown above still allows 32 K threads to co-exist, which is sufficient even for server systems.

4 Optimizing Java Lock with the KKO Lock

Synchronization in Java is based on monitors [17], which are categorized as *suspend locks* rather than spin locks. In this section, we first discuss suspend locks in general, and then explain efficient algorithms for Java locks, called *bimodal locks*. Observing that bimodal locks contain the CAS-based spin locks as described in Section 3.1, we attempt to replace them with the KKO locks. The result is a new reservation-based algorithm for Java lock.

4.1 Suspend Locks

A thread attempting to acquire a lock may observe contention. That is, it may find that some other thread is currently holding the lock. The thread must then wait for the lock to be available. Basically, there are two waiting methods, *spinning* and *suspending*.

A spin lock requires the thread to busy-wait, repeatedly performing the same steps until it has succeeded in acquiring the lock. Thus, spin locks are only suitable for short critical sections. On the other hand, a suspend lock requires the thread to relinquish control of the processor. Suspend locks are much preferred for general, multithreaded applications, including those written in Java.

A widely employed optimization of a suspend lock is hybridizing it with a spin lock [26]. We call locks optimized that way *spin-suspend locks*. When a thread attempting to acquire a spin-suspend lock finds that it is not available, it busy-waits or spins but does so only a certain number of times. After the thread has repeatedly failed in all of the spins, it relinquishes control of the processor. The upper limit on how many times precursory spins are attempted is defined by *the spin threshold*. While the threshold must obviously be one on a uniprocessor system, it is determined by a *spinning strategy* on a multiprocessor system [20].

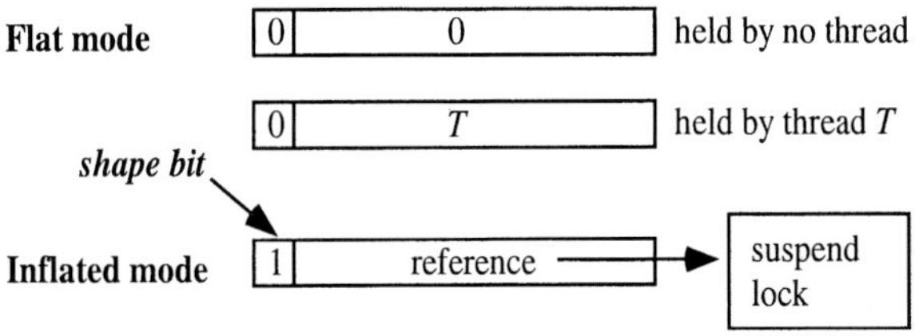

Fig. 8. Semantics of the lock field in a bimodal lock

4.2 Bimodal Locks

Space-efficiency and time-efficiency are equally important in Java locks. In general, we can make operations on objects faster by implementing them with bits in the headers. However, the real estate in an object's header is very precious, and thus the number of bits dedicated to an operation must be minimized.

A bimodal lock [6,13,25] is a space-efficient hybridization of spin lock and suspend lock, intended for use in Java. It reserves only one field in each object's header, using the field in two modes. In the *flat* mode, the bimodal lock acts as a spin lock. When the lock is held by a thread, the lock field contains the thread's identifier. Otherwise, the value of the field is zero. In the *inflated* mode, the bimodal lock behaves as a suspend lock, and the lock field contains a reference to the suspend lock. These two modes are distinguished by one bit in the lock field, called the *shape bit.* Figure 8 shows the bimodal lock's data structure. Again, we omit a well-known optimization for recursive locking here for the sake of simplifying the explanation.

The bimodal lock is initialized to be in the flat mode, and remains in the mode as long as no contention occurs. Thus, the bimodal lock is as efficient in the uncontended case as the spin lock. When the lock is contended, the bimodal lock is *inflated* and put into the inflated mode.

There are two important instances of bimodal locks, thin locks [6] and tasuki lock [25]. Both hybridize the CAS-based spin lock and the full-fledged monitor, achieving in the uncontended case the same level of performance as the CAS-based spin lock. Thin locks employ a simpler protocol, but require busy-wait on inflation, and do not allow inflated locks to be *deflated* (put back into the flat mode). Robustness is impaired by the busy-wait, while opportunities for further improvements are lost due to the lack of deflation. Tasuki lock remedies these two problems at the expense of increasing the complexity of the protocol.

In order to illustrate how the CAS-based spin lock is employed in a bimodal lock, we present an overview of the algorithm of tasuki lock using the data structure in Figure 8. For the full details of this sophisticated protocol, refer to [25]. Figure 9 shows the code. When a thread attempts to acquire a Java lock, it first does so in the flat mode, or attempts to acquire the spin lock (Line 22). Successfully acquiring the spin lock means successfully acquiring the Java lock.

If the thread has failed in the acquisition, there are two cases: the lock is in the inflated mode, or the lock is in the flat mode but being held by some other

```
 1 #define SHAPEBIT 0x80000000
 2
 3 int try_acquire(volatile word_t* lock){ return compare_and_swap(lock,0,myself()); }
 4
 5 void release(volatile word_t *lock){ *lock=0; }
 6
 7 void Java_lock_inflate(Object* obj, monitor_t* mon){ obj->lock = (word_t)mon | SHAPEBIT; }
 8
 9 void Java_lock_deflate(Object* obj){ obj->lock = 0; }
10
11 monitor_t* Java_lock_get_monitor(Object *obj){
12   word_t word = obj_lock;
13   if (word & SHAPEBIT)
14     return (monitor_t*)(word & ~SHAPEBIT);
15   else
16     /* We assume that a hashtable maintains the mapping from objects to their monitors. */
17     return find_or_create_monitor(obj);
18 }
19
20 void Java_lock_acquire(Object* obj){
21   /* flat path */
22   if (try_acquire(&obj->lock)==SUCCESS) return;
23
24   /* inflating path or inflated path */
25   monitor_t *mon = Java_lock_get_monitor(obj);
26   monitor_enter(mon);
27   while ((obj->lock & SHAPEBIT)==0) {
28     obj->flc = 1; /* set the flat lock contention bit */
29     if (try_acquire(&obj->lock)!=SUCCESS)
30       monitor_wait(mon);
31     else {
32       obj->flc=0;
33       monitor_notify_all(mon);
34       Java_lock_inflate(obj,mon);
35     }
36   }
37 }
38
39 void Java_lock_release(Object* obj){
40   if ((obj->lock & SHAPEBIT)==0){ /* flat path */
41    release(&obj->lock);
42    if (obj->flc){ /* flat lock contention has happened. */
43      monitor_t *mon = Java_lock_get_monitor(obj);
44      monitor_enter(mon);
45      if (obj->flc) monitor_notify_all(mon);
46      monitor_exit(mon);
47    }
48   } else { /* inflated path */
49     monitor_t *mon = Java_lock_get_monitor(obj);
50     if (no thread waiting on mon && contention has ceased) Java_lock_deflate(obj);
51     monitor_exit(mon);
52   }
53 }
```

Fig. 9. Algorithm of tasuki lock

thread. In either case, the current thread first obtains a monitor associated with the object (Line 25) and enters the monitor (Line 26). If the lock is in the inflated mode, the thread immediately fails in the conditional in the `while` loop, simply returning from the function. Notice that the thread has entered the monitor at Line 26, so it has already acquired the Java lock in the inflated mode.

Otherwise, the thread proceeds to the loop body and attempts to inflate the lock. It first sets a bit to indicate that *flat lock contention* has occurred (Line 28). The bit, called the *flc* bit, is allocated in a different word from the lock field, since the protocol relies on an important discipline that a lock field can only be modified without an atomic read-modify-write instruction by the thread holding the lock. The thread then attempts to acquire the spin lock (Line 29). Again, this is because the discipline requires the thread to hold the spin lock before inflating the lock. If it has failed in the acquisition, the thread waits on the monitor (Line 30). If it has successfully acquired the spin lock, the thread resets the flc bit (Line 32), wakes up all of the threads waiting on the monitor (Line 33), and inflates the lock (Line 34).

To release a lock, the current thread first tests the lock field to determine whether it is in the flat mode. If so, the current thread releases the spin lock (Line 41). Otherwise, it exits from the monitor (Line 51). Notice that releasing in the flat mode does not require any atomic read-modify-write instruction. Indeed, the discipline mentioned above is imposed for this purpose.

After releasing the spin lock, the thread actually does one more thing. It checks the flc bit (Line 42) to see if flat lock contention has occurred. Since this rarely happens, tasuki lock adds only one extra bit test to thin locks in the commonest case. When the contention has actually occurred, the thread proceeds to the body of the `if` statement, and wakes up all of the threads waiting on the monitor (Line 45). Also, just before exiting from the monitor, the thread attempts to deflate the lock. It checks that no thread is waiting on the monitor and estimates how unlikely it is that contention soon happens again (Line 50).

Readers may wonder if some thread could continue to wait at Line 30 without ever waking up. Also, they may wonder if deflation may allow two threads to execute a synchronized method simultaneously by allowing one thread to hold a flat lock and the other to hold the inflated lock. Actually, the algorithm guarantees that neither event can happen. See [25] for a discussion of the correctness.

The `try_acquire` and `release` functions are identical to the corresponding functions of the CAS-based spin lock in Figure 3. However, there are two important extensions made in the design. One is that the lock field now contains the shape bit. The other is that an attempt to acquire the spin lock always fails in the inflated mode.

4.3 Building Bimodal Locks from the KKO Lock

We now replace the CAS-based spin lock in a bimodal lock with the KKO spin lock. The resulting *spin-by-KKO* lock behaves in the uncontended case as the KKO spin lock. Thus, this new reservation-based Java lock does not require any atomic read-modify-write instructions on a reservation hit *and* does not have to stop the owner on a reservation miss.

For the replacement, we must make the abovementioned two extentions. First, we include the shape bit in the lockword as follows.

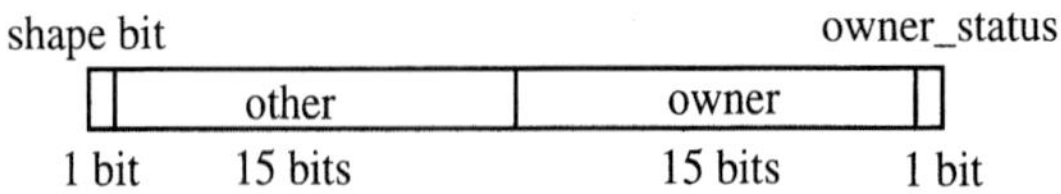

Next, we have the `try_acquire` function always fail in the inflated mode by involving the shape bit in the availability checks and state transitions. Figure 10 shows the resulting code of the extended KKO lock.

```
#define SHAPEBIT   0x80000000
#define OWNERMASK  0x0000fffe
#define OTHERMASK  0x7fff0000

#define SHAPEOWNERMASK (SHAPEBIT | OWNERMASK)
#define SHAPEOTHERMASK (SHAPEBIT | OTHERMASK)

/* The other macros are the same as the one-word KKO */

int try_acquire(volatile word_t *kko){
  word_t word = *kko;
  if ((word & SHAPEOWNERMASK)==0){ /* attempt in the initial state */
    word_t locked=(myself() | 0x01);
    return compare_and_swap(kko,0,locked);
  }
  else if ((word & SHAPEOWNERMASK)==myself()){ /* attempt by the owner */
    OWNER_STATUS_BYTE(kko) = (word | 0x01);
    if (((*kko) & SHAPEOTHERMASK)==0)
      return SUCCESS;
    else {
      OWNER_STATUS_BYTE(kko) = (word & ~0x01);
      return FAILURE;
    }
  }
  else { /*  attempt by a non-owner thread */
    word_t unlocked= (word & OWNERMASK);
    word_t locked=(unlocked | (SHIFT_OWNER_TO_OTHER(myself())));
   /* If the shape bit is set, the compare-and-swap fails */
    return compare_and_swap(kko, unlocked, locked);
  }
}

void release(volatile word_t *kko){
  /* called from a bimodal lock's release function when the shape bit is not set */
  word_t word = *kko;
  if ((word & SHAPEOWNERMASK)==myself())
    OWNER_STATUS_BYTE(kko) = (word & ~0x01);
  else
    OTHER_SHORT(kko)=0;
}
```

Fig. 10. One-word KKO extended for being employed in a bimodal lock

In inflating a spin-by-KKO lock, we store a reference to a monitor into the upper three bytes of the lockword. We avoid using the byte containing the `owner_status` field. Data race might otherwise result when a non-owner thread inflates the lock, since the owner thread is allowed to write into the byte at any arbitrary time.

Deflating a spin-by-KKO lock puts it back into the flat mode and the state of being reserved but not held. Notice that the KKO protocol requires the lock to be reserved for the same thread. Thus, we save the owner into the monitor at inflation, and restore the owner from there at deflation. We extend the monitor structure for this purpose.

5 Experimental Results

In this section we evaluate the effectiveness of our new, reservation-based algorithm in the IBM Developer Kit for Windows, Java Technology Edition, Version 1.4.0 [18]. The virtual machine in the developer kit contains a synchronization subsystem based on tasuki lock [25]. We implemented both the spin-by-KKO algorithm and the stop-the-owner algorithm [21], and compared the two algorithms, using the tasuki lock in the original virtual machine as the base algorithm.

We included a common optimization for recursive locking in the implementation of our algorithm. We allocated a counter field in each object's header to represent the recursive locking depth. The actual layout of the lockword in the implemented system is shown in the appendix.

We implemented the stop-the-owner algorithm in almost the same way as in [21]. In particular, we built it upon the original tasuki lock. Thus, when a non-owner thread of a lock attempts to acquire the lock, it cancels the reservation, and falls back to the tasuki lock.

All the benchmark programs were run under the Windows XP Professional Edition with SP1 on an unloaded IBM IntelliStation M Pro which contains two 933 MHz Pentium III processors and 512 megabytes of RAM. To enforce the program order execution where necessary, we use a software technique. More concretely, we issue the write into a byte and then the read from the word containing the byte. The write and read issued this way are not optimized through *store-buffer forwarding* [19].[5]

5.1 Micro-Benchmarks

We show the results of a micro-benchmark which clearly highlights important behavioral characteristics of the base, the stop-the-owner, and the spin-by-KKO algorithms. The benchmark creates two threads `T` and `S`, which alternately perform three rounds of computation. In each round, `T` or `S` executes the following loop.

```
for (i=0; i<MAX; i++) synchronized(a[i]){ counter++; }
```

Here the variable `a` holds a `MAX`-element array of objects. Notice that, when the loop is executed for the first time, each of the `MAX` locks is acquired for the first time.

Figure 11 shows the execution times of the three algorithms for the initial few rounds of execution, relative to that of the base algorithm in the first round. For each of the rounds, the thread which executes the round is shown under the round number.

Let us first consider the performance of the base algorithm. Although two threads are involved, the lock is not contended at all. Thus, the base algorithm shows the same uncontended performance in all of the rounds. As mentioned in Section 4.2, tasuki lock allows a lock to be acquired and released in the absence of contention with a few machine instructions containing only one CAS.

Next, we consider the performance of the stop-the-owner algorithm. As we mentioned in Section 2, the algorithm adopts the reservation policy of first acquirer. Thus, a thread attempting to acquire the lock for the first time, `T` in this case, reserves the lock for itself with a CAS. This happens in the first round in Figure 11.

---

[5] An important assumption we have made here is that blocking store-buffer forwarding preserves the write-to-read program order. While the assumption seems valid in the Pentium III, we could find no explicit mention of this in the Intel manual [19]. Thus, the performance results in this section should be regarded as showing the potential of our approach.

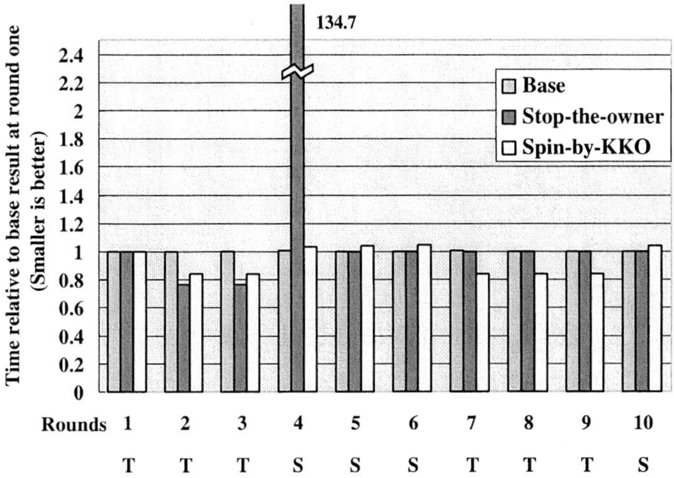

Fig. 11. Micro-benchmark results

Since the lock is now reserved for T, the performance in the second and third rounds becomes better since the thread can acquire and release the lock without any atomic read-modify-write instruction. This is the power of lock reservation.

However, when S comes into play in the fourth round, the pathological behavior of the stop-the-owner algorithm manifests itself. In this round, S stops T and cancels the reservation, making the performance in this round about 135 times worse than the performance of the base algorithm. In addition, after the fourth round, the stop-the-owner algorithm never exhibits the same level of high performance for T's rounds as for the second and third rounds, since it has fallen back to tasuki lock in the fourth round and does not reserve the lock again.

Now, we consider the performance of our spin-by-KKO algorithm. The same explanation applies for the first three rounds. In particular, we can observe a level of high performance close to the stop-the-owner algorithm on a reservation hit. The subsequent rounds show two significant advantages of our algorithm over the stop-the-owner algorithm. First, the spin-by-KKO algorithm does not show any pathology in the fourth round, since it does not stop the owner. Second, the algorithm shows the same level of high performance in all of T's rounds since it does not cancel the reservation and the lock continues to be reserved for T.

Finally, the performance of our algorithm in S's rounds is similar to the base algorithm. This is because the spin-by-KKO algorithm is a bimodal lock and the performance in the uncontended path is almost the same as the performance of the KKO lock. In each of S's rounds, the non-owner path of the KKO-lock is executed, which contains one CAS as the most dominant cost.

5.2 Macro-Benchmarks

We now show the results of more realistic applications, seven programs from SPECjvm98 [31] and two scientific applications from the SPLASH-2 benchmark

Table 1. Synchronization statistics of macro-benchmarks

Program name	Number of sync'd objects	Number of lock acquisitions	Stop-the-owner: Ratios of reservation hits	Stop-the-owner: Number of cancellations	Spin-by-KKO: Ratios of reservation hits
SPECjvm98					
`_202_jess`	12,800	14,977,053	99.353%	187	99.356%
`_201_compress`	2,462	35,382	85.764%	127	86.868%
`_209_db`	66,800	170,834,005	99.982%	52	99.982%
`_222_mpegaudio`	2,111	31,201	88.327%	91	89.028%
`_228_jack`	538,631	46,972,114	95.822%	144	95.859%
`_213_javac`	133,448	43,820,079	98.662%	1,760	99.676%
`_227_mtrt`	3,358	3,528,225	99.451%	114	99.548%
Water	858,230	4,326,541	43.668%	6,022	44.342%
Barnes	216,459	2,064,200	25.245%	78,819	34.076%

set [33]. The scientific applications are Water and Barnes which were written in Java by the authors of [30].

Table 1 shows the synchronization statistics of the benchmark programs. We collected these statistics by running a special version of the virtual machine and JIT compiler which counts the events of our interest. We ran each of the SPECjvm98 benchmarks in the application mode, specifying the problem size as 100% and the number of executions as three. As the table shows, even when JIT compiler is enabled, locks are very frequently acquired (and released) in all of the programs except `_201_compress` and `_222_mpegaudio`. Among these programs, `_227_mtrt`, Water, and Barnes are multithreaded programs.[6]

For each program, the table shows the ratios of reservation hits of the two algorithms. We compute the ratio as the number of *outermost* acquisitions by the owner thread divided by the total number of lock acquisitions. That is, we exclude recursive acquisitions by the owner thread, since they are already optimized in the base algorithm and performed without any atomic read-modify-write instructions. As shown here, both of the reservation-based algorithms can speed up the vast majority of the lock acquisitions in the SPECjvm98 benchmarks, while they can still accelerate many though not most of the acquisitions in the scientific applications. Also, as expected from the behavioral characteristics, the hit ratios are always not lower for the measured benchmarks in the spin-by-KKO than in the stop-the-owner. The difference is largest in Barnes.

For the stop-the-owner algorithm, the table shows how many cancellations of reservations occur in each program. While cancellations rarely happen in the SPECjvm98 programs, they are frequent in the two scientific applications, especially in Barnes. We suspect that frequent cancellations and the lower hit

[6] Although the virtual machine we use creates a couple of internal helper threads at start-up time, single-threaded programs are likely to result in mostly single-threaded execution.

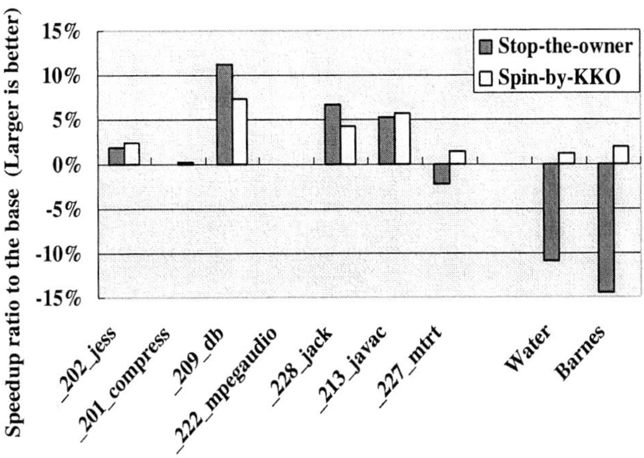

Fig. 12. Macro-benchmark results

ratios just mentioned above resulted because these two programs are translated from the C versions, and do not rely on Java's standard library very much.

Figure 12 shows the speedup ratios of the reservation-based algorithms to the base algorithm. We ran each program in SPECjvm98 in the application mode at the 100% problem size. We took the best times from the repeated runs. Let us first consider the performance of SPECjvm98. The stop-the-owner algorithm showed a maximal speedup of 11.3% in `_209_db` but slows down `_227_mtrt`. The spin-by-KKO showed a maximal speedup of 7.4% in `_209_db`, no slowdown for `_227_mtrt`, and more speedups in `_202_jess` and `_213_javac` than the stop-the-owner algorithm. Neither significantly improved `_201_compress` and `_222_mpegaudio`, since these programs involve very few synchronization operations and are little affected by the performance of Java locks.

We now turn to the performance of the two scientific programs. The stop-the-owner algorithm degraded these two programs. In particular, it causes as much as a 14.4% of slowdown in Barnes. This shows that canceling reservations by stopping the owner threads could have a significantly negative impact even on macro-benchmarks. The spin-by-KKO algorithm, on the other hand, did not exhibit such anomalous behavior, and even improved the performance of these scientific applications.

6 Related Work

There is a significant body of literature on locks. In addition, since locks are indispensable to many software systems, especially to operating systems, it is said that a large amount of unpublished work by practitioners exists. Here we consider three categories of related efforts from the literature, which are, in the historical order, locks by atomic reads and writes, locks for multiprocessor systems, and locks for Java.

6.1 Locks by Atomic Reads and Writes

Early work focused on achieving mutual exclusion using only atomic read and write instructions, leading to numerous algorithms, including Dekker's [12], Dijkstra's [11], Peterson's [28], and Lamport's [22]. However, the number of read and write instructions required in these algorithms is proportional to the number of threads (or processes), preventing them from being used in practical systems. Furthermore, academic interest in such algorithms quickly dwindled with the prevailing hardware support of atomic read-modify-write instructions.

Our reservation-based algorithm for spin lock also attempts to achieve mutual exclusion with atomic read and write instructions but only in the common case (on a reservation hit). By hybridizing the CAS-based lock and the Dekker-style lock, our algorithm only requires a few read and write instructions on a reservation hit.

6.2 Locks for Multiprocessor Systems

While the hardware support of atomic read-modify-write instructions facilitates creating locks in software, bus traffic becomes a major concern in spin locks on multiprocessor systems. Anderson [2] studied the performance of various algorithms for spin locks on shared multiprocessor systems, and discussed optimizations such as *spin on read* and *exponential back-off*. Mellor-Crummey and Scott [23] proposed a sophisticated algorithm for spin lock that performs efficiently in shared-memory multiprocessors of arbitrary size. Both of these pieces of work are orthogonal to our reservation-based spin lock, and we believe that their findings are applicable to improving the KKO lock.

Ousterhout [26] first suggested spin-suspend locks, leading to subsequent work on the spinning strategy. Karlin, Li, Manasse, and Owicki [20] empirically studied seven spinning strategies based on the measured lock-waiting-time distributions and elapsed times. As mentioned earlier, bimodal locks are space-efficient hybridizations of spin locks and suspend locks. Their findings are thus applicable to bimodal locks, including our spin-by-KKO algorithm.

6.3 Java Locks

Java created renewed interest in algorithms for locks, because very frequent and ubiquitous synchronizations caused a significant performance penalty in early virtual machines. This resulted in many techniques, both runtime and compile-time, being proposed. While runtime optimizations aim at reducing the cost of synchronization, compile-time optimizations attempt to eliminate it.

Runtime Optimizations. Bacon et al. [6] proposed the first bimodal algorithm for Java, called *thin locks*, based on the observation that most locks are not contended in Java. Thin locks reserve one field in each object's header[7], and issue only one atomic read-modify-write instruction in the absence of contention. However, thin locks require busy-wait on inflation and do not support deflation.

[7] The field is 24 bits long in their prototype.

Onodera and Kawachiya [25] proposed an enhanced algorithm, called *tasuki lock*, to solve these issues in thin locks. Allocating one additional bit in an object's header to represent a contention status, they removed the busy-wait from inflation, and enabled deflation. Importantly, they did not add any additional atomic read-modify-write instructions in the uncontended path. The SableVM [13] employs a variation of tasuki lock.

Agesen et al.[3] proposed another algorithm for Java lock, called the *meta lock*. While it only uses two bits of a word in each object's header, it requires at least two atomic read-modify-write instructions in acquiring and releasing a lock. Thus, it is not as time-efficient as thin locks and tasuki lock. Furthermore, when contention happens, it requires the full word (32 bits), and moves the 30 remaining bits to an out-of-line data structure. Thus, frequently accessed information such as a class pointer cannot be stored in the remaining bits.

Although the details are significantly different, these fast algorithms allow a lock to be acquired and released with a small number of instructions. However, the instruction sequence of each algorithm still contains one or two atomic read-modify-write instructions, which have been becoming relatively more and more expensive in modern multiprocessor architectures.

Recently, we [21] proposed a powerful runtime optimization for Java locks, called *lock reservation*. As explained in Section 2, while it significantly reduces the synchronization overhead on a reservation hit, it must stop the owner on a reservation miss. Thus, the algorithm lacks robustness and allows for pathological behaviors, which motivated the work we present in this paper. Gomes et al.[14] proposed a similar idea which they call *speculative locking*. Their algorithm also requires a heavyweight fix-up operation to be performed on speculation failure.

Bacon [5] attempted to completely eliminate the synchronization overhead in single-threaded executions. As long as the virtual machine creates and runs only one thread, it regards lock acquisition and release as no-ops. When the virtual machine actually creates a second thread, it scans the stack frames and properly recovers the lock states. Muller [24] also briefly mentioned a similar idea. Ruf [29] proposed a whole-program analysis to determine whether the program creates a second thread or not. Unfortunately, these ideas cannot be applied in most of the commercial virtual machines, since these VMs create not only the main thread, but also a couple of helper threads, at start-up time.

Compile-time Optimizations. *Escape analysis* [27] attempts to find objects only accessible by the threads creating them, thereby eliminating all the synchronization operations for such non-escaping objects. Several algorithms for Java [4,7,8,9,29,32] have been proposed with varying trade-offs between the precision and the complexity of computing.

However, these techniques are the most effective with whole program analysis by a static compiler, while they provide limited benefits for a dynamic language such as Java. When performing escape analysis for Java programs, many more objects must conservatively be determined to escape, and their synchronization operations could not be optimized away.

7 Concluding Remarks

We have presented a new reservation-based algorithm for Java lock. We obtained the algorithm by replacing a CAS-based spin lock in a bimodal lock with our new spin lock, called the KKO lock. We devised the KKO lock by applying lock reservation to spin lock for the first time, and by hybridizing a CAS-based lock and a Dekker-style lock.

We have evaluated an implementation of our algorithm in IBM's production virtual machine and JIT compiler. The results of micro-benchmarks show that, compared to the previous stop-the-owner algorithm, the spin-by-KKO algorithm achieves a similar level of high performance on a reservation hit, shows no anomaly on a reservation miss, and also yields more reservation hits. For macro-benchmarks, while our algorithm achieved up to 7.4% speedups in the SPECjvm98 benchmarks, it even improved the performance of two scientific programs which the previous algorithm degraded by more than 10%.

The new algorithm provides performance gains on those multiprocessor architectures where the cost of the CAS is higher than the cost of program-order enforcement. Hardware instructions for order enforcement are not expensive in some architectures (such as the `lsync` of the PowerPC), while they are heavy in others (such as the `mfence` of the Pentium 4). Also, software techniques for order enforcement are documented in manuals for some architectures (such as IBM 370), while they are not for others (such as the P6 family). A lightweight and certified method for enforcing the write-to-read order is valuable for many software developers, since it allows developers to create synchronization protocols to their needs.

Acknowledgments. We thank the members of the Network Computing Platform group in IBM Tokyo Research Laboratory for their useful comments and valuable suggestions. We also thank Alexandru Salcianu and Martin Rinard for making their benchmark programs available for us.

References

1. S. V. Adve and K. Gharachorloo: Shared Memory Consistency Models: A Tutorial. *IEEE Computer*, 29(12), 66–76, 1996.
2. T. E. Anderson: The Performance of Spin Lock Alternatives for Shared-Memory Multiprocessors. *IEEE Transactions on Parallel and Distributed Systems*, 1(1), 6–16, 1990.
3. O. Agesen, D. Detlefs, A. Garthwaite, R. Knippel, Y. S. Ramakrishna, and D. White: An Efficient Meta-lock for Implementing Ubiquitous Synchronization. *Proceedings of ACM OOPSLA '99*, 207–222, 1999.
4. J. Aldrich, C. Chambers, E. G. Sirer, and S. Eggers: Static Analyses for Eliminating Unnecessary Synchronization from Java Programs. *Proceedings of the 6th Int'l Static Analysis Symposium (SAS '99)*, 19–38, 1999.
5. D. F. Bacon: Fast and Effective Optimization of Statically Typed Object-Oriented Languages. Ph.D. Thesis UCB/CSD-98-1017, University of California, 1997.

6. D. F. Bacon, R. Konuru, C. Murthy, and M. Serrano: Thin Locks: Featherweight Synchronization for Java. *Proceedings of ACM PLDI '98*, 258–268, 1998.
7. B. Blanchet: Escape Analysis for Object-Oriented Languages: Application to Java. *Proceedings of ACM OOPSLA '99*, 20–34, 1999.
8. J. Bogda and U. Hölzle: Removing Unnecessary Synchronization in Java. *Proceedings of ACM OOPSLA '99*, 35–46, 1999.
9. J.-D. Choi, M. Gupta, M. Serrano, V. C. Sreedhar, and S. Midkiff: Escape Analysis for Java. *Proceedings of ACM OOPSLA '99*, 1–19, 1999.
10. D. E. Culler and J. P. Singh with A. Gupta: *Parallel Computer Architecture: A Hardware/Software Approach.* Morgan Kaufmann, 681–700, 1999.
11. E. W. Dijkstra: Solution of a Problem in Concurrent Programming and Control. *Communications of the ACM*, 8(9), 569, 1965.
12. E. W. Dijkstra: *Cooperating Sequential Processes*, 43–112. Academic Press, New York, 1968.
13. E. M. Gagnon and L. J. Hendren: SableVM: A Research Framework for the Efficient Execution of Java Bytecode. *Proceedings of USENIX JVM '01*, 27–39, 2001.
14. B. A. Gomes, L. Bak, and D. P. Stoutamire: *Method and Apparatus for Speculatively Locking Objects in an Object-Based System.* United States Patent, US 6,487,652 B1, 2002.
15. J. Gosling, B. Joy, and G. Steele: *The Java Language Specification.* Addison Wesley, 1996.
16. M. Greenwald and D. Cheriton: The Synergy Between Non-blocking Synchronization and Operating System Structure. *Proceedings of USENIX OSDI '96*, 123–136, 1996.
17. C. A. R. Hoare: Monitors: An Operating System Structuring Concept. *Communications of the ACM*, 17(10), 549–557, 1974.
18. IBM developerWorks Java Technology Zone. `http://www.ibm.com/developerworks/java/`.
19. Intel Corporation. IA-32 Intel Architecture Software Developer's Manual Volume 3: System Programming Guide, Order Number 245472-010, 2002
20. A. R. Karlin, K. Li, M. S. Manasse, and S. Owicki: Empirical Studies of Competitive Spinning for A Shared-Memory Multiprocessor. *Proceedings of ACM SOSP '91*, 41–55, 1991.
21. K. Kawachiya, A. Koseki, and T. Onodera: Lock Reservation: Java Locks Can Mostly Do Without Atomic Operations. *Proceedings of ACM OOPSLA 2002*, 131–141, 2002.
22. L. Lamport: A Fast Mutual Exclusion Algorithm. *ACM Transactions on Computer Systems*, 5(1), 1–11, 1987.
23. J. M. Mellor-Crummey and M. L. Scott: Algorithms for Scalable Synchronization on Shared-Memory Multiprocessors. *ACM Transactions on Computer Systems*, 9(1), 21–65, 1991.
24. G. Muller, B. Moura, F. Bellard, and C. Consel: Harissa: A Flexible and Efficient Java Environment Mixing Bytecode and Compiled Code. *Proceedings of the 3rd USENIX Conference on Object Oriented Technologies and Systems (COOTS '97)*, 1–20, 1997.
25. T. Onodera and K. Kawachiya: A Study of Locking Objects with Bimodal Fields. *Proceedings of ACM OOPSLA '99*, 223–237, 1999.
26. J. K. Ousterhout: Scheduling Techniques for Concurrent Systems. *Proceedings of the 3rd International Conference on Distributed Computing Systems*, 22–30, 1982.
27. Y. G. Park and B. Goldberg: Escape Analysis on Lists. *Proceedings of ACM PLDI '92*, 116–127, 1992.

28. G. L. Peterson: Myths about the Mutual Exclusion Problem. *Information Processing Letters*, 12(3), 115–116, 1981.
29. E. Ruf: Effective Synchronization Removal for Java. *Proceedings of ACM PLDI '00*, 208–218, 2000.
30. A. Salcianu and M. Rinard: Pointer and Escape Analysis for Multithreaded Programs. *Proceedings of ACM PPoPP '01*, 12–23, 2001.
31. Standard Performance Evaluation Corporation:
SPEC JVM98 Benchmarks. `http://www.spec.org/osg/jvm98/`.
32. J. Whaley and M. Rinard: Compositional Pointer and Escape Analysis for Java Programs. *Proceedings of ACM OOPSLA '99*, 187–206, 1999.
33. S. C. Woo, M. Ohara, E. Torrie, J. P. Singh, and A. Gupta: The SPLASH-2 Programs: Characterization and Methodological Considerations. *Proceedings of ACM ISCA '95*, 12–23, 1995.

A Lockword Structure of the Implemented System

We allocate three bits (the `rcnt` field) for representing the recursive locking depth. Note that we cannot have the `owner_status` field serve this purpose, since the field does not indicate anything about the lock state of a non-owner thread. We use the `misc` field for representing other object states than the lock state. To avoid data race, we only encode into the `misc` field those states which do not change after object creation.

If we could remove the `misc` field from the lockword, we could allocate 14 bits for the the `owner` and `other` fields by making the `rcnt` field two bits long.

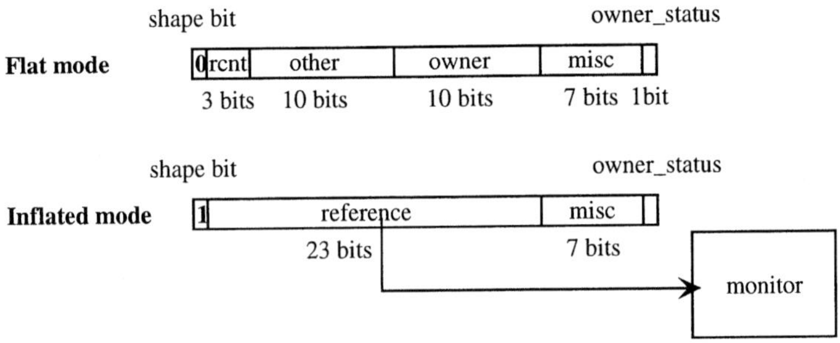

Customization of Java Library Classes Using Type Constraints and Profile Information

Bjorn De Sutter[1], Frank Tip[2], and Julian Dolby[2]

[1] Ghent University, Electronics and Information Systems Department
Sint-Pietersnieuwstraat 41 9000 Gent, Belgium
brdsutte@elis.ugent.be

[2] IBM T.J. Watson Research Center, P.O. Box 704, Yorktown Heights, NY 10598
{ftip,dolby}@us.ibm.com

Abstract. The use of class libraries increases programmer productivity by allowing programmers to focus on the functionality unique to their application. However, library classes are generally designed with some typical usage pattern in mind, and performance may be suboptimal if the actual usage differs. We present an approach for rewriting applications to use customized versions of library classes that are generated using a combination of static analysis and profile information. Type constraints are used to determine where customized classes may be used, and profile information is used to determine where customization is likely to be profitable. We applied this approach to a number of Java applications by customizing various standard container classes and the omnipresent StringBuffer class, and measured speedups up to 78% and memory footprint reductions up to 46%. The increase in application size due to the added custom classes is limited to 12% for all but the smallest programs.

1 Introduction

The availability of a large library of standardized classes is an important reason for Java's popularity as a programming language. The use of class libraries improves programmer productivity by allowing programmers to focus on the aspects that are unique to their application without being burdened with the unexciting task of building (and debugging!) standard infrastructure. However, library classes are often designed and implemented with some typical usage pattern in mind. If the actual use of a library class by an application differs substantially from this typical usage pattern, performance may be suboptimal.

Consider, for example, the implementation of the container classes such as `Vector` and `Hashtable` in package `java.util`. In designing the implementation of these containers, a large number of accesses to objects stored therein was (implicitly) assumed. Therefore, the allocation of auxiliary data structures encapsulated by the container (e.g., a `Vector`'s underlying array, or a `Hashtable`'s embedded array of hash-buckets) is performed *eagerly* upon construction of the container itself. This approach has the advantage that the container's access methods can assume that these auxiliary data structures have been allocated.

M. Odersky (Ed.): ECOOP 2004, LNCS 3086, pp. 585–609, 2004.

However, as we shall see in Section 6, it is not uncommon for programs to create large numbers of containers that remain empty or that contain only small numbers of objects. In such cases, *lazy* allocation is preferable, despite the fact that the access methods become slower because they have to check if the auxiliary data structures have been allocated and create them if this is not the case.

Library classes may also induce unnecessary overhead if an application does not use all of the provided functionality. For example, most iterators provided by containers such as `Hashtable` are designed to be fail-fast (i.e., an exception is thrown when an attempt is made to use an iterator and a concurrent modification of its underlying container is detected). Fail-fast iterators are implemented by keeping track of the "version" of the container that an iterator is associated with, and incrementing a container's version number upon each modification. This "bookkeeping code" is executed, and space for its data is reserved, regardless of the fact whether or not iterators are used. For clients that do not use iterators, a customized container without iteration support can improve performance.

A third common case of unnecessary overhead occurs when single-threaded applications use library classes that are designed with multi-threaded clients in mind. For example, many Java programs frequently concatenate strings via calls to the `synchronized` method `java.lang.StringBuffer.append()`[1]. This means that a lock must be acquired for each call to this method, which is unnecessary for single-threaded applications. Performance can improved in such cases by rewriting the application to use custom, unsynchronized `StringBuffers`.

We present a fully automated approach for generating and using customized versions of Java library classes. This approach consists of 5 steps.

1. First, type constraints are used to determine where library classes can be replaced with custom versions without affecting type correctness or program behavior. The result is a set of allocation site candidates that may allocate custom type objects instead of standard library type objects.
2. Static analysis is then used to determine those candidates for which unused library functionality and synchronization can be removed safely from the allocated types.
3. In addition, profile information is collected about the usage characteristics of the customization candidates to determine where the allocation of custom library classes is likely to be profitable. In our whole approach, selecting the training inputs and executing the instrumented program is the only manual step.
4. Based on the static analysis results and the profiling information, custom library classes are automatically generated from a template.
5. Finally, the bytecode of the client application is rewritten to use the generated custom classes. This bytecode rewriting is completely transparent to the programmer.

We applied this approach to a set of benchmark Java applications, and customized various container classes in `java.util`, as well as class `StringBuffer`.

[1] Java compilers translate uses of the +-operator on `String` objects into calls to `StringBuffer.append()`.

We measured speedups ranging from -5 to 78% (19-24% on average, depending on the VM) and memory footprint reductions ranging from -1 to 46% (averaging 12%). Moreover, the addition of custom classes to the benchmarks resulted in only a modest increase in application size: less than 12% for all but the smallest programs.

The remainder of this paper is structured as follows. Section 2 presents a motivating example. Sections 3 and 4 present type constraints and their use for determining where custom classes may be used, respectively. Section 5 discusses the steps involved in profiling and generating custom classes. In Section 6, an evaluation of our techniques on a set of benchmarks is presented. Sections 7 and 8 present related work, and conclusions and future work, respectively.

2 Motivating Example

We will use an example program that creates several `Hashtable` objects to illustrate the issues that arise when replacing references to standard library classes with references to custom classes. Class `Hashtable` is well-suited to serve as a motivating example because: (i) it is part of a complex class hierarchy in which it has both supertypes (e.g., `Map` and `Dictionary`) and subtypes (`Properties`), (ii) several orthogonal optimizations can be applied when creating custom hashtables[2], and (iii) `Hashtables` are heavily used by many (legacy) Java applications.

In order to create a customized version of, say, a `Hashtable`, one could simply create a class `CustomHashtable` that extends `Hashtable` and overrides some of its methods. Unfortunately, this approach has significant limitations. In particular, fully lazy allocation is impossible because `Hashtable`'s constructors always allocate certain auxiliary datastructures (e.g., an array of hash-buckets)[3], and each constructor of `CustomHashtable` must invoke one of `Hashtable`'s constructors. Moreover, each `CustomHashtable` object contains all of `Hashtable`'s instance fields, which introduces unneccessary overhead if these fields are unused (as was the case in the example discussed above of redundant iterator-related bookkeeping code). Therefore, customized classes will be introduced in a separate branch of the class hierarchy, as is indicated in Figure 1. The figure shows the standard library types `Hashtable`, `Map`, `Dictionary`, and `Properties`, and the inheritance relationships between them. Also shown are custom container classes `CachingHashtable` and `LazyAllocHashtable`, and an abstract class `AbstractCustomHashtable` that serves as a common superclass of customized versions of `Hashtable`.

---

[2] One particular optimization that can be applied to custom versions of class `Hashtable` is the removal of synchronization in cases where the client application is single-threaded. To avoid overhead in such cases, modern Java applications tend to use the similar class `HashMap`, in which the methods are not synchronized.

[3] While it is possible to specify the initial size of this array of hash-buckets upon construction of a `Hashtable`-object, the construction of this array-object cannot be avoided altogether if `CustomHashtable` is a subclass of `Hashtable`.

We will use the example program shown in Figure 2 to illustrate the issues that arise when introducing custom classes such as those shown in Figure 1. This program creates a number of container objects, and performs some method calls on these objects. Observe that the program contains three allocation sites of type `Hashtable` and one of type `String` that we will refer as `H1`, `H2`, `H3`, and `S1`, as is indicated in Figure 2 using comments. We will now examine a number of issues that arise when updating allocation sites to refer to custom types.

Calls to methods in external classes. Allocation site `H1` cannot be updated to refer to a custom type because the object allocated at `H1` is passed to a constructor of `javax.swing.JTree` that expects an argument of type `java.util.Hashtable`. Since the code in class `JTree` is not under our control, the type of the parameter of `JTree`'s constructor must remain `java.util.Hashtable`, which implies that the types of `h1` and `H1` must remain `java.util.Hashtable` as well. Similar issues arise for calls to library methods whose return type is a *concrete*[4] standard container, such as the call to `System.getProperties()` on line 11, which returns an object of type `java.util.Properties`, a subtype of `java.util.Hashtable`.

Preserving type-correctness. Allocation sites `H2` and `H3` may be updated to refer to, for example, type `CachingHashtable`. However, if we make this change, we must also update `h2` and `h3` to refer to a superclass of `CachingHashtable` (i.e., `CachingHashtable`, `AbstractCustomHashtable`, `Map`, `Dictionary`, or `Object`) because the assignments on lines 5 and 6 would otherwise not be type-correct. The method calls `h2.put("FOO", "BAR")` and `h2.putAll(c)` impose the additional requirement that the `put()` and `putAll()` methods must be visible in the type of `h2`, and hence that `h2`'s type must be `CachingHashtable`, `AbstractCustomHashtable`, or `Map`. Furthermore, the assignment `h2 = h3` is only type-correct if the type of `h2` is the same as or a supertype of the type of `h3`, and the assignments `Properties p1 = System.getProperties()` and `h2 = p1` require that the type of `h2` must be a supertype of `java.util.Properties`. Combining all of these requirements, we infer that allocation sites `H2` and `H3` can only be updated to allocate `CachingHashtable` objects if both `h2` and `h3` are declared to be of type `Map`.

Preserving the behavior of casts. The cast expression on line 16 (indicated as `C1`) presents another interesting case. Observe that only objects allocated at sites `H3` and `S1` may be bound to parameter `o`. In the transformed program, the cast expression must succeed and fail in exactly the same cases as before. In this case, if the type of the object allocated at site `H3` is changed to `CachingHashtable`, changing the type of the cast to, for example, `AbstractCustomHashtable` will preserve the behavior of the cast (it will still succeed when parameter `o` points to an object allocated at site `H3` and it will

[4] The use of *concrete* container types such as `Hashtable` (as opposed to *abstract* container types such as `Map`) in the signature of public library methods is often an indication of poor design, because it unnecessarily exposes implementation details. Nonetheless, this practice is pervasive. We counted 165 public methods in the JDK 1.3.1 standard libraries whose signature refers to `Hashtable`, `Vector`, or `Properties`.

still fail when `o` points to an object allocated at site `S1`). Furthermore, the assignment `Hashtable h4 = (Hashtable)o` is only type-correct if the type of `h4` is a supertype of the type referenced in the cast expression, and the method call `h4.contains(···)` implies that `h4`'s type must define the `contains(···)` method (in other words, `h4` must have type `AbstractCustomHashtable` or a subtype thereof). We conclude from the above discussion that having the cast refer to type `AbstractCustomHashtable` and declaring `h4` to be of type `AbstractCustomHashtable` is a valid solution[5].

The lessons learned from the above example can be summarized as follows: The customized program must satisfy *interface-compatibility constraints* that are due to the exchange of standard container objects with third-party libraries and *type-correctness constraints* implied by program constructs such as assignments that constrain the types of their subexpressions. Moreover, *run-time behavior* must be preserved for casts and `instanceof` operations.

Lines 5b, 15b, and 16b in Figure 2 indicate how allocation sites, declarations, and cast expressions in the original example program have been replaced with references to custom classes in accordance with the requirements that we discussed informally in this section. We will now turn our attention to a more precise treatment of these requirements.

3 Type Constraints

To determine where the types of allocation sites and declarations can be updated to refer to custom types in a way that preserves the program's type-correctness and behavior, we will use an existing framework of *type constraints* [18,25]. For each program construct, one or more type constraints express the subtype-relationships that must exist between the declared types of the construct's constituent expressions, in order for that program construct to be type-correct. By definition, a program is *type-correct* if the type constraints for all constructs in that program are satisfied. Unlike previous work on refactoring and replacing types in a program [25], our rewriting involves more than moving declared types up or down in an existing or extended class hierarchy. Instead we will move type declarations more or less horizontally: standard types in some position of the standard library hierarchy are replaced by custom types in a corresponding position in a newly added branch of the hierarchy. Sometimes vertical motion of declared types will still be useful however, because fields or variables can only hold references to both standard types and customized types if they are declared a supertype of both the standard classes and the custom classes.

In this section, we will therefore first introduce the existing constraint framework that was used in, e.g., [25]. This framework is then extended in Section 4 to accommodate the horizontal type replacements.

[5] Several other solutions exist. For example, variable `h4` and cast `C1` can both receive type `CachingHashtable`.

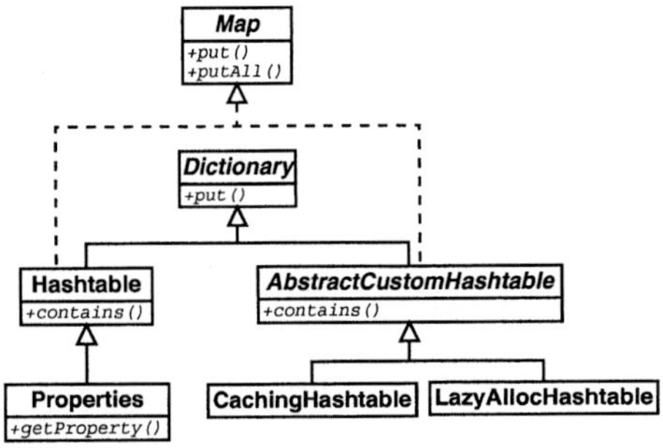

Fig. 1. A fragment of the standard container hierarchy in package `java.util.*`, augmented with several customized containers. The figure shows, for a number of relevant methods, the most general type in which they are declared.

```
1     public class Example {
2       public static void foo(Map m) {
3         Hashtable h1 = new Hashtable();   /* H1 */
4         JTree tree = new JTree(h1);
5         Hashtable h2 = new Hashtable();   /* H2 */
5b        Map h2 = new CachingHashtable();
6         Hashtable h3 = new Hashtable();   /* H3 */
6b        Map h3 = new CachingHashtable();
7         bar(h3);
8         h2 = h3;
9         h2.put("FOO", "BAR");
10        h2.putAll(m);
11        Properties p1 = System.getProperties();
12        String s = p1.getProperty("java.class.path");
13        h2 = p1;
14      }
15      public static void bar(Object o) {
16        Hashtable h4 = (Hashtable)o;       /* C1 */
16b       AbstractCustomHashtable h4 = (AbstractCustomHashtable)o;
17        if (h4.contains("FOO")){ ... }
18      }
19      public static void bad(){
20        String s = new String("bad");      /* S1 */
21        bar(s);
22      }
23    }
```

Fig. 2. This figure shows an example program P_1, which consists of lines 1–23 excluding lines 5b, 6b, and 16b. A customized version of this program that uses the custom class hierarchy of Figure 1 can be obtained from P_1 by replacing lines 5, 6, and 16, with lines 5b, 6b, and 16b, respectively.

In the remainder of this paper, we assume that the original program is type-correct. Moreover, we assume that the original program does not contain any up-casts (i.e., casts $(C)E$ in which the type of expression E is a subclass of C). This latter assumption is not a restriction, as there is no need for up-casts in Java byte code[6].

3.1 Notation and Terminology

Following [25], we use the term *declaration element* to refer to declarations of local variables, parameters in static, instance, and constructor methods, fields, and method return types, and to type references in cast expressions. In what follows, v, v' denote variables, M, M' denote methods, F, F' denote fields, C, C' denote classes, I, I' denote interfaces, and T, T' denote types[7]. It is important to note that the symbol M denotes a method together with all its signature and return type information and the reference to its declaring type. Similarly, F and C denote a field and a type, respectively, together with its name, type in which it is declared and, in the case of fields, its declared type.

Moreover, the notation E, E' will be used to denote an expression or declaration element at a specific point in the program, corresponding to a specific node in the program's abstract syntax tree. We will assume that type information about expressions and declaration elements is available from the compiler.

A method M is *virtual* if M is not a constructor, M is not private and M is not static. Definition 1 defines the concept of *overriding*[8] for virtual methods.

Definition 1 (overriding). *A virtual method M in type C overrides a virtual method M' in type B if M and M' have identical signatures and C is equal to B or C is a subtype of B.*[9] *In this case, we also say that M' is overridden by M.*

Definition 2 defines, for a given method M, the set *RootDefs*(M) of methods M' that are overridden by M that do not override any methods except for themselves. Since we assume the original program to be type-correct, this set is guaranteed to be non-empty. For example, in the standard collection hierarchy, we have that *RootDefs*(`Hashtable.put()`) = {`Map.put()`,`Dictionary.put()`} because `Map` and `Dictionary` are the most general types that declare `put()` methods that are overridden by `Hashtable.put()`.

Definition 2 (RootDefs). *Let M be a method. Define:*

$$\mathit{RootDefs}(M) = \{\, M' \mid M \text{ overrides } M', \text{ and there exists no } M'' \ (M'' \neq M') \text{ such that } M' \text{ overrides } M'' \,\}$$

[6] In Java source code, up-casts are sometimes needed for explicit resolution of overloaded methods.

[7] In this paper, the term *type* will denote a class or an interface.

[8] Note that, according to Definition 1, a virtual method overrides itself.

[9] This definition of overriding does not take into account issues related to access rights and throws-clauses. A precise definition of overriding that takes these issues into account is a topic for future work.

Figure 3 shows the notation used to express type constraints. A *constraint variable* α is one of the following: T (a type constant), $[E]$ (representing the type of an expression or declaration element E), *Decl*(M) (representing the type in which method M is declared), or *Decl*(F) (representing the type in which field F is declared). A *type constraint* is a relationship between two or more constraint variables that must hold in order for a program to be type-correct. In this paper, a *type constraint* has one of the following forms: (i) $\alpha_1 \triangleq \alpha_2$, indicating that α_1 is defined to be the same as α_2 (ii) $\alpha_1 \leq \alpha_2$, indicating that α_1 must be equal to or be a subtype of α_2, (iii) $\alpha_1 = \alpha_2$, indicating that $\alpha_1 \leq \alpha_2$ and $\alpha_2 \leq \alpha_1$, (iv) $\alpha_1 < \alpha_2$, indicating that $\alpha_1 \leq \alpha_2$ but not $\alpha_2 \leq \alpha_1$, (v) $\alpha_1^L \leq \alpha_1^R$ **or** $\cdots$ **or** $\alpha_k^L \leq \alpha_k^R$, indicating that $\alpha_j^L \leq \alpha_j^R$ must hold for at least one j, $1 \leq j \leq k$, (vi) $\alpha_1 \not\leq \alpha_2$, indicating that α_1 must not be equal to or be a subtype of α_2

In discussions about types and subtype-relationships that occur in a specific program P, we will use the notation of Figure 3 with subscript P. For example, $[E]_P$ denotes the type of expression E in program P, and $T' \leq_P T$ denotes a subtype-relationship that occurs in program P. In cases where the program under consideration is unambiguous, we will frequently omit these P-subscripts.

3.2 Inferring Type Constraints

We will now present the rules that will be used for inferring type constraints from various Java constructs and analysis facts.

Type-Correctness Constraints. Rules (1)–(17) in Figure 4 shows the type constraints that are implied by a number of common Java program constructs. For example, constraint (1) states that an assignment $E_1 = E_2$ is type correct if the type of E_2 is the same as or a subtype of the type of E_1. For a virtual method call $E.m(E_1, \cdots, E_n)$ that statically resolves to a method M, we define the type of the call-expression to be the same as M's return type (rule (2)), and we require that the type of each actual parameter E_i must be the same as or a subtype of the type of the corresponding formal parameter *Param*(M, i) (rule (3)). Moreover, a declaration of a method with the same signature as M must occur in a supertype of the type of E. This latter fact is expressed in rule (4) using Definition 2 by way of an **or**-constraint. For cast expressions of the form $(C)E$, rule (21) defines the type of the cast to be C. Moreover, rule (12) states the requirement that the type of E must be a supertype of C[10].

Rules (18)–(22) define the types of variables, parameters, fields, method return types, casts, and allocation sites in the original program.

Behavior-Preserving Constraints. The type constraints discussed thus far are only concerned with type-correctness. In general, additional constraints must

[10] In [25], this constraint for cast-expressions reads $[E] \leq [(C)E]$ **or** $[(C)E] \leq E$. We can use a simplified version here because we make the assumption that the original program does not contain up-casts.

$[E]$	the type of expression or declaration element E
$[M]$	the declared return type of method M
$[F]$	the declared type of field F
$Decl(M)$	the type that contains method M
$Decl(F)$	the type that contains field F
$Param(M, i)$	the i-th formal parameter of method M
$T' \leq T$	T' is equal to T, or T' is a subtype of T
$T' < T$	T' is a proper subtype of T (i.e., $T' \leq T$ and not $T \leq T'$)

Fig. 3. Type constraint notation.

program construct(s)/analysis fact(s)	implied type constraint(s)	
assignment $E_1 = E_2$	$[E_2] \leq [E_1]$	(1)
method call $E.m(E_1, \cdots, E_n)$ to a virtual method M	$[E.m(E_1, \cdots, E_n)] \triangleq [M]$ $[E_i] \leq [Param(M, i)]$ $[E] \leq Decl(M_1)$ **or** $\cdots$ **or** $[E] \leq Decl(M_k)$ where $RootDefs(M) = \{ M_1, \cdots, M_k \}$	(2) (3) (4)
access $E.f$ to field F	$[E.f] \triangleq [F]$ $[E] \leq Decl(F)$	(5) (6)
`return` E in method M	$[E] \leq [M]$	(7)
constructor call `new` $C(E_1, \cdots, E_n)$ to constructor M	$[E_i] \leq [Param(M, i)]$	(8)
direct call $E.m(E_1, \cdots, E_n)$ to method M	$[E.m(E_1, \cdots, E_n)] \triangleq [M]$ $[E_i] \leq [Param(M, i)]$ $[E] \leq Decl(M)$	(9) (10) (11)
cast $(C)E$	$[(C)E] \leq [E]$ if $[E]$ is a class	(12)
for every type T	$T \leq$ `java.lang.Object` [`null`] $\leq$ `T`	(13) (14)
implicit declaration of `this` in method M	[`this`] $\triangleq Decl(M)$	(15)
declaration of method M (declared in type T)	$Decl(M) \triangleq T$	(16)
declaration of field F (declared in type T)	$Decl(F) \triangleq T$	(17)
explicit declaration of variable or method parameter $T\ v$	$[v] \triangleq T$	(18)
declaration of method M with return type T	$[M] \triangleq T$	(19)
declaration of field F with type T	$[F] \triangleq T$	(20)
cast $(T)E$	$[(T)E] \triangleq T$	(21)
expression `new` $C(E_1, \cdots, E_n)$	[`new` $C(E_1, \cdots, E_n)] \triangleq C$	(22)
M' overrides M, $M' \neq M$	$[Param(M', i)] = [Param(M, i)]$ $[M'] = [M]$	(23) (24)
for each cast expression $(C)E$, and each allocation expression $E' \in PointsTo(P, E)$ such that $[E']_P \leq [(C)E]_P$	$[E'] \leq [(C)E]$	(25)
for each cast expression $(C)E$, and each allocation expression $E' \in PointsTo(P, E)$ such that $[E']_P \not\leq [(C)E]_P$	$[E'] \not\leq [(C)E]$	(26)
expression E that occurs in the libraries such that $[E]_P = T$	$[E] = T$	(27)

Fig. 4. Type constraints for a set of core Java language features. Rules (1)–(17) define the types of expressions and impose constraints between the types of expressions and declaration elements. Rules (18)–(22) define the types of declaration elements and allocation expressions in the original program. Rules (23)–(26) show additional type constraints that are needed for the preservation of program semantics. Rule (27) shows an additional type constraint needed to preserve interface-compatibility.

$$\begin{array}{ll} \mathit{PointsTo}(P_1, \texttt{h1}) = \{\,\texttt{H1}\,\} & \mathit{PointsTo}(P_1, \texttt{o}) = \{\,\texttt{H3}, \texttt{S1}\,\} \\ \mathit{PointsTo}(P_1, \texttt{h2}) = \{\,\texttt{H2}, \texttt{H3}, \texttt{P1}\,\} & \mathit{PointsTo}(P_1, \texttt{p}) = \{\,\texttt{P1}\,\} \\ \mathit{PointsTo}(P_1, \texttt{h3}) = \{\,\texttt{H3}\,\} & \mathit{PointsTo}(P_1, \texttt{s}) = \{\,\texttt{S1}\,\} \\ \mathit{PointsTo}(P_1, \texttt{h4}) = \{\,\texttt{H3}\,\} & \end{array}$$

Fig. 5. Points-to information for program P_1 of Figure 2, as computed using a variation on the flow-insensitive, context-insensitive 0-CFA algorithm [17] that propagates allocation sites rather than types. Here, `P1` represents the allocation site(s) at which the `Properties` objects returned by `System.getProperties()` are allocated.

be imposed to ensure that program behavior is preserved. Rules (23) and (24) state that overriding relationships that occur in the original program P must also occur in the rewritten program P'.

Rules (25) and (26) state that the execution behavior of a cast $(C)E$ must be preserved. Here, the notation $\mathit{PointsTo}(P, E)$ refers to be the set of objects (identified by their allocation sites) that an expression E in program P may point to. Any of several existing algorithms [20,13,21] can be used to compute this information. Figure 5 shows the points-to information that will be used in the examples below. Rule (25) ensures that for each E' in the points-to set of E for which the cast succeeds, the cast will still succeed in P'. Likewise, Rule (26) enforces that for each E' in the points-to set of E for which the cast fails, the cast will still fail in P'.

Interface-Compatibility Constraints. Finally, we need to ensure that the customized program preserves interface-compatibility. To this end, we impose the additional constraint of rule (27) in Figure 4. This rules states that the types of declarations and expressions that occur in external class libraries cannot be changed.

4 Introducing Custom Classes

The introduction of custom classes proceeds using the following steps. First, the class hierarchy is extended with custom classes and auxiliary types. Then, type constraints are computed for the program with respect to this extended class hierarchy. This is followed by a step in which all constraints are transformed into simple equality or subtype constraints. Finally, the constraint system is solved in order to determine where custom classes can be used.

4.1 Extension of the Class Hierarchy

Before computing type constraints, we extend the class hierarchy with the custom classes that we would like to introduce. Adding these types *prior to* the construction of the constraints will allow us to determine where custom container classes *may be introduced*. In addition to the custom classes themselves, some auxiliary types will be added to the hierarchy. In what follows, we use the term *customizable class* to refer to a class for which we would like to introduce a custom version. Specifically, we extend the original class hierarchy as follows:

- For each customizable class C with superclass B, a class *CustomC* is created that contains methods and fields that are identical to those in C. If B is not customizable, then *CustomC*'s superclass is B, otherwise it is *CustomB*.
- For each customizable class C, a type $C^\top$ is introduced, and both C and *CustomC* are made a subtype of $C^\top$. Type $C^\top$ contains declarations of all methods in C that are not declared in any superclass of C.
- For each customizable container C, a type $C^\perp$ is introduced, and $C^\perp$ is made a subclass of both C and *CustomC*. Type $C^\perp$ contains no methods.

Multiple inheritance is used because it allows us to express that the type of an allocation site E should be either C or *CustomC* by way of subtype-constraints $[E] \leq C^\top$ and $C^\perp \leq [E]$. It is important to note that these multiple inheritance relations are *only* used during the solving of the type constraints and that the customized program does *not* refer to any type $C^\top$ or $C^\perp$.

Figure 6 shows the parts of the class hierarchy relevant for the customization of the example program of Figure 2 after adding the classes `CustomHashtable` and `CustomProperties`, and the additional types `Hashtable`$^\top$, `Hashtable`$^\perp$, `Properties`$^\top$ and `Properties`$^\perp$. Section 4.4 describes how the *CustomC* classes can be further transformed, and turned into a separate class hierarchy such as the one shown earlier in Figure 1.

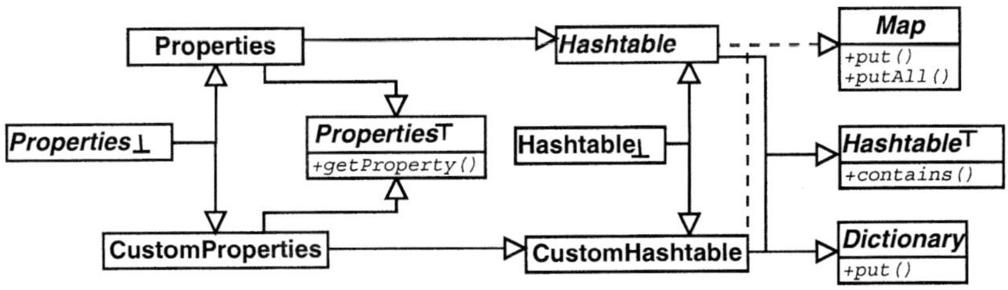

Fig. 6. Fragment of the collection hierarchy in `java.util.*` after extending it with custom classes and interfaces. For each class/interface, one or more of the methods defined/declared in that class/interface are shown.

The original program always allocates an object of type C at an allocation site `new` $C(E_1, \cdots, E_n)$, as was reflected by rule (22) in Figure 4. In the transformed program, we want to allow solutions where the allocated object is either of type C or of type *CustomC*. To this end, we replace rule (22) with rules (22)(a)–(22)(c) shown in Figure 7.

Figure 8 shows all non-trivial type constraints for the example program of Figure 2. For convenience, we have annotated each constraint in Figure 8 with the line number(s) in the source code from which it was derived, and with the number of the rule(s) in Figure 4 responsible for the constraint's creation.

program construct(s)/analysis facts	implied type constraint(s)	
expression new $C(E_1, \cdots, E_n)$ C is a customizable class	$[$new $C(E_1, \cdots, E_n)] \leq C^{\top}$ $C^{\perp} \leq [$new $C(E_1, \cdots, E_n)]$	(22)(a) (22)(b)
expression new $C(E_1, \cdots, E_n)$ C is a non-customizable class	$[$new $C(E_1, \cdots, E_n)] \triangleq C$	(22)(c)

Fig. 7. Revised type constraint rules for allocation sites and casts.

line	original constraint	rule	after simplification
3	[H1] ≤ [h1]	(1)	
3	[H1] ≤ Hashtable$^{\top}$	(22)(a)	
3	Hashtable$^{\perp}$ ≤ [H1]	(22)(b)	
4	[h1] ≤ [*Param*(JTree.JTree(),1)]	(8)	
4	[*Param*(JTree.JTree(),1)] = Hashtable	(27)	
5	[H2] ≤ [h2]	(1)	
5	[H2] ≤ Hashtable$^{\top}$	(22)(a)	
5	Hashtable$^{\perp}$ ≤ [H2]	(22)(b)	
6	[H3] ≤ [h3]	(1)	
6	[H3] ≤ Hashtable$^{\top}$	(22)(a)	
6	Hashtable$^{\perp}$ ≤ [H3]	(22)(b)	
7/15	[h3] ≤ [o]	(10)	
8	[h3] ≤ [h2]	(1)	
9	[h2] ≤ Map or [h2] ≤ Dictionary	(4)	*(removed)*
10	[h2] ≤ Map	(4)	
11	[System.getProperties()] ≤ [p1]	(1)	
11	[System.getProperties()] = Properties	(27)	
12	[p1] ≤ Properties	(4)	
13	[p1] ≤ [h2]	(1)	
16	[C1] ≤ [o]	(12)	
16	[H3] ≤ [C1]	(25)	
16	[S1] ≰ [C1]	(26)	[C1] ≤ Hashtable$^{\top}$
16	[C1] ≤ [h4]	(1)	
17	[h4] ≤ Hashtable$^{\top}$	(4)	
20	S1 ≤ [s]	(1)	
20	[S1] = String	(27)	
21/15	[s] ≤ [o]	(10)	

Fig. 8. Type constraints for the example program of Figure 2(a) as derived according to Figure 4. The rows in the table show, from left to right, the line in the source code from which the constraint was derived, the constraint itself, the rule that triggered the creation of the constraint, and the constraint after simplification (where applicable).

4.2 Constraint Simplification

Constraints of the form $[E]{\leq}C_1\textbf{or}\cdots\textbf{or}[E]{\leq}C_k$ (generated using rule (4)) give rise to bifurcations when traversing the solution space, and constraints of the form $[E']{\not\leq}[(C)E]$ (generated using rule (26)) make it impossible to define a monotone iteration step. Therefore, in order to simplify the process of constraint solving, we first perform a step in which all constraints are reduced to the simple forms $[x]{\leq}[y]$, $[x] = [y]$, and $[x]{\triangleq}[y]$.

Simplification of Disjunctions. A virtual method call $E.m(E_1, \cdots, E_n)$ to a method M gives rise to a disjunction $[E]{\leq}C_1\textbf{or}\cdots\textbf{or}[E]{\leq}C_k$ if $[E]$ has multiple supertypes $C_1, \cdots, C_k$ in which method $m(\cdots)$ is declared such that there is not a single method M that is overridden by all $C_i.m(\cdots)$, for all i, $1 \leq i \leq k$. Our approach will be to replace the entire disjunction by one of its branches $[E]{\leq}C_j$, for some j, $1 \leq j \leq k$. Note that by imposing a *stronger* constraint on $[E]$, we are potentially reducing the number of solutions of the constraint system. Nevertheless, at least one solution is guaranteed to exist: The original program fulfills each of the components of the original disjunction[11], so it will meet the simplified constraint as well.

Still, choosing the branch to replace the disjunction requires some consideration. Consider the constraint: [`h2`] $\leq$ `Map` **or** [`h2`] $\leq$ `Dictionary` that was generated due to the call `h2.put("FOO", "BAR")` in the example program of Figure 2. If we simplify this constraint to: [`h2`] $\leq$ `Dictionary`, we obtain a constraint system in which variable `h2` must be a subtype of both `Map` and `Dictionary`, as well as a supertype of `java.util.Properties`. This implies that `h2`'s type must be a subtype `java.util.Hashtable`, which, in turn, requires that allocation sites `H2` and `H3` must remain of type `java.util.Hashtable`, preventing us from customizing these allocation sites. On the other hand, replacing the original disjunction with: [`h2`] $\leq$ `Map` allows us to infer the solution shown earlier in Figure 2(b), in which allocation sites `H2` and `H3` have been customized. Clearly, some choices for simplifying disjunctions are better than others.

We use the following approach for the simplification of disjunctions. First, any constraint $[x]{\leq}C_1\textbf{or}\cdots\textbf{or}[x]{\leq}C_n$ for which there already exists another constraint $[x]{\leq}C_j$ can simply be removed by subsumption, as the latter constraint implies the former. Second, we use the heuristic that any constraint $[x]{\leq}C_1\textbf{or}\cdots\textbf{or}[x]{\leq}C_n$, for which there exists another constraint $[y]{\leq}C_j$, for some unique j $(1 \leq j \leq n)$ such that $\mathit{PointsTo}(P, x) \cap \mathit{PointsTo}(P, y) \neq \emptyset$. is simplified to $[x]{\leq}C_j$. If no constraint $[y]{\leq}C_j$ exists, the disjunction is simplified by making an arbitrary choice. The results of this approach have been satisfactory so far. If the loss of precision becomes a problem, one could compute the results obtained for all possible choices for each disjunction, and select a maximal solution.

[11] Note that the introduction of types $C^{\top}$ and $C^{\perp}$ does not affect this property, as they do not give rise to additional disjunctions.

Simplification of $\not\leq$-Constraints. Constraints of the form $[E'] \not\leq [(C)E]$ are introduced by rule (25) in order to preserve the behavior of casts that may fail. For example, in the program of Figure 2 the cast on line 14 fails when method `bar()` is called from method `bad()`, because in this case `o` will point to a `String`-object that was allocated at allocation site `S1`.

Our approach will be to introduce additional constraints that are sufficient to imply the $\not\leq$-constraint. Specifically, for each cast $(C)E$ for which the points-to set $\mathit{PointsTo}(P, E)$ contains an expression E' such that $[E']_P \not\leq C$, we introduce a constraint $[(C)E] \leq C^\top$. This additional constraint prevents the generalization of the target type of a cast in situations where that would change a failing cast into a succeeding cast.

It is easy to see that the addition of this constraint ensures that the behavior of failing casts is preserved in the customized program P'. Suppose that $(C)E$ is a cast that may fail in the original program P. Then, there exists an $E' \in \mathit{PointsTo}(P, E)$ for which $[E']_P \not\leq C$. Since P does not instantiate any custom classes, we also know that $[E']_P \not\leq \mathit{CustomC}$, and therefore that $[E']_P \not\leq C^\top$. Hence, requiring that $[(C)E] \leq C^\top$ ensures that the constraint $[E'] \not\leq [(C)E]$ is satisfied in P'.

Example. Figure 8 shows the simplified type constraints for the program of Figure 2. For the disjunction [`h2`] $\leq$ `Map` **or** [`h2`] $\leq$ `Dictionary` in Figure 8, there already exists another, stronger constraint [`h2`] $\leq$ `Map`, so it can simply be removed. Furthermore, the $\not\leq$-constraint [`S1`] $\not\leq$ [`C1`] is replaced with a constraint [`C1`] $\leq$ $\texttt{Hashtable}^\top$.

4.3 Solving the Constraints

Now that all constraints are of the forms $E \leq E'$, $E = E'$, and $E \triangleq E'$ solving the constraint system is straightforward. First, we create a set of equivalence classes of declaration elements and expressions that must have exactly the same type, and we extend the $\leq$ relationship to equivalence classes in the obvious manner. Then, we compute the set of possible types for each equivalence class using an optimistic algorithm. This algorithm associates a set S_E of types with each equivalence class E, which is initialized as follows:

- For each equivalence class E that contains an allocation expression $E \equiv$ `new` C, S_E is initialized to contain the types C and $\mathit{CustomC}$.
- For each equivalence class E that does not contain any allocation expressions, S_E is initialized to contain all types except $C^\top$ and $C^\perp$, for all C.

Then, in the iterative phase of the algorithm, the following steps are performed repeatedly until a fixpoint is reached:

- For each pair of equivalence classes D, E such that there exists a type constraint $D \leq E$, we remove from S_D any type that is not a subtype of a type that occurs in S_E.
- For each pair of equivalence classes D, E such that there exists a type constraint $D \leq E$, we remove from S_E any type that is not a supertype of a type that occurs in S_D.

Termination of this algorithm is ensured because each iteration decreases the number of elements in at least one set, and there is a finite number of sets. Moreover, each equivalence class will contain at least the type that is associated with its elements in the original program.

equivalence class	possible types
{ p1, Properties }	{ Properties }
{ h1 }	{ Hashtable }
{ H1 }	{ Hashtable }
{ h2 }	{ Map, Hashtable, CustomHashtable }
{ H2 }	{ Hashtable, CustomHashtable }
{ h3 }	{ Map, Hashtable, CustomHashtable }
{ H3 }	{ Hashtable, CustomHashtable }
{ h4 }	{ Hashtable, CustomHashtable }
{ C1 }	{ Hashtable, CustomHashtable }
{ o }	{ Object }
{ s }	{ String }

Fig. 9. Possible types computed for each equivalence class.

Figure 9 shows the sets of types computed for each of the equivalence classes in our example. The interpretation of these sets of types requires some remarks:

- Figure 9 depicts many possible solutions. In each solution, a single type in S_E is chosen for each equivalence class E.
- If type T occurs in S_E, then at least one solution to the constraint system exists in which the elements in E have type T.
- Selecting types for different equivalence classes can in general not be done independently. For any given pair of equivalence classes D and E, choosing an arbitrary element in S_D for equivalence class D, and an arbitrary element in S_E for equivalence class E may result in a type-incorrect program.
- The previous observation particularly applies to two equivalence classes associated with allocation sites A_1 and A_2. Selecting type C for (the equivalence class containing) A_1 may prevent us from selecting type *CustomC* for (the equivalence class containing) A_2. For example, if a call `bar(h2)` is added to method `Example.main()`, we have the choice of: (i) customizing both `H2` and `H3` or (ii) not customizing both `H2` and `H3`. However, customizing `H2` but not `H3` (or vice versa) will not preserve the behavior of cast `C1`.
- However, we conjecture that a solution exists in which type *CustomC* is selected for *all* equivalence classes E such that $CustomC \in S_E$.

A more precise treatment of these properties is currently in progress.

4.4 Pragmatic Issues and Further Customization

There are several issues that require straightforward extensions to our basic approach. These include the treatment of subtypes of standard library classes (e.g., an application declaring a class `MyHashtable` that extends `Hashtable`), and limiting the introduction of custom classes in the presence of serialization. Space limitations prevent us from providing more details.

Thus far, we have presented how variables and allocation sites of type C can be updated to refer to type $CustomC$. At this point it has become easy to replace $CustomC$ with a small hierarchy of custom classes such as the one shown in Figure 1 by applying refactorings [10,25] as follows:

- Split class $CustomC$ into an abstract superclass $AbstractCustomC$ (that only contains abstract methods) and a concrete subclass $CustomC$. Declarations and casts (but not allocation sites) that refer to type $CustomC$ are made to refer to $AbstractCustomC$ instead.
- At this point, clones $CustomC_1, \cdots, CustomC_n$ of class $CustomC$ can be introduced as a subclass of $AbstractCustomC$. Any allocation site of type $CustomC$ may be updated to refer to any $CustomC_i$.

The next section will discuss a number of optimizations that can be (independently) applied to each $CustomC_i$.

5 Implementation

We use the *Gnosis* framework for interprocedural context-sensitive analysis developed at IBM Research to compute all static analysis information that is needed for customization. Two nonstandard components of our analysis are:

- For customizable classes, each allocation site in user code is analyzed separately, but a single logical site represents all allocations in system code.
- Analysis is done in two passes: a conventional points-to analysis [20,13,21] is followed by a step in which additional data flow facts are introduced that model the type constraints due to method overriding, similar in spirit to [12].

Like many static whole-program analysis and transformation tools (e.g., [26]), *Gnosis* relies on the user to specify the behaviors of native library methods as well as any uses of reflection in order to compute a safe analysis result. (Note that specifying reflection entails specifying classes dynamically loaded via reflection.)

In order to gather profile information, the customization framework itself is used to replace the standard library classes created by an application with custom versions that gather profile information. This is subject to the usual limitations. In other words, we cannot gather profile information for container objects in cases where interface-compatibility constraints prevent us from applying customization. Usage statistics are gathered per allocation site and include:

1. A distribution of the construction-time sizes.
2. A distribution of the high-watermarks of the sizes of the container objects allocated at the site (i.e., the largest size of containers during their life-time).
3. Distributions of the container's size at method invocations (per method).
4. The hit-rates of search operations.
5. The hit-rates of several caching schemes for optimizing search operations.

Distributions (1) and (2) are used as a basis for deciding on an initial allocation size and on lazy vs. eager allocation. Combined with (3), they are also used to determine whether providing special treatment for singleton containers is beneficial. Distribution (3) is also used to determine whether or not we want to optimize certain methods for specific sizes, such as empty or singleton containers. Distribution (4) is used to decide on whether or not search methods are to be optimized for succeeding or failing searches. Finally, (5) is used to decide on caching schemes.

Together with the static analysis results, the gathered statistics are used by an automated decision process to determine which optimizations, compared to the standard implementation, will be implemented in the custom versions. All decisions based on static analyses are binary decisions: either an optimization is safe or is not safe. Furthermore, all customization decisions that are based on profiles use thresholds, such as hit-rates for search operations, cache schemes, fractions of containers that remain empty or singletons, etc. As such, most of the profile-based decisions in our current implementation are simple binary decisions as well. The single exception is the decision on the initial size of underlying data structures of the containers. This takes the distribution of the high-watermarks of all allocated containers into consideration. We should note that all thresholds used are very high. For example, we use lazy allocation if 75% of the allocated containers remain empty or contain only one item. Similarly, caching schemes are used only if their hit-rates are 90% or higher.

The optimizations that are incorporated into custom classes include:

1. Caching the last retrieved items in a container using different caching schemes.
2. Lazy allocation of encapsulated data structures such as a `Hashtable`'s array of hash-buckets,
3. Selecting a non-default initial size and growth-strategy for a container's underlying data structures, depending on the success-rate of retrieval operations, the distribution of the high-watermarks of the container sizes, etc.
4. Efficiently implementing frequently occurring corner cases such as container classes that often contain zero or one elements. For example, it is often possible to use a single, shared `EmptyIterator` whose `hasNext()` method always returns false.
5. Transforming instance fields into class fields if their values are identical for all objects allocated at some allocation site, or if the differences are non-critical.
6. Specialization of container classes for the type of objects stored in them, if static analysis can determine these types. Examples of such optimizations are `Integer` keys in `Hashtables`, for which we can store the `int` values instead, or `Strings` for which can exploit the fact that their hashcodes are cached.
7. Finalizing classes that have no subtypes in our program.
8. Removal of unnecessary synchronization. Currently, we only remove synchronization if an application is single-threaded. This is the case if the

`Thread.start()` method is not reachable in the call-graph starting at the program entry point[12].

These optimizations were chosen after carefully studying the existing implementations and conducting many experiments with special treatment for corner cases or access patterns. The inspiration for the optimizations originated from our own programming experience, from studying programs that heavily use container classes, and from searching the World Wide Web for manually crafted custom implementions.

In addition, static analysis information is used to detect situations where certain methods are never invoked on a container object that originates from a given allocation site A. This information is used to remove methods and fields from the custom class used at A. The bookkeeping fields used for implementing fail-fast iterators are an example of a situation where this is useful.

Java bytecode [16] is generated for each custom class by preprocessing a template implementation of a library class, and compiling the resulting source file to Java .class files. In the current implementation, this is done using the standard C-preprocessor. JikesBT[13], a byte-code instrumentation tool developed at IBM Research, is used for the rewriting of the application's class files so that they refer to the generated custom classes.

6 Experimental Evaluation

To evaluate our techniques, we measured the execution times and memory footprint of a number of Java applications on a workstation (hyperthreaded Pentium 4 at 2.8 GHz, 1GB RAM) running Linux 2.4.21 and two Java virtual machines: IBM's "j9" VM that is being distributed with IBM's WebSphere Studio Device Developer product and Sun's Hotspot Server 1.3.1 JVM. All measurements were performed using a maximum heap of 400 MB.

As our optimization technique aims at eliminating the overhead of using standard library implementations when such implementations are not optimal, we selected 7 benchmark programs that use the standard library classes in an atypical manner. Three programs are taken from the SPECjvm98 suite: _202_jess is an expert shell system, _209_db is a memory resident database, and _218_jack is a parser generator. The other benchmarks we include are HyperJ (an aspect-oriented development tool), Jax [26], PmD (a open-source tool available from SourceForge for detecting programming errors) and a chess program developed at IBM. All execution times were measured using a harness: each program is executed 10 times within one invocation of the VM, and we report the fastest time of the 10 runs. With the exception of HyperJ, for which we had only one input data set available, all measurements were performed using larger data sets than the training sets used to collect profile information.

[12] Here, "Program entry point" refers to the entry point of the actual benchmark program, and not of the harness used for measuring execution time.

[13] See `www.alphaworks.ibm.com/tech/jikesbt`

	Sun HotSpot(TM) Server 1.3.1				IBM J9 2.2			
	orig	cust1	cust2	cust3	orig	cust1	cust2	cust3
_202_jess	1.92s	1.83s *(1.05)*	1.42s *(1.36)*	1.41s *(1.37)*	1.38s	1.45s *(0.95)*	1.21s *(1.14)*	1.21s *(1.15)*
_209_db	15.04s	12.23s *(1.23)*	8.45s *(1.78)*	8.51s *(1.77)*	8.99s	8.63s *(1.04)*	6.48s *(1.39)*	6.48s *(1.39)*
_218_jack	3.23s	3.18s *(1.02)*	2.28s *(1.42)*	2.24s *(1.44)*	1.88s	1.93s *(0.97)*	1.51s *(1.24)*	1.40s *(1.34)*
Jax	21.46s	21.24s *(1.01)*	20.97s *(1.02)*	19.93s *(1.08)*	16.36s	15.04s *(1.09)*	15.00s *(1.09)*	14.90s *(1.10)*
HyperJ	13.03s	12.77s *(1.02)*	11.04s *(1.18)*	10.83s *(1.20)*	10.04s	9.63s *(1.04)*	8.68s *(1.16)*	8.58s *(1.17)*
Chess	18.07s	18.23s *(0.99)*	18.23s *(0.99)**	18.23s *(0.99)**	6.93s	6.59s *(1.05)*	6.59s *(1.05)**	6.59s *(1.05)**
Pmd	5.43s	5.33s *(1.02)*	5.33s *(1.02)**	5.33s *(1.02)**	4.37s	3.76s *(1.16)*	3.76s *(1.16)**	3.76s *(1.16)**
GEOMEAN		*(1.05)*	*(1.23)*	*(1.24)*		*(1.05)*	*(1.17)*	*(1.19)*

Fig. 10. Execution times and speedups obtained through customization. The execution times presented are of the original programs (`orig`), the programs with customized container classes, but without synchronization elimination(`cust1`), the programs with customized containers classes of which we eliminated the synchronization where possible (`cust2`), and the programs with customized and desynchronized containers classes and desynchronized `StringBuffers` (`cust3`).

	zipped archive		heap size	
	orig	cust3	orig	cust3
_202_jess	173KB	175KB *(1.01)*	1.74MB	1.77MB *(0.99)*
_209_db	6KB	21KB *(3.68)*	9.57MB	9.57MB *(1.00)*
_218_jack	70KB	95KB *(1.35)*	15.78MB	8.54MB *(0.54)*
Jax	582KB	615KB *(1.06)*	44.23MB	40.98MB *(0.93)*
HyperJ	1,767KB	1,821KB *(1.03)*	44.42MB	41.38MB *(0.93)*
Chess	135KB	151KB *(1.12)*	9.33MB	9.29MB *(1.00)*
Pmd	498KB	525KB *(1.05)*	142.51MB	123.72MB *(0.87)*
GEOMEAN		*(1.30)*		*(0.88)*

Fig. 11. Archive size increase and memory footprint reduction resulting from customization.

In Figure 10 we report execution times of four versions of the benchmarks, that were customized in the exact same way for both VMs.[14] The consequences of the customizations on memory consumption are depicted in Figure 11. An analysis of the obtained results and applied customizations reveals that:

- In _202_jess, the keys used in hashtables are either Strings or Integers, and on 2 of the hashtables all search operations fail. Depending on the VM used, customizing the Hashtable class for this usage pattern resulted in a 5% speedup or in a 5% slowdown. Eliminating synchronization, including the synchronization on very frequently used Vector objects, results in speedups between 15% and 37%.
- In _209_db, 99% of all consecutive retrieval operations on Vectors retrieve the same element (during what is essentially a column-major-order operation on

[14] In order to evaluate the customizations correctly, the original programs need to be executed with the original library classes before customization. Since all our customized classes are customized versions of IBM's jclMax implementation (which is distributed with IBM's WebSphere Studio Device Developer product), we enforced the use of the original jclMax classes on both VMs by prepending them to the boot classpath of the VMs.

a row-major-order stored array of Vectors), and the application of a caching scheme results in a 23% speedup on the Sun VM. Additionally removing the synchronization on these Vectors results in a 77% speedup on the Sun VM, and a speedup of 39% on IBM's j9.
- In _228_jack, 99% of all search operations are on empty hashtables (of which a lot are allocated), or hashtables containing one element only. Using lazy allocation and eliminating the bookkeeping data for fail-safe iteration, we can reduce the heap memory consumption with 46%. On Sun's VM, the resulting overhead in the retrieval operations can be compensated by optimizing the retrieval for the corner case of hashtables containing one element only. On IBM's j9, the overhead is almost compensated. Finally, removing synchronization results in speedups between 34 and 44%.
- In HyperJ, the same situation occurs, and lazy allocation and the elimination of unnecessary bookkeeping data for the hot allocation sites results in speedups around 2-4% if no synchronization is eliminated, and 17-20% if synchronization is eliminated. Memory consumption drops with 7%. Especially for this benchmark, we should note that our customization results are obtained on top of the already applied manual fine-tuning by the programmers via construction time parameterization.
- In Jax, most containers remain very small, and adapting the initial container size to reflect that results in speedups ranging between 1 and 3%. Memory consumption as a result drops with 7%.
- In PmD, the vast majority of a huge number of allocated HashMaps remains empty or contains only one element. Lazy allocation, the elimination of bookkeeping data for fail-safe iteration and the optimization of access methods result in speedups of 2 to 16%, and a reduction of the allocated memory with 13%. Since PmD contains a multi-threaded GUI front-end, no synchronization was removed.
- In the chess program, enumerations (over piece positions) stored in hashtables occur very frequently. Optimizing the number of hash-buckets for the number of positions (which seemed limited to the number of pieces on a board) resulted in speedups between 2 and 16%, depending on the VM. Like Pmd, the chess program contains a multi-threaded front-end. As a result, we did not yet try to eliminate any synchronization.

On average, the customizations excluding the elimination of synchronization result in speedups of 5% on both VMs. By additionally eliminating synchronization on container classes and StringBuffers in the single-threaded programs, an average speedup of 19-24% can be obtained. The elimination of synchronization is therefore clearly the dominant optimization, in particular the elimination of synchronization on container classes. There are exceptions to this trend however: for Jax the speedup following synchronization removal is insignificant on j9, and for _218_jack the removal of synchronization on StringBuffers is much more significant (10% additional speedup) than for the other programs.

The raw execution times shown in Figure 10 indicate that the two VMs have somewhat different performance characteristics. It is therefore no surprise that the obtained speedups are different for each VM as well. This indicates that the decision logic used for the customization should be made parameterizable for specific VMs.

Finally, we should note that program archive size increases only by a small amount because of the customization: as indicated in Figure 11 at most 54KB is added to the archives, for HyperJ. For all but the smallest programs the zipped archives grow by 12% or less.

7 Related Work

Yellin [28] and Högstedt et al. [14] discuss techniques for automatically selecting optimal component implementations. In [28], selection takes place at run-time, and based on on-line profiling only, while in [14] off-line profiling is used as well. In both cases, the component developer is required to provide all component versions up front, making them less viable when many orthogonal implementation decisions exist, as is the case in the present paper. Unlike our work, the approaches of [28,14] do not require static analysis because programs are correct by construction. In our setting, static analysis is needed to guarantee type-correctness in cases where objects are exchanged with the standard libraries (or other components). However, as the approaches of [28,14] do not rely on static analysis, they are incapable of *eliminating* functionality from classes.

Schonberg et al. [22] discuss techniques for automatically selecting concrete data structures to implement the abstract data types set and map in SETL programs. Depending on whether or not iterators and set-theoretic operations such as union and intersection are applied to abstract data types, their optimizing compiler selects an implementation from a predetermined collection of implementations in which sets are represented as linked lists, hashtables, or bit-vectors.

Instead of composing complex data structures from simpler ones, as is done with C++ templates or Ada generics, Sirkin et al. [24] describe how custom, optimized data structures can be generated automatically from a relatively simple specification that consists of a composition of iterators and access methods defined in a very generic container interface. To some extent this data structure compilation resembles our approach to eliminate unnecessary fields. But whereas we remove unnecessary fields when static analysis detects that access methods in the standard interfaces are not used in a program, they add fields to a data structure to allow an efficient implementation of those access methods occurring in the specification provided by the programmer.

Transformational programming [2] is a programming methodology based on top-down stepwise program refinement. Here, the programmer specifies a program in terms of very high-level constructs without worrying about efficiency. This program is made more efficient by automatically applying a sequence of finite difference transformations or by applying incremental refinement [9,19].

There is a large body of work on automatic optimization of data structures in specific domains (e.g., linear algebra kernels). For example, the Berkeley Benchmarking and Optimization Group (see `http://bebop.cs.berkeley.edu`) studies issues related to optimization and data structure selection for sparse matrix multiplication problems. In the same domain, Yotov et al. [29] compare empirical and model-driven approaches for selecting customized data structures.

Our customization approach may be seen as a type of generative programming [8], in which the program analysis and rewriting tools needed for our approach, the instrumented classes to collect profiling information, the templates to generate custom classes and the decision logic can be seen as an active library [27]. Active libraries are highly parameterizable libraries that require implementation techniques beyond what is provided by traditional compilers.

There is also work on optimizations that can be applied to specific containers such as hashtables. Beckmann and Wang [1] discuss the optimization of hashtables by prefetching the objects that are most likely to be searched for, and Friedman et al. [11] discuss the optimization of the maximal access time of hashtables to improve real-time behavior by, e.g., incrementalizing rehash operations.

The elimination of synchronization has been a very popular research subject (see for example [5]). To the best of our knowledge, all currently known solutions are either based on manual rewriting of a program to remove the synchronization or on bytecode annotations that can only be read by adapted VMs. Our approach of automatically replacing the allocation of standard types with the allocation of customized types allows to automate the existing techniques for synchronization elimination without requiring special VM support.

Based on partial evaluation and the use of aspects [15], Schultz et al. [23] specialize methods for (partially known) input data, resulting in average speed-ups by a factor of 3. While such specialization can only exploit knowledge of (properties of) parts of the input data, our customization approach is able to exploit known access patterns of otherwise unknown input data as well. Furthermore, whereas we were able to apply our approach in large real-life applications, we have not seen any indication of the scalability of program specialization through partial evaluation. The bytecode size of the largest benchmark program used by Schultz et al. [23], e.g., is only 4914 bytes. With respect to the use of aspects, we should note that some of our customizations, such as adding a cache to speed-up hashtable accesses, could be implemented with aspects as well. But other customizations, such as the removal of unused bookkeeping fields from container types, can obviously not.

A limited form of program specialization is customization, as introduced by Chambers and Ungar [4]. They used the term customization to denote dynamic method cloning in SELF compilers, in which a separate clone is generated and optimized for each of the receiver types of a method. Other cloning techniques have been applied on more traditional programming languages such as Fortran as well [7], albeit not to optimize procedures for receiver types but rather to allow other optimizations such as loop unrolling.

Besides specializing methods or procedures for statically known (properties of) input data, value profiling [3,6] has been used to produce code that is optimized for likely occurring situations. This is somewhat comparable to our profiling based optimizations. But whereas value profiling aims at lower level compiler optimization, e.g., by propagating constant values, our approach aims for algorithmic optimizations (such as caching).

During Java's short lifetime, the standard Java Library classes have been extended on several occasions. For example, the original synchronized `Hashtable` type present in JDK1.0 was complemented with the unsynchronized type `HashMap` in JDK1.2 Similarly, the type `StringBuilder` is added in JDK1.5 as an unsynchronized sibling of the synchronized type `StringBuffer`. Unlike the approach we presented in this paper, such extensions of the standard library classes can only accommodate a limited number of different implementations for each abstract data type. Moreover, such extensions do not remove the burden from the programmer to choose an actual implementation for his program. One of the main benefits of our approach is its transparency for the programmer.

Type constraints were introduced [18] as a means to check whether a program conforms to a language's type system. If a program satisfies all type constraints, no type violations will occur at run-time (e.g., no method $m(\cdots)$ is invoked on an object whose class does not define or inherit $m(\cdots)$). Type constraints were recently used to check the preconditions and determine the allowable source-code modifications associated with generalization-related refactorings [25]. The problem of determining where custom versions of library classes may be introduced is very similar to the problem of determining declarations that can be updated by the EXTRACT INTERFACE refactoring. However, in [25] the type of a declaration is only replaced with one of its supertypes, whereas our work is unique in the sense that custom classes appear in a different branch of the class hierarchy.

8 Conclusions and Future Work

We have presented an automated approach for customizing Java container classes that relies on static analysis for determining where custom container classes may be introduced in an application, and on profile information for determining what optimizations are likely to be profitable. The approach was evaluated on a set of benchmark applications, and we measured speedups of up to 78%, averaging at 19-24%. The memory footprint reductions we measured range from -1 to 46%, averaging at 12%. The cost of the applied customizations in terms of code size is limited to 12% for all of the smallest programs we evaluated.

We plan to develop a more precise formal treatment of the properties of our algorithm for determining where custom allocation sites may be introduced. Other topics for future work include more advanced program transformations (e.g, replacing a `Hashtable` with an extra field in each key object that stores a reference to its corresponding value), applications to other library classes and the use of escape analysis to determine where unnecessary synchronizations can be removed from multi-threaded programs.

Acknowledgement. Bjorn De Sutter is supported by the Fund for Scientific Research - Flanders (FWO) as a postdoctoral researcher. The research reported in this paper took place during his stay at IBM T.J. Watson Research Center in Hawthorne, N.Y. This stay was also supported by the FWO.

References

1. Beckmann, B., and Wang, X. Adaptive prefetching Java objects. manuscript.
2. Cai, J., and Paige, R. Towards increased productivity of algorithm implementation. In *Proc. 1st ACM SIGSOFT symposium on Foundations of software engineering* (1993), pp. 71–78.
3. Calder, B., Feller, P., and Eustace, A. Value profiling. In *Proceedings of the 30th annual ACM/IEEE International Symposium on Microarchitecture (ISCA97)* (1997), pp. 259–269.
4. Chambers, C., and Ungar, D. Customization: optimizing compiler technology for SELF, a dynamically-typed object-oriented programming language. *ACM SIGPLAN Notices 24*, 7 (july 1989), 146–160.
5. Choi, J.-D., Gupta, M., Serrano, M. J., Sreedhar, V. C., and Midkiff, S. P. Stack allocation and synchronization optimizations for java using escape analysis. *ACM Transactions on Programming Languages and Systems 25*, 6 (2003), 876–910.
6. Chung, E.-Y., Benini, L., and De Micheli, G. Automatic source code specialization for energy reduction. In *Proceedings of the 2001 International Symposium on Low Power Electronics and Design (ISPLED01)* (2001), pp. 80–83.
7. Cooper, K., Hall, M. W., and Kennedy, K. A methodology for procedure cloning. *Computer Languages* (may 1995).
8. Czarnecki, K., and Eisenecker, U. *Generative Programming: Methods, Techniques, and Applications.* Addison-Wesley, 1999.
9. Dewar, R. K., Arthur, Liu, S.-C., Schwartz, J. T., and Schonberg, E. Programming by refinement, as exemplified by the SETL representation sublanguage. *ACM Transactions on Programming Languages and Systems (TOPLAS) 1*, 1 (1979), 27–49.
10. Fowler, M. *Refactoring. Improving the Design of Existing Code.* Addison-Wesley, 1999.
11. Friedman, S., Leidenfrost, N., Brodie, B., and Cytron, R. Hashtables for embedded and real-time systems. In *IEEE Real-Time Embedded System Workshop* (2001).
12. Glew, N., and Palsberg, J. Type-safe method inlining. In *Proc. 16th European Conference on Object-Oriented Programming* (2002), pp. 525–544.
13. Hind, M., and Pioli, A. Evaluating the effectiveness of pointer alias analyses. *Science of Computer Programming 39*, 1 (2001), 31–55.
14. Högstedt, K., D., K., Rajan, V., Roth, T., Sreedhar, V., Wegman, M., and Wang, N. The autonomic performance prescription. Available from the author at `wegman@watson.ibm.com`.
15. Kiczales, G., Lamping, J., Menhdhekar, A., Maeda, C., Lopes, C., Loingtier, J.-M., and Irwin, J. Aspect-oriented programming. In *Proceedings of the European Conference on Object-Oriented Programming (ECOOP97)* (1997), vol. 1241, Springer-Verlag, pp. 220–242.
16. Lindholm, T., and Yellin, F. *The Java Virtual Machine Specification.* Addison-Wesley, 1997.
17. Palsberg, J. Type-based analysis and applications. In *Proc. ACM Workshop on Program Analysis for Software Tools and Engineering (PASTE'01)* (Snowbird, UT, 2001), pp. 20–27.
18. Palsberg, J., and Schwartzbach, M. *Object-Oriented Type Systems.* John Wiley & Sons, 1993.

19. PAVLOVIC, D., AND SMITH, D. Software development by refinement. In *UNU/IIST 10th Anniversary Colloqium, Formal Methods at the Crossroads: From Panaea to Foundational Support*. Springer-Verlag, 2003.
20. ROUNTEV, A., MILANOVA, A., AND RYDER, B. Points-to analysis for Java using annotated constraints. In *Proc. 16th Annual Conf. on Object-Oriented Programming Systems, Languages, and Applications (OOPSLA'01)* (Tampa Bay, FL, 2001), pp. 43–55.
21. RYDER, B. G. Dimensions of precision in reference analysis of object-oriented programming languages. In *Proc. 12th International Conference on Compiler Construction (CC 2003)* (Warsaw, Poland, April 2003), pp. 126–137.
22. SCHONBERG, E., SCHWARTZ, J., AND SHARIR, M. An automatic technique for selection of data representations in SETL programs. *ACM Transactions on Programming Languages and Systems 3*, 2 (April 1981), 126–143.
23. SCHULTZ, U. P., LAWALL, J. L., AND CONSEL, C. Automatic program specialization for java. *ACM Transactions on Programming Languages and Systems 25*, 4 (2003), 452–499.
24. SIRKIN, M., BATORY, D., AND SINGHAL, V. Software components in a data structure precompiler. In *Proceedings of the 15th International Conference on Software Engineering (ICSE97)* (1997), pp. 437–446.
25. TIP, F., KIEŻUN, A., AND BÄUMER, D. Refactoring for generalizations using type constraints. In *Proc. 18th Annual Conf. on Object-Oriented Programming Systems, Languages, and Applications (OOPSLA'03)* (2003).
26. TIP, F., SWEENEY, P. F., LAFFRA, C., EISMA, A., AND STREETER, D. Practical extraction techniques for Java. *ACM Transactions on Programming Languages and Systems 24*, 6 (2002), 625–666.
27. VELDHUIZEN, T. L., AND GANNON, D. Active libraries: Rethinking the roles of compilers and libraries. In *Proceedings of the SIAM Workshop on Object Oriented Methods for Inter-operable Scientific and Engineering Computing (OO'98)* (1998).
28. YELLIN, D. Competitive algorithms for the dynamic selection of component implementations. *IBM Systems Journal 42*, 1 (January 2003), 85–97.
29. YOTOV, K., LI, X., REN, G., CIBULSKIS, M., DEJONG, G., GARZARAN, M., PADUA, D., PINGALI, K., STODGHILL, P., AND WU, P. A comparison of empirical and model-driven optimization. In *Proc. ACM SIGPLAN 2003 conference on Programming language design and implementation* (2003), pp. 63–76.

Author Index

Lecture Notes in Computer Science

For information about Vols. 1–2989

please contact your bookseller or Springer-Verlag

Vol. 3096: G. Melnik, H. Holz (Eds.), Advances in Learning Software Organizations. X, 173 pages. 2004.

Vol. 3093: S.K. Katsikas, S. Gritzalis, J. Lopez (Eds.), Public Key Infrastructure. XIII, 380 pages. 2004.

Vol. 3092: J. Eckstein, H. Baumeister (Eds.), Extreme Programming and Agile Processes in Software Engineering. XVI, 358 pages. 2004.

Vol. 3091: V. van Oostrom (Ed.), Rewriting Techniques and Applications. X, 313 pages. 2004.

Vol. 3089: M. Jakobsson, M. Yung, J. Zhou (Eds.), Applied Cryptography and Network Security. XIV, 510 pages. 2004.

Vol. 3086: M. Odersky (Ed.), ECOOP 2004 – Object-Oriented Programming. XIII, 611 pages. 2004.

Vol. 3085: S. Berardi, M. Coppo, F. Damiani (Eds.), Types for Proofs and Programs. X, 409 pages. 2004.

Vol. 3084: A. Persson, J. Stirna (Eds.), Advanced Information Systems Engineering. XIV, 596 pages. 2004.

Vol. 3083: W. Emmerich, A.L. Wolf (Eds.), Component Deployment. X, 249 pages. 2004.

Vol. 3078: S. Cotin, D.N. Metaxas (Eds.), Medical Simulation. XVI, 296 pages. 2004.

Vol. 3077: F. Roli, J. Kittler, T. Windeatt (Eds.), Multiple Classifier Systems. XII, 386 pages. 2004.

Vol. 3076: D. Buell (Ed.), Algorithmic Number Theory. XI, 451 pages. 2004.

Vol. 3074: B. Kuijpers, P. Revesz (Eds.), Constraint Databases and Applications. XII, 181 pages. 2004.

Vol. 3073: H. Chen, R. Moore, D.D. Zeng, J. Leavitt (Eds.), Intelligence and Security Informatics. XV, 536 pages. 2004.

Vol. 3070: L. Rutkowski, J. Siekmann, R. Tadeusiewicz, L.A. Zadeh (Eds.), Artificial Intelligence and Soft Computing - ICAISC 2004. XXV, 1208 pages. 2004. (Subseries LNAI).

Vol. 3068: E. André, L. Dybkj\ae r, W. Minker, P. Heisterkamp (Eds.), Affective Dialogue Systems. XII, 324 pages. 2004. (Subseries LNAI).

Vol. 3067: M. Dastani, J. Dix, A. El Fallah-Seghrouchni (Eds.), Programming Multi-Agent Systems. X, 221 pages. 2004. (Subseries LNAI).

Vol. 3066: S. Tsumoto, R. S lowiński, J. Komorowski, J.W. Grzymala-Busse (Eds.), Rough Sets and Current Trends in Computing. XX, 853 pages. 2004. (Subseries LNAI).

Vol. 3065: A. Lomuscio, D. Nute (Eds.), Deontic Logic in Computer Science. X, 275 pages. 2004. (Subseries LNAI).

Vol. 3064: D. Bienstock, G. Nemhauser (Eds.), Integer Programming and Combinatorial Optimization. XI, 445 pages. 2004.

Vol. 3063: A. Llamosí, A. Strohmeier (Eds.), Reliable Software Technologies - Ada-Europe 2004. XIII, 333 pages. 2004.

Vol. 3062: J.L. Pfaltz, M. Nagl, B. Böhlen (Eds.), Applications of Graph Transformations with Industrial Relevance. XV, 500 pages. 2004.

Vol. 3060: A.Y. Tawfik, S.D. Goodwin (Eds.), Advances in Artificial Intelligence. XIII, 582 pages. 2004. (Subseries LNAI).

Vol. 3059: C.C. Ribeiro, S.L. Martins (Eds.), Experimental and Efficient Algorithms. X, 586 pages. 2004.

Vol. 3058: N. Sebe, M.S. Lew, T.S. Huang (Eds.), Computer Vision in Human-Computer Interaction. X, 233 pages. 2004.

Vol. 3056: H. Dai, R. Srikant, C. Zhang (Eds.), Advances in Knowledge Discovery and Data Mining. XIX, 713 pages. 2004. (Subseries LNAI).

Vol. 3054: I. Crnkovic, J.A. Stafford, H.W. Schmidt, K. Wallnau (Eds.), Component-Based Software Engineering. XI, 311 pages. 2004.

Vol. 3053: C. Bussler, J. Davies, D. Fensel, R. Studer (Eds.), The Semantic Web: Research and Applications. XIII, 490 pages. 2004.

Vol. 3052: W. Zimmermann, B. Thalheim (Eds.), Abstract State Machines 2004. Advances in Theory and Practice. XII, 235 pages. 2004.

Vol. 3051: R. Berghammer, B. Möller, G. Struth (Eds.), Relational and Kleene-Algebraic Methods in Computer Science. X, 279 pages. 2004.

Vol. 3050: J. Domingo-Ferrer, V. Torra (Eds.), Privacy in Statistical Databases. IX, 367 pages. 2004.

Vol. 3047: F. Oquendo, B. Warboys, R. Morrison (Eds.), Software Architecture. X, 279 pages. 2004.

Vol. 3046: A. Laganà, M.L. Gavrilova, V. Kumar, Y. Mun, C.K. Tan, O. Gervasi (Eds.), Computational Science and Its Applications – ICCSA 2004. LIII, 1016 pages. 2004.

Vol. 3045: A. Laganà, M.L. Gavrilova, V. Kumar, Y. Mun, C.K. Tan, O. Gervasi (Eds.), Computational Science and Its Applications – ICCSA 2004. LIII, 1040 pages. 2004.

Vol. 3044: A. Laganà, M.L. Gavrilova, V. Kumar, Y. Mun, C.K. Tan, O. Gervasi (Eds.), Computational Science and Its Applications – ICCSA 2004. LIII, 1140 pages. 2004.

Vol. 3043: A. Laganà, M.L. Gavrilova, V. Kumar, Y. Mun, C.K. Tan, O. Gervasi (Eds.), Computational Science and Its Applications – ICCSA 2004. LIII, 1180 pages. 2004.

Vol. 3042: N. Mitrou, K. Kontovasilis, G.N. Rouskas, I. Iliadis, L. Merakos (Eds.), NETWORKING 2004, Networking Technologies, Services, and Protocols; Performance of Computer and Communication Networks; Mobile and Wireless Communications. XXXIII, 1519 pages. 2004.

Vol. 3039: M. Bubak, G.D.v. Albada, P.M. Sloot, J.J. Dongarra (Eds.), Computational Science - ICCS 2004. LXVI, 1271 pages. 2004.

Vol. 3038: M. Bubak, G.D.v. Albada, P.M. Sloot, J.J. Dongarra (Eds.), Computational Science - ICCS 2004. LXVI, 1311 pages. 2004.

Vol. 3037: M. Bubak, G.D.v. Albada, P.M. Sloot, J.J. Dongarra (Eds.), Computational Science - ICCS 2004. LXVI, 745 pages. 2004.

Vol. 3036: M. Bubak, G.D.v. Albada, P.M. Sloot, J.J. Dongarra (Eds.), Computational Science - ICCS 2004. LXVI, 713 pages. 2004.

Vol. 3035: M.A. Wimmer (Ed.), Knowledge Management in Electronic Government. XII, 326 pages. 2004. (Subseries LNAI).

Vol. 3034: J. Favela, E. Menasalvas, E. Chávez (Eds.), Advances in Web Intelligence. XIII, 227 pages. 2004. (Subseries LNAI).

Vol. 3033: M. Li, X.-H. Sun, Q. Deng, J. Ni (Eds.), Grid and Cooperative Computing. XXXVIII, 1076 pages. 2004.

Vol. 3032: M. Li, X.-H. Sun, Q. Deng, J. Ni (Eds.), Grid and Cooperative Computing. XXXVII, 1112 pages. 2004.

Vol. 3031: A. Butz, A. Krüger, P. Olivier (Eds.), Smart Graphics. X, 165 pages. 2004.

Vol. 3030: P. Giorgini, B. Henderson-Sellers, M. Winikoff (Eds.), Agent-Oriented Information Systems. XIV, 207 pages. 2004. (Subseries LNAI).

Vol. 3029: B. Orchard, C. Yang, M. Ali (Eds.), Innovations in Applied Artificial Intelligence. XXI, 1272 pages. 2004. (Subseries LNAI).

Vol. 3028: D. Neuenschwander, Probabilistic and Statistical Methods in Cryptology. X, 158 pages. 2004.

Vol. 3027: C. Cachin, J. Camenisch (Eds.), Advances in Cryptology - EUROCRYPT 2004. XI, 628 pages. 2004.

Vol. 3026: C. Ramamoorthy, R. Lee, K.W. Lee (Eds.), Software Engineering Research and Applications. XV, 377 pages. 2004.

Vol. 3025: G.A. Vouros, T. Panayiotopoulos (Eds.), Methods and Applications of Artificial Intelligence. XV, 546 pages. 2004. (Subseries LNAI).

Vol. 3024: T. Pajdla, J. Matas (Eds.), Computer Vision - ECCV 2004. XXVIII, 621 pages. 2004.

Vol. 3023: T. Pajdla, J. Matas (Eds.), Computer Vision - ECCV 2004. XXVIII, 611 pages. 2004.

Vol. 3022: T. Pajdla, J. Matas (Eds.), Computer Vision - ECCV 2004. XXVIII, 621 pages. 2004.

Vol. 3021: T. Pajdla, J. Matas (Eds.), Computer Vision - ECCV 2004. XXVIII, 633 pages. 2004.

Vol. 3019: R. Wyrzykowski, J.J. Dongarra, M. Paprzycki, J. Wasniewski (Eds.), Parallel Processing and Applied Mathematics. XIX, 1174 pages. 2004.

Vol. 3018: M. Bruynooghe (Ed.), Logic Based Program Synthesis and Transformation. X, 233 pages. 2004.

Vol. 3016: C. Lengauer, D. Batory, C. Consel, M. Odersky (Eds.), Domain-Specific Program Generation. XII, 325 pages. 2004.

Vol. 3015: C. Barakat, I. Pratt (Eds.), Passive and Active Network Measurement. XI, 300 pages. 2004.

Vol. 3014: F. van der Linden (Ed.), Software Product-Family Engineering. IX, 486 pages. 2004.

Vol. 3012: K. Kurumatani, S.-H. Chen, A. Ohuchi (Eds.), Multi-Agnets for Mass User Support. X, 217 pages. 2004. (Subseries LNAI).

Vol. 3011: J.-C. Régin, M. Rueher (Eds.), Integration of AI and OR Techniques in Constraint Programming for Combinatorial Optimization Problems. XI, 415 pages. 2004.

Vol. 3010: K.R. Apt, F. Fages, F. Rossi, P. Szeredi, J. Váncza (Eds.), Recent Advances in Constraints. VIII, 285 pages. 2004. (Subseries LNAI).

Vol. 3009: F. Bomarius, H. Iida (Eds.), Product Focused Software Process Improvement. XIV, 584 pages. 2004.

Vol. 3008: S. Heuel, Uncertain Projective Geometry. XVII, 205 pages. 2004.

Vol. 3007: J.X. Yu, X. Lin, H. Lu, Y. Zhang (Eds.), Advanced Web Technologies and Applications. XXII, 936 pages. 2004.

Vol. 3006: M. Matsui, R. Zuccherato (Eds.), Selected Areas in Cryptography. XI, 361 pages. 2004.

Vol. 3005: G.R. Raidl, S. Cagnoni, J. Branke, D.W. Corne, R. Drechsler, Y. Jin, C.G. Johnson, P. Machado, E. Marchiori, F. Rothlauf, G.D. Smith, G. Squillero (Eds.), Applications of Evolutionary Computing. XVII, 562 pages. 2004.

Vol. 3004: J. Gottlieb, G.R. Raidl (Eds.), Evolutionary Computation in Combinatorial Optimization. X, 241 pages. 2004.

Vol. 3003: M. Keijzer, U.-M. O'Reilly, S.M. Lucas, E. Costa, T. Soule (Eds.), Genetic Programming. XI, 410 pages. 2004.

Vol. 3002: D.L. Hicks (Ed.), Metainformatics. X, 213 pages. 2004.

Vol. 3001: A. Ferscha, F. Mattern (Eds.), Pervasive Computing. XVII, 358 pages. 2004.

Vol. 2999: E.A. Boiten, J. Derrick, G. Smith (Eds.), Integrated Formal Methods. XI, 541 pages. 2004.

Vol. 2998: Y. Kameyama, P.J. Stuckey (Eds.), Functional and Logic Programming. X, 307 pages. 2004.

Vol. 2997: S. McDonald, J. Tait (Eds.), Advances in Information Retrieval. XIII, 427 pages. 2004.

Vol. 2996: V. Diekert, M. Habib (Eds.), STACS 2004. XVI, 658 pages. 2004.

Vol. 2995: C. Jensen, S. Poslad, T. Dimitrakos (Eds.), Trust Management. XIII, 377 pages. 2004.

Vol. 2994: E. Rahm (Ed.), Data Integration in the Life Sciences. X, 221 pages. 2004. (Subseries LNBI).

Vol. 2993: R. Alur, G.J. Pappas (Eds.), Hybrid Systems: Computation and Control. XII, 674 pages. 2004.

Vol. 2992: E. Bertino, S. Christodoulakis, D. Plexousakis, V. Christophides, M. Koubarakis, K. Böhm, E. Ferrari (Eds.), Advances in Database Technology - EDBT 2004. XVIII, 877 pages. 2004.

Vol. 2991: R. Alt, A. Frommer, R.B. Kearfott, W. Luther (Eds.), Numerical Software with Result Verification. X, 315 pages. 2004.

Vol. 2990: J. Leite, A. Omicini, L. Sterling, P. Torroni (Eds.), Declarative Agent Languages and Technologies. XII, 281 pages. 2004. (Subseries LNAI).